CHURCH DOGMATICS

KARL BARTH

EDITORS
G. W. BROMILEY
T. F. TORRANCE

THE DOCTRINE
OF RECONCILIATION

CHURCH DOGMATICS

KARL BARTH

VOLUME IV

THE DOCTRINE
OF RECONCILIATION

PART 3.2

TRANSLATOR
G. W. BROMILEY

EDITORS
G. W. BROMILEY
T. F. TORRANCE

T & T CLARK INTERNATIONAL
A Continuum imprint
LONDON • NEW YORK

T&T CLARK INTERNATIONAL
A Continuum imprint

The Tower Building   15 East 26th Street
11 York Road   New York 10010
London SE1 7NX, UK   USA

www.tandtclark.com

ISBN 0 567 09044 2 (hardback)
0 567 05149 8 (paperback)

British Library Cataloguing-in-Publication Data
A catalogue record for this book is available from the British Library

Printed and bound in the United States by the Data Reproductions Corporation

CONTENTS

vii

§ 71

THE VOCATION OF MAN

The Word of the living Jesus Christ is the creative call by which He awakens man to an active knowledge of the truth and thus receives him into the new standing of the Christian, namely, into a particular fellowship with Himself, thrusting him as His afflicted but well-equipped witness into the service of His prophetic work.

1. MAN IN THE LIGHT OF LIFE

The life to which we refer in this sub-title (cf. § 69, 2) is that of the person of Him who as true God was and is and will be true man, and as true man true God. It is the life of the Jesus Christ who was crucified and slain, but who comes again first in His resurrection from the dead, then in the promise of the Spirit, and finally in His conclusive and universal revelation, and who lives in this return of His. We do not say anything different, but the same thing, when alongside this first and personal equation we set a second and material, namely, that this life is the grace of God manifested and active in Jesus Christ and justifying and sanctifying man. And finally and comprehensively we may also say that it is God's reconciliation of the world to Himself as willed and accomplished and still being fulfilled in Jesus Christ.

Again, the light to which we refer (cf. again § 69, 2) is the light of this life and therefore the glory, proclamation, prophecy and Word of the living Jesus Christ in His coming again as it now interests and concerns us particularly in its second and middle form as His coming again in the promise of the Spirit. Personally, this is His own light, the self-declaration of Jesus Christ, and materially it is the declaration of the grace of God manifested and active in Him, or comprehensively the declaration or revelation of the reconciliation accomplished and still being fulfilled in Him.

In the preceding section we have considered the falsehood of man, namely, his attempt to escape the light of life by falsifying and perverting the Word of Jesus Christ and its whole content. We have seen that in its futility this is an intrinsically dangerous attempt, since it might entail man's condemnation, and indeed would necessarily do so were it to succeed. We now leave this behind us. Jesus Christ continually leaves it behind Him in His prophetic work wherever and in whatever form He is accepted. The most important and decisive thing to be known about the falsehood of man as the supreme form of his sin can only be that in relation to it Jesus Christ is the absolutely superior Partner, the Victor.

We now turn our attention to the positive implication for man of the fact that as the man of sin, and therefore as the liar he is, man stands willy-nilly in this light, being set in it and surrounded by it as it shines in his sphere. It does actually shine in his sphere. He is thus pricked out and encircled by it. The way is thus prepared for it to shine on him and in him and through him, i.e., for the event of his vocation (κλῆσις, *vocatio*). Defined very generally, this is the event in which man is set and instituted in actual fellowship with Jesus Christ, namely, in the service of His prophecy, in the *ministerium Verbi divini*, of the Word of reconciliation, and therefore in the service of God and his fellow-men. Even more generally, one might say that it is the event in which the grace (χάρις) of God which justifies man before Him and sanctifies him for Him finds its counterpart in the gratitude (εὐχαριστία) of man. This event, this act of God, or more exactly the one act of God in Jesus Christ in a different dimension, significance and power, is the theme of this new section. But in this first sub-section we must first consider the context of this theme, i.e., the presupposition of this event which we call the vocation of man. We must consider to what extent, irrespective of the outcome, man is actually set in the light of life and thus foreordained and predisposed for his vocation.

When we speak of foreordination and predisposition for vocation, we may perhaps be reminded, if not of worse things, of something which in the older orthodoxy of the 17th century was usually mentioned and briefly described as *vocatio naturalis, universalis, indirecta, paedagogica,* in distinction from the true *vocatio supernaturalis, particularis, directa, evangelica.* According to the *Leidener Synopsis* (1624, *Disp.* 30, 3 f.) this general calling is an invitation to know and honour the true God which is issued to all men through certain *communia documenta naturae,* by which are meant certain self-declarations of this true God which are (*a*) inward (*interna*) and impressed on the hearts of men, and (*b*) outward (*externa*) and imprinted on the whole visible creation. We are thus confronted by the well-known double thesis of natural theology for which in this context biblical support was found in Ps. 19[1f.], Ac. 17[27] and Rom. 1[20] and 2[14]. In A. Quenstedt (*Theol. did. pol.*, 1685, III, 5, *sect.* 1, *th.* 3) there is added as a third element in this general calling the *celebritas ecclesiae, sive fama de coetu quodam hominum, in quo agnoscatur et colatur verus Deus,* a preparatory form of true vocation of which biblical examples were found in the story of the visit of the Queen of Sheba to Solomon (1 K. 10[1f.]) and also in that of Naaman the Syrian (1 K. 5[1f.]).

The material value or otherwise of natural theology, and of this final additional argument from history together with all the other proofs from Scripture, has been dealt with at length in many previous parts of the *Church Dogmatics,* and need not detain us now. Nor need we dispute whether or not it was a happy thought to link this whole theory (even assuming that it is biblically and materially sound) with the concept of vocation. Quenstedt himself admits that what is proclaimed in these documents should be understood more as *invitamenta et incitamenta quaedam* than as *vocatio proprie dicta,* and that its operation can consist only in an *adductio ad ianuam verae ecclesiae.* And already the *Leidener*

Synopsis had called the knowledge of these documents a *cognitio potius theoretica quam practica.* No obvious systematic or practical gain accrued to orthodox theology from this whole notion, nor was any such expected or sought.

It is mentioned here only in order that the following warning may be issued. What we are about to consider comes at the point where the orthodox fathers stated this theory, but has nothing whatever to do with it in substance. Not even in the weakened sense of a mere *invitamentum et incitamentum* are we thinking either of an external witness of nature or an inner witness of conscience, and certainly not of a *celebritas ecclesiae,* as preparatory forms of vocation, or indeed of any preparatory form of *vocatio proprie dicta* in the sense of a *vocatio late dicta.* Without distinguishing between an improper and a proper divine speaking, we understand by the calling Word of God the one revelation and prophecy of Jesus Christ attested in the Old and New Testaments and continually attested by the Holy Spirit. Hence there can be no question of a bifurcation of the concept of vocation. In accordance with the normative New Testament word κλῆσις, vocation is solely and simply *vocatio supernaturalis, particularis, directa, evangelica,* to use the old formula. It is for this that every man as such is foreordained and predisposed. This is what has in the situation and existence of all men a presupposition or prior history established by, and to be understood in the light of, the Word of God which calls them all. It is of this that we shall first speak, and we shall speak of it as something which, again in contrast to the theologoumena of the 17th century, is of the greatest systematic and practical relevance.

In accordance with the particularity and uniqueness of the person and work of Jesus Christ, the vocation of man is a particular and unique event in God's encounter with man which is as such a history, the occurrence and coming into being of a relationship which does not exist always, everywhere and from the very first. Not all men, therefore, are called as such. They can only be called, and they can be called only in virtue of the particularity of the call of Jesus as it is issued—and for the moment we give only these two examples—to Simon the fisherman and his brother Andrew (Mk. 1[16f.]) and to Levi the publican (Mk. 2[14]). Not all men as such are called by Him, just as not all men as such are justified and sanctified by Him. On the contrary, all men as such are uncalled, just as all men as such are unjustified and unsanctified. And even those who are called are so in their particular history in which they have continually to become afresh what they are as they once became it, just as their justification and sanctification accomplished once and for all in Jesus Christ must and will find continual confirmation in their life-history as it is set under this sign by their vocation.

This does not mean, however, that the vocation of man acquires relevance and significance for him only when it takes place in his own life-history, when he is addressed as one who is called by Jesus Christ, and when he begins to know and acknowledge himself as such and to act accordingly.

Like his justification and sanctification, prior to its actualisation in his own history it has its basis, as we must say first and supremely, in his election in Jesus Christ " before the foundation of the world " (Eph. 1[4]). It has as the seed and root of its historical reality, truth and certainty the absolutely prevenient " history " which as the *opus Trinitatis internum ad extra* is in God Himself the eternal beginning of all His ways and works, namely, the election of grace of the God who loves in freedom and is free in love, in which the Son, thereto ordained by the Father and obedient to the Father, has elected Himself for sinful man and sinful man for Himself. In the light of this, the one true God is the God of man in time, yet not merely in the time in which Jesus Christ did His work and spoke His Word and thus effects man's vocation, but primarily in Himself, in His pre-temporal, supra-temporal and post-temporal eternity. In other words, He is the God who elects Himself for sinful man and sinful man for Himself. On the strength of this God and His eternal election of grace, man's justification before Him and sanctification for Him in Jesus Christ, but also his vocation to the active recognition of these and therefore to concrete fellowship with God, are first and last real, true and certain. The election is the basis of vocation. Primarily in God Himself man stands already in the light of life—each man and all men. For man's election is his election in Jesus Christ, the Son of God, whom the Father, and He Himself, has not elected for this or that man but for all men, and who has not elected this or that man but all men for Himself. In this twofold election He has taken to Himself and away from them all the rejection which applies to all men as sinners and separates them from God. Not in and of himself, but in Jesus Christ as the eternal beginning of all God's ways and works, no man is rejected, but all are elected in Him to their justification, their sanctification and also their vocation. This is the prior history which precedes and underlies the event of vocation in their own history, which is purely and totally divine, but which in intention is already divine-human.

It is of this that we must think first and supremely in relation to this event. We recall Is. 41[4]: " Who hath wrought and done it ? (The reference is to the calling of Cyrus to his work of deliverance in the service of the exiled people of God.) He who called to the generations from the beginning, I the Lord, the first, and with the last ; I am he." Of the called, i.e., Christians, we have thus to say first of all with Calvin : *Qui ad Christum accedunt, iam filii Dei erant in eius corde, quum in se hostes essent, et quia praeordinati erant ad vitam, Christo dati sunt (De aet. Dei praed., C.R., 8, 292).* Within the framework of his understanding of predestination, divorced at the crucial point from Christology, and of the vocation which follows this in time, Calvin could not, of course, speak of an election of all men to a real, true and certain vocation grounded in this election. According to him, not all men are elected in Jesus Christ, and therefore not all are called. Yet the fact remains—and this is our present point—that Calvin did speak plainly of the eternal election of man, or of certain men, as the presupposition of their vocation and not *vice versa*, and of the vocation of man, or of certain men, as the historical fulfilment of their election. For him vocation and election are indissolubly co-ordinated. Election looks forward to the future event of vocation ; vocation backward to election.

According to the New Testament norm we cannot speak of either except in this co-ordination. Christians are ἐκλεκτοί and therefore κλητοί. They are κλητοί because they are ἐκλεκτοί. And on the basis of both election and vocation they are ἅγιοι and πιστοί. All these descriptions apply to them as Christians. This is intended even in passages in which only one or two or sometimes three are expressly mentioned. If κλῆσις and ἐκλογή are not identical, they are never independent but always go together. When in 1 Cor. 1¹ and Rom. 1¹ Paul calls himself κλητὸς ἀπόστολος, he gives his own exposition by adding in Rom. 1¹ : ἀφωρισμένος εἰς εὐαγγέλιον θεοῦ. He thus traces back his calling to be both a Christian and an apostle to his election. That is why he can say in Gal. 1¹⁵ that he was separated from his mother's womb and called by God's grace. According to Rom. 8²⁸ Christians generally are κλητοί according to God's prior counsel (κατὰ πρόθεσιν). And in the famous *catena aurea* of Rom. 8³⁰ it is said of them generally that God called those whom He elected, and then that He justified and glorified them. In Rev. 17¹⁴ they are described in a single phrase as κλητοὶ καὶ ἐκλεκτοὶ καὶ πιστοί. From the very first (ἀπ᾽ ἀρχῆς) God has elected them to salvation and then called them by the Gospel, according to 2 Thess. 2¹³. It is not according to their works that God has done the latter, but in accordance with His πρόθεσις and the grace addressed to them from eternity in Jesus Christ (2 Tim. 1⁹). Finally, Jude 1 seems to point in the same direction when it says of the κλητοί that they are "loved by God the Father, and preserved in Jesus Christ."

A more difficult passage in this connexion is Mt. 22¹⁴. Jesus has just told the parable of the wedding-feast, and especially the story of the rejection of the man who appeared without a wedding garment. There is then added the independent saying : "Many are called, but few are chosen." The verse forms a *crux interpretum*, since its most obvious meaning, in analogy to the saying quoted in Plato's *Phaedo* (69c) about the few real Bacchantes among the many Thyrsus bearers, seems to be in flat contradiction with all the other passages and to speak about a calling which has no election as its presupposition. Among those who rightly thought this contradiction intolerable, and thus could not accept the obvious meaning, R. Seeberg (*PRE*³, 2, 657) took the view that in this passage ἐκλεκτοί is not a theological term but simply indicates the good and the noble of whom there are unfortunately only too few among those who are called. But if the saying is understood in this way it surely has a foreign ring in the Synoptic tradition, and no such distinction between the good and noble and the rest of the called seems to be made anywhere else in the New Testament. Indeed, how could the saying be reconciled with what is said about the called and elect in 1 Cor. 1²⁶ᶠ. ? A. Schlatter again (*Der Evangelist Matthäus*, 1929, p. 640 f.) tried to avoid the contradiction by castigating and rejecting as Greek the exposition which would " import into the supra-historical consciousness of God " the choice indicated by the word ἐκλεκτοί, Jesus and the Evangelist concentrating their attention consistently on history and therefore accepting the fact that the calling of man merely posits a beginning which contains the possibility both of apostasy and also of preservation, so that election must be separated from vocation. But if this is the case, then the rest of the New Testament is at fault, and especially Paul, who unmistakeably speaks of the election as a divine πρόθεσις and the like. Can we really isolate it from this and link it with the story of man's apostasy or preservation ? And where in the New Testament, apart perhaps from Judas Iscariot, do we have any example of κλῆσις as a beginning which carries within it the apostasy of man ? My own view is that we may and must agree with K. L. Schmidt (Kittel, II, 496) in regarding the saying as a paradox. It may thus be freely paraphrased as follows. Many are called, but there will only be few who in following the call will prove worthy of, and act in accordance with, the fact that as the called of God they are His elect, predestined from all eternity for life with Him and for His service. There will only be few who in the words of 2 Pet. 1¹⁰ are obedient to their calling and make sure, i.e., validate and confirm, their election. There will only be few who really are what they are as called, namely, elect or Christians. In this case the meaning of the redactor in Mt. 22 is this. Like so many, and indeed the majority, the man without the wedding-garment has not been or done what he could and should have been and done when invited by the king to the feast and given like all the rest the robe with which to appear before him. If this is the meaning, the saying itself then points to the fact that both the calling and the underlying election in their co-ordination have and maintain the character of a free act of grace on the side of God and a free decision on that of man. On neither side, therefore, do we have the automatic functioning of a machine. Both vocation and election are always a free event. It is to be noted in conclusion that if this verse cannot be opposed to all the others in which the co-ordination of vocation and election is so clear and unequivocal, it cannot be adduced, as it often has been, in refutation of the universality of the election which underlies the future calling of all.

If we recall the basis of vocation in the divine election of grace in Jesus Christ, it can and should serve only to emphasise and underline the fact that its basis is in the history of Jesus Christ in time. It is in this that the eternal election of man, and therefore his temporal vocation issued in it, are grounded. As in the case of his justification and sanctification, his vocation took place before it became an event in his own life, and in a way which was decisive for his situation, existence and history, in the work of God's free grace to him which in time followed and corresponded to His eternal counsel, in the divine work of reconciliation which was simply effected for him in Jesus Christ without any co-operation or even presence on his part. For this has also a prophetic character. It encloses within itself the Word of reconciliation declared to man. The vocation of man is thus comprehended within it from the very outset, i.e., before it takes place in his own life-history. In Jesus Christ it already applies to him ; it is already his vocation. For Jesus Christ did not only die for him. He also rose again and lives for him. He proclaims Himself as his Mediator and Saviour. In the promise of the Spirit He comes to him from far or near as the Prophet of the grace of God to him. No " not yet " in the life-history of man can alter the fact that it has its decisive prior history in the history of Jesus Christ . There are countless men whose justification, sanctification and vocation in the history of Jesus Christ have not yet taken place in their own history. But there is no man who can be neutral in relation to the history of Jesus Christ. There is no man whose history is not decided in the history of Jesus Christ, in the sense that whatever may or may not take place in it in whatever way will do so in relation to and according to the standard of the fact that in Jesus Christ he, too, is justified, sanctified and called. There is said to him, with no possibility of mistake, what was said to Mary in Jn. 11^{28} : " The Master is come, and calleth for thee." He calls before His call is taken up and passed on by any other men, by His prophets and apostles or the community which bears witness to Him. The truth and power of all ministerial and representative human calling stand or fall with the fact that first Jesus Himself calls, He Himself being the One who also declares Himself by means of this secondary attestation. He calls man before man hears. He calls him even when he will not hear or obey. He calls him again when He has called him already and something has already taken place in his life. Since He is risen and alive, Himself the Word of reconciliation to the world reconciled to God in Him, and Himself present in the world, calling by Him is the future of every man irrespective of the result, and as his future, even if it takes place in his own life only in the most obscure and broken way or not at all, it belongs to the historical existence and situation of every man. In it there is declared with divine power God's whole compassion for the world. Why should not His call be issued to all ? And why should it not be a supremely real determination of the existence and situation of all that His call comes to them and that they have their future in calling by Him ? He is the light of the world (Jn. 8^{12}, 9^5, 12^{46}). It is not merely that He can or should be. He has not yet to become it somewhere as conditioned by human achievements. He *is* the light of the world. And therefore to be man is always to stand already, even if with closed or blind eyes, in this light, the light of life.

What is really meant by the New Testament when it speaks of the world which God loved in giving His Son (Jn. 3^{16}), which He reconciled to Himself (2 Cor. 5^{19} ; cf. Col. 1^{20}), and the sin of which Jesus Christ bore as a sacrifice (1 Jn. 2^2) ? What is really meant when it speaks of Jesus Christ as the Saviour of the world (Jn. 4^{42} ; 1 Jn. 4^{14}) or of all men (Rom. 5^{18}, 1 Tim. 4^{10}, Tit. 2^{11}), of the conclusion of all in unbelief in order that He might thereby have mercy on all (Rom. 11^{32}), of the future outpouring of His Spirit on all flesh (Ac. 2^{17}), so that Christians, begotten of the Word of truth, may think of themselves only as the first-fruits of God's creatures (Jas. 1^{18}) and should study to show meekness to all men (Tit. 3^2) ? What is meant by Mt. 28^{18} : " All power is given unto me in heaven and in earth," or Jn. 12^{32} : " I, if I be lifted up from the earth, will draw all men unto me " ? What is meant by the conclusion of the christological hymn in Phil. 2$^{10f.}$, that at the name of Jesus every knee shall bow and every tongue confess Him as *Kyrios* to the glory of God the Father ? Or, as we might further ask, what is really the concrete meaning of so many passages even in the later parts of the Old Testament in which God the God of Israel is confessed, invoked and proclaimed as the Creator, Owner, Lord and King of heaven and earth and all men and nations, in which the latter are regarded as extremely interested spectators of the history of His people as He directs it, in which the future of salvation promised to this people is also described as and declared to be theirs too, with Jerusalem as " a name of joy, a praise and an honour before all the nations of the earth which shall hear all the good that I do unto them " (Jer. 33^9), and in which they are invited and required to fall down before Yahweh, to worship and serve Him and glorify His name ? What is meant when we read in Is. 66^{21} that Levites and priests will be taken from among them ? And the same question recurs when along the same line Paul constantly mentions Jews and Gentiles together, fully co-ordinating the Gentiles with the people of Abraham (as in Rom. 15$^{8-12}$) and unconditionally proclaiming that the wall of partition between them has been finally broken down (Eph. 2^{14}). How can reference be made in Ac. 10^{35} to men in every nation who fear God and do righteousness and are therefore pleasing to God ? In all these things we have both implicitly and explicitly a supremely positive declaration concerning the general human situation, according to which this stands in so intimate a connexion with that of Israel and the later Christian community that there are no clear boundaries between them, and the predicates of those in the narrower circles

within seem to be identifiable and actually identified with those in the wider
circle without. How are we to understand and explain this whole confession
of biblical universalism ?

There is certainly no question of the biblical writers not taking seriously
the difference or even antithesis. They do not see it bridged in terms of historical
relativism, as in Lessing's *Nathan*. Nor do they see it bridged in terms of a
general and natural presence, action and revelation of God, or an inner light
common to all men, or a continuous relationship between God and man as such,
within which the history of Israel and Jesus Christ, and therefore of Israelites
and Christians, is only a special instance with exemplary significance. Neither
the Old Testament nor the New knows of such a general continuity of the reciprocal relationship between God and man. We must not forget the role played
by the nations, with their gods and manners and customs and acts and excesses,
and their whole hostility against Israel throughout the Old Testament and elsewhere, apart from this one line. Nor must we forget the sharpness with which
the people of Yahweh is warned against mingling with them—and for good or ill
we find this no less in Deutero- and Trito-Isaiah than in the Book of Ezra. Nor
must we forget the clarity, softened by no concession, with which the New
Testament distinguishes between the being of man in the discipleship of Jesus
Christ, in His community and in the Spirit, and the being of man in the passing
world, according to its pattern and in the flesh, i.e., between walking in the light
and walking in darkness. Nor must we forget how definitely it tells Christians
not to be " unequally yoked together with unbelievers " (2 Cor. 6[14]). The
theory may seem to be good and normative and usable on other grounds, but it
certainly has no support in the Old and New Testaments. Biblical universalism
has another root and significance.

Again, we cannot understand it pragmatically as the final result of the mission
of Israel and later of the community to the world and other men. Certainly
they have the commission : " Go ye therefore, and teach all nations " (Mt.
28[19]). This is the decisive saying in which the Resurrected gives to the existence
of His first witnesses its concrete meaning and task, just as the Old Testament
Servant of the Lord (Is. 42[6]) is told that God has made him a " covenant of the
people " and " light of the Gentiles." Yet the truth of the sayings about the
world loved by God and reconciled to Him in Jesus Christ, about the knees
which will bow to Him and the tongues which will confess Him, about His title as
the Saviour of the world and therefore about God's all-embracing mercy, and in
the Old Testament about the possibility of the Gentiles glorifying God and
entering His service, is obviously conditioned in neither case by any great or
small, present or future success of the human witness to God's grace in the
surrounding world which goes its own ways with its idols and their worship
and service. The modest scope of what men actually do or can do in obedience
to their commission among the sea of peoples is not hidden from either the Old
or the New Testament witnesses, even in the stories of the Queen of Sheba,
Naaman and the Wise Men. Their comprehensive statements certainly could
not follow from any expectations in this regard. The existence and activity of
Israel and later of the community in the world could not form the presupposition
for the confidence of these statements. On the contrary, the confidence of the
statements was the presupposition or basis for what was humanly speaking
an almost hopeless enterprise, namely, their existence and activity as the servants
of Yahweh and Jesus Christ in the world.

What, then, was this confidence ? It is usually said to-day that it was their
" eschatological faith," i.e., their faith as orientated on events and conditions
in an absolute future, in a situation on the new earth and under the new heaven.
There is, of course, truth in this. But we fail to bring out this truth if we describe
their faith in tones and colours which make it appear to be a kind of heaven-
storming idealism and optimism, which suggest that its real content is a partly

despairing and partly enthusiastic projection of religious feeling into the infinite, and which thus give the impression that the whole is a flight from reality into a wonderful dream and therefore finally to be rejected with a sad shake of the head. Like so many other elements in the thought and utterance of the Bible, biblical universalism is to be understood eschatologically to the extent, but only to the extent, that its statements refer to facts and factors of present, this-worldly reality which are now concealed, and will be revealed as such only in the absolute future of the redeeming and consummating action of God. What " will be " there and then in the *eschaton* is in visibility that which really is here and now in virtue of the reconciling action of God, which constitutes the controlling sense of temporal history. That which comes finally is not a second reality distinct from a supposed first reality here and now, and therefore necessarily exposed to the suspicion of being merely ideal and therefore unreal. On the contrary, it is already the one reality which here and now still encounters us in concealment but there and then will make itself known, and will be knowable and known, without concealment. Hence we shall misunderstand the universalism of the Bible if we take its statements eschatologically and therefore (provisionally at least) unrealistically instead of supremely realistically and therefore eschatologically. They are statements the contents of which still need to be revealed in the final and conclusive future of God, which still hasten towards this future, but which in relation to it may and must already be ventured with perfect confidence in the present and in respect of that which now is. So much, then, for the universalistic assertions of the Old and New Testaments.

We have no option, therefore, but to understand extremely realistically in this sense the very positive statements of the Bible concerning the general human situation. They describe this situation as it really is in virtue of the fact that it has been altered and determined by God's action in the history of Israel and of Jesus Christ enacted within it. The authors of the Bible—and this is the basis of their confidence—clung to this action of God in and to the world and among and to men as to the one reality and the source and norm of all reality. They could do so as they believed and clung to the Word which they heard God speak with this action of His. As they attested the work and Word of God, in this respect, too, they did not coin any idealistic phrases intended and to be understood only in a religious sense. They meant what they said. Certainly they could not yet see with their eyes nor hear with their ears nor reconstruct with their understanding the altered and newly determined general human situation, the world as it really is through God's reconciling of it to Himself in Jesus Christ, that which all men really are on the basis of the fact that Jesus Christ has died and risen for them. It was concealed from them to the same degree that it is from us and all men. But as they found it possible and necessary to believe the Word spoken by God in and with His action in the history of Israel and Jesus Christ, unable to deny all this they also found it possible and necessary with the same seriousness and certainty to confess the general situation between God and man as they had to confess the particular situation between God and themselves in which they found themselves placed in the event of hearing His Word.

But what was the alteration and new determination of the general human situation ? What was the new and real being of the surrounding world and humanity in all its members as revealed in and with the reconciling action of God and known to them in faith ? They could not possibly maintain, and none of them did maintain, that the general human situation was simply the same as their own, that those without were simply within, that the uncalled were the called. This was not said to them by the Word spoken in the divine action. Indeed, the very opposite was said. As the great acts of God took place among them, and in them they could hear His Word, they were distinguished and supremely separated from all others, from the nations to whom such things did not happen. They could not be ashamed of the fact, nor deny it, that as witnesses of God's action and speech in the history of Israel and Jesus Christ they were something which in the first instance and thus far all others were not, and therefore a new and strange and highly distinctive people among them. Only as they the called encountered and even opposed the uncalled could they bear the witness which as the called they owed to the uncalled. Yet the content of the Word of God to be attested by them was not the alteration merely of their own situation by God's action in covenant with Israel and in His unity with Jesus Christ. Hence their witness—and this is the root and meaning of biblical universalism—had also, and even primarily, to be a declaration concerning others, the world and all men, namely, the declaration that the action of God in His covenant with Israel and His unity with the one man Jesus Christ was and is His gracious, judging, yet also justifying and sanctifying action for them and to them. They had thus to meet and oppose them with their witness in such a way that they did not exclude but very definitely included them, forbidding from the very outset any freedom or neutrality in relation to the content of this witness. They could not proceed on the assumption that the world and humanity around them were unaffected by the work and Word of God, but in faith in this work and Word they had to assume that they were affected by them. They had to address others in this faith, and therefore on the assumption that the Word of God received by them applied really and directly to them too, i.e., to the world and humanity which had not received it, and that they had indeed been reached and affected by it even before receiving it in virtue of its content. They had thus to address them on the basis of this alteration and new determination as already effected. They had to declare and interpret the fact of their own life as constituted by God's action. They had to draw attention to the light of life already shining around them. They could only allow that they had not yet known this life of theirs, that they had not yet been enlightened by the light of life, and that they were thus still uncalled. But they could neither acquiesce in this nor allow them to acquiesce in it. They could not let them continue to think of themselves as uncalled. They had rather to question, attack and shatter this understanding by addressing and treating them as those who were really and directly called already to a knowledge of what God had done for and to them also, and who therefore stood in the light of life even if with closed or blind eyes. For them, the as yet uncalled could only be those who were to be called. Hence their sense of obligation and joy in relation to them. On God's side, on the basis of His action and in accordance with the Word spoken in His action, all things are ready for all (Mt. 22⁴). This is the meaning of the universalism of the Bible evident in the passages adduced. The biblical witnesses could not have believed what they attested as the act and Word of God if they had thought or spoken otherwise of the world and humanity around them. But they believed what they attested, and therefore they had to think and speak of them in this way, both implicitly and explicitly confessing this universalism.

This statement concerning the human situation as universally altered and redetermined by the act and Word of God, by the existence and work of Christ ; this statement concerning the status of every man, even the uncalled, namely, that he stands already in the light of life, has to be ventured as a dogmatic tenet because it forms the indispensable presupposition of what must be developed as the true theme of this section, i.e., the doctrine of man's vocation to be a Christian.

To be sure, the assertion must not cut across or in any sense compete with the further statement that " I cannot by my own reason or strength believe in Jesus Christ my Lord, or come to Him, but the

Holy Ghost has called me by the Gospel." Our assertion concerns the foreordination and predisposition of every man for the supremely particular event of his vocation to be a Christian. If with the necessary humour and good will there may be recognised in it the element of truth in Tertullian's *anima humana naturaliter christiana*, there is obviously no reference to any immanent human capacity to be a Christian, nor to any fruit of the human work of Christian activity generally perceptible in the world, nor to any such ideal results, but to the eminently real determination of all humanity by the supreme reality of the divine act of salvation for and to it and the living divine Word evident within it. In the light of the universalistic passages of the Bible, we can say that man in every time and place stands already in the light of life. But this has no reference to the event of his vocation. It simply affirms that no man exists who is not confronted by his vocation. Hence it cannot collide with Luther's well-known exposition of the third article concerning the work of the Holy Spirit. Its reference is simply to a legitimate and necessary deduction from the second, christological article which Luther himself does not make, i.e., to the real significance and relevance of the existence and action of Jesus Christ for every man as such—a significance and relevance which always and everywhere precede the actual vocation of man to be a Christian, and are presupposed in it. It consists in the fact that Jesus Christ always comes to him with His call, that He always encounters him, that He always stands at his door and knocks (Rev. 3[20]). As in world history the history of Israel and of Jesus Christ took place with their own light and self-declaration; as among all men the man Jesus Christ also lives and proclaims Himself and the act of reconciliation accomplished in Him, the fulfilment of the covenant between God and man effected in Him, it is decided *a priori* that there is no human heart, no thinking, willing or striving which is not ordained to find its Master in Him by the work of the Holy Spirit, to be called instead of uncalled, Christian instead of pagan. This ordination is to be understood as the real historical affecting and characterising of human existence as co-existence with the existence of the God-man Jesus Christ. Whatever else it may or may not mean, the mere fact that man co-exists with Jesus Christ certainly means *de iure* a complete alteration of his situation. On the basis and in the power of his co-existence with Jesus Christ, or rather of the co-existence of Jesus Christ with him, he is virtually a different and new man. And this means in practice that from the very first and in all cases he is confronted and summoned by the fact that on this basis he is foreknown for the work of the Holy Spirit to be accomplished in him, and foreordained and predisposed, though naturally not forced, to be a hearer of the Word of God. How can this assertion question or dissolve the high particularity and autonomy of the work of the Holy Spirit and therefore the event of his vocation to be a hearer of the Word of God? In other words, how can it question or dissolve the particularity of the fulfilment of the prophetic as opposed to the royal and priestly office of Jesus Christ and to that extent of the second article of the creed as opposed to the third ? What it does—and this is its importance—is to make clear the connexion or context in which the event of calling takes place in the work of the Holy Spirit. It protects this event from having in its singularity the appearance of stupendous accident or caprice which it might assume if it were not preceded by this statement.

Certainly when the event comes it can only be described as in Is. 65[1f.] (cf. Rom. 10[20f.]) : " I am sought of them that asked not for me ; I am found of them that sought me not : I said, Behold me, behold me, unto a nation that was not called by my name. I have spread out my hands all the day unto a rebellious people, which walketh in a way that was not good, after their own thoughts ; a people that provoketh me to anger continually before my face." It is to this nation and to people such as these that God has stretched out His hands " all the day," even before they asked for Him, even before they were found by Him, even before He caused them to behold Him, even when they did not ask for Him, nor seek Him, nor call on His name, but went their own obstinate and rebellious and evil ways, provoking and challenging Him. He was always the One He willed to be for them. For Him, therefore, they were always the ones they were to be for Him.

In God's relationship to man and theirs to Him, the " before " and " after " are interconnected by the fact that in all its newness the new factor of their calling is also the fulfilment and confirmation of the old factor of their existence with a view to being called, and the old itself is a manifestation of the context or order or necessity in and with which the new takes place. Both are elements in the one free act of divine grace, our present concern being their relation in the inner context of the one work of reconciliation. Within the one free act of grace we have both the vocation of man as such and his ordination to it, both his awakening to active knowledge of the accomplished reconciliation and the alteration of the world and his own situation grounded in this event, both his actual and definitive participation, made possible and realised in the work of the Holy Spirit, and also his potential and provisional participation in the existence of Jesus Christ, in His history and the preceding history of Israel as the *prius* of his own existence and therefore his vocation, both the event itself and his foreordination and predisposition for it. The mystery of God embraces both aspects, the " before " as well as the " after." And it is clear that both may be recognised only in faith in the saving Word of God as the declaration of His saving work. But in faith in this Word they may both be recognised in such a way that they can neither be confounded nor separated, so that the recognition of the one, or its co-ordination with the other, can neither limit nor disturb the recognition of the other.

To conclude this introductory sub-section, we shall attempt a short demonstration of the extent to which our assertion is not only theoretically correct but also practically important. We have stated generally that it is important because it reveals the necessity of vocation in the context of the divine activity of grace. We must now specify three ways in which our statement brings out the practical relevance of this necessity.

1. If it is really the case that the vocation to be a Christian does not take place in the life of each individual, yet does determine the situation of each individual to the extent that his existence is directed towards vocation and he has his future in vocation, then as Christians and therefore as those who are called we are constrained to be absolutely open in respect of all other men without exception, exercising towards them the same openness as that in which alone, because the event of our calling can never be behind us in such a way that it is not also before us, we can see and understand ourselves as those who are called. If our assertion has the validity which it can have only as grounded in Jesus Christ and therefore in the work and Word of God, then we cannot view any man only in the light of those factors, e.g., the corruption of his mode of life, the perverted and evil nature of his actions, the untenability of the ideas and convictions expressed by him, which obviously seem to characterise, and in very many cases do actually characterise him, as one who is not called, as non-Christian, unchristian and even anti-Christian. To be sure, we can and should take seriously the things which mark him off with some degree of clarity from those who are already called. And there would be no point in trying to make out that he is really a Christian instead of a non-Christian in view of certain brighter aspects of his character. To the extent that we dare to confess and take ourselves seriously as Christians, we must always and everywhere count upon it that a majority, and perhaps a very large majority of our fellows, are more or less decidedly non-Christian, unchristian and even anti-Christian. Indifference in this respect has always proved the death of Christian responsibility in relation to these others. Yet the fact remains that in the existence of these others there is something which has to be taken more seriously, and indeed infinitely more seriously from the qualitative standpoint, than their blatant non-Christianity in one form or another, namely the fact that, no matter who or what they are or how they live, their vocation is before them no less surely than that Jesus Christ has died and risen again for them. This is something of unconditional significance. It is the one sure thing we know concerning them. Anything we know concerning the fact that they are not called and not Christians can finally be only a matter of more or less well-founded conjecture. And even where we think we can be most sure of the facts, the reference can only be to what they are or are not provisionally. Unconditional significance attaches only to the fact that we have always to see and understand them as those who are still to be called. This has, however, the incomparable force of the knowledge of the living Jesus Christ and of faith in His being and action for all men. In faith in Him our self-knowledge

as Christians, to the extent that we have such, has its only basis. In this faith it has an unshakeable basis. But in this faith it has a basis which means that it is possible only in constant renewal by Jesus Christ as the object and origin of faith. In other words, our calling to be Christians, as plainly shown in the New Testament in the figure of Peter, must take place again and again. No man who is called does not also have to see and understand himself as one who has still to be called and therefore as one who stands alongside and in solidarity with the uncalled. Is it not inevitable, then, that our self-understanding as Christians should constrain us on this side, together with our knowledge of the existence of Jesus Christ in its universal significance, to an openness towards others in which we reckon with the fact that they are what we ourselves still are even as Christians, namely, those who are not called but are still to be called ? For all the seriousness with which we must distinguish between Christians and non-Christians, we can never think in terms of a rigid separation. All that is possible is a genuinely unlimited openness of the called in relation to the uncalled, an unlimited readiness to see in the aliens of to-day the brothers of to-morrow, and to love them as such and not simply as men, neither the Old Testament nor the New knowing anything of a general love for humanity. Except on this basis there could be no communication between the Christian and the non-Christian, no witness or service to the neighbour. On this basis and this basis alone, but very definitely, Christian communication, witness and service in and to the world become immediately and necessarily a duty and task. To live on this basis, in this openness and readiness, in this " tolerance " towards the non-Christian, is not then a particular virtue in the Christian. He would not be called himself if he did not self-evidently and naturally (as a Christian) live on this basis.

2. If it is the case that the vocation to be a Christian, even though it does not by a long way take place in each life, determines the situation of every man to the extent that it is the future or *telos* of his existence, this implies a responsibility of every man and thus compels the Christian to see and understand not only himself but also the non-Christian in his responsibility, and to address him in terms of it. The reference is not to a general moral or human responsibility which might be interpreted as man's obligation to his conscience or character or way, or to certain supposed or real orders and forces of the cosmos. It is to the fact that every man, as he co-exists as such with Jesus Christ, stands in the light of life, that the Word of God is directed to him too, that it comes to him, that he is to be called and that he is thus made responsible to the One who calls him. He does not make himself responsible. He is made responsible by this One. To be responsible means to be ordained to see the light of life, to hear and receive the Word of God. He is able and under obligation to do this. He is free to do it. With the calling which is before him he will not go

into any foreign place but come home, come to himself, to the place where he belongs. In obeying it, he will do exactly what he ought to do. He will thus have no serious reason or excuse for not obeying. In this case he can neither appeal to the fact that he is not free to obey nor to the fact that he is free not to obey. As one who is to be called, he is free for the work of the Holy Spirit and therefore for obedience, whereas disobedience can only mean that he makes no use of the freedom which is given him. He is permitted and therefore commanded to obey. That he cannot yet see and understand this, and therefore basically himself as one who is called, is obvious. But this does not alter its truth. It does not alter the fact that he is responsible in face of his calling. And it is in this respect, and this respect alone, that he is to be taken with unconditional seriousness. It is in this respect, and this respect alone, that the Christian as one who knows what is before the non-Christian has to take him with unconditional seriousness. This is the point—and for once it may be called a point of contact if desired—which he can always count on being present in the other. And in relation to it he can and must be tolerant towards him. He cannot let go of him. Nor can he be against him as though he had to overcome him. He cannot attack him for a nature, speech and impulse only too appropriate to one who is not yet called. If he can and must cling to him, he must patiently give him plenty of rope in the quiet confidence that he cannot escape his ordination and therefore his vocation and therefore his freedom. For all that he is so unchristian in his ways, in view of this he surely can and must be tolerated and suffered, not merely as a fellow-man, which he also is, but beyond this and decisively because he is one who not for nothing can be his future fellow-Christian. This tolerance may have to be for a very long time, even his whole life, for it is not in the power of any Christian to set a term to the non-Christian course of his fellow or to actualise his vocation. So long as God does not do this, putting a stop to his present nature, speech and impulse, the Christian cannot refuse him this tolerance. But only so long as this is the case ! For obviously he cannot and will not tolerate him for a single moment in the absolute sense, but only with a tolerance full of secret but noticeable intolerance. He cannot grant him a right to be blessed in his own way, for he knows of himself that to his salvation there is no such right even for him. Absolute tolerance towards him would mean not taking him seriously, and thus causing him to fall, in the one thing in which he must always take him with unconditional seriousness, i.e., in his ordination, responsibility and freedom. And he could not do this without causing himself to fall, denying his own vocation and thus being untrue to his own vocation, responsibility and freedom. In effect, then, the Christian cannot leave the non-Christian at peace. This means that for all the sincerity of his patience with him he can only be to him in effect a most disturbing fellow-man, effectively reminding him by his existence where he also belongs and what is his own true though not yet grasped and appropriated being as his promised future. It is not surprising, therefore, if the Christian who is in some measure alive, even though he be sincerely open and patient, must always give to the non-Christian, and especially the anti-Christian, the impression of unfitting and culpable intolerance.

3. If it is the case that the event of vocation, no matter how or when it occurs, or whether it occurs at all, is the future and *telos* determinative of the situation of every man, this compels the one in whose life it has taken place, and therefore the Christian, to base his self-understanding as such finally and decisively on, and to understand himself as a Christian primarily and decisively in the light of, the One who, as He did for all His work as the humiliated Son of God and the exalted Son of Man, speaks to all in His Word uttered with this work. To be sure, this self-understanding of the Christian in the light of Jesus Christ is attainable in the first instance only in the framework of the understanding of his own realised calling. It is thus the case that I have always to look to the event of it, to the fact that it has taken place and does take place in my own life, and therefore to what Jesus Christ has done and is, has said and says, *pro me*. This may be granted. But how could I stand before Jesus Christ as the final and decisive basis of my self-understanding if it were hidden from me, or if I would not accept, that He is first *pro nobis*, the Saviour of the world, and only then *pro me*, my Saviour ? If the Christian is to understand himself in relation to Jesus Christ, and thus to be sure of his cause, he cannot try to understand himself abstractly or exclusively in the framework of his own realised calling. For it is a matter of the living Jesus Christ whose powers and possibilities he cannot think to be anywhere near exhaustion in what He is and reveals to him. Again, if he limited himself to the framework of his personal calling, even at best his knowledge of Jesus Christ, and his self-understanding even as a Christian called by Him, could be only a knowledge limited and disturbed by his personal nature or distortion and therefore deprived of the certainty which it needs. Again, and finally, his personal calling as such stands in need of constant repetition and renewal, and therefore never stands so fully behind him that it is not also before him. To be quite sure of his own cause, of the event of his calling which distinguishes him from the non-Christian, he needs to surrender every claim and to identify himself with the non-Christian, clinging to Jesus Christ who is who He is for him, yet not only or even first for him, but first for all and then also for him. This is the living Jesus Christ in the fulness of His powers and possibilities. He remains faithful to Himself and therefore to the Christian in all the imperfection and corruption of his knowledge of his personal vocation. His calling does not cease continually to take place afresh. That he may know Him is the high privilege of the Christian. And to take himself

seriously as such, and therefore as this privileged person, he is directed in his knowledge constantly to put himself where non-Christians are in their ignorance, clinging not only to his Jesus Christ but to the Jesus Christ whose work has taken place for all and whose Word is addressed to all, by whose call all are ordained to be called instead of uncalled, and therefore, whether it is heard or not, the situation of every man is altered. It is in relation to Him that non-Christians and Christians, for all their differences, are what they are, namely, men who have their calling only before them on the one side, and men who have it both behind and before them on the other. If the latter, then, are truly and surely to know themselves as Christians, they are directed to hold fast to Him as the one Mediator between God and men (1 Tim. 2⁵), whose glory as such is also one, so that no matter what comes of it He calls all men, the multitude as well as his " disciples," to Himself : " Come unto me, all ye that labour and are heavy laden " (Mt. 11²⁸). The Christian cannot be grateful for anything greater than that he, too, may stand in the light of life with all the rest, because this is the light of the world and therefore his light too.

2. THE EVENT OF VOCATION

Vocation is a specific action of the living God in the time of man determined and controlled by the work and revelation of His grace. More precisely, it is the action of Jesus Christ who in His time lived and died as the Lord humbled to be a servant and the servant exalted to be Lord, but who is also risen again and therefore lives eternally and as the Contemporary of all men, active as a Prophet among them in His Word and by His Spirit. No matter where, when or how it occurs, vocation is thus the work of God or Jesus Christ towards man in time, itself a temporal work. That it is God or Jesus Christ who calls makes the vocation of man, no matter where or when or how it occurs, an act of powerful grace and gracious power different from every other act. But it is the action of Jesus Christ—and this is where the present emphasis must fall—as the Contemporary of all men, and therefore His action in time, itself a temporal event. It takes place in fulfilment of the eternal divine counsel of grace and therefore from above, from heaven. But it comes down into history and is itself history enacted here below on earth. And on earth it takes place originally in the history of Israel and Jesus Christ. It is foreordained and predisposed here. But on this basis, as the work of the risen Jesus Christ it also takes place in many other specific histories which are not identical with this but which in their place do at least occur in time.

There was a time in the more recent history of theology—and we cannot say with any assurance that it is now behind us—when the general tendency was to see what we have called the event of vocation in abstraction from its historical and especially its supra-historical presupposition, and in this isolation to make it the true object and theme of theology and the true content of the Christian message. This isolated event could hardly be termed vocation any more because the reference to the One who calls man became ever smaller and more equivocal. The " call " in question came increasingly to bear a desperate resemblance to the monologue of the Christian concerning his faith, or, as he might prefer to term it, his piety or religion. An individual and social Christianity sought more and more to take itself seriously as such, and finally to posit itself absolutely, becoming a self-grounded and self-motivating hypothesis. To-day we usually describe a theology which looks in this direction as anthropocentric (though christianocentric would be a more exact definition), and we rightly regard Schleiermacher as its classical exponent, though we must also point to its beginnings in the Pietism and Rationalism of the 18th century and even in the spiritual movements of the Reformation and the great mystics of the Middle Ages, and also to its unmistakeable development in the modern theological existentialism influenced by Kierkegaard. This transformation of theology into an abstract doctrine of the event of vocation was an intrinsically impossible enterprise, and a reaction against it was bound to come and has in fact come. With an open exegesis of the Bible, and a new attention to the concern of the Reformation and the early Church from which it sprang, there have been proclaimed afresh the great presuppositions of vocation without which it cannot be understood, namely, the objective elements of Christian knowledge and dogmatics such as the Trinity, predestination and Christology, which for centuries were more or less despised and thrust out on the margin of theological interest. We have had to learn anew that the Holy Spirit is the Lord and Master of the Christian spirit and not simply identical with it, and that the Word of God is His Word and therefore cannot be understood merely as the self-declaration of the Christian spirit. This was good for us, and since we all have so much of the isolated *pro me* and therefore of Christianocentrism in our minds and hearts, it is as well for us to learn much more along these lines, and indeed to say much more where we see that no attention has so far been paid to this development.

Yet we also need to-day to remember firmly again that the necessary reaction should not be carried so far that the historical and supra-historical presupposition of vocation is abstracted from this as its consequence and therefore made in isolation the object and theme of theology and the content of the Christian message. The object and theme of theology and the content of the Christian message is neither a subjective nor an objective element in isolation. That is to say, it is neither an isolated man nor an isolated God, but God and man in their divinely established and effected encounter, the dealings of God with the Christian and of the Christian with God. This means, however, that the vocation of man should not be divested of its concrete historicity nor transcendentalised. We do not speak of it correctly, nor of God as its acting Subject, if we speak of it docetically, as though it became and were real, true and certain only beyond the historical existence of man in time, as the work of God which is not also His work on man, and which merely touches man's existence as it were from without. We cannot be content merely with that foreordination and predisposition of man for his vocation, as though it were not necessary for his own vocation also to take place as an event in his own life. To do this is tantamount to thinking that the star which guided the wise men to Bethlehem finally shone upon an empty manger. In opposition to the previous error, we must not present the being and work and Word and Spirit of God as an hypothesis which, even if with great majesty and glory, simply hovers over the mind and heart and life of man like a radiant ball of glass or soap-bubble, but never leads to the result that something happens, that this *prae* is followed by a real *post*, that there is a Christian ordination and disposition of man's being in time. In the vocation of man we have to do with an event in man's temporal life which to faith, but to faith very really, may be known as such. This is something which must not be questioned in any circumstances or on even the best of pretexts : not even for the sake of a dictum like *finitum non capax infiniti*, or of an infinitely qualitative distinction between God and man, or of a mistaken Christocentrism ; nor for fear of the deep problems to which the event of vocation is everywhere exposed in its historical concreteness ; nor out of a rather tiresome concern lest the non-objective will be objectivised and the non-controllable brought under control if we take them with theological seriousness ; and certainly not for fear lest we be thus betrayed into too great proximity to, or even into the very midst of, the Mystics, Pietists and friends of the community life both old and new. However justifiable the concern or threatening the danger in this respect, it should not deter us from saying what has to be said from this standpoint, i.e., with reference to that which comes upon man from God. We inevitably misunderstand the transcendence of God, the eternal election of man in Jesus Christ, the work of reconciliation accomplished without man yet also for him and to him in Jesus Christ, and therefore the great and decisive prior history of the vocation of man, and the *sola fide*, if we refuse to let B follow A, and therefore, cost what it may, to understand and describe the vocation of man as a genuine, concrete, historical event in time.

It cannot be denied nor explained away that in all the stories of vocation in the Bible, from that of Abraham to that of Paul, while we certainly have to do with works of God or of Jesus Christ towards these men according to the import of the passages in question, yet because rather than in spite of this we are also dealing in the full sense with elements in their own individual histories and therefore in the history of the more near or distant world around them. As something highly particular, yet on the same level as the other events which befell them as men, it also came about in their case that the light of life did not merely shine upon but actually enlightened them, that God called them in such a way that they had to hear him and to the best of their ability obey. Upon them, and therefore at once upon the world around them, there came something which had in their lives antecedents and above all consequences which could later be recognised, by which their further course was incisively determined, and in the power of which, wittingly and willingly or otherwise, they exercised an incisive influence on the life of the world around. Abraham, when he was called, became the ancestor of Israel, Moses its first leader and teacher. The call of God makes heroes like Gideon, watchmen like Samuel, kings like David, prophets like Isaiah, Amos, Jeremiah and others, apostles like Paul, seers like John of Patmos—and all with the most far-reaching consequences. The eternity of the basis of their vocation does not alter the fact—but rather makes it unavoidable—that something comes to pass when it really becomes an event.

Similarly, for those who came to know and could speak of vocation in the sphere of the Church, it was a work of God which came vertically from above, yet which was also just as real horizontally in their creaturely existence, so that it was an event which determined afresh their own time and that of the surrounding world. Calvin was right when he relentlessly traced back *accessus ad Christum* to God's eternal election, to His Word as filled and borne and powerful through the witness of the Holy Spirit. But for this very reason he took it seriously as his own vocation and that of other Christians, and gave it prominence in definite acts not only in Geneva but in half Europe during the 16th century. Again, John Wesley could give not only the date but the very hour of his vocation, yet rightly he understood what happened in terms of the Lutheran doctrine of justification and therefore forensically and in terms of predestination. This did not mean, however, that he was forbidden but rather required to reorientate his life completely, to commence a new period of preaching and to enter a new way on which he had so revolutionary an external influence that without any exaggeration it has been possible to write a book entitled *England before and after Wesley*. On the other hand, H. F. Kohlbrügge was also right when, to the question when and where he was converted, he gave the very different answer from that of Wesley, if basically identical, that he was converted on Golgotha ; and in his case, too, it was apparent in the Wuppertal and other valleys during the 19th century that his conversion as it had taken place there and then was a supremely real and stimulating event, in the power of which he lived and thought and spoke so vigorously and effectively as the man he was, not only in himself, but among the men and Christians of his day.

Time does not remain empty but is filled, nor does history break off but new history begins, where and when and whenever vocation takes place. Time and history as a human form of life are not neutral, but controlled and determined by the work and revelation of the grace of God in Jesus Christ. All time is potentially the time of grace, and all history the history of salvation. Indeed, we must say that they are the sphere in which, as the Lord of all men and the One to whom they belong, Jesus Christ, the Mediator and Prophet of grace and salvation, is actually on the way to His goal, namely, to His victory in His conclusive self-declaration. They are thus fulfilled time and history primarily and supremely as they are His own time and history, and have their meaning in His *parousia* in the form of the promise of the Spirit. The vocation of man is the call of Jesus in the sphere of His time and history and on the way to His goal. It is His creative call which rings out as a *Fiat*, and as it does so there comes into being that which was not but was destined to be. When this call comes to man, man's time is fulfilled and a new history begins in his history—an actual time of grace and history of salvation. This history is not merely internal but external ; it is not merely spiritual but moral, social and political ; it is not merely invisible but also visible. And in the world around him, even though its newness and particularity may not be understood but misunderstood without faith, and even though it may not be noticed, this history will at least call for notice, and, whether understood and noticed or not, it will certainly not be without relevance and significance for the history of this world around and for human history generally. It will thus be a history which itself makes history. It will not be outside space and time. It will certainly take place in the spiritual sphere, yet not in this alone. At specific points and under specific determinations and circumstances, in virtue of its origin in eternal life, it will also be a part of the corresponding though not identical earthly life, both psychical and physical. As the called or Christians may thus live this part of earthly life among others, not of themselves but by God's eternal election of grace, by the actively known grace of reconciliation and the covenant, by the power of the Word and Spirit of the living Jesus Christ, it is completely ruled out that they either should or could flee from time and history and live properly and essentially in a non-spatial and timeless beyond. In his this-worldly time and history among all other men, the Christian lives properly and essentially as one who is called. Thus any attempt to transcendentalise the vocation of man and his existence as one who is called, and therefore to understand and describe them docetically, is made impossible from the very outset.

To appreciate as such the process which takes place in this event, we must first lay down that what we have is, of course, decisively and predominantly a spiritual process which can be perceived, understood and described only in spiritual terms. This statement does not conflict with the one which we have just made, namely, that it is temporal and historical. When we say spiritual, we are not using it in the common sense which might imply the relegation of its reality to a supra-temporal and supra-historical sphere, and therefore a transcendentalising. We are using it in the New Testament sense of pneumatic, with its implication of the supreme concretion of a temporal and historical process. The process of vocation is spiritual in the sense in which it was described by Luther : " The Holy Ghost has called me through the Gospel, enlightened me by His gifts, and sanctified and preserved me in the true faith." But the Holy Ghost who does this in time and history is not an anonymous magnitude and force using the Gospel to accomplish it. As the Spirit of the Father and the Son He is the power of the Gospel itself to call and enlighten and sanctify and preserve man in the true faith. That is to say, He is the power of the One who, as the Son sent by and glorifying the Father, is not only the theme and content but also the origin, and in His person the Author, of the Gospel. He gives the Spirit who calls and enlightens and sanctifies and preserves. That is to say, as the Author of the Gospel He speaks His Word in Him with the truth and clarity and invincibility of the very Word of God. He makes it His self-witness, though not at the expense of its character as a human witness to His person and work. And as He attests Himself through the Gospel, the work of the Holy Spirit is done. His *parousia*, His personal presence and action, is the meaning, goal and substance of this work of the Spirit. He is the acting Subject of the process which we describe as vocation. It is in this sense that we call it a spiritual process. It is distinguished as such from other corporal or " spiritual," outward or inward processes which, even though we insist that God is always supremely and primarily the Subject at work, can and must be attributed directly and immediately to other and especially human subjects. Scientific discovery, artistic intuition and creation, political revolution, moral reorientation and rearmament are not spiritual processes in the sense intended, for, although we may see and understand them as lights which illumine the cosmos as such in reflection of the one light, they cannot be described immediately and directly as self-attestations of Jesus Christ. Even though as secondary lights they are genuine and authentic, and may be recognised as such, they presuppose His self-attestation as the original and true light. The vocation of man, however, is always a spiritual process, because in it there can be no question of any other subject than the living Jesus Christ acting immediately and directly in the power of His Word and by the Holy Spirit. It is for this reason that we can see and understand them only spiritually, i.e., with eyes and understanding to which this Subject, the self-attestation of Jesus Christ, and in it His spiritual work, are not alien but known after their true manner and reality. According to 1 Cor. 2$^{13f.}$, vocation as a pneumatic reality can be known only by men who are themselves pneumatic, whereas carnal men, who are blind and deaf in this dimension, do not even perceive its outline, let alone understand and interpret it, even though it takes place concretely among them in time and history. After this manner and reality which are spiritual both ontically and noetically, the vocation of man consists decisively in the fact that the living Jesus Christ encounters definite men at definite times in their lives as their Contemporary, makes Himself known to them as the One He is, i.e., as the One He is for the world, for all men, and therefore for them too, and addresses and claims them as partners in His covenant and sinners justified and sanctified in Him. He does this in the witness of the prophets and apostles. But in this witness it is He, Jesus Christ, who does it, so that these men may say with the Samaritans : " Now we believe, not because of thy saying : for we have heard him ourselves, and know that this is indeed the Christ, the Saviour of the world " (Jn. 4^{42}). The historical process of vocation is thus highly extraordinary and yet also supremely simple. It is a temporal and historical event among others, and yet it is distinguished by this manner and content.

If there is one element which we must not leave out of our description of the process, it is the objectively personal. In other words, we must maintain at all costs that the living Jesus Christ is the Subject acting in it here and now in the allotted time of the lives of specific men.

This element receded into the background in the presentation given by the older dogmatics under the title *De vocatione*. The result was that their statement became noticeably abstract and remote, and therefore not just hard to see but no less hard to understand and believe. Similarly, later and even modern descriptions of the process lack perspicuity to the extent that for varying reasons the authors concerned fail to bring out the constitutive role and significance of Jesus Christ, and instead speak more or less abstractly of the structure of the experience of the man who is called.

To be realistic at this point, we must speak quite concretely and unequivocally of Jesus Christ Himself. We do better to speak of Him in a childlike or even " mythological " way than not at all or in such sort that we give rise to the impression that mention of Him might just as well be omitted, because it serves only to indicate the objective historical reference and character, and therefore the power and profundity, of the subjective experience. If we are to speak with true relevance and clarity in this matter, we have not only to mention Jesus Christ but to name Him as the One whose sovereign action alone gives to the subjective experience the power and profundity which otherwise it could not have. It is crucial that the Holy Spirit should not in any sense be understood as a relatively or absolutely independent and independently operative force intervening between Jesus Christ and the man who is called by Him, but as His Spirit, as the power of His presence, work and Word, as the shining of the life of which He is the fulness. Only then can we speak of the real strength of the process of vocation as such. And only then, as we shall see, shall we be led directly to the materially decisive thing which is the meaning and purpose of this process.

We are safest at this point to keep to the line laid down in the New Testament. The first thing to strike us here is the remarkable fact that there is no New Testament evidence for the fine saying of Luther that it is the Holy Ghost who calls man. This does not mean that the saying is not true and valid. The presence and action of the Holy Spirit are the *parousia* of Jesus Christ in the time between Easter and His final revelation. But we certainly ought to learn from this fact that in this context the Holy Spirit is not spoken of in such a way that Jesus Christ is obscured or even completely concealed as the Subject who acts in Him and through Him and therefore truly calls.

Where the New Testament speaks generally of κλῆσις as the historical beginning of the Christian state, in obvious agreement with the Old it calls God Himself the great καλῶν. It does this explicitly in 1 Thess. 2¹² and 4⁷, 1 Cor. 1⁹ and 7¹⁵ and Heb. 5⁴, and implicitly in a much larger group of sayings. Yet this does not prevent Christians from being described as the called of the *Kyrios* or of Jesus Christ, as in 1 Cor. 7¹⁷ and Rom. 1⁶. And it is significant for our present purpose that whenever the process of vocation is described as such, especially in the stories of the calling of the disciples in the Gospels and of Paul in Acts, there is no question of an action of God the Father in which He in some sense by-passes or overlooks Jesus and deals with the person called simply as God. Nor is there any question of a corresponding action of the Holy Spirit, just as for good reasons there is no question of a vocation of Jesus Himself, since the Word obviously does not stand in any need of a prior Word of calling. On the contrary, when vocation is recounted as a history, Jesus Christ is quite plainly the One who calls. If, in those passages which speak more generally of calling, God as well as Jesus Christ is described as the One who calls, this is not, of course, an indication that the New Testament knows two kinds of vocation, the one effected by God the Father, the other by Jesus Christ, and possibly a third by the Holy Spirit. It rather corresponds to, and is even interconnected with, the fact that in the New Testament there are also two ways of speaking of the Easter event. On the one side, it is His raising up by God the Father, and on the other it is His own resurrection, and a third possibility may perhaps be seen in Rom. 1⁴ with its reference to the power of the Holy Spirit operative in this event. In both cases the statements are complementary. To the question of the concrete form in which God calls, the only answer is obviously that it is Jesus who does it in all the concreteness of His humanity. And to the question how He does it, the only answer is obviously that in what this man does God is at work in His eternal mercy and omnipotence. The New Testament does not see two or three different things here, but only one thing. And if by calling we do not wish to understand anything different from what the New Testament describes as such, our only option is also to see one thing, or rather one person, i.e., Jesus Christ, the true Son of God and of Man, alive because risen from the dead in the power of the One who raised Him from the dead, needing no calling but Himself issuing His incomparable call. What else can we do but hear and understand His call as the call of God, and the call of God as His call ?

No particular skill is needed to develop this insight if we take seriously what Jesus Christ is and what He is not. He is not a figure of the remote past, concerning whose life, acts, opinions, death and resurrection we have all kinds of reports, but from whom we are separate in our own time apart from the recollection which they make possible but not actually necessary, so that while our vocation may have a certain similarity to that of Peter or Paul it cannot be His act in any true or literal sense. On the contrary, He lives. Nor does He live only at the right hand of the Father in heaven. In his *parousia* in the form of the Holy Spirit, as the One He is there He is also on earth among us as the Contemporary of man in every age. He lives, acts and speaks as this Contemporary in a way which is different from all our other contemporaries, yet no less really than they, indeed, infinitely more really on a true understanding. And when a man is called by God to an active recognition of His grace, this Word of God is His Word, and as such concretely different from any mere feeling with which a man might regard himself as called to this or that particular action. This is a spiritual process, i.e., one in which He immediately and directly speaks to man and acts on Him through His Word. Is this really more difficult to represent and conceive than a process of calling in the description of which the question of the One who calls must be left open or can be answered only by such general terms as " God " or " Spirit " with all their possible connotations ? In the latter case, do we not finally have to look into the void, or to the man who is supposedly called, to the power and profundity of his experience ? Is there not needed a good deal of mythology, and much naivety, to understand and take seriously the vocation of man without the concrete person of Jesus Christ who as the Son of God calls him by the Holy Spirit ? In these circumstances shall we not be inclined and tempted to regard vocation as something which we can control ?

In these circumstances can we say with Paul that the God by whom we are called is faithful (1 Cor. 1[9], 1 Thess. 5[24]), and this in the sense of 2 Tim. 2[13] : " If we believe not, yet he abideth faithful : he cannot deny himself " ? In these circumstances, thrown back on the power and profundity of our own experience, can we really know what this means ? But if in the process of vocation we have to do concretely and decisively with Jesus Christ, and therefore with God and the Holy Spirit, as the One who calls man, then and then alone we know what it means, and we are joyfully relieved of the burden of being able to control our own calling.

Turning now to the process of vocation as such, our first and very concrete question concerns that which happens to man in this process, namely, the general nature of the alteration effected when it takes place

2. *The Event of Vocation* 505

not only that Jesus Christ died and rose again for him, and not only that He is present as the living One, but that He meets him in the way, i.e., in the way of his own personal being in time, as the One He is, and addresses him in the power of His Spirit in such sort that His Word strikes right home to him like lightning striking and splitting a tree, or more gently like a seed falling into the earth and there relentlessly perishing. What really happens in this encounter ? Our whole section is an answer to this question. Our present and primary concern is with the basic form of the process which involves this alteration, i.e., the form which determines and characterises the whole.

We must interject that just as surely as the one Jesus Christ is the active and effective Subject in this event, so the vocation of man is a single and total occurence in relation to him. We have emphatically described it as a temporal and historical process. This might suggest that from the human standpoint it might be divided into a series of successive events in which each is supplemented and transcended by the next. We should then have a kind of ladder, a psychological genetics of the Christian state, and vocation as the first and lowest rung would bring us to the initial point of its genesis.

Understanding the matter in this light, the later representatives of Protestant orthodoxy and the later theoreticians of Pietism, the Awakening and the modern community movement are of the opinion that there is here an *ordo salutis*, i.e., a logically and temporally differentiated series of acts in the history of salvation enacted in and on a man, or a way of salvation to be taken in a succession of ever deeper and broader and more powerful experiences. According to D. Hollaz (*Ex. theol. acroam.*, 1707, III, *sect.* 1, *c.* 4, *qu.* 3) the following stages may be distinguished in this progression of the work of the *gratia Spiritus sancti applicatrix* : (1) calling to the Church ; (2) illumination ; (3) conversion ; (4) regeneration ; (5) justification ; (6) mystical union with the triune God ; (7) renewal or sanctification ; (8) confirmation and preservation in faith and holiness ; and (9) eschatological translation into a state of eternal glory. Hollaz believed that he found all these stages in this enumeration and sequence in the saying of the Lord to Saul in Ac. 26[17f.]. But in the choice and arrangement of the stages a different procedure might obviously be followed. Points (2) illumination and (6) mystical union, which were introduced into the schema to meet contemporary enthusiasts, might be dropped. Awakening might be introduced as a special link between calling and illumination. In greater fidelity to the thinking of the Reformation, regeneration might be put before conversion instead of after. In accordance with certain tendencies in the more recent theology of the communities, a special sealing by the Holy Spirit might be asserted before confirmation and preservation or in place of it according to 2 Cor. 1[22], Eph. 1[13] and 4[30]. Such concepts as penitence, faith and works might also be introduced at suitable places. But these are only examples. The number of variations in the selection and co-ordination of all these concepts (cf. the article on " Heilsordnung " by R. Seeberg in *PRE*[3], 7, 598 f.) is almost as great as the number of the theologians who with varying degrees of originality, profundity and taste have been occupied with this matter since the end of the 17th century. Nor have there been lacking among them those who have incidentally noted that the order followed is to be understood logically rather than temporally. But how is a caveat like this to apply in practice ? If it is desired to indicate the specific stages as such and to interconnect them in their particularity, the only practical option is to present them as the different stages of a temporal process. And the essential interest in this matter has always been to outline the development of the natural man into a Christian, and the Christian into an increasingly perfect Christian, in a way which can be mastered and recounted.

The enterprise is not really a new one. John Bunyan in his *Pilgrim's Progress* (1675) was an immediate and most influential pioneer. And do we not find tendencies in the same direction in the mystical ladder of the Middle Ages (purification, enlightenment and union), which was of course so strongly combatted in substance by our orthodox Protestant fathers ? Might it not even be that Luther's schema of Law and Gospel as explained by Melanchthon in the *Loci* of 1521, and in large measure by Luther himself, gives us at least a pointer, and in practice much more than a pointer, in the same direction ? Do we not find at least the suggestion of a similar conception in the arrangement of the third book of Calvin's *Institutio* ? It would be difficult to maintain and prove these points, but they cannot be rejected out of hand. The problem of a genuinely temporal and historical understanding of the process of becoming a Christian has always confronted theology, and still confronts us to-day. It is tempting for the pragmatic thinking of modern Christianity to solve it according to the pattern of the many orders of salvation suggested since the middle of the 17th century. Yet it is obvious that even before this there were not lacking attempts in the same direction, though perhaps less conscious and consistent than in the later period. Nor need we be surprised that the Reformers themselves have largely been understood, and can be understood, in this sense.

We are well advised, however, not to embark on this venture. If we can and should do justice to the temporal and historical character of the process in question, we can do this the better by respecting its truly spiritual character and not attempting a psychological and biographical description of the evolution of the Christian. Does not even the divergent multiplicity of such attempts give us cause to doubt whether the process is rightly perceived when understood as such an evolution ? Does it not suggest that it is reinterpreted to make it more readily perceptible and manageable in practice, but at the expense of its truly spiritual character ? And is not this awkward diversity of a piece with the fact that the Bible does not offer any such schema, that the biblical witnesses were not interested in the process as a psychological and biographical evolution, that in this respect, important though it no doubt was, they had nothing to say, and that we have thus to press and extend intolerably the concepts used by them to work them up into such a scheme ? Indeed, the situation is worse than that. For the concepts are inevitably weakened and devalued when they are wrested as is done in attempts of this nature.

To revert to the example of the scheme proposed by Hollaz, what are we to think of his reduction of the κλῆσις of the New Testament to a mere *vocatio ad ecclesiam* ? Again, how can there be an illumination—the meaning of φωτισμός in the New Testament should be recalled—which is not conversion because it applies only to the intellect whereas conversion involves the will ? Again, what is conversion (μετάνοια) if it is not also the regeneration which is supposed to follow it ? And what are we to make of a justification and sanctification which have calling, illumination, conversion, faith etc. as their presupposition rather than themselves being the presupposition as already accomplished in Jesus

Christ ? What would Paul have thought of this ? Surely the Reformers must have turned over in their graves. Again, what is this mysterious special experience of a *unio mystica cum Deo triuno* which is interposed between justification and sanctification and in spite of which there is still needed a special *confirmatio* ? Can any one of the concepts really bear the meaning which it has in the New Testament when it is thus impressed into a system, and made no more than one link in a chain, one part of the answer to a question utterly alien to the New Testament, namely, that of a psychology of the way of salvation ?

The very question answered by this whole attempt implies an attack on the substance of a genuine understanding of the process of vocation. For it directs our attention away from that which in this process is done on and in man by God, by Jesus Christ and by the Holy Spirit. It turns it abstractly to the reflection of this act of God and Christ in man, to his Christian experiences and states. It does not make the concepts more precise descriptions of the one action of Jesus Christ embracing the whole history of man. Projected on this level, it is only natural in view of the sinful nature and disposition of man and the Christian that the New Testament concepts should be devalued as thus abstracted and isolated. It is only natural that they should be adopted only in relation to those which precede and follow. It is only natural that they should have to be understood as individual moments in a human evolution. It is only natural that the totality of this evolution should have to be understood as a kind of heavenly ladder consisting of such acts, none of which, in view of its particularity and its need to be completed and transcended, can permit man to be quietly confident of the Lord who calls him and of the salvation thus proffered to him as to all men, and therefore to be joyful. When we are guilty of this abstraction, and project the concepts on this level, we have already turned away from the Lord and His salvation in its unity and totality, and the only remaining comfort and admonition is the thought that these are at least stages on a way at the end of which man is sure to reach his eschatological goal and thus will finally be at rest. The relevant and important thing is no longer God's active dealing with man, but in isolation and independence the active dealing of man with God. What place is left in this picture for the truly spiritual nature of the process of vocation ? We can find no answer to this question, and therefore we must tread a very different path in our understanding of this process.

To say vocation is to speak of the one, total address to man of the living Jesus Christ, and therefore not of a mere part, a mere beginning, but of what takes place in this address in its unity and totality. It is true enough that in human existence this is reflected only in the most diverse disruption, division, differentiation and relativisation. But if we are to see what is here theologically and practically real, important and relevant, it is essential that we should understand the process of vocation as the work of the Jesus Christ who in it acts towards man. Hence we must not be led astray by considering the very dubious ways in which it is reflected in human existence. As this work of Jesus Christ the process presents itself as a totality, as the one closed and completed work of God. Thus what befalls man in his vocation is not a partial work, nor a graded series of many different acts of grace, nor the setting up of a heavenly ladder, nor the variously described organisation of a progressive alteration of man. However it may be reflected in man's existence when seen as it were from below, this alteration is his total alteration. Alongside it the unfaithfulness, arrogance, negligence and insincerity, indeed, the whole sin of the Christian, is impossible, dreadful and damnable as thus qualified. But even the worst sin of the Christian cannot alter the totality of what befalls him in the process of his vocation. He should charge his sin to his own account instead of enhancing it by thinking of his vocation, not as a perfect whole, but as something which is still being fashioned, so that its fragmentary nature explains, excuses and indeed underlies his own faults and failings.

What applies to the process of vocation as such, applies no less to each of the concepts which we may adopt to denote and describe what befalls man in this process. None of them has reference only to a part or stage of the process. In the New Testament sense which is alone adequate to the reality, each must be introduced and applied in such a way as to refer from a particular angle to the one totality of this temporal and historical but as such genuinely spiritual work of God.

This is true of the concept which, without any polemical intention, we, too, apply comprehensively to denote and describe this event in its primary form, namely, the concept of illumination (φωτισμός, *illuminatio*). In the light of all that has gone before, and on the basis of the New Testament, the choice of this concept can hardly seem to be capricious. Illumination means that the light of life carries through its work in a particular man to its conclusion. It shines on all men. But in the event of vocation it does not merely shine on a man. As established in the first sub-section, it does this prior to the event in the existence of Jesus Christ as his Contemporary, and even earlier in the eternal free election of the grace of God. The distinctive element in the event of his vocation, in which Jesus Christ in person meets him as a person and becomes a known and conscious element in his life-history, is that the light, Jesus Christ as the light of the world, illuminates this man. It does not now merely shine for him in general. It now shines for him in such a way that his closed eyes are opened by its shining, or rather his blind eyes are healed by its shining and made to see. This is the process of vocation. Man is called and becomes a Christian as he is illuminated. There is no question here of the flaring up of a light which has secretly been burning low in him already. We are confronted rather by the work of the wholly new and strange light of life shining on him wholly from without but now also lighting him within. This light imparts itself to him, making itself known in its newness, commending itself in its strangeness, becoming inward in its outwardness.

It is to the marvellous light of God that the Christian is called out of darkness (1 Pet. 2⁹). It is the light of the Resurrected which shines on him and in him as the life imparted to him. " Arise from the dead, and Christ shall give thee light," is the cry of Eph. 5¹⁴. He is " delivered " by God from the power of darkness, and " translated " (i.e., transferred from the sphere of its power) by God into the kingdom of the Son of His love (Col. 1¹³). With the once-for-allness with which Jesus Christ rose again from the dead, it comes about that the man called to be a Christian is given seeing eyes, and is turned, and has thus to turn himself, from darkness to light, from the power of Satan unto God (Ac. 26¹⁸). Christians are ἅπαξ φωτισθέντες, enlightened once and for all (Heb. 6⁴, cf. 10³²). This is their firm consolation and, of course, their immeasurable responsibility.

Illumination, however, is a seeing of which man was previously incapable but of which he is now capable. It is thus his advancement to knowledge. That the revelation of God shines on and in him, takes place in such a way that he hears, receives, understands, grasps and appropriates what is said to him in it, not with new and special organs, but with the same organs of apperception with which he knows other things, yet not in virtue of his own capacity to use them, but in virtue of the missing capacity which he is now given by God's revelation. " Jesus, give me sound and serviceable eyes ; touch Thou mine eyes." It is as He does this that they become serviceable and can be used for the function which is here ascribed to them, to which they are appointed and in which they are actually used. It is all a process which like others really implies knowledge in man. But it is all an original creation of the One who enables him to know.

" In thy light shall we see light " (Ps. 36⁹)—the saying which A. E. Biedermann caused to be engraved on his tombstone. There is a god of this world—we are reminded of the darkness in Col. 1¹³—who has darkened the thinking (νοήματα) of unbelievers " lest the light of the glorious gospel of Christ, who is the image of God, should shine unto them " (2 Cor. 4⁴). To continue the quotation already adduced : " For it is the worst evil that can befall us not to see the light." But the true " God, who commanded the light to shine out of darkness (Gen. 1³), hath shined in our hearts, to give the light of the knowledge (πρὸς φωτισμὸν τῆς γνώσεως) of the glory of God in the face of Jesus Christ " (2 Cor. 4⁶). As His God, " the God of our Lord Jesus Christ," He gives him " the spirit of wisdom and revelation " in which he may know him, " the eyes of your understanding being enlightened ; that ye may know what is the hope of his calling, and what the riches of the glory of his inheritance in the saints, and what is the exceeding greatness of his power to us-ward who believe," in short, what is proffered to man and awaits him in Him (Eph. 1¹⁷ᶠ·), and what is the structure (οἰκονομία) of the mystery concealed from all eternity in God the Creator of all things (Eph. 3⁹). Man is called as this knowledge (γνῶσις) is imparted to him. By this knowledge Christians are distinguished as the called from others who are not called.

If we are to understand this process, however, we cannot pay too much attention to the fact that in it we really have to do with a new creation. According to the speech and thought-forms of the Bible, concepts such as light, illumination, revelation and knowledge do not have, either alone or in their interrelationships, the more narrowly intellectual or noetic significance which here as elsewhere we usually give them. The light or revelation of God is not just a declaration and interpretation of His being and action, His judgment and grace, His endowing, directing, promising and commanding presence and action. In making Himself known, God acts on the whole man. Hence the knowledge of God given to man through his illumination is no mere apprehension and understanding of God's being and action, nor as such a kind of intuitive contemplation. It is the claiming not only of his thinking but also of his willing and work, of the whole man, for God. It is his refashioning to be a theatre, witness and instrument of His acts. Its subject and content, which is also its origin, makes it an active knowledge, in which there are affirmation and negation, volition and decision, action and inaction, and in which man leaves certain old courses and enters and pursues new ones. As the work of God becomes clear to him, its reflection lights up his own heart and self and whole existence through the One whom he may know on the basis of His own self-declaration. Illumination and therefore vocation is the total alteration of the one whom it befalls.

The light seen by seeing eyes becomes the light of the body, of the person of a man, in the shining of which it becomes wholly clear (Lk. 11³⁴ᶠ·) and is set wholly under the judgment and grace, the promise and command, of the One who calls him. The light thus bears " fruit " (Eph. 5⁹). There is an " armour " of light which those whom it lightens must immediately put on (Rom. 13¹²). Far from being a mere spectator of the light, man becomes and the Christian is a " child of light " (Jn. 12³⁶, 1 Thess. 5⁵, Lk. 16⁸), or " light in the Lord " (Eph. 5⁸). He is thus separated from darkness (Jn. 8¹², 12⁴⁶). For there is no darkness in God, the original light (1 Jn. 1⁵, Jas. 1¹⁷). Light and darkness, righteousness and lawlessness, are mutually exclusive (2 Cor. 6¹⁴). In the discipleship of Jesus Christ, the divine light shining in the world, it is self-evident that there should be this separation. As evil has its basis in the fact that man hates the light and will not come to it (Jn. 3²⁰), so the called and therefore the illuminated express and prove themselves to be such by the fact that the " works of darkness," to the extent that they are still implicated in them, are penally exposed by the light and cannot stand before it (Eph. 5¹¹ᶠ·). Their fellowship with God, who is light and not darkness, will be revealed in their fellowship with one another. They will be subjected to a purification of all their sins by the life of Jesus Christ offered up for them (1 Jn. 1⁷). But above all they will be noticeable to others outside, shining for them and usable towards them in the service of divine vocation as " children of God . . . in the midst of a crooked and perverse nation, among whom ye shine as lights (φωστῆρες) of the world " (Phil. 2¹⁵), proclaiming the ἀρεταί, the *magnalia*, the mighty acts of the One " who hath called you out of darkness into his marvellous light " (1 Pet. 2⁹). Their light should so shine before men, according to Mt. 5¹⁶, " that they may see your good works, and glorify your Father which is in heaven," i.e., that it will be manifest " that they are wrought in God " (Jn. 3²¹). According to the saying in Mt. 5¹⁴, which is truly awe-inspiring in view of Jesus' description of Himself in Jn. 8¹² and 12⁴⁶, they are " the light of the world " (τὸ φῶς τοῦ κόσμου).

When we bring these various points together, we can hardly fail to see that in the vocation of man, even when the process is considered in its formal character as illumination, we are not in any sense dealing with a mere part or beginning in which he becomes a Christian. For what is lacking here when we see it as God's action towards man, as that which comes on man from God ? Is not his illumination, and therefore the revelation of God which underlies his knowledge, and the knowledge established by this revelation, the one totality of his temporal and historical experience of the living Jesus Christ ? There is no doubt that in time, so far as it is his time, and history, so far as it is his history, this can take the most diverse and widely separated forms. But there is no differentiation or particularity of truly Christian experience in which we are not dealing with the one totality of the vocation of man in his encounter with the living Jesus Christ. Hence there is nothing other or higher or better, e.g., under the title of regeneration or conversion, which has still to follow vocation, which has to deepen and complete it, if it is to be true, effective and valid. There are other angles from which we have to view the one totality of this occurrence if we are to estimate and consider it aright. For the moment we ask formally concerning that which precedes. And we give a full answer to this question when we describe this occurrence in all its possible and actual modifications as the illumination which comes to man from God, which man needs with the same totality at every conceivable turn in the path if he is to be and remain a Christian, but in which he may participate with equal totality. Whether in the divine act or the human experience which makes a man a Christian, there can never be any question of anything more or less or other than his illumination, than the revelation of God which underlies his knowledge and the knowledge established by this revelation. We are guilty of a hopeless cleavage from the speech and thought-forms of the Bible if we try to deny that in the illumination of man there takes place the totality of what makes a man a Christian.

In the same sense, in our description of the process, we should set alongside the concept of illumination that of awakening, not putting it either above or below the other but side by side with it in order to gain a deeper view.

Under the influence of Pietism and Methodism this has become an important term in the Christian vocabulary. Yet it is not so compelling a New Testament word as illumination. To be precise there are only two passages which are expressly dominated by it (Rom. 13[11] and Eph. 5[14]), and even in these it appears only in the closest connexion with illumination, from which we cannot separate it materially if we are really to describe the vocation of man.

It has, however, three advantages which suggest that it may be rightly and legitimately adopted. First, awakening places that which befalls man in his vocation and therefore his illumination expressly in proximity and analogy to what befell Jesus Christ in His resurrection. In this, what man may experience as God's revelation and his knowledge of it has its model and power. It is in view of this that Jesus Christ encounters him as the One who lives eternally, speaks with him as his Contemporary, and in calling him, Himself risen from the dead, causes him to share in a new life, his life in and with that of the risen Lord. Secondly, it describes the Word which calls man, not as a mere impartation, but expressly as a call and summons which overtakes him, similar to the Word with which Jesus raised Jairus' daughter from her bed and caused Lazarus to come forth from the grave. It underlines once again that in the illumination of man we have an act of dynamic command from the standpoint of God's revelation and of equally dynamic obedience from the standpoint of man's knowledge. " Awake thou that sleepest, and arise from the dead " (Eph. 5^{14}). Thirdly, it is instructive because the reference in both the New Testament passages which mention it is not to Jews or Gentiles or children of the world, but quite unmistakeably to Christians and therefore to those who are already called but who obviously, not to the detriment but rather on the basis of that ἅπαξ, both need and are granted a new and further calling ; just as elsewhere in the New Testament Christians are continually addressed as people who are indeed awakened, roused and awake, but in such a way that they, too, are not prevented from falling asleep again, like even the wise as well as the foolish virgins who slept according to Mt. 25^5, and thus stand in constant need of, and are constantly granted, a new call to awaken. This is the extent to which the vocation of man is concerned with the establishment of the totality and not merely of a part or beginning of Christian existence. What makes a man a Christian is that the One who has wakened him once is not content with this, but as the faithful One He is (1 Thess. 5^{24}) wakens him again and again, and always with the same power and severity and goodness as the first time. What makes him a Christian is that he has a Lord who to his salvation will not leave him in peace but constantly summons him to wake up again.

As a description of the process of vocation, the term awakening cannot add materially to what is already said by illumination. As God's act to man, and man's experience of this act, it implies that there is opened up to him what was previously hidden when he was asleep and in the world of dreams. He sees what he did not previously see as a blind man, hears what he previously could not hear as a deaf man and understands and grasps what he previously could not understand and grasp because it was present to him only outwardly and not inwardly. He knows what previously, as the sleeping and dreaming fool he was, he could not know. When he awakens, life is opened up to him. He discovers it. And this life is the true life, the life created by the reconciling, justifying and sanctifying act of God, and this life given to him and therefore his own. Christ gives him light (Eph. 5^{14}), letting him know that he belongs to His day, and therefore not to the night and its darkness (1 Thess. 5^5). Behind him is his existence in a situation which was real and possible only in its perversion and could have validity and substance for him only in virtue of his ignorance. Before him is his existence in the situation which has now become for him as he knows it the only real and possible one. Awakening is the turning of many from that false situation to his true situation as effected through revelation and in the knowledge of Jesus Christ. To this extent it is nothing other than his illumination. The awakening of man in a serious sense is distinguished from anything else in the political, moral or even religious sphere which might be given this name without really deserving it, by the fact that what takes place in it is illumination, that in its innermost core and essence it is indeed nothing other than illumination, the enlightenment of the whole man by the Gospel which is the Gospel of Jesus Christ, the revelation and knowledge in the realisation of which man begins and also continues to become and to be a Christian.

We should not fail to note, however, that the concept of awakening gives to that of illumination a particularly strong accent and emphasis which it needs if it is fully to describe the process of vocation. Awakening contrasts explicitly two situations or states of man, the passing and the coming, the false and the true, his sleep and his wakening and wakefulness, his existence as determined by eyes and ears which are closed and his existence as determined by eyes and ears which are open. Awakening describes the Gospel which enlightens man as the power of God (Rom. 1[16]) in which there takes place the turning or transition of man from the one to the other. It describes the revelation which is imparted to him as effective, and the knowledge established by it as active. Awakening thus underlines again something which cannot be underlined too strongly, namely, the dynamic character of illumination and vocation as the process in which man becomes a Christian.

It is obvious that this is what caused not only the older Pietism and Methodism but also many later movements of revival to seize on the term awakening to indicate what they had in view. Rightly or wrongly, and to a very large extent rightly, they felt that they should confront and oppose a Christianity which had become static and had thus fallen fast asleep in its doctrine and its whole cultic, moral and social conduct, in the attitude of which they thus found it difficult to discern either an effective revelation or an active knowledge, in which the Gospel seemed to them to have no power of God to turn and transform, and in which the illumination of which it boasted seemed to bear no " fruit " (Eph. 5[9]). As against this, the awakened enthusiasts of every age have understood the Christianity for which they contend and which they seek to proclaim and extend as something dynamic, as a Christian thinking, speech and action which awakens out of sleep, which is itself already awake, which constantly begins again at the beginning and thus renews itself with the new hearing of a new call of its Lord. As they saw it, the churches, and Christians within them, were claiming a vocation which begins at baptism without the participation of the baptised and is thus quiescent and final, apparently failing to see the inner impossibility of this whole procedure or to fear the secularisation of Christian existence to which it unavoidably gave rise with its cessation of real activity. In place of this, they emphasised the event of divine and human vocation. In other words, they emphasised the fact that illumination is effective revelation and active knowledge, and therefore an illumination which bears fruit in the serious *praxis pietatis*.

The awakenings of which we might think were not always, and above all did not always remain, what they were meant to be and very largely were within their limits and in their own way. It was not merely that the dynamic of awakening did not always or usually last long enough, but generally passed quite quickly into a new state of slumber which made necessary new and often very different awakenings. More particularly, the dynamic of the newly experienced and proclaimed process of vocation often forced itself into the forefront as such even

C.D.—IV.–III.–II.—17

in the initial stages. In face of the static condition of popular Christianity, it could thus assume the form only of the power of generally religious and to that extent " secular " feelings, excitements and explosions, of particular experiences of the numinous in terms, e.g., of the majesty of God, the stringency of a moral commandment or fear of the judgment of God in death and hell. And in not a few cases it could even take the form quite simply of the magic fluid of specific personalities (evangelists, pastors, rulers of deaconesses etc.) and their influence, and occasionally their lust for power. In such cases there was little place for the call of the Lord, for dynamic illumination by the Gospel, or for awakening by His revelation and to His knowledge. The awakenings could become a ground of offence to both Christians and non-Christians, obscuring instead of enlightening, confusing instead of clarifying, leading away from the light of Jesus Christ instead of to it, and thus bringing new sickness to Christianity instead of restoring it to health.

Yet even in the worst cases we must not condemn or reject without asking the following question. Even in the most strange and perhaps bizarre of such awakenings, is there not concealed and borne, at least potentially, something of the genuine awakening, of the real illumination to " the knowledge of the glory of God in the face of Jesus Christ," by which we should be stimulated and reminded, and in which it is more important that we should participate than simply criticise because of the weak and confused way in which it is represented ? Even the most dreadful conceivable instances of enthusiastic extravagance surely do not alter the basic necessity of the concern which they undoubtedly proclaim and may impart in face of a Christianity, Church and theology continually overcome by slumber. What would have become of mediaeval Christendom with all its domes and altars and stained glass and scholasticism and *corpus christianum* so wonderfully represented in its spiritual and secular head, if Francis and his followers had not entered the scene and initiated such a movement with all its healthy and less healthy features ? What would have become of earlier and more recent Protestantism on the Continent and in England and Scotland, and what could it possibly be to-day, without the great and little stirrings and disruptions occasioned by dissenters and enthusiasts and sectarians of many different kinds ? It must not be forgotten that in respect of its positive substance the Reformation itself bore very clearly the marks of a revival in its early years, that Luther and Karlstadt were at first good friends, and that Calvin could talk of a *subita conversio*. Many things would have been very different and much better to-day if this forward-reaching motif had not been lost so quickly when the Reformers and their successors became afraid of their own rashness in the need to secure themselves and out of aversion to the so-called fanatics.

However that may be historically, there can be no doubt that in the calling of man by Christ to Christ, in the beginning of this calling and also its continuation, in its origin and also its renewal, we are dealing with the process which as his illumination is effective revelation and active knowledge, which is thus fruitful illumination, and which has thus to be described as awakening. How could it be the living Jesus Christ who makes Himself known to man in his vocation, if this were not his awakening and did not therefore include his awaking ?

Before turning in the next sub-section to the decisive question of the meaning and purpose of this occurrence, we must briefly consider some obvious problems in respect of its form. In so doing we may for once follow the guidance given by certain distinctions made at this point in the older dogmatics.

Within the concept of vocation a first distinction was seen between *vocatio immediata* and *vocatio mediata*. By the first was understood the summons issued directly to man, without human mediation, by

God, or by Jesus Christ through the Holy Spirit. This underlay the special ministry of witness entrusted to the prophets and apostles. The second was the vocation of all others who did and do participate in it as this takes place indirectly, mediated by the ministry of the prophets and apostles and later of other men. The possibility was not denied, of course, but even maintained *in thesi*, that in exceptional cases there might even be in the latter group an immediate calling in the course of direct dealings between God and man. This unusual exception is an indication, however, that there is a flaw in the whole conception. The intention in expressly making it was obviously to avoid setting a limit to the freedom of God for direct dealings with man. But it was asserted only as an exception. In the struggle against mystics, spirituals and enthusiasts which gave rise to the distinction, it was set as much as possible in the background and virtually excluded in practice. As against this, we do better to start with the fact that what is known as vocation in the New Testament is always and in all circumstances immediate vocation, i.e., the direct and personal work of God, of Jesus Christ, of the Holy Spirit. No men—not even the prophets and apostles—come into the picture in mediation of the call, nor are there any who are mediately called. The first to be called, the prophets and apostles, certainly have an indispensable task of mediation. But this task is simply that of witness. It is by this that the Lord who is normative for all proclaims and makes Himself known and displays Himself to others as the One who calls them too. Yet it is not their power which is at work. It is not their work. Even in Holy Scripture as such there is no inherent force. It is wholly and immediately His power and work if, attested by them, He now issues His call to others as once He did to them. The others are normatively taught and instructed concerning Him by them as the first to be called. To that extent they are bound to their witness as the criterion, though not the source, of their own knowledge. But not even mediately are they called by them. They are called immediately by Him, by God, by Jesus Christ, by the Holy Spirit. And if this has to be said in relation to the prophets and apostles as the first to be called, it applies self-evidently to all the secondary witnesses of Jesus Christ who follow them, whether we think of His community as such or of the bearers of special offices of ministry within it. There is neither an office nor an office-bearer in the Church who can even represent the one Lord who is the living Word of God, and issue a vicarious call. If we are to understand the event of vocation, it is essential that He should be understood immediately, directly and exclusively as the One who calls, and that all that can and should be accomplished in this regard by the prophetic and apostolic Scriptures, the Church and those active within it as *Verbi divini ministri* should be seen to consist in confessing Him—and in this sense themselves (2 Cor. 4[5])—as the One with whom man has to do in this event, with whom he has perhaps had to do already, and with whom he will certainly have to do in the future. The less they themselves call ; the more definitely they seek to confess and attest Him as the One who calls, the greater is the honour which accrues to them in this matter.

The second relevant distinction in the older dogmatics is related to, yet not identical with, the first. It is the distinction between a *vocatio externa* and a *vocatio interna*, the former through preaching and the sacraments and the latter through the Holy Spirit. It is not always or necessarily that the two go together, according to the older view. There may be a purely outward and ineffective vocation. But it is also maintained, with the same respect for the freedom of God and the same prudence in relation to the arbitrariness of man, that there may be a vocation which takes place only inwardly, without the mediation of preaching or the sacraments, and yet effectively to salvation, though this must always be regarded as an unusual, extraordinary instance which escapes our perception. Here again we are ill-advised to follow our forefathers. To be sure, we can and should distinguish within the one work of God an external and an internal element. But whether with or without preaching and the sacraments, it is Jesus Christ Himself who very " externally " and in all His strangeness and novelty approaches man to call him to Himself. And it is very " internally," existentially and totally man himself who through the Holy Spirit, i.e., through the power of what Jesus Christ says to him, becomes another man, called instead of uncalled. We have to distinguish these two elements, but how can we possibly separate them in such a way as to be able to speak of a purely outward calling which is not also inward and is therefore ineffective ? Is not a *vocatio inefficax* a contradiction in terms in the light of what is described as vocation in the New Testament ? Again, how can we possibly assert that the exceptional case is one of purely inward calling effected only through the Holy Spirit ? On what obscure presuppositions can the inner work of the Holy Spirit be anything other than the mighty fulfilment of that which befalls man, whether with or without preaching and the sacraments, through the Word which comes on him from without as he is confronted from without by the Lord ? There is a *particula veri* in this second distinction, namely, its indication of that which concerned us in an earlier connexion. Without being able to make any definite statements in this regard, we have certainly to reckon with the fact that the living Lord Jesus Christ who encounters and deals with man wholly from without is not bound to preaching and the sacraments in the work of His Holy Spirit seizing and altering man within, but may very well, *extra muros ecclesiae* and independently of the ministry of His community in the world and humanity reconciled to God in Him, know and tread the very different ways of very different possibilities of most effective calling. On the other hand, assuming that we are really dealing with

His calling, we certainly do not have to reckon with even an exceptional separation between His outward and inward work, and therefore with a purely outward and cultic and therefore ineffective calling on the one side and a purely inward and spiritual yet effective calling on the other.

The third distinction made by the older dogmatics is positively more instructive than the first two. It is the distinction between *vocatio unica* and *vocatio continua*. This is a distinction which could and can be made meaningfully so long as we distinguish but do not separate and therefore do not make the two into alternatives. On this assumption we can and should adopt it in the sense that the one event of vocation must be understood as once-for-all (*unica*) and yet also as a sequence of new and further callings subsequent to the once-for-all commencement. This is how we have consistently understood it in our previous deliberations. Hence we cannot and should not oppose those who insist that calling must be thought of as an event in the course of the life-history of man which takes place at a specific point and in a specific way. They should not ask of everyone an exact knowledge of the actual date, as is given to some and perhaps to not a few. And they should allow that in the impulsion to the crisis to which they or others are conscious of having been brought in these specific circumstances, they have only a beginning which must be continually followed by further developments. Granted these two conditions, however, those who stress the once-for-allness of this event are quite right. In the vocation, illumination and awakening of man we do not have a process which is in some sense immanent in the whole process of life as such and always accompanies it, just as in the incarnation of the Word, in the humiliation and exaltation of Jesus Christ, in His death and resurrection, we have, not a process which is immanent in world history and accompanies it like a thread of crimson, but a datable occurrence which determines and controls the whole from this date forwards. The theoreticians of the modern community movement have thus good cause to be on their guard against the reduction of vocation to the fact that the whole life of the Christian must be a continual penitence—to use the well-known phrase of Luther. Luther was quite right. But the baptism which inaugurates this life of the Christian was once, and is properly, the very expressive exponent of the very concrete turning in the life of man which in its singularity is expressly related to the singularity of the person and act of Jesus Christ, i.e., to His baptism, which like this is itself datable, and which means that he becomes a Christian and will continue to do so. It is the perverted ecclesiastical practice of administering a baptism in which the baptised supposedly becomes a Christian unwittingly and unwillingly that has obscured the consciousness of the once-for-allness of this beginning, replacing it by the comfortable notion that there is not needed any such beginning of Christian existence, but rather that we can become and be Christians in our sleep, as though we had no longer to awaken out of sleep. We must not allow infant baptism to induce in us this comfortable notion, nor conceal either from ourselves or others the fact that to go further in the Christian life as daily penitence this life must first begin as vocation, and has thus to be *vocatio unica* as well. If it is not, how can it be *vocatio continua*? Only when this is accepted, and therefore when an honest protest is made against the idea that there can be a sleeping Christianity and therefore a sleeping baptism, can we make and emphasise the other point which calls for notice in this connexion, namely, that even baptism properly administered in responsible consciousness cannot be more than the exponent of the turning in the life of the baptised which means his first fruitful encounter with Jesus Christ. That is, it cannot be the turning itself, or even the commencement of it. The specific time of this commencement does not have to be the matter of a specific day or experience. Without being any the less specific, it may extend over a shorter or longer period in the life-history of a man. It may be possible, but it is certainly not necessary, that he should later be able to give an account of the details and then of a decisive crisis in his "coming through" to the new life. What counts is simply that, irrespective of his awareness, partial awareness or complete unawareness of what has happened, he should live on the basis of the penetration once effected in his life, God Himself having once begun the "good work" (Phil. 1[6]) in him. What matters is supremely that this work, once begun, really begun in him, should go forward to its completion. He will never live on the basis of that penetration as though it were simply behind him and over and done with, but in such a way that it is always before him afresh. For the One who has called him, Jesus Christ, is and will be the same as He was. He is Omega as well as Alpha. He is the living One who calls again those whom He has called. And none of those whom He has called does not need and is not totally directed to be called, illuminated and awakened by Him again. None is not directed to the mercy of God which is new every morning. It would not be His vocation if it were only *vocatio unica*, only initial and once-for-all illumination and awakening, and not also *vocatio continua*. As no serious preaching of conversion can deny or even suppress, in the one event in the history of man it is a matter of the totality of his existence. Without detriment to the fact that repentance has begun once, and neither before nor after, it is indeed necessary that his life as a Christian life should consist in daily repentance.

So much, then, for what the older dogmaticians called the *modus vocationis* and tried to expound as such with varying degrees of success. And so much for the general event of vocation. But for the sake of gathering together what we have said thus far, and also of understanding what is at once to follow, it is perhaps as well that we should expressly recall the point from which we started, namely, that in relation both to the content and the form of the process thus described the event of vocation is established and determined by the Subject who acts in it. The living Lord Jesus Christ in the power of His Word and therefore in His Holy Spirit is the Subject who acts in this event.

It is not in view of what we Christians, or even the most excellent of Christians, have experienced, let alone felt as our vocation, but in view of the One who has honoured us with His vocation, that we venture, and must venture, to speak of this process with the distinction which we have accorded it, and must continue to do so. In itself this human process, which is so ambiguous, feeble and even perverted, has so much in common with other human processes, especially of a religious character, that we are continually tempted to understand it only as one such process, to regard its particularity as only relative, and thus to reject the idea that in the process in which a man becomes a Christian we have a radically distinct occurrence. There is only one compelling reason why we should not reject this idea but rather assert the doctrine of vocation as an integral article in the Christian faith which overcomes the world, even the religious world, and all that is in it. This is regard for the One who is present and at work to call. But this is a compelling reason. The One who calls the Christian is certainly in the world. But as the true Son of God and Man He also confronts it. He does not live and work only within it, but also on it and for it. And this gives to His whole work, and therefore to the event in which His call is issued to man, an absolute distinction as well as a relative particularity. To see Him is to see the absolute distinction given to a man when he becomes a Christian.

In its distinction as a spiritual process, however, we have understood the process as one which is temporal and historical and therefore real in the fullest possible sense. It is certainly illumination, and therefore the event of divine revelation and knowledge. Yet it is not restricted to a special sphere of the noetic which the being of man can confront neutrally and without being really affected. Rather, it is an event of revelation and knowledge by which the being of man is not only affected but seized and refashioned so that it becomes his new being. There is always a temptation to regard it otherwise, namely, as a purely intellectual and ideal illumination and enlightenment of man's being and not as a temporal and historical reality. Indeed, this temptation is finally irresistible if from the very first and continually the vocation of man is not seen and understood in the light of this decisive element, namely, Jesus Christ as the One who calls. In relation to Him it cannot be more than a temptation. For in Him we are not dealing with any light, but with the original and eternal light shining in the world, and therefore with the fulness of temporal and historical reality. Only if we abstract from Him as the One who acts on man in his vocation can we fail to see that the process in which man is enlightened by Him has a share in the fulness of His reality and that it is only *per nefas* that it can be understood in that restricted sense.

There is nothing else to hinder a purely ideal understanding of the
event. He alone prevents this misunderstanding. But He does so
truly, definitely and conclusively.

Again, the validity of what we finally said in relation to the distinctions of the older dogmatics in respect of the form of this process
stands or falls by whether or not our gaze is concentrated on the One
who is here the the acting Subject who calls man. If we openly admit
that there is only one calling, that this is only *vocatio immediata*, and
that as such it is to be understood as both *externa* and *interna*, both
unica and *continua*, these statements are meaningless in themselves,
i.e., except as descriptions of the call of Jesus Christ. To call them
paradoxical or dialectical does not help to clarify them. They have
to be made and can be understood, however, if we remember to whose
vocare we refer. The One who calls is the one Mediator between God
and man who needs no vicar but acts and speaks directly. We speak
of another calling than His if we set alongside or in opposition to it
a *vocatio mediata*, even though it be that of the prophets and apostles.
But He calls man through His Word which comes from without with
inwardly victorious power. His vocation is thus *vocatio externa* and
interna. And in its once-for-allness His calling is continuous, yet
continuous without denying its once-for-allness. It is thus *vocatio unica
et continua*. Whether or not we call these statements paradoxical and
dialectical, this whole *modus vocationis*, which is apparently so
contradictory, is obviously necessary once we consider, and do not
cease to consider, that we are concerned with the *vocatio* which is
nothing other than the function and work of Jesus Christ in His
prophetic office. This *vocatio* of His takes place in this *modus*.

3. THE GOAL OF VOCATION

What is at issue when the extraordinary thing takes place that the
living Jesus Christ is not merely present for a man as He is—significantly
and powerfully enough—for all men but when He comes to him and
addresses to him the Word of grace in the power of the Holy Spirit,
and does so in such a way that he cannot evade it or obstinately
resist it but is both caused and liberated and therefore spontaneously moved to hear it ? What is the meaning and purpose of this
occurrence ? What is the *telos* of the alteration which befalls a man
when, in addition to all that he is or might be, he becomes a hearer of
this Word and in illuminated, awakened and set in motion by it ?
What is the extraordinary thing which is willed for him and from him
in and with this extraordinary occurrence ? What is the form of
existence at which his vocation aims and to which it moves ? This is
the question to which we must now try to give first a basic and compre-

hensive answer, in order that on this general foundation we may describe rather more concretely what is really at issue in the three final sub-sections.

The mystery of vocation, of the fact that there takes place this calling of man within human time and history, is very great. In its own manner and place it is no less than the Christmas mystery of the birth of the eternal Word of God in the flesh in which it has its primary basis. And the miracle which denotes this mystery, i.e., the miracle of calling, of its possibility, of the way which God takes with man when He causes his calling to take place, is also great. In its own manner and place it is no less than the Christmas miracle of the birth of Jesus Christ of the Virgin Mary in which it has its pattern. Those to whom Jesus Christ in calling them gives the freedom (ἐξουσία) to become the children of God, so that His call does not return empty but reaches its goal, are not those who are born of blood, nor of the will of the flesh, nor of the will of man, but of God (Jn. 1^{12-13}). When we put our question, we do not violate either the mystery or the miracle of vocation. Good care is taken that we shall always be astonished afresh as we contemplate it. Yet this does not alter the fact that God knows what He wills in the vocation of man, and that this cannot be hidden for a moment from the man who is called. We are concerned with a lofty event, yet not with one which is without meaning and purpose, but with one which is controlled by an intrinsically clear *ratio*, like the primary event of Christmas. Our question concerning its *telos* is not then unanswerable. And if in our attempt to give a right answer we cannot look too high or dig too deep, the right answer will be basically very simple.

In its very simplest form we have already anticipated it in our previous deliberations. The purpose of a man's vocation is that he should become a Christian, a *homo christianus*. In this event it is thus a question of the creation of the Christian and then, in the sense of a *creatio continua*, of his preservation and nurture. Whatever may have to be said in the matter can consist only in a series of elucidations of the simplest answer. But it certainly stands in need of radical explication.

Apart from all else, there is no sure agreement that in the vocation of man Christian existence as such is really in view. Can we really say that Christian existence as such, the nature which characterises and distinguishes the Christian, stands or falls with the fact that he is called, that he is made a Christian, becoming what of himself and previously he was not, in the mystery and miracle which correspond in mode to the Christmas story, and which are the mystery and miracle of the special event of his illumination and awakening by the living Christ as by the Word of God specifically directed to him and victoriously reaching him ? Before we precede further, we must firmly establish this basic assertion. Serious objections might be brought against the necessary linking of vocation with the Christian status, and the Christian status with vocation. It might be argued that the real place and validity of vocation is as the special basis of a particular form of Christianity and not as the indispensable basis or *conditio sine qua non* of Christian existence as such.

There is a prevalent understanding of Christianity which makes this objection not only possible but necessary. Long before there was any such thing as its modern secularisation, at the time of its supreme historical triumph, did not the name of Christian become one which was accepted and even claimed by almost innumerable people who neither knew anything nor thought that they should know anything of any special vocation to be bearers of this name, or of the need for any such event to enable them to be and to be called Christians ? As they saw it, to be a Christian was to live in the tradition which was shaped, or partially shaped, by Christianity. It was to be brought up and educated in the context of the history in which, side by side with the ancient world and the different national traditions, side by side with ancient and modern learning as it grew and blossomed and bore fruit on this soil, Christian influences also helped to shape and determine society in a more or less penetrating way. To be a Christian was thus to share the inheritance visible in the variously described complex of Christian ideas, principles, habits and customs, or in the circle of the Christian Church. It was to take these seriously and to find nourishment also in these elements of the native background. It was to be reached as a Western man by that which is above or beyond the world, by that which is unconditioned, and to that extent by God according to the Christian conception and impression of the divine, without necessarily having to enquire into any other commitment or responsibility towards Him than that of private opinion, but rather in basic if not always practical freedom to decide what attitude should be adopted to the given historical and contingent reality and what could and should be made of self, others and the world on this assumption. It is clear that within the framework of this conception we have a very positive relationship to Christianity which may be that not only of Liberal Protestantism but also of Orthodox Protestantism—so far as there still is such a thing—and especially of Roman Catholicism.

Now obviously to be a Christian in this sense no vocation is required. All that is needed is to have, not a new, but a given and present attachment, implicitly and secondarily to Jesus Christ, but explicitly and primarily to a family, nation, culture and civilisation. All that is needed is some kind of fixed participation in the historical and intellectual context of the West. Within the framework of this understanding of Christian existence vocation is not ruled out as a special phenomenon. A place may be found for it even in a partially or totally institutional form. In Roman Catholicism it may be vocation to the priesthood or to an order. In the Evangelical world it may be calling to the office of preaching, or to the mission field, or the diaconate, or some other special activity, or perhaps to a higher or deeper or some other special form of Christianity such as that of the communities or even some of the Free Churches. This special calling—to the extent that those who think they receive it do not make themselves unpleasantly conspicuous—may be one which in the eyes of other Christians is not only respectable but valued as necessary and perhaps supported in virtue of its complementary and even representative function. The proponents of this view are forced to concede, not perhaps very willingly, that outside the framework of the Christian tradition, on the so-called pagan mission fields of the South and East, some kind of special vocation is necessary to become a Christian. But those who have a special calling—if they are not to make themselves unpleasantly conspicuous—must not give the impression either tacitly or vocally that the

Christian as such, and therefore every Christian in every time and place, can become and be called a Christian only by vocation. The assertion must never be made that those who are not called cannot be Christians.

The objection is in its own way well-founded. If it were right that we can be Christians only on the basis of the calling of Christ, every supposed and ostensible Christian would have to test whether and how far, in what he regards as his Christianity, there is a completely non-traditional element which is other than the given realities of his existence, which is not a heritage to be accepted and used to the best of his knowledge and conscience, which is not a determination of Western man naturally passed on with his mother's milk and the water of baptism. He would then have to consider whether as a Christian, in distinction from something merely handed down and taken over, and quite outwith his own sphere of control, he really is something which can be understood only as the work of a new and strange promise and claim directed to him. He would then have to ask whether he can and should take himself seriously and make himself out to be a Christian except on this basis and therefore in the light of his vocation. He would then have to understand his Christianity, not implicitly and secondarily, but explicitly and primarily as his attachment to Jesus Christ, and this attachment as the work of His free decision concerning him which he in his existence as a Christian can only follow with his decision. This would be positively the dreadful demand made of everyone who regards himself, and wishes himself to be regarded, as a Christian, if vocation and being a Christian were indeed inseparably connected. And there is also a negative aspect. It might be that he does not know or want to know anything of this element in his Christianity which is so non-traditional and so very different in kind from all his other attributes as Western man. It might be that he does not know or want to know anything more than a Christian heritage under his own control and at his own disposal. It might be that he cannot discover or know himself and therefore take himself seriously as one who is called and therefore as one who is explicitly and primarily attached to Jesus Christ. Assuming that there is that connexion between vocation and being a Christian, would not this necessarily mean that he is invited to renounce all claim to Christianity ? Would not the number of those bearing the name of Christian melt like snow before the sun ? And would there not be many who for various reasons regard it as their right and honour to bear this name, and who would thus take this invitation very badly, being quite unprepared to be part of the melting snow or to be excluded from the society of Christians ? We need have no illusions concerning the quiet or more violent energy of the objection to the thesis that vocation and being a Christian are mutually conditioned. In adopting and championing this thesis, we cut to the very quick, not the world as such, but the Christian world and Western man. Dogmatics will make itself even more unpopular in Western Christianity than it is already if it recalls and insists that the goal of vocation is not a special Christian existence but the existence of the Christian as such, and that the existence of the Christian is either grounded in his vocation or not at all.

This dangerous but inescapable thesis is at least negatively confirmed, though not, of course, established, by the modern development of the relationship between Christians and the world around. The assumption which underlies the notion of a Christian existence growing out of and to be taken over from a Christian tradition was never genuinely present. It has now become quite impossible, and with it the notion itself.

The picture of a man who is a Christian solely on the ground of his historical situation as determined or partially determined by Christianity could only arise and have any real meaning or dominance in the society of the middle period of the history of the Church *post Christum*, i.e., after Constantine and before the Renaissance and the Reformation. It rested on the unity which was taken for granted in this society, even by Christian theoreticians, between the antiquity of Greece and Rome and the various European national groups on the one side and Christianity on the other. It presupposed the practical concurrence between civilisation, culture and political power on the one side and the Church on the other. Yet even in this society, in the *corpus christianum* which later Romanticism so yearningly accepted as an ideal, it could not actualise and assert itself without disruption. Even in this happy period there was never any true or assured peace between the *sacerdotium* here and the *imperium* there, between the saints here and the knights and wise men (or fools) there. There could never be any effective amalgamation of the themes and concerns prosecuted on the two sides. The primitive and heathen Swabian, German, Saxon, Frank, Briton, Italian, Spaniard or Hungarian, though he might dress up in priestly or even episcopal robes, did not cease to lead his own virile life and go his own ways in this society in spite of his baptism. It also had certain disruptive results that the Christian and secular scholarship of the time tried to build so explicitly on the blind heathen Aristotle who had been passed on to them as a very dubious gift by the Arabs. It was also inevitable that from the niche carefully and respectfully found for the called Christian, namely, monasticism, there should be confusing incursions into the sphere of general Christianity supposedly dispensed from any special vocation. Hence the heritage of the Middle Ages was brittle even before it passed into the hands of those who came after. The rise of the new age which commenced at the end of the 15th and was completed at the beginning of the 18th century thus carried with it no more than the explicit manifestation of a conflict which had never really been settled because it was implicit in the *corpus christianum* from the very first. What happened was simply that the two partners conjoined in this union—antiquity and the nations on the one side and Christianity on the other—rose up in revolt against being understood in terms of that bold but totally immature synthesis. In the so-called Renaissance, learning, art, social and individual ethos, and above all political power, and in the Reformation and Counter-Reformation the Church, and increasingly within it the individual Christian, awakened to an awareness of their autonomy and particularity. If Christianity could not and would not deny its existence in connexion with non-Christian humanity, nor free itself from the problems of this humanity, just as this humanity rather strangely would not wholly or radically free itself from Christianity with a few well-known exceptions, the individual Christian found himself more and more compelled to consider his own specific characteristics and to set himself on his own feet.

This age—which I now prefer to call that of the self-understanding of the Christian rather than of *diastasis*—is no longer new. But it is still our own age. The idea of a Christianity which is automatically given and received with the rest of our inheritance has now become historically impossible, no matter how tenaciously it may linger on and even renew itself in various attempts at restoration by the Church and the world. The Christian West, i.e., the society in which Christian and non-Christian existence came together, or seemed to do so, no longer exists either in the city or in the peace of the remotest hamlet. Even in Spain it no longer exists. Hence a man can no longer be brought up as a member of it. His Christianity can no longer derive from the fact that he is a member of it. Whether he likes it or not, therefore, he is asked to-day whether or not this Christianity of his has some other basis than the scrap of tradition which may still remain as an anachronistic relic. It may thus be argued that to-day even from the historical standpoint there can be no escaping the startling recognition that a man's being as a Christian is either grounded in his vocation or it is simply an illusion which seems beautiful perhaps in the after-glow of a time vanished beyond recall. And it is perhaps surprising that the most radical of the surviving Liberal theologians are the very ones who in a very old-fashioned way have been trying to deduce and explain the Christianity of self-understanding faith in terms of a Christian tradition supposedly still present and normative for us.

Our present concern, however, is not with spiritual development but dogmatics. In this type of historical analysis, therefore, we may find only a confirmation and not a proof of the necessity of this thesis of ours, which is still not generally recognised and is so unpopular in content. It can be proved dogmatically only if we examine the name " Christian " in relation to its origin and meaning, understand it strictly and take it seriously in this sense, and thus see it in its necessary connexion with the concept of vocation.

As is well known, the term Christian occurs very seldom in the New Testament (1 Pet. 4¹⁶ ; Ac. 11²⁶, 26²⁸). The so-called missionary command (Mt. 28¹⁹) is not that the disciples should make the nations Christians, but that they should make them disciples (μαθητεύειν) like themselves. And with the exceptions mentioned, the men who become disciples and are gathered in the various ἐκκλησίαι, are always in the Epistles called πιστοί, ἅγιοι, ἀγαπητοί, above all ἐκλεκτοί, and therefore κλητοί. It is not that some of them who are specially endowed or commissioned for special service in the community are given this latter title, but all of them without difference or exception. There can be little doubt that in the three passages in which it is used the term χριστιανοί is to be filled out by the other concepts, and not least, but primarily indeed in relation to the question how a man becomes a χριστιανός, by the concept κλητός. The Christian is a man to whom the call to discipleship has come through the ministry of the disciples, and who has followed it as the call of the One who called, accepted and treated these as His disciples. If he is in the community, he is a κλητός. If he is not a κλητός, he is not in the community. Only as such is he what is denoted by the other concepts. The new master concept χριστιανός, however, is intrinsically and as such so full of content that we need not regret that it later prevailed, and we shall find it supremely rewarding and indeed necessary to take it in all seriousness. It is surely not insignificant that in Ac. 11²⁶ the emergence of this name (" And the disciples were called Christians first in Antioch ") is linked with the one-year stay of Paul in this community. If it is not stated in so many words, it is surely obvious that the disciples, i.e., those who have become disciples through the disciples, are men who have come to faith in Christ, who have placed themselves under His name, who already here and now have recognised in this name (Phil. 2⁹ᶠ·) the name which is above every other name, who already here and now in this name bow the knee to the glory of God the Father and confess that the One who bears this name, Jesus Christ, is Lord. It is as such, as those who are called, that they are Christians : μέτοχοι τοῦ Χριστοῦ γεγόναμεν (Heb. 3¹⁴).

Taking the word in its most obvious sense, a Christian means one who belongs in a special way to Jesus Christ, i.e., in a way different from that in which, since He died and rose again for all, and all are to bow the knee to Him and join in that confession, all men belong to Him and on the basis of His election and mission are His own, His possession and people according to John 1¹¹. The special way in which Christians belong to Him, however, is that their existence among all other men is determined, according to the commonest New Testament expression, by their faith in Him, by their liberating and yet also binding and active knowledge that all men and therefore they themselves belong to Him. In the active knowledge of this faith of theirs they anticipate the form of existence which one day is to be that of all men. In this special sense all men do not belong to Him here and now, but only Christians belong to Him and are His own, His possession and people.

But how do they come to belong to Him in this special sense ? In the light of our most general material definition we obviously cannot say that they do so in virtue of their existence in the continuity of a situation which is determined or partially determined by Him. It cannot be contested, but has to be maintained, that there is indeed a time and history continuously controlled and determined by Him, i.e., by His personal presence and action. That this is so is confirmed by the fact that within this time and history there is a kind of Christian tradition in which every man participates or may come to do so. It is not at all the case, however, that by existing in this time and history and participating in this tradition or coming to do so, a man belongs to Christ in this special way, namely, as a Christian. The active knowledge of faith in Christ, which makes a man a Christian, does not grow naturally out of the continuity of his situation as this is determined or partially determined by Christ. According to 2 Thessalonians 3² " all men have not faith." And the saying in Luke 18⁸ is even sharper : " Nevertheless when the Son of man cometh, shall he find faith on the earth ? " No, Christian ideas and principles and habits and customs may well be handed down and received by tradition with other ingredients of the spirit of the age, but not the active knowledge of faith in Jesus Christ.

Another possible meaning of attachment to Jesus Christ may also be mentioned and briefly discussed. Does it perhaps consist in the fact that Christ is the central supporting and symbolical figure in the particular culture of Christians and their particular doctrine of God, the world and man ? Formulated thus or in some other way, and critical or even sometimes positive in intention, this understanding has found many supporters. It certainly means, of course, that Christians do not so much belong to Christ as Christ to Christians. He is not the Creator but the supreme creature of faith. It might well be asked historically whether faith like that of the Christian in an accomplished reconciliation of the world to God, in a concluded and fulfilled covenant between God and man, and in a specific person in whom this has taken place and is revealed, could really have arisen autochthonously. But this question smacks of apologetics. The crushing objection to this understanding is a reference to the simple fact that there has never yet been a living Christian who has recognised himself in it and who has therefore understood and expounded his attachment to Jesus Christ as the attachment of Jesus Christ to his faith and cultus and doctrine. To do this, he would either have to cease to be a Christian or to lose sight of himself and thus forget himself as such. At any rate, he could adopt this interpretation only in the profoundest ignorance of what is involved. The ignorance of the non-Chrisitan, which may, of course, lurk in the heart and mind of the Christian and occasionally declare itself, can naturally explain Christian existence in such a way that Jesus Christ becomes its creature rather than its Creator, its exponent rather than its essence, its predicate rather than its Subject. But no one who really knows Christian existence can be guilty either in fact or in speech of such aberration. Such an interpretation cannot even call for notice or discussion, let alone be accepted as a norm. For those who are really competent to know and judge in this matter, the only serious explanation is that which rests on the clear assumption that the Christian belongs to Christ, and that it is only on this basis and in this way that Christ also belongs to the Christian and is his Christ.

It is by recalling the description of Jesus Christ as the Lord, which is so important throughout the New Testament, that we can move forward decisively to a proper understanding of the relation between Him and the Christian and the Christian and Him. In the well-known and clear-cut phrase of Luther, " I believe that Jesus Christ is my Lord." This includes and expresses everything that he is and does specifically for the Christian, and the whole relationship of the Christian to Him. According to Matthew 7[21] not every one who—perhaps very zealously—says : " Lord, Lord," does, of course, belong to Him. But we can at least say by way of delimitation that everyone who belongs to him certainly cannot and will not refrain from confessing that He is his Lord, that he himself belongs to Him as his Lord, and positively that in active knowledge he knows what he is saying when he maintains that he definitely belongs to Him. In the light of the Old Testament as well as the Hellenistic provenance of the word *Kyrios*, however, this means that his attachment to Him rests on a personal action, and is the work of a personal act of lordship, on the part of the One whom he may and must address in this way. He does not belong to Him of himself. He is set by Him in this attachment to Him. He is one who is won over to it. We have a lord when we acquire and maintain him as such in virtue of his lordly power. This is how it is in attachment to Jesus Christ. " Ye have not chosen me "—whether by accepting a tradition or exercising your own judgment—" but I have chosen you " (Jn. 15¹⁶). His very name as Lord implies and declares this higher origin of Christian existence in Jesus Christ.

What is entailed by this attachment to Him, and therefore by Christian existence, will occupy us later. But first we must ask how a man is placed in it by Jesus Christ Himself according to His name as Lord.

There can be no question of an act of compulsion on the part of this Lord. The forces of nature assert themselves in this way. This is how death snatches away all living creatures. Fate rules thus according to the conception of many heathen religions and the terrifying descriptions of several Christian theologians. Human lords acquire and exercise their dominion by the use of superior physical force. Demonically gifted individuals are able to master, control and sway even whole masses and peoples by their physical vitality, intensity and dynamism and the corresponding magical power of persuasion. But this is not what happens when Jesus Christ makes Himself known as Lord, and acts as such towards man, placing him in the particular attachment to Himself which makes him a Christian. He certainly exercises power, putting down the mighty from their seat and exalting them of low degree (Lk. 1⁵²). Nor is there any power in heaven or earth comparable with or superior to His. But it is not a blind, brute power working causally and mechanically. He does not force or suppress or disable in His exercise of it. He is not the rampaging numinous which strikes man unconditionally so that he can only be petrified and silent before it, yielding without really wanting to do so. He does not humiliate or insult man. He does not make him a mere spectator, let alone a puppet.

If we are to boast of His power, we should boast of the particular nature of this superior power rather than of the power as such, in the depiction of which we may even with the most laudable of intentions be betrayed into the magnifying of a supernatural power of compulsion. We should boast of the omnipotence of God—with which we are really concerned in the power of Jesus Christ—in terms of *potestas* rather than *potentia*. Above all, if we for our part wish to serve Christ our Lord dynamically, we should see to it that we do not seriously and whole-heartedly, to His glory and the supposed salvation of our fellows, practise towards them any crude or refined form of the power of compulsion. The charge of the lord and host in the parable (Lk. 14²³) : ἀνάγκασον εἰσελθεῖν, might well be rendered *compelle*, as in the Vulgate, but it cannot be rendered *coge* (*cogite*) *intrare*, as was later supposed in justification of some curious methods of converting the heathen and instructing heretics. A yoke which is not easy, a burden which is not light (Mt. 11³⁰), so that those who bear it cannot draw their breath properly (ἀνάπαυσις, Mt. 11²⁹), is certainly not the yoke or burden of Christ which He lays on those who come unto Him. And we have always to remind ourselves that so long and so far as we find no relief in being Christians or even theologians, but do so only at bottom with sighs and complaints, like the Saxons so harshly baptised by Charlemagne or the Indians brought to baptism in no less cruel ways by the 16th-century Spaniards, to this extent we should quietly admit that we are not really Christians or theologians at all, and have only reason to look about for the proper way in which we may finally become such. A forced Christian is not a Christian.

The power in which Jesus Christ sets a man in attachment to Himself is the liberating power of His Word which is opposed to all compulsion and eliminates and discards it. It is the power of the free grace of God revealed in Him. When He who is Himself the Resurrected from the dead exercises His power on man, this man may breathe and live and rise and stand with Him. It is the power in which He illuminates man as the light of life, declaring Himself to him, enlightening his eyes and understanding, so that he sees and understands and recognises Him in his own freedom. It is the power of His prophecy in which He awakens him to faith in Himself which is rooted in this recognition, and therefore to obedience. It is in doing this that He sets him in the attachment to Himself which makes him a Christian and distinguishes him from other men. No compulsion brought to bear upon him, even though it were supernatural and exercised in the name of the supreme God, could awaken him to faith rooted in that free recognition and therefore set him in attachment to the One who is light and not darkness, to the living Jesus Christ. What similarity could there be between the resignation and capitulation of a compelled, defeated and subjugated man and the free recognition which is the root of faith in Him? This would never make him the prisoner or slave of Jesus Christ as Paul describes himself. There is a true subjection to Him. But this does not consist in his being crushed and trampled underfoot. It consists in the opening of his eyes, in the acquiring of the courage, exalted by Kant as the essence of true enlightenment, to use his own understanding, in finding himself placed on his own feet and set in motion on his own path. " Where the Spirit of the Lord is, there is liberty " (2 Cor. 3¹⁷). This is an indispensable criterion by which the seizure of power by Jesus Christ may be distinguished from all others.

The lordly power in which a man is set in attachment to Him is the power of His Word. This means concretely that it is the power of the promise given by Him, the claim made by Him and the address personally directed by Him, which consist in the fact that He reveals and truly makes Himself known to man as the One He is for all and therefore specifically for him, thus liberating him to know Him and therewith to be awakened to faith in Him. He calls him, and calls him quite simply to Himself. He calls him without anxiety whether he can and will hear and obey. He gives him the confidence that he can and will do so. It was thus, with no question as to their will or ability, but with the gift of very literal confidence in this will and ability, that He called His first disciples to Himself. He never calls in any other way. When He calls, He thus calls with power. For in this confidence in which there is no anxiety, He calls with liberating and creative force, summoning non-being into being, giving Himself unreservedly to the one whom He calls, delivering Himself up to him, really calling him to Himself, enabling him to hear and obey self-evidently and without argument like the first disciples, and on no other basis than the obviously all-sufficient basis of His call. This call of His : " Come unto me," awakens man to faith in Him as by it He makes Himself known. It calls him out of a form of existence in which he lived as though Jesus Christ were not the One He is for all men and therefore for him, into another form of existence in which this stupid " as if " is left behind, in which he makes use of the free-dom given him, and in which he therefore lives on the clear assump-tion that Jesus Christ is the One He is for all men and therefore for him. The life of man in this second form of existence, awakened by His creative Word and the confidence placed in Him, is the particular attachment to Him which makes a man a Christian. Hence the vocation of man is the special enduement of grace which distinguishes him and marks him off from others.

We are thus brought back to the point from which we started. Our task was to show that Christian existence as such is grounded only in vocation. Having shown this, we can take up again our original thesis that the purpose, meaning and goal of vocation is Christian existence. What Christian existence is, what it means for a man to be a Christian, we have defined only in a very general way in speaking of the special attachment to Jesus Christ in which a man is set by his vocation. We still face the larger task of defining and describing more precisely the goal of vocation.

Where shall we begin ? For the sake of honesty and safety we had best begin by stating that Christians too, and therefore those who are set in this particular attachment to Jesus Christ, are men, with all the good, doubtful and bad things which this implies. The second and new form of existence which is the goal of vocation is not an angelic, let alone a divine form. It is one which is divinely fashioned, i.e., especially determined and shaped by the special active Word of God. But it is still a human form. " I pray not that thou shouldest take them out of the world " (Jn. 17^{15}). The new creation fulfilled in vocation (2 Cor. 5^{17}) does not mean the cancellation or destruction of the old, but the investing of man, of the child of Adam, with the new clothing or armour of God of which Paul loved to speak as of the great transformation which has come to the Christian but which is also still to come on him without any grasping of his own. Christians are in no sense freed from their union with humanity. They have not left this union. On the contrary, they are its most genuine and loyal members to the extent that, in contrast with all others, they know what kind of a union it is both for good or ill, under the judgment of God or under His grace as Creator, Reconciler and Redeemer, and to the extent that they also know what they owe to the union itself and, in full solidarity with them, to their fellow-members.

In his fine hymn on the inward life of Christians, Christian F. Richter has beautifully described this relationship to others : " In all other things they are children of Adam, Bearing the image of earth and decay, Suffering in flesh like all other sinners, Eating and drinking as needed each day, In bodily matters like sleeping and rising, Distinguished from others by nothing surprising, Only the world and its pleasures despising "—although we might add that like other sinners they do not consistently despise the world and its pleasures, but in their own way do sometimes discreetly or indiscreetly take part in them, just as their humanity extends to a good deal more than bodily matters.

As plainly revealed in the life of Peter and the teaching of Paul, e.g., in Romans 7 and 8, the new creation of man by the call of Jesus Christ does not exclude the fact that, although his sin and guilt are indeed behind him, they are behind him in such a way that they are still a potent factor in the present, so that he must continually receive afresh his freedom from them and allow himself to be set forward on the road ahead. Nor should we forget what we learned in the preceding section, namely, that falsehood in its fully developed form, in which it is also the culmination of all human sin, is the falsehood in which man tries to escape the Word of God spoken to and heard by him by falsifying it. We should not forget that falsehood in its fully developed form is Christian falsehood. Who but the Christian knows the nature of the condemnation hanging over man in respect of this culmination of his sin ? Of all creatures he is the very last to be able to boast to his human fellow-creatures that he is not as they are. Death is in the pot once he makes the slightest movement in this direction like the Pharisee in the temple (Lk. 18[11]).

The particularity of the Christian is his particularity within the general union of humanity. As such it cannot, of course, be given too sharp or radical emphasis. He is undoubtedly set apart from the others in company with whom he is a man and therefore like them. Hence it must also be said that he is not like them, but different from them. In our description of the process of vocation we have seen how this comes about, namely, by his illumination to active knowledge which as such is his awakening. Since this is an act of God, of Jesus Christ, of the Holy Spirit ; since it is the active Word of God effectively spoken to him, it is established that his distinction from others is definitely not grounded in himself, nor put in his own hands, let alone made over to him as a possession and as it were placed in his pocket. His distinctiveness stands or falls with the fact that it is freely given him, and that he receives it as a grace with the pure gratitude which advances no claim. But given and received in this way it is a very real distinctiveness. Incomparably great though it is, and misleading and even dangerous though its application necessarily appears, we cannot escape the saying that the Christian, as a child of light, is a child of God who is Himself light. This truth is far too impressively suggested to us by the New Testament, and materially far too close to the centre of its message, for any such evasion. Now we desire that this truth should apply to all men. There can be no doubt that it ought to do so. We hope that it finally will. But it cannot be said to apply to all men unless we arbitrarily wrest it.

It is to be noted that in Rom. 8¹⁹⁻²³ the κτίσις, which also includes humanity, is set over against the υἱοὶ τοῦ θεοῦ. Both are waiting and sighing for a future revelation. But it will be the revelation of what the children of God are hic et nunc, of the freedom which, even though its glory is hidden from them too, is already granted and proper to them hic et nunc. It is to the manifestation of what distinguishes them already within the rest of the cosmic and human world that, in harmony with their own necessary expectation, the ἀποκαραδοκία of the κτίσις generally is directed. With their future there stands or falls that of the whole cosmos and all men. 1 Jn. 3¹⁻² is to the same effect : " Behold, what manner of love (how particular, great and extraordinary, ποταπὴν ἀγάπην) the Father hath bestowed upon us, that we should be called (literally, called to be) the sons of God," and then the clear-cut statement : ἀγαπητοί, νῦν τέκνα θεοῦ ἐσμεν. To these assertions there are added the delimiting but not in any sense weakening sayings : " Therefore the world knoweth us not, because it knew him not " ; and then : " It doth not yet appear what we shall be," i.e., in the light of the final revelation of God. No one is by nature, nor has the power to be, what Christians are. Not all receive the Logos come into the world. All belong to Him, but not all believe in Him (Jn. 1¹¹). And it is to those who receive Him, who believe in Him, who are granted to do so by Him, that power is given to become the sons of God as they are born of God (Jn. 1¹²). There thus takes place the most extraordinary thing that at the very point where it was and is to be said to all men : " Ye are not my people," it is to be said of these men : " Ye shall be called the children of the living God " (Rom. 9²⁶). They are this διὰ πίστεως, not because they believe, but as they do so. And they are it ἐν Χριστῷ Ἰησοῦ, as by faith in Him they belong together with Him and participate in what He is (Gal. 3²⁶). They are it as the Spirit of God, who is the power of the Word by which Jesus Christ calls them to Himself, and who is thus the πνεῦμα υἱοθεσίας, of His sonship but also theirs in Him, impels, permits and commands them to cry with Him : " Abba, Father," and to pray with Him : " Our Father." They are it as His Spirit attests to their spirits, praying in this way, what their spirits praying in this way also attest : ὅτι ἐσμὲν τέκνα θεοῦ (Rom. 8¹⁴⁻¹⁶).

According to the obvious tenor of the statements of the New Testament, the distinctive feature of the being of Christians as the children of God thus consists decisively and dominatingly in the fact that, as those whom Jesus Christ has called and calls to Himself in the work of His Spirit, they exist in particularly proximity to Him and therefore in analogy to what He is. He is originally—not merely in the counsel of God but in the eternal being of God, and then in time, in the flesh and within the world in virtue of the counsel of God—that which men become as they are called to be Christians. That is to say, He is originally the Son of God. And in analogy and correspondence, which means with real similarity for all the dissimilarity, they may become sons of God. Their new and distinctive being as Christians is their being in this real similarity, for all the dissimilarity, to His being as the Son of God. They may become and thus be what He is originally and does not have to become. They are secondarily, as those who are called by Him, as those whom He adopts as His brothers and sisters, as those who become such, the children of God. Yet they are this with full reality. Secondarily they are no less really the sons of God that He is primarily the eternal Son of the eternal Father. Thus the statement : " Ye are all the children of God " (Gal. 3^{26}), is never to be expounded as though it were not meant strictly. The strict meaning is that, inasmuch as they become and are Christians, they have their basis and origin (analogously to the One by whose call they become and are this) in the will and act of the eternal God, who has not only made the world, but in the giving of His Son has also loved it, and does and will continue to do so. Like Christ, who sets them in fellowship with Him as their first-born Brother, they are the handiwork of this fatherly love of God. In this they are His new creation. In this consists their freedom in the glory which *hic et nunc* is still hidden from the world but *illic et tunc* will be revealed to it. In this they are different men from all others, not separated but differentiated from them. And in this, in their divine sonship, consists the goal of their vocation. When it takes place, it is with this end in view.

Now their being as the children of God is not empty ; it does not have to be accidentally or arbitrarily filled out. It is not idle ; it does not have to become active. It implies from the very first and therefore unavoidably a definite situation and position in which they are placed, a definite character which they are given, a definite function which is committed to them, a definite action which they are commissioned to perform. Their nature is fashioned and characterised by the fatherly basis and origin of their existence. If only in analogy to the existence of Jesus Christ, yet very really in this analogy they, too, as the children of God exist in repetition, confirmation and revelation not only of the manner but also of the will and act of God as the One from whim they derive.

Here, too, the mode of thought and speech found in the Bible will prove our surest guide. In the New Testament it is Jesus Christ, the Son of the Father, who with supremely concrete and active fulness is called the Son of God, not as the One who has to become this, but as the One who is so from the very first. According to the particularly rich declarations of John's Gospel in this regard, He is the One who, sent by the Father and one with Him, does the will and works of the Father and reveals and glorifies Him. He is the Son of God as He is also His being and act, His being concretely as His act and His act as the expression of His being, as these are disclosed in the being and act of the One who is called the Son of God.

To understand what must be said even concerning this model of all divine sonship, we must bear in mind that whenever Scripture speaks of sonship, in accordance with Oriental ideas and terminology it has in view not merely the relationship of descent but also the fatherly characteristics, determination, commission, and practical mode of life as continued in the sons or children concerned. The sons of Aaron (Lev. 1[5] and *passim*) are not merely his descendants, but as such those who take up and continue his priesthood. The sons of Korah mentioned in Ps. 42 and at the commencement of other Psalms are obviously a distinct family but as such they seem also to have been a kind of guild of poets and musicians. The children of Israel are the 10 + 2 confederated tribes not merely in view of their common descent from Jacob-Israel but decisively in view of the promise which according to the stories of the patriarchs was given to Abraham, Isaac and Jacob, and therefore as the people of the covenant as whose partner their common ancestor lived his eventful life. And if we often read of the children of men (or Adam), especially in the Psalms, this description implies even in its most attenuated form the co-inherence of all men in this first of the race, and the nature and corruption, the blessing and cursing, in which they participate as his descendants. It is possible, and not improbable, that when we read of the children of Sion or Jerusalem, as in the well-known lament of Jesus in Mt. 23[37], or of the children of Babylon, as in Ezek. 23[15], we are to give the term " children " this wider, functional significance. And in a very striking way this can sometimes crowd out and replace the narrower sense, so that when someone is called a child or son there is no further reference at all to a human father or forefather, but simply to the fact that for good or evil he is determined from the very outset in a particular way, and will thus inherit the resultant curse or blessing. He may be a child of transgression (Is. 57[4]), or of death (1 Sam. 26[16], 2 Sam. 12[5]). But it is in the New Testament that the word is most frequently used in this sense. Here he may be a child of this world (Lk. 16[8]), of wrath (Eph. 2[3]), of corruption (2 Thess. 2[3]), or even of the devil (Ac. 13[10], 1 Jn. 3[10]). But he may also be a child of the prophets and the covenant (Ac. 3[25]), of promise (Rom. 9[8]), of peace (Lk. 10[6]), of a spirit which distinguishes him from others (Lk. 9[55]), of the resurrection (Lk. 20[36]), of the kingdom (Mt. 13[38]), and, of course, of light (Jn. 12[36f.]).

In the phrase " child of God " the two meanings are most emphatically reconciled. Those who bear this name are men whose being reaches beyond its creatureliness to its origin in a particular act of God, so that in its particular acts it is analogous to the being and act of Jesus Christ, the original Son of God, and in distinction from other human being manifests the particular will and work of the One who is their Father as well as the Father of Jesus Christ.

In the light of this term, and in concrete development and amplification of it, we return to our question concerning the goal and purpose of vocation. To what does Jesus Christ call those whom He calls ? What kind of a being is that of the man called by Him, of the Christian ? If, as we have laid down, it is the being of a man who by the call of God is called a child of God, and in the strength of this call really is a child of God (1 Jn. 3[1]), then a second basic assertion is demanded before anything specific can be mentioned. The one who is called by Him, and thus called by Him a child of God and made a brother or sister, is set in fellowship with Him in a way which seriously distinguishes though it does not separate him from other men. For this is something which happens to him but not to all. All are elected and ordained for fellowship with Jesus Christ. All move towards it. It is waiting for all. But it is one thing to be elected for it and another to be set in it. The latter is the distinctive thing which takes place in the calling of man and makes him a Christian. As certainly as this calling aims at his becoming and being a child of God, its goal is very simply but powerfully his fellowship with its source, i.e., with the One who calls him. Whatever we may have to say in detail about this goal is all included and enclosed in the fact that Jesus Christ does not call those whom He calls merely to any place, but He calls them to Himself, to attachment to Himself as we have previously said, to fellowship with Himself as we must now put it much more strongly. All that they are to become and be as those who are called stands or falls by whether they come once and continually to fellowship with Him.

" God is faithful (i.e., in His continuing βεβαιοῦν), by whom ye were called unto the fellowship of His Son Jesus Christ our Lord (δι' οὗ ἐκλήθητε εἰς κοινωνίαν τοῦ υἱοῦ αὐτοῦ Ἰησοῦ Χριστοῦ τοῦ κυρίου ἡμῶν, 1 Cor. 1⁹). If we compare this text with the many others which speak of the goal of calling, it is easy to see that it is a *locus classicus* which sums up all the rest. In the language of the New Testament, κοινωνία or *communicatio* is a relationship between two persons in which these are brought into perfect mutual co-ordination within the framework of a definite order, yet with no destruction of their two-sided identity and particularity, but rather in its confirmation and expression. We have such a relationship, such fellowship and therefore mutual co-ordination, in unique perfection in the relationship of man to Jesus Christ in which he is set when his vocation takes place.

The simplest description of this fellowship, which reveals at once its distinctive order and perfection, is that which is preferred in the Gospels, namely, that he is called to discipleship of Jesus Christ. He becomes his *akoluth* or follower. In the present context we can give only a brief indication of what this implies as demanded for our purpose (cf. *C.D.*, IV, 2, § 66, 3). Discipleship very properly describes the relationship between Him and His followers as a history which in this way is proper to Him and to Him alone. Jesus goes, and the disciple accompanies Him on the same way. It is Jesus who chooses the common way, and treads it first. The Christian follows Him on the way which He has chosen, treading in His steps (1 Pet. 2²¹). He believes in Jesus, not in a theoretical and general way, as in a good leader alongside whom there might be others, but in such a way that He is the inescapable Leader who leaves him no option but to go after Him on the way which He has chosen. And believing in Him, he obeys Him, again not in a general or theoretical way which enables or even perhaps constrains him to think and speak and act in detail according to some standards of his own, but in such a way that his own sovereignty is completely forfeit and he does exactly as he is told even in detail. And obeying Him, he confesses Him, again not just theoretically—and whether or not in words is only a secondary question—but quite unequivocally by publicly entering the way which is chosen by Him, by irrevocably and bindingly accepting his own relationship to Him, by thus compromising himself with Him, by making himself a fool for His sake, as we must add for the sake of clarity. Hence he does not belong to Jesus in a purely general way. He lives his own life in a fellowship with His life which is not ordered by himself but by Him. His discipleship, which is the history of the relationship of the Christian to Him, embraces the whole life of the Christian. The fact that His call is the call to this discipleship, and therefore to fellowship with Him, thus shows us particularly clearly that vocation is not merely *vocatio unica* but also *vocatio continua*.

But we must characterise more sharply the order in this fellowship. Jesus has the right to call man to Himself and therefore to His discipleship because He is his Lord and because man is engaged and bound to Him as such. Hence His call is simply the exercise, and the confession of the man called to Himself and His discipleship is simply the recognition, of His right of lordship. We have seen that its establishment has nothing whatever to do with the application of any power of compulsion on man. The power in which Jesus Christ establishes it is the free and liberating power of His Word, the power which is proper to, commensurate with and worthy of light as the light of life, manifest truth, the proclamation of the justification and sanctification of man effected in Him. In this free and liberating power, however, He directs upon man His right which is steadfast from all eternity and now demonstrated in His work in time. In virtue of this right He validly and authoritatively claims man for Himself, and man is validly and authoritatively claimed for Him. The validity and authority in which this takes place is quite unambiguous, and absolutely superior to any validity and authority which man might ascribe to his claims, because the right of lordship exercised by Him and recognised by man is the right of the owner to his property. It is in this sharpness that the order of the relationship between the Christian and Jesus Christ as his Lord in manifested in the relationship of discipleship. In the terminology of John's Gospel (esp. 17[6f.]), Christians are those whom the Father has given to the Son, unreservedly entrusting and committing them to Him. And the goal of the vocation of man is the man who actively knows himself as one who is given into the hands of the Son of God, and who thus lives in the knowledge that he does not belong to himself but to his Lord. In the event of vocation he is led to this insight. And in it he is made over and freely delivers himself *de facto* to the One to whom He belongs *de iure*, as he is also transferred and freely escapes *de facto* from the one to whom he does not belong *de iure*, namely, himself. He finds himself placed, and thus places himself, in the hands of the One to whom as owner there belongs the sole and total responsibility and care for his existence and its guidance and direction, since He has taken it upon Himself by electing Himself from all eternity for him, by electing him from all eternity for God and His salvation, and by fulfilling this election in intervening and offering up Himself for him in time. And he also finds himself taken out of his own hands and freed from the useless concern of responsibility for providing for and governing his own existence, by recognising himself, and being able to exist freely, as the possession of the One who long ago, indeed, from all eternity, came forth to restore what he had ruined, and could only ruin, as his own owner and lord. In this self-understanding to which he is awakened by his vocation, the super- and sub-ordination in his fellowship with the One who calls him, the structure of this fellowship as revealed in the fact that He calls him to discipleship and he himself allows himself to be called to discipleship, can only be natural and self-evident. In this structure the fellowship of the Christian with Christ is solidly grounded and ordered yet also free, because it is a fellowship which is rooted in the free grace of the Word spoken to him, which grows and renews itself from this, which never gives rest without a holy unrest, nor unrest without a holy rest.

Ὑμεῖς δὲ Χριστοῦ is the clear and succinct formula which Paul uses in 1 Cor. 3²³ to tell Christians who and what they are. They belong to Christ just as surely and in the same perfection as Christ belongs to God. Not in spite of, but in virtue of and in their appropriation to Him, which includes their own expropriation, they can and should be refreshed and vivified and established. For strangely yet incontrovertibly it is in the fact that He is their Owner and they His possession that their freedom is powerfully secured, whether in relation to their human teachers such as Apollos, Cephas or Paul himself, or in relation to the world around, or in relation to their life and death and future: πάντα ὑμῶν (1 Cor. 3²¹f.). This also follows from Rom. 14⁷f. : " For none of us liveth to himself, and no man dieth to himself. For whether we live, we live unto the Lord ; and whether we die, we die unto the Lord : whether we live therefore, or die, we are the Lord's " (τοῦ κυρίου ἐσμέν), and belonging to Him we are obviously at a place which is superior to life and death. Similarly, it is both with the deepest humility and yet also the greatest pride that Paul says of himself : " By the grace of God I am what I am " (1 Cor. 15¹⁰), and that in the very first words of introduction to Romans he calls himself a slave of Christ and yet as such a fully credited ambassador (Rom. 1¹). In this sense Christians (Jn. 10¹⁴, 13¹ ; 2 Tim. 2¹⁹)—and indeed (Jn. 1¹¹) virtually and prospectively all men—can quite simply be called His own (οἱ ἴδιοι, τὰ ἴδια, τὰ ἐμά). In this respect the *Heidelberg Catechism* gives the well-known answer to its first question : " What is thy only comfort in life and death ? That I, with body and soul, both (with both ?) in life and in death, am not my own, but belong to my faithful Saviour Jesus Christ." This is the comfort of the Christian. That is to say, he hears and accepts this as a promise and yet also a claim both to establish and to direct him. It is his only comfort, but his total and lasting comfort. He becomes and is a Christian as he finds this comfort, as he cleaves to and accepts all the implications of the fact that he is the possession of Jesus Christ.

It is the power of the Word of Jesus Christ which impresses upon man His right of lordship, the right of the owner to his property, awakening and impelling him to a spontaneous recognition and acceptance of this right, in which he gives himself to the discipleship of Jesus Christ, becoming obedient in his freedom and free in his obedience. The Word of Jesus Christ has divine power to accomplish this. But this divine power is the Holy Spirit. As Jesus Christ speaks with man in the power of the Holy Spirit, His vocation is *vocatio efficax*, i.e., effective to set man in fellowship with Himself. For the gift and work of the Holy Spirit as the divine power of His Word is that, while Jesus Christ encounters man in it with alien majesty, He does not remain thus, nor is He merely a strange, superior Lord disposing concerning him in majesty from without. On the contrary, even as such, without ceasing to be the Lord or forfeiting His transcendence, but rather in its exercise, He gives and imparts Himself to him, entering into him as his Lord in all His majesty and setting up His throne within him. Thus His control, as that of the owner over his possession, becomes the most truly distinctive feature of this man, the centre and basis of his human existence, the axiom of his freest thinking and utterance, the origin of his freest volition and action, in short the principle of his spontaneous being. The gift and work of the holy Spirit as the divine power of the Word of vocation is the placing of man in this fellowship with Him, namely, with the being, will and action of Jesus Christ.

The κοινωνία τοῦ ἁγίου πνεύματος in the well-known Trinitarian formula of greeting and benediction in 2 Cor. 13¹³ does not differ, then, from the κοινωνία . . . ᾽Ιησοῦ Χριστοῦ of 1 Cor. 1⁹, but the latter is grounded, maintained and continued in and by it. It is indeed essential to the latter : " Now if any man have not the Spirit of Christ, he is none of his " (Rom. 8⁹). " No man can say that Jesus is the Lord, but by the Holy Ghost " (1 Cor. 12³). As the grace of the Lord Jesus Christ and therefore the love of God are effective in man as well as towards him in the impartation of the Holy Spirit ; as fellowship is effected between the divine power of the Word of Jesus Christ and this man ; as man becomes a " temple " of this divine power of the Spirit (1 Cor. 6¹⁹) in which the Spirit " dwells " (Rom. 8⁹) ; as there is freedom where the Spirit of the Lord is (2 Cor. 3¹⁷), it takes place that Jesus Christ Himself " dwells in your hearts by faith " (Eph. 3¹⁷). Apprehended by the grace of our Lord Jesus Christ and therefore by the love of God (" shed abroad in our hearts by the Holy Ghost which is given unto us," Rom. 5⁵), man is placed in the most direct fellowship with this Lord of His, and as a Christian he becomes a man who may exist in this fellowship with Him. That this should be achieved is the goal of his vocation, illumination and awakening.

Not by way of addition, but to give the most precise expression possible to what we have already stated in various ways, we must now take a further step. This is not merely because certain passages of the New Testament clearly direct us beyond the point already reached, but because the matter itself imperiously calls for further reflection. What is the nature of this fellowship of Christians with Jesus Christ if we have correctly understood it as the relationship of discipleship and possession, and finally as the powerful work of the Holy Spirit ? Are we not justified in asking whether the word " fellowship " is not too weak to embrace everything that is involved between Jesus Christ and the man called by Him, whether the word is not transcended and thus rendered unusable by the content which it acquires at this point ? Yet this is not the case. From all these different angles the relationship is always one of fellowship because, for all the intimacy and intensity of the connexion between them, there can be no question of an identification of the follower with his preceding leader, the possession with its owner, or the life of the one awakened by the Holy Spirit with the One who gives him this Spirit. There can thus be no question of an identification of the Christian with Christ. We have still to show, however, to what extent the fellowship of the Christian with Christ is one which is uniquely close and direct in the perfection of the mutual address of the two partners, so that it cannot be interchanged with any other.

We may begin by stating that it belongs to the perfection of this fellowship, and must not be overlooked or denied, that in it Christ does not merge into the Christian nor the Christian into Christ. There is no disappearance nor destruction of the one in favour of the other. Christ remains the One who speaks, commands and gives as the Lord. And the Christian remains the one who hears and answers and receives as the slave of the Lord. In their fellowship both become and are genuinely what they are, not confounding or exchanging their functions and roles nor losing their totally dissimilar persons.

A delimitation is required at this point. In particular relation to its perfection, the fellowship here described, which is the goal of vocation, has often been linked with the concept of mysticism both in exposition of the relevant New Testament texts and elsewhere. As is well known, even Calvin referred once to a *unio mystica* (*Instit.*, III, 11, 10). But we should never do this unless we state precisely what we have in view when we speak of " mysticism "—and it would have to be a mysticism *sui generis* in this context. There can certainly be no question of what is usually denoted by the term in this relationship. That is to say, there can be no question of an experience of union induced by a psychical and intellectual concentration, deepening and elevating of the human self-consciousness. For while it is true that in his fellowship with Christ, now to be appreciated in all its perfection, the Christian acts as well as receives, neither his receiving nor his acting in this fellowship is the product or work of his own skill, but both can be understood only as the creation of the call of Christ which comes to him. Again, there can be no question of a disappearance of the true confrontation of God and man, of the One who addresses and the one who is addressed and answers. There can be no question either on the one side or the other of any depersonalising or reduction to silence. There can be no question of any neutralising of the distinction between Creator and creature or of the antithesis between the Holy One and sinners, nor of any establishment of the kind of equilibrium which may exist between things but can never obtain between persons, and especially between the divine Jesus Christ and the human person. Even as a child of God, and therefore in the analogy of his existence to that of the eternal Son in the flesh, the Christian is not what the latter is, and alone can be. His fellowship with the latter thus has and maintains the character of an encounter in which the grace of Jesus Christ in all its fulness, but His grace and therefore a grace which is always free, is addressed to him. Nor does this grace fail to include a judgment passed on man. It does not cease to demand that he keep his distance. In face of it even his supreme and most joyous gratitude must always have, and continually acquire, the character of adoration. It is also important to notice that precisely in this fellowship of encounter there is not merely safeguarded the sovereignty of God, of Jesus Christ and of the Holy Spirit, but also the freedom of the human partner is preserved from dissolution. Indeed, it is genuinely established and validated. Unless we consider, safeguard and expressly state these things, we do better not to speak of " Christ-mysticism " when there is obviously no compelling reason to do so.

Having made this point, we may now proceed to state that the fellowship of Christians with Christ, which is the goal of vocation, is a perfect fellowship inasmuch as what takes place in it is no less than their union with Christ. The terms " attachment " and " co-ordination " are inadequate if they are not expressly understood in the sense of " union," i.e., the Christian's *unio cum Christo*. As we have shown, union does not mean the dissolution or disappearance of the one in the other, nor does it mean identification. It does not mean a conjunction of the two in which one or the other, and perhaps both, lose their specific character, role and function in relation to the other, the reciprocal relation being thus reversible. The union of the Christian with Christ which makes a man a Christian is their conjunction in which each has his own independence, uniqueness and activity. In this way it is, of course, their true, total and indissoluble union : true and not ideal ; total and not merely psychical and intellectual ; indissoluble and not just transitory. For it takes place and consists in a self-giving which for all the disparity is total on both sides. In this self-giving Christ and the Christian become and are a single totality, a fluid and differentiated but genuine and solid unity, in which He is with His people, the Lamb on the throne with the one who recognises in Him his Lord and King, the Head with the members of His body, the Prophet, Teacher and Master with His disciples, the eternal Son of God with the child of man who by Him and in Him, but only thus, only as His adopted brother, may be called and be the child of God. Like His own unity of true deity and humanity, this unity is *hic et nunc* concealed. It may be known in faith but not in sight, not by direct vision. The revelation of its glory has still to come. But even *hic et nunc* there can be and is no question of creating it or giving it force, but only of making definitively and universally visible its possibility, nature and reality as something incomparably great and totally new. This, and this alone, is what the whole of creation, with all men and Christians too, is waiting and groaning for. The purpose for which Christians are already called here and now in their life-histories within universal history is that in the self-giving of Jesus Christ to them, and theirs to Him, they should enter into their union with Him, their *unio cum Christo*.

For the sake of practical perspicuity in our definition of the Christian we first spoke of his humanity in common with all men, then of his divine sonship, then, in description of his fellowship with Jesus Christ, of the relationship of discipleship, his existence as the possession of this Owner, and the powerful work of the Holy Spirit within him. It is only now that we have reached the heart of the matter in his union with Christ. In view of what we said about the problem of the *ordo salutis* in the preceding sub-section, there is obviously no question here of a description of the genetic sequence of the states of the Christian, nor is it to be assumed that in the *unio cum Christo* we reach the culminating point of such a sequence. Our present concern is not with the event of vocation at all, but with its meaning and goal. And our supreme and final definition of this as the union of the Christian with Christ describes the most essential element in it which underlies and comprehends all the others, so that from the purely material view we really ought to have put it first. This is what Calvin actually ventured to do (*Instit.*, III, 1) when he opened his whole doctrine *De modo percipiendae gratiae* with a depiction of this *unio*. If we have not followed him in this, and for the sake of clarity have thus departed in some sense from the matter, it is to be noted expressly that only now have we reached the central point which supports all that precedes and is tacitly presupposed in it.

If we are to understand the nature of this union, then, in relation to the emphasised independence, uniqueness and activity of Jesus Christ on the one side and the Christian on the other, we do well to begin, not below with the Christian, but above with Jesus Christ as the Subject who initiates and acts decisively in this union. We do well to begin with the union of Christ with the Christian and His self-giving to the Christian, and not *vice versa*. It is here that the union and self-giving of the Christian have their roots.

That Jesus Christ in calling man to be a Christian unites Himself with him means first from His own standpoint that He is unique as the One who in His life and death was humiliated and exalted in the place and for the sake of all, as the One in whom the reconciliation of the world to God and the justification and santification of all were accomplished. In all this He has no assistant nor fellow-worker to accompany Him, let alone any *corredemptor* or *corredemptrix*. He is absolutely isolated from all others. Without them, He intervenes for them. But as this One, when it is a matter of the revelation of this work as inaugurated in His resurrection from the dead and continued in the work of His Holy Spirit, when it is a matter of His work in its prophetic dimension, He cannot and will not remain alone, nor can He be solitary in the reconciled world on His way to His future, conclusive and universal revelation. He cannot and will not be the Master without disciples, the Leader without followers, the Head without members, the King without fellows in His people, Himself without His own, Christ without Christians. The fact that the One who is disclosed in His resurrection from the dead and the outpouring of the Holy Spirit is really the omnipotent God who stooped down in unmerited love to man, the Lord who became a servant, has in the time which moves to its end in His final revelation a counterpart in the fact that as the Proclaimer of the act of God accomplished in Him, in His prophetic office and work, He does not go alone but wills to be what He is and do what He does in company with others whom He calls for the purpose, namely, with the despicable folk called Christians. He attests to the world the reconciliation to God effected in Him, the covenant of God with man fulfilled in Him, as He associates with Christians, making common cause and conjoining Himself with them. He does not merely do this ideally or partially, but really and totally. He does not merely comfort, encourage, admonish or protect them remotely or from afar. But as He calls them to Himself in the divine power of His Spirit, He refreshes them by offering and giving Himself to them and making them His own. That He wills and does this is—in analogy to the mystery and miracle of Christmas—the true *ratio* of Christian existence as this is celebrated, adored and proclaimed within the community of Christians in the common administration of the Lord's Supper, instituted to represent the perfect fellowship between Him and them which He has established —an implication which we cannot do more than indicate in the present context.

We now turn to what must be thought and said concerning this union of His with Christians from their standpoint. There is, of course, no one, apostle, saint or the Virgin, who can contribute in the very slightest to what is accomplished for all by the one Jesus Christ in His life and death. In relation to His high-priestly and kingly work even a Paul can only know what has been done for us by God in Him (1 Cor. 2¹²). But those to whom He reveals and makes known this life and death of His as the act of God for their salvation and His own glory do not confront this act of revelation, this work of atonement in its prophetic dimension, as hearers and spectators who are left to themselves and ordained for pure passivity. What kind of vocation, illumination and awakening would it be, what kind of knowledge, if they were merely left gaping at the One who discloses Himself to them ? No, as surely as He does not will to tread alone His way as the Proclaimer of the kingdom, so surely they for their part must be with Him, companions of the living One who are made alive by Him, witnesses in His discipleship to that which He wills to reveal to the world as having been effected in Him, namely to the reconciliation accomplished and the covenant fulfilled in Him. This is what He makes them as He calls them to Himself, as He does this really and totally, as He does not leave them to themselves, as He does not remain outside them, as He gives Himself to them, as in the divine power of His Spirit He unites Himself with them. That they may become and be those with whom He unites Himself by His Word ; that they may be those who are born again from above by His presence and action in their own lives ; that they may be continually nourished by Him—this is, from their standpoint, the *ratio* of Christian existence. Here again we are naturally reminded of the mystery and miracle of Christmas, and must make provisional reference to the Lord's Supper.

" I in you " (Jn. 14²⁰, 15⁴). " I in them " (Jn. 17²³, ²⁶). " I in him " (Jn. 6⁵⁶, 15⁵). According to Jn. 15¹ᶠ· He is the vine which produces, bears and nourishes the branches, or according to the even stronger expression in Jn. 6³³ He is the " bread of God which cometh down from heaven, and giveth life unto the world." He gives them His flesh and blood, imparting and communicating Himself to them, giving Himself to nourish them, in order that as He lives they also may and will live to all eternity (Jn. 6⁵³). The same teaching is found in Paul. " Know ye not your own selves, how that Jesus Christ is in you ? " (2 Cor. 13⁵ ; cf. Rom. 8¹⁰, Col. 1²⁷). He is the One who has apprehended the apostle (Phil. 3¹²), putting His power in him (2 Cor. 12⁹), setting His truth in him (2 Cor. 11¹⁰), speaking in him (2 Cor. 13³), and always magnifying and glorifying Himself in his person (Phil. 1²⁰). And in relation to other Christians He is the One who dwells " in your hearts by faith " (Eph. 3¹⁷), or who seeks to be formed in them (Gal. 4¹⁹). Whether they are Greeks, Jews, Barbarians, Scythians, slaves or freemen, Christ is in them all (Col. 3¹¹). Χριστὸς ἐν ὑμῖν is the great mystery of God among the nations (Col. 1²⁷). In the strongest possible expression (Gal. 2²⁰), Christ lives in the apostle in such a way that he has to say of himself that he no longer lives, i.e., in himself and apart from the fact that Christ lives in him, but that he now lives in faith in Him who gave Himself for him, this being his own most proper life to which, as one who still lives in the flesh, he can do justice only as he believes in Him. In Col. 3⁴, however, " Christ our life " is also said in relation to Christians generally, and again in relation to all those who by the Spirit have been given to know what is given them by God there is made the immeasurable claim : " We have the mind of Christ " (ἡμεῖς δὲ νοῦν Χριστοῦ ἔχομεν, 1 Cor. 2¹², ¹⁶), i.e., in virtue of His life in us we have His reason.

It has always involved an unwise and, on a proper consideration, an attenuating exposition of these verses to speak of an extension of the incarnation in relation to the Christian's *unio cum Christo* and then in relation to the Lord's Supper. We are concerned rather with the extended action in His prophetic work of the one Son of God who became flesh once and for all and does not therefore need any further incarnation. We are concerned with the fact that He as the one Word of God takes up His abode in the called, that His life becomes their life as He gives Himself to them. This is the mystery and miracle of His union with them. Similarly, we do well to refrain from describing the Christian in relation to his fellows (Luther, *De libertate*, 1520, W.A., 66, 26), or, as Roman Catholics do, the priest in the mass in relation to other believers, as an *alter Christus*. In this perfect fellowship the one Christ as the only original Son of God, beside whom there can be no other, is always the One who gives, commands and precedes, and the other, the *homo christianus*, whom He makes His brother and therefore a child of God, is always the one who receives, obeys and follows. The former is the Word of God in person ; the latter, like John the Baptist in the Fourth Gospel, is His witness. In this distinction, of course, neither remains alone. Both become a totality. For it is not too great or small a thing for Christ to give Himself to the Christian, to cause His own life to be that of the Christian, to make Himself his with all that this necessarily implies. This is the high reality of His vocation to the extent that this takes place and is to be understood as His union with the Christian.

In the reality and power of the union of Christ with the Christian, however, their fellowship has also the meaning and character of a union of the Christian with Christ. Their fellowship would not be complete if their relationship were actualised only from above downwards and not also from below upwards, if it were not reciprocal. A justifiable concern for the unconditional predominance of the freedom, grace and decision of Jesus Christ which establish the relationship should not mislead us into suppressing or minimising the fact that His action has its correspondence in an action of the Christian. According to the guidance of the New Testament the declaration concerning the communication of Christ with the Christian necessarily includes a complementary declaration concerning the communication of the Christian with Christ.

That Christ links Himself with the Christian settles the fact that the latter, too, does not go alone. To do justice to Christ as his Counterpart he is not directed to believe in Him and to obey and confess Him on his own initiative or resources. He is certainly summoned to believe, obey and confess. And both as a whole and in detail this will always be the venture of a free decision and leap. It will always be a venture in which no man can wait for or rely on others, as though they could represent him or make the leap for him. Even in the community and therefore with other Christians, he can believe, obey and confess only in his own person and on his own responsibility. But does this mean on his own initiative and resources ? No, for the act of the Christian is not to be described as a leap into the dark or a kind of adventure. We have only to consider what kind of a free decision or leap is involved to see that, if there is any action which is well-grounded and therefore assured in respect of its goal, it is the faith, obedience and confession of the Christian. The Christian undertakes these things as through the Spirit he is called to do so by the risen One in whom he believes and whom he obeys and confesses. And in the knowledge given him with his calling, he is not merely required but empowered to do it. In Jesus Christ he knows and apprehends himself as a member of the world reconciled to God in Him, as a man who is justified and sanctified in Him in spite of his sin, as a legitimate partner of the covenant fulfilled in Him. Believing in Jesus Christ and obeying and confessing him, he simply does the natural thing proper to him as the man he is in Christ and therefore in truth. He simply realises his true—the only truly human—possibility. He simply exercises the freedom given him as the man he is in Christ and therefore in truth. The decision or leap of his faith, obedience and confession consists in the fact that he takes himself seriously as the man he is and recognises himself to be in Jesus Christ instead of immediately forgetting his true self (who and what he is in Christ), like the man who looks at himself in a mirror and then goes on his way (Jas. 1[23f.]). It consists in the fact that he begins to act on this basis, i.e., on the basis of Jesus Christ and as the man he is in Him. He believes, obeys and confesses as, now that Christ has united Himself with him, he unites himself with Christ, giving himself to the One who first gave Himself to him, and thus choosing Him as the starting-point and therefore the goal of His thinking, speech, volition and action, quite simply and non-paradoxically because this is

3. *The Goal of Vocation* 545

what He is, because there is no other starting-point or goal apart from Him, because in truth he is not outside Him but within Him.

Here again, however, we must consider the opposite side and therefore add that as the Christian unites himself with Christ it is also settled that he cannot part from Christ. In his relationship with Him He alone is the One who gives, commands and leads, and the criterion of the genuineness of all the faith, obedience and confession of Christians will always necessarily consist in their allowing Him alone to be what He alone is, neither openly nor secretly trying to subject Him to their own dominion, in the exercise of which their faith would at once become unbelief, their obedience, disobedience and their confession denial. This does not mean, however, that they can refrain from immediately and directly recognising their own cause in His cause, i.e., in the occurrence of His prophetic work in the world. For as they recognise Him, they can and should recognise themselves in Him, what they themselves are in truth. Except by the self-deception of Jas. $1^{23f.}$, how could they break their solidarity with Him ? As those they are and know themselves to be in Him, as members of the world reconciled to God in Him, as justified and sanctified sinners, they cannot possibly leave Him in the lurch instead of following Him. In the freedom given them as those they are, they have only one option, namely, to believe in Him, to obey Him and to confess Him, and in so doing, in making this movement, to unite themselves with Him as He in His turning to them, in calling them and making Himself known to them, unites Himself with them. Called, illumined and awakened by His prophetic Word, for this Word they can only be in truth the men they are. What other can they do, then, as those to whom Christ has given Himself, than to give themselves to Him, to exist as His, and therefore continually to seek and find their life in Him, in whom it is their truest life ?

The New Testament gives us every reason to draw very distinctly this line from below upwards. For rather strangely, but quite unmistakeably, it is not merely no less but much more noticeable in the New Testament than the opposite line which is original and must thus be regarded as decisive in our description of the whole relationship. It certainly receives more frequent mention. While the authors of the New Testament presuppose the being of Christ in the Christian, with no fear of injuring the supremacy of the divine initiative they do in fact look more in the opposite direction, namely, to the being of the Christian in Christ. The whole emphasis of the speech concerning the vine in Jn. $15^{1f.}$ is obviously laid on the fact that, as the branches can bear fruit only as they abide in the vine, so the disciples, if they are to be what they are fruitfully, must abide in the One who speaks to them. This is brought home in many different ways, and it is impressively repeated in the First Epistle of John ($3^{6, 9}$, 4^{16}). For χωρὶς ἐμοῦ, "without me ye can do nothing" (Jn. 15^5). That they are called to abide in Him presupposes that the free and responsible participation of Christians in their status is envisaged in the description of the fellowship between Christ and them. It presupposes that they are already in Him, and obviously because first and supremely He is in them and has made their being a being in Him. " I in you " (Jn. 14^{20}), comes first, but secondly and on this basis it must

C.D.—IV.—III.—II.—18

also be said : " Ye in me." That Christians are in Christ, that their Christian existence is everywhere realised in the fact that it unites with His in which it has its origin, substance and norm, is the insight which in the New Testament dominates especially the thinking and language of Paul, though it also finds expression in the First Epistles of Peter and John. The statement usually has an indicative character. But we have to remember that even indicatively it speaks of the history in which the union of the Christian with Christ takes place, so that we need not be surprised that it may become the imperative so characteristic of the Johannine passages. Christians are now quite briefly described as οἱ ἐν Χριστῷ Ἰησοῦ, or usually even more simply as ἐν Χριστῷ or ἐν κυρίῳ (Rom. 8¹, 2 Cor. 5¹⁷, Eph. 2¹³, 1 Pet. 5¹⁴). And they are described in this way because they are in Him (ἐστέ, 1 Cor. 1³⁰, 9¹, ²; ἐσμέν, 1 Jn. 2⁵). And they are in Him because Christ has adopted them into unity with His being (Rom. 15⁷), which means that in virtue of their baptism they have put Him on like a covering garment (Gal. 3²⁷), and must continually do so (Rom. 13¹⁴). This historical being in Christ is decisively determined, of course, by the fact that first and supremely God was " in Christ " reconciling the world to Himself (2 Cor. 5¹⁹). It is thus determined by their election made and revealed in Christ (Eph. 1⁴, ⁹, 3¹¹), by their redemption accomplished and manifested in Him (Col. 1¹⁴), by the grace of God addressed to them and recognisable in Him (1 Cor. 1⁴), by His love (Rom. 8³⁹), by His peace (Phil. 4⁷), by the eternal life of which they are assured in Him (Rom. 6²³). As they are in Christ, they acquire and have a direct share in what God first and supremely is in Him, what was done by God for the world and therefore for them in Him, and what is assigned and given to them by God in Him. But their being as thus determined by God is a concretely active being. In the one reality ἐν Χριστῷ God and man do not confront each other abstractly as such. On the contrary, there is a direct and concrete confrontation of the divine and corresponding human action, the former kindling the latter and the latter kindled by it. Conscious of being an ἄνθρωπος ἐν Χριστῷ (2 Cor. 12²), Paul is very definitely activated as an apostle. He can be absolutely certain of his convictions " in him," as in respect of the distinction of meats in Rom. 14¹⁴. He can have " in him " the joy with which he confidently makes his request of Philemon ⁽v. 8⁾. He can be sure " in him " of speaking the truth both from God and before Him (Rom. 9¹, 2 Cor. 2¹⁷). " In him," too, he can be quietly confident in respect of His communities (2 Thess. 3⁴, Gal. 5¹⁰) and thank God that He always causes him to triumph in Christ and to spread abroad the savour of His knowledge (2 Cor. 2¹⁴). Nor does Paul ascribe here to himself anything that he does not also basically ascribe both indicatively and imperatively to all Christians and to the whole community. " In him " he makes his boast in respect of them (1 Cor. 15³¹). Has not he Paul as an apostle begotten them again in Christ Jesus through the Gospel (1 Cor. 4¹⁵) ? Called " in Christ," are not all Christians " in him " saints (Col. 1²) and believers (Col. 1⁴, Eph. 1¹⁵), hoping " in him " (1 Cor. 15¹⁹) and " in him " called to obedience in their own particular situation (Eph. 6¹ᶠ⁻) ? " We all, with open face beholding as in a glass the glory of the Lord, are changed into the same image from glory to glory, even as by the Lord who is the Spirit," without whom it would be impossible (2 Cor. 3¹⁸ᶠ⁻). Hence Paul can see in one or another his fellow-labourer (Rom. 16³) or fellow-servant (Col. 4⁷) " in Christ," and in Epaphras his fellow-prisoner " in him " (Phil. 23). They are all light " in the Lord " (Eph. 5⁸). They can and should all glory " in the Lord " (1 Cor. 1³¹, 2 Cor. 10¹⁷, Phil. 1²⁶). They can and should all rejoice " in the Lord " (Phil. 3¹, 4⁴, ¹⁰). The apostle greets them " in him " in his letters (1 Cor. 16¹⁹, Phil. 4²¹). And " in him " he also admonishes them, here too presupposing that they are " in him," that as Christians they are within and not without, so that they have only to be told to continue to walk " in him " (Col. 2⁶, 1 Pet. 3¹⁶) and to be reminded of the mind which is self-evident " in Christ Jesus " (Phil. 2⁵) and of that which is " fit in the Lord " (Col. 3¹⁸). To what can those who are in

Him be meaningfully admonished, invited and summoned but—in a rather different expression—to stand as who and what they are (1 Thess. 3⁸, Phil. 4¹) ? In relation to the historical character of this being of theirs, however, it is indeed meaningful to admonish, invite and summon them to do this. How could they be what they are in Christ if they did not continually become it ?

This is not by any means a full list of the New Testament references to the εἶναι ἐν Χριστῷ. To give such a list it would be necessary not only to mention and co-ordinate many others, but also to introduce a series which we have left aside, namely, the passages which, without any basic alteration of meaning, substitute διὰ Χριστοῦ or ἐν ὀνόματι Χριστοῦ for ἐν Χριστῷ. But we have certainly adduced sufficient to show what powerful witness there is in the New Testament to the union of the Christian with Christ which is our present concern.

It is perhaps relevant to our purpose to add a brief linguistic enquiry into what has been said both materially and in the biblical discussions concerning the two aspects of this union, i.e., that of Christ with the Christian and that of the Christian with Christ. What is meant by the word " in " when we say that Christ is in the Christian and the Christian in Him ? Is this a mode of expression which demands demythologisation because of its evident localising ? We may confidently reply that the word certainly has in all seriousness a local signification. If, in the fellowship between Christ and the Christian and the Christian and Christ, it must be maintained—for this is the limit beyond which there can be nothing more to demythologise—that we have an encounter in time between two personal partners who do not lose but keep their identity and particularity in this encounter, then the " in " must indeed indicate on both sides that the spatial distance between Christ and the Christian disappears, that Christ is spatially present where Christians are, and that Christians are spatially present where Christ is, and not merely alongside but in exactly the same spot. Hence we say that Christ is in Christians and they in Him. Yet while this is true, it has surely become obvious both in our material presentation and in our survey of the biblical evidence that in this context the word " in " transcends even though it also includes its local signification.

The first statement, namely, that Christ is in the Christian, has the further meaning that Christ speaks, acts and rules—and this is the grace of His calling of this man—as the Lord of his thinking, speech and action. He takes possession of his free human heart. He rules and controls in the obedience of his free reason (2 Cor. 10⁵). As a divine person it is very possible for Him to do this in the unrestricted sovereignty proper to Himself and yet in such a way that there can be no question whatever of any competition between His person and that of the Christian, whether in the attempt of the latter to control His person, or conversely in its suppression or extinction by His person. It is very possible for Him to do it in such a way that the human person of the Christian is validated and honoured in full and genuine freedom, in the freedom of the obedient children of

God. That Christ is in the Christian means, then, that as the Mediator between God and man He does not exist merely for Himself and to that extent concentrically, but that in His prophetic work, in the calling of His disciples and Christians, with no self-surrender but in supreme expression of Himself, He also exists eccentrically, i.e., in and with the realisation of the existence of these men, as the ruling principle of the history lived by them in their own freedom.

The second statement, namely, that the Christian is in Christ, has not only the local but also the higher meaning that his own thinking, speech and action has its ruling and determinative principle—and herein it is the work of his gratitude corresponding to grace—in the speech, action and rule of Christ. His free human heart and reason and acts are orientated on Him, i.e., on agreement with His being and action. In the power of the Word of God which calls him, and therefore in the power of the Holy Spirit, this orientation is his only possibility, already in process of realisation. Again, there is no rivalry between the human person and the divine. There is thus no danger that the former will be overwhelmed by the latter. There is no danger that it will necessarily be destroyed by it and perish. Rather, the human person, experiencing the power of the divine, and unreservedly subject to it, will necessarily recognise and honour it again and again in its sovereignty, finding itself established as a human person and set in truly human and the freest possible movement in orientation on it. That the Christian is in Christ means *mutatis mutandis* for him, too, that as one who is called by the one Mediator between God and man in the exercise of His prophetic office he cannot exist for himself and to that extent concentrically, but that, without detriment to his humanity, awakened rather to genuine humanity, he also exists eccentrically, in and with the realisation of his own existence, being received and adopted as an integral element in the life and history of Christ.

This, then, is the Christian's *unio cum Christo*. We recall that in this high view and doctrine we are not presenting a climax of Christian experience and development in face of which the anxious question might well be raised whether we have reached the point, or will ever do so, where in respect of our own Christianity we can sincerely say : " Christ in me, and I in Christ." On the contrary, we are presenting the last and most exact formulation of what makes us Christians whatever our development or experience. We have seen that Paul particularly in the New Testament does not think of restricting his insight in this regard to himself and a few other Christians of higher rank, but that as he speaks of himself he also speaks of the generality of Christians, not excluding the very doubtful Christians of Galatia and Corinth and not excluding the doubtful nature of their Christianity. If, as we have attempted in concentric circles, we think through what it means that the goal of vocation, and therefore of Christianity as divine sonship, is always attachment to Christ, co-ordination and fellowship with Him, discipleship, appropriation to Him with the corresponding expropriation, life of and by the Holy Spirit, then we are infallibly led at last to the point which we have now reached and described, namely, that a man becomes and is a Christian as he unites himself with Christ and Christ with him. And we remember that from the purely material standpoint this is the starting-point for everything else which is to be thought and said concerning what makes the Christian a Christian.

The final question might be raised whether it is altogether necessary to express the general answer to our enquiry concerning the goal of vocation in this way which is so pointed as to seem at first glance rather too bold, open to misconception and even fraught with danger.

It has to be conceded, and is worth pondering, that in the New Testament as a whole it is only Pauline and Johannine passages which give us direct sanction for pursuing the line to this point. Explicitly we encounter neither the idea nor the concept of *unio cum Christo* either in the Synoptic Gospels, the Epistle to the Hebrews, the Epistle of James, or the Book of Revelation. It may be said in reply, of course, that when we seek to define the Christian we probably have to push on to this point even on the basis of the specific message of these other parts of the Canon and in their exposition. Yet the texts themselves hardly constrain us to do this directly. Indeed, we might almost say categorically that they do not do so. It is thus easy to understand the restraint—and some material justification might also be found for it in the disturbing boldness of the whole enterprise—which may be discerned in both ancient and modern theology in relation to this matter. A particular concentration on Paul and John was always demanded, and for all the great respect which might be shown to these authors, not everyone could proceed so confidently on the very edge of mysticism as Luther did in the age of the Reformation, and as Calvin also did, probably treading in the footsteps of Bernard of Clairvaux in this regard.

In the *De libertate* of 1520 (*W.A.*, 7, 54, 31 f.) Luther maintained that in the incomparable grace of faith the soul and Christ are coupled together in a marriage far surpassing the *tenuis figura* of what passes for such among men, since in it the soul may possess and glory in everything that Christ has, i.e., His grace and life and salvation, whereas Christ makes His own everything that belongs to the soul, i.e., its sin and death and damnation. In the *De libertate* he amplifies this view by referring to the fact that there is a corresponding eccentric being of the Christian in relation to his fellows also : *Christianum hominem non vivere in seipso, sed in Christo et in proximo suo, aut Christianum non esse . . . per fidem sursum rapitur supra se in Deum, rursum per charitatem labitur infra se in proximum* (*ib.*, 69, 12 f.). It is in this context that he makes the statement already quoted that the Christian must become to others a second Christ. In his exposition of John's Gospel (1528) Luther's comment on the saying in 17[24] : " Father, I will that they also, whom thou hast given me, be with me where I am," is to the effect that we should all inscribe this text on our minds and hearts in large letters (*W.A.*, 28, 193, 11). On 17[11] (" that they may be one ") he says that this " one " does not merely imply *concors* or harmony, but *una res*, that they should be one thing, one cake, one body (*ib.*, 151, 7). On 17[21] (" that they also may be one in us ") he remarks that " everything is linked like a chain and forms a great circle or a beautiful crown " (*ib.*, 184, 32). On 17[23] (" I in them, and thou in me ") he says that *sicut Pater et Filius* are *unum divinum* being, *sic Christus cum sua Christianitate* is one Christian being (*ib.*, 187, 19). In all these passages we see a horizontal extension, except that instead of the neighbour we now have *christianitas*, in and with which emphasis is laid on the unity, grounded in that of Father and Son, of Christ with the Christian and of Christians with one another, so that by the interposition of Christianity a circle or crown is indeed made out of the simple sequence of God, Christ, man and fellow-man. The situation is rather different in his exposition of Galatians (1535). Here his concern is almost exclusively with the question of the justification of the sinner. A consequence of this is that—at least in the relevant passages—the reference both to the neighbour and to Christianity seems to be weakened, and there is a stronger insistence on Christ and the Christian. The circle of which Luther now speaks is the ring of faith (*W.A.*, 40¹, 165, 3), which contains (*apprehendit*) as its stone, not love as the Scholastics maintained, but Christ, so that the Christian possesses (*possidet*) Him in faith. Gal. 2²⁰ is thus paraphrased as follows (*ib.*, 283, 30) : *Christus ergo, inquit, sic inhaerens et conglutinatus mihi et manens in me hanc vitam, quam ago, vivit in me, immo vita qua sic vivo, est Christus ipse. Itaque Christus et ego iam unum in hac parte sumus.* Luther knows that it is a *mirabilis loquendi ratio*, yet he cannot avoid saying : *Christum et me esse coniunctissimos.* Whatever there is in me of grace, righteousness, life, peace or salvation, is His. What is His is actually mine : *per conglutinationem et inhaesionem, quae est per fidem, per quam efficimur quasi unum corpus in spiritu.* If faith is not just a *historica fides de Christo* such as the devil and the ungodly may also have (*ib.*, 285, 20), then the Christian and Christ become *quasi una persona. Hic oportet Christum et conscientiam meam fieri unum corpus* (*ib.*, 282, 21). In view of this unity the certainty of faith as such is certainty of salvation, and indeed unconditional certainty, whereas any return to the Law would inevitably entail despair and destruction, Christ being viewed and understood as the One enthroned in heavenly majesty, and oneself, apart from Him, in the light of one's own life and works. *In causa iustificationis*—this is the basic thesis which emerges clearly in the *Commentary on Galatians—unio cum Christo* is the decisive factor.

It is astonishing that precisely *in causa iustificationis* the successors of Luther did not speak more frequently and incisively of this matter. Was not the righteousness of the sinner before God something alien imputed to him ? Was it not in this way an unconditionally real righteousness ? Did they not strictly repudiate any co-operation of human works in its attainment ? Did they not also reject any idea of a *gratia infusa* ? Did they not maintain the *sola fide*, and the *simul iustus et peccator*, or however else we might describe the paradoxes of the Lutheran doctrine of justification ? Did they not also cling to the *propter Christum* which had come to have so dominating a role from the time of Melanchthon ? But how else could they establish or explain these things except on the basis of the union with Christ ? This truth might well have set the Reformation doctrine in so radiant a light that, quite apart from misunderstandings on the Protestant side, perhaps even the fathers of Trent would have been prevented from their unfortunate resistance to it in *Sessio* VI. We cannot say, however, that this took place in the 16th century or after in a way which was incisive and unmistakeable to friend and foe alike. Nor did the Lutherans particularly put another question, namely, whether the Christianity of the Christian, if it really has its basis and essence in his union with Christ, is really exhausted by his justification before God ; whether his faith really consists in no more than faith in the remission of sins ; whether *unio cum Christo* does not include with the same dignity and power the sanctification of man and therefore his obedience. We cannot avoid the impression that a source of comprehensive knowledge was discovered at this point, but that it was not exploited as it might have been, to maintain at least the inner unity of Protestantism and perhaps that of the whole Western Church. So much, then, for what we can learn from Luther in this matter, and for the further lessons which are also suggested.

But the same line of teaching is found quite definitely in Calvin as well. We say " quite definitely " because according to an ancient legend still current to-day Calvin was the great champion of distance between God and man, so that we should not expect to find in him a notion or teaching which so obviously overcomes this distance as does that of the *unio cum Christo*.

Yet when we turn to Calvin we first note that this is the central and dominating concept in his definition of the gift and fruit of the Lord's Supper. This consists (*Conf. fidei de Eucharistia*, 1537, *Op. sel.*, I, 435) in the *communio* and *participatio* of the Christian with the whole Christ exalted at the right hand of the Father, with His *caro vivifica*, as Calvin emphasised in opposition to Zwingli, indicated and offered under the signs of bread and wine and actualised in the elect by the Holy Spirit who unites them with Him. From first to last in his utterances on the Lord's Supper, Calvin maintained that Christ's impartation of Himself to us as *notre vie unique* (*Petit traité de la S. Cène*, *Op. sel.*, I, 504) is the *materia sacramenti*, the *res ipsa*, with which we are concerned. With incomprehensible mystery it is attested to us that we are to grow up to be one body with Christ, to become one with Him, so that what is ours is His and what is His ours, He being the Son of Man with us and we sons of God with Him, He lowly weak and mortal with us and we exalted, strong and immortal with Him, He invested with our unrighteousness and we with His righteousness (*Instit.*, IV, 17, 2).

Perhaps on the basis of his understanding of the Lord's Supper, but certainly in a much wider context, this notion has a comprehensive and basic significance for Calvin. Indeed, we might almost call it his conception of the essence of Christianity. This first emerges, if I am not mistaken, in the *Institutio* of 1543 (in the chapter *De fide*, C.R., I, 462 f.) when he is contesting the semi-Papal theologoumenon which had been advanced at the period, perhaps by Cardinal Contarini, according to which the Christian can have perfect assurance of salvation in relation to Christ but none at all in relation to himself, and is therefore forced to live, as Calvin comments in what is perhaps something of a caricature, in a constant state of dialectical alternation between supreme trust and supreme despair. Against this Calvin appeals expressly to Bernard of Clairvaux, and quoting extensively from this author he argues that we are to view and understand Christ, not as *veluti procul stantem*, but as dwelling in us, so that we are to view and understand ourselves, not as separated from Him, but as those to whom He has imparted not only all His goods but supremely and decisively Himself : *utraque manu fortiter retinere oportet eam qua se nobis agglutinavit societatem*, the *mirabilis communio* in which Christ has not only inseparably (*individuo nexu*) bound Himself to us but in which He grows with us from day to day, so that we find our merited damnation absorbed by His salvation present in and with us, and we are thus fully delivered from that dialectic. Again, in his *Commentary on Galatians* of 1548, and especially in the verse in 2[20] which naturally caught his attention too (C.R., 50, 199), Calvin refers in the first instance to the problem of justification. Like Luther, he emphasises that there is a freedom from the Law, *quam dum efficimur unum cum Christo*, like the shoot of a plant which can share in the nourishment given through the roots only to the extent that it forms a totality with them. To believe is to exist outside oneself in Him in a *vera et substantialis communicatio cum ipso*. That is to say, it is to live one's life *iure unionis* together with the life of Christ received into our consciousness (*conscientia*) by the power of the Spirit, and thus *vitam habere cum ipso communem*. But already there is a new feature as compared with Luther. This is the assertion that the *unio* has two aspects. It is first and comprehensively the sanctification (*regeneratio*) of man. As He lives in us, He rules us by His Spirit and directs our actions. Within this, it is also his justification, the *gratuita iustitiae acceptio* as the presupposition of His lordship. Plainly what we have here is the comprehensive signification of *unio* as it perhaps hovered before Luther in his *De libertate* and especially his sermons on John, but then disappeared in his *Commentary on Galatians* with its concentration on justification. As yet, however, Calvin did not draw out the consequences of this twofold meaning of *unio*, and he obviously did not perceive its central significance, though there are naturally hints in this direction in the appropriate sections of his *Commentary on John* of 1554. On Jn. 14[1], for example, we read that Christ is the true Emmanuel *qui simul ac fide quaeritur, intus nobis respondet* (*C.R.*, 47, 322). Or again on Jn. 14[19] : *Cum Christi vita etiam nostra coniuncta est, atque ex ea non secus atque ex fonte sua manat* (*ib.*, 330). On Jn. 17[21] he is careful to point out, against Osiander, that His proper being does not become ours ; he maintains that by the power (*virtus*) of His Spirit He gives us a share in His life and thus in all that He has received of the Father (*ib.*, 387). On Jn. 16[7] he makes the notable observation that the reference is to a kind of presence that is far more salutary and desirable for us (*longe utilius ac magis expetenda*) than one in which He might be physically present to our eyes, but only to our eyes (*ib.*, 358).

These are only isolated glosses, however, which hardly reveal the basic reach and significance which the matter increasingly came to have in Calvin's thinking. The real advance has obviously been made when we come to the *Institutio* of 1559, in which *unio cum Christo* has become the common denominator under which Calvin tried to range his whole doctrine of the appropriation of the salvation achieved and revealed in Christ. For now in the Third Book, before he can speak of faith, of conversion and renewal, of the *vita hominis christiani*, of *abnegatio nostri* as its sum, of the necessary bearing of the cross, of the relation between this and the future life, then—and only then—of justification, of Christian freedom and prayer, of eternal election as the ultimate presupposition of the whole, and finally of the future resurrection, according to the view attained in 1559 he has first to make it plain how it can come about at all that what God has done for us in Christ, as declared in the Second Book, can apply to us and be effective for us. The answer given in the noteworthy opening chapter of the Third Book is to the effect that it comes about through the *arcana operatio Spiritus*, which consists in the fact that Christ Himself, instead of being *extra nos*, outside the man separated from Him and therefore irrelevant to us, becomes ours and takes up His abode in us, we for our part being implanted into Him (Rom. 11[17]) and putting Him on (Gal. 3[27]). This does, of course, take place in faith. But it takes place in faith—and one of the distinctive features of Calvin as compared with Luther is that he never speaks of faith or the *unio* except in this context—through the Holy Spirit as the *vinculum quo nos sibi efficaciter devincit* (Christ). Without the Spirit, i.e., without what Christ Himself does to us through Him, we could only indulge in frigid and unprofitable speculation concerning Him. Through the Holy Spirit, however, He achieves the *coniunctio* between Himself and us and us and Himself. Calvin, too, speaks of a *sacrum connubium* in this connexion. That is, Christ achieves a union in which we become flesh of His flesh and bone of His bone (Eph. 5[30]), *adeoque unum cum ipso*, He embracing us and we appropriating Him, and in Him our justification and sanctification. It certainly takes place in faith, but, no matter how zealously the *doctores* might summon us, we could never come to faith were it not that, before and with our faith, *Christus ipse* as the *interior magister* opened our eyes for Him by the *Spiritus intelligentiae*, illuminating us, drawing us to Himself and making us new creatures in Him.

Hence the theme of the Third Book, as W. Niesel has rightly observed (*Die Theologie Calvins*, 1957, p. 121), is " again Jesus Christ." My only qualification would be that this is so at least in arrangement. It is now clearly shown on what basis alone we can meaningfully consider and describe the totality of what makes the Christian a Christian. " Fellowship with the Mediator brings about the change in our lives " (*ib.*, p. 122). Indeed, in the doctrine *De modo percipiendae gratiae* as developed in the Third Book, there are not lacking occasions when Calvin expressly recalls this basis. Yet we cannot really say that the totality is projected and worked out in the light of it. The *Institutio* of 1559 was not a reconstruction in this sense. In this last as in the preceding editions his work was for the most part that of a very skilful and careful sifting in which he took over all the main parts of his earlier writings and then formulated and enriched and illumined them by all kinds of major or minor alterations and additions. One such addition, though in detail it incorporates earlier features, is this first chapter of the Third Book, which thus reminds us to some extent of the new patches of Mk. 2^{21}. In the result, there can be no doubt that the basic significance of the *unio* doctrine is well brought out both intrinsically and especially in virtue of its position as an introduction to the whole. Yet we are then astonished to find that it is not exploited very differently in what follows, but for long stretches is concealed again by lengthy deliberations of an earlier origin and resting on a very different basis. It is true that in the great chapter on faith (III, 2, 24–5) Calvin leaves unaltered the section in the 1543 edition to which we referred, including the quotation from Bernard. Yet we cannot possibly say that his definition and explanation of faith are unequivocally determined by this. The same is true at a later point in his doctrine of justification. Here again powerful and most effective reference is made to the *unio* in rebuttal of Osiander (III, 11, 10), but this has little bearing on the positive presentation of the doctrine and certainly does not have any determinative influence. Hence in the form which he gives it, it can no more have the power of penetration, which this centre might have given it, than it can in popular Lutheranism or in its Romanist opponents. Similarly, in the doctrine of sanctification which dominates the Third Book, in the two eschatological chapters (9 and 25) and in the return to the doctrine of election, there are occasional references but not the illuminating penetration we might have expected. To this extent we are forced to say that in the Third Book Jesus Christ is again and most impressively the theme of Calvin from the standpoint of arrangement, but only from the standpoint of arrangement.

The same is true of the Reformed theology which followed in the 16th and 17th centuries. One of the features which distinguished this from contemporary Lutheranism was that under the obvious influence of the *Institutio* of 1559 it opened its whole doctrine of the appropriation of salvation with the special and basic doctrine of *insitio* or *insertio in Christum*. In this regard it should be noted how untenable is the statement that Lutheranism laid greater emphasis on the fellowship between God and man and Calvinism on the distance. As the older Reformed set everything from the very first under this standpoint, it became unnecessary for them at a later stage to speak of a mystical union of the soul with the Lutherans of the later 17th century in response to one of the concerns of Pietism. In Reformed theology, and already in Calvin himself, regard was had and justice done to this concern at the very outset. And when we remember that even such strictly Reformed areas as the Lower Rhineland and Holland saw the development of a pronouncedly mystical Pietism, it can hardly be denied that this distinctive theological feature seems to have had very practical origins and consequences, though it must also be admitted that against the sinister background of the Calvinistic doctrine of predestination—we have only to think of G. Tersteegen—there might easily be suspicious aberrations in the direction of a generally religious divine immanence for which the *unio cum Christo* might well be no more than the exemplary schema of an anonymous " I in Thee, Thou in me." Indeed, it is not impossible that in the well-known definition of Schleiermacher (also of the Reformed tradition), namely, that Christianity is a mode of believing in which everything is related to the redemption accomplished by Jesus of Nazareth (*Der Chr. Glaube*, 11), we have a distant and, of course, severely distorted echo of that basic Calvinistic proposition. However that may be, Reformed theology has kept alive the recognition that the vocation of the elect consists essentially in his *unio cum Christo*, and therefore in all its aspects is to be understood accordingly. In Reformed orthodoxy as in Calvin himself there was no systematic outworking or exploitation of this insight in relation to the whole doctrine of vocation. But we may be grateful that it brought it out strongly at least from the standpoint of arrangement.

The purpose of this historical excursus was simply to show that we are not isolated but in good company in making this matter the central point in our answer to the question of the goal of vocation. In intention at least, we definitely have Luther and then Calvin and his followers behind us. To show this is not, of course, to prove that we have adopted the right procedure.

If we are asked how far it is necessary to give this final point to the definition of the Christian or his Christianity, the only proof is to be found in the first place in the counter-question whether we can desist from following the compellingly clear voice of at least the Johannine and Pauline if not the whole of the New Testament witness, regardless of the perilous depths of mysticism by which it leads us. But then, materially, the goal of vocation, with which we are concerned in its general form in this sub-section, can be the object and content of a serious statement of faith only in the perfection in which it confronts directly, and is directly comparable with, the mystery and miracle of Christmas, constituting a single totality with it. A perfect being of the Christian in this sense, i.e., a being in which he can and should believe with the same clarity and distinctness as he believes in God, in Jesus Christ, in the Holy Spirit and in all the works of God, can take place, however, only in the fellowship in which God always and in every respect intervenes for man, and man always and in every respect is free for the venture of relying both in life and death on God. It is a being in this fellowship which is disclosed to man as he is called to be a Christian. In his being in this fellowship he can and should believe in the full sense of the word. Recognising it, he can and should wholly count upon it, and live unconditionally in the confidence that it is his true being. The truth of his being in this fellowship, however, is the declaration of his union with Christ. And this is what makes this declaration materially necessary.

4. THE CHRISTIAN AS WITNESS

In this and the next two sub-sections, we have now to show and develop in detail what the goal of vocation is in detail, namely, what it means practically and concretely to become and be a Christian.

The Christian who is called by God in Jesus Christ through the Holy Spirit, exists in an apparently endless multiplicity of different forms in his specific freedom, orientation and determination. As no

man is simply identical with another, so it is with Christians. And
the decisive reason for this is not to be found in their natural human
individuality, nor in the particular temporal and spatial preconditions
of their existence. These form only the framework in which each is
this particular Christian and not another. The basis of the particularity
of each Christian existence consists in the fact that the vocation of
each Christian is particular. It thus consists finally in the particular
thing which the Lord who calls is for him and has in view for him.
But this multiplicity of the actual goal of vocation in the case of individual Christians should not mislead us or cause us to conclude that
the last word is one of a *laissez-faire* in which anything is possible,
legitimate, demanded and in its own way right, so that there can be
no investigation of what makes all of them Christians as distinct from
the rest. The Lord who calls them all, and is in His own specific way
above them all, is one Lord. Hence it is surely impermissible to accept
an ultimate disparity of individual Christian forms. It is obvious,
rather, that we should ask concerning features common to all the forms,
concerning the law which they all follow and the norm by which they
are all measured. If they all exist by the Word of the one Lord,
then there must be lineaments, outlines and contours of the Christian
which more clearly and accurately in some cases, and with greater
distortion and inaccuracy in others, impress themselves upon all and
are visibly the same in every case. In its connexion with the One by
whom it is established, the manner of the Christian does not distinguish itself from that of all other men, or from a perverted or
degenerate Christianity, in such a way that as applied to individual
men it can be made otherwise than with a strict reference to the final
judgment of the Lord who calls them. But it does distinguish itself
in such a way that we can clearly know, indicate and describe what is
and what is not the manner of the Christian in accordance with the
adequate and binding standard of our own provisional judgment.
The multiplicity of His ways with individuals may be recalled. The
fact that He alone is the final Judge of individuals may be respected.
Yet since the Lord who calls all of them is one, it is not only legitimate
but imperative that we should ask concerning the one goal of the calling
of all Christians, concerning the law of the freedom which they will
none of them resist but to which they will all correspond if they are
genuinely Christians.

We have learned to know the decisive content of this law in the
propositions of the third sub-section which is now behind us. In all
circumstances we understand by the Christian a man whom Jesus
Christ has called to attachment to Himself, to His discipleship and to
living fellowship with Himself, and whom, as we finally say, He has
bound and indeed conjoined with Himself. In the power of the Holy
Spirit it takes place and is the case that he is in Christ and Christ in
him. Anything more special, practical or concrete than that could

hardly be said concerning the manner of Christian existence, concerning what makes all Christians Christians.   If we now ask further concerning the law of freedom valid for all and binding on all, this cannot mean that in the doctrine of vocation we are only now reaching that which is special, practical and concrete.   It can mean only that we find it necessary and desirable to know how far this insurpassably special, practical and concrete attachment of the Christian to Christ proves and expresses itself in the existence of Christians, of each individual Christian.   We ask concerning the structure of the Christian as it is determined by his attachment to Jesus Christ, as it reflects this attachment, and as it is controlled by a definite principle.   If only we keep strictly before us the decisive content of that law as the general thing which in this context is supremely particular, practical and concrete, then in the attempt at a narrower and more precise answer to our question we cannot and shall not be led into obscurity but we shall follow a clear and definite line.

But where are we to begin if we are to tread surely, consistently and meaningfully along the lines of our previous conclusions ?   If it is really to be a matter of the structure of Christian existence, whatever else may need to be said, our first and supreme concern must be with the controlling principle.   In describing this we shall seize only on that which is essential.   Many ultimate or penultimate things may seem to us great and important, but they must not be made primary.   This or that among them may be legitimate and apparently necessary in the light of a common denominator, but we must not substitute it for the common denominator which underlies and controls all the rest.   To be sure, that which is secondary is not to be passed over or suppressed.   On the contrary, it is to be given its true dignity and validity.   But the fact remains that what is primary must be recognised and represented as such, as the common denominator for all the rest.   How else are we to discern the lineaments, outlines and contours of the manner of the Christian ?   How else is there to arise a true picture of the Christian ?   This needs to be emphasised because in the preaching and instruction of the Church, and indeed in the systematic theology of all confessions and trends, different prejudgments have been and are reached and executed, with the best of intentions but far too hastily, which seem in some sense to be self-evident and necessary, which are even characterised by definite elements of truth, but which, as prejudgments in respect of the principle which controls the structure of Christian existence, have had and still have the consequence of obscuring and confusing the picture in a way which seriously threatens the orientation and understanding of the Christian message.   There is need of basic reflection on what is the primary thing, the common denominator, in the existence of the Christian.   We must not try to evade this.

We may begin by considering the situation as it arises out of the conclusions of the previous sub-section. In the world, among all other men, as the first-fruits of the prophetic work of Jesus Christ, illumined and awakened by His Word in the power of the Holy Spirit, there are Christians. And whatever else this may imply, it certainly means that there are in the world men who, as distinct from all others, and in their relationship to them (more badly perhaps than well), exist at the side of the God who acts and reveals Himself in Jesus Christ. They have not placed themselves at His side. They do not stand there on their own merits. They do so only in the power of the call of His free grace as it has come to them and been received by them. But they do stand there : in the world yet over against it ; like it, yet unlike it ; with it, yet in solidarity with God against it. They may be few or many. They may declare and express themselves among the rest either appropriately or inappropriately in their human qualities as Christians. But their existence as such is a small yet completely new factor characterising and helping to determine the whole world situation *post Christum*. And as such it reflects, however imperfectly and distortedly, the great, pure and perfect new factor of the fulfilment of the covenant between God and man accomplished in Jesus Christ to whom they belong and who belongs to them, and of the revelation of this fulfilment which is the basis of the reflection. Like the great factor, the small can also be forgotten, overlooked, unrecognised and denied. But grounded in the former, it cannot be reversed. It is an integral and determinative factor in the world situation which cannot be expunged. The God who has reconciled the world to Himself is not alone as the true Witness and Proclaimer of this event. The world and men within it are not only dealing with Him. Because with Him, even though in a very different way and in co-ordination with and subordination to His presence and action, they are also dealing with these people who in all the equivocal character of their humanity are called by Him through His Holy Spirit. As they respond to His call, well or badly believing in Him, loving Him and hoping in Him, for all their feebleness they really stand at His side as His own. But the question arises as to the significance of this small new factor of the existence of the Christian. What is its meaning and basis ? For what purpose do these people exist as those who are called to Him, who are called to His side, and who thus confront the world in the world ? In rather more banal terms, what advantage is it to the world, to themselves, and last and supremely to the God who acts and reveals Himself in Jesus Christ, that they are present as such ?

We shall first consider an answer commonly given in our time. It is a rather thin and unsatisfying variation on older and relatively more impressive and substantial answers. Yet this does not alter the fact that it undoubtedly merits consideration by reason of its concentration on one single point of the new being of the Christian in and in face of the world. It is to the effect that Christians are those who, as recipients of the *kerygma* of the eschatological divine act accomplished in the death of Jesus Christ, recognise, affirm and grasp within the world the possibility of their own non-worldly being, and therefore transcend and leave behind the world even as they still exist within it, and to this degree improperly. According to the passage usually adduced as *locus probans*, they have wives as though they had none, weep as though they wept not, rejoice as though they rejoiced not, buy as though they possessed not, use this world as though they had no use for it (1 Cor. 7$^{29f.}$). This freedom which is to be maintained in the world, but in face of the world, is what is thought to be envisaged in the calling of a man to be a Christian.

Now we cannot contradict the apostle Paul. Nor can we fail to see that the dialectic of Christian freedom, the great ὡς μή, stated in this passage, is in its own place a significant element in Christian existence and therefore calls for expression. It is important to refer to it because in it particularly there is impressively revealed the characteristic antithesis of the standing of the Christian in and in face of the world.

The question arises, however, whether even on the basis of this passage, let alone the rest of the Pauline and the New Testament witness generally, the being of the Christian may be centrally represented in terms of this dialectic of worldliness and unworldliness and therefore of eschatological tension. Can this ὡς μή really be understood as the decisive characteristic, and even the substance and final goal, of Christian existence ? Is even Christian freedom itself adequately described in terms of this dialectic ? Has Jesus Christ really lived and died and risen again (allegedly in the *kerygma* of His death) only in order to present and offer to the recipients of this *kerygma* a being in this antithesis, only in order to make such a being possible for them ? While it is not disputed that this ὡς μή has in a specific context its own validity and importance, can it really be understood and advanced as the ultimate description of what Paul called the being of the Christian in Christ and of Christ in the Christian ? Is this really the principle which controls the structure of Christian existence ? Is this really the final goal of vocation ? Does it bring before us the totality of the manner of the Christian ? Surely this would imply a lack of proportion between the mountain-moving power of the revelation and knowledge of Jesus Christ and its supposed and relatively trivial result. It is this disproportion which does not permit us to be satisfied with this answer.

We come nearer to the heart of the matter if with the moralism of all Christian epochs we think we see what makes a man a Christian, and therefore the goal of vocation, in a distinctive ethos. On this view, the call of Jesus Christ is decisively an invitation and demand that the men to whom it comes should adopt a particular inward and outward line of action and conduct of which we have the basic form in the twofold command to love God and our neighbours and a normative description in the imperatives of the Sermon on the Mount or the admonitions of the apostolic Epistles. And the Christian is the man who gladly accepts this invitation and demand as a binding Word of the Lord, and stirs himself to obey and to do justice to it. He is essentially a doer of the Word of Jesus Christ which calls him to a new order and orientation of his life.

There can be no doubting the theological importance and absolute indispensability of the content of this answer. No discussion of the antithesis between Moses and Christ or the Law and the Gospel should cause us to overlook or even contest the fact that in His relationship with Christians as His own Jesus Christ is their Commander, their supreme and indeed true and only Lawgiver, with a power and authority incomparably greater than that of Moses. The particularity in which Christians stand at the side of God in and in face of the world consists quite indisputably in the rendering of the obedience of life which they owe Him as their Lord. Hence in our consideration of what essentially distinguishes the manner of the Christian from that of other men, the voice of Christian moralism must also be heard, and its pronouncements must in no circumstances be suppressed or weakened in the context of the total discussion.

On the other hand, this justifiable and necessary concern should not be made the bracket within which everything else, the totality of Christian existence, is to be seen and understood. We should at least be warned by the fact that, so soon as the Christian ethos is divorced from its natural context, considered abstractly as an absolute magnitude and declared to be a controlling principle as such, it loses the distinctiveness, originality and uniqueness which mark it off from the type of ethos common to the rest of the world and humanity and thus make it an appropriate designation of the distinctive manner of the Christian. Even outwith the Christian sphere and its presuppositions, in a way which is often an example to Christians, and puts them to shame, there is much sacred commanding and pious obedience very similar to and apparently identical with that which is Christian. The Christian ethos can stand apart from all this only in its connexion with a principle which is anterior to it and which controls and determines it along with the whole structure of Christian existence. It cannot do so in itself and as such. A self-glorifying Christian moralism, which tries to be such a principle itself, has always resulted in a relativising and levelling down of the difference between Christian and non-Christian existence and the practical sterilisation of the former, i.e., the loss of its offensive and defensive power. Here too, however, the decisive point is that, if we have in the Christian ethos an absolute magnitude and therefore the controlling principle of Christian existence, we do not merely ask in vain, but do not really ask at all, concerning

the meaning and basis of this ethos. That the Christian is commanded
to love God and his neighbour with all that this implies, and that he
has to render obedience to this command as a binding Word of His
Lord, can only be maintained, accepted and acknowledged as a given
fact ; it cannot be understood and explained. It seems we cannot
avoid the question why and for what purpose this command is made
upon the Christian, and why and for what purpose he should obey it.
The content of the question is self-evident, because *per se* neither
the directions of Jesus and the apostles, nor the commandments
previously given to Israel, nor the sum of them in the twofold command of love, can be described as perspicuous and compelling.
Why and for what purpose, with what basis and meaning, is the
Christian summoned to this line of action and brought under this
prescription ? Who can answer this question ? But if the reference
to the Christian ethos were really the first and final word concerning
what makes a Christian a Christian, the Christian ethos would
obviously be an end in itself, and it would not only be impossible
to answer such a question but impermissible to raise it at all. For
example, if the rigorism of the Kantian moral concept in particular
were to be normative in this matter, then the Christian ethos, in
which we also have a nexus of commanding and obeying, would
have to be understood as indeed an end in itself, which would thus
exclude from the very outset any counter-question as to its meaning
and basis or any enquiry concerning its Why or Wherefore. What
is demanded of the Christian would simply be demanded because
it is, and he would have to obey simply because he has. Jesus Christ
would thus be his Lord only in virtue of a formal authority to command
certain things without any obligation to disclose their purpose. We
need hardly show in detail how often the relationship between Jesus
Christ and the Christian has in fact been understood and described
in terms of a triumphant moralism of this kind. But is it theologically
legitimate to allow it this triumph ? In other words, can the specific
relationship between the specific commanding of Jesus Christ and
the specific obedience of the Christian, and therefore the Christian
ethos, really be interpreted according to the norm of the Kantian
concept ? Certainly we have here in the strict sense an unconditional
commanding and an unconditional obedience. But both take place
in the light and not in darkness, however majestic or worthy of respect.
Both take place with a meaning and basis which are self-revealed
and therefore knowable. Hence it is not only not illegitimate but
imperative to ask concerning this meaning and basis. The Christian
ethos does not allow itself to be understood as an end in itself. It
is not a first thing, but follows from what Jesus Christ and Christians,
what He who commands and they who obey, are in themselves and in
their mutual relationship prior to their commanding and obedience.
The commanding on the one side is more than the assertion of a formal

authority, and the obedience on the other is more than formal subjection to the authority of the One who commands. The " more " consists in the fact that the Christian ethos has its origin, its creative and therefore separate meaning and basis, in the particular being of Jesus Christ in Christians and of Christians in Jesus Christ. Without this meaning and basis it cannot arise or exist at all. But the meaning and basis may be known as they make themselves known. Hence to ask concerning them, and to orientate ourselves by them, is not only not illegitimate but imperative if the ethos is to be and continually to become Christian. It is in view of this meaning and basis that the Christian ethos is from the very first distinct from every other. The form of this or that other ethos may be very similar to and even apparently identical with the Christian, but the origin of the latter in the being of the One who commands and the one who obeys in their unity is characteristic of it alone. This means, however, that the reference to the Christian ethos, while it is indispensable in its own place, cannot be the first or final word in a relevant definition of the manner of the Christian, of what makes a Christian a Christian, of the goal of vocation. However greatly we may honour the Christian ethos as a determination of the Christian manner, it cannot be the common denominator which we seek.

We now come to the answer which is the most important, which is in fact classic, and which we are therefore constrained to treat in great detail. All ancient and modern dogmatics of all confessions and schools, in so far as they have not surrendered to Christian moralism, have gravitated to this answer as though it were self-evident and there could be no question of any other. It does in fact seem to commend itself at once as the simplest and most obvious answer to our question. If it is agreed that in the Gospel as the Word of God which calls man we are concerned with an invitation and demand addressed to men ; if it is further agreed that in it we are also concerned with the placing of man in a freedom which he has to express in the world yet also in face of the world ; and if it is agreed that we are concerned with these things only in connexion with the offer and impartation of a divine act of grace and favour, then there can surely be nothing more obvious than to define the Christian as the man who is distinguished from others by the address, reception, possession, use and enjoyment of the salvation of God given and revealed to the world by God in Jesus Christ. Christians, we are told, are those who are the recipients of grace. They are illumined and awakened by the work of the Word and Spirit of the Lord. They are born again and converted. They have peace with God. For them the reconciliation of the world to God in Jesus Christ, and the justification fulfilled and sanctification established in Him, have not taken place in vain as for all the rest. They have their own personal share in the fruit of this divine action—a share which is effective in their lives and experienced by them. As they repent and believe, and continue to do so, they have the forgiveness of their sins and are also introduced to and empowered for a life corresponding to this liberation. They are the beloved of God who may love Him in return. They have the freedom as His children to converse with Him as their Father. On the basis of the resurrection of Jesus Christ they have the sure and open prospect of their own resurrection, and are already granted a foretaste of the eternal life of which they now know themselves to be the heirs. They may continually find new confidence, take new courage and stir themselves to new obedience. They are and have and may do all these things, not in their own power but in that which is given them by God in Jesus Christ through the Holy Spirit, nor because they have deserved to receive them but by the free prevenient grace of God, nor without temptation and assault and conflict and tribulation but in the fire of all the ills of humanity which they are not spared, in the manifold afflictions which come upon them particularly as Christians, in the shadow of the transitoriness of this world and in the darkness of the death which overtakes them. Yet in and through all this they are what they are, have what they have and may do what they may do. And according to the classic answer to our question, it is the fact that they are and have and may do these things specifically which makes them Christians and thus constitutes the distinctive feature or principle of Christian existence and the essential goal of vocation. As those who in distinction from others are and have and may do these things, and rejoice in the fact, Christians are in the world and yet they confront the world, standing at the side of the God who acts and reveals Himself in Jesus Christ.

Vocatio ad regnum Christi est actus gratiae, quo Spiritus sanctus hominibus extra ecclesiam constitutis voluntatem Dei de salvandis peccatoribus per verbum divinum manifestat et ipsis beneficia a redemptore Christo acquisita offert, ut ad ecclesiam adducantur, convertantur et aeternam salutem consequantur (D. Hollaz, *Ex. theol. acroam.*, 1707, III, sect. 1, cap. 4, *De gratia voc.*, qu. 1).

Gratia vocationis est voluntarius et immeritus ille Dei favor, quo is ab aeterno electos et in tempore per Christum redemptos, natura peccatores plerosque simplices et ignobiles, supernaturali et potente vi sua per praeconium verbi externum et Spiritum sanctum ad communionem gratiae et gloriae suae ita invitat et trahit, novos creat et regenerat, ac simul fide in Christum donat et per eam Deo unit, ut Deo sic vocante infallibiliter adducantur et ad communionem ejus postliminio perveniant (H. Heidegger, *Med. Theol. chr.*, 1696, 21, 2).

However it may be explained, deepened or amplified in detail, is not this the comprehensive and exhaustive answer, the *non plus ultra* of what is to be said concerning the Christian as such? There can be no doubt at least that the remarkable fact that Christians are and have and may do all these things is the practical and even the theoretical point of much of the best preaching and instruction and the most zealous evangelistic and pastoral effort, as it is also the theme in many different languages of the finest and not so fine hymns and other poetic compositions of the Christian Church and community, and apparently the most solid bond of Christian fellowship, and the strongest and perhaps the only genuine and effective motive for Christian apologetics. In all the organisation and work of all churches, fellowships and sects, is it not the purpose in some form and with some degree of urgency to save human souls, to show men the way of redemption, to cause them to become Christians for the sake of their personal salvation and the experience of salvation, and with the same end in view to confirm and strengthen and nourish them as such, to maintain, protect and more deeply establish them in their Christianity ? What is meant by edification in its more customary and rather un-biblical sense, if not continuing instruction and equipment for the specific being, possession and capacity of the Christian ?

Now there can be no disputing that something true and important is meant and envisaged in all this. There can be no doubt that in respect of the goal of vocation we may and must also speak most emphatically, earnestly and joyfully of that which is appropriated to the Christian, or to the one called to Christianity, by the goodness of God, of his personal experience of grace and salvation, of the endow-ment, constitution and position in which man is put as there takes place in his life the mystery and miracle of his vocation, illumina-tion and awakening to Christian existence. There can be no doubt, therefore, that in the delivering of the Christian message it is also a matter of saving souls, of inviting and helping men to personal being, possession and capacity in the kingdom of grace and salvation, and therefore to participation in the supreme good and all the other goods which it includes. And since this appropriation and personal experience is the most obvious, illuminating and impressive thing to catch the attention of Christians when they consider the great alter-ation and singularity of their status, it is certainly not difficult to understand, but only human, that they should give this so great if not exclusive prominence, making it the inner goal of their vocation, as has been the case with thousands of witnesses in every age and right up to the present day. Who is not decisively interested in the vocation of man—and modern theological existentialism has again lent powerful support to this self-evident presupposition—to the extent that it concerns and reaches him personally in this happy way ? But if we are not wide awake, we shall rush on to the tempting con-clusion that what vocation promises and implies and effects for man personally in terms of the *beneficia Christi* is in fact the decisively and dominatingly relevant, essential and central factor in the goal of vocation. What could be more relevant than that which in supreme and ultimate matters concerns me ? But then another conclusion might so easily be drawn, namely, that that which concerns and affects and reaches me, my gracious visitation and salvation, the saving of my soul, and to that extent my reception, possession, use and enjoyment of the *beneficia Christi*, is the only thing which is relevant, essential and important in the goal of vocation, that this goal, and therefore my standing at the side of God, consists absolutely and exclusively in my Christian being, possession and capacity. Is this a false deduction from the classic answer which now occupies us? The fact remains that it has not infrequently been drawn, and not by the worst of people. The fact also remains that from it—who knows? —perhaps even more pregnant deductions (e.g., along the lines of Feuerbach) might well be drawn in respect of the total conception of Christianity. It is not easy to avoid either the first or the resultant conclusions if we accept this answer.

All things considered, however, we cannot accept this answer any more than that which refers to the freedom of the Christian in and in face of the world, or that which points to the Christian ethos. Yet in view of its obvious importance we must obviously give the most careful reasons for rejecting it, and these reasons will finally yield us quite naturally our positive answer.

While it does not give us solid ground for rejection, it will perhaps serve as an indication that something is wrong if, without any claim to completeness, we first draw attention to some of the difficulties in which we are entangled if we assume that this answer is right.

1. Even though we recognised its indispensability, we could not regard the reference to the Christian ethos as the decisive word on the distinctively Christian manner of existence because it has in itself no recognisable basis and meaning, is not therefore an end in itself, but can be understood as the Christian ethos only in the light of its origin in the particular union of being between the One who commands and the one who obeys. Now if with the classic answer to our question we understand the being of Jesus Christ decisively as that of the One to whom the Christian owes the grace of God addressed to him and therefore his salvation, and the being of the Chriitian decisively as that of the man who approves and accepts this benefit, then it is here that we have the meaning and origin of the Christian ethos and from this point that we should understand it. But while light is here shed on it, as by the fine reference to the relationship between grace and gratitude, it cannot be understood from this point in its necessity. How does Jesus Christ as the pure Benefactor of man come to be also his Commander, and how does the Christian as the recipient of His benefit come to be one who is committed to obedience to Him? As is well-known, it has often been contested or doubted that there is here any serious question of commanding and obeying, appeal being made to the absolute primacy of the Christian experience of grace and salvation and objection being taken to Christian moralism. On this view it is, of course, possible to maintain and illustrate the necessity of the Christian ethos. It is not possible, however, to understand or

genuinely to demonstrate it. But where this is so, then secretly and often blatantly there will have to be accepted a confusing juxta-position, dangerous to the whole practice of the Christian life, between the divine gift and the divine task, Gospel and Law, justification and sanctification, the Christian experience of salvation and Christian service to the glory of God and the benefit of one's neighbour. Even at best the two will seem only as it were to be glued together. This dualism can be overcome only if the Christian experience of grace and salvation is no more an ultimate than the Christian ethos, but both have a common origin in the conjoined being of Jesus Christ and the Christian, so that we have to reckon with a basis and meaning of Christian existence superior to both.

2. The classic answer gives rise to a further difficulty when we ask how it is possible on this presupposition to maintain the dis-tinction between the Christian and the non-Christian. May it not be that the Christian has to admit quite honestly that in respect of his glorious experience and existence, which he knows well enough and of which he can and should boast, he is often enough, and perhaps in some dark recesses permanently, either very near to zero or even well below it ? And does he not sometimes come across non-Christians—pious Hindus or Buddhists, or the valiant, cheerful and often very serious children of the world whom we often meet in the West—who do not merely say but demonstrate in astonishing fashion that even without the benefit of Jesus Christ, and in a very different language, conceptuality and terminology, they have something analogous to or even identical with his Christian being, possession and capacity, namely, that they are not strangers to, but enjoy to an astonishing degree, something of the same peace and patience and trust and discipline and freedom in and in face of the world ? May it not be that the magicians of Pharaoh can change their rods into snakes, and that he does not have Aaron's rod to swallow them up (Ex. 7$^{11f.}$) ? Does not this make it impossible to speak of an absolute uniqueness of the Christian ethos in itself and as such ? Does it not involve a fatal interchangeability of at least the aspects under which the Christian and the non-Christian experience of life may be undeniably represented ? If his being, possession and capacity as such were the *rocher de bronze* of his Christianity, how could the Christian know himself as a Christian, and confidently maintain himself as such, in relation to something which is both inwardly and outwardly so vulnerable ?

3. If it is really the case that the true and ultimate goal of my vocation is that I as a Christian may exist so well and gloriously for Christ's sake, then in practice everything depends upon my strong or feeble awareness of this with invincible definiteness. Everything depends upon my personal assurance of salvation triumphantly dispelling the constant obscuring of my experience. Now there can

be no doubt that the Christian can and should have assurance of his faith and salvation. But can his salvation as known by him be the principle which dominates his Christian existence, the nail on which everything else is hung ? Does he do right to be persuaded, or to persuade himself, that he can and must think on the basis of his personal assurance of salvation ? Is it really the supreme work of the impelling and constraining Holy Spirit to help him to this assurance of his own standing in grace ? If this is really the Alpha and Omega of vocation, if the assurance of faith, grace and salvation is the basis on which he stands at the side of God in and in face of the world, will not insistence that this is the true work of the Holy Spirit necessarily mean a wild illusion either in respect of himself or in respect of the true moving of the Spirit ? Can there be a real assurance of salvation, a genuinely peaceful and happy awareness of our good and glorious existence, so long as we regard this, and therefore our assurance of it, as grounded in some way in ourselves, so long as we see in it the main purpose of our Christian standing, so long as we do not see that our personal Christian existence, like our Christian ethos, is a second thing which follows and results from something else which is really first, being secured in this and not in our own experience ? Only as it is grounded indirectly, and not directly or in itself, can our assurance of the experience of faith, grace and salvation be genuine and unshakeable. These, then, are some of the difficulties the solubility or insolubility of which we must take into account if we accept this answer.

There is also a material difficulty which, while it should not be adduced as a reason for rejection, does carry real weight and must be overcome if the answer is to be accepted. We have pointed out as a notable fact in favour of the answer that it is genuinely human and therefore understandable that the Christian should be supremely interested in the goal of vocation from the standpoint of its personal or " existential " relevance to himself. But this merit of the answer reveals also its limitation. Expressing a human insight, might it not be unfortunately only too human ? Can it be so self-evident for the Christian as such to regard the benefit addressed, revealed and imparted to him, his own temporal and eternal salvation worked out and applied to him in Jesus Christ, as the content and even the heart and substance of the Word which calls him ? Can it really be the inner end, meaning and basis of my Christian existence, and therefore the goal and end of the ways and words of God to me, that I should be blessed, that my soul should be saved, that I should participate in all the gifts of reconciliation, that my life should be one of reception, possession, use and enjoyment of these gifts, that I should finally attain to eternal bliss, that I should not go to hell but to heaven, and that each of the few or many others who might accompany me should also know the extraordinary exaltation of his human

existence mediated in the benefits of Christ, and therefore the satisfaction of his deepest needs and the fulfilment of his most lofty and
necessary desires ? Does not this wholly possessive being seem to
smack of the sanctioning and cultivating of an egocentricity which
is only too human for all its sanctity, of a self-seeking which in the light
of what is at stake renders every other form of self-seeking quite
innocuous ? To be sure, there is a very legitimate and necessary
Christian " I " and " mine." But does this mean that it can be made
the last word on what makes a Christian a Christian ? It gives us a
very strange relationship if on the one side we have the selflessness
and self-giving of God and Jesus Christ in which the salvation of the
world is effected and revealed, and on the other the satisfaction with
which Christians accept this and are thus content to make use of the
very different being and action of their Lord. Can this be really all, can
it be the true and essential thing which distinguishes them, that
within a world which in all the folly and impotence of its pride,
sloth and falsehood already hastens through such indescribably
great suffering to its end, there is a handful of men whose particular
existence has only the meaning and basis that, called, illumined and
awakened thereto by Jesus Christ, they may rejoice in the little faith,
love and hope of their being in the light of His grace which He has
given them, which is so superior to their prior being, which is so
glorious in the surrounding darkness, and in which, snatched from the
massa perditionis, they have simply to move on to heavenly felicity ?
Did the Son of God clothe Himself with humanity, and shed His
blood, and go out as the Sower, simply in order that He might create
for these people—in free grace, yet why specifically for them and only
for them ?—this indescribably magnificent private good fortune,
permitting them to obtain and possess a gracious God, opening to
them the gates of Paradise which are closed to others ? Can this really
be the goal of His calling and therefore of His ongoing prophetic
work ? Can it really be the goal of the work once and for all accomplished in His death ? Can it really be the meaning of His election
and sending ? Is it legitimate and even imperative for Christians to
be content that they may thankfully understand themselves as those
who are reconciled, justified, satisfied and blessed because elected
from eternity and called in time in Him ? Can the community of
Jesus Christ—we shall have to take up this question in the next
section—really be only, or at any rate essentially and decisively, a
kind of institute of salvation, the foremost and comprehensive *medium
salutis*, as Calvin self-evidently assumed and said ? Is not every form
of egocentricity excused and even confirmed and sanctified, if egocentricity in this sacred form is the divinely willed meaning of Christian
existence and the Christian song of praise consists finally only in a
many-tongued but monotonous *pro me, pro me,* and similar possessive
expressions ? It can hardly be denied that the piety, teaching

and practice of Christianity in every age and place—and particularly in the strongest movements and most impressive champions—has disclosed an almost sinister and irresistible bias in this direction, as though it were really inevitable that man—in this case the experience and existence of the Christian—should be the measure of all things. It is this bias or tendency which make the classic answer to our question so deeply suspect irrespective of whether we explain the tendency by the answer or *vice versa*. I use the term " suspect " because I do not regard the difficulty of the Christian *sacro egoismo* to which it perhaps unavoidably gives rise as a true, theological reason for rejecting this answer. For after all, egocentricity may not be its unavoidable consequence. If a strict warning is issued against the danger which threatens in this regard, the answer itself may still be acceptable.

It will perhaps be helpful to give a few indications of how complex the matter is in the actuality of Church history. In this way we may be kept from over-hasty judgments and also confronted more sharply with the question whether this answer can stand or must be replaced by another and better.

If within the sphere of the classic answer there has been and still is a deeply suspect pious egocentricity, it must also be noted that it is only with comparative infrequency that this has been able to work itself out and find expression in a pure form, and that it has almost always been resisted by a tendency in the opposite direction. In the strict sense, it is only Christians of a pronouncedly quietistic mystical type who have sought to understand, explain and express themselves as pure recipients and possessors of the salvation addressed to them in Jesus Christ, and even in their case, as we see from such leading representatives as Madame de Guyon, Pierre Poiret and Gerhard Tersteegen, it was found impossible to refrain from at least pastoral and sometimes very extensive literary activity. They certainly sought to find complete satisfaction in being pure recipients and possessors of salvation : " Who hath Thee, May quiet be, Who to Thee in spirit cleaves, Other craving leaves . . . Deep in Him abiding, In covenant residing, Quiet we may be . . . If to more Than Thee I soar, I can only shake my peace And my bliss decrease." Yet in reality they were not at all quiet. For they could not refrain from talking about these things with those who shared them and from extolling and commending them in word and writing to those who did not, as though they, too, could not be content with Augustine's *Deum et animam scire cupio*. The same picture emerges even more clearly and in even sharper contours in the 17th and 18th century Pietists, who originally aimed quite decisively in the same introverted direction in opposition to orthodoxy. For immediately their new personal experience of salvation overflowed into endless conversations with those like-minded and those who found it impossible to share their views, into pious activity with a heavenly orientation, into preaching and poetry, into the formation of groups amongst the cultivated and less cultivated, and in the higher and lower strata of society. Indeed, in A. H. Francke, their greatest leader after Philipp Spener, while the original impulse was not denied, it was certainly transmuted into a well-considered and powerfully executed programme of pedagogic, social and missionary activity which for all the reservations of individual observers demanded the respectful notice of the whole century even in circles outside the Church and Christianity. And it was the older Pietism itself which produced its great counterpart in Count Nicholas von Zinzendorf, who was educated and fashioned by Halle, who then outgrew it, and who from the very first understood his particular vocation both as a call to a supremely personal and direct intercourse and life with the Saviour and also as a call to His service, to the passing on of what he had received from Him, and finally as the commission to form a free ecumenical community of those united in and committed to Him. Again, we are forced to admit that the Awakening of the Napoleonic and post-Napoleonic period, which in contrast to Francke and especially to Zinzendorf implied a certain constriction, did not carry with it any desire on the part of those who participated in it to keep their materially very private Christianity to themselves, but rather impelled them to proclaim it *urbi et orbi* and to seek to assert it both in Church and society. It was this movement which gave the real impulse to evangelical mission. And it was from it that its counterpart emerged as Zinzendorf had done from Pietism, namely, J. C. Blumhardt, in whose message of hope, which in the name of Jesus embraced the body as well as the soul and the world as well as the community, and in whose expectation of an outpouring of the Holy Spirit on all flesh, the old Gospel acquired a freedom, freshness, breadth and significance for which there are hardly any previous parallels. And the same may be said of the English-inspired social and evangelistic movement of the later 19th and our own centuries, which for all its orientation on a personally committed Christianity largely aimed from the very outset, not at the mere formation of groups, but at the preaching of the Gospel to those not yet reached by it. On the left wing of this movement stands the Salvation Army, which had its origin in Methodism, and the activities of which leave nothing to be desired from the standpoint of the extrovert. Mention may also be made of the resolute John Mott, who shortly before the catastrophe of 1914 felt that he could proclaim the slogan : " The evangelisation of the world in this generation." And if in this particular sphere there has not yet emerged, so far as may be seen, an even greater counterpart corresponding to Zinzendorf and Blumhardt, this is hardly the fault of the movement, which is no less adapted than the older Pietism and the Awakening some day to transcend and seriously to point beyond itself. What may be said of these specific movements, in which concentration on the personal ex-perience of salvation has played and plays so emphatic a role, applies also, of course, to the wider sphere of Christianity in the Church, to its whole piety, in-struction and practice as these were constantly and very deeply influenced by the specific movements and contributed to them in countless cross-connexions and personal links. Even theological Liberalism as impressively represented by Alexander Vinet, and at the turn of the century by the dominating figure of the Genevan Gaston Frommel, does not constitute an exception. Here too, of course, although generally to a lesser degree, the constricting attention paid to the individual life of faith was not without its dangers. But here too, where there was less chance from the very first of making Christianity a private matter, the dangers were not so great as they might have been, and there were many fortunate inconsistencies.

If we are to avoid over-hasty and unjust conclusions, we have thus to consider the fact that in the historical actuality of Christianity, of which we have given the more modern examples, there never has been, except possibly in the case of individuals, any pure or strict concentration on the personal experience of grace and salvation which is supposed to make a Christian a Christian. This has not proved to be possible, again with isolated exceptions, even in the contemplative orders of the Roman Catholic Church. The tendency inwards, i.e., to the in-wardness of the individual Christian, has always in fact been paradoxically opposed by a more or less explicit and powerful urge for expansion. Is it not the case that striving in this one dimension—however high the emphasis we lay on its primacy—is not usually practicable without being completed and accompanied by striving in what seems to be the opposite dimension, i.e., by a centrifugal striving for expression and impartation, or at least for the discovery of others with whom Christians engaged in the first striving are already united in fellowship, and beyond this for the winning of those who are not awakened to participation in the first striving, and then for particular fellowship, with a view to mutual confirmation, with those who are encountered, or it is hoped will be encountered, in that first striving, in the true reception and enjoyment of grace and salvation ? It is obvious that this implies at least a disturbance of the egocentricity by which Christians are threatened, and indeed to a large extent dominated and not just threatened, when the personal experience of salvation as such is regarded as the principle and essence of Christian being. Yet it seems as though there must always be at least this relative opposite. It seems as though the pious egocentricity of the individual must always broaden out into at least a kind of collective egocentricity. This is always unexpected, since in itself it is hard to see why it should not be easier and more effective to express it individually than collectively. There must have been many who, impervious to the lessons of history, have believed this and therefore withdrawn not only from the life of the Church but also from participation in these particular movements, living wholly in the strength of their private experience of the supreme good. And because in a sense they are self-consistent, it will always be difficult to teach them anything better. In fact, however, the first striving is confronted by one which is at least relatively new and different, and the personal experience of salvation presses to its limits as such, where it is not content to remain individual but demands and seeks expression, impartation and fellowship. And it must obviously be stated as a simple fact that the coming of this relatively new and different and heterogeneous factor, of which we have a clear example in the ancient transition from anchoretic to cenobitic monasticism, seems to follow a rule for all that it is so paradoxical, and thus to constitute *de facto* if not *de iure* the norm. This has to be taken into account and reckoned in its favour even though we do have to criticise the classic answer to our question in view of the threatened danger, and perhaps to reject it altogether on other grounds. The answer can hardly be given without carrying within itself a certain corrective, opposing a centrifugal striving to the centripetal which alone corresponds to it in the first instance.

Yet even when this is taken into account—so complex is the matter !—it cannot be conceded that the shadow of egocentricity which makes the answer suspect is dispelled by the fact that historically it hardly ever confronts us in a pure form except in certain cases for which there is little if any documentation. The shadow is dispelled only in the very few cases in which the answer as such is consciously or unconsciously, logically or illogically, questioned and even overcome, in which the personal experience of salvation in the form of the second and additional striving seems not only to point but actually to move beyond itself, in which it is prepared not to be any longer the measure of all things but to measure itself by a superior standard, as happened in the case of J. C Blumhardt and even, with some reservations, in that of Zinzendorf. For the most part, however, it insists on positing itself absolutely, and therefore the shadow pursues it even where it does not merely express itself concentrically but also expansively according to the paradoxical rule, thus moving in a direction which is relatively opposed to that of pious egocentricity. Where it regards itself as the Christian *non plus ultra*, can even this rule have any sure validity ? Is there not always the possibility of what is perhaps a fairly solidly grounded lapse or retreat into a purely private Christianity ? And even when the rule is kept, will the movement ever be more than a variation on, and to that degree a challenge to, the suspect basic principle ? Can it possibly represent its suppression and replacement by another ? Out of the solitariness of the first and true striving a plurality emerges in the fulfilment of this movement and the addition of the second and expansive striving. But while this process is full of hope, it accomplishes nothing decisive towards the dispelling of the shadow. Indeed, in the event might it not entail a strengthening and concentration of the pious egocentricity if, instead of isolated individuals, many Christians and even whole groups and corporations concern themselves in concert with the reception and enjoyment of the *beneficia Christi*, and thus concerned try to stand at the side of God in and in face of the world ? Might not the egoism of salvation find even more forceful expression in this expansion ? Supposing the whole Church and the whole of Christianity were to become one powerful community and office of salvation ? Do those isolated individuals realise what they are missing by trying to live out their egoism in this form ? Might it not even be inferred from the rule that this egoism is even better asserted when the second striving is introduced than in a purely private Christianity ? If this is a possibility with which we have at least seriously to reckon, this surely means that the difficulty in relation to the classic answer as disclosed by the existence of the shadow is not only not eased but actually intensified when we consider this hopeful movement. The answer is not undermined nor is it to be dismissed for this reason. A historical presentation and discussion such as that which we have now attempted cannot possibly achieve this result. But it certainly cannot be denied that from this standpoint, too, we are led to see that the exaltation of the personal experience of salvation into the principle of the structure of Christian existence is not quite so inviolable as might appear at a first glance.

We now turn to the two theological arguments which both lead us beyond this questioning of the classic answer to the conclusion that it is actually untenable, and in the development of which there emerges the answer to the question of the controlling principle of the structure of Christian existence which is here demanded, which is consonant with the matter, and which is thus to be given.

Our primary concern is with the answer which is given in Holy Scripture. What kind of goal, according to the Old and New Testament tradition, does the event have which is there described as the calling of specific men ? What does calling mean decisively, centrally and constitutively for those who according to the biblical narratives are placed by it in a new position ? In the first instance we must keep to the biblical records which actually speak of this translation, and draw from them the basic meaning and purpose of the event. But when we do this, we cannot mistake the fact that what should be the Alpha and Omega in these records according to the classic view, namely, the personal *esse* and *bene esse* of the called, is not, of course, disputed or absent, but certainly does not play any constitutive role, being for the most part tacitly implied, or it may be merely indicated, as obviously and most decidedly a secondary element according to the meaning and intention of the tradition.

We certainly do not have in the Bible stories of conversion such as that which Augustine recorded in his autobiography, or the numerous legends of the saints stimulated by Augustine in the Middle Ages, or the Christian portraits of which the first half of the 19th century was so particularly fond, or the testimonies given in gatherings of the Salvation Army and Moral Rearmament by those who at first were not interested in personal salvation, then sought it in the wrong place and finally sought and found it in the right place. There can be no contesting the significance of an experience like that of Luther in the cloister. But where do we find even the remotest likeness to it in the Bible ? Certainly there was no question of Paul finding a gracious God in his conversion.

To be sure, there are places in the Bible, especially in Luke and Acts but also in the typical stories of calling, where we can glimpse something of the fact that such a personal experience was directly or indirectly linked with the decisive thing, i.e., with what came upon the called from the hand of God, so that in and with the true thing which re-determined their life on the basis of their vocation there took place an illuminating and salutary alteration in their own being and status. Yet we can hardly speak of more than glimpses. The personal history of the called and its happy outcome never become a real theme, not even in the stories of the publican Zacchaeus and the Philippian gaoler. The killing and eating of the fatted calf is as little the burden of the parable of the Prodigal Son as is David's dancing before the Lord when the ark was brought up to Jerusalem the burden of his vocation.

There can be no doubt, of course, that in other parts of the Bible we find not only indications but rich and lively communications on the state of grace of the pious and righteous man who fears God, who believes, and who is justified before God and sanctified for Him. " Blessed is the man . . . ! " " Blessed are they . . . ! " Yet in connexion with the calling of man, and in the typical stories of calling, even where this takes place at all, it never does so in such a way that the reader is led to think that the existence of the man placed in this state of grace, or this state of grace as his personal experience, is the purpose of the event of vocation recorded, or of the divine action within the framework of which it happens. We surely have to read a great deal into the passages which speak of the calling of Abraham, Moses and the prophets, or in the New Testament of the disciples and later the special calling of Paul, to gather from them that their chief concern is with the saving of their souls, or their experience of grace and salvation, in short, with the establishment of their personal well-being in their relationship with God. It is true, of course, that at other points and in other connexions we are told of some of these men, though not all, that these things were their portion, and that in respect of them they learned to glory in the fact that as those called to the side of God they were continually summoned to repentance, and that they could therefore stand at His side humbly yet joyfully, rightly directed by Him in their standing and falling and standing again, in good days and in bad, richly comforted and endowed by Him, and having a final expectation of the " crown of life." But the fact that this was so, while it definitely belonged in some form to the goal of their vocation, did so only incidentally—and indeed so incidentally that when the story of their vocation is told it is completely concealed by the decisive point at issue, being only indicated even if mentioned at all. It is an encouraging and consoling confirmation of the distinction imparted to them by the fact that in and in face of the world God has called them to His side as His own and His friends. If we may calmly express it in this way, it is a superabundant and undeserved reward, dispensed in overflowing kindness, for the obedience and faithfulness with which they are content to stand and remain at

His side. It is their preparation for the work entrusted to and demanded of them as those who are set in this position. It is a radiance, a *doxa*, a glory, by which they are actually surrounded to their own astonishment, without expecting or seeking it, and without being able to contribute to it.

In this sense, i.e., to summon the called to a recognition of their distinction and to gratitude, to remind them of the resultant position, and especially of the enlistment and commitment indissolubly bound up with their experience of salvation as its presupposition, their calling can occasionally be related in the New Testament to the benefit which is subordinate to and necessarily follows it, but which is only subordinate and only follows. In this sense, it can thus be said of Christians that they are called by the Gospel to sanctification through the Spirit and in faith in the truth (2 Thess. $2^{13f.}$), or that they are called to freedom (Gal. 5^{13}), or to the peace of Christ (Col. 3^{15}), or to the marriage-feast of the Lamb (Rev. 19^9), or to reception of the promise of the eternal inheritance (Heb. 9^{15}), or more directly to eternal life (1 Tim. 6^{12}) or eternal glory (1 Pet. 5^{10}). The meaning of all this is brought out in Phil. 3^{14}, where Paul says the final and supreme thing along this line, namely, that his personal participation in the resurrection of the dead is the βραβεῖον or prize of the calling from above which has come to him and in obedience to which he finds himself engaged in the irresistible forward movement described in this chapter.

Yet the fact remains that little mention need be made of all this, or attention paid to it, in the concrete descriptions of vocation. In no story of calling in either the Old or the New Testament does it stand in the foreground or the centre. Strangely enough, it plays no part even in the accounts of the calling of Paul. And from the standpoint of the Old and New Testaments it is quite impossible that this confirmation, reward, preparation and *doxa* should be transformed into the true point and meaning of the distinction of the called and their existence at the side of God.

If this assertion is correct, we are already carried a decisive stage beyond our previous deliberations. For the classic answer is not only challenged. It is shown to be contrary to Scripture, and is thus to be rejected for this theological if in the first instance formal reason. In its description of what makes a Christian a Christian, this answer gives to the element of his personal experience of grace and salvation, to his reception and enjoyment of the *beneficia Christi*, an abstract significance and weight which it does not have in the thinking and utterance of the Old and New Testaments. It allows itself to make an emphasis which necessarily means that the picture of Christian existence visible in Holy Scripture can be recognised in its own picture only in obscure and distorted form.

But this critical assertion gives us implicitly the positive answer which rightly and necessarily forces itself upon us in the light of what is called vocation in the Bible. It is common to all the biblical accounts of calling that to be called means being given a task. And for those who are called according to these stories vocation thus means existence in the execution of this task. Existence in its execution is how we must phrase it. It is not the case, then, that when the called have received the task they can continue to exist in some way in and for themselves and devote themselves to other things than its execution. Acquiring it, they are consecrated to it. Hence their existence can be controlled only by their readiness to discharge it. Everything that they have and are and will and do as men must take second place and be subordinated to and made to serve the execution of their task. As they acquire it, they are distinguished from the ordinary ranks of men in the sense that for them all the generally recognised individual or collective aims are basically relativised. Their habits, customs and orders lose their obviousness and unshakeable validity. They can respect them and take them seriously only in the framework and context of the execution of their task. They are thus set in genuine confrontation with others, though not wholly separated from their life and activity. As they no longer belong to themselves, they no longer belong to the human society to which they do not cease to be attached. This is how it stands with all those who are called according to the biblical accounts. But this is directly linked with the fact that none of them has received his task from other men or from human society, but each has received it from God. This means, however, that none of them has sought or chosen it for himself. For each it is something absolutely new and strange which takes possession of him. And of more than one of them we read that he shrank from being apprehended in this way, that he regarded himself as ill-equipped, unable and unworthy to execute the task, and yet—for the task laid hold of him before he did of the task—that he had to execute it and was ready and able to do so. None of them, then, receives it only incidentally, *ex officio*, or temporarily. Even the notion of an impressed *character indelebilis* is too weak to denote what came upon them as the claiming for service of their whole being in time. When this had happened, they could live only for their commission. It was from God, however, that they received it, and received it in the form of this total claim. Hence there can be no question as to the power or skill necessary for its discharge. Not in vain does God call them to His side. He involves Himself by commissioning them. He makes His cause theirs, and therefore He makes their cause His. He Himself legitimates, authorises, instructs and nourishes them. His presence is the secret of their existence among other men. His action is the hidden but powerful sustaining basis and impelling motive of theirs. It is here that we catch a glimpse of the fact that their vocation does actually include their personal blessing, experience and endowment as something secondary and accessory, which certainly will not pass them by, but which remains linked with the primary and proper element in their status and can have its own power and constancy only in this relationship. The true substance of their standing, that which distinguishes them decisively from others as the called, consists absolutely in their existence in execution of the task which God has laid upon them. This makes them what they are. Their personal being, possession and capacity, the honour, joy, assistance, comfort and encouragement, the whole exaltation which they themselves enjoy as this task is given them and they can and should execute it, all these constitute the indispensable periphery which is not actually withheld from them. But the task is the centre of their existence.

What is this task? It is to be noted supremely that it is a divine and therefore a pure and genuine task. In no sense, then, can it be referred back to some lack or longing, belief or desire of their own, however profound, necessary, justifiable or sacred. In no sense can it be understood as the expression and exponent of such. It does not grow out of the inner necessity of an immanent creative force, a discovered idea, an apprehended conviction. Its execution, then, is not the satisfaction of a need to do justice to a supreme or basic indwelling ultimate, to express and impart it, to find for it interchange and fellowship, to propagate and proclaim that which inwardly moves it, to secure its acceptance by others. The task does not arise out of the men themselves. It comes wholly and most astonishingly upon them to be taken up and fulfilled by them. It is a pure and genuine task because it is laid upon them. As some of them actually call it, it is a burden which they have to carry.

And it consists in the fact that with their whole being, action, inaction and conduct, and then by word and speech, they have to make a definite declaration to other men. The essence of their vocation is that God makes them His witnesses. Only indirectly and by implication does this mean that He makes them witnesses of the fact that He is, or of who and what He is in and for Himself in His hidden Godhead. He makes them witnesses of His being in His past, present and future action in the world and in history, of His being in His acts among and upon men. They are witnesses of the God who was who He was, is who He is and will be who He will be in these acts of His. They are witnesses of the God who in these acts of His, and therefore as God, as God with us, Emmanuel, was, is and will be with His creation, the world and all men. These who are called according to the biblical narratives are men to whom, in the event of their calling, He has made Himself known as this Emmanuel, whose eyes He has opened to Himself, to His being in His acts, in His past, present and future activity in history. He is concealed from the rest, from the majority, from all men normally and in themselves. His activity certainly takes place before their eyes and ears. But they do not see, nor hear, nor perceive. They do not know what happens to them. They do not realise that in what takes place before their eyes and ears they have to do with Him. Hence they do not know what they do. No man discovers or knows this of himself. The called—and this is the gift of vocation—come to know it by the action of the One who alone can enable them to do so. They are shown it by God. Hence they are made by Him His witnesses, i.e., those who are not blind and deaf as His will is done, but are present with open eyes and ears, He being to them no longer a stranger but their well-known Neighbour, the closest Neighbour of all, who is beside them as the One He was and is and will be in His acts. They are made His witnesses : not idle spectators merely watching and considering ; not for the enjoyment of a spectacle granted to them ; not for the vain increase of their knowledge of men, the world and history by this or that which they now come to know of God ; not inquisitive reporters ; but witnesses who can and must declare what they have seen and heard like witnesses in a law-suit. Their calling embraces not only the fact that God gives them knowledge concerning Himself and the doing of His will, and that He calls them to this knowledge, but also the fact that He summons and equips them to declare what He has given them to know. In other words, their calling means both that He reveals Himself in His action and also that He summons them into the witness-box as those who know. As God speaks His Word to these men in and with what He does, and as He is heard by them, He gives them the freedom, but also claims and commissions them, to confess that they are hearers of His Word within the world and humanity which has not heard it but for which His work is dumb, and in this way to make the world and humanity hear. This is their *raison d'être*. In vocation, then, it is a matter of God on the one side and the world on the other. It is a matter of the service of God in the form of a service to be rendered by them in and to the world. The Word of the work which God does in and on them is to be sounded out and heard in the world. What God has done and does and will do is to become a message directed to it and to be spoken in its ears. In the biblical narratives those called by God are men who are summoned, commanded and empowered to declare this message. They are responsible for addressing the message of God to His creatures. As witnesses they have to repeat what God Himself has first said to them. This is the task laid upon them in their calling and to be discharged with their whole existence. This is the point of their particular existence. This makes them what they are in distinction from all others. Whatever else they may be, and especially their being, capacity and possession graciously granted as their particular experience of salvation, the ethos especially required of them, and all that they might have to undergo in the way of particular suffering—all this depends upon and stands under the common sign of the fact that they are entrusted with this declaration and message and have to discharge this commission. They are witnesses. They are *Verbi divini ministri*. Hence they are called the prophets of Yahweh in the Old Testament and the disciples and apostles of Jesus Christ in the New.

According to the simplest meaning of the terms, a prophet is one who has to declare something and an apostle one who has to deliver a message. According to this simplest and most general meaning of both terms, which meet in that of witness, all those who are called in the Bible are thus both prophets and apostles. There is disparity in respect of what the prophets of the Old Testament have to attest as compared with the apostles of the New, and *vice versa*. On the one side it is a matter of the acts of God in the history of Israel as it moves forward to Jesus Christ, whereas on the other it is a matter of His acts in the history of Jesus Christ which is the goal of the former history. These are two different things. Yet there is parity in respect of their function as witnesses. In both spheres, of course, they are all different from one another. For all the common features, the biblical accounts of vocation and the commissions disclosed in them are all specific and are not therefore interchangeable. This is of a piece with the fact that the work of God, the Word of which the called have to hear and attest to others, is an ongoing and at all points differentiated history in the course of which God continually wills and does particular things and therefore has always something particular to say, even though He always speaks of His present, past and future rule and action. It is for this reason that He calls so many different witnesses at specific times and in specific situations. It is for this reason, too, that the form and content of their witness are so rich and varied.

According to Gen. 12¹ (and cf. 20⁷ where he is also called a prophet) Abraham is a witness of God, i.e., of His action as it moves towards its far distant and therefore totally hidden goal, not only to the men of his home town and kindred and to the inhabitants of Canaan, but also to the estranged Sarah, to the unsuspecting Isaac and to all those implicated in his particular history. He is this quite simply by doing what he is told to do in strict obedience and blind trust. He emerges as one who is called by God to represent and reveal by way of anticipation what God wills to do and will do, even though He begins to do it in great concealment. This is his " righteousness " (15⁶), the exemplary character of which for Christians is emphasised by both Paul (Gal. 3⁶, Rom. 4³) and James (2²³). As God gives him this task, his name becomes a term of blessing (12²) for all the nations of the earth (12³). And as he takes up this task, he cannot be worsted and does not need to fear, since Yahweh is His shield and he lives with the promise of the richest reward (15¹).

When we turn to the call of Moses (Ex. 3¹⁻¹⁴), we find that Yahweh comes in strange, mysterious and terrifying form to a man who unsuspectingly stumbles upon Him, i.e., upon the portent of the burning bush which is not consumed. This man is one who has already committed an abortive act of violence on behalf of his people oppressed and tortured in Egypt. He has been the adopted son of the king's daughter. He is now the shepherd of his Midianitish father-in-law, and has no fixed programme for the rest of his life. What does this encounter mean for him ? Lo, it is the God of Abraham, Isaac and Jacob—the work begun in their time is being carried a stage further—who as such, as the God of the people descended from these patriarchs, has seen their sufferings and heard their cry in Egypt, and has come down to save them and to lead them into the land promised to their fathers. His concern is wholly and utterly with this people and His further plans for it, and only for this reason is He also concerned with Moses, who by divine commission is first to go to Pharaoh and then to lead out the Israelites to the place appointed. " Who am I," asks Moses, that I should undertake and execute such a task ? The question is futile. He is the one ordained to do this by Yahweh. " I will be with thee "—this can and should be enough. And if the Israelites ask who has sent him, he must make the bold answer : " The God of your fathers hath sent me unto you." And if they ask the name of this One who has sent him, and therefore of the God of their fathers, e must tell them that He is called and is " I am, who I was as the God of your fathers and will be as your God." The second period in the life of Moses, which begins with this encounter on the mountain of God, is absolutely filled and claimed by active attestation of the work of this God as expressed in its fulfilment and as it points both to the past and present. Moses has heard its expression. He must now attest and re-attest it in difficult circumstances to Pharaoh and in even more difficult circumstances to the people of God. This task and its execution are the goal of his vocation. And the personal reward which will certainly not be lacking (Ex. 33^{11}) is that God will speak with him, with the man who is bound and committed to him, "face to face, as a man speaketh unto his friend." Can a man demand more? Has any mystic, Pietist or Romantic experienced anything higher? It was in the fulfilment of his *ministerium Verbi divini*, however, that he had this supreme experience.

According to the Deuteronomically conceived Book of Joshua (1$^{1-11}$), the calling of Moses was followed by the special but related calling of Joshua. The work of God still goes forward. The land is wide open before the people and is already given them. "Every place that the sole of your foot shall tread upon, that have I given unto you, as I said unto Moses." Joshua has to lead the people in, and therefore across Jordan. The occupation—a term which is meaningful only if it is understood as supremely active acceptance—is now to commence. Its execution is the task and active witness of Joshua. Is it not greater than that required of his more illustrious predecessor? But rivalry is expressly negated: "As I was with Moses, so I will be with thee (in all thy ways, as is said later): I will not fail thee, nor forsake thee." Joshua has thus nothing to fear, for no one can withstand him. "Only be thou strong and very courageous (this is said three times), that thou mayest observe to do all the law, which Moses my servant commanded thee: turn not from it to the right hand or to the left, that thou mayest prosper whithersoever thou goest." He is to speak of this law and meditate in it day and night. No doubt this precise statement can be attributed to a later stratum of the tradition. But Israel's self-understanding in respect of its origins is here rightly in substance explaining that calling as active calling to witness—it is the Lord of the whole history of Israel who calls—takes place in a continuity even though it is new in each case, and that in this continuity the work and Word of God yesterday cannot be separated from His work and Word to-day, but the two belong together and form a single whole for all the differentiation in detail. The particular task of Joshua in continuation and completion of that of Moses is the motive which according to the Deuteronomic presentation controls his particular existence.

Gideon is called in the same way according to Jud. 6$^{11-24}$. He, too, is summoned, and after initial hesitation impelled, to the specific active witness of repulsing the desert tribes which constantly threaten Israel: "Thou shalt save Israel from the hand of the Midianites: have not I sent thee?" It is to this mission that he must devote his life, and he does so. Again, Samuel is called in the same way according to 1 Sam. 3$^{1-21}$. The task given him in early youth is specifically that of proclaiming the divine judgment on Eli and his house, but this is obviously extended as he grows up: "The Lord was with him, and did let none of his words fall to the ground. And all Israel from Dan even to Beersheba knew that Samuel was established to be a prophet of the Lord." According to the tradition, he then exercised this prophecy supremely in connexion with the rise and fall of Saul, the first king of Israel, and then the elevation of David and his house in place of Saul. Again, David's unexpected anointing by Samuel (1 Sam. 16$^{1-13}$) is to be understood as a calling, and his assumption and discharge of the royal office are thus to be regarded as his own specific witness to the fulfilment of the will of Yahweh for His people, and indeed for all peoples, as distantly revealed already in the great extension of his dominion. It is surely no accidental coincidence that the greatest record of the confession, not lacking even in the Old Testament, of the individual and collective experience of salvation, the Book of Psalms, has been brought into such close relationship with the name of this hero and ruler who was the most forceful of all the active witnesses to the Word of God's action in the history of Israel and therefore in the world, and that in certain detailed passages it is perhaps to be understood as an effective parergon of the historical mission of David. In the very Psalms devoted to the active praise of the divine action in the sphere of creation, it could and should also be stated *expressis verbis* what it meant personally for all God's witnesses that their human activity as such was accompanied by the repeated promise : " I will be with thee." We must not read the Psalms, as Christians unfortunately so often do, in abstraction from their Messianic setting, and therefore from the witness to God's kingdom so powerfully given in the life and acts of David. Otherwise we may well misinterpret the unforgettable things which they say concerning the existence of the called in all its dimensions, misapplying them in the sense of an individual and collective egoism of salvation.

Again, we have to think of the calling of the prophets in the narrower sense. Except in the cases of Moses and Samuel, it is only with them that word, speech and writing, i.e., declaration in the more literal sense, may be said to stand in the forefront of their task and sending. Of course, their witness, too, consists decisively in their existence as those who are called by God. But their spoken word now becomes the typical expression of their existence and form of their witness. God speaks to them as to all their predecessors. He tells them what His will and act were and were not, are and are not, will be and will not be, in world-occurrence and particularly in events within the sphere of Israel and Judah. Hence the formula : " Thus saith the Lord "—their acceptance of what God says being the basis, authorisation and power of their own human preaching, teaching, proclamation and (in the appropriate place) writing in the service of the divine Word. What they do in this service usually has symbolic significance, not merely in representation of what they say, but in depiction of the fact that they do not refer to timeless truths but to the past, present and future occurrence in which the will and action of God are declared to them. They are certainly called to declaration in the literal sense. But it is seldom that this is not presented in their writings, or in later accounts, as an event in their lives which is in many cases dated. The Word of the Lord came to them. It imperiously entered their lives like an unexpected guest. Even where there is no such reference, it may be naturally assumed. In effect, the Old Testament gives us actual accounts of calling only in the cases of Isaiah, Jeremiah and Ezekiel. All of these have distinctive characteristics. Yet for an understanding of what is meant by vocation they all point in the same direction.

The calling of Isaiah, like that of Moses, begins with a divine theophany (Is. 6^{1-13}). In this case, however, it is on a much grander scale than the appearance in the bush, and it is immediately recognised for what it is by the one who is called. He sees a King so high and lifted up that his train fills the great expanse of the temple in Jerusalem. Above Him and around Him, representing the heavenly cosmos within the earthly, are the seraphim with their threefold *Sanctus*. At the continuation of this hymn or ascription, the posts of the door are moved and the whole house is filled and enveloped by the smoke of what is clearly an invisibly threatening fire. The words of the continuation should be noted, for they constitute a historical declaration which goes beyond anything previously said to the called. They are to the effect that " the whole earth is full of his glory." It is not merely that the temple, which can hardly accommodate His train, is full of His glory, nor indeed Jerusalem, nor Judah, but the whole earth. It is thus that He is the thrice holy. This is what is sung and said by the seraphim. This is something which is resolved and settled in relation to King Yahweh whom Isaiah sees majestically enthroned. This is what is proclaimed by the stroke of the historical hour of this prophet. Isaiah is the man who sees King Yahweh in this way, who hears the *Sanctus* with this addition, continuation and extension. But we misread the situation as he himself saw it if we expect that a word along these lines, the proclamation of the universal rule of Yahweh as such, will be his task and the purpose of his mission. So far there has been no mention of any commission. What shatters and seizes Isaiah in face of the exalted King and as a hearer of the hymn or ascription of the seraphim is a recognition, which pierces asunder to the very joints and marrow, of the total disparity and discrepancy between the being and rule of Yahweh, as disclosed to him by the declaration articulated in the saying of the seraphim, and himself as a member of the temple community and the people of Jerusalem and Judah. The contrast is a mortal blow : " Woe is me ! for I am undone ; because I am a man of unclean lips, and I dwell in the midst of a people of unclean lips." It is to be noted that he does not speak of the unclean heart, but of the unclean lips of himself and his people. It is thus clear to him from the very first that what he has seen and heard demands to be expressed and proclaimed. It must go out as a human word on human lips, to be sounded forth and heard in its immeasurable positive and negative significance among all men throughout the earth. But he knows of no human mouth which is able and worthy to form and express that which corresponds to the matter. He must confess that he is a member of the community and people in which there are only unclean lips which contradict rather than correspond to the matter. He thus knows that what he has seen and heard must be expressed and yet cannot be expressed by a human mouth. It is in view of this dilemma that he cries : " Woe is me ! for I am undone." And the distinctiveness of his calling is to be found in the fact that his own commissioning is thus delayed and he himself must first be made able and worthy. There thus follows at the hands of one of the seraphim the touching of his mouth with a live coal taken with tongs from off the altar : " Lo, this hath touched thy lips ; and thine iniquity is taken away, and thy sin purged." There must be no mistaking the fact that the remission and purging which he is granted—whatever personal or private significance they might have—relates strictly to his enabling, to his being made worthy, for a service of his lips which is not yet but obviously will be required. Its purpose is strictly to make him free to render this service in distinction from the other members of his community and people. It is a further surprise that this is not followed at once by his commissioning and sending as such but by a kind of general promulgation of the task as though it might be accepted by others : " Whom shall I send, and who will go for us ? " There then follows the further unique feature of the free offer of Isaiah. Being freed for the purpose, he is free to attempt the task without presumption : " Here am I ; send me." There then comes a final and truly confusing and astounding surprise. Isaiah is commissioned, but for what ? He is sent, but to whom ? It might have been supposed that like Paul he would have been sent to the nations to tell them that the whole earth is full of the glory of thrice holy King Yahweh. But like all his predecessors, apart from Moses' commission to Pharaoh, he is sent only to Israel, and indeed with even greater restriction to this people of Jerusalem and Judah. And if we might have been expected that he would be sent to them to speak to them the wonderful Word of Yahweh and His royal dominion, and to call and direct them to a joyful acceptance of the special mission among and to all peoples, we are again disillusioned, for the dreadful task of Isaiah is as follows : " Go, and tell this people, Hear ye indeed, but understand not ; and see ye indeed, but perceive not. Make the heart of this people fat, and make their ears heavy, and shut their eyes, lest they see with their eyes, and hear with their ears, and understand with their heart, and convert, and be healed." This is a dreadful message for the hearers, but even more dreadful for the speaker who has nothing to impart to the people of God among all the peoples but that it is too late to receive any other word, and that it cannot and will and shall not understand any other. " Lord, how long ? " is the startled cry of the man who is given this task. How long will this Word apply ? How long will the appearance of the enthroned King and the saying of the seraphim mean this and this alone for the people chosen and beloved by Him ? How long is it to be told only that God passes it by and has no more to say to it ? The answer is given : " Until the cities be wasted without inhabitant, and the houses without man, and the land be utterly desolate " ; until even the tenth of the people which is yet spared is destroyed ; until only a stump remains of the felled terebinths and oaks ; until the judgment of the King of whose glory the earth is full has been executed to the bitter end on this people. It belongs to another chapter that the stump will still be a holy seed, and that the history of the acts of God among and to this people will not come to an end with this judgment. The clock has now struck twelve. The axe is laid to the root of the tree. Isaiah, the witness of the will and act of Yahweh in this hour, has to attest this and this alone to his people. It is for this that Yahweh has appeared to him. It is for this that he has heard the seraphim magnify Him as the King of the whole earth. It is for this that his lips are purged. It is for this service that he has freely and readily offered even though he did not suspect its nature. It is in order that he may discharge it that he is separated from the community of the temple and from the people, and set over against them as the messenger of Yahweh.

The hour of the calling of Jeremiah as described in Jer. 1⁴⁻¹⁹ is different again. The universality of the lordship of Yahweh over His people and the other nations has taken very concrete form in the history of his time, and so, too, has its recognition as this is granted to Jeremiah. The judgment intimated by Isaiah now stands at the very doors in the form of the overwhelming Babylonian threat. This is the meaning of the visions of the almond tree and the seething pot. " I will hasten my word to perform it," and : " Out of the north an evil shall break forth upon all the inhabitants of the land." This is not just a political situation which can be remedied by diplomatic or military means. Yahweh is about to make irresistible use of His power as the Ruler of the world. There can be no averting the fall of Jerusalem, of the temple and of the house of David. This is what Jeremiah has to tell the people of Jerusalem, the political and ecclesiastical leaders, and all members of the people, through all the changing circumstances of the reigns of Josiah, Jekoiakim and Zedekiah, in flat opposition to all optimistic prognoses, constantly swimming against the stream, suspected of defeatism and even treason, and constantly provoking irritation and hostility. His account of his calling to deliver this message reflects the irresistibility of the happening but also the dreadful nature of the task of proclaiming it as the will and act of Yahweh. Yahweh had chosen him for it before he received it, indeed, before he existed, before Yahweh formed him in his mother's womb. He had sanctified and ordained him, before he came forth from the womb, to be a " prophet unto the nations " in this strict sense and as the unwelcome bearer of this message. He would have to abandon himself to abandon this task and therefore to cease to be a prophet in this sense. In other parts of the Book (20⁷⁻¹⁸) we find his complaints and accusations in respect of the impasse to which Yahweh has brought him. Yahweh has deceived him, and he has let himself be deceived. Yahweh has overwhelmed and subjugated him. In terms even sharper than the sharpest words of Job, he curses the day of his birth and the man who announced it to his father. It would have been better if he had not been born to tread this unavoidable path. For the Word of the Lord has become to him a daily reproach and derision. He admits, of course, that he cannot actually be untrue to his election and ordination : " Then I said, I will not make mention of him, nor speak any more in his name. But his word was in mine heart as a burning fire shut up in my bones, and I was weary with forbearing, and I could not stay." In his vocation this outer and inner conflict is still before him. The account gives us only the sigh : " Ah, Lord God ! behold, I cannot speak : for I am a child." But this is dismissed. The answer is made :

" Say not, I am a child : for thou shalt go to all that I shall send thee, and whatsoever I command thee thou shalt speak." Thou shalt go ! Thou shalt speak ! He can only do as he is told. For in his case too, though no detailed description is given, there is a touching of the mouth which constitutes the decisive moment in the act of calling : " Behold, I have put my words in thy mouth. See, I have set thee this day over the nations and over the kingdoms, to root out, and to pull down, and to destroy, and to throw down, and to build, and to plant." Finally, in relation to the power granted with this ordination, like so many of his predecessors he is given the promise : " Be not afraid of their faces : for I am with thee to deliver thee," and then even more explicitly : " Be not dismayed at their faces, lest I confound thee before them. For, behold, I have made thee this day a defenced city, and an iron pillar, and brazen walls against the whole land, against the kings of Judah, against the princes thereof, against the priests thereof, and against the people of the land. And they shall fight against thee ; but they shall not prevail against thee ; for I am with thee, saith the Lord, to deliver thee." In accordance with this Jeremiah can confess even in the sombre retrospect of that later passage : " The Lord is with me as a mighty terrible one : therefore my persecutors shall stumble, and they shall not prevail." It is noteworthy that this promise, which is lacking in Is. 6, should be present in the case of Jeremiah, who later treads such a desolate and afflicted path, so that even on this path there gleams through a final personal assurance, security and triumph which he particularly is granted. At the same time it is even more obvious that this promise is absolutely bound up with his task and mission, that it is co-ordinated with the difficult action of his witness, and that it is not in any sense the theme of his history.

The most explicit and bizarre of all the biblical accounts of vocation is that recorded of Ezekiel in the first chapter of his Book (vv. 3–27). Our attention will not be directed to the features which it shares with earlier callings, but rather to that which gives it its own colouring and has perhaps a useful and important contribution to make to the total picture. A strange circumstance in this case is that the true act of calling consists in the fact that, when Yahweh appears to him in a splendid vision, Ezekiel is given to eat a roll which is written on both sides (2⁹ᶠ·). This obviously emphasises the precision with which he must simply accept and pass on that which is most objectively given him by God. Nor should we overlook the fact that this extraordinary food is said to be as sweet as honey when he puts it in his mouth (3³). Concerning the content of the writing, and therefore the message which Ezekiel has to deliver, we are given only three words. These are " lamentations," " mourning " and " woe " (2¹⁰). While Jerusalem moves forward to its destruction, and the work of Jeremiah to its critical point, the younger Ezekiel must join hands with the latter and with Isaiah before him in proclaiming the accusation and judgment of Yahweh to the exilic community in Babylon which has not yet been instructed by the catastrophe which has already engulfed it. The whole house of Israel (3⁷), whether Samarian or Judean, whether in exile or in the homeland, presents a hard forehead and a stony heart to God and His Word : " They will not hearken unto thee ; for they will not hearken unto me " (3⁷). Hence the divine equipment of the prophet (3⁸ᶠ·) can only consist in making his face as hard as theirs and his forehead as adamant : " As an adamant, harder than flint, have I made thy forehead." His task thus seems to be simply to embody God's defiance of the defiance of man and to stand like a sharp and impregnable rock among them. He must spring to his feet and cry " Thus saith the Lord " among these impudent and stiffhearted children (2²⁻⁴). But what does the Lord say ? One of the strange features of these chapters is that the mission of the prophet seems to consist simply in attestation of the fact that Yahweh speaks. The question of the practical goal and effect of his witness is thus left completely open. As is continually impressed upon him with increasing sharpness, he has simply to give it, to represent the Word of Yahweh among them " whether they will hear, or whether they will forbear " (2[5, 7], 3[11]). The purpose of his mission is simply that they should " know that there hath been a prophet among them " (2[5]). In Ezekiel we have obviously reached a final point which also seems to indicate a critical point in the history of Old Testament prophecy. Even the witness of Isaiah, Jeremiah and the other prophets cannot really be understood pragmatically, i.e., from the standpoint of a practical, moral or even religious goal obvious to the prophets themselves and to the hearers and readers of their histories. And basically are we not forced to say the same of the call of Abraham, Moses and the rest, even though we may discern in detail certain subsidiary aims such as the formation and existence of the people, its liberation and direction, its entry into and security in the land, and the reference to ways in which it must walk in virtue of its election ? What is the real purpose of the whole history of Israel ? What is the real purpose of the Word of Yahweh spoken in and with it and attested by the called ? It becomes increasingly improbable that either the history or the Word can have any inherent meaning or purpose as more and more they assume the pronouncedly negative character of a history and Word of pure judgment which emerges unmistakeably from at least the time of Amos and Isaiah. In the sphere of the Old Testament there is no answer to the question of the goal of the history of Israel or the final purpose of prophecy. This is what seems to be confirmed and sealed in the calling of Ezekiel. What is made clear in this is simply the naked fact that the history of Israel is the interconnected work of Yahweh, who is not dumb but speaks in its occurrence and therefore in His action. What is made clear, then, is simply the necessity and consistency of what is said and done in the sphere of the Old Testament. What is made clear in the inscrutability of its goal and purpose is the fact that what is said and done here points beyond itself.

When we turn to the New Testament we must begin by stating that there neither is nor can be any history of the calling of Jesus. As is particularly emphasised in John's Gospel, but occasionally in Matthew and Luke as well, He is sent. As the Son of God, He is sent by the Father to the world, to earth and among men. He has come as One who is sent. In at least one passage He can thus be explicitly called an " apostle " (Heb. 3[1]). But He is also a " prophet," charged with an incomparable task, and expressly described as such in several places in Matthew, Luke and John. Yet there is no becoming of Jesus which underlies and precedes this being and can be narrated as such. There is thus no account of the coming into being of His prophecy and apostolate. There is a voice from heaven in the story of His baptism and again in that of His transfiguration on the mount, but this is not a calling in virtue of which He becomes what He was not before after the pattern of those commissioned by Yahweh in the Old Testament. It is His proclamation as the One who as the Son of God is the Prophet and Apostle *per se*, and is to be heard as such. It describes and confirms Him as the One who needs no calling because He is called essentially. But in saying this we say rather more than the New Testament, which does not apply the concept of vocation to Jesus at all. Of Him it can only be said and told that He Himself calls. He is the foundation of the apostles and prophets (Eph. 2[20]), and only as such is He Himself to be called Apostle and Prophet. He stands at the point where in the Old Testament Yahweh confronts those who are to be called and are actually called by Him. This is the new starting-point with which we have to reckon in the New Testament stories of calling. The Subject who calls with the authority and efficacy of the Old Testament Yahweh is a man, this man, who as such encounters other men, calls them to Himself and His service, and constitutes, equips and sends them forth as His witnesses. The existence of the man who may and must do this, and actually does it, is the new factor which is the origin and theme of the New Testament. This is the act of God at the goal and end of the history of Israel and its prophecy.

" As thou hast sent me into the world, even so have I also sent them into the world " (Jn. 17¹⁸). " As my Father hath sent me, even so send I you " (Jn. 20²¹). This καθώς includes the fact that the historical work of God and the spoken Word of God are no longer two things but one, the former as the transparency which is illumined by the light of the latter. Hence the work of God, i.e., the fulfilment of His action in the history of Israel by the existence of the man Jesus sent forth by Him, no longer stands in need of any special Word to reveal it as the work of God, since it speaks and is itself the Word of God as such. The Word spoken by this man, as distinct from that of all the Old Testament prophets, can and must, therefore, consist simply in the self-revelation of this man and the proclamation of His own existence as the Son of God. He Himself is the work of God in the fulfilment now attained and effected. Through Him, the Son, God " who at sundry times and in divers manners spake in time past unto the fathers by the prophets," has now spoken at the end and goal of all times (Heb. 1¹ᶠ·). But can the Son, as Witness of the work of God now accomplished in His own existence, bear testimony to anything other or higher than Himself ? And if He for His part, unlike any of the Old Testament prophets, calls and sends out others, what charge can He give them, or to what can He commission them, except to be witnesses of the work of God accomplished in Him, and therefore His witnesses, i.e., witnesses of His existence, proclaimers of the Word of God spoken in His existence ? In correspondence and accordance with (καθώς) His own sending, He sends them. Neither together nor individually could the Old Testament prophets be witnesses of the fulfilment of the work of God " when the fulness of time was come " (Gal. 4⁴), namely, of the fulfilment in which this work having reached its goal in the existence of the man Jesus, is both a fact and a saying, in which it is also the Word of God as such. Hence their genuine witness concerning the work and Word of God in the history of Israel could only be incomplete. It could not finally be perspicuous in itself. It could only point beyond itself. But in so far as the work of God attested by them moved in fact to this completion ; in so far as the history of Israel moved in fact to that of Jesus Christ ; in so far as it was the indispensable presupposition, preparation and intimation of it, their witness, too, had reference to the One who was to come and did come, and therefore the witnesses of this One who came, the apostles sent by Him, were not mistaken when even in the provisional word of the prophets of the One who had not yet come they found genuine witness to Christ, and even placed it as such before their own direct witness, basing their own witness on that of the fathers and respectfully taking their place behind them.

If we are to understand and estimate the New Testament accounts of calling as such, our best plan is to start with the account of the calling of the disciples in the Fourth Gospel (Jn. 1³⁵⁻⁵¹). A first point to catch our attention is that the distinctive call of Jesus in the Synoptic stories : " Follow me," while it is addressed to Philip in v. 43, is now exceptional and almost occasional. It is, of course, known to the Fourth Evangelist (cf. 8¹², 12²⁶, 21²²). But in the reciprocal relationship of Jesus and the disciples it seems to have more of the character of a deduction from the presupposition which really underlies this relationship and not to be itself the underlying presupposition. When we turn to the others mentioned in this account, we find that Andrew comes first, so that with reference to this passage, and not without rivalry against Peter and Rome, he is celebrated as the πρωτόκλητος in the Eastern Church. Together with Andrew is an unknown disciple, who is surely identical with the unknown disciple who appears frequently in this Gospel. Then comes Andrew's brother Peter, then Philip and then Nathanael, who is brought by Philip after some resistance and who cannot be identified for certain with any of those mentioned by the Synoptists. None of these, however, is called verbally ; we are told of one after the other that as soon as they saw Jesus, in some cases brought by the others, they spontaneously followed him. The two first (v. 35 f.) seem originally to have been disciples of

John the Baptist who met Jesus in company with John and attached themselves to Him when they heard the Baptist's cry : " Behold, the Lamb of God ! " Simon came when he was told by Andrew : " We have found the Messias " (v. 41), and Nathanael was similarly brought by Philip (v. 45 f.). Whether with or without this mediation, they all seem to take the decisive step of themselves with an astonishing freedom and necessity. In the case of none of them do we have express reference to any task or mission. Is this really an account of calling at all ? In the intention of the Gospel, it undoubtedly is, and exactly as it is narrated. The basic importance which this Evangelist ascribed to the coming of the disciples may be seen already from the exact statement in v. 39 that it began at the tenth hour of the third day of the fellowship of the Baptist with Jesus. Again, on a closer examination there can be no mistaking the fact that in this coming of the disciples to Jesus the decisive acting Subject both in His own sight and theirs is Jesus Himself. For this Evangelist, too, Jesus is thus the One who calls. The only point is that, except in the case of Philip, the calling is not verbal according to this presentation. It is rather the underlying presupposition of verbal calling. This is the concern of the Fourth Evangelist. There can be no ignoring the difficulty and indeed the impossibility of harmonising his account with that of the Synoptists from the standpoint of the historical pragmatics of the process. But even if we prefer to follow the Synoptists for this reason or in this respect, we have to allow that from the purely material standpoint the Johannine account constitutes a strangely original statement which is needed alongside that of the Synoptists to point to their background. It tells us that it needed only the initial impulse of the saying of the Baptist, and certain men had to follow Him, and did follow Him, and were thus called, commissioned and sent by Him, without any verbal summons on the part of Jesus and with supreme objective necessity. According to the view of the Fourth Evangelist there existed between Him and them a kind of predestinarian, and as such highly efficacious, bond which was simply disclosed, confirmed and actualised in their encounter. Thus Simon was immediately addressed by Jesus (v. 42) not only with his full name but also with the surname Cephas, which according to the Synoptists was given him only at the climax at Caesarea Philippi, and which denotes his future function. Again, Nathanael is at once described as " an Israelite indeed, in whom there is no guile." Again, one after the other is simply found (v. 41, 43, 45), and they for their part declare : " We have found the Messias " (v. 41), or : " We have found him of whom Moses in the law, and the prophets did write, Jesus of Nazareth, the son of Joseph " (v. 45). Again, Jesus saw Nathanael under the fig tree even before Philip called him (v. 50). And the mere declaration : " I saw thee," together with the recognition that Jesus knew him, was enough to evoke from Nathanael the confession : " Rabbi, thou art the Son of God ; thou art the King of Israel " (v. 49). What the Johannine account obviously intends to say is that the encounter of these men with the man Jesus is in itself and as such strong enough to bring into effect their relationship of discipleship to Him as something already resolved concerning them. He calls them as they become aware of His existence and of the determination of their own existence for discipleship. He speaks, calls and summons by His presence. And what they are called to—there is no mention of personal salvation or perdition in this story—is highly practical recognition of His existence and commitment to it. The confessions of Andrew, Philip and Nathanael show that with their actual calling to this recognition—the concept of believing occurs in v. 50—they also acquire and have taken up their task and are already engaged in discharging it. What is still ahead according to the concluding verse of the story is simply the fulfilment of the confession already made and the task already accepted and undertaken : " Ye shall see heaven open, and the angels of God ascending and descending upon the Son of man." It is certainly tempting and possible to regard this Johannine account as a theological commentary on the Synoptic records which are so much shorter and more explicit. In any case, it is legitimate and indeed necessary to see in it an indication and description of the basic process enacted between Jesus and the disciples when He came to them and they to Him, and to derive from the Synoptic accounts the explication of this basic process, in which the man Jesus did not in the first instance need to call other men verbally because in His being as the One He was, as the completed work of God, He was also the Word of God which as such had both the content and the power of calling.

When we come to the Synoptists, we shall take first the story of the calling of Levi (Mk. 2¹³⁻¹⁷ and *par.*), who is called Matthew in the First Gospel, because this gives us the explication of the basic process in its simplest and therefore its most eloquent form. For all that it is so astonishing, the decisive event in the story is as simple as possible and is described in a single verse in all three versions. All emphasise the apparently casual nature of the occasion. Jesus is passing through Capernaum on His way to the lake-side, and in passing (παράγων) He sees Levi the son of Alphaeus sitting in his tax-office, which is apparently open to the street. Whether Levi sees Jesus is irrelevant. Jesus sees Levi. According to the context Levi is a rich man. But he is more than suspect to the strict Jews of the city on account of his calling, the collection of taxes being a lucrative business farmed out by the alien rulers to large-scale operators who then committed it to lesser middlemen like Levi at a lesser profit, and also probably on account of the harshness and trickery which were almost inseparably bound up with the operation of the system and to which Levi probably owed his wealth, like the more highly placed Zacchaeus in Jericho (Lk. 19⁸). In any case, Levi belonged to those who in exercising this calling excluded themselves *ipso facto* from the national and religious society of the Jews, and could only be reckoned as transgressors before the Law and in the eyes of its commissioned expositors and representatives. This is the man whom Jesus sees in passing. He says to him : " Follow me." And he arises, and leaves everything (Lk. 5²⁸), and follows Him. On the side both of the One who calls and of the one who is called, it is all quite unequivocal, totally unprepared, and highly improbable, and yet the records tell us with great sobriety that it happens. How does Jesus come to call this man ? He does so. How does this man come to obey Jesus ? He does so. In this simple event which is so astonishing on both sides and yet which happens, there arises the mastership of Jesus on the one hand and the discipleship of this man on the other. And the context gives the happening a specific note which is most significant. For in the continuation Levi invites Jesus and the disciples who are already following Him to a feast in his house, to which he also invites a great company of worthy or less worthy associates in his unhappy calling and reputation, " many publicans and sinners " who " sat together with Jesus and his disciples." This table fellowship of Jesus with " publicans and sinners " arouses the serious displeasure of the Pharisees, and in relation to them Jesus introduces the comparison of the doctor in his dealings with the sick' and the well, and says : " I came not to call the righteous, but sinners to repentance." What does this mean ? The fact that in all three versions it is related to the earlier incident, and that Jesus speaks expressly of καλεῖν, makes it plain that in the light of the calling of Levi Jesus is here saying something decisive and well worth pondering concerning the meaning and purpose of His calling generally. " I came not to call the righteous." The righteous are those who in their own judgment and that of other righteous people, who are never lacking in the world even without the intervention of Jesus, are standing in the right place as distinct from others, namely, at the side of God. Apart from their reconciliation to God effected in Jesus, and therefore apart from His prophecy, there is a relatively large minority of men who see in themselves and one another those who are already placed at the side of God, who are already called, who seem in some sense to form God's party in the world, and who can advance many good reasons for claiming to do so, in contrast to the majority of the godless with whom as such they are in conflict. The Pharisees belong to this party of those who are already righteous and called. The publicans and sinners obviously do not, but belong to the party of the godless assailed by them. And now Jesus comes to the scene of battle and finds the righteous on the one side and the ungodly on the other. To whom does He belong ? To whom does He issue His call ? The righteous seem not unwilling at first to hail Him as one of them. Does not He call men out of the *massa perditionis* to set them at God's side within the world ? Surely this implies a welcome confirming and strengthening of the already flourishing and militant divine party of the warriors of light against darkness. Surely it holds out the prospect of their overwhelming and definitive victory against all opponents. But there now comes the great disappointment and alienation. It is astonishing enough that Jesus calls a notorious publican to be His disciple. But this may be condoned on the natural assumption that He is calling him out of the great company of worldlings and ungodly and leading him into their camp. To make proselytes has always been a fine occupation for the righteous. Yet this is not what happens. What happens is that Jesus seems to follow the one who is called by Him rather than *vice versa*. He accepts his invitation, goes to his house, sits down at table not only with him and the existing disciples but with a highly dubious company of worldlings, eats and drinks with them, and in this way openly and publicly dissociates Himself from the righteous and associates with the ungodly. Is this what it means to call and set Levi at the side of God ? Can a righteous man, one who is himself at the side of God, do a thing like this ? " A man is known by his company." Who, then, is Jesus if this is His company ? Can a man who does this be righteous and call to righteousness ? The astonishing answer of the three Evangelists is that this righteous man, this man who calls to righteousness, the man Jesus, actually has to do this. He does not stand in the camp of those who are already righteous. He does not take their righteousness seriously. He has no intention of leading the one who is called by Him into that camp or integrating him into the phalanx of the party of God in opposition to the godless. He goes before him, and His existing and future disciples, by first following him into his house, sitting at table quite unreservedly with a great company of publicans and sinners, and very peacefully and non-heroically holding a celebration with them. He has not come to call the righteous, those who in their own judgment and that of those likeminded are already righteous and stand at the side of God. Why should He ? In regarding themselves as such, and conducting their party politics as such, they obviously do not need to be called by Him, any more than the physician by those who are well. Nor has He come to strengthen them in their righteousness or to give validity and new thrust to their party politics. Nor can He use them in His discipleship for what He has in mind for those who are called by Him. They are the very last who can become and be His witnesses. As those who are already righteous, they can never be this. As His disciples, as Christians, they could only cause confusion and offence by understanding and representing His Gospel as a new and higher kind of Pharisaism. He, Jesus, is not against publicans and sinners at the side of God. He is for them. He is for the worldlings and ungodly. He conducts their case at and from the side of God. This is His righteousness which He calls and sends out His own to proclaim. Those whom He calls to Himself He calls to the side of God where they, too, cannot be against but only for the children of the world. Those who are already righteous, and thus contend against the ungodly, He can only pass by. He can only wait until perhaps one day they step down from their lofty pulpit or platform and abandon their righteousness and therefore their contest. He has not come to call them, but to call sinners. Levi is a notorious sinner and nothing more. As such he is usable as a witness of Jesus. As such He calls him. And in confirmation and proclamation of the full seriousness of the calling, commissioning and sending of this sinner, he sits down with him and all his fellow-publicans and fellow-sinners, eating and drinking with them in celebration of his calling, the meaning and goal of which, since it is the act and Word of the free grace of God, can consist only in the attestation and proclamation of this free grace. To know, to receive and therefore to attest and proclaim this grace, a man must be a sinner, and know himself as such, and allow himself to be known by others as such. In no sense and in no circumstances, then, can he regard himself as already righteous, or conduct himself accordingly. This is clear enough in the case of Levi. It is for this reason that his calling can and must be an event which is as unexpected and improbable as appears at the beginning of the account. Nor should we miss the basic significance of the passage. In this respect the calling of Levi is not exceptional but typical. The calling of Jesus is never a calling of those who are already righteous. All those who are already righteous, and remain such, are *per se* the uncalled from whom He can only dissociate and whom He can only pass by, turning instead, and most surprisingly, to the sinner in the tax-office. His calling is always a calling of sinners, because, as calling to Him and to His discipleship, it is always calling to the proclamation of the free grace of God which as such can take place authentically, credibly and acceptably only in the mouth of sinners, of those who are wholly directed to it.

The calling of the four fishermen, Simon, Andrew, James and John, comes at the beginning or immediately after the beginning of the whole Gospel narrative in the three Synoptists. The Synoptic tradition agrees with the Johannine in a presentation which first presupposes a Jesus who exists alone, e.g., in his baptism, in the temptation in the wilderness and in the assumption of His teaching office, but which is then rapidly broadened by the calling of the disciples, in this case of these four as the first, before the idea of a Jesus without disciples can harden and establish itself. Other callings must have followed these first, as may be seen from the lists of apostles adduced later ; though only that of Levi is narrated, unless we refer to the incident in Lk. 9^{59}, where Jesus called an anonymous figure to be His disciple, but he wanted first to go and bury his father, and was told in reply : " Let the dead bury their dead : but go thou and preach the kingdom of God." When we turn to the calling of the four, one thing stands out plainly in the essentially similar accounts in Mk. 1^{16-20} and Mt. 4^{18-22} and also in the Lucan version in 5^{1-11} which obviously follows a special tradition and purpose. This is that this first calling, which is the most important to the community on account of the persons involved, stands in direct connexion with the beginning of the public proclamation by Jesus of the fulfilled time and the imminent kingdom of God, and of His call to be converted and believe in view of this good news. Throughout the Gospel narrative which follows, this prophetic action will always be His, and will consist in words personally spoken and deeds personally performed by Him. It is only in Acts that we shall be concerned with the words and deeds of the disciples. But according to the presentation in all the Gospels this prophetic action always has as its aim that it should be taken up and continued by His disciples. From the very outset it demands their presence as witnesses who see and hear. They are to go along with Him on His way through Galilee and later to Jerusalem. They are to accompany Him, whether they understand or not. According to Mk. $6^{7f.}$ and *par.* they will indeed be sent out a first time in distinctive anticipation of their later execution of their commission, and although we are given no details they will thus go into action both in word and deed. But almost from the very first, when Jesus Himself makes His debut as Prophet, His call to discipleship implies commissioning to their own future speech and action. Hardly has His own Word gone forth concerning the fulfilled time, the kingdom, conversion and faith, before they must attach themselves to Him and in some sense tread on His heels. In Mark and Matthew we are introduced to a group consisting of two pairs of fishermen who are obviously engaged in very different tasks. The first two, Simon and Andrew, are casting their nets ; the others, James and John, assistants of their father Zebedee, are mending theirs. In this case, too, the text emphasises the casual nature of the encounter. It is as Jesus is walking (περιπατῶν) by the sea that He meets the first two, and as He goes a little farther (προβάς) that He finds the second. He might well have overlooked either the first, the second, or both. But He sees them as He later saw Levi, and this differentiating and electing seeing decides their fate according to the Evangelists, being followed at once by a call which can hardly be translated in its dramatic intensity : δεῦτε ὀπίσω μου, and in the power of which they cease to be what they were and become what they were not. Why should they come and follow Him ? In contrast to the story of Levi we are here given an explanation which is formulated rather clumsily in Greek : " I will cause that you become fishers of men " (Mk. 1¹⁷). Jesus will make them fishers of men instead of ordinary fishers. " He made twelve, that they should be with him, and that he might send them forth " (Mk. 3¹⁴). They will have to give up any further exercise of their previous calling, but their previous calling is made a similitude of the goal of their vocation. It may well be that their own salvation, the saving of their souls etc., are part of this goal. But there is no mention of these things in this important passage. No, the concern is supremely and finally with the men themselves, and with others near and distant. It is a matter of seeking them out, of reaching them, of encircling them, of gathering and fetching and winning them, not for any selfish end, but for the sphere of lordship and light of the One whom they have now to follow as He goes before them in Word and deed. It is to do this, as once they did it in the careful casting, the wider and bolder throwing and the steady drawing in of their fishing nets, that they are now called and have to follow Jesus, i.e., to become His disciples. Now, at once, is intended, and now, at once, they do what they are told as Levi was to do later : " And straightway they forsook their nets (and their father in the case of the second pair), and followed him." It is to be noted that there is no discrediting of their previous honest, modest and very useful work. Indeed, even the prior occupation of Levi is not disparaged. The fishermen might well have continued quite confidently in their job for the rest of their lives. But their material service is now transformed into service in and to the broader world of men. Their gaze and concern are to be with people. For the gaze and concern of Jesus are not directed on things, though these are not despised nor rejected, but on people. He is the Saviour of people, of ἄνθρωποι. The whole effort of those who are called to His discipleship must be concentrated, therefore, on the winning of people, not to themselves, but to Him. This does not mean that their previous calling is devalued. Their calling to a material ministry is made a parable of their new activity and thus given a new and higher value.

We now turn from Mark and Matthew to Luke, who is obviously seeing, understanding and depicting the same incident in his own way. The prior history of Jesus without His disciples is much more extended in his case. Did He wish to emphasise the special, peculiar and gracious character of the first and of every event of vocation by postponing its description and first recording at some length the visit and sermon of Jesus in his own city of Nazareth, the story of an exorcism, a case of healing, and a summary account of many such incidents ? The idea that Jesus needed His disciples in the sense that He had to turn to them and their discipleship is certainly very effectively excluded by the Lucan account. And in the depiction of the actual event of their calling he treads a distinctive path which makes it a waste of time to attempt harmonisation with Mark and Matthew. According to Luke, it is the pressure of the crowd in its eagerness for the Word of God preached by Jesus which brings Him to the lake-side and therefore to the two ships, one of which belongs to Simon, no mention being made of Andrew in this account. Simon and his two partners in the other ship are washing their nets after an unsuccessful night outing. It is worth noting that we are not actually told that Jesus " saw " the two ships, and that His first interest seemed to be in Simon as the owner and pilot of one of the vessels. At the request of Jesus, Simon places the boat at His disposal, in order that He may address the crowd on the shore from a suitable distance. It might appear as though another person could just as well have given Him this minor technical assistance. But Jesus now gives him in return comparatively much greater technical assistance by telling the surprised and hesitant fisherman to launch out again and causing him to experience the miracle of the enormous draught of fishes. This means—and everything points to the fact that this is Luke's intention—that the boat of Simon becomes in quick succession the scene (1) of an action of the Word of Jesus, and (2) of a σημεῖον accompanying His Word. It means, therefore, that Jesus enters the sphere of this man's life and work, that He requisitions him, that He draws him into His sphere of action, though not without twice demanding that Simon should have a part. But what is to become of Simon ? As Luke obviously sees it, it is the σημεῖον of the miraculous draught of fishes which opens his eyes to what has happened, namely, that with the ship as his sphere of life and work he himself is requisitioned, that he is claimed by Jesus for Himself, that he is drawn into His sphere of action, and therefore—for how else are we to express it ?—that he is called by Jesus. He is obviously called to participate in that which Jesus has enacted there before his eyes and ears, in the proclamation, fulfilled and to be fulfilled in speech and action, of the work and Word of God, the Word of His kingdom drawn near and of all the consequences of its approach. Jesus calls him by invading his own sphere and speaking and acting in it. How can he fail to understand that this implies a call to act with Him ? If we understand the incident in this way, then, and only then, are we able to understand the distinctive expression with which Simon, like Moses, Isaiah and Jeremiah, first tries to escape his calling : ἔξελθε ἀπ' ἐμοῦ, i.e., depart from this sphere of mine. Why does he want Him to depart ? Because he does not feel worthy for what is assigned to him with this entry of Jesus, nor does he regard himself as capable of it, " for I am a sinful man, an ἀνὴρ ἁμαρτωλός, and not one of the rigl.teous who might perhaps be considered for co-operation with Jesus in His work. His partners, too, undoubtedly understood the miraculous catch, which they helped Simon to bring in, as an entry of Jesus into their sphere which directly included in itself their calling, and Luke records that they were gripped by a similar astonishment (θάμβος). They, too, are called like Simon and Levi. The saying of Jesus at the conclusion of the incident is addressed to them as well as to him : " Fear not." Once the call of Jesus has gone forth, it is too late and unnecessary to fear it as flagrant sinners or to try to evade it by confession of sin. As we learn from the story of Levi, Jesus has come to call sinners and not the righteous. The fate of the sinful man is decided, and he must act accordingly. As Jesus says in exercise of supreme sovereignty : " From henceforth (ἀπὸ τοῦ νῦν, now that I have come to thee) thou shalt catch men." Thou shalt, as Jeremiah was once told when he pleaded that he was too young. Now that I have come to thee, thou sinful man art made worthy and able to be my witness. Thou art given thy commission in association with My own speech and action and in its service. Thou hast no option but to accept and discharge it. It was in the sense of this ἀπὸ τοῦ νῦν that Simon and his partners, who are now identified as James and John (with no mention of Andrew), experienced and understood the incident : " When they had brought their ships to land, they forsook all, and followed him." This is the result in which the Lukan account agrees again with those of Mark and Matthew. This is the outcome which according to all three Evangelists constitutes that of the story of Levi too. From the standpoint of historical pragmatics, it is no more possible to harmonise Luke with Mark and Matthew than it is the Johannine version of the calling of the disciples with that of all the Synoptists. Yet the New Testament picture of the event of the calling of the disciples is so enriched materially by this distinctive account, and the material agreement with the others is so significant, that discrepancy from the standpoint of historical pragmatics is a trivial price to pay. To conclude the series of typical biblical accounts of calling we must naturally consider that of Paul. There can be little doubt that it towers above all those recorded in the four Gospels, not only in respect of the person of the one called, but also in respect of the uniqueness of the story and *telos* of his calling. In this story we are not dealing with a man who belongs to the disciples of Jesus in the narrower sense. He himself acknowledges this. As he says, he entered the group " as one born out of due time " (1 Cor. 15⁸). And yet he became the chief of all, who impressed himself upon the later Church—if only it had listened to his witness more carefully !—as the apostle *par excellence*. Nor is there any story which brings out more plainly than his the sharpness of the transition and the basic and dominating purpose of the event of vocation in which a non-Christian becomes a Christian. We shall not attempt any detailed analysis of the story because it has already claimed our attention in an earlier context on p. 198 f. of this volume. Repetition of this analysis could only confirm the main features, and underline the typical significance, of the picture which has already emerged of what is meant by vocation in the Bible, and particularly of what constitutes the goal of vocation. We may simply recall how Paul himself understood the purpose of his existence as a man personally called by Jesus Christ. It pleased the One who separated him from his mother's womb, like Jeremiah, to call him by His grace by causing His Son to be revealed to him and in him (ἐν ἐμοί, Gal. 1¹⁶). Why ? In order to endow him personally with temporal and eternal blessings ? This was included, for otherwise where would have been the grace which he experienced in his calling ? Yet he does not mention this. By the revelation of His Son God has called him to proclaim this Son of His, and therefore the Gospel, the good and indeed the best news, among the Gentiles. Hence in the parallel passage in 1 Cor. 15⁹ᶠ· : " By the grace of God I am what I am "—I, the least of the apostles, who am not worthy to be called an apostle, because I persecuted the Church of God. What were Simon Peter and the publican Levi compared with a sinner of this nature ? Yet the fact remains that " his grace upon me was not in vain." In what respect was it not in vain and therefore effective ? Because he was saved, justified and sanctified by it ? Of course ; yet this is not what Paul says, but rather that by the grace of God " he laboured more abundantly than they all " (i.e., the other apostles), and therefore became in fact the most active of the apostles. To be κλητός means for him (Rom. 1¹) quite self-evidently and naturally to be κλητὸς ἀπόστολος, to be separated for service to the Gospel of God promised by the prophets in Holy Scripture, and as such to be a debtor (ὀφειλέτης) both to the Greeks and the barbarians, the learned and the unlearned, indeed, the whole human race (Rom. 1¹⁵). " Grace and apostleship, the address of Jesus Christ to him and his own sending to fashion " obedience of faith " to His name among the Gentiles, are one and the same thing (Rom. 1⁵) rather than two different determinations of his existence. God has committed to him the λόγος καταλλαγῆς, preparing for it an abode in his person (θέμενος ἐν ἡμῖν), so that he is the ambassador of Christ and exists in order to plead with men in His stead that they should be reconciled to God in correspondence with the reconciliation of the whole cosmos in Him (2 Cor. 5¹⁹ᶠ·). He does not gain anything, any καύχημα, nor does he make any claim for himself, in preaching the Gospel. He has no option. Necessity (ἀνάγκη) is laid upon him to do so. " Woe is unto me, if I preach not the gospel " (1 Cor. 9¹⁶). In Phm. 9 and Eph. 3¹ he describes himself as the δέσμος Χριστοῦ Ἰησοῦ, and in both passages he surely means not only that he is a prisoner for Christ's sake in Rome but also that he exists as one who is held captive by Jesus Christ. His personal salvation was no doubt very dear to him, but it was only secondary, as we see from the almost frightening passage in Rom. 9³, in which he says bluntly that he would be ready to be personally accursed (ἀνάθεμα) from Christ if he could thus benefit his brethren in Israel, to whom he knows that he is continually bound even as an apostle to the Gentiles. And in this true ministry of his to the Gentiles he regards himself not only as a λειτουργὸς Χριστοῦ Ἰησοῦ who as to such is ordained to " celebrate " (ἱερουργεῖν) the Gospel in order to present the Gentiles as a worthy offering to God (Rom. 15¹⁶), but he also regards his own life with joy as a drink-offering to be poured out with the offering of the faith of his congregations (Phil. 2¹⁷). This is the kind of man he has become with his conversion from Saul to Paul. All the three accounts of this event in Acts agree with his self-understanding and self-testimony in this respect. It was for this that he was called or converted before Damascus. His conversion meant his calling, commissioning and sending. Its purpose was that Jesus meant to have this enemy as His friend and apostle. Without asking him, He made him this, just as He made those men in Galilee His disciples according to the accounts in the Gospels.

The first argument is thus presented and developed which not only challenges, but proves to be theologically quite untenable, the classical answer to the question of the controlling principle of the structure of Christian existence, and which at the same time reveals the better and true answer to this question. To be sure, Holy Scripture which we have just consulted, and in which there are not lacking the most varied stories of calling, makes it quite plain that the calling of man by God and to God alters his situation radically and comprehensively in the sense also that he is personally set by it in a new and positive relationship to God, that he is placed in a position no longer ruled by sin but by the grace of God, that personal salvation comes to him, and that he may be glad and sure of this salvation as he grasps and clings to the promise thereby given him. Yet according to Scripture this alteration of his situation is not the principle which controls the structure of the existence of a man called by and for God. It is more or less clearly visible in many of the biblical stories of vocation. It must be supplied even in those in which it does not seem to be visible. But in none of them does it have the basic and central significance ascribed to it in the classical answer to our question. Where this refers to the *status gratiae et salutis* of the called man, Scripture always speaks of the commissioning and sending of the called man, and sees him set in a function to be exercised between God and other men, between God and the world. In its exercise he must surely be important to himself, since God treats him as so important. And he can hardly come to any harm. But the principle which controls the structure of his existence as one who is called is that God on the one side and the world and his fellows on the other have become more important to him, and indeed qualitatively more important, than he can be to himself : God who discloses Himself to him in His work and gives him his corresponding task in relation to the world ; and the world to which he is bound and committed as he knows the divine work and has to discharge the task which God has given him in relation to it. The called man in the biblical sense is in fact a witness in the twofold sense that he has seen and heard the acts of God, or in the New Testament His one consummating and conclusive act, which is also as such God's Word directed to and received by him, and that he is called to the work of declaration, faithfully, if without any claim, addressing, imparting and proclaiming to others that which he has seen as God's act and heard as His Word. As a witness of this kind he may confidently let well alone and things will definitely go well with him. Basically and finally all things will work together for good to him both in time and eternity (Rom. 8²⁸). But these things are only incidental and secondary, and he will be prepared to hazard them and treat them lightly to the extent that his main concern is with his function as a witness. As such he stands under the command to love God and his neighbour, in which there is no question of self-love, even the highest and finest. His regard must be first (πρῶτον, Mt. 6³³) for the kingdom, i.e., the establishment of the lordship of God in the world and the righteousness of this kingdom, i.e., what is right in the light of its coming. This regard is the principle which controls him. Caught up in it, he may rest assured that " all these things," both great and small, will be added to him.

But if Scripture is normative and is to be followed in this matter, where else are we to seek that which makes a Christian of the man called to be a Christian except along the lines of the mode of existence of the biblical prophets and apostles ? And in what can it be found or consist but that in his own order and place, and therefore without aspiring or being able to be a Moses or Isaiah, a Peter or Paul, he will be very clearly and definitely set in the ranks with these, being made a witness in analogy, however distant, to them ? It is for this that the Christian can and should continually believe and obey. It is for this, i.e., to be serviceable in this function, that in free grace, justified before God and sanctified for Him, he receives the forgiveness of his sins and light and power for a liberated life. It is for this that he can and should daily ask all things, and for this that God daily hears and answers and grants his requests. The promise given to and to be grasped and held fast by him, and the fulfilment which constantly commences with its reception, apply to him in his quality and function as a witness. He, the witness, may and can and will live by it, and do so joyfully for all his incompatibility, defiance and conflict with the pious and less pious world, and above all with himself. As and to the extent that he exists as a witness, even in his weakness and corruption he stands on solid, eternal ground and need not fear nor hate anyone, even himself, since he has God on his side. For God, in making him His witness, has set him at His own side as that of the One who need not fear or hate anyone who resists Him, who loves man even as He chides him, who chides him only because He loves him so much that He has to withstand him on the ways which he has begun to tread apart from and in opposition to Him. Because and as and to the extent that he becomes and is the man called by this God, a Christian and His witness, he exists in covenant with Him and therefore with men and himself—the peace which passeth understanding (Phil. 4⁷). This is what we have to learn in the question at issue if we are ready to be taught by Scripture.

The second theological argument which must be applied at this point both critically and positively presupposes as a basis the scriptural demonstration adduced in the first. But in distinction from the first it is to be worked out in the form of a material discussion in which our concern must be to set the question quite radically in the light of relationship between Jesus Christ as the One who calls and the Christian as the one who is called by Him, and to answer it accordingly.

To do this, we recall the general definition of the goal of vocation which we reached at the end of our third sub-section. Not without the stimulation and confirmation of certain important New Testament passages, we there finally maintained that this goal, and therefore the true being of the Christian, when given its supreme and yet also most precise definition in a way which reveals it to be not unworthy of comparison with the mystery and miracle of Christmas, is to be understood as the perfect fellowship and even unity of the Christ who calls man with the Christian called by Him, or conversely of the latter with the Christ who calls him.

That Christ should live in the Christian by the Holy Spirit is the purpose of his vocation. " In Christ " means that Christ lives where this man, the Christian, is, in his time and place, in the sphere of his free thinking, volition, resolution and action, in such a way that He takes up His abode in what is most proper and remains most proper to him, in his innermost being or heart, being present there as the Lord of the house and understanding him better than he understands himself. Or, seen and stated conversely, the purpose of the vocation of the Christian is that he should live in Christ by the Holy Spirit. " In Christ " means where Christ is, with Him in His time and place, in the centre of His intention and action, in such a way that in the use of His distinctive sovereignty, which remains proper to Him, Christ is not a stranger but his best known and trusted Neighbour whom he understands better than he does himself. In sum, the self-giving of Christ to the Christian and the Christian to Christ is the goal of vocation, the true being of the Christian.

We have emphasised the indissoluble differentiation and irreversible order of this relationship. The life of Christ in the Christian does not mean that in giving Himself to him He loses Himself in him, but that He, the Lord, finds him as one who belongs to Him and takes possession of him. Hence it does not mean the surrender but the exercise of His supreme sovereignty over him. Similarly the life of the Christian in Christ does not mean that the former takes over His control, but that he knows that he is subject to it, and thus places himself at its disposal, not in forfeiture but in exercise of his own most proper freedom. According to the measure and within the limits of this order the relationship between the Christ who calls and the Christian who is called by Him is a perfect fellowship and indeed unity, real and not just ideal, total and not merely partial, indissoluble and not just temporary. What is the bearing of this on our understanding of the principle which controls the structure of Christian existence, on our reply to the question as to the essential, decisive and distinguishing feature which makes the Christian a Christian and characterises him as such ?

Does it mean, as the classical answer would have us believe, that what makes the Christian a Christian is decisively that which accrues to him personally as he is called by Christ, i.e., the present or future consequences for his own life ? Presupposing that the true being of the Christian really consists in that perfect fellowship between Christ and him, and him and Christ, is this how it is to be interpreted ?

If so (1) Christ living in the Christian would obviously be for him decisively the Mediator, Dispenser and Giver, present in and with his own existence, of a good ascribed by God to man and to be received, appropriated, used and enjoyed by the man called by Christ—the supreme good of his liberation, restoration, renewal and exaltation to fellowship with God. As the supreme and in the true sense only means of grace, Christ would then be where the Christian is, dwelling and reigning in his heart, his thoughts, his needs and aspirations, his seeking and finding, his being and possessing. There is not the slightest doubt that Christ is and does all this as well. This belongs to the fellowship or unity to which He gives Himself with the one called by him. How could He give Himself if in Him there were not given everything that is His, the fulness of all His goods ; if He did not cause him personally to partake—each in his own measure and manner—in the benefits which God has granted to the world in Him ? But is the fact that he becomes the recipient of these benefits the decisive thing, the principle which determines the existence of the Christian ? What would it make of Christ Himself ? A supreme and unique means of grace ? If Christ were in truth only this, or primarily and essentially this, then the fellowship granted the Christian by His presence in his life would not consist properly and essentially in fellowship with Him, but in participation in the goods mediated by Him. What would really count would not be His self-giving to the Christian, but the blessings procured for the Christian by Him. He would dwell in the heart of the Christian, not as the Lord of the house, but as the Disposer and Distributor of these blessings, of the forgiveness of sins, sanctification, power for a new life, the promise of eternal life, and the accompanying consolation and assurance. And the faith, love and hope of the one called by Him would not really be directed to Him as the Giver, but to the goods and gifts appointed for his own consumption, and to Himself only to the extent that what is truly desired and valued, i.e., grace and salvation in all these forms, is not to be received and enjoyed without Him, but only through Him. The thought might then arise more or less acutely whether the Christian, perhaps desiring His gifts all the more as he enjoys them, might not find the gifts enough and have only incidental need of Him as their Giver, Vehicle and Dispenser. And even if things did not become as bad as this, He might well become for the Christian no more than the instrument which is serviceable for the attainment of this high and important purpose but subordinate to it. To this we cannot agree. For in what serious sense could we then say that Christ the Lord has sought and found the Christian as the one who belongs to Him, that He has taken possession of him and dwells within him in exercise of His sovereignty? Should we not have to say conversely that the Christian has sought and found Christ as the man who is indispensable for that which He alone can do for him, who is present at bottom only as the guarantee of that which he personally needs in the deepest and final sense, and who lives in him only as the epitome of the satisfaction of his most serious needs? But what is left of Christ the Lord, who gives Himself to man but does so as the Lord, if this is His life in the Christian? Yet this is what His life must be if the classical answer to our question is true and valid. For the Christ who reigns in the Christian there would be no room in this inn. But this means that the true Christ would always stand without, and the one within under His name would not be the true Christ. What, then, are we to make of the answer?

According to this answer again (2) the Christian living in Christ would not be truly orientated to Him, interested in Him, claimed by His intention and action, or participant in His work. In that which makes him a Christian he would live in a world of his own apart from Christ, being occupied with his own concerns and their best satisfaction instead of with the concerns of Christ. He would will what Christ wills, but only to the small degree in which it benefits himself. He would definitely be His client, receiving His benefits and enjoying His work. And it certainly belongs also to the goal of His vocation that he should be. As one called by and to Him, to be where He is, he certainly can and should be personally glad from the very heart, holding fast to the promise: " How shall he not with him also freely give us all things? " and therefore being quite simply His client. The Christian, too, belongs to the world reconciled to God in Him. He can and should be comforted and confident that he personally is justified before God and sanctified for Him in Him. But what a stranger Christ must be to him, and how radically he misunderstands Him whom he ought to understand better than himself as he lives in Him, if it is really the decisive thing that, as one who lives in Him, he may profit by the fact that He lives for him and is his Saviour ! Can he really give himself to Him in this way ? Will he not rather snatch Him to himself as a prey ? Instead of subjecting himself to His control, will he not rather try to control Him ? Instead of letting himself be used by Him, will he not finally try to use Him ? As one who lives in Christ, can he really deal with Him or harness Him in this way ? If this is his attitude, is he not elsewhere than Christ, and therefore not really one who lives in Him and is called by Him ? Of what avail, then, if subsequently it does sometimes occur to him that there is something lacking, that as the privileged client of Christ he owes Him something, that as the grateful recipient of His bounty he must consider His interests and do certain things to further them ? Is that man really a disciple, a pupil, a follower and companion of Jesus Christ, and therefore one who lives in Him, to whom what Christ thinks and wills is only a matter for subsequent and occasional reflection and action, whereas truly, essentially and decisively he is occupied with himself, i.e., with what it means for himself to be with Him ? Quite apart from what it means for him personally, should not that which Jesus Christ thinks and wills be the principle which controls the existence of one who is called by Him ? The classical answer to our question with its *pro me* speaks otherwise. What, then, are we to make of it ?

In the light of what constitutes the true being of the Christian, i.e., the life of Christ in him and his life in Christ, we can only say on both sides that this answer does not correspond to the presupposition but contradicts it. It does not follow from the presupposition, but is quite impossible and untenable in the light of it and is thus to be rejected. From the standpoint of its critical or negative content our second and material theological argument thus leads us to the same result as our first and biblical.

But what does really follow from the presupposition ? We now come to the positive content of the second argument, and we may first say generally that, if the true being of the Christian consists in the life of Christ in him and his life in Christ, then it follows that the principle which controls Christian existence, provisionally formulated, consists in the community of action determined by the order of the relationship between Christ and the Christian. We have in view divine-human action in divine-human sovereignty when we speak of the being and life of Christ, and human action in human freedom when we speak of the being and life of the Christian. Christ is engaged in a work, and in perfect fellowship with Him so, too, is the Christian called by Him. The latter works, but he does so in perfect fellowship with the working of Christ. Everything else which takes place in this relationship, and especially the giving of Christ and receiving of the Christian, takes place relatively to this community of action, within the context and in furtherance and consequence of it. And since the fellowship as a fellowship of action takes place in this definite and irreversible order, the action, work or activity of Christ unconditionally precedes that of the man called by Him, the Christian, and that of the latter must follow. Their fellowship of life thus finds realisation as a differentiated fellowship of action in which Christ is always superior and the Christian subordinate. Hence the principle controlling Christian existence, which is our specific concern, will always necessarily result from the fact that the Christian, as he lives in Christ and Christ in him, exists in this fellowship of action and its order. Whatever else may distinguish it, it is to be understood primarily and decisively from this standpoint.

We come nearer to the heart of the matter when we go on to say that the action in fulfilment of which Christ and the Christian are one, He preceding in His own way and the Christian following in his, takes place in a great context as part of the history of salvation, of the history of God in and with the world, in which the point at issue is the divinely willed and accomplished renewal, restoration and fulfilment of the covenant which He made with the world in creating it, the irruption, dawn and lordship of His glory in it, and therefore its deliverance, salvation and peace. The starting-point common to Christ and the Christian is the will of the gracious and merciful God as a true Creator and omnipotent Reconciler. That which from this starting-point constitutes the meaning of the life of Christ in the Christian and the Christian in Christ, and the meaning of their common action, is obedient to the work of this faithful, omnipotent and gracious God in correspondence with His will. And the common standpoint and outlook of Christ and the Christian in their action and therefore in obedience to the work of God, the object of their concrete interest, is the world created and loved by God, the man re-established by Him in his status as a covenant-partner and thus affirmed anew by Him in his creatureliness. What Christ does, He does not do out of any need or lack or desire of His own, nor to His own advantage, nor in His own interests, but by the free choice and decision of His free love for the world, for the son lost without Him but found again in Him, for man generally and for all men. And if He does not will to be alone in this action of His for the world and men, but to call certain men to His side, to invite and summon them to participate in what He does ; if He wills to live in these men and to awaken them to life in Him, this necessarily means that the starting-point and goal of these men can only be the same as His. Wherever it may lead, their starting-point can only be the will and work of God, and their goal the world. The man in whom Christ lives, and who lives in Christ, has no option but to confirm in His action the living relationship in which God and the world are held together in the work of Christ, the self-determination of all men for God. These together and in their totality, identical with the person and work of Jesus Christ, are called in the New Testament the kingdom of God, the gracious and saving establishment of the lordship of the holy, merciful and almighty God in His creation. This kingdom alone can be the principle which controls the structure of the existence of the Christian. To be sure, it will not be to his loss but to his salvation. But in his human action, in the fulfilment of his life, he can seek first only the kingdom of God. If Christ has given Himself to live in him, and if he has given himself to live in Christ, there is no alternative. The cause of Christ, the relation of God to the world and the world to God, quite naturally and self-evidently takes precedence in his life over all other concerns, not least his own, even though these include his personal beatitude or damnation.

We now take a third step. If the action which decisively determines and characterises Christian existence takes place together with that of Jesus Christ Himself, this means in fact the true and concrete participation of the Christian in the great context of the history of God with the world, and therefore of salvation history. It is evident that in saying this we must not say too much. We must not say anything which would even in the slightest degree equate the Christian with God and thus declare him to be the subject of the history and therefore himself the reconciler or co-reconciler of the world. We must not say anything which would imply a constriction or replacement of the One who calls by the one who is called, of Christ by the Christian in whom He lives and who lives in Him. We must not say anything which would assert, entail and actually include a divine humanity and therefore a divinity of the Christian. In short, we must not say anything which would deny or even challenge the indestructible differentiation and irreversible order of their relationship. The participation of the Christian in that history, his function in that great nexus, can only be such as is proper to him as a man who is not a God-man like Christ. Again, it would naturally be far too much to regard and expound the action of Christ in that nexus as conditioned by the action of the Christian and therefore as bound and referred to this and limited by it, as though the action of the Christian were necessary to complete it. On the other hand, it is equally obvious that we must not say too little. We must not conceal, let alone deny or even question, the fact that the true being of the Christian does in its own place and manner have a true, significant and effective part in that history. If Christ lives in him and he in Christ, if this common life is not just the action of Christ but his own action, then, although the Christian is certainly not the subject and in no sense the author of the history of salvation which takes place in the action of Jesus Christ, although he is not himself the reconciler or even the co-reconciler, although he is in no sense an independent promoter of the kingdom of God, yet he certainly has a part in that history as a co-operating subject, and in its own place and manner this part is not merely apparent but real, nor is it meaningless and superfluous, but significant and effective. But can and should we really describe him as a co-operating subject ? We certainly cannot describe the term as absolutely impossible, and therefore we cannot reject it out of hand. Yet, since it might so easily imply too much, it is as well for us to look around at once for another term which will give its precise meaning.

The notion of a co-operation (*cooperari*, συνεργεῖν) of man in his relationship with God, of the Christian in his relationship with Christ, has been given the well-known title of synergism, which is normally used polemically and critically to denote the Pelagian and semi-Pelagian doctrine of a *liberum arbitrium*, i.e., of man's co-operation in the attainment of grace and salvation in virtue of a free power of decision unaffected by sin. A warning that in speaking of co-operation we enter a danger zone in which we must be careful what we say is to be found in the great reserve and obvious selectivity with which the New Testament handles the terms συνεργεῖν and συνεργός. The word συνεργεῖν can be used fairly freely when there is reference to the relationship between the faith and works of the Christian (Jas. 2²²). It can also be said without fear of contradiction in Rom. 8²⁸ that to those who love God τὰ πάντα συνεργεῖ εἰς ἀγαθόν. And not infrequently nor inappropriately Paul called his younger fellow-workers his συνεργοί. But the statement that the *Kyrios* co-operated with the disciples sent out by Him, confirming their word with signs following, is to be found only in the later ending to Mark (16²⁰). And as concerns a co-operation of man with God, the most commonly adduced passage in 1 Cor. 3⁹ : θεοῦ γάρ ἐσμεν συνεργοί, is most uncertain, since in the context the συν probably refers, not to God, but to the fellowship of teachers in Corinth, and especially to Paul and Apollos : " We are fellow-workers in the service of God " (W. Bauer). The description of Timothy as συνεργὸς τοῦ θεοῦ in 1 Thess. 3² is equally uncertain because the best manuscripts have διάκονον rather than συνεργόν. On the other hand, it is at least possible that in 2 Cor. 6¹, where Paul says that as " working together " (συνεργοῦντες) he beseeches the Corinthians (in the sense of the preceding words in 2 Cor. 5²⁰ᶠ·) that they " receive not the grace of God in vain," the context demands, or at any rate makes possible, an amplifying (σὺν) θεῷ. The most certain passage is to be found in Col. 4¹¹, where Aristarchus and others are called συνεργοὶ εἰς τὴν βασιλείαν τοῦ θεοῦ. At a pinch 3 Jn. 8 might also be mentioned in conclusion, where Christians are recommended to receive and further certain brethren from abroad on the ground that they will thus be συνεργοὶ τῇ ἀληθείᾳ. The findings hardly justify us in saying that we are encouraged by the New Testament to use the expression in the present context. On the other hand, we cannot say that its use is forbidden.

Is there any other term which would avoid the misunderstanding against which the language of the New Testament was perhaps trying to guard, but which would still say what has to be said ? For the fact remains that the Christian in whom Christ lives, and who lives in Christ, does participate as a subject, and indeed as an active subject, in the action of Christ and therefore in the history of salvation, doing things with Christ even if not himself effecting them. This is something which cannot be suppressed but has to be said.

There is in fact an expression which does not say too much nor yet too little, which is much more relevant in its content, and which is closer both to the matter itself and to the language of the New

Testament. This is quite simply the term " service " or " ministry."
In the present context it is more illuminating and helpful because it
denotes not only the action of the Christian who is called but primarily
the preceding action of Jesus Christ Himself as the One who calls him,
and therefore that which is common to the life of both. Moreover,
it brings out and explains the order which the action of the Christian
must necessarily follow in relation to that of Christ.

In the New Testament the first and original minister, servant or slave—the
form of the ' *ebed Yahweh* of Isaiah 53¹³ᶠ· now revealed in its fulfilment—is not
the disciple, apostle or Christian, but Jesus Christ Himself. To be a man like
all other men meant for Him, to whom it was proper to exist in the form and
majesty of God, to exist rather, in a way which is exemplary for all men and
especially for His own, in the form and lowliness of a δοῦλος engaged only to
obedience, in order that as such He might be distinguished by the name of *Kyrios*
which is absolutely superior to all other names (Phil. 2⁶ᶠ·). He is the ἅγιος παῖς
'Ιησοῦς (Ac. 4²⁷·³⁰, cf. 3¹³·²⁶). He became the διάκονος of the people of the circum-
cision (Rom. 15⁸). The disciple who would be great or first among his fellows
must be the minister and servant of all, since " the Son of man came not to be
ministered unto, but to minister, and to give his life a ransom for many " (Mk.
10⁴⁵). " I am among you—not as he that sitteth at meat, but—as he that
serveth " (Lk. 22²⁷). And we are obviously reminded, too, of the story of the
foot-washing in Jn. 13²ᶠ·, which characteristically takes the place of an account
of the Last Supper in this Gospel. It is in virtue of this subjection of His that
He is preferred before them and they are subjected to Him. Followed by others,
His greatest apostle will make it both his all-consuming and dominating task,
and a title of honour, to be the servant (δοῦλος) of this Servant of God (Rom. 1¹ᶠ·).

Christ establishes the order of His relationship to His own, not
by an authoritarian decree but with inner necessity, by going before
them as the One who is first and originally subject to this order, and
therefore as One who serves. They can follow the One who serves
God and man only as those who also serve, i.e., as those who, since the
cause of God and man has been victoriously prosecuted in His service,
serve Him as His ministers and slaves, and thus serve God and men.

In addition, the term service is particularly well adapted to denote
the fellowship of action between Christ and Christians in view of its
inner distinctiveness. Where service is rendered, two very different
active subjects are obviously at work together in different ways, but
with a clear differentiation of function. The One is the Lord, who
quite apart from the superiority of His person is also superior in the
fact that in the common work it is wholly and utterly a matter
of His cause. The other is the servant, who quite apart from the
littleness of his person is also subordinate in the fact that in his
participation in the common work it can only be a matter of renounc-
ing his own cause and treating that of the Lord as though it were his,
or rather of really making it his own. In meaning and purpose, in the
form of its execution and in relation to its scope, what takes place in
the fellowship of action of the Lord and His servant is the work of
the Lord and not of His servant. Whatever may be his own ideas,

tendencies, aims or plans, the servant has to do only with the work of his Lord. But he really has to do with Him. Hence he is no mere spectator of his Lord, nor is he a dead instrument moved and used by Him. He, too, is a living and therefore an active subject, wholly occupied in the cause of his Lord, wholly concentrated upon it, according to his own deliberation, resolve and responsibility. In his own place and function he is no less free than his Lord. But he is free only to obey and serve Him, just as his Lord is free and sovereign to claim, accept, direct and approve his service. His free action as servant consists in the fact that he accompanies his sovereign Lord in His action, assisting, seconding and helping Him. This is the action of the Christian.

To use for once the imagery of Roman Catholic worship, the Christian is not a priest, nor does he read the mass, nor have anything to do with the transformation, the sacrifice and the dispensing of communion ; he is only the server or altarboy who carries the missal backward and forward and swings the incense and rings the bell at the decisive moment. Yet he is this, and assists in this way. He is called to this ministering presence. What makes him a Christian, and distinguishes him as such, is that he also acts as minister in what Christ does. In this sense we may well say that he co-operates in the work of Christ.

When we understand the term in this sense, neither too much nor too little is said of him. Too much is not said, for the work is Christ's and he can only assist in total and not just partial subordination. Nor is too little, for as this co-operating assistant in the work of Christ he does acquire and take and have his own share, to be responsibly fulfilled.

In this sense service is the basic determination which in the New Testament makes the disciple a disciple, the apostle an apostle and the Christian a Christian. The two Greek equivalents διακονία and δουλεία are both expressive in their own ways, and, since their meanings are very close and merge into one another, both must be used for a full understanding of the matter. Originally a διάκονος is a servant or assistant or waiter in the direct sense, as in the διακονεῖν τραπέζαις of Ac. 6². It is after the manner and with the attitude of such that the Christian must serve his Lord. For the rest, διακονία emphasises particularly that which constitutes his service, the order as such within which he finds himself in his own place in relation to his Lord. It is no accident that from the earliest days (Phil. 1¹) διάκονος rather than δοῦλος was used to describe definite officials in the Christian community. To render δοῦλος as servant is in most contexts, if not all, too weak. A δοῦλος is usually a servant who is not a paid employee (called ἐργάτης, as in Mt. 20¹) but the property of his lord and therefore his slave with no rights of his own. We might say in addition that δοῦλος emphasises better than διάκονος the personal nature of the relationship of dependence in which he finds himself with his action in relation to his lord. This relationship is brought out sharply and clearly in Lk. 17⁷ᶠ·. When the δοῦλος returns from the field in the evening, will his master invite him to sit down ? No, he will say rather : " Make ready wherewith I may sup, and gird thyself, and serve me, till I have eaten and drunken ; and afterward thou shalt eat and drink." Nor will he thank him " because he did the things that were commanded him." " So likewise ye, when ye shall have done all those things that were commanded

4. The Christian as Witness   603

you, say, We are unprofitable servants : we have done that which was our duty to do." For the rest, in distinction from the fairly consistent sense of διάκονος, δοῦλος has a critical sense, as shown by Mt. 6²⁴, which speaks of the possibility, or rather the impossibility, of being the δοῦλος of two lords. Instead of serving God as his true Lord, which he is summoned to do again in vocation, a man may serve sin (Gal. 2¹⁷ ; Rom. 6⁶, ¹⁷, ²⁰), the Law (Rom. 7²⁵), elemental spirits (Gal. 4⁹), mammon (Mt. 6²⁴), even the belly (Rom. 16¹⁸), or indeed wine (Tit. 2³), in short φθορά (Rom. 8²¹ ; 2 Pet. 2¹⁹). Or again, in the wrong sense he may be the slave of men (1 Cor. 7²³). The true Lord, whom the called man serves as διάκονος or δοῦλος (there being no material difference in the terms), is God (Mt. 6²⁴ ; 1 Thess. 1⁹ ; 1 Cor. 3⁵ ; 2 Cor. 6⁴ ; Rom. 6²²), of whom even temporal rulers are also " deacons " (Rom. 13⁴), or more concretely Christ the Kyrios (Jn. 12²⁶ ; 1 Cor. 7²² ; 2 Cor. 11²³ ; Rom. 12¹¹, 14¹⁸, 16¹⁸ ; Col. 1⁷, 3²⁴, 4¹² ; Eph. 6⁶). It is as the δοῦλος Ἰησοῦ Χριστοῦ that Paul stands in the service of the new covenant and therefore of the Spirit (2 Cor. 3⁶), of righteousness (2 Cor. 3⁹), of reconciliation (2 Cor. 5¹⁸). It is as such—as a free man he has become the slave of all (1 Cor. 9¹⁹)—that he stands in the service of his communities and their members (2 Cor. 11⁸ ; Col. 1²⁵). And it is on this basis that he can and must tell them that the fundamental rule for a proper use of their own freedom is that they should subject themselves one to another and serve one another in love (Gal. 5¹³), which comes to much the same thing as all that is said by him under the concepts of ταπεινοφροσύνη and ὑποτάσσεσθαι.

In conclusion we should not forget to mention expressly the important person in whose history the whole complex of words associated with δουλεύειν is brought out in a single term not used elsewhere in the New Testament. We refer to Mary's answer to the angel : ἰδοὺ ἡ δούλη κυρίου (Lk. 1³⁸). God has seen her lowliness (ταπείνωσις) as this handmaid (v. 48). It is as such that she utters the remarkable saying : " Be it unto me (γένοιτό μου, fiat mihi) according to thy word," and as such that she is addressed expressly as the mother of the Lord (v. 43), a phrase which makes it impossible to dismiss the θεοτόκος of Ephesus as unbiblical. May she also be described as mediatrix omnium gratiarum, or corredemptrix, or regina coeli ? Surely it is flagrantly too much to build this on the fiat mihi and the motherhood of the Lord, when the person thus glorified and set by the side of the one Mediator, Redeemer and King is specifically informed by the angel concerning the kingdom of her Son, when she herself is told only that she has found grace with God and that He is with her, and when she explicitly acknowledges herself only as the handmaid of the Lord. In any case, does not the same Gospel in which we read all this tell us in the passage already adduced from 17⁷ᶠ· what is implied in the δουλεία of the Lord even when we have done all that we are commanded to do ? The present context, which only very arbitrarily can be made the basis of a whole Mariology, neither commands nor permits us to see in Mary more or other than a model and example for all Christians called and ordained to faith and therefore to obedience and service, for a Christianity which unequivocally serves its Lord, and therefore neither directly nor indirectly reigns with Him, but works together with Him only in the form of its service. In contrast, it is only by ignoring the true Mary that there has arisen the possibility and actuality of Mariology.

We now take a last step which brings us back to the results of our previous biblical and theological discussion. In what consists the service which is entrusted to the man called by Christ and which thus makes the Christian a Christian ? What kind of an action is it in which he assists the action of Jesus Christ and thus has an active part in the history of salvation ? To answer this last and decisive question we must first turn to the sovereignly preceding action of

Christ Himself which the Christian can never do more than follow with his action. The nature of the life of the Christian in Christ and therefore of his co-operation in the action of Christ may obviously be known only in relation to the life of Christ in him in which his life in Christ has its basis. To what extent, then, does Christ so live in the Christian as to establish an active life of the Christian in Him and the co-operative assistance of the Christian in His action ? At this point above all a clear distinction is necessary.

Christ lives indeed in Christians, as He also lives in non-Christians, as the Mediator, Head and Representative of all, as the new and true Adam. He is simply the Son of God and Man in whose life and death the whole world is reconciled with God, in whose person and work every man is justified before God and sanctified for Him. Since He is the man in whom this has taken place for all men, there is none who exists wholly without Him, who does not belong to Him, to whom—whether he realises it or not and whatever his attitude to it— He is not present as his Lord and Head in whom decision has already been made concerning him prior to all his own decisions, who is more present indeed than he can ever be to himself. As this new and true Adam Christ lives in the Christian as in every man. And as the Christian, in distinction from the non-Christian, may recognise Christ as this new and true Adam who lives in all men and therefore in him too, he sees in Him, in this form as Saviour of the world, the deepest and final basis, support and consolation of all creation and therefore of his own existence, and constantly returns to Him as the One who lives for him and in him in this form, continually looking and moving forward from this place and this place alone. The Christian's only consolation in life and death is that He lives for and in him as for and in all men in this form, that He is his justification and sanctification as He is the justification and sanctification of all men. But with the opening of his eyes to the Christ who lives in him in this form, he must also recognise, no, he may joyfully recognise, that he is dealing here wholly and exclusively with Christ Himself, with God's act for the world and therefore for himself, so that there can be no more question in his case than that of others of any co-operation, or even co-operative assistance, in what Christ Himself does in this form. For how could there be active co-operation in God's reconciliation of the world resolved and accomplished in free grace, and therefore in the action of Jesus Christ the humbled Son of God, who as High-priest in the place of all men has accomplished once and for all their justification, and the exalted Son of Man, who as King in their place has accomplished once and for all their sanctification, introducing the new and true Adam in His person ? How could any man, including the Christian, give even the co-operation of an assistant in the action of the One who as the man of Golgotha lives also in him ? At this point we are concerned with the work accomplished by God Himself without any human assistance. There can be no server at the side of this Priest. There is no place for any other alongside the One who works here. There is no place for the work of any other, however generous or modest. " Be it unto me according to thy word," says Mary (Lk. 1³⁸), and it is only in her willingness and readiness to accept what is told her by the angel that she is the handmaid of the Lord and may describe herself as such. In relation to the One who is at work in this happening, the Christian knows and accepts the fact that every other can be only the one to whom it happens. To live in the One who is here at work, and at work in him as the one High-priest and King, can mean only for the one who recognises, trusts and loves Him as such, and therefore for the Christian, that he acknowledges Him as such with adoration and gratitude, and accepts His action without trying either to do any part of it or to add to it. In Christ's action for the world and the Christian as fully completed in His passion, he can participate only passively, in pure faith in Him, love for Him and hope in Him, without making even the slightest or most incidental contribution. Even the suggestion of Christian co-operation in this respect, let alone any attempt at it, could only be evil, because it would arbitrarily question and finally deny the ultimate foundation, support and consolation of the whole world and therefore of the Christian.

There is another form, however, in which Christ lives in the Christian. In this form, too, He lives for the world and for all men, as their Mediator, Head and Representative, as the new and true Adam. But in this form He does not live in all men. He lives only in those called by Him, in Christians. And in relation to this other form of Christ living in the Christian, more may be said of this life of Christ in him. That is to say, the question of the Christian's co-operation in what Christ does is not to be set aside. It is most definitely to be given a positive answer in a sense now to be determined. We are not dealing with another Christ, but with the one Christ in whom and by whom the work of the reconciliation of the world with God, completed in His crucifixion on Golgotha, took place once and for all. But the point is that this work of His is not exhausted in the action of His passion as then undertaken once and for all by Himself alone and with no co-operation by anyone. The point is that His work goes forward in presentation of what took place then. He has risen from the dead as the self-declaration, actualised in His person, of the work of divine grace then accomplished in and by Him. As the Resurrected, He lives as the One who not only then, but then once and for all, was humiliated and exalted, offered up and triumphant, for the justification and sanctification of all men, living not only in His own age but in every age as the Lord of all time. He lives in every to-day as the One in and by whom there took place yesterday, in His time, the reconciliation of the world to

God. As such, however, He does not live in idleness, but actively in the enlightening power of His Holy Spirit as the Revealer of that which took place in and by Him alone. The work of God—and this is the great presupposition of the whole of this third part of the doctrine of reconciliation—has also the dimension of the Word of God. Commencing in His resurrection, continuing in the presence and activity of His Holy Spirit, and moving towards the completion of this whole economy in His final, universal and definitive appearance and revelation, Jesus Christ is also the Proclaimer of His being and action as the one High-priest and King. He is also the one Prophet of the kingdom of God drawn near in Him. That is to say, He is not content with what He did once and for all. He also imparts Himself as the One who has done it. He also tells the world that it is the world reconciled in Him. He also declares to men that they are justified before God and sanctified for Him in and by Him. The light of His life shines also among them. This shining, revealing and declaring of His is also a free divine act of grace and the divine-human work of Jesus Christ. He alone is competent and authorised to perform it. He alone is the Speaker of the Word of God as well as the Doer of His work. But in exercise of this prophetic office of His, even though it is He alone who controls it, He does not will to be alone. Controlling and exercising it, He calls certain men to His side and commissions them to be His disciples or pupils, i.e., Christians. In His form as the one Speaker of the Word of God, He not only makes Himself known to them in the power of His Holy Spirit ; He also takes up His abode in them, living in them in order that they for their part may live in Him as the One who works in this form. That they may and should do this is the special characteristic which marks them off in the world from the world, distinguishing them as men from other men. But what does this mean for them ? It certainly means also that they should hear and be told in person the Word of the covenant of grace. They must let themselves be told this like all others. And it is told them like all others. Unless they are told it, how can they be fit and ready and willing for the specific task to which Christ calls them ? Yet this *conditio sine qua non* is not the *ratio* of their life in Him. It is not the specific thing with a view to which He calls them. This specific thing results from the fact that they for their part cannot possibly live in idleness in the One who as a Prophet is not idle to-day in their time but is active as the living Speaker of the Word of God in the world. Being called by and to the Christ engaged in the exercise of His prophetic office, they have no option but to attach themselves to Him with their own action, to tread in His steps, to become with Him proclaimers of the reconciliation of the world accomplished in Him, heralds of His person and work. With Him does not mean as His peers. They do not become Christs in their action. They can only follow Christ.

He alone is always the Lord, the authentic, original, immediate and direct Speaker of the Word of God—He who is also alone the Doer of His work. It can and will be enough for them to be like Him, to copy or repeat His revealing and proclaiming, to approximate to Him as His representatives. The herald is not the king. He summons them, however, to be His heralds. He calls them—and it is in this sense that we may really speak of their co-operation in His prophetic work—to the *ministerium Verbi divini*, to the service of God and His Word. This then, the divine Word, the Word of Christ, is the *telos* and meaning of their service.

Does He have to bring and summon them in this way? Does He have to live in them in order that they for their part should live in Him and serve Him? Apart from the prophetic work of Jesus Christ Himself, does there have to be this ministry of His Word, the Word of God, by these men? Do there have to be Christians to render this service? The question is important because on the answer to it there depends the answer to our present question, namely, in what consists this ministry of the Word and therefore the action which constitutes the distinctive feature of Christian existence. Now we are certainly well advised not to maintain that disciples, Christians, are in this sense indispensable to their Lord, that He could not tread His way as the Revealer and Proclaimer of the kingdom of God, of the reconciliation of the world to God accomplished in Him, without their assistance. It is they who need His assistance, not He theirs. Men who were indispensable to Christ in this sense, so that His work was conditional on their assistance and could not be accomplished without being supplemented by them, would obviously have to be as it were Christs themselves. Only God Himself acting and speaking in Christ is indispensable to the occurrence of the work of God— none else. Nor should we forget that the work of Christ even in this prophetic form in which it is actually accompanied by the work of man is not less a free act of grace than it is in His action as High-priest and King here revealed by Him as Prophet. In this respect, too, it is thus free from any need or necessity of a human co-operation or assistance without which it could not occur or reach its goal. " The word of God is not bound " (2 Tim. 2⁹) any more than the work of God declared in it, and it is certainly not bound to the herald ministry which Christians can render to it and which is so infinitely feeble in relation to it. The question arises indeed whether God and the world would not be far better served by a " word of reconciliation " (2 Cor. 5¹⁹) spoken by Jesus Christ Himself and alone, without any cc-opera-tion on the part of Peter and Paul, let alone the rest of us. May it not be that Christians with their assistance actually do more to com-promise, disrupt and hinder the prophetic action of Christ than to further it? If this co-operation of theirs is actually demanded by Christ in their unity with Him as the meaning and principle of their existence as Christians, and if it is not ordained in vain, this is to be established and explained only by the fact that the free action of Christ even in this prophetic form, being bound neither to anyone nor to anything, is in a supremely specific sense the action of free divine grace, and as such it does not exclude but includes this human co-operation. It certainly does not need it. But it expresses its freedom in it. In a distinctive overflowing of divine grace it would have it so. He thus calls Christians to Himself, to His side, to His discipleship, to His service, and uses them as His heralds.

We recall how frequently and plainly Paul traces back his ministry to a demonstration of divine mercy freely and undeservedly made to him. And strangely but quite unmistakeably this is the reason why it has for him, not a less, but a supremely distinctive importance. It was in relation to this fact that he undertook and executed it with all the zeal and self-awareness so characteristic of him.

Hence it is not out of any need, but in this special demonstration of mercy, that Christ calls His people. In this way, however, He does call them truly and seriously. Their ministry of the Word, and they themselves as Christians, are necessary in this sense. Superfluously in this glorious sense, they live only by the fact that Christ permits and commands their ministering co-operation which He might well despise and dispense with, allowing it to run its course, indeed, making use of it and even acknowledging it, not denying but granting it His own assistance. And they do in fact live by this as those who are called by Him in fellowship with His life and in the fellowship of their action with His. Nor do they do so in vain, nor without meaning and purpose, even though their action can never match up to His, nor their word to His authentic, original and direct proclamation of the work of God, and even though it is only as a necessity grounded in His free grace that they can understand their commission. On this basis their word and action can and should always be concerned with Him, with His Word of the kingdom and of reconciliation. Their word can and should reflect the light of His prophetic work. It can and should be the sign which accompanies and confirms His self-revelation—no more, but also no less. As they are called and appointed to be this sign in what they do in their all too human fashion, their ministry of the Word of God is undertaken and executed in obedience, and for all its dubiety as a human work it is a work which is well-pleasing to God in His relation to the world and promising for the world in its relation to God. In its own place and manner it takes place in participation in the history of salvation, and it may be incontestably described as the co-operation of the Christian in the work of Christ.

The introduction of the concept of sign has already told us, however, in what this ministry of the Word, and therefore the action which constitutes the specific feature of the existence of the Christian, consists. The Christian is called to be the accompanying and confirming sign of the living Word of God. It thus follows that he must indicate and attest this Word in the act of his whole existence. He never can nor will speak it himself. But as he is called, awakened and enlightened by Christ in the power of the Holy Spirit, it will be effectively spoken to him in a way in which he can and does receive it. And in this way a living seed is sown and a fruitful fact created. The Christian is thus liberated but also summoned to manifest, indicate and attest what is said to him and received by him as a Word of reconciliation directed not to him alone but to the whole world and all men. That he should do this is the concrete goal of his vocation, the meaning of the life of Christ in him and his life in Christ, the *ratio* of his Christian existence. He may be a hearer of the Word to become a doer. But his doing of the Word can consist decisively only in the fact that, commissioned and sent by Christ and himself existing in the world as man, he may turn to the world and other men who have not yet heard this Word, and make known to them what he was enabled to hear. He can do this only as a man, i.e., as a sinful man. He cannot bring to this action more or other than his human, sinful existence and its possibilities. His ministry cannot be more or other than a human indication and attestation of the Word of God, disrupted and burdened by the sinfulness of his human existence. If Christ did not bear witness to Himself, of what avail would be even the best witness with which the Christian can serve Him ? And if the Christian has the power to make perceptible the self-witness of Christ as its echo in the world, this power is Christ's and not his human power. To the Christian and his fellow-men it is always a miracle when his witness has this power. More than his human witness, then, is not demanded of him. But the service of his human witness is demanded. Nor is too much hereby demanded. As one who is called to do it, and set in fellowship with the life and action of Christ, he can and should achieve it. The question is not, of course, whether he regards himself as able or worthy, nor whether he is willing, nor whether he can guarantee specific results. In our biblical discussions we have established that these questions do not arise in relation to the calling of any prophet, disciple, or apostle. " Ye shall be witnesses unto me " (Ac. 1⁸)—this is enough for the one to whom Christ speaks and who has heard Him. Whether strong or weak, willing or unwilling, successful or unsuccessful, the Christian is a witness, irrespective of whether the miracle occurs, or whether it occurs visibly or invisibly. In all circumstances and with his whole existence he is a responsible witness of the Word of God. He is called to be this. As such he is set at the side of God in the world, and therefore set over against the world. As such he is bound both to God and men. He exists in this engagement, but he is also invested with the honour which it implies to be bound in this function. It is in this way that he and his service, his very existence, are the appointed sign of the living Word of God and therefore of its substance, of the kingdom of God drawn near in all its concealment in the person and act of the One who alone can and does reveal it.

It is obvious that the concept of the Christian as the witness of Christ, which we have reached by way of this basic discussion, needs to be explained and filled out more concretely. We shall not consider its wider significance in the present context. More must be said about it in the sub-sections which follow. We shall then have to take it up more broadly in the section devoted to the sending of the community. Above all, as implicitly decided already, it will be the basic concept in the doctrine of the command of God as we return to it in the context of the doctrine of reconciliation. In other words, it will be the controlling principle of the second form of Christian ethics.

Our only remaining task at the end of this most important sub-section of the doctrine of human vocation is to make it clear that the New Testament concept of ministry or service presses us in the direction which we have taken and which has led us at length to a provisional conclusion in the concept of the witness.

The three phrases with which Paul describes himself in the particularly instructive verse Rom. 1¹—" servant of Jesus Christ," " called to be an apostle,": and " separated unto the gospel of God "—all obviously say the same thing with mounting precision. The word " servant " or " slave " tells us that Paul stands in a service or ministry which is laid upon him and binds him absolutely. The phrase " called to be an apostle " explains that the service of this slave consists in a mission. The " gospel of God " denotes the meaning, content and goal for the sake of which he is separated, elected and called to this service as an apostle. And if we ask further concerning the " gospel of God " we learn in vv. 2–3 that it is the message of God, previously proclaimed by the prophets, περὶ τοῦ υἱοῦ αὐτοῦ, the news of His Son, of Jesus Christ, as the servant of whom Paul introduces himself in the first designation. To proclaim Him is the *telos* of the service to be rendered by Paul His slave as an apostle called by Him. This is expressly related in Col. 1²³ and Eph. 3⁷ to the Gospel to be proclaimed by him to the whole world. What else is at issue in the " ministry of reconciliation " (2 Cor. 5¹⁸ᶠ·) entrusted to Paul but the declaration of the " word of reconciliation " ? Nor can Paul be understood in any other way when he speaks (2 Cor. 4¹) of the διακονία granted to him by the mercy of God and demanding his energetic fulfilment, or of his ministry as an apostle to the Gentiles (Rom. 11¹³), which he would magnify by winning at least a few of his Jewish compatriots. The same is true of the many other passages in which he describes as a ministry either his own work or that of his fellow-labourers. In Ac. 6⁴, too, the ministry which has fallen as their lot (1¹⁷) to the re-established twelve in Jerusalem is characterised as διακονία τοῦ λόγου, a ministry of the Word. And if to their *ministerium Verbi* there is immediately opposed a ministry in the exercise of which the particular concern is material care for the widows of the Greek-speaking portion of the community in Jerusalem, it is noteworthy that it is one of those expressly charged with what seems to be a very different ministry, namely, Stephen, who comes into the forefront in a far wider sphere as a man who is " full of the Spirit and power " (v. 8), who works " great miracles and wonders," who then above all speaks powerfully in the Hellenistic synagogues (6⁹ᶠ·) and finally before the Sanhedrin (6¹²ᶠ·), and who in the ministry of the Word, as a highly

critical expositor of Old Testament history, is indisputably the first of the disciples
who has to seal the ministry of Christ by giving his life, thus becoming a witness
or martyr in the sense which later became classical.

Some more specific statements are now demanded concerning the New Testament use of the term " witness." The first is the general one that there is hardly
a single instance of the use of μάρτυς in what became the usual sense from the
2nd century onwards. Even Stephen " is not called a martyr because he dies ;
he dies because he is a witness of Christ " (H. Strathmann, Kittel, IV, p. 498).

According to the general meaning of the term in the New Testament, a μάρτυς
is one who is present at an occurrence with eyes and ears open to its course but
also with insight and understanding for its meaning and significance, so that he
is in a position to affirm, indicate, declare and make it known to others both
as an occurrence and in respect of its scope, there being very little difference
in the New Testament between witness to fact and witness to truth (Strathmann,
op. cit., passim). Μαρτυρεῖν is this declaration of his as such. Μαρτυρία can indicate
either the process or event of this declaration or its content. We have always
to keep in view (a) the difference between the witness and his witness on the one
side and the One to whom he bears witness on the other, there being no μάρτυς
whose speech and attitude do not contain the respect due to this Other as the
origin or theme of witness ; (b) the secondary character of his position and
function in relation to the superior reality and truth of the One attested by
him, there being no μάρτυς who claims to speak the basic Word or any more than
a kind of prologue or epilogue ; (c) the special empowering which he needs for
his declaration and which characterises him in it, there being no μάρτυς who dare
attempt it either on his own resources or on an authority with which he is not
invested for the purpose ; and (d) the historical importance of his action, there
being no μάρτυς whose word does not have its own relative necessity, dignity
and significance as spoken within the sphere of a high historical order and context.

The prototype of the New Testament witness who measures up to all these
requirements is the figure of John the Baptist, especially as he emerges in the
Fourth Gospel, where the Evangelist is perhaps contending against a particular
sect which could be traced back and which appealed to the Baptist, but where
he also and above all brings out most clearly his distinctive position and function
in relation to the Jesus portrayed in his Gospel. Who is this " John " ? According to Jn. 1⁶ he is a man, but he is a man—and the Prologue is very solemn at
this point—who came, existed or became (ἐγένετο)—the same expression is used
of the making of all things in v. 3 and of the incarnation of the Logos Himself in
v. 14—as sent by God εἰς μαρτυρίαν, namely, to bear witness to the light, that
all men through him might believe (v. 7). There then follows the express delimitation (v. 8) : " He was not that Light, but was sent to bear witness of that Light."
A further delimitation is to be found in his testimony or cry (κέκραγεν) in v. 15 f.
(cf. v. 30) : " This was he of whom I spake, He that cometh after me is preferred
before me : for he was before me. And of his fulness have all we—it is to be
noted that this John does not speak only in his own name—received, and grace
for grace." And again in reply to the question of those sent to him from Jerusalem
(vv. 19–23), he says that he, John, is not himself the Messiah, nor Elias come
again, nor the promised prophet, but only a voice crying in the wilderness to
prepare the ways of the Lord. And finally, when asked concerning the significance of his baptism (vv. 25–27 and 29–33), he answers that, as distinct from the
baptism with the Holy Spirit to be expected from the Messiah, it is only a baptism
with water. The Baptist bears witness to the Messiah, as indicated by the
constantly pointing finger of his οὗτος (to be found already in v. 2 and then
again in vv. 15, 30 and 34), and he does so realising and confessing that he is
not worthy to unloose the latchets of his shoes (v. 27). He bears witness to
Him as " the Lamb of God, which taketh away the sin of the world " (v. 29).
He bears witness to the fact that, although he knew Him no more than others

(v. 26), he saw the Spirit descending from heaven like a dove and abiding upon Him (vv. 32–33). He bears witness that He is the Son of God (v. 34). He will confirm and sum up the meaning and structure of this witness in a speech reproduced later in which he calls his disciples to bear witness for their part that he said : " I am not the Christ, but am sent before him " (3²⁸). And he then expands : " He that hath the bride is the bridegroom : but the friend of the bridegroom, which standeth and heareth him, rejoiceth greatly because of the bridegroom's voice : this my joy therefore is fulfilled " (3²⁹⁻³⁰). He is thus praised by Jesus Himself in 5³³ for having borne witness to the truth, i.e., confirming the content of the witness of Jesus Himself. We must remember this structure of this first witness preceding Jesus and then surpassed by Him when we are told later that the disciples of Jesus, because they have been with Him from the beginning (ἀπ' ἀρχῆς), should and will bear witness to Him (15²⁷), and particularly when one among them is singled out in virtue of his veracity as an eye-witness of his death (19³⁵) and finally as a true witness of the whole content of the Gospel (21²⁴).

We have heard already of the " voice of the bridegroom " which the friend of the Bridegroom rejoices to hear. According to the Johannine, and not merely the Johannine, view, the One attested by this friend, who is only the friend and not the Bridegroom, is in no sense a dumb object of witness, nor is he introduced only in this witness. The truth is rather that He Himself is primarily, originally, immediately and directly the Witness who introduces the voice of the friend and makes him His witness by His own attestation. What the seer on Patmos attests (Rev. 1²) is " the word of God, and the testimony of Jesus Christ." He is " the faithful witness " (Rev. 1⁵), or " the faithful and true witness " (Rev. 3¹⁴). The μαρτυρία, the course and content of the witness, is in the New Testament primarily, and as the basis of all other μαρτυρία, that of Jesus Christ Himself. " To this end was I born, and for this cause came I into the world, that I should bear witness unto the truth " (Jn. 18³⁷). Even the Septuagint description of the Old Testament tabernacle as the σκηνὴ μαρτυρίου, which according to Rev. 15⁵ is not without importance even for the Christians and authors of the New Testament, is an extension of the Hebrew concept of *'ohel moed* (the place of conversation or *rendezvous* between Yahweh and Moses) to that of the self-attestation or revelation of God in His directions given to Israel by the hand of Moses. It might well be consonant with this view that in Jn. 1¹⁴ the dwelling of the Logos among men is described as a σκηνοῦν, which reminds us also of the reference in Rev. 21³ to the " tabernacle of God with men." This would mean that already in Jn. 1¹⁴, as immediately suggested by the identification of Jesus with the Logos of God, we are concerned indirectly with the description of this incarnate Word of God and therefore of Jesus as the One who attests, reveals and proclaims Himself and therefore the truth. At any rate His self-attestation is in fact the absolutely dominating theme of the Gospel of John. Jesus not only is the light of the world, but as He is and shines as such, He also says that He is (Jn. 8¹²). And if the Pharisees argue that this is μαρτυρία περὶ σεαυτοῦ which as such cannot be true (v. 13), they are told in reply that precisely as self-witness His witness is true because He knows what they do not know, namely, whence He comes and whither He goes (v. 14). Like all other men, they can attest only their existence as confined between beginning and end if they speak of themselves. Hence they certainly cannot speak the truth, as Jesus also says of Himself quite definitely in 5³¹. Yet when Jesus speaks of Himself, He speaks as well of the hidden whence and whither of His own and all human existence. Thus, speaking of Himself, He speaks the truth. According to the saying put in the mouth of the Baptist in Jn. 3³², as the One come from above He attests what He Himself has seen and heard " above " (cf. also 3¹¹). And materially the meaning is the same when He appeals to the witness of the Father which directly and indirectly—through the works which He causes Him to do as the One sent by Him—confirms His own self-witness, as also when He appeals to the fact that it is confirmed by the Old Testament Scriptures (5^{39}), and that the " Spirit of truth " (15^{26}) will always confirm it. For this reason He does not need any human witness, as is expressly stated in 5^{34} and 1 Jn. 5^9. Bearing witness to Himself, He speaks the words of God (the ῥήματα τοῦ θεοῦ, Jn. 3^{34}). He is the truth (14^6). To this " voice of the bridegroom " which precedes the voice of the friend, i.e., the Baptist and every other witness, awakening it only as its echo, reference is also made in 1 Tim. $2^{5f.}$, where it is said of the man Jesus Christ as the one Mediator between God and man that in giving Himself a ransom for all He has given the testimony of which Paul has been ordained a herald and apostle. We may also think of 1 Tim. 6^{13}, where the warning reminder to Timothy concerning his own confession is reinforced by a reference to the witness which Jesus Christ Himself made before Pontius Pilate with the " good confession " of His mission and as a Witness of the truth. We are also reminded of this self-witness by the μαρτύριον τοῦ κυρίου of which Timothy is not to be any more ashamed than Paul is as the prisoner of the Lord (2 Tim. 1^8). And in a way which is at least relevant to the relation between Jesus Christ and those who proclaim Him, there belongs to the same series the expression used in Ac. 14^3, namely, that in causing " signs and wonders to be done by their hands," the *Kyrios* Himself added His testimony to the " word of grace " preached by Paul and Barnabas in Iconium.

Above all, however, we have to think of the way in which the witness laid upon and given by the apostles in Acts is continually described as the witness of the resurrection of Jesus Christ or of Jesus Christ as the Resurrected (1^{22}, 2^{13}, 3^{15}, 4^{33}, 13^{31}). Indeed, all the speeches of the apostles to both Jews and Gentiles in Acts refer explicitly to the Easter event. It is as the " testimony of God " that Paul proclaims the crucified Christ and Him alone (1 Cor. 2^1), attesting Him as the One raised by God from the dead (1 Cor. 15^{15}). It was as the One who is alive in this unprecedented sense that God called him too and particularly before Damascus. Here, and therefore in the evangelical and Pauline accounts of the appearances of the Resurrected, the self-witness of Jesus Christ which underlies all the witness concerning Him has its true locus and origin. Here— and we may confidently take this to be the meaning of the Fourth Evangelist— the " friend," i.e., the whole Christianity of the New Testament, heard the " voice of the bridegroom." As the meaning of His resurrection is decisively His self-revelation, so His self-revelation takes place decisively in His resurrection. This is what distinguishes His self-witness from that of all others. This is what characterises it as the witness of God Himself which admits of neither doubt nor counter-question. This is what gives to it its liberating yet also compelling authority. It is in view of this that Old Testament Scripture, the witness of the Law and the prophets (Rom. 3^{21}), is shown to be the witness concerning Him already intimated in the history of Israel. And it is again in view of this that the " Spirit of truth " can and will always bear witness to Him and to Him alone. It is in view of this that His self-witness demands the secondary, subservient and merely confirmatory witness of the friend, of each to whom it is perceptible as the witness which is unmistakeably distinct from any witness that man can give and is itself the power in which this witness may be attempted, and in obedience has to be attempted, by him. In the light of His resurrection Jesus Christ is manifest as the One who does not need to be called but simply calls. He is manifest in His high-priestly and kingly action, and therefore in the authority and power of His prophetic action. He is manifest in the free power of the grace of God to make men His disciples, apostles and prophets, i.e., Christians and therefore counterwitnesses. " I am he that liveth, and was dead ; and, behold, I am alive for evermore " (Rev. 1^{18}). As such He is the One in relation to whom even the angel of the Apocalypse (19^{10} ; cf. 22^8.) can acknowledge that he is only the σύνδουλος of the seer and his brethren the prophets

(22⁹), i.e., of all those who have received the μαρτυρία or self-witness of Jesus, so that he has to forbid the adoration of the divine with the admonition : " Worship God."

But according to the clear-cut conclusion of Revelation, 19¹⁰ the μαρτυρία 'Ιησοῦ as His self-witness is (ἐστίν) the πνεῦμα προφητείας. The " voice of the bridegroom," the self-witness of the Jesus risen again from the dead, is as such both the theme and content and also the divinely motivating and impelling power of prophecy, which in the language of Revelation and according to the context means the origin and force of the human witness of the seer and his brethren, Christians. Hence the concept of the witness and his speech and action, wherever it is implictly or for the most part explicitly used in the New Testament in the theologically relevant sense, refers to a man who bears witness to Jesus in word and act and attitude. He does not bear witness abstractly to benefits and gifts which he may point out to those around as one who knows and has received them, but concretely to Jesus as the Lord, the Son of God, the Messiah, the Saviour of the world, in short, as the Subject, source and fulness of the grace which God has manifested to the world and all men and which includes as such all the benefits and gifts which may be seriously regarded as such. The focus of interest is not the man himself, the witness or friend. It is the One to whom he bears witness, the Bridegroom. " He must increase, but I must decrease." And if we go on to ask how a man can become this kind of witness, whether we consult the Pauline, Synoptic or Johannine writings, or Acts or Revelation, the only possible answer is that the self-witness of Jesus, directly or indirectly addressed to him, has not only called him to be His witness but appointed and made him such, and finally motivated him as His creation. In himself as a man and a sinner, even though his name is Peter, Paul or John, he is simply a rock-face in his relation to Jesus, and in no sense adapted of himself to give back even àn echo. He is simply a reflector such as we have on our roads, with no intrinsic power of illumination. It is the voice of Jesus which brings sound from the rock-face and His light which brings light from the reflector. It is the μαρτυρία of Jesus Christ Himself which makes possible and actual the μαρτυρία of His own, which makes all the μάρτυρες, the prophets and apostles, indeed, all Christians, fellow-labourers in His work, συνεργοὶ τοῦ θεοῦ, and *ministri Verbi divini.* But as the πνεῦμα προφητείας (Rev. 19¹⁰), the self-witness of Jesus does actually do this. It is the sowing of the divine seed, the genesis and divine-human principle of Christian existence and its structure. The self-attestation of Jesus Christ is the vocation of man reaching its goal.

5. THE CHRISTIAN IN AFFLICTION

In explanation of the title, the word " affliction " stands for what is called θλίβεσθαι and θλῖψις in the New Testament. It signifies the experience of pressure which is exercised on a man from without by relationships or by a hostile and menacing environment, over the development, power and duration of which he has no control, which simply comes upon him as " tribulation," and which he has simply to endure as long as it lasts. The inner constriction corresponding to and consequent upon this pressure, the anxious concern engendered by it, is called στενοχωρία in the New Testament. In the majority of cases the concept of θλῖψις, of the affliction or pressure which a man has to suffer from without, is used in the New Testament for that which Christians as such have to suffer from the world around them. In a few instances (2 Thess. 1⁶, Rev. 2²²) θλῖψις signifies the affliction which God brings upon the ungodly as a punishment. In some cases it is more neutral, as when Jas. 1²⁷ speaks of the θλῖψις of widows and orphans which it is " pure religion and undefiled before God and the Father " to relieve, or Jn. 16²¹ of the θλῖψις of a woman in labour, or 1 Cor. 7²⁸ of the θλῖψις of the flesh which according to Paul is to be expected by those who think they should marry contrary to his advice. For the most part, however, the word signifies the external pressure to be endured by Christian existence as such. The Christian has to suffer under this pressure. He is assailed by it. It leads him into temptation. He can and should prove himself a Christian under it. His way is a ὁδὸς τεθλιμμένη (Mt. 7¹⁴). We are obviously reminded of Dürer's rider between death and the devil. This is what is meant by the title " The Christian in Affliction."

Our concern is with the Christian in his specific affliction, i.e., under the pressure which is exerted on him by the world, which according to its purpose and nature can fall only on him, which is to be endured by him alone. Naturally as a man like all others, and in solidarity with them, he comes under all kinds of other external and internal pressures which in some degree fall on him too in one form or another. Our present reference, however, is to the additional, specific pressure to which he is exposed because he is a Christian and in the quality which distinguishes him from other men as such. To be sure, it strikes him in human fashion, in his vitality which is not basically different from that of others. How could it be otherwise ? It is as man that he is called to be a Christian, and even as a Christian he is still man and therefore exposed to human suffering. We refer, however, to the pressure or affliction which he has to suffer as a Christian man, and which does not affect others, no matter how severely they may be afflicted in other respects. Again, even in the affliction which strikes the Christian as such we do not have finally or basically a private affair, but one which is of public and even universal interest. What is at issue in the existence of the Christian as such, in his witness, is the relationship between God and the world and the world and God. As the action in which, called by God, he must intercede for the world is one of ministry, so his passion or suffering under the affliction caused by the world must be one of ministry. Ultimately and basically, therefore, it does not concern himself alone but in a very real sense all other men, even those who cause it. Yet this is true only ultimately and basically, *sub specie aeternitatis*. In the first instance it is he and he alone who has to undergo and endure his affliction, whereas others, even though they do not in practice directly or indirectly cause it, can only be present as more or less sympathetic spectators, not suffering it themselves, but watching how he undergoes and wrestles with it.

How does there arise this specific affliction of the Christian ? We now assume as quite plain that according to his essential and basic and not just incidental or subsequent calling the Christian is a witness set in the service of Jesus Christ in and in face of the world. It is just because he is a witness of Jesus Christ, and to the extent that he is active as such, that affliction comes upon him from without, from the world in face of which he stands. It is not the affliction which makes him a Christian. Like his personal experience and assurance of salvation, of which we shall have to speak in the last sub-section, this is a secondary determination of Christian existence. Yet like his personal experience and assurance of salvation, even though it is secondary, it is necessary. The primary determination of the Christian witness unavoidably brings with it the two secondary, and above all the experience of affliction.

With regard to the relation between these secondary determinations, we first note that the personal experience and assurance of salvation could not and would not as such expose the Christian to affliction from the world around. As distinct from the ministry of witness, this has in itself and as such a purely inward character. In itself and as such, therefore, it would belong to the many and varied inner states and movements of certain men which may perhaps in some measure be noticeable to others but which do not on that account lose their essentially private character, which do not have any effects or exert any pressure without, and which cannot therefore provoke any counterpressure on the part of others. Since it does not disturb the world, in the name of religious freedom it might well be tolerated and even respected and regarded as an important cultural factor as the private affair of these men. Where Christian existence moves and presents itself only with this inwardness, it need fear no pressure. Hence it is not surprising that when Christians are threatened or already visited by affliction, they should be assailed by the treacherous thought, which must inevitably arise where the personal experience and assurance of salvation is regarded as the essence of Christian existence, whether it is not permissible in face of the storm of affliction, and even perhaps imperative for the sake of general and not least of individual peace, to retreat into an island of inwardness where the Christian will give offence to none and will thus be not unfavourably regarded by many, and where he may fairly certainly count upon it that he will be safe from the painful counterpressure of the external world. There can be no absolute certainty, of course, for even the Christian who withdraws and saves himself in this way, even the coward who has already found happy refuge in this retreat, cannot altogether succeed in hiding his light under a bushel or concealing the fact that he is a witness in the enjoyment of his personal experience and assurance of salvation. Adept though he may be in camouflaging himself, those around might well be disturbed and challenged by his existence, and he might not escape affliction at their hands. It is as well for him, indeed, if his attempted evasion does not succeed. For he would be brought into mortal danger if his calculations were correct. Assuming that the Christian succeeded in retreating to that island and really found peace there in the abode of his inner life and experience, his withdrawal could only mean the renunciation of his ministry of witness and therefore of his Christian existence of which it is the principle. If he discharges his ministry of witness, however, he cannot avoid disturbing those around, exerting upon them by his witness a pressure to which they can and will react with counter-pressure. When he makes his declaration as a witness, he will neces-sarily expect it to be heard irrespective of its content. If he does this, then affliction becomes unavoidable. But if he does not, and thus renounces his ministry of witness, this is not a minor omission which he may make in order the more peacefully and surely to enjoy his personal experience and assurance of salvation, or perhaps even to strengthen and consolidate this experience and assurance if he regards it as the true essence of his Christian existence. On the contrary, such renunciation means quite simply and terribly that he denies and suspends the life of Christ in him, his life in Christ, and therefore his vocation. To the extent that he really carries through this renunciation, he ceases to be a Christian. And he cannot then try to find consolation in his personal experience and assurance of salvation. For in such circumstances this is an illusion in which he might perhaps rejoice for a time but not for long. For this is wholly dependent upon his being a Christian, and his being a Christian is dependent upon his being a witness of Christ who discharges his ministry as such and is not a deserter for the sake of avoiding affliction. His inner experience and assurance is the glorious fruit of his ministry of witness which will not be withheld if he discharges it. But if he does not discharge it because he will not accept the other and less glorious fruit of affliction, he will lose the very thing which he thinks to preserve in that island kingdom of inwardness. This wonderful plant, flower and fruit blooms only *in actu*. But the act is not an abstract act of faith, love and hope to be performed in that inner world, but concretely the act of the Christian in relation to the external world, the act of his witness, in fulfilment of which he has to endure and must not try to escape the affliction which will be heaped upon him by the world.

" And when he thought thereon, he wept," is written concerning Peter in Mk. 14[72] when the cock crew for the second time after his nocturnal exchanges with the household of the high-priest. Why did he really weep, and weep " bitterly " according to Matthew and Luke ? Had there been even the slightest change in what Jesus meant and was for him ? Was he not the man who had gone to Him over the waves and been held up by Him when he began to sink ? Had he not sat at table with Him, and been directly assured of fellowship with Him, with His body and blood, and therefore of the expectation of his participa-tion in the eternal festal meal of the coming kingdom ? Was it such a bad thing that he was not prepared to cast pearls before swine, to make use of his acquaintance with Jesus before that chattering household ? Yet he went out and wept bitterly as though all were lost. All that had really happened was that, in the moment when the affliction inseparable from his commission had met him in a relatively harmless form as the called disciple, apostle and witness, he had preferred not to be what he was or to confess himself to be such. But in so doing he had denied the One who called him and thus jeopardised, forfeited

and lost himself and all that Jesus meant and was for him. In his case the
illusion did not last longer than the time between the first cock-crow and the
second. He had good reason to go out and weep. He had lost everything when
in his ministry of witness he had tried to escape the affliction inseparably entailed
and thus renounced his ministry and become a deserter. Obviously he was still
the " sinful man " he had been when called, except that now he did not stand
in any sense in the place in which he had then been set as a sinful man. In the
same way we all fall from grace if we try to regard it as a private affair.

A further general warning is indispensable before we turn to the
matter itself. If the ministry of witness is the primary determination
of Christian existence, and if the ministry of witness unavoidably
brings the Christian into affliction, then we have to say that none can
be a Christian without falling into affliction. To be sure, we have
not to desire or seek or provoke it, as martyrdom or the so-called
baptism of blood was coveted in some circles in the early days of
Christianity. This could only rest on misunderstanding, as though
the bearing of affliction made the Christian a Christian. In fact, it
is only the call of Christ, as His calling to the ministry of witness,
which can constitute Christian existence as such. Yet such a view
would also miss the true reality of the specific affliction of the Christian.
To this belongs the fact that it comes upon him from without as an
occurrence over which he has no power, which he cannot escape, but
which he has not to desire or bring upon himself. Just as the other
secondary determination of his existence which necessarily follows
his ministry of witness, namely, his experience and assurance of
salvation, is not his work but can only come to him as a gift from
God, so affliction can only be the work of the surrounding world and
cannot in any sense be brought about by himself. As willed and
caused by himself, it could have nothing whatever to do with his
Christian existence. It could only be an arbitrarily conjured evil
such as all men bring on themselves and have to suffer. On the
other hand, since the vocation to be a Christian is essentially and
decisively the vocation to be a witness, a man cannot possibly become
and be a Christian without having to experience and endure affliction
as the work of the surrounding world. Real Christians are always
men who are oppressed by the surrounding world. The pressure
exerted on them can take very different forms. Its form will not
necessarily but only relatively seldom be the spectacular one of persecution or something similar. Often the affliction of the Christian
may consist only in isolated conflagrations of greater or lesser severity
which break out and then die down again. It may often consist in
a continual and relatively tolerable habit, in a latent tension which
has perhaps almost become an institution, which is the reaction of
the surrounding world to his witness and which he has thus to endure.
This will particularly be the case where the surrounding world for its
part in some form makes itself out to be a Christian or even perhaps a

highly Christian world, so that the pressure which the Christian has to suffer is not exerted with the violent force of heathenism and godlessness, but, as in the case of Paul in Rome (Phil. 1[17]), with the soft and muffled but for that reason all the more intensive force of a kind of Christianity. The distinctive affliction of the Christian may indeed be concealed and equivocal as a determination of his existence as such. And we have also to take into account in conclusion that the individual Christian may from the purely human, constitutional and nervous standpoint live so secure a life that he is not so sharply conscious of the affliction which comes on him, that it does not weigh so heavily on him as it might, and that he can thus fortunately show a comparative robustness in his endurance of it. There can be no doubt, however, that it will come, that it will not be lacking to him in his character as a Christian. For the Christian nature of his existence would be doubtful to the degree that it experienced no affliction and perhaps had even the good fortune to enjoy not merely the toleration but the recognition and even the applause of those around, to the extent that he became wherever possible a popular figure, e.g., a well-liked parson, coming to terms with the world by means of appeasing compromises and even concordats, to the extent, therefore, that he seemed to be spared the need of wrestling with and isolating himself from it. But supposing the world itself spared him this need ? Supposing it really gave him little or no trouble ? There might be legitimate reason for this in the fact that, while it was not ready to receive his witness, this made upon it in passing a positive impact in some respects and to some degree, creating for itself a kind of respect, as seems to have been in some measure the case with that of the apostles according to Luke. But the reason for this peace of the Christian within the world might also consist illegitimately in the fact that the salt of his witness had lost its savour in the sense of Mt. 5[13], he himself no longer standing, and perhaps never having seriously stood, where he ought to stand as one called by Christ, no longer or not yet confronting the world but resembling all others within it, not in any sense discharging his function in relation to it, not saying anything but having nothing really to say, and not therefore unsettled by it because not unsettling it. If, then, a man is not oppressed by his environment, if he has nothing serious to fear or to suffer at its hands, he has reason carefully to ask at least whether and how far he is genuinely a Christian at all and not fundamentally self-deceived in this respect.

Leaving these general considerations, we now tackle our initial question how the Christian comes into the specific affliction which falls on him particularly as a Christian. We shall try to answer it along three lines. The world as it is must cause him this affliction as the witness of Christ. He himself must bring it upon himself with his witness. And originally, finally and decisively, it is his fellowship with Christ which unavoidably plunges the Christian into this affliction.

His affliction derives first (1) and in some sense inevitably from the situation and manner of the world to which he belongs as a man but over against which he is set as a Christian and in his ministry of witness. It is the world which was created good and is seriously loved by God, which to its own loss has turned away from Him but to which, as the One who loves faithfully and sincerely, He has turned to its salvation, which in confirmation of the covenant made with it in and with its creation He has reconciled to Himself in Jesus Christ, yet which has not yet grasped and appropriated—and this is the decisive aspect of its situation and manner in relation to our question— this reconciliation and therefore its salvation, and which cannot and will not do so of itself. It is the world which stands in urgent and painful need of the revelation of Jesus Christ in the power of His Holy Spirit as the revelation of its own true reality. Now it is this revelation which the Christian has to attest to it in the service of His prophetic action and as called by Him. He has to proclaim the name of Jesus Christ as the word of reconciliation, as the good news of the kingdom, of the saving *coup d'état* of God within it. And the world would not be the world which has not yet received this name and word and news, which has not yet grasped and appropriated the work of which it speaks, if the proclamation which comes to it through the witness of Christians, and the import of which it perceives at least in blurred outline, did not have for it the appearance of monstrous presumption and insolent demand to which it must react accordingly.

We recall what it is actually told by the witness of the Christian. Its sorry state is not one which has taken place by chance and may be made good in the same way. It is a result of the guilt which it has contracted in its apostasy from God. Its alienation from God as such is not a possibility for which it was free and in the realisation of which it can thus understand itself. It is an enterprise which as a plunge into nothingness is already judged, is impotent from the very outset and irrational because devoid of either meaning or purpose. Its salvation is not a supreme goal which can be reached or at least attempted in its own rapid or gradual progress ; it is the perfect good which is already shown and granted in God's *coup d'état*. Its understanding, appraisal and evaluation of its own reality does not correspond even approximately to the truth, but is one long error which it may bewail but which can only lead it into fresh error and finally confound it. Its future is not an ever-extending time of indefinite content, but the future of the end of its own and all time, of an end which will consist in the revelation of the grace of God addressed to it but also and therewith of its own judgment. And finally, summing up and focusing all the other offences, its origin and goal and centre are not its own desire and power to counsel, help, order, liberate and correct itself, but a completely new factor in relation to its whole being and action, namely, the man Jesus Christ who alone interceded, acted and suffered for it in demonstration of the love of God, but whom it crucified, and who in this death of His has become its peace, wisdom, righteousness and hope : He who, judged by it, will be its Judge yet also its only Advocate and Guarantor at the end of its time ; He who is all this really and truly, yet He alone. It is with all this that the witness of Christ has to confront the world, whether implicitly or explicitly, whether in words or in acts or attitudes, yet unequivocally and resolutely, pledging it in his own person. He has to tell it openly to a world which can obviously receive it as good and therefore welcome, consoling and helpful news only when it has grasped and appropriated it, but before it has done so must inevitably see in it only a series of negations which radically challenge its own foundations. Unless the Christian is to renounce his own existence, however, he cannot spare it this witness in his proclamation of the name of Jesus Christ.

His affliction arises quite simply from the fact that the world cannot accept this demand and challenge, and the less so the more clearly it realises what is at issue. Let there be no mistake ! The world can tolerate, approve and value a good deal in the way of religion. Religious dogma, ritual, faith and personalities are phenomena which do not have to be alien or unsympathetic, but which may well be basically integrated with its picture of human reality in both past and present. Religious freedom is a universal principle which like all other freedoms is often sadly violated but can still triumphantly assert itself. Radically anti-religious notions, attitudes and enterprises undertaken on a broad scale and with great emphasis have always proved to be more or less accidentally occasioned, have usually emerged as the muted or open attacks of one religion on another, and in the long run have been impracticable as the true denial of all religion. The transcendence at issue in religion may often have gone out of fashion, but other ages have followed in which it has again become the latest novelty. It has always been the case—and neither the atomic age nor iron curtains can alter the fact—that there is no serious reason to prevent the world itself from being religious and perhaps even deeply religious in some imposing or remarkable form. And so long as it can understand Christianity, too, as a form of religion, or so long as Christianity perhaps represents and evaluates itself as such, the world will be well able to integrate Christianity into itself, i.e., into the picture which it makes of its reality, and it will thus have nothing really to fear from it. So long as it is not felt to be an attack, and perhaps does not really make any attack, the little commotions and conflicts which unavoidably arise at times in defence of its position can never be more than the proverbial storm in a tea-cup. The situation is radically altered, however, if in the circle of a basically tolerated and respected Christianity there suddenly emerges from this relatively innocuous background the existence of the authentic Christian and therefore of the witness, i.e., of the Christian as the reflection and echo of the prophetic Word of Jesus Christ. It is not a matter of the special movements which he may or may not make as such. Perhaps only very seldom will he engage in the great gesture of contentious proclamation. Certainly this will not necessarily stamp him as the one he is. Perhaps only on occasion, and then more indirectly than directly, will he act critically and polemically as an aggressor. Perhaps he will more often be recognised by his absence on certain occasions than by his counteractions, by his silence than his words. But he will always stand out as the one he is, plainly different from the world even though he is in it. He will be different because determined, stamped and contoured by what is said to him in and with his calling in such a way that he can neither forget nor conceal it. He will be different because by the Word of Christ he is made, not a second Christ, but one who points to His Word and therefore to His work, to His existence, to the act of God effected in Him, and therefore to the revolutionary alteration of the whole reality of the world as it has been accomplished in Him. In face of the world the Christian is the one who shows it its own reality to which its own eyes are closed, yet into whose dark depths it still desires to enter. The Christian becomes and is to it the witness of the great Yes which God has spoken to it in total renewal and definitive liberation. This Yes which God has spoken to it is its own truth. The Christian is the messenger who tells the world this truth to its face. Whether loudly or softly, in words or works, he declares to it this Gospel by his existence.

It is the world, however, which perhaps cannot and will not but certainly does not grasp and appropriate the Gospel, the gracious Yes of God spoken to it and therefore its own truth. For how can it comprehend and expound the indication made to it by the existence of the Christian, assuming that it is made, not in the innocuous form of tolerable Christian religion, but in the form of the authentic Christian as the witness of Jesus Christ, and assuming also that it cannot fail to hear it but must wrestle with it as a fact? One thing it certainly cannot conceal from itself. One thing it will certainly hear and understand even though it does not really hear and understand. And that is the supremely provoking No pronounced against it in and with the Yes. Not simply much but everything would be gained if it would accept this No as the No of God, and therefore as the reverse of God's Yes, which, even though it is naturally dark, accusatory and scorching, is not devoid of grace and help, but conceals the grace and salvation of the kingdom. Everything would be gained, in fact, if it would accept the Law as the form of the Gospel. But it is quite unable to accept His Law and therefore His No in this way as the Gospel. What it hears is merely the painfully wounding word of a man who presumes to contradict its self-understanding and therefore to speak of perdition instead of misfortune and of sin and guilt instead of imperfection, who contests its freedom to take up different attitudes in relation to God, who resolutely questions its progress and any positive goal to be attained by it, who tells it quite plainly that it has erroneous views of itself, who proclaims its end as the judgment which comes upon it, who insists—and this is the most galling thing of all—that the name of a man who lived and died in the years A.D. 1–30 is the new thing in which alone there is enclosed all salvation and hope. What it hears is merely the arrogant voice of a braggart who in his witness says something different from the representatives, sages, priests and prophets of all the known religions recognised with comparative respect, and even dares to question and set aside all these religions both individually and as a whole. What the world perceives when it hears the witness of the Christian is the opinion of a fanatic who has obviously broken his bridges and burned his boats behind him, and demands that it should do the same. Of what avail is it, then, if the witness of the Christian is perhaps given in fact in a positive way and in what the Christian himself believes to be a compelling, constructive and peaceable form? In it all, the other hears only the No, and this is for him simply the wild, fantastic and inhuman No of a man. Shocked and enraged, he can only wonder what this will mean for what the world knows as the True, the Good and the Beautiful. The world usually wonders in what diluted form it might tolerate all this. But if the Christian with all his positive and peaceful intentions can offer no tolerable dilution of his No, it finds the matter far too serious to allow him to utter it. His existence within it is not merely disturbing but threatening and dangerous. Something must be done to forestall any further utterances on his part and to silence his witness, which it regards merely as his arbitrarily morose invention. To his No—for he is the aggressor who has begun it all—there must be opposed a much more energetic No, to his pressure an oppressive counterpressure.

This is the simple and natural way in which affliction comes to the Christian from the world. It may take many different forms. The counterpressure of his environment may be exerted in the name of the society whose customs and ordinances are disturbed by his witness, or occasionally in the name of the state with its particular interests, or in the name of conservative, liberal or even socialist ideologies and forces, or by the representatives of accepted morality or a dominant piety or churchmanship, or sometimes quite simply by the mob. It may have its particularly dangerous origin in the Christian's own family. He may find himself suppressed as a witness by a decidedly non-Christian or even a far too decidedly Christian individual. The world's counter-attack may be directed

against his witness as such, but more frequently it may take the
indirect way of charges levelled against the Christian himself and
attempts to eliminate his existence under various heads. And in
accordance with its multiplicity the affliction of the Christian at the
hands of the surrounding world may be open or secret, it may give
to him a painful prominence or treat him with a no less painful dis-
regard, it may be crude or refined, it may work out in the form of
material or " only " spiritual and moral maltreatment. Whether it
is heavier or lighter does not depend on its source or form. It may be
relatively light when public, and very heavy when most private.
It may be light when crude, and heavy when refined. It may be
light when material, and direct and heavy when hardly perceptible
in the spiritual and moral sphere. But the converse, of course, is
also true. In every form the really oppressive feature is the defamation
and ostracism to which the Christian is exposed as a witness. He is
accused of *odium humani generis*, and he is also the target of *odium
humani generis*. As the witness of Christ he has only good things,
indeed, the very best, to say to the world, and he finds himself regarded
and treated not only as the bringer of bad news, of that No which is
all the world can hear, but also, since for good or evil he must identify
himself with what he says, as a malicious disturber of the peace.
In attesting Jesus Christ to the world, and therefore its reconciliation
with God, he might well think that he is the best and most loyal and
useful citizen, but to all his fellow-citizens he is necessarily an odious
stranger and foreigner who is best expelled. He is their friend—for
who could be bound in greater solidarity with the world than the
Christian as witness ?—and yet he must undergo the experience of
being treated as their worst enemy. This is the affliction of the
Christian. All else might be borne, but how is he really to endure
the misunderstanding which lies at the root of all else ?

We have been trying to describe that which in the New Testament is called
the hatred of the world or man that falls on disciples or Christians and has to
be endured by them. It is always Jesus Himself who speaks of it, except in 1 Jn.
3¹³, where the readers are told not to be surprised that the world hates them.
This, too, is according to the tenor of the declarations of Jesus as reported in the
Gospels. The one who is the target of this hatred has indeed no reason to be
surprised at it. In the words of 1 Pet. 4¹², we are not to be afraid of their terror
as though something strange had come upon us as Christians. Hence all that
is said on the subject is distinguished by a soberness which is free from all senti-
mentality and which treats the hatred as something necessarily bound up with
the existence of disciples. Ἔσεσθε μισούμενοι ὑπὸ πάντων διὰ τὸ ὄνομά μου is what
we read both in the sending out of the disciples (Mt. 10²²) and in the final eschatological address (Mk. 13¹³, Lk. 21¹⁷). Luther's translation : " Ye must be hated
of all men," is materially correct. The ἔσεσθε is just as categorical as the ἔσεσθέ
μου μάρτυρες of Ac. 1⁸. It describes an accompanying circumstance of the execution of their task which they can as little avoid as the task itself. No less categorical is the ὑπὸ πάντων. The hatred which will fall on the disciples is not an
accidental nor exorbitant phenomenon ; it corresponds to the general rule. The

remarkable tense of Jn. 17¹⁴ points in the same direction : " I have given them thy word ; καὶ ὁ κόσμος ἐμίσησεν αὐτούς." That is, in His giving them the Word of God, it was decided and took place already that the world hated them. It is to be noted that in the New Testament the word " hatred " nowhere seems to have, and does not have here, the sense of a personal emotion of personal aversion for the object of the hatred. The Christian is not hated as a human individual who is repulsive to the one who hates him on account of his personal being and action. He is hated as the bearer and representative of a specific claim and cause. Only in this sense can it be said to the disciples by Jesus that no one can come to Him unless he hates father and mother, wife and children, brothers and sisters (Lk. 14²⁶), i.e., unless he is determined not to be bound by these persons, not in their individuality, but as the representatives of the power of the family and domesticity dangerously clinging to him and hampering and thwarting his ministry. It is thus that the disciples are hated by all men and the world, being regarded and treated as outlaws—not because they are Peter, Paul or John, but because they represent to all men and to the world the alien and intolerable cause of the kingdom, the *coup d'état* of God. According to Mt. 10²² and *par.*, this comes upon them, not because of what they are personally, but διὰ τὸ ὄνομά μου, quite simply for the sake of the name which they preach, and of its import. It comes upon them because He has entrusted the Word of God to them (Jn. 17¹⁴), because as those who are sent and commissioned by Him they are no more ἐκ τοῦ κόσμου than He is, because they can have no part in the self-understanding of the cosmos but can only contradict it. But since it is a matter of this basic and material thing, the New Testament μισεῖν signifies a disproportionately sharper reaction than even the worst that might happen when one man cannot tolerate another for personal reasons. On the same ground the command issued to the disciples that they should do good to those who hate them (Lk. 6²⁷), that they should love their enemies, that they should bless those who curse them etc., cannot meaningfully be understood as the demand for an extraordinary exercise of moral virtue, but only as the marching order never to allow the rejection and opposition which they encounter to divert them from their accepted role as witnesses of the kingdom in which they cannot cease to love, to do good and to bless—for how else could they be witnesses of the kingdom ?—even though they meet with nothing but enmity, hatred, cursing and therefore affliction. Again, it is only in this light, and in relation to the service in which they stand and which brings them this reward, that we can understand what they are told in Lk. 6²²ᶠ· (cf. Mt. 5¹¹ᶠ·) : " Blessed are ye, when men shall hate you, and when they shall separate you from their company (ἀφορίσωσιν ὑμᾶς), and shall reproach you, and cast out your name as evil (ἐκβάλωσιν), for the Son of man's sake. Rejoice ye in that day, and leap for joy ; for, behold, your reward is great in heaven ; for in the like manner did their fathers unto the prophets." As those who are hated they are to be regarded as blessed, and on the day when they experience hatred they are to rejoice, because when this happens it shows in what order and ministry and cause they exist in the world. For it would not happen if as disciples they did not exist in the order of the prophets. As it happens, they are thus to count themselves blessed. The First Epistle of Peter is particularly eloquent in this regard : " If, when ye do well, and suffer for it, ye take it patiently, this is acceptable with God " (2²⁰) ; " The spirit of glory and of God resteth upon you " (4¹⁴). But that to which the blessing relates is quite uncompromisingly the fact that even those of our own household become our enemies (Mt. 10³⁶). For " think not that I am come to send peace on earth : I came not to send peace, but a sword " (10³⁴). The context makes it quite clear that this is not a sword which the disciples have to draw but the sword which is sharpened and drawn against them, the sword which Paul mentions in Rom. 8³⁵, where he then goes on to quote Ps. 44²² : " For thy sake are we killed all the day long ; we are counted as sheep for the slaughter."

We need hardly say more concerning the affliction brought to bear on the Christian by the world around. We must now consider and answer our question from the standpoint (2) of the oppressed subject, namely, the Christian. An external pressure is certainly exerted on him in this happening. But it would not strike him as it does if he had not to expose himself to it in a way which makes him a fit object for it. We are thus forced to say that his affliction has an inner cause and is conditioned by himself.

We first recall that the Christian cannot evade it by ceasing to be a witness or to be active as such, since this would be a denial or renunciation of his vocation and would ineluctably carry with it the forfeiture of the personal knowledge, experience and assurance of salvation which distinguish him from other men. In this respect his back is to the wall. He cannot do that which would spare him affliction.

Nor can he escape by changing his situation in accordance with circumstances, for even though he might then avoid one form of affliction, i.e., the men or relationships of the previous surroundings in which it seemed quite impossible in practice to continue his witness, it would only break out afresh in the new situation and surroundings. This type of evasion has been called exile for the sake of faith.

The exodus of the Bernese Baptists to Catholic Jura, the Palatinate and elsewhere, the flight of Puritans threatened by the Church of England to North America, the departure of the Huguenots from France under Louis XIV, as also of the Salzburg Protestants from Catholic Austria, and the movement of certain German Separatists to Russia are famous examples of this type of possibility. On a small scale the same kind of problem has also arisen for many ministers in the form of the question whether it is not sometimes legitimate and even necessary for them to make a new beginning in a new communion when the situation becomes too sterile in the old.

The possibility of such local evasion was already familiar to New Testament Christianity. " And whosoever shall not receive you, nor hear your words, when ye depart out of that house or city, shake off the dust of your feet " (Mt. 10¹⁴). And later (v. 23) : " When they persecute you in this city, flee (φεύγετε) into another." According to Mt. 2¹³ᶠ· this is just what Joseph did with the young child and his mother at the express command of the angel of the Lord that they should flee into Egypt. Again, in Mt. 12¹⁵ we read of Jesus Himself that He became aware of a plan to destroy Him on the part of the Pharisees and left (ἀπεχώρησεν) Capernaum, although in Lk. 13³¹ He was not prepared to follow similar advice when told of the threat of Herod to kill Him. Again, we read in 2 Cor. 11³³ and Ac. 9²⁵ that Paul escaped from Damascus by being let down in a basket through a hole in the city wall, and he was obviously fleeing from his persecutors, whoever they might be. Again, at the end of the great enumeration of the " cloud of witnesses " (Heb. 11³⁸) we read of those who in flight found refuge in dens and caves and holes and clefts. Again, in Rev. 12⁶ we read of the woman clothed with the sun and moon and twelve stars that " she fled into the wilderness, where she hath a place prepared of God, that they should feed her there a thousand two hundred and threescore days." David's flight from Saul must have made a particular impression on the New Testament community in this regard. There is a genuine point here. Yet we cannot conclude that all such evasion is always and in all circumstances legitimate or even required. One thing we certainly never find in the New Testament is a legitimate flight from dangerous proximity to Jesus to another and safer place, the kind of flight engaged in by all the disciples in the garden of Gethsemane, including an anonymous youth who ran away as naked as when he was born (Mk. 14$^{50f.}$). This flight was immediately followed by the denial of Peter.

In relation to this possibility the Christian must ask who and what it is that calls him from the one place to the other. Is the pressure which he has to endure of such a character that it constitutes an expulsive force which puts a term to his ministry? Has he really fulfilled this ministry to such a degree that he is free to break it off and commence again elsewhere? If he has not soberly faced and answered these and similar questions concerning the responsibility of his action, then it may well be that escape by removal is not legitimate but quite definitely forbidden as a desertion of Jesus. Jesus Himself did not flee in Gethsemane, nor did the apostles allow themselves to be driven out of Jerusalem by the persecution which followed the stoning of Stephen. It would certainly constitute denial if such removal meant for the Christian that he ceased to minister, that he did not immediately resume his ministry in the new surroundings, and thus discover that its discharge inevitably means a new form of pressure. Exile for the sake of faith does not mean that the Christian can live elsewhere an undisturbed life of faith with no obligation of witness. If, however, he resumes his witness in the new place, his flight does not imply denial, and sooner or later he will there too experience the world as the world, so that finally he will have no option but to stand with his back to the wall. Whatever his surroundings, he will always be a man who is threatened by affliction and in some form already overtaken by it.

And in different respects he is a man who is notably helpless and vulnerable in face of it. For one thing, he is in no position to make easy and cheap for men the hearing and receiving of what he has to attest. No self-evident friendliness, humanity and serenity with which he turns to them will deceive them. The glorious divine Yes which he may attest to them as the Gospel, and will perhaps do so in a way which is impossibly hard and cheerless and humourless, is necessarily enclosed in the No which they never like to hear because it not only gets on their nerves but touches them on the raw, radically challenging and overthrowing their existence. Not even in the name of love can he, to make it more acceptable, blunt either edge of the two-edged sword of the Word of God (Heb. 4$^{12f.}$). He cannot make the free grace of God a comfortable grace, nor transform the good Lord into a good man. He cannot disguise from them the fact that, where the kingdom or *coup d'état* of God is recognised and acknowledged as such, it is a matter of losing one's life to gain it, of making a right-about turn. Above all he cannot disguise from them the fact that in this turn we are not concerned with the familiar religious experiment the fulfilment of which means the strengthening and heightening of their self-consciousness. He cannot conceal from them the fact that on their side it can only be a matter of the willingness and readiness, which must constantly be renewed and which is contrary to all human self-consciousness, to allow themselves, together with the freedom necessary for that turn, to be limited by the Holy Spirit who is so alien to their own spirit, so that the turn is taken quite naturally in all humility and with no claim or pretension. They can thus understand themselves only as those who are permitted and commanded not to exist otherwise than in fulfilment of that turn. They cannot, then, be either invited or conducted to any kind of moral rearmament. The last ground is cut away from under their feet. The freedom of grace which is always at issue necessarily makes those who proclaim it unsympathetic, unsettling, uncomfortable and therefore basically odious to men. The impossibility of making the witness of the Christian tolerable as it stands thus includes the impossibility of evading the rejection and ill-will with which the surrounding world must react against it. He would necessarily be a denier if directly or indirectly, unintentionally but in fact, he did not provoke its counterpressure and all that this involves. Necessarily, therefore, he makes himself vulnerable.

Again, he cannot ward off the affliction which strikes him in his character as a Christian, and therefore as a witness, in the same style and with the same means as would a normal man when he is attacked, i.e., in the manner in which he might within limits be permitted and even required to defend himself if on the level of general human society it were a matter of defence of his rights and honour or protection in the pursuit of his calling etc. When as a Christian he finds himself persecuted because of his witness, he cannot oppose severity to severity, force to force, cunning to cunning or tactics to tactics. He cannot speak back or hit back. Why not ? Certainly not because the use of severity, force, cunning or tactics is in itself and in all circumstances a possibility which must be rejected. On the level of general human relationships the Christian can make a very limited use of these possibilities even in relation to what he has to attest. But to the extent that he is concerned with his specific service as a witness—and the borderline will often be difficult to fix and will never be rigid—he cannot make any use of them at all. In so doing he could only compromise his ministry as a witness. All these possibilities and their actualisations rest on the presupposition which he must contradict and contest as a witness, namely, that of a world which has not grasped and appropriated its reconciliation to God and can thus exist only in constant contradiction and conflict not only with God but also with itself. In the measure that he, too, lives as a man among men, the Christian cannot wholly escape this presupposition. Hence he cannot refrain from making a very cautious, provisional, incidental and temporary use of the doubtful means of protection of a humanity not yet aware of its liberation. Nevertheless, he can never do so to protect himself as a witness of Jesus Christ. He would make himself quite unconvincing and impossible as such if to ward off those who afflict him in this function he were to place himself on the basis of this presupposition and act accordingly. His witness as such is his only instrument of justice and force. His whole strategy and tactics, his whole cleverness and politics, can consist only in being faithful, courageous and cheerful in his testimony to the Gospel. It is as well for him if he is conscious of the secret strength of this position of his. But his persecutors cannot operate otherwise than on the ground of that presupposition and therefore even in relation to him with the weapons whose use he must himself renounce. Hence they have an immediate advantage and he a disadvantage. They are the stronger and he the weaker. They are armed and he is defenceless and vulnerable. He must be prepared, therefore, to accept what they may do and thus to be initially on the weaker side. In the first instance he confronts them like the boy David facing Goliath.

A third and decisive point is that the Christian can confront the world only as a witness. His action is wholly dependent on the truth and reality of what he attests. He can only point men to the speaking of Jesus Christ, drawing attention to the fact that He speaks. As we remember from the exemplary figure of John the Baptist, he cannot come and speak among them as a second Christ, as if Christ spoke through him. He can encounter them only as the friend of the Bridegroom. If Christ speaks through him, giving to his witness the power of His own self-witness, as He can and will, this is not in the Christian's hands and he cannot boast of it to the world. He has no power to baptise with the Holy Ghost, for, even though he may receive and have Him, he does not control Him. Hence it does not stand in his own power to cause the Gospel so to shine that it must enlighten the world, to create and give men the freedom to grasp and appropriate the kingdom of God and therefore their reconciliation, to recognise and confess Jesus Christ as Lord. The Christian is allowed to co-operate in this as a minister, but it is all the prophetic work of Jesus Christ Himself which the Christian with his work, constantly referred to Jesus Christ and His action, can only precede and follow. Any ignoring or transgression of the appointed limit can only be evil and imply a failure to play his own part and do his own work. He may thus speak only with the authority and intensity proper to him as a sinner serving the Word of God as witness. He may not act as though he were a revealer. He may not himself usurp and exercise the judicial and gracious office of the Gospel. He may not in any sense try to speak as though from heaven. Good care is taken that he cannot do so even if he tries. But he should not try. He should not act as though he could. Every attempt in this direction, every outreaching of his own power, means that he unpardonably does too little rather than pardonably too much. For he fails to discharge the ministry entrusted to him, namely, that of humble but for that very reason steadfast reference to the power of the Gospel, of attesting Jesus Christ as the Lord who attests Himself. Indeed, he actually hampers this Lord who attests Himself, casting his own shadow on His light. But this means that he cannot and should not try to avoid being defenceless and vulnerable in this respect too, and precisely in this respect. If he cannot transgress this limit, the implication is that he may not deny but has to confess that in his action he is absolutely dependent on that of Jesus Christ, that he can do nothing without Him, that he is referred to Him as is an echo to the voice which calls or a reflection to the presence of the original mirrored in it. Only in relation to Jesus Christ is the Christian strong. In relation to himself he can only know and admit that he is weak. And he would be doubly weak if he did not know and admit this. He is not given the weapon whose splendour and power would consist in the truth, wisdom and substance of his own being, speech and action. He cannot regard his existence as a witness as protected by the magic of his own power. This is particularly true in face of his oppressors, who know nothing of the power which secretly sustains and upholds and activates him, who cannot respect this power, who, knowing that this is his only protection, treat him as one who is truly defenceless. It is plain that for them he is as it were left hanging in the void.

What we have said concerning the defencelessness of the Christian under assault may be regarded as an attempted exposition of the saying in Mt. 10¹⁶ : " Behold, I send you forth as sheep (Lk. 10³ has ' lambs ') in the midst of wolves." It may be noted in passing that they are not sent out as shepherds who have to feed the sheep, though this is indeed their function (Jn. 21¹⁵ᶠ·), but as themselves sheep in the midst of wolves. Nor are they sent out as wolfhounds who can bite no less powerfully than the wolves themselves, and are a good match for them, but as creatures who have no power to fight them and by human reckoning can only be chased and devoured by them. This is not a very heroic or comforting aspect of Christian existence. There is nothing here for Nietzsche. But the fact remains that it is as ill-equipped and helpless creatures like this that Christians are to go out into the sphere where wolves exist and will enjoy making short work of them. The addition (which is lacking in Luke) : " Be ye therefore wise as serpents, and harmless as doves," is hardly to be understood as a direction as to the way in which they might perhaps help themselves in this terrible situation by superior skill. Taken alone, the first picture could only give us that of serpents seeking and finding their ways with subtlety and their hiding-places with caution. We should thus be left with advice which is hardly conceivable in the context of Mt. 10 or in the mouth of the New Testament Jesus, namely, that the disciples should show themselves to be particularly skilled diplomats. But the first picture does not stand alone. And if in the second the disciples are told to be as harmless as doves, this is not to be regarded as a second piece of advice which is rather surprising alongside the first. For here, as so often, the καί shows us that we are dealing with an intensifying and transcending of what precedes by what follows. In other words, we are given an interpretation which has to be understood dialectically. In contrast to the normal pattern, your serpent wisdom, your way of escaping from difficult situations, your diplomacy, can consist only in the most undiplomatic harmlessness of doves. Your serpent wisdom is to have no illusions about the evil world into which I send you, and yet to go into it without fear, encountering it in spite of the consequences simply as what you are, as what you have to be as my disciples and witnesses, because I have made you such. A further commentary on Mt. 10¹⁶ is to be found in the direction in Mt. 10⁸, which has certainly to be understood also, but not exclusively, in its most immediate and literal sense. According to this saying, the disciples are to give out δωρεάν, without expectation of or claim to recompense, that which they have received δωρεάν, as the free and unmerited distinction and endowment of their own persons. And in rather a different direction the same is true of the injunction in Mt. 10⁹ᶠ· that they are not to procure gold, silver or brass to carry in their purses to provide against all contingencies, that they are not to take a scrip, neither two coats, neither shoes, nor yet staves, but to go out into that alien world as those who from the human standpoint have nothing with which to back their cause. They are even to settle it in their hearts not to prepare beforehand their answers to the charges of the world (Lk. 21¹⁴).

Important in a very different respect is the saying in Lk. 22³⁶, which according to the third Evangelist was spoken by Jesus immediately before the commencement of His passion, and according to which the disciples were to take their purses and scrips, and if they had no swords they were to sell their coats and buy one, whereupon the disciples produced two swords and Jesus broke off with the little sentence : ἱκανόν ἐστιν. Boniface VIII tried to establish on this passage the doctrine presented in the bull *Unam sanctam* concerning the twofold power of the sword, i.e., the spiritual and the temporal, with which the Roman See is invested. Now the saying of Jesus is undoubtedly parabolic. But the reaction of the disciples with their two swords, which engaged the attention of that pope, does not rest on an understanding of the parable, as he obviously supposed, but on a very bad misunderstanding. Schlatter has pointed out that we have here a formal parallel to Mt. 16⁵⁻¹², where Jesus speaks no less parabolically of the leaven of the scribes and Pharisees against which the disciples are to guard, but the disciples think that He is referring to the fact that they have not brought enough bread. When they voice their misunderstanding of the present statement, they receive by way of answer the little saying which is not necessarily to be understood ironically or sadly but which certainly breaks off the parable. The instruction imparted to them is for the time being at an end. What follows later in Luke is Gethsemane and the arrest of Jesus. The purses, scrips, cloaks and above all swords of which Jesus speaks are obviously pictures for a definite determination of the situation *in extremis* which with His passion now breaks not only on Himself but also on His disciples. It is to be noted—and we have here a warning against too one-sidedly direct an exposition of Mt. 10⁹ᶠ·—that purses and scrips are here spoken of in a very different and even contradictory sense. The disciples are now to find and take and carry these things as those setting out on a journey on which they will need them. It is also assumed that they have the cloaks they were not supposed to have according to Mt. 10¹⁰. And if they are to sell these and with the proceeds buy swords, this signifies that their journey will plunge them in a conflict for which they must be fully prepared, cost what it may. Obviously, then, there is no reference to a sabre of iron or steel, as we rather strangely find in the Göttingen Bible, nor to the kind of weapon with which two of his disciples evidently proved to be armed. Obviously there is no reference either to sword-play, nor, as Bengel thought, to at least a show of resistance to sword-play. Yet we are also well advised not to think of the sword of the Spirit or of the Word of God, but simply and most emphatically of the unconditional preparation of the disciples for a situation in which, if they were not witnesses of Jesus Christ, they could only give blow for blow, i.e., in which they are brought under extreme attack and have thus to be ready for supreme ventures. Of the nature of the extremity we are not told in the parable. All that we know, as indicated by the misunderstanding of the disciples with their production of two swords, is that it does not consist in what is called the use of force.

That it is impossible to expound it along these lines is made quite incontestable by the immediate context in which it is adduced by Luke. For immediately afterwards he tells the story of the arrest of Jesus, and like the other three Evangelists he includes the episode of the unfortunate stroke of the sword with which one of the disciples (identified as Peter in Jn. 18¹⁰) so painfully injures the ear of one of the servants of the high-priest (also identified by John as Malchus). What has Jesus to say concerning this ? According to Jn. 18¹¹ He says : " Put up thy sword into the sheath : the cup which my Father hath given me, shall I not drink it ? " According to Mt. 26⁵²ᶠ· He gives the same categorical order, and then adds : " All they that take the sword shall perish with the sword. Thinkest thou that I cannot now pray to my Father, and he shall presently give me more than twelve legions of angels ? But how then shall the scriptures be fulfilled, that thus it must be ? " According to Lk. 22⁵¹ He simply says quite briefly : ἐᾶτε ἕως τούτου (" Thus far and no further "), and Luke gives added emphasis to this by telling of the accompanying healing of the wounded man as the last modest but highly significant miracle of Jesus. No less eloquent in its own way is Mark's treatment of it as an incident which aroused no comment from Jesus (Mk. 14⁴⁷). The repudiation of the action of the disciple is everywhere unequivocal. It does not belong to the ministry of witness. It contradicts it. Jesus cannot be defended in this way. Dreadful though it is, there is nothing surprising in the fact that they come out against Him with swords and staves as against a robber. But the very notion of a corresponding offensive on the part of Jesus and the disciples is wholly absurd. Similarly, the witness quite obviously cannot defend himself in his quality as such. Even if he were in a position to call down fire from heaven on his adversaries and consume them, he should not do so (Lk. 9⁵⁴ᶠ·). Even if he possessed a sword, he should put it in its sheath and not use it (Mt. 26⁵²). But how then should he defend himself when attacked ? Should he not do so at all ? Everything seems to point to the fact that he should not do so, but should be prepared to be sent out as a sheep among wolves. He, too, stands under the order that the Scriptures must be fulfilled and therefore these things must happen to him.

It is in Paul especially that in this context we find a strong awareness of the fact that as a preacher of the Gospel he is not allowed to secure worldly strength or advantage by presenting it in an acceptable or tolerable form. He cannot— and this tells us everything—preach himself (2 Cor. 4⁵). He cannot go around with cunning (ἐν πανουργίᾳ) and handle the Word of God deceitfully (2 Cor. 4²). He cannot corrupt it (καπηλεύειν, 2 Cor. 2¹⁷). He can commend himself to other men's consciences only " by manifestation of the truth " (2 Cor. 4²). What he means by falsification on the one side and the truth on the other we learn with particular clarity from the first and second chapters of the First Epistle to the Corinthians. It is falsification to try to give to the Gospel the form of a word of wisdom (1¹⁷, 2¹, ⁴). Faith cannot be based on human wisdom (2²). Why not ? Paul is quite definite—and this is the truth—that he has to proclaim only Jesus Christ and Him crucified (2²). But this origin, theme and content of his witness prevent him from satisfying either the Jews who ask for a sign or the Greeks who demand wisdom (1²²). The crucified Christ is the power of God to Jews who are called, like Paul himself (Rom. 1¹⁶), and He is also the wisdom of God to Greeks who are called (1²⁴). But the apostle's proclamation as the Word of the cross can only be an offence to Jews who are not called and folly to Greeks who are not called (1²³). Paul would have to make the cross of none effect if he wished it otherwise or tried to act as though it could be otherwise (1¹⁷). This folly of God, however, is wiser than men, and this weakness of God stronger

(1^{25}). For by this folly, which is wisdom for those who come to the goal of their calling (2^6), those who believe are saved (1^{21}), and the wisdom of the world is made folly (1^{20}). Thus Paul can come to Corinth only " in weakness, and in fear, and in much trembling " (2^3). And to this there corresponds the aspect of those gathered by his ministry of witness : " For ye see your calling, brethren, how that not many wise men after the flesh, not many mighty, not many noble, are called : but God hath chosen the foolish things of the world to confound the wise ; and God hath chosen the weak things of the world to confound the things which are mighty ; and base things of the world, and things which are despised, hath God chosen, yea, and things which are not (τὰ μὴ ὄντα), to bring to nought things that are (τὰ ὄντα) : that no flesh should glory in his presence " (1$^{26-29}$). This then—necessarily shaped by the content of his witness—is the not very imposing figure of the apostolic witness of Christ, and indeed of the Christian generally, that emerges from our final citation. In more than one passage, indeed, Paul speaks very dramatically of his vulnerability, weakness and abandonment as an apostle and Christian. In the context of the well-known saying that he bears the treasure of the knowledge of Christ in an earthen vessel (2 Cor. 4^7) has reference to the fact (vv. 8–10) that he is troubled, perplexed, persecuted and cast down—the expressions all indicate external pressure rather than inner temptation, uncertainty, doubt etc.—and that, even though not distressed, despairing, forsaken or destroyed, he is so radically oppressed that, inwardly appropriating the external pressure, he can describe the totality of it as a repetition in his own person of the dying (νέκρωσις) of Jesus. There is not an hour in which he is not in danger, not a day in which he is not delivered up to death (1 Cor. 15^{30}). In 2 Cor. 6$^{4-10}$, and then again and more explicitly in 2 Cor. 11$^{23-27}$, we are given a formal list of the provoking and painful experiences which he underwent, including some which are not mentioned in Acts, e.g., that he five times received the conventional Jewish punishment of forty stripes save one, that thrice he was beaten with rods and once stoned. It is worth noting that among the different perils listed in 11^{26} he expressly mentions those occasioned by false brethren. Whether the expression used in 1 Cor. 15^{32}, namely, that he fought with wild beasts at Ephesus, is to be understood literally or figuratively may be left open. But we are certainly told comprehensively in 1 Cor. 4^9, and with more than a personal reference, that he thinks that God has set forth the apostles as utter rejects (ἐσχάτους) and doomed them to death, since they " are made a spectacle (θέατρον) unto the world, and to angels, and to men." And immediately after he says even more strongly : " We are made as the filth of the world, and are the offscouring of all things unto this day " (1 Cor. 4^{13}). Hence the weakness which he contrasts in 2 Cor. 12$^{1-10}$ with the lofty revelations which he has enjoyed is quite definitely not the mysterious ailment of which he seems to speak in vv. 7–8 but, as is shown by the conclusion (v. 10), the weakness of the witness oppressed in the place of Christ. That in confirmation of Mt. 10^{16} the existence of the Christian stands *de facto* under this sign emerges elsewhere in the New Testament and especially in the First Epistle of Peter and the Book of Revelation. Particular note should be taken of 1 Pet. 5^9, where the persecuted readers are told that " the same afflictions are accomplished in your brethren that are in the world." Μέλλομεν θλίβεσθαι is the general statement of Paul in 1 Thess. 3^4. In the light of this declaration we are forced to speak of a *de iure* or inner necessity of the affliction which overtakes the Christian and therefore of a " weakness " of his position and situation. He takes pleasure (2 Cor. 12^{10}) in existing in it, for when he is weak he is strong. He boasts of his weakness (v. 5, 9). The *Kyrios* has said to him : " My grace is sufficient for thee : for my strength is made perfect in weakness " (v. 9). All in all, we have in Paul not merely an explicit and illustrated confirmation but an emphatic affirmation of the inner necessity which makes Christians those who are oppressed from without, or sheep in the midst of wolves.

The first and last and true basis of the affliction of the Christian is (3) Jesus Christ Himself, His fellowship with the Christian and the fellowship of the Christian with Him. First and last his affliction is not grounded in the manner or perversion of the world which confronts him, nor in his own constitution as a Christian man, but in the affliction of Jesus Christ Himself in which it is impossible for the one who is called, for the man in whom Jesus lives and he in Him, not to participate. There is justification for the statements which we have made under (1) and (2). But it is only relative justification. They are justified only to the extent that they themselves are grounded in the superior assertion to which we now turn. Jesus Christ Himself leads those who are called by Him into the situation in which they come into collision with the world, in which they expose themselves to this collision, and in which they have thus to suffer the pressure brought to bear on them. Christ Himself leaves the Christian no other choice than to accept this mortal risk.

The world would not be the world which has to oppose him, which has to be for him a world of wolves, were it not that it is already shaken and threatened to its foundations, and thus challenged to withstand and resist, by the self-witness of Jesus Christ, by His resurrection from the dead, by the revelation of what He is and has done for it. Its opposition and resistance detected by the Christian in affliction is its reaction to the action of Jesus Christ in fulfilment of His prophetic office. It is no more, and therefore it is not an action independently ventured and realised. But it is not less, and therefore it is not accidental but a necessary action reacting against the action of Jesus Christ by which it is provoked.

Similarly, the Christian would not be what he is apart from the self-witness of Jesus Christ by which he is not only shaken and threatened like the world but also called, enlightened to knowledge and confession, made a witness, and commissioned and sent out as such. If he cannot be more than this, he cannot be less. He can only respond to the Word of the Lord. But when he hears it, he must respond to it. Ordered and determined by Him, his action and its necessary consequence in affliction are not accidental but necessary.

Thus the outer and inner necessity of the affliction of the Christian have first and last a single root. It is not merely because he cannot escape the world as it is, nor because he cannot without self-betrayal be otherwise than he is, that it is impossible for the Christian to avoid it. The nature of the world and the Christian, and the painful collision between the two, are an ineluctable accompaniment and consequence of the presence and action of Jesus Christ as the living Word of God, of the ongoing of the history of salvation in its form as the history of His prophetic work enacted between the Easter revelation of Jesus Christ and His final appearing. As this history moves from its commencement to its goal in the power of the Holy Spirit of the living

Lord, the world has necessarily to oppress Christians and Christians must be ready to accept and endure affliction.

Why does this have to be so ? It has to be so because the guiding, controlling and deciding factor in this history is called Jesus Christ. It is with Him that in their different ways the world which oppresses Christians and the Christians oppressed by it have to do. And He was and is the One who is primarily and properly oppressed, not merely by the world, but first by God. It is as such that He is the Lord and Saviour of the world which does not know Him and of Christians who are enabled to do so. Paul knew what he was talking about when he declared in 1 Cor. 2^2 that he wanted to know only Christ and Him crucified. It is because He is the Crucified that the world has to persecute Christians and Christians must be prepared for persecution by it.

It is as the Crucified that He has risen from the dead and appeared to His disciples, and that He lives and reveals Himself right up to our own time. He reveals Himself in His prophetic Word, spoken in the power of the Holy Spirit, as the One who then suffered under Pontius Pilate for the reconciliation of the world to God. He speaks as the One who then, not because the world but because God so willed and ordained, gave Himself up to the assault and invasion of the world, accepting the bitter cup of its hostility, not from its own hand, but from the hand of God, and draining it to the last drop. He now speaks of Himself as the One upon whom there came the great and absolutely unique and unrepeatable passion in which the world which brought it upon Him according to the will of God was judged and overcome but also saved and set right in His person, in which the kingdom of God was set up within it, in which the covenant between God and man was confirmed and fulfilled, in which the justification of man before God and his sanctification for Him were accomplished. His prophetic Word to-day is thus the self-witness of the Son of God and Man who was then supremely and once-for-all afflicted. The Word of the cross is the Word of reconciliation, the good news of the salvation of the whole world, of each and every man. It is as this Word that it works and calls and enlightens and convinces in the power of the Holy Spirit, and is grasped and appropriated.

But how can and should and will the world, which has not yet grasped and appropriated this self-witness of His, act in relation to it ? It is immediately apparent that it cannot encounter His Word, i.e., Himself in His prophecy, otherwise than it encountered Him in His work. The questioning and indeed shaking of its foundations by the dawn of a new era as it then took place in the great affliction which came upon Jesus Christ and was borne by Him, obviously still proceeds in a most unsettling way in this Word which reveals His work. The offence which He caused and which the world then took at Him is repeated to-day as He meets it in His Word. So long and so far as His Word is not grasped and appropriated, how can it fail even to-day, and to-day especially, to meet Him with the same alienation and aversion, and for the sake of self-preservation with the same active resistance, as it did then? It is also apparent, however, that since the good will of God was then fulfilled in its own best interests, there can be no question of a new surrender of the Son of God and Man into its hands, that it cannot impose upon Him to-day the great affliction which it imposed then, that it cannot crucify and slay a second time the One who is risen again from the dead and lives in the power of the Holy Spirit. Crucified and slain then, and attesting Himself to-day as the One who suffered then, He is now outside the sphere of its control, and no matter what it may do, it can never do anything directly to Him. In trying for what it thinks to be good reasons to break free from Him, it can only seek to hurt Him indirectly. It will not cease to do this, however, so long and so far as it has not yet grasped and appropriated His Word. And, impotent in face of Himself and His self-witness, it brings all possible force to bear against the witness to Him, and therefore against His witnesses or disciples, i.e., against Christians living within it. It oppresses Him, their Lord and Head, by turning against them. They are still in its sphere of control. And since, as the world sees clearly, Christ lives in them and they in Him, the worst that it can do is to oppress Him in this secondary form, but really to oppress Him in this form. In accordance with the relationship of their witness to His self-witness, what it can do to Him in this form, what Christians come to suffer at its hands as affliction, cannot be the great affliction which the world imposed on Him. It would be sheer exaggeration to speak of a Gethsemane and Golgotha to be borne by Christians. Nevertheless—and this is the result of their enterprise—the world can remind them, and in their persons their Lord, of that great affliction in sharp and painful reflections and analogies. It can plunge Christians into a darkness which, if it is certainly not that of the crucifixion of Jesus Christ, is quite unmistakeably that of the shadow of His cross. It can cause them to feel what it means to belong to Him if only as His disciples and witnesses. In this secondary form, but in it no less seriously, Jesus Christ is not, therefore, merely the man of the passion of yesterday. In this form of the little passion of His disciples His own passion goes forward. Since it, too, can take place only according to the will of God, it is primarily and properly He who is to-day oppressed by the world, yet not only by the world, but also by God.

On the other side, however, Christians are also confronted by the self-witness of the living Jesus Christ and therefore by the Word of the cross. Yet, though they belong to the world and are in solidarity with it, their attitude to this Word is very different from that of the world. As distinct from the world, the Christian may understand, grasp and appropriate it as the Word of reconciliation, as God's gracious and liberating Yes to man. He is the man who is called and enlightened by this Word. He may live by and with and in it. And so the One who speaks this Word lives in him, and he in Him. Hence Christ is where the Christian is, and the Christian where Christ is. But this ineluctably means that in face of the world he stands at the point to which it can look only with the profoundest mistrust, aversion, ill-will and finally hatred, as the target of its resistance and counter-attack against the new reality and truth of Jesus Christ by which it is threatened. No matter how it happens, he is betrayed into fellowship with Him and compromised by Him, so that the sharp finger of the serving-girl of Mk. 14[67]—a notable counterpart to the pointing finger of John the Baptist—points plainly to him : " Thou also wast with Jesus of Nazareth." This means, however, that, belonging to Him, thou art entangled in His affliction and passion, thou shalt have a share in it, and therefore thou must suffer with Him in thine own place and manner. The very Word of the cross grasped and appropriated by the Christian makes this unavoidable. He would not only deny it outwardly but throw it off inwardly if he could escape this consequence. But if he cannot throw it off no matter how often he denies it, he necessarily has his share in the suffering of Christ, and in his own place and manner is brought under the shadow of His cross. We repeat that in his own place and manner he is brought under the shadow of His cross, and not therefore under the great affliction and passion of Jesus Christ Himself, not under a fellow-suffering of the atoning suffering endured once and for all by the one Son of God and Son of Man, not under the task and claim to achieve again by what he endures that which He achieved for all times and men, not under the dreadful, isolated responsibility in which He did it, not under the final and supreme extremity which this fulfilment entailed for Him, not under the agony of the question of Mk. 14[34] : " My God, my God, why hast thou forsaken me ? " Even in the last extremity the Christian realises that he is spared this question, this affliction and passion, because it has been borne by the suffering of this One. And he must realise this if he is to avoid that wild exaggeration. On the other hand, he certainly does suffer, and has to do so, as a witness of the suffering of this One. He has to bear the lesser, yet for him no less severe and bitter, suffering which inevitably overtakes those appointed to be witnesses of this One. This suffering of his is suffering in reflection of and analogy to the suffering of the one man of Gethsemane and Golgotha. It is suffering under the shadow of His cross. And in this secondary form appropriate to His follower and disciple, it is suffering in real fellowship with Him and with His suffering. The Christian has not sought fellowship with Him. Like all others, he has tried to block the way to fellowship with Him. And if there is the slightest spark of sincerity in him, he will have to admit that he still tries to do so. But elected by Him, he is set in fellowship with Him by this One Himself, by the fact that, in calling him, He willed to have and established fellowship with him. Hence, whatever he makes of it, he does in fact exist in fellowship with Him. Nor can he prevent or alter the fact that this fellowship includes his fellowship with the suffering of the One to whom he bears witness, so that in his own place and manner and portion he, too, must suffer.

It is not, therefore, the disposing of the world, nor that of the Christian, but primarily and finally Jesus Christ Himself who is the true reason for the necessity of His affliction.

Concluding here, too, with a glance at the statements of the New Testaments, we may begin with two Johannine passages which speak of the world's hatred for the disciples and which reveal its true basis in a way which is particularly instructive. " If the world hate you, ye know that it hated me before it hated you (ἐμὲ πρῶτον ὑμῶν). If ye were of the world, the world would love his own : but because ye are not of the world, but I have chosen you out of the world, therefore the world hateth you " (Jn. 15¹⁸ᶠ·). With this we may compare Jn. 7⁷ with its even stronger, and according to the literal wording exclusive, emphasis on the direction of this hatred against Jesus Himself : " The world cannot hate you ; but me it hateth "—the meaning obviously being that the world would not hate you, would have no cause to do so, would not even be allowed by God to do so, were it not that I am the true object of its hatred. In the light of this we can understand in what sense 1 Pet. 2¹⁹ᶠ· regards it as a danger threatening Christians that as the doers of good deeds they should be affected by this hatred and should thus have to suffer. You are called to do so—this is the only passage in which the line from the concept of κλῆσις is expressly drawn in this direction— because Christ has suffered for you and has left a ὑπογραμμός (literally, a model for a writer or artist to copy), that you should follow in His steps (1 Pet. 2²¹). That He has died for them implies their suffering with Him. A similar passage is to be found in 1 Pet. 3¹⁸, although here the ἅπαξ of the preceding suffering of Christ is emphasised. The fact that He has suffered once and for all means that in their own place and manner they, too, have to suffer, participating (κοινωνεῖν) in His sufferings (1 Pet. 4¹³). The unity of Christians with Christ for all their difference from Him is just as clear in this passage as is their differentiation from Him in this unity.

In the same sense Paul speaks of an abounding (περισσεύειν) of the sufferings of Christ in him (2 Cor. 1⁵), or of the wounds (Gal. 6¹⁷) or dying (2 Cor. 4¹⁰) of Jesus which he has to bear or bear about in his body or person, or of his κοινωνία with His sufferings (Phil. 3¹⁰, cf. 1 Pet. 4¹³), or of the fact that he is made conformable (συμμορφιζόμενος) to His death. To the same group there obviously belongs also the much quoted Col. 1²⁴ where he speaks of his sufferings ὑπὲρ ὑμῶν (for his readers) in which he fills up (ἀνταναπληρῶ) that which is still lacking of the afflictions of Christ (τὰ ὑστερήματα τῶν θλίψεων τοῦ Χριστοῦ) in his flesh for His body's sake namely, His community, of which he was made a διάκονος, according to the dispensation (οἰκονομία) of God. The introduction of the concept of διακονία ought to have served as a warning against the hazardous exposition which would have it that the apostle here represents himself as not merely participating in the atoning sufferings of Christ but as continuing and completing them. That he could be crucified for his communities in this sense is expressly denied in 1 Cor. 1¹³. How else are we to understand the ὑστερήματα, the afflictions of Christ which are still lacking or outstanding, except as the secondary form in which His once-for-all passion is after His resurrection, and in the power of His resurrection according to Phil. 3[10], reflected, analogically copied and to that extent repeated on the very different level of the sending out and existence of His disciples. On this level we find ourselves in the sphere of the οἰκονομία of God in which it is a matter of the Word of God as the revelation to the saints (to the apostles and Christians) of the mystery now realised within the Gentile world (Col. 1[25f.]). It is here that the apostle and his suffering have their place and function. It is here that we may say of his affliction that it had to be borne in the service of the gathering, upbuilding and sending of the community as the body of Christ and to that extent for them. It is not in any sense in realisation of the mystery of reconciliation, which has been already and definitively realised, but in the service of the revelation of this mystery among the Gentiles, that the apostle in and with his affliction fulfils the great affliction of Jesus Christ Himself. There still lacks its reflection or likeness in the attestation to be accomplished by the apostle or the Christian generally, and in this attestation the affliction of the apostle is unavoidable. In the same context we may finally refer to the passages in which Paul in relation to himself and Christians generally speaks of being crucified or dying with Christ (Gal. 2[19], 6[14] ; Rom. 6[3, 6, 8] ; Col. 3[3] ; 2 Tim. 2[11]). " We thus judge, that if one died for all, then were all dead : and that he died for all, that they which live should not henceforth live unto themselves, but unto him which died for them, and rose again " (2 Cor. 5[14]). It is true that these passages do not belong only to this group. But it is also true that they do belong to it. The reference to dying with Christ, and especially the forceful reference in Rom. 6[5] to the Christian's being planted in the likeness of the death of Christ, are in some sense set in the context of the notion of the suffering of the Christian as a witness, and therefore they cannot be so abstractly mystical, speculative or sacramental as many interpretations assume. And there can certainly be no question of the death of Christ first achieving actuality in the dying of the Christian as that which transforms it from a mere fact into an event of existential significance and as such ripe for proclamation. On the contrary, it is only in the light of the death of Christ, which according to the New Testament view is in itself and as such of existential significance, and which forms the content of the *kerygma* ; it is only by way of participation in the existential significance of this death, as dying with the dying of Christ, that in analogical correspondence and order there can be in the life of the Christian a dying worthy of regard and consideration, and His great affliction can be succeeded by the little affliction of the Christian in fellowship with Him and His. It is also to be noted that this happening in the life of the Christian is expressly spoken of as a μορφή (Phil. 3[10]) or ὁμοίωμα (Rom. 6[5]) of the death of Christ. It actually has a share in it as its other form or likeness. It does not do so in any other way. But it really does so in this way.

The teaching recalled from John, 1 Peter and especially Paul refers us back quite unmistakeably to a fact which emerges with equal clarity in the Gospels, namely, that the little passion of the disciples is grounded in the great passion of the Lord. We have seen this already from Lk. 22[35-37], where it is the immediate proximity of His own death and passion which causes Jesus under the images of the purse, scrip, garment and sword to issue that warning cry to the disciples, to draw their attention to the supreme affliction which menaces them, and to demand their uttermost readiness for it. As Scripture is fulfilled in Him, as He is numbered among the transgressors, as what is ordained concerning Him must reach its end (v. 37), it is decided that a corresponding severity must be their portion too. " Lord, I am ready to go with thee, both into prison, and to death " (v. 33), was the assurance of Peter, though later—there was good reason for the warning cry of Jesus—he proved in his own person that such readiness can never be taken for granted even though there is genuine willingness for it. We are also told (Mt. 26[53f.]) that the vulnerability of the disciples in the difficult times which await them is grounded in the fact that Jesus Himself, in order that Scripture should be fulfilled, does not pray in His affliction for the despatch of the angel legions, let alone think of other possible measures, since He cannot refuse to drink of the cup which is given Him, not by Caiaphas or Pilate, but by His Father (Jn. 18[11]). Following Him in this order, the disciple has to sheath his sword. The same context is in part at least referred to again in a figure in Mt. 10[24f.] : " The disciple is not above his master (i.e., not secured against that which befalls his master). . . . It is enough for the disciple that he be as his master, and the servant as his lord. If they have called the master of the house Beelzebub, how much more shall they call them of his household ? " The same thing is stated plainly in Jn. 15[20f.] : " If they have persecuted me, they will also persecute you. . . . All these things will they do unto you for my name's sake, because they know not him that sent me." He will have to deny them before His Father in heaven if they will not confess Him before men (Mt. 10[33]). They will not be worthy of Him if in confession of Him they will not bear their cross too and follow Him (Mt. 10[38]). They can find their own lives only as they lose them for His sake (Mt. 10[39]). This is clearly the point of departure for all the other statements of the New Testament relevant to this theme.

The propositions of this sub-section on the Christian in affliction, which we must now draw to a close, are not to be understood as a complaint. They must be made quite definitely, and their content must not be lost to view. It will have been noted that what the New Testament says on this theme is always much more severe and menacing than we might say of ourselves. At the goal, or at least at the provisional goal, of vocation we can always expect affliction. Thus the man called to be a witness, and therefore the Christian, is always the Christian in affliction. The question which arises in this respect is whether we who call ourselves Christians in our own time and circumstances recognise ourselves in the Christian in affliction whom we have been describing. Is it really so dangerous for us to be Christians ? If not, it is a suspicious symptom, not of the untruth of what we have been saying, but of the unreality of a Christianity which is perhaps not Christianity in affliction, but a comfortable Christianity, because it does not even remotely takes its appointment to the work of witness with the seriousness appropriate to something in which the very principle of Christian existence is at stake. Where the Christian has taken seriously his existence as a witness, he has never failed to be engulfed in affliction for the reasons given and described. And we must make this point the more emphatically because it is only against this background that what will have to be said in the sixth and last sub-section concerning the Christian and personal salvation can be said meaningfully and forcefully, and understood accordingly. The point at issue will not be the salvation of an imaginary Christian individual, but the salvation of the Christian as a witness and therefore the salvation of the afflicted Christian. Nevertheless, in relation to all that has preceded and to what will follow, what we have considered in this sub-section cannot in any event be understood as a sorrowful and pitiable lament that it is made so hard for a man to be a Christian in this world. Not only will it be out of keeping, but a Christian will in fact disavow himself and display his unreality as such, if he raises a lament or complaint of this kind. And in order to cut it short in case it might insinuate itself, we must now bring out with no less clarity the positive, bright and joyful background which gives meaning and justification to the serious, stern and to a large degree dark picture which we have just drawn. In this respect, too, we must now try to say what falls to be said.

1. To begin with the most general feature, is not an evil but a good, for all the unmistakeable difficulties, to become and to be a Christian in affliction. The sheep sent out in the midst of wolves are in truth better off than these wild beasts, and infinitely so, for all the perhaps desperate circumstances in which they are set. It is not they but their enemies who need the serious sympathy of the love, benediction and intercession directed to them. In all the undeniable stress and pain which his vocation and therefore his ministry of witness entails, the Christian may and should be finally and basically well off. He would vindicate his tormentors, and not himself, if things were otherwise. What he experiences in and with what the world does to him is simply that he really stands at the side of God, or rather that God unquestionably stands at his side. It is simply that the origin, theme and content of his witness are present and active in his person, and that the world is aware of this even though it does not see and grasp them but can only reject them. If this were not so, why should he be afflicted by it? The very fact that he comes under its aversion thus testifies to the reality and aggressive power of the Gospel. Is it not good for him, then, to come under affliction?

Thus Paul cannot possibly be ashamed of the Gospel in a hostile world (Rom. 1¹⁶). He can only glory in the θλίψεις which fall on him (Rom. 5³). He can say that in all his afflictions he is abounding (ὑπερπερισσεύομαι) in joy (2 Cor. 7⁴). Similarly James can summon his readers (1²) to count it all joy to be brought into various kinds of tribulation. Similarly the suffering of Christians can be called χάρις παρὰ θεῷ (1 Pet. 2²⁰). Similarly those who are persecuted for righteousness' sake are called blessed : " for the kingdom of heaven is on your side " (Mt. 5¹⁰); " for the spirit of glory and of God resteth upon you " (1 Pet. 4¹⁴, cf. 3¹⁴). Similarly, the war which Paul is leaving behind him (2 Tim. 4⁷), but Timothy has still to face (1 Tim. 1¹⁸, 6¹²), can be quite unequivocally called a good fight.

2. We have seen that it is first and last Jesus Christ Himself who brings the Christian into affliction. It is for His sake, for the sake of His name, in fellowship or union with Him, as Christ lives in the Christian and the Christian in Him, as the Christian bears the stamp of the Crucified, in His reflection and image, in analogy to His great passion, that the Christian suffers. But again it is first and last Jesus Christ Himself who makes the war which the Christian has to wage as His witness in his own little passion, a good fight which he will not

be sorry but will rather rejoice to have fought. To be united with this Crucified is to participate in the existence of the One who as such, in His death and passion, not only humbled Himself to be a Servant but was also exalted to be Lord, and who in His death and passion strode forward to the Easter revelation of His indestructible life as the One who was humbled and exalted in this way, as the Servant of God and the Lord of all men and the whole world. Thus those who, like Christians, suffer something corresponding in their little passions, as a reflection and likeness of His great passion, may rest assured that their suffering takes place in the light of the Easter revelation towards which He moved in His great passion. It thus has a goal and horizon in a future analogous to the Easter revelation of Jesus Christ. Hence they can and may expect no other than their existence in fellowship with the One who rose again and lives as the Crucified and Slain. They do not suffer absolutely, but in this expectation, in movement to this future, on the way to the revelation of their life with His, in participation in His life. This is the decisive reason why the Christian cannot be ashamed of the Gospel as the Word of the cross, why he may glory in afflictions, why he may rejoice in them, why he may know and experience them as a grace. Those who fight as witnesses of Jesus Christ and in fellowship with His suffering may fight under the promise of His resurrection and therefore in glorious hope. Their fight becomes and is necessarily a good fight.

" In the world ye shall have tribulation : but be of good cheer ($\theta\alpha\rho\sigma\epsilon\hat{\imath}\tau\epsilon$) ; I have overcome the world " (Jn. 16³³). " But rejoice, inasmuch as ye are partakers of Christ's sufferings," i.e., with a foretaste of the joy or happiness which will be your portion too in the manifestation of His glory (1 Pet. 4¹³). For " whosoever shall confess me before men, him will I confess also before my Father which is in heaven " (Mt. 10³²). " Planted together in the likeness ($\delta\mu\omega\dot{\omega}\mu\alpha$) of his death, we shall also be planted in the likeness of his resurrection " (Rom. 6⁵). Why are we constantly in this mortal body given up to death for Jesus' sake ? " That the life also of Jesus might be made manifest in our mortal flesh " (2 Cor. 4¹¹). " For as the sufferings of Christ abound in us, so our consolation also aboundeth by Christ " (2 Cor. 1⁵). These statements make it perfectly plain why there is no passage in the New Testament in which the affliction of the Christian is spoken of in terms of protest or complaint.

3. As the difficulties of the Christian in the world arise out of his fellowship with the crucified but also the risen Christ, they acquire from the very first the character of what we might almost call an ecstatic forward movement beyond himself to that horizon and goal. It cannot be otherwise, since the theme and content of the testimony which brings the one who gives it into affliction is the Word, proclaimed by him in ministering repetition of the self-witness of Jesus Christ, of the reconciliation of the world to God effected in His death. He is called to announce the general and definitive revelation of this reconciliation in which it will be known by all creatures and will

thus take effect for all creatures. The Christian with his witness anticipates the penetration of the light of the fulfilled covenant of grace into the darkness which still surrounds it. Necessarily, therefore, as a witness of this Word he can acquire and have a part in the dynamic of this Word even in all the terror of the surrounding darkness. Deriving from the death and passion of Jesus Christ, he finds that even in the storm into which he is plunged as a witness of this Word he is engaged in movement and transition towards the future of that revelation and therefore that penetration. He is still in the night, but he moves towards the day when " God shall wipe away all tears from their eyes ; and there shall be no more death, neither sorrow, nor crying, neither shall there be any more pain : for the former things are passed away " (Rev. 21⁴). He is necessarily carried as on a powerful wave, through and beyond all that the world can do, by the hope which he may proclaim to a world which does not yet see and grasp it, himself begotten again unto this lively hope (1 Pet. 1³).

It is only through much tribulation that he can enter the kingdom of God (Ac. 14²²). But in this tribulation he is engaged in transition and entry into the kingdom of God. He humbles himself as he suffers, not before the forces of the world, nor before the men who cause his suffering, but " under the mighty hand of God, that he may exalt him in due time " (1 Pet. 5⁶). He recognises in his afflictions—and this statement is found only in the strange context of 1 Pet. 4¹⁷⁻¹⁸—the judgment which falls on him too, which must indeed begin at the house of God, and in the terror of which he may still do good, committing himself to God as his faithful Creator. He lets men spoil him as they will, knowing that he has " a better and an enduring substance " (Heb. 10³⁴). Indeed, with the inheritance of eternal life he will receive back many times over that which he must lose for the name of Jesus in the way of human relationships and possessions (Mt. 19²⁹). He reckons " that the sufferings of this present time are not worthy to be compared with the glory which shall be revealed in us " (Rom. 8¹⁸). " For our light affliction, which is but for a moment, worketh for us a far more exceeding and eternal weight of glory, while we look not at the things which are seen, but at the things which are not seen," and towards which we hasten through the things which are seen (2 Cor. 4¹⁷ᶠ·). " Ye will greatly rejoice, after that now for a season ye must needs be in heaviness " (1 Pet. 1⁶) Indeed, " ye shall weep and lament, but the world shall rejoice : and ye shall be sorrowful, but your sorrow shall be turned into joy. A woman when she is in travail hath sorrow, because her hour is come : but as soon as she is delivered of the child, she remembereth no more the anguish, for joy that a man is born into the world " (Jn. 16²⁰ᶠ·).

4. Between the glorious future arranged for the Christian through the resurrection of Jesus Christ, and his present in the affliction which is unavoidable in fellowship with the Crucified, there is, however, no gulf separating the two situations and making the hope of the Christian in affliction a lofty but empty because unfulfilled expectation which illumines from afar but does not alter in practice his situation in affliction. On the contrary, that future already determines and shapes the present of the Christian in his affliction. He does not merely

sense and yearn for, but actually "tastes" the powers of the future world (Heb. 6⁵).

To be sure, he cannot anticipate and therefore count on certain results which will accrue here and now from his affliction and his endurance in it. Nor can he look to and claim the future glory which will follow his affliction in fellowship with Jesus Christ, the "crown of life" (Rev. 2¹⁰), as an appropriate result of his suffering. As he has not sought his existence under the cross, so he can understand and expect his life with the Resurrected only as a gift which is made to him in free grace. In the same sense there can be no question in his present of any fruits deriving from his situation as determined and shaped by Christ except in virtue of the free goodness of God. In virtue of this goodness, however, there are such fruits, and as they are seen they form important indications of the future which does not merely illumine from without but transforms from within the present of the witness oppressed in the world. They are transformations of the evil which befalls him into a good which is already actualised here and now and is more or less plainly recognisable. They are provisional, little fulfilments, anticipatory and indicatory of the great, comprehensive and definitive fulfilment to be expected in that future revelation.

Paul was thinking of such when he summoned Christians to be steadfast and immovable, always abounding (περισσεύειν) in the work of the Lord, and when he could thus encourage them : "Your labour (κόπος) is not in vain in the Lord " (1 Cor. 15⁵⁸). He also speaks of the fruits of θλῖψις, which may already be gathered in the inner life of the oppressed Christian, in Rom. 5²ᶠ·, where he says that he glories not only in the hope of the glory of God, but also in affliction, because, when suffered in the service of Jesus Christ and therefore with Him, it awakens, creates and produces patience (ὑπομονή), patience fashions experience (δοκιμή), and experience—the circle will be noted—confirms hope, which does not make ashamed. The argument in Jas. 1²ᶠ· is rather different. In the testing of faith by temptation there arises Christian patience, and in this the orientation to the appointed goal of τελειότης. Obvious reference is made to another provisional fruit when Paul says in 2 Cor. 1⁶ (cf. 2 Tim. 2¹⁰) that his affliction, which is particularly severe according to v. 8, works out, not to his own strengthening and deepening as in Rom. 5²ᶠ·, but to the "consolation and salvation" of the Christians in Corinth. For, as we are told in v. 3 f., the God of all comfort has comforted him in all his affliction in order that he may also comfort those who find themselves in affliction with the comfort which he himself has experienced. The text 1 Pet. 2¹² seems to point us in yet another direction when it tells us that the continuance of Christians in the good works which have first brought on them the calumniation of the heathen around them will on a closer inspection cause them to give glory to God.

5. The true analogy of the resurrection of Jesus Christ in the existence of oppressed Christians, the true might and power of the future which already in their present is appointed for them in their fellowship with Jesus Christ, does not consist, however, in the inner or outer fruits which, however valuable or worthy of thanksgiving they may

be, are only isolated, fluctuating and variable indications of the existential determination which is thus given to oppressed Christians, and cannot claim to be the determination itself. The determination itself is a continuous and invariable whole which simply consists in the fact that the Christian in affliction is a man who is absolutely secured by the goal appointed for him in Christ. This is not because the world which afflicts him is not powerful enough to shake and even vanquish him. It is not because he himself is strong enough to resist it. The security of the Christian is not that fancied by the Stoics. The Christian is secure, absolutely and essentially secure, because his life is hid with the risen Christ in God, i.e., with the One who was not overcome by the world but overcame it (Col. 3³). Assailable and assailed though it is, it is not exposed to any threatened overthrow or destruction, nor to any serious disturbance. Its continuation is assured even though there breaks upon it the storm of every worldly force. " If God be for us, who can be against us ? " (Rom. 8³¹). This is the existential determination given to the oppressed Christian by the resurrection of Christ. This is the defiant question which he may fling out in virtue of his belonging to Him. This is the answer already presupposed and given in it. No one and nothing can be against us, or do us true and serious harm, or finally overcome us—not even the last thing which may threaten, namely, death. For the Christian lives in the power of his fellowship with Christ, in the power of what he has perceived and may attest, even though he dies (Jn. 11²⁵). It is in this basic way that he is secured. He has no reason to pay serious respect to any power. Above all, he has no reason to regard his human opponents as great figures because of what they can do to him. The wolves which threaten the sheep are not secure, for God is definitely not for them. The sheep threatened by the wolves are unconditionally and totally secure whatever the latter may do. And they are thus infinitely superior in spite of their inferiority. In their inviolability they can and should summon the wolves to them. Is this foolhardy ? No, because for them there can be no question of anything other than this inviolability in face of them. If they are Christians, and therefore witnesses, and therefore oppressed, then without any particular ability or daring they exist in this inviolability and therefore superiority as those who are absolutely secure. This sovereignty of the Christian in affliction is the true because total, continuous and invariable analogy of the resurrection of Christ in his existence.

" It is a faithful saying (in this context, order ?) : For if we be dead with him, we shall also live with him : if we suffer, we shall also reign with him " (2 Tim. 2¹¹ᶠ·). This future reigning with Him not only throws its light but also works forcefully in the present of the Christian. " Who is he that will harm you, if ye be followers of that which is good ? " (1 Pet. 3¹³). Are not the disciples of much more value to God than many sparrows (Mt. 10³¹) ? Must not all things work together to them for good (Rom. 8²⁸) ? It will be given them what to say to their accusers : " For it is not ye that speak, but the Spirit of your Father which speaketh in you " (Mt. 10²⁰). " Whatsoever is born of God overcometh the world " (1 Jn. 5⁴). But the faith of Christians is born of God, and therefore faith is the victory already won (νίκη νικήσασα) over the world. When it is kept, it is more precious than gold tried in the fire (1 Pet. 1⁷). For by the Lord Jesus Christ in whom Christians believe and with whom they are one in faith, God gives them even now the victory which has been won by Him and which they are to win as His disciples (1 Cor. 15⁵⁷). Not in our own strength but in His, " through him that loved us," by the love from which none of the known or unknown forces of the universe can separate us, we not only triumph, but triumph gloriously (ὑπερνικῶμεν, Rom. 8³⁷ᶠ·). How this occurs is unforgettably described by Paul in the self-portrayal of 2 Cor. 6⁴⁻¹⁰ (cf. 4⁸⁻¹⁰) : " But in all things approving ourselves as the ministers of God . . . by the word of truth, by the power of God, by the armour of righteousness on the right hand and on the left, by honour and dishonour, by evil report and good report : as deceivers, and yet true ; as unknown, and yet well known ; as dying, and, behold, we live ; as chastened, and not killed ; as sorrowful, yet always rejoicing ; as poor, yet making many rich ; as having nothing, and yet possessing all things." This is what is meant by the security of the Christian, his defiance in the midst of the affliction for which he shows himself a match, indeed, to which he is sovereignly superior.

6. We do not weaken or question the unconditional givenness and certainty of the sovereignty imparted to the disciple, the witness, the Christian, but we rather lay necessary stress on the existential character of this determination of his existence by fellowship with the Crucified and the Resurrected, if we refer finally to the imperative dynamic of this indicative. The being of the Christian in this sovereignty is demonstrated in his exercise of it. He is hidden in God as he does what he who is hidden in God has to do, and does not do what such an one cannot do. Our concern is with the determination of the present existence under the cross which is proper to him in virtue of the future assigned him in fellowship with the Resurrected. How is this to be realised unless in his present as *christianus viator*, like the runner so graphically described by Paul in Phil. 3¹²ᶠ·, he moves with effort and energy and haste towards this goal, following its own irresistible movement ? There is no alternative ; what is unconditionally and unassailably given has to become a task. In accordance with the nature of the gift, it necessarily becomes a task. The good fight in which the Christian finds himself must be accepted and fought. He must really lay hold on the eternal life to which he is called (1 Tim. 6¹²). What is meant by the terms " fight " and " lay hold " ? He is to be what he is, namely, a disciple, a witness, a Christian. He is to remain, and continually to become again, what he is. In affliction, in face of it and through it, he is set in the ministry laid upon him, and summoned, engaged and challenged to discharge it, in order that in so doing he may be and become that man who is absolutely secure. This is the imperative which must be our final word in this connexion.

In the New Testament its content is summed up in the concept of ὑπομένειν, of ὑπομονή, of loyal endurance, perseverance, or persistence (which Luther renders rather too weakly as patience). Directly or indirectly, this is always related to the attitude of the Christian in affliction. Ὑπομονή is his action, orientated on but also demanded and permitted by his fellowship with the Resurrected, in the passion which he has to undergo in fellowship with the Crucified. Hence in Rom. 12¹² : τῇ θλίψει ὑπομένοντες. Hence also ὑπομονή in Rom. 5³ as a direct consequence of the θλῖψις which assails the Christian. The concept denotes the most obvious thing, that which is not just in some way laid upon or ascribed to the Christian from outside in affliction, but that which is most natural, immediate and self-evident for him. He is to be and remain and become, not something new and strange, but who and what he is. He must not allow himself to be jostled out of his function as a disciple and witness, as his enemies intend. He must not allow himself to be shaken by them, or caused to vacillate (σαίνεσθαι, 1 Thess. 3³). " Behold, we count them happy which endure " (Jas. 5¹¹). He cannot and should not cast aside or throw overboard the confidence (παρρησία) which is given him on his way as a disciple and witness of Jesus Christ, and which carries with it so great a reward (Heb. 10³⁵). He must not be afraid. He has no reason to be. " Fear not " (Mt. 10²⁶). Why not ? Because there is " nothing covered that shall not be revealed ; and hid, that shall not be known." For this means that nothing can arrest, suppress or conceal the revelation of what you are charged to attest, that the sun will in any case bring it to light, and that there is thus no sense in abandoning the ministry of its attestation in face of that which now seems to try to impede its manifestation. Therefore speak in light that which I say to you in darkness, and preach from the house-tops that which you hear in your ear. This is the ὑπομονή of the Christian which rests on the fact that he has no cause to fear. Why should he fear those who may kill the body but can do nothing against the soul, i.e., against his existence as the man he is ? God alone is to be feared as the One who can destroy him eternally in his existence and therefore in his totality (Mt. 10²⁸). But if he fears Him he need have no fear of others. Or more positively (Lk. 12³²) : " Fear not, little flock." Why not ? " It is your Father's good pleasure to give you the kingdom." Hence you need not fear. The whole πανοπλία of God mentioned in Eph. 6¹¹ᶠ·—His truth, His righteousness, the Gospel, faith, salvation, the Spirit or Word of God—stands at the disposal of the called, the disciple, the witness, the Christian, " that ye may be able to withstand in the evil day, and having done all, to stand " (Eph. 6¹³). Has he still to put it on ? Has he not long since put it on ? He is to put it on again and again. According to Heb. 10³⁹, however, he is one who has already put it on : " But we are not (οὐκ ἐσμέν) of them who draw back unto perdition ; but of them that believe to the saving of the soul." This " we are " may fittingly form the conclusion to what must be said concerning the Christian in affliction.

6. THE LIBERATION OF THE CHRISTIAN

We now come to the final topic of the section. Our concern is with what the vocation of man means for him, and therefore for the Christian, from the purely personal standpoint, as what we may for once describe as a determination of his private existence. In it he himself is also in view. We cannot accept the widespread view that in the vocation of man it is primarily, decisively, predominantly or even perhaps exclusively a matter of this personal aspect, of the private Christianity of the Christian. The existence of the Christian is not an end in itself. As fellowship with Christ it is in principle and essence a ministry. It is witness. We emphasise this point even in the order of the section. Only now at the very end do we turn to the personal aspect, significance and effect of vocation, just as in the doctrine of the divine election of grace (*C.D.*, II, 2, *c. 7*) we had first to speak of the election of Jesus Christ, then of the Old and New Testament community and only in conclusion of the election of the individual which has almost completely dominated all previous discussion. The personal significance of vocation for the Christian is a phenomenon which only accompanies the ministry of witness which properly makes him a Christian. This we must always, and at the very end explicitly, remember. Nevertheless, the personal aspect must not be ignored nor dismissed too summarily. The Christian does have his own existence in relation to what he has to attest as such. In co-ordination with his ministry as a witness, like the unavoidable affliction which we have just considered, he himself belongs to the goal of vocation, with the peculiar determination of his own existence corresponding to the content of his witness. There is a particular *status gratiae et salutis* of the Christian man.

No special prominence is given to this aspect in Holy Scripture. As we have seen, the biblical stories of vocation and conversion are different from those which have usually been recounted in the later days of Christianity. They tell us how certain men were ordained to be prophets and later apostles ; i.e., were claimed, made responsible and activated for the proclamation of the Word of God in their more immediate or more distant human environment without any question as to their willingness or ability. What this meant for them personally can at very best be only gleaned from the stories or occasionally ascertained from the content of the witness, as in the case of Paul in Rom. 7–8. Yet while this is true, neither the Old Testament nor the New is wholly lacking in direct references to this aspect. When Yahweh says to Abram : " I am thy shield, and thy exceeding great reward " (Gen. 15[1]), or when it is said of Him that He spoke with Moses face to face as a man speaks with his friend (Ex. 33[11]), or when Jeremiah in his bitter complaint at the burden of his calling can say that Yahweh is with him " as a mighty terrible one . . . that seest the reins and the heart " and to whom he has " opened my cause " (Jer. 20[11f.]), these are obviously promises which, even though included in the first instance in their official signification, are also personally given to these witnesses and received by them. And in many of the best known Psalms there is such impressive reference made to the personal experiences of the individual believer that it is not surprising that in a later Christian period many readers were tempted to understand them primarily as pious self-expressions and completely to miss the fact that in large measure we have in them attestations of the work and Word of the God of Israel, and that only incidentally are they concerned with the particular part which outstanding Israelites played in this work and Word in their own life-stories. There can be no question that according to the Psalms there is in fact a supremely personal participation of the witness in that to which he bears witness. This is also indicated in Jn. 10[3], where we are told that the Good Shepherd calls His own sheep by name, or in Col. 3[15] and Rev. 19[9], where His people are described as those who are called to the peace of Christ or as guests at the wedding-feast of the Lamb, or in 1 Pet. 3[9], Heb. 9[15], 1 Thess. 2[12], 2 Thess. 2[14], 1 Pet. 5[10] and 1 Tim. 6[12], where the receiving of blessing, or the promise of an eternal inheritance, of the glory of Jesus Christ or quite simply of eternal life, is called the goal of vocation, or in Mt. 5$^{3f.}$, where every good, and first and last no less that the kingdom of heaven, can be ascribed to the spiritually poor, the mourners, the meek, those who hunger and thirst after righteousness, those who are pure in heart, those who are persecuted for righteousness' sake. Indeed, the term kingdom, which originally and properly means the seizure and exercise of power by God on earth, is frequently used (cf. Mt. 25^{34}, Lk. 12^{32}, Heb. 12^{28}, Jas. 2^5, Rev. 1^9) to denote the epitome and fulness of that which is personally and specifically assigned and promised to the Christian as one who is called by Jesus Christ. Thus the foolish question of Peter : " What shall we have therefore ? " (Mt. 19^{27}, but omitted by Mark and Luke) is not set aside but given the very positive answer of a reference to the superabounding wealth marked out for them in the new aeon. We must not divorce any of these passages from their biblical context. It does not constitute the essence of the vocation of these men that they will participate in a life in which they will receive and enjoy such grace. But as they are called to be witnesses they will in fact—and this is the unmistakeable teaching of these passages—participate in such grace. We must not try to avoid exploring this aspect of the matter.

Let us begin with the simplest and most obvious fact that from the formal standpoint the vocation of man takes place in such a way that for the called it necessarily carries with it a supremely personal endowment and equipment. The Word of God goes forth indeed to all men, for Jesus Christ who speaks it is the Head of all men, and what He declares, the gracious act of God accomplished in Him, has taken place for all men, for the whole world. In the event of the vocation of His witnesses, however, it comes to these men in such a way that they enjoy a special liberation, namely, that it is given to them to receive it, its content disclosing itself to them and they themselves being opened to its content. It does not remain concealed from them. They hear, see and recognise it, and to that extent each in his own manner and measure shares and appropriates it. The gracious act of God for the whole world and for all men, reconciliation, the covenant, the justification and sanctification of man, the promise of eternal life, all that has been accomplished in Jesus Christ and is now presented and disclosed to them, is now no longer an unknown or improperly understood magnitude, nor is it merely an external and therefore alien phenomenon ; it is something known and properly understood, a part of their own experience, i.e., an element in their own life. This can perhaps mean many different things. They may have more clear or obscure perception. They may take it more or less seriously to heart. They may handle it with more or less loyalty. They may allow it to speak to and work in them with greater or lesser willingness and with greater or lesser power and consistency. But as those who are called by the Word of God, so that they have some measure of knowledge and experience in respect of its content, they are no longer the men they were. The reality disclosed and imparted to them in the Word of God has become a factor in their own personal existence. The fact that they have actively perceived distinguishes them from other men and is peculiar to them. They have perceived this reality, and it was given to them to do so, because they are to attest it, and in order that they may be able to attest it. It was in fulfilment of this essential determination that this distinction, endowment and equipment were imparted to them, that this new element came into their life, that the gracious act of God in the power of His calling Word, which is the power of His Holy Spirit, became a factor in their existence. Nevertheless, the fact remains that the distinction, endowment and equipment have come to them in their own lives, in their supremely personal human existence. They personally have become those who know instead of those who do not, those who have experience instead of those who have not, those who see and hear and walk where once they were blind and deaf and lame, those who are freed from uncertainty and error for the truth, those who are freed from an existence which lacks that reality for one which participates in it. All this is in and with their commissioning for service and with a view to their service. But it all applies to themselves. As they have entered on their service as those who are freed and qualified in this way, they are men who may themselves live by the Word which has opened itself up to them and for which they themselves are opened, by their experience of its content. Incidentally perhaps, but unavoidably, all these things are also to their own judgment and salvation, to their own support, comfort and impulsion. Thus they are not in vain for them too. To their supreme advantage they are made different from what they were, and from all other men, by the power of the Word which calls them, being marked off from all others as those who are now ahead of and have the advantage over them. The far-reaching purpose behind their enlightenment to knowledge does not alter the fact that in the process they themselves are actually brought out of darkness to light. And the higher intention behind the knowledge and experience of the *beneficia Christi* does not weaken but rather confirms their own participation in that which is entrusted to them.

We shall now consider the same insight from another and more intimate standpoint. The vocation of man is indeed more than his enlightenment to knowledge of the Word of God in the power of which he becomes another man, experiencing what the Word declares, i.e., the gracious act of God accomplished in Jesus Christ. The vocation of man implies and creates a distinction and alteration of the being of the man who is called. As Jesus Christ Himself is God's gracious act of salvation effected for the whole world, so He is the Word which calls certain men to the attestation of this act. It is He who makes men Christians, and He does so by calling them to Himself, to His discipleship, to a life in direct fellowship with Him. In the power of His Word He sets them exactly at the point in and in face of the world at which He Himself stands. He sets them in the service of His own prophetic office and work. He makes them other men by making them His own men in this sense. This is not merely the subjective but the objective and essential distinction and alteration of these men. We remember what was said in the third sub-section concerning the mutual union of Christ and the Christian. Where Christ is as the Lord who proclaims Himself to be the fulness of grace and salvation, there the Christian may also be as His servant, i.e., His witness. Conversely, where the Christian is as His servant and witness, there Christ also wills to be as the Lord who proclaims Himself. Vocation does not imply the obliteration of the distinction between the Lord and His servant or their respective functions, but it certainly means a removing of the distance which separates the Caller and the called and an establishment of full communion and concord between the being and action of the former and those of the latter. What the Christian as a man called by Christ may believe, and in faith recognise, acknowledge, experience, understand and grasp, is finally and decisively this union of Christ with him and himself with Christ. He believes and confesses Christ in him and himself in Christ, and in this union God's gracious act shown to the world, the whole reality of reconciliation, the covenant, the justification and sanctification of man, the promise of eternal life which he is given. But this union, preceding and superior to his faith, knowledge and experience, by which it is not bound but of which it is the basis, is the being of Christ with and in him and his own being with and in Christ. This is the power, depth and scope of the vocation to a ministry of witness which has come to him. This is the final necessity of the obedience which he has to show in this ministry. The meaning and *telos* of this union is clear, and must be seen clearly, unadulterated by the various mystical and speculative notions which so easily suggest themselves at this point. It is a matter of the common action of the Lord and His servant which derives from and corresponds to their common being. It is thus a matter of the self-proclamation of Jesus Christ and of the confirmatory witness of Christians. But since it is a matter of these in their essential union, from this standpoint, too, it is clear that the Christian cannot possibly go away empty in the subordinate function appropriate to him. If Christ in calling men makes them His men, if they are given this special function in a fellowship of their being with His, then obviously the self-proclamation of Christ does not come last, but first and directly, to those who have to serve Him as His witnesses. How could they be His witnesses if Christ did not disclose and impart to them Himself and the fulness of the salvation enclosed and actualised in Him? And if this takes place in the immediacy of the union of the Caller and the called, if the Christian really is where Christ is and Christ where the Christian, then we have to say that the Christian is as it were from the very outset, namely, in the fellowship of his being with that of Christ, the recipient of His revelation and a participant in the benefits which Christ has won for the whole world and for all men, and which the Christian as a witness has personally to attest to the world and to all men. He can do this, and does so, as they are made known and mediated to him at first hand. The Christian—and the same term again forces itself upon us—is liberated, i.e., liberated from the concealment in relation to these benefits which afflicts all other men, and liberated to recognise and gratefully to accept them as benefits won for him too. He is directly freed in this twofold sense because there is now no alienation, distance or tension between him and the One who is the source and epitome of these benefits, so that the revelation and mediation of these benefits to him can be no problem. Again incidentally, but necessarily, the personal knowledge, reception, possession and enjoyment of the *beneficia Christi*, personal participation in the marriage-feast of the Lamb, appears and is, as we may well say, self-evidently assured to the one who, like the Christian as His witness, is with Christ in this way.

To consider the same insight from yet a third standpoint, we return to our main thesis that the Christian is a witness, a witness of the living Jesus Christ as the Word of God and therefore a witness to the whole world and to all men of the divine act of grace which has taken place for all men. Thus in what makes him a Christian the first concern is not with his own person. He is referred, not to himself, but to God who points him to his neighbour, and to his neighbour who points him to God. He does not look into himself, but in the most pregnant sense outwards, i.e., to the fact that Jesus lives, rules and conquers, and to all that this fact includes. In the measure that he is engrossed in himself, rotating about himself and seeking to assert and develop himself, he alienates himself from what makes him a Christian. And in the same measure he curiously hazards and forfeits the very thing which does in fact personally accrue to him as a Christian, as a witness referred to God and his neighbour.

The man who loves his life (Jn. 12^{25}) and tries to keep (Lk. 17^{33}) or save it (Mk. 8^{35}, Mt. 16^{25}), will lose it. But the man who loses it for the sake of Christ or the Gospel, will save or keep it. This is put even more paradoxically in Mt. 10^{39}, which tells us that the man who finds his life loses it, and he who loses it for Christ's sake will find it. As indicated by the different forms in which it is handed down, and especially by the different settings which it is given in the Gospels, the saying points in different dimensions. In the contexts of Mark, Matthew and Lk. 9^{24} it might well be paraphrased : The man who is concerned about himself in My discipleship will miss the very thing which is assigned to him in My discipleship ; but he will receive what is assigned to him in My discipleship if he loses all concern for himself in My discipleship. It is quite possible that an understanding of the saying that there will be given to him that hath, and taken away from him that hath not even that which he hath, is also to be sought along these lines. In Mk. 4^{25} and Lk. 8^{18} this is brought into connexion with the light set on a candlestick, and in Mt. 25^{29} and Lk. 19^{26} with the Parable of the Talents, so that it might also, although again not exclusively, be taken to mean that to the man who without any regard to himself is made a disciple by the task which he is given, there is added to his ordination a personal possession, but that he will necessarily miss this to the extent that he does not keep quite strictly and selflessly to the execution of the task laid upon him.

We may thus say that in the standing of the Christian we have a model of supreme objectivity. But as appears in the positive application of the sayings adduced, there is also more to be said. Even though the Christian as a witness of Jesus Christ is not concerned with himself, even though he turns away from and abandons himself in this sense, even though he concentrates his attention strictly on God and his neighbour, yet he certainly cannot and will not fail also to have a place for himself personally in his psycho-physical existence which is his and his alone, in his life-history between his birth and death, in the ebb and flow of its outer and inner movements. On the contrary, precisely as he is in the first instance unreservedly claimed for God and his neighbour, precisely as he can be concerned only with the ministry required of him, he will incidentally, without any desire, longing or effort, yet quite infallibly, have a care for his own best interests. It is inevitable that in receiving, accepting and discharging this ministry he should at once and continually be also affected, moved, determined and altered by the matter at issue. As he is called, he himself comes to have dealings with the reality of the omnipotent, holy and wonderfully gracious God whom he can and should represent to the world and other men. There opens up for him a prospect of the height and depth and breadth of the good creation of God, but also an insight into the abyss which has been opened up by the transgression of man between man on the one side and the good God and His good creation on the other. He must confess, therefore, that he himself is the first and greatest sinner in most profound solidarity with the great and little sinners by whom he finds himself encircled. From the very first and continually he must put to himself the question thereby posed how he, the puny and contemptible figure which he presents, can ever be or become even remotely usable in the service of God and his neighbour. He himself is compelled to cry after the God who will have him as His witness and will not let him go as such, like a little child which has lost its mother. But even as he has to do so, he himself will constantly come to taste and feel again that God has not lost sight of him, that He heard him even before he cried, that His mercy towards him obviously has no limits, that in willing to have and use him continually as His witness He incomprehensibly yet very really keeps faith with him, the unfaithful. In virtue of the constant faithfulness of his Lord and Commander he himself may rise afresh each morning after every troubled night to take a few steps forward on the path of his little life-history. He himself may thank God that he may again and again summon all his feeble resources to do either well or badly the most immediate of the many things laid upon him by way of witness. He himself, hemmed in between God and his neighbour, yet not broken nor choked nor perishing nor dying, but living, may emerge again and with good hope for his next steps and the steps beyond, and may enjoy peace and joy, and even great peace and great joy. He himself may count upon it that the great *Christus pro nobis* which he has now to attest contains within it a *Christus pro me*, i.e., that God willed to be and is in Christ not only the God and Saviour of the whole world but his God and Saviour, that He has given and continually gives to his little being a comprehensive meaning which He will finally disclose to his eye which as yet can hardly perceive it, and indeed to the whole cosmos. He himself, if only he does not cease to live for his ministry, may definitely see in and around him certain little lights which announce the coming great light and confirm the whence and whither of his way. He himself may know, and hold by and be satisfied with the fact, that not only in his good and strong and filled and fruitful hours but also in his bad and weak and empty and sterile, in life and in death, he is held in the right place, hungering and thirsting but also nourished with food and drink, tired but also alert, rich even in misery, justified and sanctified even as a sinner, elect even as rejected, the beloved child of God even as His unprofitable servant. Of course, all this, even the very best of it, is only incidental. It is only a sure and certain addition to his being and action as a Christian and a witness to which he is called and created anew as a Christian. The liberation which also comes to him in his personal history with the God who calls him can never be the goal and end of the ways of God. God's concern is with His name, His kingdom, His will, His glory in His creation and therefore the salvation of the world and all men. And this, and this alone, can and should be the concern of the Christian too. But as this is God's concern, and the only possible concern of the Christian, it is inevitable that in some form all these other things should come spontaneously to the Christian, and that the history of his ministry should become as such the history of his own liberation. The Christian himself cannot make it his business to see that this happens, that these other things do come to him. He can work out his own salvation with " fear and trembling " (Phil. 2¹²) only because it is the good-pleasure of God to work in him the corresponding willing and achieving, i.e., because the content of the witness laid upon him, namely, reconciliation, the covenant, justification, sanctification, the living Lord Jesus Christ, reflects and stamps and reproduces itself with divine power in his little life as that of His witness, and to that extent expresses itself in his action and attitudes. It is a special grace that the Christian may come to have his own particular part in the grace of God which he has to attest, that he may live out the great history of liberation as his own little history. Nevertheless, he can and will experience this special grace of his own liberation.

We shall now attempt to describe this grace in a few strokes. But first it will be rewarding to consider as such the statement that a personal *status gratiae et salutis* of the Christian man is included in the order of his vocation. We have defined and understood this as something incidental and additional, as a by-product of the real thing which makes him a Christian, of his appointment as a witness. But this cannot mean that it is an unimportant or even dispensable determination of Christian existence. If for the most part indirectly rather than directly, the Christians of the New Testament refer far too often and plainly and impressively to this incidental feature, to their personal faith and knowledge and experience, to their own responsible participation in the *beneficia Christi* which they have to attest as Christians, to their own liberation, to the necessity that they should gratefully work it out. And there has always been good reason that in times when there was danger of overlooking or forgetting this aspect of calling a reaction should follow, dangerous like all reactions, to lay the appropriate emphasis upon it. The Christian could not be the essential thing which makes him a Christian if the content of the witness which he owes the world did not reflect itself in and impress itself upon his own life, or if he tried to evade or resist being personally affected, determined and altered by it.

This brings us to the problem of ecclesiastical and doctrinal orthodoxy in every age. Orthodoxy means zeal, watchfulness and loyalty in relation to the content of the Christian witness as such, an emphatic appreciation of the objective superiority with which this precedes all human faith, knowledge and experience as their origin and confronts them as their theme, a scrupulous concern for the true and correct and perfect understanding of this content, for the demonstration of its validity, for the purity of its presentation and proclamation. In itself it is a good thing. It represents a concern which there is no legitimate reason not to satisfy. But it ceases to be good when it is linked with indifference to or a depreciation of the incidental but necessary question of the existential determination of the Christian by the content of his witness. However carefully the content is investigated and presented, however resolutely and competently it is conserved in one or another form and protected against misunderstandings and errors, it will harden into a possibly impressive but undoubtedly lifeless idol, and the Christian will find neither joy nor power in attesting it, if it tries to ignore the fact that the living God in Jesus Christ, who is indeed the content of Christian witness, necessarily touches and apprehends the man who is called to attest Him, engaging him in his whole being, making disposition concerning him, finding reflection in his life in the form of personal liberation. We cannot ignore nor abstract away this accompanying phenomenon. We cannot overlook nor suppress nor only partially declare this aspect and significance of vocation. Otherwise even the most conscientious, the sincerest and the strictest orthodoxy becomes an idle pursuit. Otherwise it works in a vacuum in which it quickly becomes alien even to its own supporters because no one can live in it, let alone render service as a Christian witness. Even the trinitarian God of Nicene dogma, or the Christ of the Chalcedonian definition, if seen and proclaimed in exclusive objectivity and with no regard for this accompanying phenomenon, necessarily becomes an idol like all others, with whom one cannot live and whom one cannot therefore attest. And there is something menacing and dangerous in an orthodoxy of this kind. For against its will, but inevitably, it evokes all kinds of reactions and correctives which are relatively justified in their main concern but which will sooner or later lead to a neglect of, or perhaps a wrong answer to, the question of the content of Christian witness. To the fatal orthodox picture of Christ without living Christians there is almost always opposed the no less fatal mystical, liberal or existential picture of Christians without Christ, the incidental being regarded as the essential and *vice versa*. An orthodoxy which does not know this incidental element, or which does not take it seriously and honour it in its relative necessity, has never failed to oppose, destroy and make itself impossible in the form of the heterodoxies which it invokes. We must be careful not to take even the first steps towards this kind of orthodoxy.

To be sure, the personal liberation of the individual Christian man, his own reception and experience of the *beneficia Christi*, the particularity of the fact that this too marks and fashions the Christian life and the singularity with which in different ways it does so—all this necessarily seems a small, indeed, the very smallest problem in relation to the great liberation of all creation which God has undertaken and accomplished in Jesus Christ, and in relation to the revelation and proclamation of this liberation. What does it really matter, in face of the content of Christian witness, whether or how there is this reflection and impress in this or that individual Christian?—especially when we remember that in all these reflections and impressions there can never be more than a very fragmentary and indeed distorted and confused reproduction of what is really to be expressed. What importance can be attached to your or my Christianity compared with the great cause of God and man?

In answer, the following is to be said. The majesty, holiness and power of this cause, its superiority to all other powers and in face of all contradiction or resistance, its victory already won in Jesus Christ and to be definitively and universally demonstrated in His final revelation, fortunately do not depend on your or my personal Christianity. The love of God does not await my response to love to become eternal and omnipotently saving love. Nor is it the case that the truth is conditioned by the fact or manner of its expression in your or my existence. It would be the truth even if it had no witnesses. It is the truth even though all its human witnesses fail. It does not live by Christians, but Christians by it. On the other hand, it is also not the case that God wills to tread without us, as He might so well have done, the path which He has entered in prosecution of His cause in the world. Jesus Christ, who is both the reality of this cause and its truth, its Prophet and Revealer, does not will as such to be alone, to be without His own, His disciples, Christians as His witnesses. Even in His final manifestation He will not appear alone but with all His saints (1 Thess. 3[13]). And so even here and now He wills to rely on, to make common cause and to compromise Himself with these curious saints called Christians by calling them as the Lord to His service. This service is the point at issue in the question of the personal liberation of the man who is called. Indeed, in relation to his service it is no longer a small but a very big and even in its own way decisive question. To be sure, it is not a matter of the majesty and victory of the great cause of God and man, nor of the truth of its revelation and of the Christian witness concerning it. Nevertheless, it is a matter whether the Christian appreciates the mercy shown him by the fact that in his calling he is summoned, drawn and awakened to this participation as an active servant in the cause of God and man, of Jesus Christ. Hence it is a matter whether he personally is grateful or ungrateful for this undeserved personal distinction, whether he does honour or dishonour to his Lord as a witness, whether he remains a witness or not. It is a matter whether the witness to the truth on his lips rings out in the world and finds credible expression as such, whether it is spoken as a word of man to men, whether it affects them as such, in short, whether it can accomplish its ministry as a proclamation of the great liberation and therefore as a true ministry of God and man. In this respect, however, his little personal liberation, his own faith, knowledge and experience, are an indispensable prerequisite, a *conditio sine qua non*.

The point is, in general terms, that only on the lips of a man who is himself affected, seized and committed, controlled and nourished, unsettled and settled, comforted and alarmed by it, can the intrinsically true witness of the act and revelation of God in Jesus Christ have the ring and authority of truth which applies to other men. This means, however, that, himself receiving and activated, he must continually participate in what he has to attest to others, to the world. It makes no difference whether his witness is actually accepted or even understood. He must accept the fact that the success of his witness is not in his own hands but in the hands of the One whom he has to serve in it. Yet the fact remains that it can be accepted or even understood only to the extent that he himself has accepted as well as understood what he attests, that he can attest it in his own faith, knowledge and experience as one who has himself been overcome, subdued and determined by it, so that it has taken and continually takes form in his inner and outer life. He cannot, then, be satisfied merely to confess the act and revelation of God as objective truth, and to declare them as such in his speech and conduct. He should naturally do this. But he must show that they are objective truth by attesting them as one in whose subjectivity they prove their superiority and in whose humanity they find a reflection and impress. He cannot simply refer and appeal to the faith, knowledge and experience of others, e.g., of Christians either before or around him, nor can he simply refer and appeal to the dogma and *kerygma* of the Church, nor the original testimony of the biblical prophets and apostles. He neither could nor would be a Christian if he despised this school, nor could he continue a Christian if he left it. But he must not imagine that he

can be a Christian and therefore a witness on the authority of Paul
or John, of Luther or Augustine, of pious elders or friends. If he
hears them, if he goes to their school and remains in it, then he will be
led by them to a personal part in the act and revelation of God. And
it is in vain that he will shelter under the wings of their authority
if he will not let them conduct him to their source and thus be instructed by them in his own responsibility in relation to this source.
However else it may be with him, less than his own person is not
enough if his true witness is to be declared as true by him, if it is not
to be on his lips as sounding brass or a tinkling cymbal, and if therefore, in spite of its truth, it is not to be futile and even false witness
with which he dishonours rather than honours his Lord, neither
serving Him nor helping but only hindering the world and other men.
He cannot be a herald to others and himself a castaway (1 Cor. 9²⁷).

There are in the main three characteristics of Christian witness in
which the indispensability of the liberation of the Christian to his
ministry as a witness may be plainly seen.

1. He has to attest to the world that the light of the act and
revelation of God in Jesus Christ is not a dream, nor an illusion,
nor a subject of mere theory, but a fact, and indeed a fact which is
relevant and significant for each and every man, which applies
directly to every man, so that he has not merely to reckon and
wrestle with it as a given factor, but to give it place and freedom to
work as such in his life. The One who introduces this relevant factor
and gives it the power to speak for itself is not the Christian; it is
Jesus Christ Himself working by His Holy Spirit. But the Christian
has to follow Him in this. He has to serve the omnipotent self-witness
of Jesus Christ. And he has to do this in such a way that in his
action, his human words and attitudes and conduct, he brings before
the world a phenomenon which corresponds and therefore points to
the self-witness of Jesus Christ and therefore to the act and revelation
of God, reflecting at least the light of this powerful self-witness and
thus confirming it as used by Jesus Christ for this purpose. But if
human words and attitudes and conduct are to be able to do this,
if they are to be at least serviceable in this ministry of the prophecy
of Jesus Christ Himself, there is needed the personal illumination
of the Christian by His light. Whoever, whatever or however the
Christian may be, he must be himself a man for whom the act and
revelation of God are neither dream nor illusion nor the subject of
mere theory, but a reality believed, known and experienced either in
power or in weakness. It is not in his own hand or power to emerge as
such. But to be a Christian and a witness he must be such, i.e., a man
who can emerge as such. The name, kingdom and will of God must
be for him a relevant factor which determines his life. Otherwise
even his best action cannot reflect the self-witness of Jesus Christ.
It is not the action of the Christian which is serviceable in this

ministry, but he himself in his action. Nor is it he himself in a measure of Christian rectitude or excellence, but as a man whose heart has found its Master and Lord in Jesus Christ and whose life has acquired in Him a new centre. If he himself were lacking, or if his heart did not have this lordship and his life this centre, his whole action might seem to be Christian but it would not be so. It would not be a phenomenon pointing the world to the act and revelation of God in Jesus Christ. It would not be a witness. To be this phenomenon or witness, his action must also have in its own way and within its limits the character of a self-witness. It must be the word of a man who speaks, who represents in what he does and refrains from doing, that which he believes, knows and experiences, that which determines his own existence. He must be a Christian in order to be able to do as such that for which he is ordained if the Lord is pleased to use him. He must encounter the world as one in whose life the factuality and relevance of the great liberation has its analogy and counterpart in the factuality and relevance of his little but very personal liberation.

2. It is to a new and strange light astounding in its majesty, to the two-edged sword of an inescapably impending judgment, that the Christ has to refer and point his fellow-men as a witness of the self-attestation of Jesus Christ, of the act and revelation of God effected in Him. He has thus to make known to them the command of a supremely radical decision, and to approach them with a harsh demand. He has to attest to them reconciliation, the covenant, the grace of God active and knowable in Jesus Christ, as the only deliverance and security of all. He has thus to attest their radical need, their utter dependence on the fact that God is undeservedly for and not against them. He has to see and address them all as sinners living only by the mercy of God. And in his witness he has to invite and summon them not to say No, nor Yes and No, but in faith to say Yes to God as their only Helper, but also therewith to their own helplessness. He has to attest to them this way of faith, not as one possible way among many others, but as the one to which all without exception are directed, which is open to all, and which must necessarily be followed by all. This is obviously a great deal even as expressed in this summary fashion. But there can be no question of anything less in the task laid upon the Christian in relation to his fellow-men, no matter in what form he may receive, accept and execute this task. Any subtraction or dilution of any aspect means a denial of the whole and therefore utter disloyalty. The Christian, however, can correspond to this hard task only when he is compelled and authorised to undertake it by the fact that the blinding light which discloses both the grace of God and the misery of man has first struck his own eyes. He can measure up to it only when he first sees himself set in judgment and under the command of the radical

decision of faith, when from him first every hope is taken away save hope in Jesus Christ, when to him first every way is bolted and barred except the way of faith. The yoke whose acceptance he must attest to others as unavoidable must first lie on his own shoulders. The mortal conflict to which he calls them must have become, and must continually become again, his own conflict. Does he know, not the great dereliction of Golgotha, which it can never be his business to know, but at least the shadow of this dereliction in his own life as a disciple of the Man of Golgotha ? If he does not, how can he know what he is talking about when he imagines he can speak to others about the Lamb of God which took away the sin of the world in that great dereliction ? And if he does not know this, what has he to say at all ? Even his most earnest indication and proclamation, in work and attitude and action, of the God who is so stern in His goodness and the man who is so plainly and pitilessly judged in the work of His grace, can only be mock thunder. He himself must have been and be involved if he is to be able authoritatively to indicate to others what it means to be involved in this matter.

The little boy of an African parable, who had played for long enough with a prettily and faithfully carved wooden lion—it might have been an excellent dogmatics !—was dreadfully frightened one day when he saw a real living and roaring lion approaching. If we have never seen the Gospel approaching as a real and living lion, we must not even imagine that we can ever point others to, or prepare them for, that astounding light, that two-edged sword, the decision which is forced on them or the unequivocal way in which it must be made. How can they be expected to take seriously what we ourselves have not taken seriously, or have done so only in the form of a lion which, however savagely it speaks and acts, is only carved out of wood ? And if we have not taken it seriously, how can we be usable in the service of Jesus Christ ?

To be sure, it is not the shock of our own little liberation which gives truth to our witness to the great liberation of all men, and to the judgment which ineluctably overwhelms them in it. This is true in itself. But this true witness can and will be spoken as such only on the lips of men who have experienced, and still do so, the shock of their own little liberation.

3. We now come to the point which is genuinely and finally decisive. What the Christian has to represent and indicate to all men is the self-witness of Jesus Christ, the Gospel of the act and revelation of God accomplished in Him as the good, the unambiguously glad and gladdening news of God's omnipotent and merciful Yes to His creation. What has taken place in Jesus Christ is the removal from the world of the curse under which it arbitrarily placed itself, its redemption from the bondage in which—piling one sin on another, heaping guilt on guilt, adding always to its own misery—it seemed inextricably to have entangled itself, the ending of its campaign against its Creator which inevitably brought it into internecine and

inner conflict. It is thus the breaking of the thraldom under which man could only vacillate between tyranny and anarchy, between secular falsehood and religious falsehood, between impotent carnal lust and even more impotent spiritual pride, between anxiety and defiance, so that either way he was condemned always to introduce more sin and therefore more evil. What has taken place in Jesus Christ is the breaking of this *circulus vitiosus* and more positively the birth of a new man at peace with God, his neighbour and finally himself, and therefore the appearance of a new heaven and a new earth wherein dwelleth righteousness. It is to this work of peace that Jesus Christ bears witness in His self-witness, to this divinely accomplished alteration of the situation and constitution of creation by the passing of its old form and the coming of its new. And it includes the fact that man for his part may accept this immeasurable benefit, that on the basis of the affirmation of the new form of his being as introduced by God he may say a confident, bold and hopeful Yes to his being as the creature of God, that he may thankfully breathe and run and rest and work in the new sphere of life which he is given, that in the best sense of the word he may be satisfied with it. It can only be joy for man to accept what Jesus Christ says to him—Christmas joy, Easter joy, Whitsun joy—and all as a fore-taste of the joy of consummation at His final appearing for which he waits and to which he looks and moves, no longer in a circle but forwards. The Word of the living Christ alone can and will give this joy to men and set them on this joyful course. The calling, ministry and task of the Christian, however, in his assistance of the Lord, consists in the fact that in his modest and limited way, yet very definitely, he confirms this Word of joy by what he may say and be and do, so that he draws the attention of his fellows to this Word, to its content and meaning, to the reality of the immeasurable benefit conferred on all, thus preparing them at least for the great joy of peace on earth which awaits them and is to come to them. He can and should make them yearn for this joy. But again we are brought up against the presupposition of the fulfilment of this Christian task. How can the Christian undertake and execute it if the great joy has not yet come to himself? How can he bring it if he has not himself received it? A gloomy, morose and melancholy Christian can obviously attest only a gloomy, morose and melancholy Gospel. But this would contain an inner contradiction which certainly does not correspond to the Word of the living Jesus Christ and which cannot, therefore, serve to attest it. It could only give the appearance that Jesus Christ has not made things, or not made all things, new, that man has not become in the very least a new creature in Him, that his liberation in Him has either not taken place at all or only in part. Such a Gospel could only confirm the bondage, the conflict, the vicious circle, in which man exists and may still try to exist outside Christ. It would be the gloomy, morose and melancholy Gospel, not of Christ, but of the world without Him, of a God who is not for us but against us. It would not be witness for Jesus Christ, but against Him. But this means that it would not be good or glad news but bad or sad news—the saddest of all. It would not be *Euangelion* but *Dysangelion*, not inviting anyone to expect the great joy which is to come to him, but strengthening the world in the gloom and bitterness and melancholy which is in any case its hardly concealed mystery. But how can a Christian ever come to attest such a *Dysangelion*? Obviously only on the assumption that he himself has not received it as the Word of the living Jesus Christ and therefore as *Euangelion*, so that it has not given him the joy which it includes within itself and without which no man can receive it. But if this is so, how can he have been called by the Word, by the self-attestation of the living Jesus Christ? How can he be a disciple of this Lord? How can he be a Christian at all? A troubled Christian is *per definitionem* not a Christian, because as such he is definitely not in a position to be a witness of Jesus Christ. To be sure, it is not his personal joyousness which makes him a witness. For this is not what makes his witness true. But he can be enabled to give the true witness entrusted to him only when its content, which makes it true witness, gives him personal joy, making him a bright and merry Christian, i.e., only when he can give it as one who has received the Yes of divine grace said also to him, who can therefore live personally by the power of this Yes in spite of the old man which still rumbles within him and the old world which still startles him, and who in virtue of the penetration of the vicious circle accomplished for him and not by him may take a few steps forward, himself liberated and therefore a bright and cheerful Christian.

So much, then, by way of establishing and explaining the statement that for all its incidental and relative character the personal liberation of the Christian is an indispensable presupposition, a *conditio sine qua non*, of his existence as a witness of Jesus Christ and therefore of his Christian status.

We shall now try to make clear by a few concrete instances what is at issue in this liberation. To be complete we should have to return at some length to the concepts of justification (§ 61), sanctification (§ 66), faith (§ 63) and love (§ 68) already discussed in the first and second parts of the doctrine of reconciliation. Already at these points we were unable to understand the divine act of atonement effected in Jesus Christ without considering its meaning and scope in relation to the man, i.e., the Christian, to whom it is given, as he comes to know it, to participate in it, not merely *de iure* like all others, but *de facto*. From this standpoint the liberation of the Christian consists quite simply in the fact that what has taken place for all men in

Jesus Christ becomes the concrete determination of his own existence and the dominating factor in his own life-history, that he may exist as a man who is justified before God and sanctified for Him, that he may believe and love for all his sin and guilt and need. With express reference to our earlier discussions, we must here content ourselves with a few cross-sections and individual glances.

But first a formal clarification is demanded. In the doctrine of vocation which we now conclude, and again with reference to the Christian's personal qualification, we have spoken more than once of the status of the Christian, of his *status gratiae et salutis*. Now we can and must understand the special grace addressed to the Christian to mean that it is given to him personally, as the witness of Jesus Christ, to stand at a certain place which is uniquely illumined, full of promise and especially blessed, i.e., to stand at the same place as Christ, for all the difference from Him. This is his status. But this leads us on at once to consider that Christ does not find Himself indolently resting at this place, but that in fulfilment of His prophetic work in the power of His Holy Spirit He strides through the ages still left to the world until His return in its final form. Hence we have to understand the Christian's standing at the point where Christ is as an element in the movement in which he is set in fellowship with Christ and which in this fellowship it is his task in his own time to fulfil. The embracing concept of vocation describes a history, namely, the history of the Christian in connexion with that of Jesus Christ Himself as engaged in His prophetic work. And we are concerned with an element in this history in the personal participation of the Christian in the salvation addressed to the world in Jesus Christ, so that to describe it we have deliberately preferred the dynamic term " liberation " to the more static " freedom." In the course of his vocation there also takes place the fact that personal liberation comes to the Christian as the man called to be a witness of Jesus Christ. And it is as this happens that he stands in freedom at that special place. We must now try to consider this event of his liberation. And in so doing we must remember that in its full and serious sense the word " liberation," like " freedom," does not signify merely a release from some authority or power which illegitimately binds man and dominates him to his own destruction, but also a redemption to responsibility to a very different court which demands his attention and obedience and which has a genuine, valid and saving claim upon him. Liberation is the one movement and history in which there takes place inseparably the transition of man both from a false commitment and to a true, and to that extent both from an old and perishing being and to a new and saving. As the existence of the Christian takes place in this small and imperfect transition, it becomes and is an image and analogy of the great and perfect transition, namely, of the liberation of the world and all men which God has accomplished in Jesus Christ, and the Christian acquires and has his own share in the grace of God addressed to the world and all men, being personally qualified for that which primarily and properly makes him a Christian, for service as a witness of Jesus Christ.

We shall now give some indication of what takes place in this special history, not with any claim to completeness and naturally not in the sense of drawing up a genetic sequence of the points treated, but in an attempt to present and clarify the totality of this history from certain specific standpoints.

The liberation of the Christian takes place (1) as he is drawn out of solitariness into fellowship. The glories and miseries of isolation, of self-dependence, of loneliness, are now over for the Christian. As a witness of Jesus Christ he has nothing more to seek or find in this dark cavern. With every step which he takes as such he moves further out of it, leaving it behind and moving over and into fellowship, into fellowship with Jesus Christ, which at once opens up in two dimensions as fellowship with God, who also sends him out as His servant in and with Christ, and as fellowship with men, to whom He is sent in and with Christ as His servant. When he is addressed and claimed by Jesus Christ for His service, both his relationship with God and his relationship with his neighbour are personally assigned to him with superior power and force. He has ceased to be lonely. He is in any case brought into conjunction with God as his Father and his neighbour as his brother. In relation to himself and the way in which he realises it, the relationship in both its aspects may and will be very doubtful and vulnerable, being often broken in both dimensions. The old desire for a purely private existence, and therefore for reserve and resistance to both God and neighbour, may and will continually arise again in the Christian. The cavern of a fatherless and brotherless isolation will continually be for him an enticement and threat and temptation and danger. But there can be no question of a malign fate driving him back thither and thus disrupting the relationship with God and his neighbour. There is no such fate for the one who is in Christ and Christ in him, as is true of the Christian as His witness. For all the relapses into his old, private being, it is once and for all established that that cavern is behind him and the open country of fellowship before him. In its conjunction with the history of Jesus Christ his life-history moves in this and not the opposite direction. He may not be very comfortable in the established order. He may wrongly and senselessly transgress it. But he must always have beside him the God who sends him and the fellow-man to whom he is sent. He cannot, therefore, live alone, He must always reflect and express the relationship of his existence to the covenant which he has to attest. This is one aspect of the liberation which comes to him and which cannot be too highly estimated.

It also comes to him (2) as his deliverance from the ocean of apparently unlimited possibilities by transference to the rock of the one necessity which as such is his only possibility. It is really a matter of deliverance. That ocean spelled his destruction. The Christian as such is saved from this destruction. There can be no more question for him of an existence without horizon, contour or shape, open on all sides, exposed to every wind and thus a prey to disintegration. There can be no more question of the pride and misery of unrestricted thought and aspiration. He has awakened from the dream or nightmare of a freedom of choice in which he might always in all respects do different things, loving, choosing, grasping and executing now one thing and now another according to fate or preference, chance or caprice. Called to be a witness of Jesus Christ, he finds a Lord and becomes His servant, and thus finds that he is given a definite task and definite orders. He may and will often forget or neglect these. He may and will misunderstand them and execute them in a wrong sense. But he has them. He lives with and by what is entrusted to and demanded of him. The desire may and will often come to him to think of God as a Don Giovanni and himself as his Leporello, to make himself the lord and to cease to be a servant. Woe to him if he tries, for it can only lead to trouble! But he cannot and will not succeed in the attempt. His Lord is not one of the lords whom a man may accept or leave according to his own wishes, and therefore he is not one of the servants whose resistance has any prospect of success against their lord. To be sure, it is not external constraint, but his own freedom, which he owes to the grace of his Lord electing him in divine freedom, which prevents him from emancipating himself from this Lord. He is elected continually to elect this Lord and His service. He may renounce or fall short of this determination and characterisation of his existence, and if he does he will quickly reap the bitter fruits of what he sows. But he cannot in any event escape this determination and characterisation. He can frustrate them, but he cannot break free from them. Called by Jesus Christ to be His witness, he belongs to Him and not to himself. He is His man. This means however—and this is his deliverance, his indescribably great salvation—that the beginning and end of his course, and therefore its direction, are already fixed. He can be unfaithful to this direction, but he cannot reverse it. He has been deprived of all possibilities but one. He can only remember and never dream again that old dream of unlimited freedom of choice. The corresponding existence without horizon, contour or shape lies insubstantially behind him. It is not that he has not to choose in the future towards which he moves as a Christian. Every step on the way marked out before him will in fact be his choice. But every element of chance, and above all of caprice, will be taken out of his choice, so that it can no longer be a burden and anxiety and embarrassment to him, nor lead him to destruction. He has only to choose as the called and elect man he is, and he can enjoy certainty, even in regard to his past and future mistakes in detail. His way may have many turns, but since he can and must tread it according to the unambiguous sense of his vocation, he can and will always take his bearings by the compass which is thus given him and which he can never lose. Hence he cannot go astray at least in general direction. He can always move ahead. For all its inner contradiction, his life will thus be orientated on the one thing which is the one necessary thing and which constitutes a relatively restricted whole—in this respect, too, not without reference to the concrete unity and totality of the act of deliverance accomplished in Jesus Christ which he has to attest, reflecting and expressing it in his existence on this way. That his life is in movement in this sense is the second aspect of his liberation.

It is (3) his transition from the forcible dominion of things to the free territory of man and the human. To reconcile the world to Himself, God in Jesus Christ became a man and not even the most important or resplendent of things. And He did what He did *propter nos homines*. Hence the smallest sigh or laugh of a man is surely more important to Him than the support of the most important institutions, the construction and working of the most marvellous apparatus, the development of the most lofty or profound ideas. Similarly, it is for the sake of men and not of things that the Christian, himself a man among men, is called to be a witness and exists as such. It might almost be said that there cannot and should not be anything else for him but man. This is the decision which separates his past and his future. In the light of it, by the Word of God which he has to serve, and in relation to himself as well as others, it is only man, his mystery as such, his gifts and tasks, his heights and depths, his true and corrupt features, his genuine and false needs and aspirations and joys and sorrows—it is men near and far, in isolation and plurality, who are set in the centre of his attention and who constitute the problem of his own being and action. To be sure, there is also a periphery with its own apparently independent facts and factors and problems. There are things which are necessary to the life of man, which make life easier or more beautiful, which are means of life, or helps to it, the material, spiritual, technical, civilising or cultural goods, contrivances, machines and gadgets whose presence and operation man has to take into account in virtue of the psychophysical, individual and social structure of his being in time. It would be radically mistaken to assert that it is legitimate or even imperative for the Christian, in his exclusive orientation on God and his neighbour, not to be concerned about these things. They belong in some form to all human life. Man could not be without them. Hence the Christian cannot ignore them even though his central concern must be with God and therefore with man and the human. His sincere and zealous co-operation is obviously demanded even on this periphery of human existence. If he lost sight of this periphery, of things, he would obviously lose sight also of the centre, of man and the human. His pure humanity would lead to inhumanity. It is not things, either small or great or the greatest of all, which are broken and ended, but the lordship, the tyranny, the fatal dominion over man of things both great and small, the autonomous, abstract and absolute estimation and worship of things, of institutions, machines and furniture, even of ideas as such, the reversal of the order that they are to serve man and not man to serve them. The Christian cannot take seriously or love or cherish any one of them for itself but only in relation to man and the human. In case of conflict he will always prefer man and the human to machinery and gadgets, and if need be he will joyfully renounce most if not all of the latter. As he stands on the basis of the decision for man taken in Jesus Christ, and can no longer set this aside, in all circumstances man takes precedence of things, and things—however great or even sacred —can never be preferred to man. It is under the sway of this rule that the Christian moves in his individual thoughts and acts and modes of conduct, though here too there are, of course, unfortunate inconsistencies, deviations and contradictions of all kinds which at once avenge themselves, yet in such a way that he does not move elsewhere than in the sphere of this rule, that he cannot possibly contest, weaken, remove or even impede its validity for him even by the most contradictory fulfilment of the wonderful liberation in which he participates in this sphere. In this respect, too, his personal existence has a definite and irreversible orientation. In this " humanistic " respect, too, he is fashioned by and made conformable to that which he is charged to attest, the loving-kindness of God for man (Tit. 3⁴). This is, then, another aspect of the personal liberation which comes to him.

It comes to him (4) in the fact that he no longer has to desire and demand, but he may now receive. As a witness of Jesus Christ the Christian is a model of the man born again to be a pure recipient. He is not liberated as such from vigorous activity and action, but from all the wishful thinking, self-justification and demanding which do not further this but rather poison and impede it. The Christian has neither the right nor the possibility of a claim to become the distinguished man he does become as a witness of Jesus Christ, nor to maintain and assert himself as such. " What hast thou that thou didst not receive ? " (1 Cor. 4⁷). To become and be this man is something which he could and can only receive. And in this receiving without any prior desire or demand, his existence as a Christian corresponds exactly to what he has to attest as such, to the reconciliation of the world to God accomplished in Jesus Christ, to the freedom with which God has justified man before Him and sanctified him for Him in Jesus Christ quite apart from any desire or demand on his part. This original of grace necessarily finds reflection—to his salvation—in the personal life of the Christian. What applies to him as a Christian applies to him also as a man living in time and under its conditions. He has absolutely nothing to postulate. But this means that he is delivered from the torturing necessity of always having to postulate, e.g., the limited success and results of his action, the acknowledgment, encouragement and estimation of his person and efforts by those around, or reasonably consoling prospects for the confused history of humanity in which he is both actively and passively entangled, a relatively clear understanding of his own existence, an inner conquest at least of its limitations and contradictions, an attainment outwardly of something palpable, a measure of assurance in the possession of the promise of an eternal content and future for his life in time, a certain degree of inward cheerfulness. We have intentionally described all these objects of desire and demand as modestly as possible. For the Christian has no claim to them even in this modest form. He does not have to claim them. Even in relation to these modest things he is delivered from the unholy compulsion of having to desire and claim them. This deliverance does not come by the frenzied way of an enjoined or self-imposed asceticism. It results quite simply from the fact that as a Christian he is born again a pure recipient, so that the great and little things, the external and the internal, which may be good but to which he has no right or claim, are accepted by him contentedly in the form in which they come. He may live, not by resignation, but by the assured grace of God to him. He knows as a Christian how it comes about that God's sun, the shining of which none can postulate or claim, rises and breaks through the clouds, how God's grace very simply but very really came to him, how he could very simply but very really become and be the man he is in virtue of it. How could he fail to know this as a man and in relation to his human situation with its needs and difficulties and aspirations? But knowing it, he can take it seriously and abide by it, not folding his hands and idly waiting, but waiting for what comes to him with the hastening, active waiting of the Christian. Yet for all its haste and activity his waiting is without anxious desire. Neither openly nor secretly does he blink after that which he regards as good, without which he cannot be, which he must therefore think to be necessary. Rather, he confidently awaits that which cannot fail to come, that which will be given him as his true good in a familiar or perhaps very unfamiliar form. He would not be a man if he did not know the temptation to fall back into desiring, postulating and claiming, with the consequent non-receiving. And he would not be a sinful man if he did not continually succumb to this temptation. Yet no temptation which comes upon a Christian, nor weakness in face of it, can alter the fact that he has been taken out of an existence of desire and demand and set in one of receiving. He can never free himself from the sway of the rule that he may indeed ask for what he is to receive, but may not demand it, and therefore does not need to do so. The fact that he has been appointed a witness of Jesus Christ, and may exist as such, means that it is written in his heart. In this sense, too, liberation is and always will be afresh his personal share in the great liberation which he is summoned to attest.

His personal liberation consists further (5) in the fact that, borne as with eagles' wings above the abyss, he is delivered from indecision and set in action. His indecision is closely bound up with all the four points under which we have thus far described the sphere from which the Christian is delivered and which he may leave behind. What ought man to do, what can he do, when God and his fellow-man are absent for him, when his existence has no horizon because of his unlimited freedom of will, when he is set under the dominion of things and has to serve them, when he thinks he has to live by the leave and under the compulsion of desire and demand? Under these fatal and mutually interwoven presuppositions, what is he to grasp as the first or most essential or best or even the right thing joyously to decide on and confidently to accomplish? Who is to advise him in this regard? How can he advise himself? Instead of indecision we might speak of confusion, because the man who is unadvised or ill-advised can never refrain from doing something, and by reason of the variety of his undertakings his experimentation necessarily betrays him into hopeless confusion. But the Christian as a witness of Jesus Christ leaves the presuppositions behind, and with them he also leaves the indecision and confusion which they inevitably produce. He does not know, of course, what it would be meaningful or right or even profitable to do on those presuppositions. He knows only that there is no way from them except to indecision and confusion. As one who is called by Jesus Christ, however, he may proceed on the basis of the fact that the presuppositions have been set aside by the Lord who, in calling him, has set him in fellowship with God and his fellow-men, in the reality of the only possibility, in the midst of men and the human, in a pure receiving free from all desire or demand. On this basis, and moving towards the future thus disclosed, he cannot be without advice, nor can he try to help himself by mere experimentation. To be sure, the counsel which he is now given is not a theory of life. It is in his indecision, not when he has left it behind, that man constructs and has theories. Delivered from indecision, the Christian is led at once beyond all theory to practice, to action. By his Lord, and as His servant, he is not called or engaged to, nor empowered for, either theorising or experimenting, but rather obedience. It is always in the most immediate act of obedience that he knows and proves himself to be a man, the new man, who has found what is in fact good advice—the very best. But the most immediate act of obedience is always the step in his service as a witness which is now demanded of him, which may indeed be small, even infinitesimally small, but which has to be taken resolutely. As he takes this step, even in his humanity he definitely moves out of the sphere of confusion, and out of the confusion of his personal life. This may break over him again like a mountainous sea. But if he is engaged in the act of a called witness, he cannot and will not wholly succumb to it. He will emerge again—*non omnis moriar*. In spite of it, he will give what is perhaps a very small, yet also perhaps a greater, demonstration of the Spirit and of power, expressing in lively fashion, even though in narrow limits, that which he has to attest, namely, that God has had mercy on His world and man, and that man has found in Him his Lord. Each act of obedience by the Christian is a modest proof, unequivocal for all its imperfection, of the reality of what he attests. And as he may demonstrate this in his action, he himself lives in the power of the liberation which has come to him too.

This leads us on at once, however, to the further point that the liberation of the Christian consists (6) in the fact that he no longer has to exist in the dialectic of the moral and the immoral, but may now exist in that of forgiveness and gratitude. Or, as we might also put it in the more familiar terms, he no longer has to live under the Law, but may now live under the Gospel. What do we mean by what we have called the Christian's act of obedience? Even as the act of a witness of Jesus Christ it is a human act, and as such, in distinction from the act of the Lord Himself, it is fallible and sinful. To what extent, then, is this act of obedience a good act in the execution of which he may experience, taste, feel and practise liberation? The answer often seems to suggest itself that it is a genuine act of obedience to the extent that, even though it is stained by his immorality, by the virulent self-love and resistance to the claim of his Lord which have not disappeared but still work powerfully even in the Christian, this is counter-balanced, and it is made a good and obedient act, by his morality, by his willingness to satisfy the claim of his Lord which is also at work in him and is superior to his reluctance. Setting aside all other questions or reflections, we advance at once the decisive objection which makes this answer quite impossible. If the act of the Christian were really good and obedient in this sense, it would correspond exactly to what every serious and careful Jew, Hindu, Mohammedan, pedagogue or psychologist usually describes as a good act, but it would not correspond in the very least to the divine act of reconciliation, to the justification and sanctification of the sinner accomplished in Jesus Christ, the knowledge and attestation of which are what makes the Christian a Christian. It would then be quite inexplicable as a specifically Christian act of obedience. Surely the victory of the Spirit over the flesh as described by Paul cannot be equated with the supposed or actual prevailing of human morality over human immorality. Naturally, the Christian did once exist in the latter dialectic, namely, before he was called to be a Christian. And to the degree that he is unfaithful to his vocation he may and will sink back into it and have to live in it, finding the goodness of his action in the fact that his morality does in fact resist his immorality and finally prove superior to it. But on the basis and in the power of his vocation he can no longer regard this as a problem. He cannot think that the character of his act as an act of obedience is any longer dependent on the supposed or real superiority of his good willingness to his evil reluctance. He has been awakened from this fantastic dream. The real dialectic of the new life to which he has been awakened as a servant of the Lord and on the basis of His address is as follows. In all his activity as His witness he may rest on the victory over sin, over the hostility between God and man, which has been already won for him, which is active both in his willingness and his reluctance, and which is the power that dominates him in his totality. He may move forward from the forgiveness which even as a Christian he wholly and utterly needs in his willingness and morality no less than his reluctance and immorality, but in which as a Christian he may participate. And for the fact that he may thus participate he can only be grateful. For it is not he who is the Victor in this conflict ; he must admit that in it he could of himself only be defeated whether in his morality or his immorality. He can be thankful, however, for the fact that he may move forward from the forgiveness of all his sins only by continually taking the next step, by continually moving, irrespective of the relationship of his morality to his immorality, to the next action demanded, trusting not in the immanent goodness of his own action but in the revealed goodness of God in Jesus Christ. Done on the basis of the forgiveness which has come to him, and therefore in gratitude, in the new dialectic unknown even to the best and noblest of Jews and Gentiles, his act is a good act, an act of obedience. It is good and obedient in the fact that it is done in the light of the merciful act of God accomplished and also revealed in Jesus Christ, in the fact that it thus reflects and represents the occurrence which the Christian has to attest to the world both good and bad as its only salvation. In the transition from that false to this true dialectic the Christian may live. Hence from this special standpoint, too, his vocation is his wholly personal liberation.

His liberation is finally (7) a liberation from anxiety to prayer. In prayer he may move towards his Lord and therewith out of anxiety, thus expressing and reflecting that which God has caused to take place for all men and for the whole world in Jesus Christ. Anxiety is the shrinking of man, of the man who is not at peace with God, his neighbour or himself, from the compulsion under which, like one who is buried alive, he has to exist, wills to exist, yet cannot exist. It may take the form of fear of life, of the world or of death, but it is always the same in essence. It may express itself pathologically in sheer panic or very normally in ironic nonchalance, or somewhere between in the familiar alternation between elevation and depression, between partial and passing triumph and partial and passing defeat. It may stimulate to apparently fruitful exertion, or it may result in apparently the severest of overthrows. It may be more grievously felt by some, more lightly by others ; more sincerely admitted by some, anxiously or defiantly silenced and stifled by others. But at some point and in some way this great fear of the necessity or impossibility of existence arises and operates in all men. Even the Christian can know anxiety. Who is so at peace with God, his neighbour and himself that he does not have some measure of anxiety, or is not possessed by it ? And when it does possess a man, even a Christian, it does so totally. Whether he perceives and admits it or not, it embraces, darkens and calls in question not only his natural dispositions but even his Christian faith, love and hope, even his ostensibly assured knowledge, apprehension and appropriation of the revealed truth of God, even his ministry of witness. It makes everything uncertain in the whole circle of his experience, feeling and consideration of the many liberations which have come to him already, and do so continually, from God's great work of liberation and its revelation. It shakes his whole relationship to this work. What then ? And since anxiety in some form lurks in every man, even in the Christian, and snatches at him to possess him, what indeed ? Well, even though the Christian certainly knows anxiety, he can and should always remember that, no matter how powerful its attack, it is limited by the authority and strength of the Lord whom he is summoned to attest. Did not the Lord call him irrespective of the state of his relationship to God, his neighbour and himself, irrespective therefore of his worthiness or ability, and irrespective therefore of the fact that he might know and be possessed by anxiety ? Thus, even though it presses his most inward being, it cannot prevent him from thinking of his Sovereign who is also its own. Again, no matter how great it may be or seem to be, he need not regard it as so great that the lordship of his Lord in face of it can consist only in a static superiority and not one which dynamically sallies out against it at the point where it contains it. He can and should count and build far more on the fact that this Lord of his has in the place of all and therefore in his place, for the sake of all and therefore for his sake, resisted and indeed overcome in His own person the anxiety which threatens all and therefore himself as a consequence of their and his estrangement from God, their neighbours and themselves, disarming it and depriving it of all basis or relevance. At any rate, even though it does still totally embrace, darken and call in question his human and even his Christian being, it cannot prevent him from crying to Him like the sinking Peter :

" Lord, save me." It cannot prevent him from running to Him even in the midst of his anxiety like a child on the dark street running to meet its father as he returns home in the evening. He can and should pray to the God who encounters him in this Lord of his. His vocation is a vocation to prayer : not to particularly pious, fervent or beautiful prayer—the prayer of Peter could not be described as such—but simply to prayer. Nor can any anxiety, however great, impair, arrest or reverse this liberation for crying to God. It is not that by his prayer he liberates himself from anxiety, but that in prayer he confesses the dynamic lordship of God over all things and therefore over anxiety as his particular anxiety, and that he may trust the One who has only to stretch out His hand and grasp him to rescue him from anxiety, and of whom he may expect nothing other than that He wills to do this, and will do it. As the Christian prays, he actually anticipates his own liberation from anxiety even when engulfed by it. Praying to God, he can no longer have it, nor be possessed by it. If only he does not cease to pray, he necessarily breaks free from its embrace, chases its shadow and renders problematical, impotent and insubstantial its own evil problematising of his human and Christian being. In praying he gives evidence already that, though it may have shaken many non-essential and equivocal things, it has never shaken, nor ever will, his Christian existence as such, so that even though he may often despair and stumble he can never be reduced to desperation or completely laid low. As he prays, he comes to himself again in face of anxiety, finding the solid ground and the appointed path of his vocation. It is true enough that as often as I cry and pray all things yield before me. This is not because the Christian cries and prays, nor in the strength in which he does so. It is because he cries and prays to God who is greater than his anxiety and who does not will to leave him in it and will not do so. Liberated for this action he receives and has a real assurance that his liberation from all anxiety in all its forms is in process of accomplishment, so that even in the midst of it he can no longer be one who can and must succumb to it but rather one who strides out of the sphere in which it might become and be triumphant.

We may conclude by clarifying, underlining and confirming certain points as obviously demanded by the series of concrete indications just given.

First, in none of the contexts mentioned can we describe the liberation of the Christian otherwise than as an event which is just commencing and not in any sense complete. It may be that occasionally we have painted a little too strongly the renewal which comes to a man when he is called by Jesus Christ to be His witness. It may be that occasionally we have not painted it strongly enough. We are undoubtedly concerned with a most radical alteration if it is true that the content of Christian witness emerges in the Christian life of him who has to attest it, if it is true that the great history of salvation attested by him, the history of the living Lord Jesus Christ, begins to reflect itself in and impress itself upon his little life-history, which is what happens in his particular liberation. We can never stress too strongly the radical nature of what commences when it is a matter of this liberation of his. On the other hand, we cannot be too careful or modest in what we think and say concerning it, because even in what seem to be the most ideal manifestations our concern is always with the mere commencement. The life of the Christian is a life in transition. The Christian is a pilgrim. Indeed, he is a pilgrim between two worlds. His dark past is behind, his bright future before. The status of the Christian has often and rightly been denoted and described as that of a pilgrim. The alteration which takes place in and characterises him is clear and definite and unequivocal enough in itself. But it is not yet accomplished. It is in process of accomplishment. Its outworking will always have limits which cannot be passed. For there is an eternally irremovable difference between the Lord and His servant, between the incarnate Son of God and the witness taken up into fellowship with Him. Again, the alteration takes place in each and every Christian under certain specific outer and inner, historical, psychical and even somatic preconditions. Again, the time allotted to the Christian, as to all men, is so brief, even though it may exceed the normal portion (Ps. 90[10]). Again, his possibilities are so limited. Above all, even to the very end, whether it comes soon or late, he is not only a brother of Jesus Christ and child of God but also a descendant of Adam and therefore a sinner, a creature engaged in all kinds of transgressions and with every cause, not only to leave it to others to say this, but to " groan within himself " (Rom. 8[23]) for the full revelation of his divine sonship, awaiting the redemption which has not yet come to him in person. Hence the reflection and expression of the great history of the Lord Jesus Christ in the little history of the Christian will always be provisional. What takes place in his life in the form of his being, thinking, speaking, conduct and action can never be more than an *analogatum* which is not only incomplete but which only commences in relation to its *analogans*, and which is quite inadequate to it. It can never be more than a replica which indicates and suggests the original only very distantly and indistinctly. It is still a wonderful distinction and endowment that it is given to the Christian to be " changed into the same image " (2 Cor. 3[18]) and to become the replica of Jesus Christ as His witness. The *status gratiae et salutis*, which is not to be doubted in itself but joyfully demonstrated, will always be even at best and in every stage of life, including the last, a *status nascendi*. There is no biblical precedent for seeing or understanding it otherwise.

Secondly, we have spoken and speak of the liberation of the Christian. But this has exemplary significance. For all that it is so incomplete and provisional, it takes place not only in anticipation of its own awaited completion but also in anticipation of what is truly and finally purposed in what God has done and revealed in Jesus Christ, namely, the liberation of all men. For what else does the God who acts and is manifested in Jesus Christ desire of all men than that they should praise Him, that they should become His witnesses, and that they should thus exist in transition along the lines which we have tried to indicate ? According to the glorious saying in James 1[18], which ought to have been enough in itself to prevent Luther from calling James an " epistle of straw " : " Of his own will begat he us with the word of truth, that we should be a kind of firstfruits of his creatures." This is what Christendom and every Christian is in terms of what he may have before others in his own personal life in virtue of his vocation. He is a firstborn of God's creatures, a first-fruits reaped and gathered from the field of the world. He is truly great as such. But he is no more. The greater thing is that one day we shall hear " every creature which is in heaven, and on the earth, and under the earth, and such as are in the sea, and all that are in them " (Rev. 5[13]), singing the praises of Him that sitteth on the throne and of the Lamb. The Christian has to see himself as the firstfruits of this host. He has not only to know in faith, but actually to perceive, that the creaturely world, that men whose transgression and misery are no more but also no less clearly visible to him than his own, are called and liberated with him in Jesus Christ, who is the Word of God spoken to the whole world. He has to consider the ministry of witness to which creation as a whole is ordained. He has to have in view the joy and peace of the reconciliation which is revealed to it too in its totality, and which is to be realised by it too in the same totality. He has to keep clearly before him the whole harvest. This is the ineffable and incomprehensible goal and end of the ways of God. We can appreciate it only in the light of its beginnings. Nor will it be attained except through many judgments, and finally not in time, but with and in its end as it comes down in the consummated " regeneration " (Mt. 19[28]), in the final manifestation of Jesus Christ. There can be no doubt, however, that in the liberation which comes to the Christian here and now, in that which is personally and speci-fically disclosed and given to him in and with his calling, the Christian himself is not the end of the ways of God but only the preliminary sign of this end. Hence he can see and understand his Christian existence only as a prophetic existence. What will finally be at issue in the coming of Jesus Christ to the last judgment of the quick and the dead, in the resurrection of the flesh and the manifestation of the life everlasting, will be not merely the consummation but the univer-sality of the renewal which has come to him here and now. Hence even on its personal side his Christian existence can be only proleptic and prefigurative. It can be only a first and tiny opening of the doors through which God has ordained that he should go first as a member of the people elected and called to be His witnesses without any merit or co-operation of their own, but through which He has ordained that all creation and not merely he and the other members of this people should finally go. In this respect too, therefore, it becomes the Christian to be modest in relation to his liberation, not only in his dealings with God, but, because with God, with all other men and indeed with the whole of creation.

Thirdly, the liberation of the Christian is a phenomenon which necessarily accompanies his vocation, and therefore an indispensable presupposition of his ministry of witness. Its purpose consists strictly and unequivocally in giving to his voice as a witness of Jesus Christ that ring and note of veracity without which his witness, its inner truth notwithstanding, could not gain credence. Or positively it consists in giving to his witness an orientation to the man himself, to the transition for which the life of the Christian and the lives of others who receive his witness are ordained. The personal liberation of the Christian can and should fit him for this ministry of witness. But it cannot and should not become the content of his witness. The servant has to proclaim his Lord and His work and Word, not himself nor the processes by which he has become His servant nor the privileges which he has come to share as such. He is a *minister Verbi divini*. But the *Verbum divinum* is not the expression of his own experience however great or profound. It underlies this, and thus makes possible the Christian's ministry of witness. But it has its own theme which is independent of and superior to all Christian experience, and this alone can constitute the content of Christian witness. It must be noted rather than proclaimed that liberation has come to him too, and to him specifically. Inevitably this will in fact be perceived in his witness, not merely in the convincing note and ring of his voice as a witness, but also in the fact that it is made explicit that the work of God is the Word of God, and that as the Word of God it is the Word which calls, which summons man personally to the service of God, and which thus liberates him personally, that it is a Word whose truth may be experienced in his own life by each of those to whom it is attested. Witness without this personal edge, relevance and commitment would not be witness to the Word of God, to the living Lord Jesus Christ. This does not mean, however, that the Christian as a witness has to declare or even indicate the fact or extent that the Word of God has become a Word which calls and liberates him personally. It is obviously technically impossible to speak of this with any precision or in a way which will be illuminating and useful to others. He is necessarily hampered by the insurmountable limitations of all and therefore of his own personal liberation. He is also supremely restrained by the concentration demanded of him upon the true and overriding theme of the Word of God which

he can certainly guarantee to those around only by his personal liberation, but from which he can only deflect them if he interests them
additionally, let alone centrally, in his own life-history in its connexion
with the saving history of God, or in this saving history in the form
in which it reflects itself in and impresses itself upon his own life-
history.

One of the many false propositions which Evangelical theology championed
at one of its acknowledged peaks in the 19th century is that I myself as a Christian
am the most proper object of knowledge to myself as a theologian. To be sure,
I myself as a Christian, in my regeneration, conversion and renewal, am an
indispensable instrument to myself as a theologian, as a preacher and pastor,
as the witness which I am called to be like others. But I am not a theme or
object. I am not the object of my knowledge and proclamation, nor of my witness,
in any conceivable form. I and my personal Christianity do not belong to the
kerygma to be declared by me.

I could only obscure the light of the real theme of my witness
if I tried to put myself forward as a transparency, no matter how fine
or profound my experiences. The Christian is to attest the Word
of God with the veracity of one who is himself called and therefore
liberated, and in so doing he is to bring out as such the application
in the calling and liberation of each and every man. But if he is not
to cause offence, but rather to bring honour to God and to be serviceable to Him, he must spare his fellows any direct information concerning himself and the way in which the Word of God has become
significant and effective in his own life in some such application. It
need hardly be indicated against what kind of proclamation this
delimitation is directed.

Fourthly, and finally, we may mention something which brings
us back to the beginning of the sub-section and its relationship to the
whole doctrine of vocation. The liberation of man is undoubtedly
a theme which is particularly interesting and stimulating for Christians,
or for those who take it seriously. The notion seems almost necessarily
to force itself upon them that in their concern with it, at the moment
when at long last the person of the Christian himself, his own individual
life and existence, are discussed and set in the forefront, there is
brought about very possibly a basic crisis in their Christian existence
and situation. Has this liberation really come to us ? Are we engaged
in this transition, in all these transitions ? Are we in fact regenerated,
converted and renewed ? Are we Christians ? The question cuts
deeper and is in fact more menacing than any which might unsettle
a Christian in the light of a philosophy or world-view, or of criticism
of the Bible, dogma or the Church on the basis of such a philosophy or
world-view. For as distinct from such questions it has a personal
application. " Brother, how does it stand with thy heart ? ", as the
ageing Tholuck used to say *privatissime* to his students. And we may
hope that in the course of our present deliberations something of

the urgency of this question will have been perceived. Yet we must not forget that, urgent though the question of the personal liberation of the Christian is, this liberation is only an accompanying theme which even in practice can be rightly understood and grasped only in connexion with the main theme which dominates it. It is not rightly grasped if the answer to this burning question is sought in the form of an expectation, project or attempt in which there is an autonomous concern for the liberation of the Christian and therefore for that transition or those transitions, so that the liberation from isolation to fellowship, from lack of horizon to concentration on the one necessary thing, from anxiety to prayer, and therefore the actualisation of becoming a Christian by personal reception of the *beneficia Christi*, is considered in independence and isolation. There are no legitimate expectations, projects or attempts which can have as their theme the abstract and autonomous actualisation of the personal liberation of the Christian. The attempt to experience and achieve one's regeneration, conversion and renewal in a vacuum can be compared only to the attempt to build in the air rather than on solid ground. No Christian has ever experienced or achieved them in this way. The man is self-deceived who thinks that he can. Where they have been experienced and achieved, where the liberation of the Christian has taken place in all those transitions, it has taken place in the context of his vocation. But this is his vocation to discipleship of Jesus Christ as a disciple and witness. In it he is not in the first instance asked concerning his personal life and existence, as all the biblical examples show. In it he is impressed into service irrespective of his personal qualification, fitness or ability. In it, therefore, the first concern is not with the alteration of his personal life and existence which we have now tried to describe as his liberation. This cannot and will not be left out. His calling to service includes within itself the fact that there is given him the needed renewal by the Lord who calls him, and that he may practise and realise this renewal as His gift. But he can do so only in this context. It cannot, then, be an object of primary interest. Thus the question whether or not a man is a Christian is not put in relation to what he thinks he has experienced as his regeneration, conversion and renewal, and even less in relation to what others think they can know and say concerning his being and action in those transitions and therefore concerning his personal liberation. Thus the really basic crisis of Christian existence comes with the prior question of his call to service and its realisation. Has the living Lord Jesus so encountered me, and is He so present to me, that voluntarily or involuntarily I must recognise, acknowledge and accept in Him the merciful and omnipotent decision of God in relation to his whole creation and universe, the Word of His work in which the totality of all that is distinct from Him, i.e., all things are renewed, and in this first and final Word the factor which is actually and incomparably at work in my own life also ? Do I so recognise and acknowledge and accept it that voluntarily or involuntarily I am claimed by and for this Word, that I cannot therefore keep to myself that which I have received, burying it in my own little corner in creation and the world of humanity, but I am constrained to confess it, declaring, representing and attesting it with my whole being ? Do I believe in such a way that I have no option but also to speak ? Do I stand under that constraint (1 Cor. 9^{16}) under which I must say : " Woe is unto me, if I preach not the Gospel " ? Whether I like it or not, irrespective of who or what or how I am, whether I am worthy or unworthy, skilful or unskilful, am I forced to live for this Word and its declaration to all men ? Is this what I do, or something quite different ? Am I free perhaps to do something quite different ? Is the Word of God which demands my word, whatever the results, an unknown magnitude ? Can I neglect or leave to others what it seems to ask ? Yes or no ? This is the question, the question of primary relevance, the truly provocative question, in relation to my Christian status. It is when this question is raised that I am plunged into the basic crisis in which the Christian always latently finds himself and which from time to time becomes extremely acute for him. It is in and with the answering of this question that there arises necessarily, urgently and unavoidably the question of his personal life and existence as well. If his answer to the first question is in the negative, then he is obviously not called and he cannot seriously raise the second. And all the torture he gives himself in his desire to be converted and become another man is irrelevant and futile. His existence cannot possibly be the theatre of those transitions. But if he can and may and must give a positive answer, if without any merit or co-operation or religious glory of his own it is the case that he cannot evade the living Lord Jesus Christ and His call, but only accept and appropriate them, necessarily taking up the ministry in which He sets him, then for the man who is thus called a positive answer is also spontaneously given to the question of his personal liberation, regeneration, conversion and renewal. In and with his vocation it is settled that his existence becomes a theatre of those transitions. A radical end is put, however, to any self-consciousness in the consideration of this question. All self-torture in relation to his personal transition from darkness to light, from death to life, is made quite impossible and done away by the positive fact that he cannot live his life in the ministry of witness for which he is enabled by his Lord except in this movement and transition. The order of God embraces on the one side the reconciliation of the world to Himself as He has resolved and accomplished it, and the revelation of this work, and on the other his own function as its witness. And in this great order he can and must and will be personally brought to order, finding and working out his own personal salvation on the basis of the fact that it is God who will incidentally but most assuredly and definitely work in him to will and to do of His good-pleasure. Does it not in itself mean a liberation, namely, from a whole sea of unnecessary and dangerous questions and problems and concerns, that the Christian may thus see and understand and experience his personal liberation in this context and order ?

§ 72

THE HOLY SPIRIT AND THE SENDING OF THE
CHRISTIAN COMMUNITY

The Holy Spirit is the enlightening power of the living Lord
Jesus Christ in which He confesses the community called by Him
as His body, i.e., as His own earthly-historical form of existence,
by entrusting to it the ministry of His prophetic Word and therefore
the provisional representation of the calling of all humanity and
indeed of all creatures as it has taken place in Him. He does this
by sending it among the peoples as His own people, ordained
for its part to confess Him before all men, to call them to Him
and thus to make known to the whole world that the covenant
between God and man concluded in Him is the first and final
meaning of its history, and that His future manifestation is already
here and now its great, effective and living hope.

1. THE PEOPLE OF GOD IN WORLD-OCCURRENCE

As in the first and second parts of the doctrine of reconciliation,
so here, and with particular directness in this third part orientated
on the concept of the prophecy of Jesus Christ, we come up against
the reality of the Church, being led unavoidably from κλῆσις to
ἐκκλησία. As we have tried to explain and affirm in the preceding
section, the vocation of man is his vocation to be a Christian. But
we must now continue that vocation to be a Christian means vocation or calling into Christendom or the Church, i.e., into the living
community of the living Lord Jesus Christ. It is impossible to be
called first into the Church, and then, in and by the Church, to be a
Christian. On the other hand, it is equally impossible to be called
to be a Christian and then subsequently to be called, or possibly not
to be called, into the Church. As Christian existence is not a mere
complement of existence in the Church, so existence in the Church
is not a mere complement of Christian existence.

Our present emphasis is on the latter point. From the very
outset Jesus Christ did not envisage individual followers, disciples
and witnesses but a plurality of such united by Him both with Himself
and with one another. To be sure, He was thinking in terms of
individuals and not of an anonymous number, collection, conglomera-
tion or collective. But His purpose in relation to the individual
was not just to set him in a kind of uni-dimensional relationship to

Himself. It was to unite him both with Himself and also, if in a very different sense and under very different conditions, with the other individuals whom He has called, and wills to call, and will call. " All ye are brethren " (Mt. 23⁸). This does not mean, as it has often been understood and depicted in recent years, that a social impulse derived from their common situation, faith and community sense brings Christians together and makes them brothers. Other religious unions and fellowships of all kinds may arise in this way. And the strength of the social impulse which constitutes them is the more or less sure guarantee of their continuation. But Christianity, the community of Jesus Christ, neither arises nor continues in this way. It does not rest on the natural need of union and co-operation felt by those who share a common aim. As the individual himself does not come to Jesus Christ and thus become a Christian under the impulsion and in the power of his religious and moral disposition, but only in virtue of the fact that Jesus Christ calls him and thus unites him with Himself, so it is Jesus Christ Himself, not in a second but in and with the first calling of the individual, who calls these individuals in their plurality and unites them with one another. He would not be who He is if in the truth and power of His one Word He did not do both these things, and therefore the second in and with the first. He is the man in whose person God has, of course, elected and loved from all eternity the wider circle of humanity as a whole, but also, with a view to this wider circle, the narrower circle of a special race, of His own community within humanity. He is the man who on this account has offered Himself first for this community of His (Eph. 5²⁵). If this man for His part calls certain men to be His disciples and witnesses, and therefore Christians, in so doing, and always with a view to all humanity, he constitutes them a special people. Hence He does not put them in a place which is occupied in immediate proximity to Himself but otherwise empty. He sets them among and alongside others who are also His own and therefore with Him in this special sense. He places them in His community. There is no *vocatio*, and therefore no *unio cum Christo*, which does not as such lead directly into the communion of saints, i.e., the *communio vocatorum*. The same truth emerges when we think of the concrete sense in which Jesus Christ calls each individual and therefore leads him to *unio cum ipso*. He wills to have him as His witness, and appoints him such. Whatever his personal experience may be in this respect, in the personal liberation which comes to him the Christian will certainly find that at particular points on his way he is brought into touch with some and perhaps many of the called, that he finds in them his brothers, that he is encouraged and challenged by them, and that he must proceed in company with them. But in his ministry of witness—and it is this essentially which makes him a Christian—he is from the very outset, by his very ordination to it, united not only with some or many, but—whether or not he knows them and their particular situation—with all those who are charged with this ministry. He is united to them by the simple fact that, since there is only one work as the Word of God and only one Mediator between God and man self-declared in His activity, the content of his witness cannot be other than that of theirs, nor the content of theirs other than that of his. He and they may have received, and may take up and discharge, their ministry of witness in very different ways. But they cannot possibly be apart in this ministry. They cannot be monads or private disciples operating in their own strength. They are always linked in a common and therefore a mutual responsibility accepted and borne together. They are always members of the same distinctive people, set in the sphere of the one brotherhood constituted by their Teacher, in the one community founded and maintained by Him as the Lord who calls them all.

In the New Testament Gospels there is no passage which refers directly and explicitly to the foundation or establishment of the ἐκκλησία by Jesus of Nazareth. What are we to make of this fact ? One might suppose that if there had been an event of this kind in the course of the history of Jesus it would have been important enough to the community living by the tradition of this history to find a distinctive and even, it might be thought, a prominent place in the Gospel records. And if it was really important or even indispensable for the New Testament community to look back on such an event, it is surely a matter for surprise that it never seems to have struck anyone to have enriched the tradition by a corresponding aetiological narrative throwing light on the question of the origin of the community. But in fact there is not to be found in the context of the occurrence from which the New Testament tradition derives and which it records any foundation or establishment of the community corresponding, e.g., to the institution of the Lord's Supper, nor did the community which lives by this tradition see any lacuna at this point nor think it necessary to know of such an event and therefore to add to the evangelical narrative in this respect.

What are we to conclude from this fact ? Are we to accept the theory which has sometimes been advanced, and found no little support, that the reason why no basic connexion is to be found in the texts between the existence of the Jesus of the Gospel tradition and the existence of a Christian community is the very simple one that there never was any such connexion ? Is it the case that the self-declaration of Jesus, which is identical with His proclamation of the kingdom of God drawn near, has nothing whatever to do with the rise of the Church, nor *vice versa* ? Is the story of Jesus quite distinct from that of the growth of His community, belonging to a completely different level and demanding independent study and evaluation ? It is surely obvious that those who try to work with this theory fall into the old error of being unable, and perhaps unwilling, to see the wood for the trees.

The reason why the establishment of the community by Jesus Himself could not emerge as a definite and distinctive event in the Gospel tradition is rather that this is the theme of the whole Gospel narrative as an account of Jesus, the whole of the Gospel narrative as an account of Jesus necessarily being an account of the birth of the Christian community, of the development, corresponding to and consummating the unification of the twelve tribes of Israel in the exodus from Egypt, of the people of God of the last time which has been inaugurated with the coming of Jesus Christ. We can, of course, point also to more detailed aspects of this happening, i.e., to particular elements in the texts which attest this happening where the birth of the community seems to be sketched in fairly clear outline. For instance, when Jesus calls His first disciple He at once adds another and then more still. Again, we are told of the appointment of twelve messengers (Mk. 3[14f.]) in an account which recalls and is surely connected with the beginning of the history of Israel. Again, there is the mission of the twelve (Mt. 10[5f.]). There is also the mission of the seventy (Lk. 10[1f.]). There are also the well-known words to Peter in Mt. 16[17f.]. There are the beatitudes at the beginning of the Sermon on the Mount (Mt. 5[3f.]). There is the institution of the Lord's Supper, or the feet-washing which replaces it in Jn. 13[1f.] There is the missionary command of the Resurrected, and finally the outpouring of the Holy Spirit at Pentecost (Ac. 2[1f.]). But why should we pick out these passages, or give them more emphasis than others ? On due reflection are we not forced to say that, while we cannot use any single text as a *locus classicus*, all of them in different ways speak of the origin of the Christian community as the people of God of the last time, and indeed of its origin in the will of Jesus and His act of vocation ? Indeed, do we not have to go further and say that the whole Gospel record at least from the baptism of Jesus in the Jordan to the story of Pentecost is implicitly also an account of the origin of this people, of its beginning in the words and acts of Jesus, of its gathering, maintaining, upbuilding, ordering and sending by Him ? It is not for nothing that the oldest history of the community finds unmistakeable reflection in the history of Jesus Himself as recorded in the Gospels, so that it is quite impossible to keep the two histories apart, to find a Jesus who prior to and apart from the community exists by His Word in the community, to study, portray and evaluate this Jesus in isolation, and thus to try to write first a life of Jesus and only then a history of the primitive Church. Everywhere, as we are forced to say, the texts themselves speak of a Jesus who founds His community and of the community founded by Him. And it is for this very reason that there can be no special account of this foundation. It is for this reason that there can be no point in trying to find such an account, or, if no such account is found, in adopting the desperate hypothesis that there was once a history of Jesus which was not also as such the history of the foundation of His community by His call.

The phenomenon and problem, the reality of the Church concerns us in this third part of the doctrine of reconciliation from the particular standpoint of its mission or sending, i.e., as the " apostolic " Church.

In this first and basic sub-section, we shall consider first, in preliminary isolation from its function, the sheer fact of its existence as the people of God in world-occurrence. There co-exists with it as this people, and *vice versa*, the whole cosmos both in its wider sense as the cosmos of all the reality distinct from God and created and ruled by Him, and also in its narrower and concrete sense as the cosmos of men and humanity. Its history as it takes place is surrounded by the history of the cosmos, and everywhere affected and in part determined by it. Conversely, it is not without significance for the cosmos and its history that its own history takes place.

Three questions demand our attention : 1. What is, from this standpoint, that which takes place without in its historical environment ? 2. How should it see and understand itself in this environment ? and 3. How does it live and persist in this environment ? These are the questions which we must first answer in preparation for the true theme of the section, namely, the question of the task and function of the community in its relation to the cosmos, or the question of its sending.

In the first instance, then, we have to consider theologically the world-occurrence as such within which and surrounded by which the community has its own being. What takes place in this other history which accompanies the community of Jesus Christ in its whole course, which partly determines it, and in the course of which it constantly participates ? What is meant by the term " world history " ?

It is expressly presupposed that for us there can be no question of any other than a theological consideration. It might well be argued that all things considered and in the last resort this is true for others as well. For the moment, however, we are content to maintain that for us, along the lines of discussion and investigation which we have taken up and pursued in responsibility to the Word of God revealed to the Church in the witness of Holy Scripture, and to be attested by it, there cannot possibly be any other. Others who on the basis of different assumptions may think that they should accept different responsibilities must look to themselves. Those who know who is the καλῶν and what the κλῆσις and ἐκκλησία, the latter being directly established by the former, cannot possibly believe that they are free according to their own wisdom or preference to select the standpoint from which to pose and answer the question of world-occurrence around them. Thus, even while we recognise and presuppose that the community created by the call of Jesus Christ exists in world-occurrence and in constant connexion with it, we cannot attempt to sketch a world-view or philosophy from some point discovered in the environment of the Christian community and to the exclusion of the prophetic witness entrusted to it, making this, and therefore world-occurrence itself, the basis of our understanding and interpretation. There are, of course, many points from which this can be done. But for the adoption of which of them are there more than hypothetical reasons ? For the adoption of which of them is there any necessity or indisputable authorisation ? And if we do adopt one or another of them, how can we avoid—for no man can serve two masters even in the realm of thought—an ultimate understanding and interpretation of the community within world-occurrence from this alien standpoint rather than in the light of its vocation ? If we take seriously its basis in vocation, and therefore take seriously the Lord who calls it, then we must renounce all attempts to think from other standpoints, whether in relation to the community itself or to the world-occurrence around it. Our only option is truly to see and understand world-occurrence as the environment of the people of God and its history, recognising that it cannot be understood or interpreted in terms of itself but only of the community, or more strictly of its vocation, or more strictly still of the Lord who calls it and of the prophetic witness which He has entrusted to it, but recognising also that when it is understood in this way it is seen for what it really is, in its truth and actuality.

This obviously means, however, that we must begin by stating that in the voice of the Lord who calls it the community of Jesus Christ does not perceive the voice of any lord but the voice of the Lord of all lords, of the absolute Lord, of the Lord of all men and all things. Nor does it hear merely *a* word, but *the* Word, the Word which was in the beginning with God, and which was God (Jn. 1¹), the Word which was spoken in the depths of time from the height of eternity, the Word of God which cannot be compared with any other because it is the Alpha and Omega which are sought and intended in all words, which are lacking in all, but which are also the mystery and promise behind and above and before them all. What is heard by it distinguishes its hearing from that of the human peoples around. The One who precedes it and whom it follows, who is present and acts among it as its Head in the power of His Holy Spirit, is seated " on the right hand of God the Father Almighty." But in relation to the cosmos around it and not yet enlightened by His Word, this means that it does not belong to a man, or to itself, or to any other lord, but that in its own perverted way it is unconditionally the property of the God who makes covenant with man in Jesus Christ and continually reveals Himself in Him as the One who does so. Even the world without, which seems to be and is so very different, belongs to Him, the King of Israel. As such He is its King too. To Him it owes its existence and nature. Without Him it would not be what it is, nor how it is. Indeed, without Him it would not be at all. He has created it too. It, too, is wholly and utterly from Him and by Him and to Him (Rom. 11³⁶). And this means further that what takes place without in the cosmos in distinction from the history of the community of Jesus Christ is not occurrence which is alien to this one God, which evades or escapes the will of His love, the omnipotence of His mercy and forbearance, or His gracious over-ruling, which is finally and properly directed by man or by itself or by some other lord. To be sure, it is not as such Christ-occurrence, and therefore it is not the history of salvation, nor the prophecy of Christ, nor the revelation of salvation, which tread their own path within it in supreme actuality yet also in supreme concealment. And there can be no doubt that world history as such contains within itself a whole sinister stream of the history and revelation of the very opposite of salvation. It is thus distinct enough from the history from which the Christian community derives, and therefore from the history of this community. On the other hand, the community of Jesus Christ has a very inadequate view of its Lord, the King of Israel who is also the King of the world, if it is not prepared to recognise that even world-occurrence outside takes place in His sphere and under His governance, or if it tries to imagine that in this occurrence we are concerned either with no God at all, or with another God, or with another will of the one God different from His gracious will demonstrated in Jesus Christ, and therefore with another kingdom on the left hand directed by God to another end and in another spirit. That which really takes place on the left hand of God, not outside but in hostility and opposition to His will, can only be nothingness and the devil. But on the right hand with which He masters and beats back the devil, the principle of His positive will is Jesus Christ alone, the one Word by which He has created, and preserves, accompanies and overrules in its course, all the reality distinct from Himself. Even in relation to what takes place without, to the history of the cosmos as it is distinct but not separate from the history of the community of Jesus Christ, there can thus be no question of the real sway of any principle independent of the God who acts and is revealed in Jesus Christ, whether it be the autonomous rule of man, the overruling of fate or chance or of a freedom or necessity immanent in world-occurrence, or the control of any of the powers, forces or divinities which continually appear with their demands for fear, love, trust, and obedience. The one God who acts and declares Himself in Jesus Christ is the One who rules and holds the sceptre—He and He alone. His will and action precede cosmic occurrence, and it can only follow. His will and action accompany it, so that in neither little things nor great, neither as a whole nor in detail, neither in its relative necessity nor relative contingency, neither in its coming nor going, neither in its possibilities nor its actualisations and fulfilments, can it take place without Him. His will and action determine its future, so that it can take place only with a view to Him and the goal which He has set, the eyes of all waiting upon Him alone that He may give them their meat in due season (Ps. 104[27]).

To be sure, the history which takes place there without is astonishingly different. It is different in its darkness in respect of the reconciliation and relationship between God and man accomplished for the whole world and for all men. It is different in its concealment of its own true basis, meaning and goal. It is different because it does not yet disclose either a basic, radical and thoroughgoing contradiction of man's contradiction of his Creator, his neighbour or himself, nor a basic, radical and concrete hope. It is different because in it the creature, left to itself, imprisoned in its good and bad dreams and illusions, involved in stolid quiescence or disturbing unrest, implicated in the most disruptive conflict with itself and with others, seems to plunge headlong to its own destruction. It seems to do so, yet it is actually held and restrained in its fall. It is not yet left to itself, for God has not let go of it. It is not yet allowed to pursue its contradiction to the bitter end. As its dreams and illusions testify, it exists as if there were still some hope for it. Plainly God has not yet turned away His face from it, nor withdrawn His hand. Even this other history still takes place under His fatherly providence. What takes place cannot be a wholly and absolutely different history. The community would be guilty of a lack of faith and discernment if it were seriously to see and understand world history as secular or profane history. In so doing it would in fact concede to this history the right to see and understand itself as such, and therefore as a history which is an independent and very different history in relation to the history of salvation and the Church. If it is not to bear some of the responsibility for its corruption, it cannot possibly allow it any such independence. The thought of God's royal lordship and fatherly providence overruling even world-occurrence must be the first and decisive step of all Christian thinking about world-occurrence, the positive sign before the bracket of whatever else may have to be considered, the point to which the community of Jesus Christ will always have good reason to return. It proves unfaithful at the very first step to itself, i.e., to its calling and the Lord who calls it, if it tries to see things otherwise.

The doctrine *De providentia* which we have briefly sketched in this way, and which found more explicit development in *C.D.*, III, 3 § 48–49, has nothing whatever to do with an optimistic evaluation of the world. In the sense indicated it follows very soberly from the necessity of understanding the first article of the creed in the light of the second, which refers in closing to the *sessio Filii ad dexteram Patris omnipotentis.*

We have a concrete example of this necessity, and therefore of the meaning of our statement concerning the providence of God overruling world history, in the distinctive Old Testament picture of the situation and role of the nations co-existing with Israel as the one people of God. The theme of the Old Testament is not the general history even of Israel as a spatial and temporal sphere. It is its history as constituted by the specific acts and revelations of its God, yet this in all its particularity as occurrence in and with the world-occurrence around it. Though significantly marked off, it is not separated from the latter. It is rather caught up in relationship and interaction with it as the inner circle in an outer which, though it never acquires any thematic significance of its own, is present with the inner from the very first, and continually demands notice, not merely as the background or setting, but as a factor which for all its difference belongs to the history of Israel, which stands out in it, and in which it for its part also stands out.

It is not with the calling of Abraham and therefore the formation of the inner circle, but long before in the wider circle that we have the beginning of the Old Testament narrative, namely, with the primitive sagas, which are not, of course, neutral, but which are unmistakeably understood and fashioned in retrospect of the guidance and experience of Israel and therefore in the light of the inner circle : the sagas which tell of the beginning of the cosmos, of the creation of heaven and earth and all creatures by the God who is called Elohim in Gen. 1 and Yahweh in Gen. 2 and who is identical with the covenant God of the patriarchs, Moses, David and all the prophets ; the sagas which speak of the very first men, of their determination by the gracious command of God, of their catastrophic fall, of the first representatives and generations of their progeny, of their universal corruption, of their initial destruction, of the preservation of a remnant from which there develops and spreads a second humanity placed by the same God under the promise of a second covenant ; and finally the sagas which narrate the new Titanism of this second humanity ; the ensuing destruction of its unity hitherto maintained by means of a common speech, and the confusion and scattering of the nations as sealed by the loss of this unity. Now in what is recounted in the first eleven chapters of the Bible we do not yet have either the history or revelation of salvation. We do not yet see to what general occurrence will lead or how it will end. We obviously still find ourselves in the outer circle where good and evil, and more evil than good, are engaged in constant alternation and interfusion. But is it true that we are only in this outer circle ? The remarkable thing about this outer circle is that it seems to presuppose and to move towards an inner of which there is as yet no trace, anticipating and prefiguring it in features which it would be difficult to mistake. The remarkable thing is that even here, if only diffusely and in the forms, well-known among many peoples, of a world of saga not lacking in mythical elements, we seem to be concerned with God and men, with the revolt of men against God and their mutual conflict, with the wrath and judgment of God, but also with His grace and faithfulness and covenant. These chapters cannot possibly be read merely as secular history. How, then, are they to be read ? Obviously as world history which already has its future, even though concealed as yet from itself, in the history and revelation of salvation commencing within it, and which is already stamped and determined by this future, so that in spite of its own lack of wisdom it can and must be prophecy in virtue of the wisdom of God which rules it. At the end of the eleven chapters the stream of its presentation then becomes all at once noticeably narrower. The one descendant of Noah, i.e., Shem, comes prominently into the foreground, and then finally, as a descendant of one of the lines of this family, the one man Abram is introduced, and with his history there comes to light the inner circle of the history of God with His elect people and the history of this people with its God, i.e., the special history and revelation of salvation as the sphere which will now form the centre of the whole presentation. Now obviously world history will not be lost to view as one of the outer circles surrounding the inner. It is self-evidently not the intention of the transition from Gen. 11 to 12 that there should be no more overruling of God, of the one true God Yahweh-Elohim. On the contrary, in the broad and unmistakeable canvas of the first chapters of the Old Testament, and therefore of the whole Bible, it is brought before us in typical fashion that the one true God of the covenant was and is and will be the Lord of this history which is different and yet not entirely so. And the Old Testament narrative which follows takes gcod care that the people of God does not lose sight of this environment and of God as its Lord and Ruler.

Immediately after the calling of Abram it is said that in him " shall all the families of the earth be blessed " (Gen. 12³). And then in Gen. 16¹f. and 17²³f. it is emphasised that even Ishmael, " a wild man " whose hand is " against every man, and every man's hand against him," was also the son, and indeed the elder though not the promised son, of Abraham, and that as such he was to be circumcised and to enjoy special divine protection. Again, in Gen. 19³⁷f. we have a rather dubious derivation of the neighbouring and later very hostile peoples of Moab and Ammon from Lot, and therefore from a near relative of Abraham. And finally in Gen. 33 the dispute between Jacob and his elder brother Esau, who in many ways resembles Ishmael, ends in a reconciliation, so that in Gen. 36 the race of Edom, later to be another unpleasant neighbour of Israel, is given a place in the account of the patriarchs. In this prelude to the true history of Israel, in which the patriarchs are already present, even if only as strangers, in the land of Canaan as the land promised to Abraham when he was called out of Chaldaea, it is thus plain that those who are without, the men who surround Abraham, Isaac and Jacob, are certainly men of different and strange peoples which are not elected and called, that they do not belong to the people of God with which we are concerned in the patriarchs, yet that they are not completely cut off from this people, but that they are conjoined with it, so that in their own manner and place they, too, are in the sphere and hand of its God as the one God.

The immediate worldly counterpart to the people of God, related to it from the time of Noah and yet more sharply differentiated from it, is naturally Egypt. This is briefly mentioned in the story of Abraham (Gen. 12¹⁰f.). It then forms the sphere in which Joseph, hated and betrayed by his brethren, rises to great dignity and power. It is the place where Jacob and his other sons find refuge in the hour of need, but where another Pharaoh who " knew not Joseph " (Ex. 1⁸), who not unjustifiably feared that this family which had now become a nation would gain control, and who could not exterminate them, reduced them to slavery. It is finally the territory from which, when this Pharaoh is overtaken by the judgment of God, the people is led by Moses into the wilderness, and then through the wilderness to possession of the land promised to the fathers. The native Canaanites, the Midianites and other border peoples in the East and the Philistines in the West then become their often mortally dangerous neighbours up to the time of the kings. And even well on into the time of the great prophets Egypt still constitutes the great southern horizon of their history, while Syria first forms the northern horizon, and then the nations of Mesopotamia when their growing power comes to overshadow and constrict all other peoples. Under the pressure of these nations we first see Israel and then Judah collapse. The greater part of the people of God loses its land for good. The smaller part returns under Persian suzerainty, and is then tossed like a ball from the hands of one nation to another until at last it loses the tiny fragments of independent existence in its futile conflict with Rome in A.D. 70, being then apparently lost in the nations around in total self-alienation. Yet only apparently, for in fact no nation in world history, when it has come to the end of its independent existence, has been so little assimilated, or has been able so mysteriously and yet so genuinely and distinctly and continuously to maintain its identity in the sea of surrounding, overflowing and absorbing alien peoples, of *goyim* old and new with their own histories and languages and cultures, as has the people of Abraham, Isaac and Jacob. And it may well be— indeed, according to current events there are good grounds for thinking—that with or without the new state of Israel this people will outlast the modern powers no less radically that it has outlasted the greater and smaller powers of antiquity and the Middle Ages, in spite of all that has been done to it. In our own time the people of the Old Testament has certainly outlived a " thousand-year " Reich which was set up in conscious opposition to it. It seems as though world history is ordained always to be the framework for the history of this people.

What does the Old Testament know and say of these nations around Israel ? This question is to be answered from two standpoints, one subordinate and pro- visional which stands in the foreground, and one primary and definitive which stands in the background.

The first proposition which we are forced to make is to the simple effect that the nations around Israel interest the Old Testament only in this capacity, i.e., in their relation to the existence and history of Israel. It is only very incidentally and indirectly, and with a very foreshortened perspective, that we learn anything concerning the Orient of that time or the history, culture and religion of other nations. They are always in the picture, but only to the extent that they impinge on Israel in some way. We are then led to the further proposition that their contact with Israel always means for the latter, according to the view and presentation of the Old Testament, either temptation or threat or both together : temptation particularly to religious but also to practical adjustment and relativisa- tion, and therefore to apostasy from the covenant God and disobedience to His commandments ; and the threat of physical robbery, violence, suppression and extermination. Apart from a single instance, there are only individual exceptions to this rule, as, for example, Melchizedek, King of Salem, who is introduced as a " priest of the most high God " and who brought forth bread and wine to Abraham (Gen. 14¹⁷ᶠ·), Abimelech, King of Gerar, who is shown by his dealings with Abraham to be a God-fearing and upright man (Gen. 20¹ᶠ·), and who later concluded a compact with Isaac (Gen. 26²⁶ᶠ·), Jethro, the wise Midianite father- in-law of Moses (Ex. 2¹⁶ᶠ, 3¹, 18¹ᶠ·), the Moabite Balaam, who was supposed to curse Israel, and wished to do so, but could only bless (Nu. 22–24), the Canaanite harlot Rahab who was so helpful to the spies (Jos. 2[1-20]), the Moabitess Ruth, who was so important to the Old Testament tradition as the great-grandmother of David that a whole book was devoted to her history, the Kenite Jael, who served the cause of Israel so well with her underhand trick (Jud. 4[17f.]), King Hiram of Tyre, who helped Solomon to build the temple (1 K. 5[15f.]), the Queen of Sheba, who visited Solomon that she might be personally convinced of his wisdom and riches (1 K. 10[1f.]), Naaman, the Syrian general, who when he was healed of leprosy by Elisha recognised and confessed " that there is no God in all the earth, but in Israel " (2 K. 5[15]), and the Persian king Cyrus as presented in Deutero-Isaiah. Only in one instance, namely, the account of the effect of Jonah's preaching in Nineveh (3[5f.]), do we read of the repentance, accepted by God, of a whole foreign nation. For all that there is this exception, the first and decisive impression which we gain of the nations surrounding Israel from our reading of the Old Testament is the negative one of an evil and dangerous world in face of whose enticements Israel is sometimes strong but more often weak and in the long run extremely weak, and in face of whose physical assaults it is often victorious, and even gloriously so at the great points in its history, but more often defeated, and in the end catastrophically overthrown.

But this is not the end of the matter as the Old Testament sees and states it. It may seem to catch our attention, since it stands in the foreground, but it is only subordinate and provisional. And in relation to the primary and definitive teaching which stands in the background the exceptions mentioned have no doubt a greater significance than that of breaches which establish the rule. It is indeed the case, and cannot be otherwise, that it is only in co-existence with the people of God, and not as the subject of independent or neutral interest, that the nations appear on the canvas of the Old Testament. But the meaning of this co-existence of theirs is not by a long way exhausted in what they mean or do not mean for the people as such. For what is this people itself apart from what it is only by the electing grace and in the service of its God ? The decisive point for the nations, too, is what the same God is also for them, namely, that they, too, in their critical function in relation to His people are not governed and directed by themselves or by fate or chance, but, unknown to themselves yet very really, by this God whose will ordains in relation to them too. It is He who makes a place for His people among them. It is He who conducts the wars of this people and gives it peace. It is He who makes these nations its neighbours to test it by their nature and corruption. It is He who causes it to experience their power and vitality the more compellingly to remind them of and to pledge them to Himself. It is He who causes it now to conquer and triumph, now to be defeated and despoiled. It is He who works and speaks in the weakness and strength of these peoples in relation to it. It is His cause which is at issue in what they have to do and suffer. It is He who introduces Pharaoh and the potentates of Assyria, Babylon and Persia. It is He who uses them either to execute His judgments, or, as in the case of Cyrus, as the instruments of His faithfulness and goodness. It is He, too, who assigns limits to their action. It is He who causes their empires to rise and flourish and fall. It is He who is also their Judge, and acts towards them as such. It is He who destroys every re-current manifestation of a competition of their will, ability and achievement with His own. It is He, and He alone, who is truly great in them. Their own gods do not count at all beside Him. Even these worldly nations exist in fact by Him and for Him, for that which He Himself and not His people wills and establishes in the history of His people. They too, just as they are, tempting and menacing to His people, are in His hand. The fact that this is so is the bracket within which there develops all that takes place between Himself and His people, including the apostasy which they cause, the destruction which they bring about, and the preservation apart from independent existence which they cannot prevent. That God is their Creator, Lord and Ruler too is the first and final meaning of their co-existence with His people, binding them to this people for all that they are so different, strange and hostile. And this is what the Old Testament really has to see and state concerning them in harmony with its first eleven chapters.

This is the basis of the many antitheses in the Old Testament in which it speaks at once of the lordship of God over His own people and yet also over all peoples, of the latter because of the former, or *vice versa*. " Ye shall be a peculiar treasure unto me above all people : for all the earth is mine " (Ex. 19⁵). Or in the Song of Moses : " When the Most High divided to the nations their inheritance, when he separated the sons of Adam, he set the bounds of the people. . . . For the Lord's portion is his people ; Jacob is the lot of his inheritance " (Deut. 32⁸ᶠ·). Or at the beginning of Ps. 24 : " The earth is the Lord's, and the fulness thereof ; the world, and they that dwell therein " (v. 1), which is followed by the more specific question : " Who shall ascend into the hill of the Lord ? " (v. 3), and then by the answer : " This is the generation of them that seek him, of them that seek thy face, O Jacob " (v. 6), and finally, in what are obviously more universal terms, by the great hymn concerning the entry of the Lord of glory through the everlasting gates which open up before Him (v. 7 f.). Or again in Ps. 148, where all creation is summoned to the praise of Yahweh, and then expressly towards the end : " Kings of the earth, and all people ; princes, and all judges of the earth. . . . Let them praise the name of the Lord : for his name alone is excellent ; his glory is above the earth and the heaven " ; but then the concluding verse goes on to say : " He also exalteth the horn of his people, the praise of all his saints ; even of the children of Israel, a people near unto him." Or in a particularly pregnant way in Ps. 117¹⁻² : " O praise the Lord, all ye nations : praise him, all ye people. For his merciful kindness is great toward us : and the truth of the Lord endureth for ever." Or in Ps. 67, where we can glimpse the teleology of this juxtaposition : " God be merciful unto us, and bless us ; and cause his face to shine upon us ; that thy way may be known upon earth, thy saving health among all nations. Let the people praise thee, O God ; let all the people praise thee. O let the nations be glad and sing for joy : for thou shalt judge the people righteously, and govern the nations upon earth (vv. 1–4). . . . God shall bless us ; and all the ends of the earth shall fear him " (v. 7). Nor should we overlook the fact that behind the nations, and constituting as it were a third and outermost circle, all creaturely and cosmic occurrence is seen in the same way and set in the light of the same juxtaposition. We may again refer to Ps. 148, but also to Deut. 10¹⁴ᶠ· : " Behold, the heaven and the heaven of heavens is the Lord's thy God, the earth also, with all that therein is. Only the Lord had a delight in thy fathers to love them, and he chose their seed after them, even you above all people, as it is this day." We are also reminded of Ps. 19, in which verses 1–6 speak of the heavens and the sun declaring themselves and therefore the glory of God, but there then follows a magnifying of the Law of Yahweh, with a final prayer for His forgiveness and direction. In Ps. 147, too, the praise of God as the Lord of all nature is everywhere interwoven inextricably with His praise as the Deliverer of Jerusalem. To be sure, these statements are not made in terms of historical analysis, but from an eschatological standpoint. Yet all of them look through and beyond the present aspects of world-occurrence to their future and determination which are their true meaning and purpose. And eschatological means supremely realistic. From the standpoint of the history of God with Israel attested in the Old Testament, world-occurrence has not yet to acquire, but already has, this future and determination, and with it its true essence, contradicting, transcending and integrating its present aspect. It has been summoned by God, and concretely by the existence of Israel as His people, to add its voice to Israel's praise of God. This is its reality. God has created the nations (Ps. 86⁹). In fact He is already their King (Ps. 47⁸). Hence their raging against His people is already futile (Ps. 2¹). His eyes are already upon them (Ps. 66⁷). This is the decisive thing which the Old Testament sees and says concerning them in the light of its own theme and centre.

Recollection of God's rule is certainly the first, decisive and comprehensive thing which we have to say and continually to recall theologically in relation to world history. But it cannot be the only thing. *Hominum confusione et Dei providentia regitur.* If the *confusio hominum* does not escape the *providentia Dei*, but is subject to it, and in the long run is completely impotent and subordinate in relation to it, yet as *confusio* it is not grounded in it, nor in its corruption can it be deduced from it. In a way which is most unsettling, it stands before us as an obscurely and even absurdly distinctive reality which we can neither overlook nor deny as such, but which we must clearly grasp in all its inexplicability, because otherwise all consideration *sub specie aeternitatis* would show a fatal inclination in the direction of mere optimism. Superficially perhaps, but very directly, the community of Jesus Christ has to do with this distinctive reality of the *confusio hominum*, even though it recognises and confesses God as the Lord of all men and all things, and, come what may, relies on the power and wisdom of His governance. Whatever may be the significance of the fact, it is closely bound up with the great and small and smallest world events directed by this *confusio hominum*. This is the aspect under which it presents itself from day to day and from century to century. It is the power of whose apparently unlimited play it must be conscious in every sphere of the human life around and whose pressure it has always and in continually new forms to detect. And it will be constantly tempted to wonder whether after all the *confusio hominum*, perhaps against the background of what is if possible an even more dreadful cosmic disorder, is not merely the reality but the inner truth of world-occurrence, with which it has to reckon as the final word in the matter, to which it has to return, and in the light of which it has thus to understand and direct itself. It has also to be noted that even on this view the community has always been able to create and maintain for itself a peculiar inner life, as it has often enough done on the assumption of this understanding. But if it does, the theme of the present section is meaningless from the very outset. There can be no serious question of a " sending " of the community into the world and to the world. Its task is simply to attest its obvious futility and to proclaim its sure and certain destruction. As the community of those to whom Jesus Christ has entrusted the word of reconciliation, it cannot possibly understand itself in this way. Hence it cannot possibly accept either human confusion or a cosmic confusion perhaps concealed behind it as the final meaning of world-occurrence. The temptation in this direction is so great and pressing, however, that we are surely obliged at least to consider the underlying facts of the situation.

We cannot fail to see or realise that humanity appears strangely lost in its history. The community can make no mistake : " The whole world lieth in wickedness " (1 Jn. 5^{19}). It is indeed true that in the light of the prophetic witness entrusted to it its history has always had this aspect, and always will, in the continuity of its situations and destinies, of its commissions and omissions, in the repetitions and cycles which are so much more important in its main line of forms and developments than the occasional progress which is also seen. What has really happened, and does happen, in what is called world history ?

What has really happened, and does happen, for example, in the sequence of the different kingdoms of Egypt, or the dynasties of ancient China, or the monarchies of the Book of Daniel, or the history of England from Julius Caesar to Churchill, or in that of France from Charlemagne to General de Gaulle, or in that of Germany from Hermann to Adenauer, or in that of the United States from the Pilgrim Fathers to John Foster Dulles, or in that of Russia, India and Africa from primitive times to our own day, or in that of the Swiss Confederacy from the Fathers who bound themselves in the name of God to modern Switzerland ?   We think of the many links in these stories, and the many similar chains of events, and all the possible continuations, and the innumerable relationships, intersections and conflicts.   We recall all the few or many things that we know of all the great and little powers which here rise and fall, of all the civilisations that come and go with all their transmutations, of all the treaties concluded and broken, and above all of all the wars which were fought, and ended, and then broke out again, of the great names, eminent for a time and in a restricted area, of individual princes, statesmen, generals, poets, thinkers, scholars and inventors, and of the acts associated with them.   We remember, too, the hopes and disappointments and sufferings and joys, more felt than known, of the anonymous millions of individuals recorded by history only in partial selection and brief outline, yet also participating and contributing as they also live and die in the limits and under the pressure of the conditions imposed upon them. Whence and whither and to what end is all this ?   To take both a great example and a small, where is there, for instance, in the history of the Second World War, or in that of the separation of the Canton of Basel in 1830–1833, a single constant point on which the eye can focus and find with even approximate certainty any more than *confusio hominum* ?

We are now obviously thinking and speaking from a lower standpoint. But here, too, our concern must be with the theological aspect of the world-occurrence which surrounds the community. *Hominum confusione et Dei providentia. Et ?* Is not this a very dubious word ? But how are we to avoid the dubiety ? Is it not theologically unavoidable that we should see things in two different ways ? God rules. From above He rules over all things and in all things. But here below, in the sphere and under the prior dominion of this higher rule, yet in its own way very really and quite unmistakeably, there also " rules " this other principle. And as *Dei providentia* is the appropriate expression for the first and higher and decisive aspect, so is *hominum confusio* for that which is to be seen below from the theological angle, i.e., from the standpoint of the Christian community or its prophetic witness, for the view which is to be taken of surrounding world-occurrence as such.

It is to be noted first that *hominum confusio* does not indicate a state in which men find themselves, but an action, an activity and work, in which they are engaged. They wander and collide and get confused. It is as they do so, as they always seem to have done and presumably always will, that world history takes place. Attention should also be paid to the word *hominum*. Men are the subjects of this action. It is another matter that God rules them from above. But it is not He who gets confused. What He wills, and has already achieved, is the unravelling of historical confusion. On the other hand, it is wiser and more consoling not to call the devil the subject of this fatal action. All honour to him, but he can be abroad only where man is abroad, i.e., exiled from God and his brother. It is men exiled from God and their brethren who create confusion and therefore a world history which seems to be so strongly bedevilled. Finally, the expression *hominum confusio* is theologically appropriate because it says neither too little nor too much. *Confusio* undoubtedly denotes something very questionable and indeed wholly evil. It opens up a vista of folly and wickedness, of deception and injustice, of blood and tears. But it does not pronounce any absolute sentence of rejection. It does not describe world history as a night in which everything is black, as an utter mad-house or den of criminals, as a graveyard, let alone an inferno. It simply says—and this is serious and severe enough—that men make and shape and achieve confusion. And confusion does have also a positive element. Here below there can be no theoretical significance in the fact that it takes place under God's providence. But where there is confusion, there have to be at least two different elements at work, which, instead of being kept apart, are intertwined and thus become entangled. It is the fact that man entangles them, but only this, which determines and characterises world-occurrence as seen from below.

Now from the theological standpoint the relevant factors are the two elements of world history which are always entangled by man. On the one side there is the good creation of God, which is not in any sense robbed of its goodness, which does not lose it, which is not broken or defaced, which is just as glorious as it was on the very first day. And this creation of God includes not only man himself, who in respect of all that makes and marks him as a creature—whatever may have to be said of his action—is good and not bad. It also includes the surrounding cosmos, created as the *theatrum gloriae Dei*, in all its explored and unexplored dimensions, with all its known and as yet unknown or only suspected possibilities and powers, with a nature which God Himself has given no less than in the case of man, and which can neither shift nor change. Creation does not cease to extol its Creator, and it is therefore far more sensible to extol creation itself in respect of its Creator than to deplore its puzzling and difficult features. " For every creature of God is good, and nothing to be refused, if it be received with thanksgiving " (1 Tim. 4⁴). In none of its forms or developments has world history ceased to have a share also in that which God created good and even very good, and has maintained as such. On the other side however—and it is here that we may seriously think of the devil—there is the reality and operation of the absurd, of nothingness, grounded in no possibility given by God, neither elected nor willed by the Creator, but existing only *per nefas*. What is this ? It is nothing other than the negation of the good creation of God, which itself can only be negated, excluded and rejected by Him, which the creature of God too, and man at the centre and as the keypoint of the creaturely world, could and would only negate, exclude and reject if he lived at peace with God, his brother and himself. But world history in all its forms and developments has a most radical share in this basically futile negation as well as in the good creation of God. How can this be ? The answer is : *hominum confusione*, i.e., as the action of men implies neither an unequivocal and decided negation of the good creation of God nor an unequivocal and decided affirmation, as it implies neither an unequivocal and decided affirmation of nothingness nor an unequivocal and decided negation, but consists in the inextricable intertwining or confusion of these two elements which are so totally antithetical and cannot be united. It is to be noted that what is at issue is no more than equivocation and indecision, and therefore confusion. This is the most of which men are capable under the limiting rule of the providence of God. But they are actually capable of this as sinners against God, their neighbours and themselves.

Now the confusion of the two elements which men constantly achieve may be analysed as follows. They think that they can and may and should ignore the fact that these elements are so absolutely antithetical, and accept both of them together, relativising the one by the other, i.e., the good creation of God and therefore the creaturely reality elected and willed by Him on the one side, and its negation as rejected by God and therefore that which is intrinsically impossible on the other. They count upon both where, with appropriate seriousness, and to the exclusion of the other, they ought to count only upon the one, and therefore, with a consistency appropriate to a mere intruder, not to count upon the other. Hence it is not the glorious or shameful acts, but their compromises, which give to their history its distinctive aspect from the human standpoint. Their eye is shifty (Mt. 6²³). It squints, as a good eye neither would nor could. It is with this squinting eye that they try to live. But they cannot do so unless they try to bring into some sort of impossible relation these two elements between which there is intrinsically no relation, believing that there cannot be any question of mutual exclusion, that the two can both be accepted simultaneously, and that they ought thus to be somehow asserted in concert and brought into conjunction. But is not the only form in which there can be achieved any such co-ordination between them a form which involves the reversal of their proper dignities and roles ? In fact the good creation can only be placed absolutely above nothingness as the reality which is opposed to and thus excludes the impossible. And in fact nothingness can only be absolutely subordinated to the good creation of God as its negation, as the impossible which is excluded by reality. In the *confusio hominum*, however, everything has to be reversed. Nothingness is not thought to be nor treated as excluded, and it is thus given the primacy over the good creation of God. The good creation of God is not thought to be nor treated as excluding, and it is thus merely co-ordinated with and therefore subordinated to nothingness. *In concreto*, therefore, the inter-relating of the two elements means that nothingness, the negation of the good creation of God, becomes the master, controller and ruler of this creation, and the good creation of God is set in the service and under the control of its own negation, of nothingness, to be subjected, guided, used and despoiled by it. This is the great confusion, intermingling and jumbling of the two elements which characterises world-occurrence. The metaphysics and logic here at work are those of the man who has fallen from God and therefore fallen out with his neighbour and himself. This man cannot think or act in any other way. He is consistent in overlooking the absolutely antithetical nature of the two elements, in seeing them both together, in counting on both, in living with both simultaneously, in bringing them into relationship, in being able to co-ordinate them, and actually doing so, only with that complete reversal of their dignities and roles, in short, in bringing about that great confusion. Giving place to nothingness as the enemy of God, his neighbour and himself, neither he nor his whole cosmos ceases to be the good creation of God. But it is settled that for him, in his heart and thinking and action, nothingness is given that precedence over the good creation of God, and the good creation is to its own destruction betrayed into that position of subservience and subordinated to nothingness.

The consequences are of such a kind, and just as incalculable, as we actually discover in world history. In our more bitter moments we are tempted to think that they entail wholesale confusion—no more, but surely this is bad enough. Yet there is another side ; for if through the confusion with nothingness which man has brought about the goodness of the creation of God can be attained and discovered only in part, it declares itself the more plainly where it cannot be touched by man. In every age and place throughout world history, there has always been also the laughter of children, the scent of flowers and the song of birds and similar things which cannot be affected by any confusion with nothingness. Nor have there been lacking poets and musicians and other noble spirits who have been able to look past or through the creation confused with nothingness and thus to perceive, and to make perceptible to others, its form as untouched by this confusion. Nor should we try to maintain that there is no more than confusion even in the darkest phenomena of world history in which this confusion is quite incontestable, as though we really had to reckon with a bedevilment which would necessarily have as its presupposition a withdrawal of the Creator in face of the confusion of His creation brought about by man. Whatever else may be the consequences of the *confusio hominum*, there is no such withdrawal on the part of the Creator, and therefore no removal of the goodness of His creation. In spite of the *confusio hominum*, Ps. 104²⁴ is still valid : " O Lord, how manifold are thy works ! in wisdom hast thou made them all : the earth is full of thy riches." There are no forms, events or relationships in the world-occurrence unmistakeably confused by man in which the goodness of what God has created is not also effective and visible, the only question being how this is so. On the one side, there is the inexhaustible plenitude of the supply of the cosmos surrounding man, the forms and forces and materials of which seem to be in mysterious agreement with man's capacities and to wait only to be seen and known in their particularity to become fruitful and of assistance to him in his life. On the other side, there is man himself with his obviously inexhaustible ability to make use of this supply, not finding in the cosmos an alien antithesis, but understanding, comprehending and apprehending it as his own cosmos, making it human, and acting as the subject of this object. The interplay of cosmos and man, of man and cosmos, could and should be orderly. This is not yet the case. But it would be foolish to close our eyes to the glory of creation which is manifest—and terrifyingly so—even in the confusion of world history. It would be an act of blindness not to see it even here with open eyes. What is world history ? Even in its obvious and dreadful confusion, it is also the ongoing history of the good creation of God which cannot be destroyed by any confusion of man. It is also the history of the supply given to man in the cosmos around him, and of man's ability to recognise and use it as such.

The only point is that, as the history of the man who has fallen away from God and fallen out with his neighbour and himself, it is also and simultaneously the history of the confusion continually caused by him. All the forces of the cosmos and his own spirit may be turned by him, as one who is himself the first to be entangled in confusion, to further that inversion. He thinks that he can handle them as though he who has really fallen away from God and fallen out with his neighbour and himself were really their creator, as though they were the sinner's possession, as though it were self-evident that they should be at his disposal as instruments of his unbridled caprice. He thus forfeits the simplicity, reverence and gratitude with which he might and should use them as gifts of God's grace and therefore in peace with his fellows and himself, seeing in them merely aids to fuller living. His desire for more and more is roused and satisfied and roused again by them in the sorriest possible imitation of God, who is God in the fact that, wholly self-sufficient, He wills to give and does actually give more and more, without any self-seeking. To his mistrust and hatred of his fellows as rivals who are obviously animated and impelled by the same desire, they offer means of defence and attack, where it would be so much simpler and more obvious to use them concertedly in the service of life. To the deep anxiety which he feels in relation to himself, to his inward emptiness, they offer a hasty escape to even more hasty acts which are not determined by any necessary goal, where he might peacefully enjoy their use and use them with enjoyment. There is thus forfeited, not the good creation of God, but its meaning for man as it becomes to him merely the valueless material impelling him to the senseless circling to which he has condemned himself, and condemns himself again and again in this fall, to the wholly alien pursuit of knowledge for the sake of knowledge, of power for the sake of power, of possession for the sake of possession, of glory for the sake of glory, of enjoyment for the sake of enjoyment. When the good creation of God is confused by man with the service of nothingness and therefore its own negation, when it is used by him in this way and thus misused as a means to this end, what can be the result but a work of destruction which finds its full fruition in war? It is not for nothing that constant wars, representing the extreme possibility of the man involved in this fall and his extreme misuse of cosmic and personal powers, have always determined and characterised the course and form of world-occurrence from the days of Cain onwards. But war is only the extreme point, the worst and constantly re-emerging representative, of the work of destruction which *hominum confusione* goes on even in what is called peace, and which makes peace a continual preparation for war. On the other hand it is simply a warning sign of the plunge into a final, total and definitive destruction towards which man moves as the "humanising" of the good creation of God, undertaken by him in this fall, has as its upshot his sinning, not only against God, his fellows and himself, but also against this creation, against its wonderful supply and his no less wonderful capacity to use it.

It is, however, the glorious and yet also the terrifying feature of all world history that the good creation of God is not removed, destroyed or set aside by what man does to it, by his confusion of it with nothingness, but that, even if in the form and outworking determined by this confusion, it still maintains itself and persists. Since it is itself a creature, whether from the standpoint of the outer cosmos or of man himself, it does not share the inviolable majesty of God and is thus exposed to co-ordination with and even subordination to nothingness and therefore to its own negation. But even in this humiliation and shame it remains what it is and how it is. As a creature which God does not let fall, it cannot break under the negation which it suffers, nor can it be dissipated by it. Its objective and subjective power, the cosmic supply and man's ability to use it, do not stop nor diminish nor alter when man subjects them to that alien service. This is glorious, for it is a clear proof of the superiority of the Creator even in and in face of the history of man's confusion of His creation. But it is also terrifying, for the power of the good creation of God, which cannot disappear nor even diminish as such even in that alien service, can now work only negatively instead of positively. The reason which characterises man becomes nonsense. The grace addressed to the creature of God now becomes judgment. The benefits objectively and subjectively assigned and displayed to man becomes plagues. As *corruptio optimi*, of the optimum of the opportunity afforded man, the confusion caused by him works out as *corruptio pessima*. Man would not be able to insult his creator so coarsely, nor do so much injury to his fellows and himself, nor fill his sphere with so much of the " savour of death unto death " (2 Cor. 2[16]), nor lead himself and his world with such vehemence to a final and definite plunge into the abyss, as he continually does, were it not that he does these things in all the power of the good creation of God which he has, of course, perverted. Even in its perversion it is this creation which punishes him when he sins against it, which causes to recoil on his own head the stroke which he delivers with its help, which threatens him with even severer negation when he ventures to negate it. In the unhappy circle trodden by him, in the situation thus created by him, he is dealing superficially with a host of dangerous because demonised powers and forces. More basically and properly, however, he is dealing even in these powers and forces with the constancy of the good creation of God which must be his enemy because he has made alliance with its enemy. And therefore indirectly but very palpably he is dealing with the living God Himself, who will not be mocked, but in great things and small alike causes man to reap exactly what he has sown. God will not be unfaithful either to himself or to man. He will not throw man over. He will not withdraw what He has given. But neither will He let Himself be mocked (Gal. 6[7]). When man for his part is unfaithful to God and therefore to his fellows and himself, it is inevitable, since he himself will have it so, that what God has given him should not be a means and instrument of salvation but rather of perdition. This negative operation of the good creation of God consequent upon *confusio hominum* is the truly terrifying element in the form and picture of world history.

Our modern period suggests a final illustration of the connexion indicated, namely, the history of modern physics in its development from atomic research to the discovery and creation of atomic weapons. All the elements of *confusio hominum* meet at this point : the good creation of God in the form of a newly discovered and glorious cosmic supply and a newly developed and no less glorious human capacity ; man himself, who after a brief period of hesitation combines it with nothingness and places it in the service of the latter ; and the recoil in which it becomes in all its glory an enemy threatening man with destruction. Robert Jungk (*Heller als tausend Sonnen*, 1956) has described this cycle in a way which is both factual and generally comprehensible. But we can see with seeing eyes, yet not perceive. Universal shrinking from the atomic death which unmistakeably impends is one thing, but it is not enough to arrest the cycle. Quite another is recognition of *confusio hominum* as such, which in this case means recognition of atomic sin. So long as this does not confront both those who advocate atomic armament in their concern either for Socialism or the " free world," and also those who oppose them, or so long as it does not do so more distinctly than is as yet the case, world history will have to proceed under this sign, though even so, to our comfort, it must still conform to the providence of God.

But the time has now come to turn the page. We had to begin, as was only proper, by recalling the royal and fatherly world governance of God. Then in this bracket and under this presupposition we had to consider the great human confusion in which world history unfolds and displays itself. Both standpoints were and are theologically imperative and necessary. Who God is in the height, as the good Creator and Lord of His good creation, and what He wills and does as such, has obviously to be the first and comprehensive theme for our serious attention. But secondarily, yet no less seriously and necessarily, we had also to consider man and his action, the *confusio hominum*. World history takes place in this strange co-operation of God and man, which is so clear when seen from above, so obscure when seen from below. This is how the Christian community sees and understands it in the light of the prophetic witness with which it is entrusted and commissioned. But is this all ? Does it not see or know anything more concerning world history than what may be conjoined and distinguished in the twofold concept : *Hominum confusione et Dei providentia* ?

We must be clear what it would mean if this were really all. The Christian community would then have to accept the fact of being forced to exist, in relation to its environment, in an irrevocable tension or dialectic of faith in God's unconditional overlordship as commanded and authorised by the Word which underlies it and its knowledge of human confusion which is unavoidable in the light of the same Word. It would then have to look seriously upwards on the one side, yet no less seriously downwards on the other. It would have to look courageously and confidently to the Lord of history on the one side, yet very fearfully and anxiously to history itself on the other. It would have to look to the seriously and definitively certain factor of its goal and meaning on the one side, yet also to all kinds of less certain actualisations of a good or better which may perhaps be perceived or deduced here and there in the midst of human confusion. Is it really the case, however, that this must be the existence of the people of God within the world-occurrence around it ? It has often been depicted in this way, sometimes with a gentle or more vigorous sigh and shaking of the head, sometimes with the pathos of a very sober and realistic Christianity, sometimes with the kerygmatically declared assurance that it is the specific gift and task of the community in relation to the world to exist in this tension or dialectic of its faith and knowledge, in the two spheres which may be delineated in this way. But is this in fact a genuinely and specifically Christian view or solution ? To test this, let us try for a moment to divest the two aspects of the theological meaning and character in which we have understood and depicted them. The twofold concept might then in fact be described as the view which with more or less confidence or despair almost all men of all ages have had and will have, namely, that man exists and world history takes place under the sign of the contradiction between a higher, primary and therefore predominant principle and a lower principle which persistently maintains itself and has thus also to be taken into account. Everything lies and takes place, then, in the twilight of light and darkness, which it is hoped will be that of the morning and not the evening, in which the demand to be on the side of light seems meaningful and illuminating, but in which it must be constantly affirmed that it is not so simple to do this, that it can be done only with great labour and step by step, since darkness is present very actually and actively, so that the last word must be an appeal to oneself and others that they will dare to take and to keep to this side in spite of everything. The last word ? Will it not perhaps be that the supposed last word will continually fluctuate between these counsellors whom others might admit to be right in theory, and these others themselves whose gaze is no less steadily fixed below and whom we usually describe as practical men standing on solid earth ?

If we think at all, and are not guilty of sheer stupidity or malice in our thinking, are we not confined within these limits ? Does not the Christian community, with its distinctive theological forms and terminology, think within these limits ? And, if we may anticipate the main theme of the section, does not its mission and task in the world consist in saying precisely this to the world, and thus in singing again, and if possible commending, the old song of the tension or dialectic of the two principles or kingdoms and of the attitude to be desired on the part of man, the main accent being sometimes placed on the theological equivalent of an ideal and theoretical outlook, and sometimes on the theological equivalent of a realistic and practical ? As if all the birds in their different ways were not voicing the same song from every roof ! And as if in these circumstances we need be surprised that the voice of the Church in the world at large does not seem to be received as one which has anything urgent or significant or at any rate noteworthy, because decisively illuminating and helpful, to proclaim ! But is it really so that its message is only a duplicate of that which might be said without its aid, and is in fact usually said, though with no very outstanding results ? Does it really think and say no more than that there is a higher and a lower, a theoretical and a practical truth, that it is certainly good to think more of the higher and give it greater scope, that it is better in world history if men resolve and act accordingly, but that it is unavoidable and quite imperative that we should not lose sight of the other aspect, that we should take it very seriously, and that in this respect we should diligently avail ourselves of the wise counsel of our so-called statesmen and political experts ? Is this really the view and message of the Christian community as well ?

If this is how it is understood, there can be no doubt that even what it says concerning the two aspects is misunderstood. The mere fact that, so long and so far as it even faintly remembers its special commission, it has to say very differently, i.e., theologically, the same thing as so many others, is not a matter of chance or caprice, but indicates at least that in reality it sees and understands the two antithetical aspects in its own very distinctive way, and that what it says concerning them cannot really be equated with what is said elsewhere with respect to similar contradictions. But is it really clear enough itself to make this clear to the world around, and thus to remove the misunderstanding, so long as there is no more to its view than a consideration of the two aspects, and therefore a recognition of both the providence. of God and the confusion of man, its own thought and utterance in relation to world history thus falling within the framework of that tension or dialectic ?

Great caution is demanded, however, if we go on to assert that, while the two modes of consideration which we have adopted thus far are both necessary, yet they cannot have ultimate significance or validity for the Christian community, since a third view, which, if it does not negate them, is superior to and comprehends them, is not only possible but obligatory for the Christian, and since it is only in the light of this view that we can see what must be the true and specifically Christian word that it has to attest to the world.

Why is caution demanded at this point ? What we have said concerning the *providentia Dei* and then the *confusio hominum* might so easily be regarded as Hegelian thesis and antithesis, and the third and superior view or decisive word which is to be sought at this point might then be envisaged or understood as the Hegelian synthesis which takes the contradiction into itself, integrates the two sides and thus overcomes it. But then—to consider for a moment the tempting path which opens up before us—our concern would be to grasp and indicate a point, already foreseen if possible in and behind all that precedes, from which the two sides of the contradiction can be seen and comprehended together. From this point the relative value and justification of the two factors in world-occurrence seen on this twofold view could then be assured by undertaking to disclose a positive connexion between them and in this interconnexion to interpret them as the two factors or elements of one and the same reality. But when it is a matter of seeing and understanding world history, is it really the special gift and task of the Christian community to do this ? For what would this undertaking imply ? First, it would obviously mean the divesting of both the providence of God and the confusion of man of the mystery which in very different ways is characteristic of both. But in this case we could not seriously speak either of a mystery of God over world history or a mystery of iniquity within it. Both the providence of God and the confusion of man would have to be seen and handled, and indeed harnessed, as moments of history which are intrinsically perceptible, understandable and explicable. But then both would also lose their absolutely distinctive antithetical character. The providence of God could no longer be regarded as the factor which must be absolutely affirmed, honoured and adored, nor the confusion of man as that which must be absolutely negated and abhorred. Decision between the two could no longer be stated to be the irrevocably last word in matters of the consideration and understanding of world-occurrence. A positive relation between the two would have to be sought and found and maintained ; a relationship of basis and dependence demonstrated. We should then have to speak of what is finally a positive and not a negative will of God as the ultimate meaning, not merely of creation, but of sin, of the human confusion of creation with nothingness. And this confusion could not be spoken of only as an actualisation of the impossible which has intervened *per nefas*, as a work of apostasy and disruption, but rather as a factor in world history which, in virtue of its basis in a positive will of God, demands positive evaluation, and therefore as a possibility which is at root respectable. Even distinctively Christian consideration and understanding would then mean bringing the providence of God and the confusion of man under a common denominator, estimating the one as the basis of the other and the other as filled with meaning in virtue of this basis, and therefore approving and validating both in their higher unity. The sure and certain result would be that in extolling this unity Christians would in practice be compelled, with sighs perhaps but also perhaps with cheerfulness, to affirm the human confusion justified and sanctified by its connexion with the providence of God. But of what does all this remind us ? Obviously of the only too human procedure which according to our previous deliberations has given rise, and always does give rise, to human confusion. Once more then, though now in a higher chorus and in the garb of a Christian evaluation and position, we should be concerned with the procedure in which man brings together, combines, intermingles and confuses the good creation of God and nothingness, rejoicing in both, seeking to control both, and thus unavoidably giving precedence to nothingness, and to his own loss placing the good creation of God in its service. In the search for a superior principle transcending and dissolving the antithesis of God and man in world-occurrence, the Christian community would then have found a place above the antithesis, and therefore a synthesis and reconciliation, in which human confusion, which has itself originated in such a synthesis, would be supremely established and affirmed and therefore definitively justified and sanctified. Christ Himself would then have been brought into agreement and harmony with Belial (2 Cor. 6^{15}). And the proclamation of this agreement and harmony would be the glad tidings which Christianity has to transmit to the world. As though the world had any need to listen to such tidings! For is it not the familiar confusion of men which in this message comes to it in the form of the confusion of Christians? Is not this a wholly superfluous confirmation? Obviously, this is a path which we must avoid at all costs when we too, commencing with that twofold view, must try to look beyond it.

But what really is this path which we must avoid? It is in the light of its end that we have been forced to say that it is impossible for the thinking of Christians. We must now look back, however, to its beginning. For what is forbidden obviously does not take place at the end, but already at the beginning. If the attempt to go beyond that twofold view, even while recognising its inevitability, and the elements of truth in it, is not to end so fatally by leading back, as Christian confusion, to the confusion of man, then we must start in a very different way from that adopted at the beginning of the path indicated. If we are really to attain to the overarching view of world-occurrence which is both requisite and permissible for the Christian community, we must not begin by thinking that any of us can go beyond that twofold view in his own strength or by his own choice, finding and fixing a supposedly superior point in the void, ostensibly establishing himself there by a bold resolve, and then looking back on the contradiction and antithesis and seeing it as a unity. It is in this way, with this kind of mastery over the problem, that man generally and not merely the Christian, occupied always and everywhere in some sense with his own version of the twofold view, constructs his world-pictures in an attempt to understand the cosmos and himself, or himself in the cosmos. And if he begins with this attempt at mastery, the usual result is not a real overcoming of the antithesis but a regression to the affirmation of the human confusion which competes with divine providence. The most deeply confusing aspect of the confusing action of man is that he thinks he can set himself above both God and himself at a point beyond the creative will of God and the opposing nothingness, where he can and should see the two together and combine them. It is in the very arrogance of this speculation and disposition that he betrays and confirms the fact that he is the man who has fallen away from God and fallen out with his neighbour and himself. Beginning in this way, and proceeding accordingly, he can and will only confirm and confuse one confusion by another. The wisdom of serpents will always produce the work of serpents. The will and intention may be good, but the result will necessarily be further confusion. This, then, is the way which must not be taken by the Christian community as it is required to go beyond that twofold view. It is for this reason that here, too, we must begin very differently.

The alternative is clear and childishly simple. Our main task is simply to realise and grasp its clarity and simplicity as the only possible alternative. And it is simply that the reality and truth of the grace of God addressed to the world in Jesus Christ is the third word which the Christian community is both required and authorised to consider and attest beyond and in integration of the first two as it turns its gaze on world-occurrence.

Looking back on what has been said thus far, we note first that there is no question here of any arbitrarily seen and fixed point in the void making possible no less arbitrary speculation and disposition concerning the antithesis arising on that twofold view. Jesus Christ is not a concept which man can think out for himself, which he can define with more or less precision, and with the help of which he can then display his mastery over all kinds of greater or lesser problems and therefore over the problem of this antithesis too. On the contrary, Jesus Christ is a living human person who comes and speaks and acts with the claim and authority of God, and in relation to whom there can be no question whatever of controlling and using Him to grasp or master this or that even in the sphere of thought. Hence the grace of God shown to the world in Him is not a principle which man can perceive, affirm and appropriate as such, and then logically develop and apply to transcend and overcome all possible antitheses, and therefore the one which now concerns us. It is rather a free and sovereign power and a free and self-disclosing truth. It is free because it finds actualisation in the sovereign, divine-human acts of the life and death of Jesus Christ. It is free because it is revealed in the resurrection of the same divine-human person of Jesus Christ. It is free as a Word spoken in the power of His Holy Spirit, who blows where He lists. What is there here to see and fix, to be the object of speculation and disposition? The grace of God addressed to the world in Jesus Christ is that which exists supremely, but quite uniquely, only as on the basis of God's eternal love and election and faithfulness it was and is and will be event, inaccessible to all human or even Christian *hybris*, recognisable only in gratitude for the fact that it is real and true, and in prayer for ever new recognition of its reality and truth. If we treat it otherwise than as an object only in the character of a supreme subject ; if we regard it as if it were a product of our own thinking, a concept and principle and therefore an instrument with the help of which we can master and solve any problem, including a problem of the order of the antithesis of divine providence and human confusion, then we merely show that we are deceived in thinking that we are dealing with grace. We think and speak like poor heathen, no matter how earnestly we may imagine that we think and speak of it. Where grace is actually present and active, it is enveloped by the mystery of its royal freedom. For good or ill we who exist in this mystery must consider this when we describe and proclaim this grace as the third word which is entrusted to the community within world-occurrence and in relation to its course. Only then shall we avoid the confusion which means falsification from the very outset in the attempt to press forward to this third word.

We note further that there is no question of introducing into the discussion a kind of *Deus ex machina* or marvellous supernatural solution when we try to think further in terms of the grace of God addressed to the world in Jesus Christ. We do not introduce this element at all ; we simply affirm that from the very outset it has been the presupposition of our question as to the Christian understanding of world-occurrence, and that it must now be brought into the forefront or the limelight if a correct and valid answer is to be given. From the very outset our concern is not with any view, but with that view which is disclosed and given to the people of God in world-occurrence as a required and legitimate view. If it were only that in the general terms of the philosophy of history, and on a neutral basis, we were discussing the relation of the two familiar principles of good and evil or light and darkness or whatever else we like to call them, then the introduction of what we term the grace of God addressed to the world in Jesus Christ would certainly mean the introduction of a *Deus ex machina* which would alienate the other participants in the discussion and rightly cause them to shake their heads and say that they can make nothing of the notion. But we are not in fact engaged in any such discussion. From the very outset we have been seeking the specifically Christian or theological view of world history, the view which has as its presupposition the prophetic witness entrusted as a commission to the people of God. But the unequivocal burden of this witness is that in Jesus Christ the grace of God was and is and will be addressed to the world. It is from the place which is appointed by the witness entrusted to it, which it has not chosen for itself, at which it cannot maintain itself, in which it was set and to which it is continually recalled, that the community looks first into the heights and thinks of the royal and fatherly overruling of the God at whose right hand Jesus Christ is seated, and then looks down into the depths and surveys the confusion of the men for whom the same Lord Jesus Christ has lived and died and risen again. From this standpoint it is not any antithesis but this particular antithesis which has engaged us. And from the same standpoint we are now quite right, indeed, we find it simple and self-evident, expressly to affirm and disclose this presupposition, understanding the view of history which concerns us, precisely its twofold aspect, in the light of this presupposition which is so peculiarly our own, leading it to its goal in the form most proper to it, and in so doing at least provisionally sketching to the world the witness which the community owes to the world engaged in that general discussion. To be sure, it will seem to the world that we are introducing a kind of *Deus ex machina*. But this need not trouble us, since it rests on the mistaken view that we, too, are engaged in that general discussion in which there is no place for the present line of argument. We can easily understand the world's attitude in this respect, for even to our own thinking, let alone that of the world, our presupposition always implies and is a new thing which as such may easily suggest a marvellous supernatural solution. We may even be confident in spite of this misapprehension, since we believe that this new thing has the power to break through the illusion and to disclose itself, as to us, so also to the world, and finally not merely to individuals but to all men, as the reality and truth which speaks for itself.

What does the people of God see in world-occurrence around it ? To be sure, up above it sees first and last the glorious spectacle of its God, the Creator of the world and man, who as such is the Lord and Ruler of this occurrence. To be sure, down below it sees the dreadful spectacle of the man who has fallen away from God and fallen out with his neighbour and himself—so that he can and does achieve only confusion. To be sure, it sees the contradiction, the conflict, the *diastasis*, the riddle of this occurrence. And accordingly, to be sure, it sees no real synthesis resolving the riddle, no harmony between above and below, no relation between the positive will of God and the confusion of man, no possibility of understanding the one as the basis of the other, or the other as grounded in it. It accepts the two-fold view. But it also sees that there is more to be said. What the Christian community has to think and say of world history in accordance with this twofold view cannot be its final thought or word. For the assertion of this antithesis and contradiction cannot possibly be its first thought or word in relation to world history. That by which it is itself created and sustained within world-occurrence as the people of God charged to bear witness to the work and Word of God, its own basis of existence, is a new thing in relation to that antithesis and contradiction. Originally and primarily it has to think on the basis of this new thing as its distinctive *a priori*, and it is only in this light, therefore, that it can see and understand the antithesis and contradiction of above and below. It is precisely because it sees it from this point that it must take it so strictly and exclusively, regarding the lordship of God as so glorious and the confusion of man as so dreadful, and finding it quite impossible to see them together or to reduce them to a common denominator. It derives from this new thing. It does not itself create it. It is what it is as and because this new thing has introduced itself into world-occurrence and is of itself so actual within it as its meaning and goal. It has not itself discovered this new thing. It has no more discovered it than other men or peoples. It cannot, then, master or control it. This new thing—and this is what makes the community what it is as the people of God created in world history —has revealed and made itself known to it as the work of God for the world and His Word to it. The task entrusted to the community is to attest this new thing to the world. It did not come to it. On the contrary, the new thing came to the community. It showed itself to it. It opened its eyes that it might and should see it. Hence it does see it as the new thing which is beyond the antithesis, yet also new within it. In relation to the world-occurrence around it, it is this new thing which is its final as it is already its first word.

Materially and to that extent neutrally we can and should describe it as the new thing. But this new thing which is manifest to the community in the world around it is the grace of God addressed to it. It sees the world in a new light to the extent that it knows that, while the contradiction or antithesis is not removed and does not lose its seriousness, it is relativised, loosened and in a definite sense broken through by the fact that God not only confronts the world as its Creator, Lord and Governor, but in this great superiority of His has turned to it as gracious Father, that apart from and even in spite of its deserts He is kind towards it in the free omnipotence of His mercy, which necessarily means for the world that it is not just obscured by the confusion of men who have fallen away from God and fallen out with their neighbours and themselves, but that in spite of this confusion of theirs the world is not bereft of grace but exists under this gracious address of God. As described in this way, the new thing which is event and revelation within world-occurrence may be known as such. Neither in relation to God's sovereign lordship nor to man's confusion can it be called self-evident, and yet it is incomprehensibly valid. What opposes that antithesis and contradiction, preventing the disruption of the cosmos and shining over the abyss as the promise of peace, is the grace of God, this grace alone, but this grace truly and effectively as the grace of God, and therefore this grace as it implies a new heaven, the manifestation of the heaven from which God not only rules the world but in so doing has turned and continually turns to it in loving-kindness, and also under this heaven, in virtue of the loving-kindness with which God turns to it, a new earth. Even when it is stated in this way, we are thus given a new and positive sign under which the community may see God and the world and therefore history.

But is not this description perhaps too general and pale to denote unmistakeably the new thing which discloses itself to the community in relation to history, and which the community has to attest to the world ? Indeed, if it is described in this way, is it not possible that this new thing will easily give rise to the misunderstanding that, if the Christian community is really to appreciate the new thing disclosed to it, its gaze must still continue to vacillate, even under the new promise, between God on the one side and the world on the other, with the inevitable consequence that it can never come to rest on either side, that it can attain only a dialectical and not a simple assurance of the grace which unites God and the world ? Indeed, how can the community really know it as the new *thing* if this material description is exhaustive ? When described in this objective and neutral way, might not the concept of a God who has turned to the world in grace, and of a world which is participant in this gracious address—grace itself being obviously the overarching concept—easily give rise to the suspicion that after all it only denotes the product of further human speculation ? Might it not represent yet another of the many bridge-building attempts which lead into the void ? Might it not be simply giving a new and more hopeful name to the gulf between above and below, the gulf being hidden under the name grace, but still remaining open in fact, so that it is concealed or closed only in the dubious way already familiar to us ? Under the biblical and Christian concept of grace, we might still have merely the play of a synthesising the product of which will certainly not be the new thing perceived by the people of God in world-occurrence. The new *thing* ? Unquestionably the grace of God addressed to the world, and therefore a world which is participant in this grace, is the new thing perceived by the people of God. But do we not describe it in a way which is perhaps too equivocal, general, innocuous, dialectical, and therefore exposed to that suspicion, so long as we call it the new *thing*, however right we may be in fact to fill it with the concept of grace ?

The new thing which the people of God perceives in world-occurrence is the new, unique person Jesus Christ. It is the grace of God addressed to the world in Him. And this " in Him," the name of Jesus Christ, indicates more than the means, instrument or vehicle used by God in addressing His grace to the world. We cannot therefore look past Him, or look through Him as through a glass, to the true point at issue, namely, God's gracious address to the world as the true and proper thing intended under this name. He, the person who bears this name, is Himself God, the Son of the Father, of one essence with Him. He is Himself God in His gracious address to the world. He is Himself the grace in which God addresses Himself and which He addresses to the world. He is Himself the work of God in and on the world, and the Word in which this work declares itself to the world. He is Himself the true matter at issue. And it is as it looks at Him that His community in the world can see and understand world history in relation to Him. Once we realise this, the darkness and ambiguity in which we have been moving lighten and disperse. Looking to Him, the community does not look to a concept which intellectually removes the antithesis and contradiction of that twofold view, whether it be a concept invented by man on the one side or a concept supra-rationally introduced under the biblical and Christian title of grace on the other. It looks to the concrete event, once and for all in time, of His life and death and resurrection. Looking to Him, it is neither constrained nor enabled, neither commanded nor authorised, to look about excitedly either upwards to God on the one hand or downwards to man on the other. On the contrary, it calmly concentrates its gaze on the single place of this event. Looking to Him, it has to do with more than even the most glorious of promises and its fulfilment, with more than a positive sign of its thinking about God and the world, with more than a bridge over the gulf between them, with more than a new and more hopeful illumination of the human situation. It has to do with the true and radical alteration of this situation. This is what is meant by the grace addressed to the world in Him, by the new thing which is known by the community and which it has to attest to the world. This new thing is the event which alters the whole human situation and therefore world history. It is His existence, He Himself. It is He, the new person.

The new thing in Jesus Christ, in the power and truth of which He is the new person, consists quite simply in the fact that in Him— as the people of God in the world may know even though the world itself does not—we are concerned in the strictest sense with God, with His work and Word. This means, however, that we are concerned not only with God but also directly with humanity, and not only with a pure and ideal humanity but with the very impure, historical and sinful humanity which has fallen away from God and fallen out with itself, with the " flesh of sin " (Rom. 8[3]), and therefore with the subject of the great confusion of world history. The event indicated by the name of Jesus Christ and identical with His person is that the true Son of God, of one essence with the Father, has in this One assumed humanity, and very concretely this humanity, to unity with Himself, that He not only became one with it and adopted its creaturely nature but took to Himself its whole sin as though He had committed it and were its Author, that in His death He bore it away instead, thus achieving in its place the obedience to the Father which the humanity of the first Adam had refused and still refuses. The reconciliation of the world with God, the justification and sanctification of man, of all men, before Him and for Him, the cutting off of human confusion at its root, the restoration of order in world-occurrence, is thus the event in question, the work and Word of Jesus Christ. The Christian community hears this Word, sees this work and knows this person as it hears and sees and knows the One whose call is the basis and meaning of its own existence. Hence what it perceives in this One is not merely an illumination of world history but its correction and reformation. The gulf is not merely bridged ; it is closed. Man is not just comforted and admonished ; he is rescued from destruction and renewed in the being assigned him by his Creator.

The hymn does not exaggerate : " Now to God His saints are pleasing ; Now prevails a peace unceasing ; Now all conflict is concluded." Nor does the other hymn : " All claim the devil once might make, Against the race for Adam's sake, Is hazarded and forfeit." How blind is the Christianity which sings such things but acts as though everything were otherwise !

For the open secret of what has happened in Jesus Christ is that in Him the transcendent God who yet loves, elects and liberates the world, and lowly man who is yet loved, elected and liberated by Him, are indeed distinct and yet are not separated or two, but one. In Him the covenant between God and man has not merely been kept by God and broken by man, but kept by both, so that it is the fulfilled covenant. In Him there is not the clash of two kingdoms, but the one kingdom of God in reality. This is the new thing which the Christian community has not sought and found at random, let alone invented in a fit of inspiration, but which has disclosed itself to it and by which it has thus been found as the Word or call of Jesus Christ has come to it and has been received by it. This then—and we may return to our general description with no fear of finding ourselves on the way of new speculation—is concretely the grace of God addressed to the world which stands before the Christian community as it is confronted by world-occurrence around it. This is the final thing which it has to think and say in relation to this occurrence, because it is already the first thing, because it is the source from which it derives its own existence and life.

The point to be grasped is that in Jesus Christ we do really have the new reality of world history. The great test of the relationship of the community and individual Christians to Him, of the genuineness of their existence, is whether they see and are sure and keep to the fact, and with childlike confidence avouch to the world, that it is in Him that world history really and properly takes place. This is not just a new opinion, view or theory about it which has opened up before the community ; it is the work of deliverance and liberation which God Himself has accomplished and completed in and on the world, its reconciliation to Him, the fulfilment of His covenant with man, the justification of man before Him and his sanctification for Him, and therefore, as a result of the existence of Jesus Christ, the new reality of the world and man. It does not see in Jesus only what might be, or ought to be, or one day will be ; it sees what is, what has come into being in Him and by Him. How could it attest Him or believe in Him or know Him, what advantage would it have over the world or what would it have to say to it, if Jesus Christ were not unconditionally and unreservedly for it the One in whom there has taken place once and for all this alteration, the coming of the kingdom ? Everything else the world knows just as well as and perhaps better than the community. What would it have to say to it if, perhaps because it did not know it, it did not have this to say, attesting the absolutely new thing of the lordship of God already established within it ? It can and must realise that Jesus Christ is the new person in whom this new thing has already happened and is constantly shown to have already happened. It can and must keep to the fact that what has happened in Him has the dignity, power and validity of the first and last thing in world-occurrence. Hidden though it may be from the world and even the community, it will come to light as the reality of all history. It is He, and therefore what has taken place in Him, which will emerge as this reality rather than other things which claim its attention, and exclusively so in the case of the world.

This does not mean that the twofold aspect of world-occurrence— *hominum confusione et Dei providentia*—is dissolved or dispersed. It does not mean that Jesus Christ has merged into world-occurrence and world-occurrence into Him, so that we can no longer speak of them as separate things. This would be Christomonism in the bad sense of that unlovely term. What it does mean is that according to the true insight of the people of God the twofold form of world history loses the appearance of autonomy and finality, the character of an irreconcilable contradiction and antithesis, which it always seems to have at a first glance. The twofold view loses its sting. It acquires a good and natural sense, being indissoluble and indestructible simply because God and man are still different even in their unity in Jesus Christ. It no longer points us to a menacing abyss. Hence we are no longer tempted either to invoke a *Deus ex machina* or to bridge it by speculative or dialectical juggling. It becomes relative to Jesus Christ, to what has already taken place in Him. The one Jesus Christ has already represented God to man and man to God. He has already championed the cause of God with man and the cause of man with God. He has already executed the decisive act of the fatherly and royal providence of God by the removal of human confusion. He has already restored order between God and man and concluded peace between them. He, and that which is accomplished in and by Him, is already the reality of world history precisely in its twofold form. His cross and empty tomb are already the sign of its true meaning. His Word already declares this meaning. His life is already the reality which takes place in it. His community knows this. It is unknown to the world, but already known to His community. For His call, which underlies and sustains it, has already made it known to it, and continually does so.

The restriction now to be made is not obvious, since it is connected with the by no means obvious fact that neither the world nor the people of God within it is at the end and goal of God's work, that even after the appearance of Jesus Christ and what has taken place in Him there is still time and history : time for the community to proclaim the Word of Jesus Christ and what has taken place in Him ; time for the world to receive this Word ; space for the history of the prophecy of Jesus Christ. The resulting restriction is that the reconciliation of the world to God, the fulfilment of the covenant, the reconstituted order between God and man and therefore the new reality of world history, is known even to the community only in Jesus Christ and cannot therefore be known to the world which does not participate in the knowledge of Jesus Christ. It cannot be known. Hence the restriction is not in respect of the new reality of world history as such. This has been created and introduced, and is present. It is lacking in nothing. In the life and death and resurrection of Jesus Christ everything has been accomplished and made new. This is what the community cannot and must not forget, let alone deny, but recognise and confess in spite of every appearance to the contrary. It can do this only in faith, not in sight ; but the point of faith is to be aware and certain and confident of it. What would it mean to believe in Jesus Christ if it were not believed, and known and confessed in faith, that this has taken place in Him, that in and by Him world history has acquired this new reality, and that to this extent it has become the new history of a new world perfectly reconciled to God ? The restriction applies rather to the revelation and knowledge of this new reality. Apart from Jesus Christ Himself it is still the hidden reality of world history. In this history itself, i.e. in its visible form, in its events, movements and relationships, in its rising and falling and intercrossing lines and series, it cannot be seen nor deduced even though we be dealing with what is called the history of the spirit. The form in which world history appears to us is at best only the twofold form of the antithesis and conflict of above and below. To blind eyes it is not yet the new reality, and to no eyes at all is it yet the new form of this new reality.

There are signs (cf. *C.D.*, III, 3, pp. 198 ff.) of this new reality. There are distinct histories and historical constants in its history which stand in particularly close relationship to the event of the grace of God addressed to the world in Jesus Christ. There is, for example, the history of Holy Scripture, of the Church and of the Jews. Nor is the new reality of world history prevented from occasionally intimating itself as the first and final meaning of the whole even at what seems to be the farthest remove from the occurrence of the specific history of salvation. Perhaps it is only because of our stupidity that we do not more often and more strikingly see such intimations of its new reality. But these intimations are not declarations. If they can be the basis of meaningful gropings, they cannot form the foundation of knowledge. And in any case they are relevant only for those to whom the new reality of history has already made itself known directly in a very different way, though even by these, let alone by others, they are not to be overlooked nor interpreted differently. When we come to the other and more usual events of world history, we can only say that they may give both Christians and non-Christians cause for many suspicions concerning its meaning and interconnexion, but that these suspicions can never reach into the depth of its true reality nor have as their theme anything more than a variation on its familiar twofold aspect. In the light of what is seen in and may be deduced from world history, neither Christians nor non-Christians could suspect the reconciliation of the world to God in which the distinction between them is robbed of the sting of division, nor the divine covenant with man fulfilled by God Himself, nor the reconstituted order between the two, nor the kingdom of God inaugurated. If any do have inklings of these things, they are not to be restrained. But the Christian community in every age would be well advised not to erect its tents, let alone its houses, and especially not the temple, on inklings of this kind, if it is not to be guilty of the radical defection of attempted Christian philosophies of history and the related practical experiments, but to continue to see clearly that the transition from faith to sight is not in its own hands, that it is not therefore required, and that, since it is not required, it is not permitted. Sight is that which is not yet granted either to the world or to itself, namely, the perception of the new reality, of the one kingdom of God in world-occurrence itself. For the moment, even in the best of circumstances we can see this kingdom only in that twofold form and not in its true and proper sense.

The coming of the kingdom for which we now pray will be its manifestation, the final, universal and definitive manifestation of Jesus Christ and of what has already taken place in Him. For the community this will mean the transition from faith to sight. As yet however—and this is the restriction which now concerns us— He Himself, and what has taken place in Him, and therefore the kingdom, is known only to the community, and to the community only in His appearance and person and not in world-occurrence as such, so that even the community must pray for the coming of the kingdom. To be sure, it is enough and more than enough that the new reality of world history is not hidden but is actually revealed and knowable in Him. Already, believing in Him, it does actually see in Him, in His appearance and person, the first and the last, the atonement already made in Him, the covenant already fulfilled, the order restored. This knowledge of the new heaven and the new earth already given in relation to Him distinguishes it, for all the restriction of its vision, from the rest of humanity which does not yet participate in the knowledge of Jesus Christ and what has taken place in Him. And it is this distinction which capacitates it for witness to the world, and commits it to this witness.

But knowing the new reality of world history even if only in Him and as hidden in Him, it is not merely enabled and authorised but also compelled and commanded to see world history as such very differently from the way in which the rest of humanity can see it. This is not because, in relation to the events of yesterday, to-day and to-morrow, it has certain higher or deeper insights than others which it can weave into a Christian theory of the meaning and course of world history and then teach to others. We are thinking of something much more solid. As the new reality of world history is made known to the people of God in Jesus Christ, it is enabled, permitted and commanded to see things very differently in practice, to participate in world history very differently in its own attitude and action, than is the case with those who do not yet have knowledge of this new reality. Knowing Him whom others do not know, it sees it very differently to the extent that it now exists and participates in it very differently. And when we say " very differently " we do not mean this hypothetically, in the nature of an " as if," but in full and true reality on the basis of its knowledge of the true reality. Its faith may be only faith and not sight. But it is faith in Jesus Christ and therefore knowledge of what has taken place in Him. It is also obedient faith. It thus anticipates the appearance of that which already is but is not yet manifested. In its faith, which is both knowledge and obedience, it affirms already the transformation in which world-occurrence will be presented to it and to all humanity in the final, universal and definitive revelation of Jesus Christ, accepting the fact that this transformation has already taken place in His life and death and resurrection. Nor is this faith and anticipation an idle speculating and gaping. As obedience it is a resolute being and attitude and action. It is in this resoluteness that its view of world history will display the distinctiveness which makes it so different, so unique, as the Christian view. It is in this resoluteness that the people of God is already in its existence in world history a witness to the kingdom which it can see to have come already in Jesus Christ but towards the coming of which in direct and universal visibility it still looks forward. It is only in this resoluteness that it can and will properly discharge its ministry as a witness of Jesus Christ to the rest of man, as a people of those who see among the blind.

This is the resoluteness of a definite confidence. We refer to confidence in Jesus Christ and Him alone. But as such, in all its exclusiveness, this is true and total confidence. In world-occurrence the people of God sees no more than others. Even more soberly than others, it sees in it the great rift between above and below, between light and darkness. With even sharper eyes than others it recognises here the antithesis between the rule of God and the confusion of men. But it sees the same things differently. And the difference is real and indeed total to the extent that it always begins with the confidence, and may return to it, that in spite of everything the history which takes place is that of the world already reconciled to God. In spite of everything, the man who acts and postures on this stage, who in wickedness and folly, being blind to what he already is in Jesus Christ, thinks and speaks and acts, and arranges his sorry compromises, and sins, and causes so much suffering to himself and others, is the man who stands in the covenant with God which is already fulfilled. The order which is now so shamelessly and with such pregnant consequences attacked and violated, but which cannot be overthrown, is that which has been already and irrevocably restored. The people of God has no illusions about what goes on beneath its eyes, and not without its own participation. But it knows that in what takes place it is dealing with the passing and vanishing of a form of the world which is already judged, removed and outmoded by the coming and secret presence of the kingdom, so that, although it takes it seriously in all its consecutive and fading pictures, in none of them can it take it with ultimate, but only, as is proper, with penultimate seriousness. Or more positively, it knows that under, behind and in all that will be and is seen, there is concealed, and presses towards the light, the new form of the world which alone must be taken with first and final seriousness. Hence it can share neither the enthusiasm of those who regard the old form as capable of true and radical improvement nor the scepticism of those who in view of the impossibility of perfecting the old form think that they are compelled to doubt the possibility of a new form. It need judge no man either optimistically or pessimistically because in relation to all, whatever their virtues and accomplishments or their faults and blasphemies and crimes, it is sure of the one fact that Jesus Christ has lived and died and risen again for them too. In face of the disorder of historical relationships and interconnexions it can yield neither to reactionary spasms on the one hand nor to revolutionary on the other, because in relation to the reality of history already present in Jesus Christ it knows how provisional and improper is all the construction and destruction of man, or more positively how definitive and proper are the demolition and rebuilding which have already taken place in Jesus Christ and only wait to be manifested in the world on behalf of which they have been accomplished. This is the confidence with which the community confronts world history and the rest of humanity which does not share it. In world-occurrence it can neither fear for it nor be afraid of it, nor can it fear for nor be afraid of the humanity which acts within it as if it still had ground or presupposition on which to do so. But just because it cannot fear, it cannot hate, and therefore basically, whether it finds it easy or difficult, it can only love. At bottom and in the long run it can only be *pro*, i.e., for men, since God in Jesus Christ is and has decided for them. It cannot be *anti*, i.e., against even individuals. Obviously, it does not discuss or ponder its confidence. Nor does it experiment with it. What would become of it if it were regarded as marketable in this way ? Nor does it resolve to maintain it. Since it is the community which has been called by Jesus Christ and which therefore knows Him, the decision has been made for it. It has no option but to maintain it. In all the necessity of its commitment to and orientation on Him, it can do no other. It thus maintains it, and it lives within world-occurrence with this great confidence.

But the resoluteness with which in Jesus Christ it sees what is and what is not, is necessarily also the resoluteness of definite decision. This brings us to the test whether it really believes in Jesus Christ or in a synthesis which is supposed to interpret and explain history and artificially to bridge the gulf which threatens in it. Faith in such a synthesis always has as its basis the desire to find escape from decisions in the supposed freedom of the Yes and No, of the As-well-as, of the neutrality which is fatally active in the origin of the combination of the good creation of God with nothingness and then again in the combination of this confusion with the world government of God. As the community sees and knows, the decision has been made in Jesus Christ which makes quite impossible the idle contemplation and assessment of world-occurrence from a spectator's seat high above the antithesis between God and sinful man. All mere meditation or discussion for discussion's sake is now ruled out. Serving both the glory of God and the salvation of man, the decision taken in Him in unequivocally and definitively a decision for the world government of God and therefore against the confusion of men, for the good creation of God and therefore against nothingness. In Him, in His obedience to the Father, God is unequivocally and definitively glorified as the Creator and Lord of the world. And in His self-offering for men the power of nothingness and the confusion of men are just as unequivocally and definitely set aside. The man who has fallen away from God and fallen out with his neighbour and himself, and who has thus surrendered to nothingness and caused confusion after confusion, has been crucified and done to death on the cross, and a new man, free in obedience to God, has been born and introduced. The act of God in Jesus Christ is a clear decision for this new man living at peace with God and therefore honouring the goodness of His creation. It is a clear decision for the new form of the world actualised in His existence. It is thus a clear decision against the old man and the old form of the world, which can only disappear now that they have been set aside. The community of Jesus Christ sees this decision taken in Him. It keeps to it. It follows it. It follows it in world-occurrence and therefore within the limits of its own possibilities. Yet it does follow it, not as an idle spectator, but in active obedience. It follows, not in one great absolute step, but in several small and relative steps.

But it really does follow it. It cannot and will not accomplish the coming of the new man and his world and the perishing of the old man and his. It can only attest this coming. But it does this in resolute decisions for and against. It cannot and should not be otherwise than that where it does there should be provisional clarifications anticipating the great and conclusive clarity towards which it and the whole cosmos are moving. It is here that there is a cleavage of minds and ways and possibilities so far as this is possible prior to the last judgment of Jesus Christ. It may be that where two apparently equal and illuminating possibilities seem to offer, it will not mince matters but decide for the one and not the other, and therefore against the other. Conversely, it may not accept what seems to be the only possible course but pursue or seek a third way. But in any case, whether by declaration or impressive silence, whether by partisanship or rejection of partisanship or even the formation of its own party, it will resolutely participate. And in so doing it will always have regard to the decision taken in Jesus Christ ; it will always look back to the triumph of the cause of God and man championed by Him ; it will always seek to respect and assert His great Yes and No as it freely speaks its own little Yes and No ; it will always look forward to the future, perfect manifestation of His victory, of the Yes and No spoken in Him. Looking backwards and forwards in this way, it will exclude any compromises in the little Yes and No which it can speak ; it will refrain from excusing itself by its own uncertainty, ignorance and impotence ; it will avoid all regressions into hesitation ; and it will always be responsible and prepared, either engaging, or on the point of engaging, in resolute action within general world-occurrence. It can neither execute its decisions with a view to certain results, especially such as might seem good to itself, nor can it refrain from doing so in view of the unpleasant consequences which are always entailed, and least of all when these might seem to constitute a threat to itself. What it has been given to know in a certain situation on the basis of the new reality of history in Jesus Christ, it can never wrap up nor conceal nor keep to itself nor treat as if it were something indifferent, a mere matter of faith which can remain purely inward and individual and need not be followed by any specific conclusion or action. On the contrary, in concrete obedience and confession it will always do in world-occurrence that which men who do not yet know Jesus Christ neither do nor can do. It will take concrete account of the atonement made in Jesus Christ, the covenant fulfilled in Him, the order re-established in Him. It is always expected to do or to refrain from doing specific things. And as it executes its decisions in world-occurrence, it will undoubtedly change it. " Resolves genuinely taken change the world " (C. F. v. Weizsäcker). They do not do so absolutely conclusively or unequivocally. What the community can say and do in relation to the decision taken in Jesus Christ and in attestation of this decision, will always be relative. It can never consist in more than the erection of a sign. But the point at issue is that there should be this relative alteration of world history by the erection of signs. The community cannot and must not evade this if its faith is not an indolent or dead faith, if it is faithful with the little possibilities entrusted to it in relation to the new reality of history. No more than this is demanded. But this is unconditionally demanded. If it does not perform it, then it cannot have its true confidence in relation to world-occurrence. Indeed, the question whether or not it performs it is the test whether it believes in the living Jesus Christ or in the cheap grace of a synthesis which it has itself invented with a view to evading decision. If it believes in Him, it exists in the resoluteness of definite decisions in world-occurrence.

It exists finally in the resoluteness of a definite hope for world-occurrence. In the light of the grace of God addressed to the world, i.e., of Jesus Christ as the new reality of world history, and therefore unencumbered either by optimism or pessimism, it looks forward to the goal appointed, namely, to the revelation of the new reality of history which is as yet concealed. The confidence with which, right through whatever else it sees, it keeps to what it sees in Jesus Christ, is a quiet confidence in relation to what has already taken place in Him, but also a very lively confidence in relation to what applies and is, and to what does not apply and is not, on this basis. Otherwise it would not work out in the resoluteness of the decisions which it must constantly execute. Yet it is not exhausted by the movement in which it tries to follow, in relation to the immediate temporal future, the decision which has been taken in Jesus Christ. It is a resolute confidence even in relation to the future, to the goal of the totality of world history. The Christian community dares to hope in Jesus Christ and therefore it dares to hope for the world. It waits for Him who came once and for all yesterday, and who is and lives always and therefore to-morrow. In relation to Him it knows that the form of the world which now confronts it cannot last but will one day perish and be seen no more, and that its new reality will then appear and alone be seen by itself and all men—the world reconciled to God, the covenant fulfilled by Him, the order reconstituted by Him. It waits for Jesus Christ. It waits for Him to emerge from His concealment in world-occurrence and to show Himself to it and to the men of every age and place as the One He already is as its Lord. It yearns for this. It rejoices in it. For it sees it coming as the goal and end of world history. In relation to it, it hopes for history, not merely individual benefits, but the very best. And it does so with the same resoluteness with which it maintains its confidence and ventures and executes its decisions in relation to its present form. Resolute in its confidence and decisions, it cannot but hope, looking for the coming of Jesus Christ in His glory. Only in so doing, and therefore only in the resoluteness of its distinctive hope in Him and therefore its hope for the world and all men, can it and will it be capable of equally resolute confidence and decision.

In sum, when we ask what is world history we may say that for the people of God it is simply the sphere in which it has to exist with this resoluteness. In Jesus Christ this people sees it in the form of its new reality. In this form it is manifest to it in Jesus Christ from whom it derives, who is its Lord, and whom it has to attest to all other men. Apart from this one picture of Jesus Christ, the new reality of history is still concealed from it as from all men. What it sees as world history apart from this picture consists of the many pictures of a form which does not correspond to but contradicts its new reality, i.e., the form in which there is still a wide gulf between the providence of God which overrules it and the confusion of man which rules in it, the form of the history of a world which is as yet unreconciled and far from the kingdom of God and alien to it, of a man who is as yet unjustified and unsanctified. But already the Christian community sees it differently even in this form. For it is not deceived. It realises that in all these pictures in which it presents itself it does not have its true reality but a being which is already outmoded and condemned to perish in virtue of the new reality even now present within it. Hence it cannot fix its gaze on these pictures, however exciting they may be for good or evil, as though in any of them it had to do with first or final things. It is free in relation to all of them. It can take them in earnest only transitorily in their coming and going, knowing that they are all pictures of a transitory being. Again, it sees them all differently in the positive sense that, no matter how the pictures may change from day to day, it takes them seriously as the field where it must maintain the resoluteness to which it has been called and for which it has been empowered by the new reality revealed and not concealed in Jesus Christ, and which it has to express as the confidence grounded in Him, in the decisions determined by Him and in the hope directed to Him. The sphere in which it may do this is world history as seen by the people of God.

We must now turn to the second question how the Christian community is to understand itself within world-occurrence. " Within world-occurrence," i.e., participant in and confronted by it, is in this context the particular standpoint from which we must raise and answer the question of the nature of the Church. And in the light of what we have just said the answer can and must be decisively very simple, namely, that the Church or the Christian community is the people which exists in the divinely given knowledge of the new reality of world-occurrence concealed in Jesus Christ, and in the resultant and distinctive resoluteness of its confidence, decisions and hope. It understands world-occurrence as the sphere in which it has to exist with this resoluteness. We may thus continue that it understands itself as it exists with this resoluteness. It must be underlined that in so doing it defines and understands itself as what it is. Not otherwise, for how else can it define and understand itself as what it is ? Yet this answer obviously stands in need of a certain differentiation, as it also needs in some sense to be deepened. What kind of a people is it which exists with this resoluteness and understands itself in so doing ? And when we have cleared up this point to some extent, there still remains our third and final question on which both its view of world-occurrence and its self-understanding ultimately depend, namely, how it can and does come about that it actually exists with this knowledge and therefore with the resoluteness based upon it.

As in relation to the first question, we must begin by noting that our consideration of the nature of the Christian community in world-occurrence must be strictly theological. It is true that we can pose and answer the question in the setting of a general phenomenology and sociology of fellowship, and especially of religious fellowship, as Schleiermacher did in his own brilliant fashion in the context of his ethics and philosophy of history, and as lesser minds are tempted to do in accordance with the historicist habit of thought. It is to be seriously doubted, however, whether there can be even an approach on these lines to that which constitutes the particularity of the Christian community. But however that may be, our responsibility to the Word of God disclosed to the community in the witness of Holy Scripture, and to be attested by it to the world, cannot be evaded at this point where it is a matter of the community itself. In our treatment of the world-occurrence which surrounds the community, we cannot abstract from our recollection of the καλῶν by whose κλῆσις the community is constituted His ἐκκλησία. Hence in the problem of the nature of this community we cannot look in any direction or take any steps other than in the circle indicated by these three terms. It is from the standpoint to which we are directed by them that the Christian community understands itself truly, i.e., in accordance with the truth which underlies it and therefore in its real essence.

We start off with the general observation that it is not improper but proper to the Christian community to be visible, and indeed basically and virtually to be so to every eye in every possible aspect of human affairs. The Christian community is a phenomenon which all men may perceive and assert like all others in the sphere of history and indeed of creation generally. It is an empirical and rationally comprehensible magnitude " like the kingdom of France or the republic of Venice," as they used to put it in the 16th century. It is another question whether or to what extent and with what precision it is actually seen by men at a given time and place, whether or to what degree it is thus a known magnitude. It may not have become and it may not be this to many men. Yet the fact remains that it did and does become this, and is this, to countless others to some extent and with some degree of precision. And our present concern is with the basic and virtual fact that it can be a known magnitude to any man, and that it is visible in this sense. To be sure, it is also not improper but highly proper to it to be also invisible, i.e., not to be visible to every eye, not to be a phenomenon like all others, not to be an empirical and rationally comprehensible magnitude, and to that extent to be a magnitude which, for all that it is known, is in principle and not merely in fact unknown to countless thousands. It is not the case, however, that only to the extent that it is invisible, i.e., an unknown magnitude to countless thousands, is it the real Christian community, as if its invisibility were essential and its visibility non-essential or accidental. On the contrary, it is no less essential to it—and this is our present concern—to be visible as well as invisible, i.e., to be a magnitude which may be known by all. Even what it is invisibly, i.e., as it is not visible to all men, is not separated or apart from its being as visible to all, but lies in the mystery, or the disclosure of the mystery, of its visible being.

But if it exists essentially in the sphere of visibility, this implies that it exists essentially *ad extra* within world-occurrence, and not behind or above it, nor after the manner of a transcendent idea or *civitas platonica* or angelic dominion, let alone after that of the purely transcendent God who may be called God only if it is forgotten that His Word became flesh. The community which was created and lives by this Word, the people of Jesus Christ, also exists in the flesh, *ad extra*, within world-occurrence. And we must be more precise and say that it does not do so like an embedded foreign body, like a meteorite which has fallen from a distant sphere or a pearl in its shell, but as itself a genuinely and thoroughly worldly element participating in world-occurrence. There is an ecclesiological as well as a christological Docetism which we must carefully avoid at this point. The Christian community does not merely resemble the other elements, magnitudes and factors in world-occurrence ; for all the particularity of its structure and situation it is of like manner with them. It does not hover over them ; it exists on the same level. It can thus be seen together with them, and critically and constructively compared with them. It is itself a people like so many others. There can be no excluding the attempts made to understand it in the categories of general sociology as a union or society or more specifically a religious fellowship, and therefore historically as a link in, or possibly as the supreme product of, the history of the development of such unions, and therefore as part of the history of religion, or the history of the spirit, or even secular history as a whole. Indeed, where it is thought that its essence is exhausted by that wherein it is visible to all, this course will seem to be demanded as the only sober way of understanding. Devastating misunderstanding will undoubtedly result. The Christian community is not merely *ad extra* and visible. But it would not be the Christian community if it were not also wholly visible, *ad extra* and worldly ; if it were so completely different from other historical factors ; if it did not also have this other aspect ; if it were not exposed to this misunderstanding.   Under this aspect it is indeed exposed to it with no means of defence, just as the incarnate Word of God which underlies and sustains it, even the man Jesus Christ, was and is also exposed to it.   It would not be His community if offence could not be taken at it too.

It is not non-essential but essential to it to exist wholly *ad extra* in a visible and worldly manner, and therefore to the very end and goal of all temporal history to be exposed without means of defence to the offence or misunderstanding of its nature.   We need not bewail this, nor wish it otherwise, nor try to suppress or artifically to conceal it as a *pudendum*.   In its visibility we do not have a disturbing appearance which does not belong to the true community of Jesus Christ, which attaches to it only temporarily as perhaps one of the implications of the post-Adamic state of humanity to which it is subject, which will finally disappear, and which may thus be regarded so far as possible as accidental, co-incidental and indifferent, so that no primary or ultimate significance need be seen in it.   This is the kind of gross or refined theoretical and practical ecclesiological Docetism which the Christian community must avoid if it is rightly to understand itself and to exist with the resoluteness appropriate to it.   As surely as its Lord Jesus Christ was elected from all eternity, not as the λόγος ἄσαρκος, but as the *Verbum incarnandum*, in His concrete humanity and visibility as the man Jesus of Nazareth ; as surely as He came and lived and suffered and died " in the flesh " (1 Jn. 4²) ; as surely as He did not lay aside His concretely human nature but in it rose again from the dead, and ascended into heaven, and, clothed in it, sits at the right hand of God ; as surely as the condescension of God to flesh, to concrete Adamic humanity, does not imply any diminution, but rather, as the work of His grace, the triumph and fulfilment of His eternal, pre-temporal, supra-temporal and post-temporal glory and majesty, so surely in the same Jesus Christ God has also elected His community in its very being *ad extra*, in its visibility and worldliness, in its likeness with other peoples, and so surely it will not be divested of this being, but will be manifested in its visibility and worldliness at the fulfilment of His return, when it will, of course, be no more exposed to misunderstanding, but in the unequivocal radiance of the totality of its being will share eternal life in fellowship with God.   But if it is essential to it as the community of Jesus Christ from and to all eternity to exist also wholly *ad extra* as a visible and worldly people like others, then obviously this is particularly so in the temporal history which takes place during this intervening period.   It would necessarily be ashamed of the God who acts and speaks in Jesus Christ if it were to be ashamed of itself existing also *ad extra*, visibly, in likeness with all other historical and creaturely elements and factors.   And any attempt artificially to transcend or secretly to set aside this likeness with the world, even though such attempts are all foredoomed to failure, would inevitably entail its separation from this God, from the Lord by whose Word it has been created and lives. It can be faithful to Him only in exact and honest and sober correspondence to His coming in the flesh. In accordance with His example, it can meet the world only on its own level, as itself visible to the world and wholly and utterly worldly. How else can or will it be for the world a witness of Jesus Christ and of the reconciliation to God effected in Him? It can be this only as it is utterly like the world. To be this now is to be exposed to the danger of the same misunderstanding and offence to which in His humanity its Lord was and is also exposed. But in its being *ad extra*, in its visibility and therefore its likeness and solidarity with the world, it can be to it His witness. Hence it belongs to its essence also to be *ad extra*, to be visible, and therefore to be like the world and in solidarity with it. Hence also we need not bewail this nor entertain any illusions in relation to it, nor deny it. Sheer gratitude is called for in face of the astonishing fact that in correspondence with the coming of the Son of God in the flesh, in His discipleship, there may be a people like others which precisely as such is His people and may exist in His service.

It is only in the setting of this basic likeness that we can understand the election and calling of the Old Testament covenant people, and its wonderful distinction and mission among all peoples. Implicitly and explicitly the prophets were constantly reminding Israel of this fact. " You only have I known of all the families of the earth " (Am. 3²). But this is not because Israel has any natural or acquired advantage over others. It is as " Not my people," like all others, that it is called " My people " by Yahweh (Hos. 2²³). " Are ye not as children of the Ethiopians unto me, O children of Israel ? saith the Lord. Have not I brought up Israel out of the land of Egypt ? and the Philistines from Caphtor, and the Syrians from Kir ? " (Am. 9⁷). Similarly the people of Jerusalem are shown in Ez. 16³ᶠ· how the Lord found this nation in the open field as an exposed and abandoned infant : " Thy birth and thy nativity is of the land of Canaan ; thy father was an Amorite, and thy mother an Hittite." In these conditions the Lord said " Live," and continually received it to Himself, and heaped His favours on it and decked it with honour, only to experience shameless infidelity at its hand. We may also recall the prayer for the bringing of the first-fruits of the harvest in Deut. 26⁵ᶠ·, which begins with the confession : " A Syrian ready to perish was my father," who went down into Egypt, and there became " a nation, great, mighty and populous," which has finally been given the fruitful land in which it may now rejoice. Relevant, too, is the saying in Is. 63¹⁶, which sharply cuts off any confidence in historical tradition and succession : " Doubtless thou art our father, though Abraham be ignorant of us, and Israel acknowledge us not : thou, O Lord, art our father, our redeemer ; thy name is from everlasting." So, too, is Is. 64⁸ : " But now, O Lord, thou art our father ; we are the clay, and thou our potter ; and we all are the work of thy hand." Of this people as seen in itself and as such it might always be said : " They shall return to Egypt " (Hos. 8¹³, 9³). And the New Testament confirms this aspect : " Many shall come from the east and west, and shall sit down with Abraham, and Isaac, and Jacob, in the kingdom of heaven. But the children of the kingdom shall be cast out into outer darkness " (Mt. 8¹¹). Nor can there be any doubt in relation to the members of the people of God elected and called from the nations, that as the branches of a wild olive, while they are grafted into the good olive and come to have a share in its rich root, they might just as well, and perhaps more easily, be cut off again as so many of the original branches (Rom. 11$^{17f.}$). The saying in Mt. 3^9 is even stronger, namely, that it is by awakening them from the stones that God makes them children of Abraham. God has called them from darkness to His wonderful light (1 Pet. 2^9). Those who once were Gentiles in the flesh, without Christ, aliens from the commonwealth of Israel, strangers to the covenants of promise and without God (ἄθεοι) in the world, have now been made nigh, being included in the peace in which they and Israel are one new man, one body, and have access by one Spirit unto the Father (Eph. 2$^{11f.}$). This, then, is how the community of Jews and Gentiles is constituted and exists. It is a people of those who were dead (Eph. 2$^{1f.}$) and have been awakened to life. There is a people like this, a people of Jesus Christ, elected and called by God. But there are no men who have any right or claim to be this people. They can be what they are, namely, this particular people, only by free grace. In themselves and as such, i.e., in abstraction from God's free grace, they are not a particular people, but one among many others and like all others. Neither the Old Testament nor the New Testament community can have it otherwise, nor try to understand itself in any other way.

We now move on to a second general statement which complements the first. Like Israel in the Old Testament, the Christian community is not just a people in world-occurrence but this people. It is just as essential to it to be this people as to be a people. And it is just as essential to it to be not merely visible as one people among many but also invisible as this people, i.e., to be a phenomenon which cannot be grasped and asserted by all, a magnitude which cannot be comprehended and therefore known by all in empirical and rational terms. As this people it might well be a magnitude which is totally unknown to all. Hence it is both visible and invisible in the one essence.

Only after fully revising and clarifying the Platonic doctrine of the relation between idea and appearance—a task which we cannot undertake in this context —might it be possible at a pinch, but only at a pinch, to describe the one essence of the Christian community according to these categories, as we ourselves prefer not to do.

It is not that according to its proper nature on the one side the Christian community is invisible, and according to its improper nature on the other side visible. Rather it is totally and properly both visible and invisible. The christological background should be remembered. Jesus Christ is not visibly but improperly true man and properly and invisibly true God. In the one being He is both visible as true man and invisible as true God, and both properly. Thus it is in the totally visible being of the community that the totally invisible lives and moves as its secret. And the totally invisible calls for manifestation and declaration in the totally visible. It is as this particular people that it is one among others. And it is as one among others that it is this particular people.

Just as it is one among others in that it is wholly *ad extra* and like all the other elements, magnitudes and factors in world-occurrence, so it is this particular people in that it is from within and unlike all others. Nor does this mean that it is unlike only as one example in a species, or one species in a genus, or one genus in a class ; it means that it is unlike because it is unique and incomparable, an example, a species, a genus, a class apart. It is for this reason that disastrous misunderstanding necessarily results when interpretations are attempted which assume that it is to be reduced to a common denominator with such analogous phenomena as Islam or Buddhism or even Communism, and considered together, and perhaps conceived in historico-critical terms, probably under the master concept of religion, as either a link in historical development or the particular actualisation of a general possibility. As in the total visibility of its being it is exposed without means of defence to the inevitable misunderstanding which threatens from this quarter, so in its total invisibility it cannot be even remotely affected by this misunderstanding, the interpretation being so totally devoid of any substance of truth. To the extent that it does not exist only *ad extra* and in likeness with all the other elements in world-occurrence, but also from within and in complete unlikeness, it is essentially invisible, i.e., it is not visible to the eyes of each and all. Hence any interpretation which abstracts from this fact, keeping only to what is visible to all, can only miss and misunderstand its being, and indeed its total being, including that wherein it is visible. Therefore, no matter what the interpretation may be, we can be sure that the community of Jesus Christ is not in any case or in any sense what it is there stated to be.

That which makes it, as one people, this incomparable people ; that wherein it is totally from within, and therefore invisible, i.e., not visible to all eyes, is, however, the fact that it is the community of Jesus Christ and therefore as such the people of God in world-occurrence. It may be granted that without His election and calling, without His will and work and Word, it would not exist even visibly, *ad extra*, in worldly form and to that extent in likeness with the various elements and factors of the world. It exists at all, and therefore in this sense, only in the power of the divine decision, act and revelation accomplished and effective in Jesus Christ. Yet in this power, and therefore as the community of Jesus Christ, it also exists from within, uniquely and therefore invisibly, i.e., in a way which is visible to some, though not all. At this point we are brought up against the same limit as in our answering of the first question concerning the new reality of world history created and revealed in Jesus Christ, namely, who can see, accept and affirm what the Christian community is on the basis of its election and calling, as the work of divine decision, act and revelation, except by knowledge of this divine work, of the Lord who elects and calls His community, and therefore of Jesus Christ. It is eyes that are opened for Him and by Him which see what His community is as grounded in Him. They see it, of course, as the mystery of the one being which is sealed and which reveals itself in its visibility. They see the establishment of the community as it has been and is accomplished by the invisible God in Jesus Christ. They thus see it exist as this incomparable people. Hence for all its likeness to other elements they see it as unique. For the community, to whose seeing eyes we refer, there is revealed and not concealed in Jesus Christ the will and work and Word of God by which it is called into and sustained in being. Hence it cannot go wrong in its understanding of its invisible essence, nor indeed of its visible. For what it is from within is what calls for expression *ad extra*. What it is invisibly wills as such to become generally visible, and has the promise that one day it will do so. Hence even what it is *ad extra* and visibly is not only like but unlike other world elements to the extent that it bears within it the mystery of what it is from within and invisibly, to the extent that this is to be disclosed and declared in it. What it is from within is what it is to become outwards. For this is the hidden distinction of its visible being. It cannot understand itself otherwise than as the living community of its living Lord Jesus Christ, i.e., as the people in and with whose existence He Himself is actively present and at work in world-occurrence. He has elected and called it. He underlies its being both in its invisibility and also its visibility. He directs it as He controls this its one being. And He controls it as He leads and impels and presses it from within outwards, from invisibility to visibility. In world-occurrence, and in all its worldliness, it is His community, the elect and called people of God, as in this sense it is directed by Him and obedient to His direction.

Its being, then, is invisible, but its impulse is from within outwards, from invisibility to visibility, from particularity to universality. Even as visible, it bears the promise of invisibility within it. This means, however, that, even though it is like the world and in world-occurrence, yet it is distinct from the world and different, individual and unique in relation to it, being set over against and in confrontation with world-occurrence. The existence of the Christian community thus corresponds to the existence of Jesus Christ to the extent that He first came in the flesh, so that in His human nature He is the eternal Son of God, and as such different from the world in spite of His solidarity with it, confronting world-occurrence unequivocally as its Lord even while He inconspicuously integrates Himself into it. His community follows Him as it must understand and therefore express its own being as one which is wholly worldly and yet also as a being in encounter with world-occurrence.

At this point, of course, a certain reservation or delimitation is necessary. The invisible being of the community which presses from within outwards for visibility, and in which for all the likeness it is different, individual and unique in relation to the world and its elements, magnitudes and factors, is something which, together with its confronting of world-occurrence, it cannot realise of itself, but which it owes wholly and utterly to its election and calling, to the divine decision, act and revelation enacted in Jesus Christ. What it is invisibly is its being by grace and not by nature. It is promised and allotted to it as a free gift. It is only with the greatest surprise and gratitude that it can understand it as a being which is truly its own. Between its invisible being and that of Jesus Christ, between its distinction from the world and His, its confrontation of world-occurrence and His, there is indeed correspondence but no parity, let alone identity. Even in its invisible essence it is not Christ, nor a second Christ, nor a kind of extension of the one Christ. The supreme and final thing to be said of it—and this brings us back in another context to a familiar theme—is quite simply that it is His body, His earthly-historical form of existence. It is indeed in the flesh, but it is not, as He is, the Word of God in the flesh, the incarnate Son of God.

Thus to speak of a continuation or extension of the incarnation in the Church is not only out of place but even blasphemous. Its distinction from the world is not the same as His ; it is not that of the Creator from His creature. Its superiority to the world is not the same as His ; it is not that of the Lord seated at the right hand of the Father. Hence it must guard as if from the plague against any posturing or acting as if in relation to world-occurrence it were an *alter Chrisus*, or a *vicarius Christi*, or a *corredemptrix*, or a *mediatrix omnium gratiarum*, not only out of fear of God, but also because in any such behaviour, far from really exalting itself or discharging such functions, it can only betray, surrender, hazard and lose its true invisible being, and therefore its true distinction from the world and superiority to world-occurrence.

Its true invisible being, and therefore its real distinction from and superiority to the world, is that it is elected and called to be a people alongside and with Jesus Christ and with a share in His self-declaration, that it is given to it to be appointed His witness, to be set in the service of the eternal Word of God spoken in Him, to be ordained to follow the Son of God incarnate in Him. This is its incomparable glory and dignity which it would be mad to surrender by grasping at anything higher. This is what makes it unique among all peoples. Its particular structure and situation do not make it this, for they might be similar to or like others. The crucial point is that it exists on the basis of the call and summons of Jesus Christ, that His commission and command are the meaning of its structure, that it belongs to Him and is His possession in this particular sense. These things cannot be said of any people or society which has come into being by natural or historical means. In virtue of them, it cannot be understood only in historical and sociological terms. In virtue of them, even though it participates at every point in it, it is also opposed to world-occurrence, and indeed opposed in a way which is teleologically meaningful, in a fruitful antithesis. It cannot possibly receive the particular grace freely addressed by God to it, nor rejoice in nor boast of this grace, without being at once aware of the prophetic task therewith implied, without taking up this task, without giving itself wholly to it. To recall the starting-point of the discussion, it can understand itself as the community of Jesus Christ only as it ventures to exist with that resoluteness and therefore to bear the witness entrusted to it.

What we have been attempting positively to sketch is the self-understanding of the Old and New Testament community.

It is to be noted above all that in relation to its concretely historical being and nature in space and time the people of both parts of Holy Scripture understands itself in its particularity to be the people of God. It is its being as fundamentally visible to all which it takes to be determined, in a way which is, of course, invisible, i.e., which is not visible to all, by this its particularity. In so doing, it does not look into the heights or depths of an idea, of a metaphysics distinct from spatio-temporal physics, of a transcendent essentiality in which it really exists, so that in its present form it is what it is only improperly, incidentally and transitorily. It does not understand itself with visionary reference to a myth, nor its historical existence as the transparency of a myth. Even its historical existence it regards as determined by the divine decision, act and revelation. It is the very fact that its historical existence in all its spatio-temporal and human concreteness is determined by the will and work and Word of God which constitutes the invisible essence of the people of God. We are thus dealing with its invisibly determined visible being even when mythological notions, images and expressions are used, as they often are in both Testaments, to state its self-understanding. How could it take any other course when it has to denote the determination of its visible essence by its invisible, of its historical existence by the action and speech of God? But even and precisely when it does use the language of mythology, what it expresses is its historical existence as thus determined and not a distinct world behind or above this in which alone it is properly that which within world-occurrence, in likeness to and solidarity with the world, it can be only improperly. Precisely what it is properly, it is in virtue of the presence of its invisible essence in its visible. Here in time and space, where it is only one people among others, there takes place within it the action and self-declaration of the invisible God. As one people it is His people and therefore this people. This is the most succinct and comprehensive way in which we can state the self-understanding of the Old and New Testament community.

As one people it is His people. It is one people. As such, under the name of Israel, it was first a confederation of more or less consanguineous tribes, not unlike the many others in the Near East and elsewhere, which emerged from small and obscure beginnings to tread the stage of history for a time and then to be reduced to a small remnant. And then again as such, it became the plurality of Jewish and Gentile societies of life and worship which arose in the days of Hellenism and took their name from the supposed Messiah Jesus. In both cases we have one people among others arising more or less naturally on the one side and freely on the other. But in both cases this one people is the people of God. For in both cases what takes place invisibly in its concretely visible existence and history is the determination which it is given and which is proper to it, namely, that it is God's people. Is ? Yes, as it becomes this, as it is given the determination to become and to be it, it is. It becomes it, for no human society could or can become and be it of itself. But by the decision, act and revelation of God, by His will and work and Word, this people is freely elected, fashioned, called, nourished, maintained and directed to be His people, the people of God. It is so only and exclusively in this way, but in this way truly. We recall the unheard of events of its origin. We remember first the descendants of Jacob-Israel, their escape from Egypt, their nomadic life in the desert and at Sinai, their fruitful settlement on the eastern shores of the Mediterranean, their expansion, their rise to modest glory and subsequent fall. Is this, then, the people of God ? Yes, it recognises and confesses that it is ; indeed, it cannot but do so : " Blessed is the nation whose God is the Lord ; and the people whom he hath chosen for his own inheritance " (Ps. 33^{12}). " O come, let us sing unto the Lord : let us make a joyful noise to the rock of our salvation. Let us come before his presence with thanksgiving, and make a joyful noise unto him with psalms. . . . O come, let us worship, and bow down : let us kneel before the Lord our maker. For he is our God ; and we are the people of his pasture, and the sheep of his hand " (Ps. 95$^{1f.,\ 6f.}$). And therefore : " The Lord of hosts is with us ; the God of Jacob is our refuge " (Ps. 46^{7}). Then again, we remember the ἐκκλησίαι which were formed after the manner of sects in Judaism, which then emerged from Judaism, which were gathered and spread after the manner of sects in the Roman Empire, and which for all the fact that they were so unimpressive, as freely admitted by their greatest apostle in 1 Cor. 1$^{20f.}$, were not ashamed of their so-called Gospel but sought to proclaim it everywhere. Is this, then, the people of God ? Yes, it recognises and confesses that it is : " Blessed be the God and Father of our Lord Jesus Christ, who hath blessed us with all spiritual blessings in heavenly places in Christ : according as he hath chosen us in him before the foundation of the world, that we should be holy and without blame before him in love : having predestinated us unto the adoption of children by Jesus Christ to himself, according to the good pleasure of his will, to the praise of the glory of his grace, wherein he hath made us accepted in the beloved " (Eph. 1$^{3-6}$). Thus, it is of God alone, but of God truly and effectively, that the community of the Old and New Testaments is His people. This is how it understands itself. It is thus that it recognises and confesses its invisible being in and with the visible.

We must now say further, however, that only in the fact that it is the people of God, that God lives and acts and speaks as its God, is it this people. Here alone the singularity of its existence and nature has its basis and may be perceived. It is indeed a unique people. It alone is what it is. It alone exists as it does. " Happy art thou, O Israel : who is like unto thee, O people saved by the Lord, the shield of thy help, and who is the sword of thy excellency ! " (Deut. 33^{29}). This is really appreciated by the New Testament community : " For whatsoever is born of God overcometh the world : and this is the victory that overcometh the world, even our faith " (1 Jn. 5^{4}). The God who elects and calls this people, however, is the One who lifts it up so high, who imparts and guarantees and maintains its uniqueness, its radical distinction and superiority in face of all around. He really does this, but He alone does it in the omnipotence and freedom of the grace addressed to it. To be sure, it also has its relative individuality marking it off visibly from other nations. It treads its own historical paths, has its own structure of faith, its own consequent form of tradition, its own doctrine and cultus, its own manner of life first in Israel and then in the Christian communities. Nor should we forget the obvious connexion between the first form and the second, which marks them off in common and most significantly from other historical phenomena. Nor can there be any doubt that the visible particularity of each is not accidental, but is itself determined and impressed upon it by the divine election and calling. Yet the fact remains that it is only the electing and calling God Himself who makes it in its own particular way this people, who imparts, guarantees and maintains its particularity, and who makes this visible. Apart from Him, i.e., from His living, personal presence and action, it would be only one people and not this people, unique in relation to all other historical phenomena, even in its relative individuality. Apart from God, even the distinctive contours in which it exists and is seen within world-occurrence would not shine out in their uniqueness as those of the people of God, but might very well be seen together and compared and interchanged with the contours of other historical phenomena. In the self-understanding of the people of God it is thus ruled out that it should rejoice and glory in the distinction and superiority revealed in its particular form and history except in the gratitude, penitence and praise of prayer to the living God who has elected and called it ; it is ruled out that it should try to have the free grace of its election and calling, and therefore existence as His people distinct from and superior to all others, except by direct reception each new day from the hand of the free Giver. As it asks Him for it, it does receive it from Him and have it in Him. By Him it really is distinguished from those around and exalted above them. By Him, as is brought out with particular vividness in the Old Testament but strongly enough also in the New in obvious reminiscence, it is permitted and even commanded to take seriously and to assert its uniqueness and distinction from surrounding nations, not to intermingle nor confuse its way of life with theirs, to keep itself free and uncontaminated in relation to them, to follow its own law and maintain its own direction. What is at issue is not the preservation of its own way of life, the keeping of its own law or the maintaining of its own direction as such, but the grateful obedience which it owes to the will and work and Word of its God, to His election as indicated in its uniqueness. For all its loyal, zealous and bold self-assertion on the way of obedience to which God has directed it would be quite futile if God Himself did not tread this way with it, if in His preservation and direction of it He did not graciously maintain and express Himself on its behalf.

Thus " I will not trust in my bow, neither shall my sword save me. But thou hast saved us from our enemies, and hast put them to shame that hated us. In God we boast all the day long, and praise thy name for ever " (Ps. 44$^{6f.}$) " From whence cometh my help ? My help cometh from the Lord, which made heaven and earth " (Ps. 121$^{1f.}$). Or again in relation to the past : " If it had not been the Lord who was on our side, now may Israel say ; if it had not been the Lord who was on our side, when men rose up against us : then they had swallowed us up quick. . . . Blessed be the Lord, who hath not given us as a prey to their teeth " (Ps. 124$^{1f. 6}$). Or in relation to the future : " Turn us again, O God, and cause thy face to shine ; and we shall be saved " (Ps. 80^3). For obviously : " Not unto us, O Lord, not unto us, but unto thy name give glory, for thy mercy, and for thy truth's sake. Wherefore should the heathen say, Where is now their God ? " (Ps. 115$^{1f.}$). In every respect, therefore, " our soul waiteth for the Lord : he is our help and our shield. . . . Let thy mercy, O Lord, be upon us, according as we hope in thee " (Ps. 33$^{20f.}$). Yahweh ! His mercy ! " Except the Lord build the house, they labour in vain that build it : except the Lord keep the city, the watchman waketh but in vain " (Ps. 127^1). This is the self-understanding of the Old Testament community. By a slender and indeed invisible thread it clings to its God, standing with Him and His living will and work and Word. Without Him it could only fall. But it is not without Him, for He is not without it. He, however, does not fall. Hence it cannot fall. The slender, invisible thread shows itself to be an unbreakable chain. It alone holds. But it really does hold.

When we turn to the New Testament community, we find it said of it (Mt. 13^{17}) that it is given to see and hear what many prophets and righteous men had in vain sought to see and hear, to perceive things (1 Pet. 1^{12}) which even the angels desired to look into. It is called the house or community of the living God, the pillar and ground of truth (1 Tim. 3¹⁵), the elect nation, the royal priesthood, the holy people, the people of possession (1 Pet. 2⁹, cf. Rev. 1⁶), and the light of the world, the city set on a hill (Mt. 5¹⁴). It can be said of it (Eph. 3¹⁰) that by it the manifold truth of God will be declared to heavenly powers and forces. It is promised (Mt. 16¹⁸) that even the gates of hell shall have no power to swallow it up. This is how it can and should understand itself. This is the high point on which it finds itself placed and where it can and should maintain itself.

We must not forget, however, the story of the crossing of the lake as told in Mk. 4³⁵⁻⁴¹. Inevitably the New Testament ἐκκλησίαι find their own story here. But what serious or final relationship is there between this and their high position in relation to other worldly structures ? For what does it imply ? To be sure, the ship is impressively manned by the disciples whom Jesus has already chosen and called to be His apostles. Carefully attired, according to mediaeval fancy, in the correct episcopal vestments, they are the rowers. According to the Markan context, Jesus has just spoken of the light set on a candlestick, and the seed which grows of itself and becomes a great plant, and to them alone, as we are expressly told, He has expounded these parables. They are not, then, a motley group of inexperienced novices. Nor are they alone with a mere tradition or recollection of the words and person of their Lord. Jesus Himself is with them. But " he was in the hinder part of the ship, asleep on a pillow." And when the great storm arose, and " the waves beat into the ship, so that it was now full," these men who were elect and called, who had already received so many promises and consolations in respect of their own existence as His people, who had indeed the assurance of His own presence, seemed to be cast back upon their own faith and in the last resort upon its bold action in exercise of their seamanship. But lo ! their apostolic office, their episcopal habits, their experience, their tradition, even the living but sleeping Jesus among them, all appear to be useless. The storm is too violent. The pillar and ground of truth totters. The gates of hell are menacingly open to engulf them. They are terrified that the ship and they themselves and Jesus will all perish, that it will be all up with them, as the community has often since had cause to fear and has actually feared. Basically, of course, it has never had any true reason, but it has certainly had occasion enough. The situation is obviously too much for the disciples. Similar situations have always been too much for the community, as has, indeed, its whole situation in the world. If Jesus were not in the ship, it must inevitably have gone down. But He is in the ship, and for this reason, if for this reason alone, it cannot go down. His disciples will necessarily be preserved with Him. They need not have wakened Him. They are not praised for doing this. On the contrary, they are rebuked for their fearfulness, being asked : " How is it that ye have no faith ? " (" Where is your faith ? " Lk. 8²⁵). Even if the storm had increased rather than abated, and even if they themselves were helpless in face of it, that which He had made them, that which they had received of Him, their freedom and power in view of the kingdom of God relentlessly drawn near, their instruction concerning the light on the candlestick and the mustard seed, and decisively the living presence of Jesus, should have been enough to assure them that this ship could not and would not go down, nor we, this people, perish. *Fluctuat, nec mergitur.* But Jesus tells them this only after He has rebuked the wind, and bidden the raging sea be still, and therefore dismissed all cause for fear, revealing how groundless it is, and showing Himself to be the sure basis of their existence as His people and therefore the unassailable basis of their tottering faith. " There was a great calm," for in the living presence of Jesus there was revealed His living action, His self-declaration in deeds. He not only was what He was for them, their Lord and Deliverer ; He made Himself known to them as such. He made peace for them. No doubt His people could and should have clung simply to the fact that through Him alone, but genuinely through Him, it had peace and would be and was sustained. But supposing it did not do what it could and should do ? Supposing its faith was feeble ? Supposing that in spite of all that it was through Him and had received from Him, and even in spite of His tangible presence, it was miserably afraid for itself and for Him in the midst of world-occurrence ? He Himself gave the answer to this sorry defiance with His superior and joyful defiance. He upheld it, yet also revealed Himself as the One who did so. He was its unassailable basis, and showed Himself to be so. The story ends with the noteworthy statement that when the wind dropped, when the cause of their fear was removed, when Jesus not only was their Preserver but visibly showed Himself to be such, " they feared exceedingly (ἐφοβήθησαν φόβον μέγαν), and said one to another, What manner of man is this, that even the wind and the sea obey him ? " We recall that according to the same Gospel (16[8]) the women were seized by fear and trembling at the empty tomb of the Resurrected, and dared tell no one what they had seen, for " they were afraid." We also recall the Bethlehem shepherds, who were so terrified (Lk. 2[9], using the same word as Mk. 4[41]) when the angel of the Lord appeared to them and the glory of the Lord shone round about them. What was this fear ? It was the great and necessary and legitimate fear of the Lord which, as the beginning of wisdom, began with the end of the little and unnecessary fear which could only lead the community to despair of itself, its apostolate, its faith and indeed its Lord. And the end of the little fear came with the fact that Jesus not only was its Saviour but manifested Himself as such and therefore as the sure foundation of its existence as His people, of its apostolate and of its faith. " What manner of man is this ? " Could the community do any better, or show itself in any better way to be the people placed at that high point, than by letting itself be gripped and moved by this great and holy and joyous fear in face of His self-declaration ? It became and was indeed the light of the world, the pillar and ground of truth, by letting itself be seized with this fear when it saw Him as the One who showed Himself to be its Lord within world-occurrence. This was the decisive happening on the crossing. It is always on such a crossing, in the power of the active self-declaration of its Lord, and as it is plunged into fear by this self-declaration and the knowledge it brings, that the New Testament community has achieved and does achieve its self-understanding in relation to its distinctive and unique existence. There is no other way. And it is obvious that in this respect its self-understanding is coincident with that of the Old Testament people of God.

An attempt must now be made under various heads to describe more concretely what we have sketched of the existence of the people of God in world-occurrence both in its visibility and likeness to other historical magnitudes and its invisibility and distinction from them.

1. The Christian community, as one people among others and yet also as this people, i.e., the people of God, exists in total dependence on its environment and yet also in total freedom in relation to it. Neither its dependence nor its freedom is partial ; they are both total. For its visibility and invisibility, its likeness and distinction in world-occurrence, are the twofold determination of its one and total being, just as Jesus Christ, in whose discipleship it exists in this twofold determination of its one existence, is with the same totality both true man and true God, and as such the one Jesus Christ. Indeed, when we remember Him we are forced to say that it is not a lamentable defect, but legitimate and in order, that in relation to the world around it should not merely be totally free

but also totally dependent, and not merely totally dependent but also totally free. By dependent we mean that for all its freedom it is bound to it, orientated on it, determined and conditioned by it. And by free we mean that for all its dependence it is sovereign in relation to it, having its own law, and therefore its own will and power, so that it is not only determined and conditioned but also determines and conditions.

In considering its dependence and freedom, we think on the one hand of the important sphere of speech.

The Christian community has its own message to impart, but it is dependent on the world around in the sense that it does not have its own language in which to impart it. In its utterances, even in the strictest service of the attestation of the Word of God with which it is entrusted, even in the necessary work of probing reflection on its witness, even in its theology, therefore, it can only adopt the modes of thought and speech of its spatial and temporal environment more near or distant, more ancient or modern. It has thus to subject itself to the implied conditions and restrictions. Even though it speaks with tongues, it cannot really transcend human speech. No other form of utterance stands at its disposal. Its speech may be eloquent or powerful, but when it speaks it stands on common ground with the world around, nor can it leave this common ground in any circumstances. There can thus be no question of its having at its disposal, alongside the exoteric speech suitable to the world and therefore improper, an underlying esoteric speech which is reserved for inner use or for discussion with the more particularly enlightened of those without, which more nearly touches and expresses the heart of the matter, and which may thus be described as proper. Whether externally or internally, to informed or uninformed, exoterically or esoterically, it can use only human speech. It is not God. It can and should bear good witness to His Word. But it neither can nor will speak it as God does. It can only serve it with its own word. It has no vocabulary of its own, nor grammar, nor syntax, nor style, by which even to approximate its expressions to the Word of God, let alone to give an adequate rendering of it.

There have often been pointless tensions between, e.g., what is called religious and what is called non-religious language. But all religious language is also and indeed primarily non-religious, having in itself no less but also no more to do with what the Christian community has to say than non-religious. Whatever the Christian community has to say, it can say only after worldly fashion, each term being worldly at root and each expression worldly in its original meaning. It cannot, then, escape being secular, nor does it have to try to escape from a sacred sphere of language—for there is no such thing—into a supposedly more secular realm in order to achieve perhaps a better or easier understanding.

The fact that it has no language of its own carries with it the perpetual risk of misunderstanding, as if it were merely saying in rather a peculiar way what is or could be said by others in other ways. But it also carries with it the possibility of self-deception, i.e., that in its use of language conditioned by the world around it should forget that in this language it has something of its own to say which is very different from what is or could be said by others.

It naturally appears that there really does exist such a thing as a sacral speech peculiar to it. But this is only an appearance. It arises from the fact that in every age the Christian community has to understand itself as ecumenical in time as well as space, i.e., as the fellowship of saints of both to-day and yester-day, and that it has to act accordingly even in the language of its witness. Its speech cannot, then, be like the mere buzzing of a fly. It will always and every-where follow the language of the Old and New Testaments, and constantly return to it as the source and norm of its witness. But it must also formally adopt and appropriate the language of the early Church and the fathers. This is necessary because, even though it must put what it has to say in contemporary terms, it has always to say it in company with the prophets and apostles as the first guarantors of the Word of God and therefore of their own witness, and also in company with those who have preceded it as witnesses. It cannot do this, nor really speak ecumenically, unless it accepts with love and under-standing the speech of the Bible and the early Church. What seems to be peculiar in its speech is in truth only this older or old element in it. The fact is that even these older and old elements in its speech, even when it is a matter of the most concentrated language of Canaan, have once been themselves elements of secular speech which through the years have acquired a particularly respect-able and even quasi-sacral ring, though they have not altogether lost their secular character. There is no reason to avoid the use of these elements on the foolish view that we thus use secular modes of speech and are more readily understood. For what authority have we for thinking that as themselves elements of wholly human speech they may not become or cannot be at least as easy to understand as the corresponding elements of certain modern idioms ? On the other hand, there is also no basis for the illusion that in making use of them the community is employing a specifically religious and intrinsically holy and proper language more adequate to the theme of its witness. For even the language of Canaan, being itself wholly secular in the last resort, is just as open to misunderstanding as modern modes of speech, and may just as easily conceal rather than reveal what the community has to say. The Christian community never can nor should speak only in that older or old language. But whatever language it uses, it lives only on alien or rather on common property. Quite obviously and inescapably it is limited and conditioned on every hand by the human forms of expression which it has in common with its more near or distant, more ancient or modern environment. It can speak only in secular terms.

The freedom of the Christian community in this sphere of speech has its origin in the free omnipotent Word of the grace of God which it is charged to attest. It has no control over this Word. But this Word has supreme control over it, and in the exercise of this control this Word makes its word a free word. It has simply to serve and attest the Word of God. In the bearing of this testimony it is restricted and conditioned by its secularity, by the possibilities of expression of its more near or distant environment, beyond which it has no other. Yet not for nothing is it elected and called to this service. Not for nothing is the free and omnipotent Word of the grace of God which it has to attest, and of which it has to speak in human words, the meaning and task of its ministry. For this Word of God which it can and should attest with its human speech is not itself hampered or restricted by the conditions and limitations of its own and all human speech. It is God's omnipotent Word, which as such can very easily make itself perceptible even in the witness of humanly conditioned and limited words, or, to put it more plainly, can very well make use even of these humanly conditioned words.

Assuming that it does this, this implies for the human words which are claimed that, without losing their secular character or undergoing any inner transformation, without any question of transfiguration or transubstantiation, they acquire a function and capability as thus exercised which they did not have in themselves as elements of general human speech, but which they may now receive and have as they are claimed by the omnipotent Word of God. *Ceteris imparibus*, we are reminded of the eating and drinking of bread and wine, which do not have in themselves, but which, without ceasing to be what they are, acquire and have in the Lord's Supper, the function and capability of indicating and confirming the fellowship of the community with its Lord, its participation in His body and blood and its attachment to His person. Thus, even though these human words do not cease to be elements of general human speech which may be used and understood or misunderstood by all, nevertheless, not by the men who speak them but by the omnipotent God who calls these men to the service of His Word and uses their secular words, they are given the power to bear testimony to His Word. Pronounced by these men in the service of His Word, they do not merely say what they might say in their secular sense ; beyond this they speak of God and His will and work revealed in His Word, calling Him to mind, pointing to Him, drawing attention to Him, mediating His promise and claim. For why should it be impossible for God as the Lord of His creation and especially of His people to do this, to dispose of human speech in this sense ?

Does He really do it ? Yes, inasmuch as by the omnipotent Word of His grace He calls His people to proclaim it to all peoples, this is exactly what He does. He puts His word on the lips of the men of this people. That is, He gives to their lips, to their human knowledge and confession, to their human voice, the power to attest His Word, and by His Word His work, and by His work Himself. The grace of God in which He is omnipotent is that He wills to take all men to Himself in Jesus Christ, that He has done this, that in Him He has made it manifest to all men, and that He has resolved and already begun to indicate and make this known to them by the ministry of His community. In this grace of His He actually disposes in this sense of the speech of the men of His community. It thus took place, and still takes place, that He actually does what He as the Almighty can do, namely, that He puts His Word on their lips, that He sanctifies their profane language, that He gives them the power and freedom to speak of Him in their humanly secular words and expressions and sentences, and therefore to become and to be His witnesses to other men. It is their freedom as to these men, appointed the witnesses of God and His Word, there is entrusted under the conditions and within the restrictions of the general possibilities of human speech something which they alone can say as and because they are elected and called to the exercise of this power—they exclusively, yet genuinely, on this presupposition.

It is their freedom because, disposing of no sacral speech of their own, they are not bound to any such speech. The whole sphere of human speech and wealth of its possibilities is open to them, so that as they go to different men they can use their own modes of speech, simple in the case of the simple and complicated in the case of the complicated, to declare to them what the community has to declare as the witness of God and His work and Word. It is their freedom because in this whole domain they can and should really choose, preferring one possibility to another, alternating between them, transferring from the one to the other, making regular or frequent use of some, less use or no use at all of others. It is their freedom because they can play or rather work without bondage to the secular meaning of the words and expressions which they use. For in their selection and usage they are strictly responsible only to one court, i.e., that of the Word of God which must always be attested by what they say, and for the rest they are independent of all the laws of speech and thought grounded in the various theories of knowledge or schools of logic, semantics or metaphysics, as they are also and quite naturally independent of any strivings for particular solemnity, piety or unction, or for particular modernity, ingenuousness or worldliness, in their utterances. They are compelled to seek none of these things; they may avail themselves of any.

The only root of their freedom is its self-evident limit, namely, that God gives it to them and they enjoy it for the attestation of His Word. It is in attestation of His Word and not in the pursuit of their own whims that they use it. This means that it is with gratitude for the distinction imparted by their high calling, and therefore with humility and reverence, with strict commitment to it, with constant reflection on the content and purpose of the message entrusted to them, with the recurrent question how they can protect it against misunderstanding and falsification, in short, with obedience, that they will also and particularly act in this field of speech, electing and deciding, playing and working, in this whole territory. That God wills to use human speech for the proclamation of His Word necessarily means for the community to whom He has entrusted it that it is responsible to Him. Its high freedom is given it for the fulfilment of this responsibility. Nor should we forget—for this is not merely the infinitely consoling element in the whole matter freeing the fulfilment of this heavy responsibility from any legalistic anxiety, but also the material pivot of the whole to be constantly recalled by the community—that the self-witness of God neither depends on nor lives by their witness, but that their witness depends on and lives by the self-witness of God. Hence, when to the best of their ability they have done all that they should do in the service of His Word, after all the exertion imposed by their endowment with this freedom, they should keep silence again, enjoying their

Sabbath and leaving it to the Word of God to speak for itself. What they say can and should in any case only precede the Word of God as a herald making an opening and creating respect for it. And when they have tried to do this as skilfully and conscientiously as they can, once again they can and should rest from their labours in this field of speech too. If they take their responsibility seriously in this sense also, then for all its dependence, limitation and restriction they can and should exercise the freedom of their Christian word as their royal freedom.

In respect of both the dependence and the freedom of the community we must also consider on the other hand the question of its sociological structure. And here, too, it is guilty of misunderstanding if it does not perceive, accept and express both its total dependence and its total freedom.

First, it cannot deny its dependence in this respect. To the distinctiveness of its calling and commission, and therefore to the form of its existence as the people of God in world-occurrence, there does not correspond in the first instance or intrinsically any absolutely distinctive social form. Notwithstanding peculiarities in detail, in every age and place its constitution and order have been broadly determined and conditioned by political, economic and cultural models more or less imperatively forced on it by its situation in world history. Either in part or virtually in whole, it has had and still has to adopt or approximate itself to these in order to maintain itself, or, no less subject to the law of its environment, it has had and still has to evade or oppose them in respect of the form of its existence, again in order to maintain itself. Either way, it has never been fashioned with absolute spontaneity or originality, but always and everywhere in open or secret, conscious or unconscious, positive, critical or negative relation to the events, changes and conditions in the contemporary world, to its particular tendencies and interconnexions. More or less plainly, it is always in some way subject to the dictates of this world. Even where this is less clear, and it opposes these dictates in some sense, the fact that it, too, was and is only one people among others emerges in the fact that the possibilities for which it decides are always in thoroughgoing correspondence with those which seem unmistakeably to have suggested themselves to others in respect of the social structuring of their life and relationships. Even in the decisions of the community we have never had nor have more than selection within the comparatively small and measurable circle of variant answers to this common human question. There has never been anywhere a distinctive answer penetrating this circle, an intrinsically sacred sociology. Obviously there is no such thing, just as there is no absolutely distinctive or intrinsically sacred language. In this respect, too, the people of God exists in worldly fashion within world-occurrence.

Here, too, the appearance of the contrary might be suggested by the fact that from time to time the community has found good reason to hail and accept with particular gratitude—gratitude, it is to be hoped, to its Lord—one of the many courses offered to it from without, or, conversely, with particular emphasis —the emphasis, it is to be hoped, of an act of obedience to its Lord—to refuse such a course and to seek and adopt a less obvious. It is inevitable that in such situations the form and structure actually selected should be seen to be invested with a particular glory which makes it seem to be the form and structure of Christian society which is absolutely Christian, and therefore generally necessary, and therefore sacred. That this is an illusion is seen only when the community sooner or later becomes less sure of its decision, and is inclined in respect of the possibility selected at least to make compromises with others in the sphere of the possibilities presented. But the illusion persists in even more drastic form where there is a supposedly definitive hardening and ossifying in the choice of one of these possibilities, as in Roman and Eastern Catholicism. For where does there shine out more clearly the inextinguishably secular character, in origin, of all sociological forms—in these cases the Roman Empire and the Byzantine State with its ceremonial—than where it is thought that one such form should be absolutely and consistently preferred to all others and proclaimed as the Christian and ecclesiastical form *par excellence* ? But it obviously shines out no less plainly where the community finds a pattern for its social form, not in a βασιλεία of antiquity, but in the constitutional monarchy, enlightened aristocracy, or finally the democracy of more modern times, insisting more or less tenaciously that this is the model which it must follow. In this respect, too, the community obviously lives on alien, or rather on common possessions, i.e., in forms which it assumes either by following the world around or opposing it. In this respect, too, it can be misunderstood, or compared and confused with other historical constructs. For, as it can speak only in worldly terms, it can follow only worldly orders and structures.

Yet in this respect, too, the freedom of the people of God rests in the freedom of the omnipotent Word of His grace. As the Word of God addresses itself in different places to different men at different times, it summons them out of their isolation, calls, brings and binds them together, and unites them both invisibly with God and visibly with one another. As it appoints all these men its witnesses, reminds them all of their task and leads them to and equips them for its execution, it establishes and forms a new and peculiar human society set at its disposal and existing under its control. Again, as it is God's omnipotent Word, it cannot be hindered by the obvious secularity of all human forms of society from creating within these a society which in the first instance is not distinct from them, yet which is still this specific society, the people of God, the Christian community, nor can it be prevented from maintaining, accompanying and ruling this society as such. And, as it can use the secular possibilities of human speech, to establish this particular society it can use the secular possibilities of social structuring, not changing them essentially nor divesting them of their secularism, but giving to them as they are a new meaning and determination. Establishing, preserving, accompanying and ruling the community, it can command and permit the community, and give it the power, to exist in various sociological forms, none of which is better adapted for the purpose than others, and in these forms to be visibly what it is invisibly, namely, the Christian community or the community of Christ. And this is what the Word of God actually does as not merely His omnipotent Word but also the Word of His grace. This is what actually takes place in the power of this Word. Intrinsically unholy possibilities in the structuring of man's life in society are sanctified and made serviceable to the gathering and upbuilding of the people of God in the service of its commission and for the purpose of its election and calling. The free God gives to this human people, which still cannot do anything more or different in this respect than what others can also do, the freedom to adopt its own form, i.e., the form corresponding to its calling and commission, in the sphere of general human possibilities.

It is above all its wonderful freedom to recruit across the frontiers of nations, states and other natural or historical unions and societies, not removing the distinctions or boundaries but transcending them, not identifying itself with any but being one and the same *ecclesia una catholica* in all, existing within them as a universal people, indeed as *the* universal people. It is thus its freedom in more than one sense to select its form, preferring and grasping some possibilities and rejecting others. It may follow as its principle of order a monarchical, aristocratic or liberal and democratic constitution, or the model of a free association. In certain situations it may find itself pressed to adopt towards the states by which it is confronted and the society and culture around it a closer or looser, a predominantly positive or predominantly critical relationship, which it must assume with full awareness of what it is doing. It is compelled to do none of these things ; it may do any of them. There is no sociological possibility—for all are intrinsically secular—which it must always select, nor is there any which it must always refuse.

Again its freedom is limited only by its source. But its source really is its limit. It is born of the omnipotent Word of God's grace in Jesus Christ. It cannot, then, hear the voice of a stranger (Jn. 10[5]). For all its dependence on the world and world-occurrence, it cannot be ruled and determined by these. The wonderful freedom with which it may assemble itself from all human societies and across all their frontiers, and with which its members, i.e., Christians, are commanded and permitted to exist also as members of these societies, must always show itself in the fact that no matter where these Christians may be, or what else they may be, they must always see themselves and act first and decisively as Christians, and only then as members of this or that nation, citizens of this or that state, participants in the work of this or that cultural or other society.

Their responsibility as members of the Christian community will take unequivocal precedence of all their other responsibilities. And all their free selection as the community among the different possibilities of form and structure will always be that of obedience and not of caprice or externally motivated opportunism and convenience. In the exercise of their freedom they will not be able in practice to select all things or even many things, but only one thing. And as, driven to this or that decision *hic et nunc*, they make their choice, they can do so neither autonomously nor under the pressure of alien force, but only in correspondence with what is commanded them in this particular time and situation by the Word of God which rules them. Their service of God, and within it their prayer and preaching and the living fellowship and action of their members, must always be a fulfilment of their commission and therefore their witness to the world around them. Thus the rightness or wrongness of the constitution and order adopted will always depend upon whether the Word of God entrusted to them and ruling them is thereby honoured or dishonoured in a given time and situation. Their Church may thus be a national Church, a state Church or a free Church, but its invisible essence must always be made visible in the fact that it is a confessing and missionary Church which leaves those around in no doubt as to whom or what it has to represent among them.

In all these possibilities it is free to elect and determine itself for the service of God in conformity with and in loyalty to His election. Hence it need not fear the secularity of any of them, nor is it bound to any as if this were invested with a peculiar sanctity. In face of them it is not free to act as if it had any particular desire for any, nor is it free to subject itself to any of the alien powers which lurk in all of them. Freed by the calling Word of God, it is free to elect, and to be and do, that which it must elect and be and do in responsibility to the Lord known from His Word and in obedience to His will. If it elects and exists at the point thus indicated and circumscribed, then even in and in spite of all its dependence, conditioning and restriction, it can and should understand and exercise the freedom of its sociological structure as its truly royal freedom.

2. In order to make concrete the existence of the people of God in world-occurrence as determined by both its visible and its invisible being, we shall now consider it from the second standpoint of its total weakness and its total strength in relation to this occurrence. Here, too, we have totality on both sides. Hence it is quite in order and need not be deplored that, while we may speak quite confidently of the strength of the Christian community, we must also speak quite openly of its weakness. If we did not speak of its weakness, what we might say of its strength would be hollow and unconvincing. For it is the strength of which Paul says in 2 Cor. 12[9f.], and with more than a personal reference, that it is made strong and perfected in weakness. Even the strength of Jesus Christ neither was nor is strong except in supreme weakness. It is the glory of the community to follow Him in this too, and therefore to be totally strong only as it is totally weak, but to be really strong, of course, in its weakness. Strength means ability. Weakness means inability. Of the Christian community in world-occurrence we have to say both that it can do nothing and that it can do all things.

In both respects we think first of the problem of its place in world-occurrence. Its weakness consists in the fact that it undoubtedly has its place, but that this is not one which belongs to it self-evidently, that it is not a firm and assured place as foreseen to be necessary and therefore grounded in the creaturely disposition of human existence. It cannot be said of it as of the state, or work, or trade, or the different forms of culture, that it belongs to the essential constants of human existence and therefore of world-occurrence.

This may well be said of what is called religion, as maintained by Schleiermacher and finely expounded to the cultured among its despisers. But the existence of the people of God cannot be subsumed under the concept of religion, or can be so only in the sharpest antithesis to its self-understanding. From the standpoint of religion as of other constants of human existence and history, the Christian community is a purely contingent phenomenon arising at its own point in the economy of human affairs but not really belonging to these for all its humanity. In other words, it is an alien colony for the nature and existence of which there are no analogies in the world around, and therefore no categories in which to understand it, and therefore no real use.

Even in its worldly visibility it cannot deny that it is not of the world, even though this be understood as God's good creation. Badly deformed and confused as they are by the *confusio hominum*, the origins at least of other stable or perennial elements in history, including what is called religion, do belong to this. But the people of God, even though it be one people among others, does not have its origin in creation nor live by one of the forces of creation. Neither it nor the world around can understand it in the light either of innocent man or particularly of sinful man fallen victim to destruction. The people of God elected in Jesus Christ and called to be His witness owes its nature and existence to the new divine act of reconciliation resolved and executed in the sphere of creation and man for the sake of creation and man. It belongs to the order of grace established within the order of nature for its restoration and direction, Jesus Christ Himself being its basis, centre and goal. He Himself, God's grace to the world in person, is the first and supreme Guest and Stranger who found no room in the inn and still cannot find any. How could the community be His community if it were present in any other way, if it had holes like the foxes or nests like the birds, if it had somewhere to lay its head (Mt. 8²⁰)? It must share with Him His weakness, which also consists in the fact that He has no such abiding place. Naturally it means weakness for it too, and indeed it means total weakness in face of the other elements in world-occurrence and the whole world of humanity around, that it has no such place, that it is nowhere at home on the earth, that it can only lodge and camp here and there as the pilgrim people of God, that at best it can only be permitted to stay but not granted any rights of settled citizenship. Yet how could it be what it is or do what it has to do if it were otherwise, if it could be rid of this weakness and act accordingly?

It is never more than an appearance when its alien character is temporarily concealed, when it seems to be just as much part of the community as industry and agriculture, as the school and the centre of government, as the university and the theatre, when it is recognised and accepted with varying degrees of friendliness as one of the constant factors, when it is impressed into the economy of human affairs. The world should be aware of what might be involved with the incorporation of this stranger and its humanity. Yet the world knows well enough that it cannot really trust it. Even at best, therefore, it treats it with no more than respectful but cautious toleration, taking good care not to become too deeply implicated. In practice, if not perhaps in theory, it has a basic awareness that the community does not really belong. Again, it is no more than a sorry appearance if the community itself postures and acts as if it were one of the constant factors and therefore not a stranger, as though it could impose upon and commend itself to the world around by building houses and cathedrals, and even basilicas to Peter, instead of camping, and by thus attaining a likeness or at least a similarity to other elements and factors in world-occurrence in the role either of a venerable religious institution or even of a holy state within the state. This role is quite unsuitable and indeed impracticable. In attempting to play it, it will either, to its own destruction, become what it plays, i.e., a competing secular construct, and thus lose its birthright, or, as it doggedly persists in the role, to its shame but also to its salvation it will be seen by the world for what it really is, i.e., an alien and disruptive body, and treated accordingly in spite of all the skill with which it plays its role. If it is genuinely true to itself, i.e., to its election and calling, then it is quite unavoidable that willy-nilly it should confess its character as the pilgrim people of God. And the power of its election and calling is always great enough, even when it is unfaithful, sooner or later to call and incline it to conversion, i.e., to movement away from that false appearance to the homelessness, the marginal existence and the confession of this true reality which alone are appropriate to it as the witness of the new Word of the new work of God, but which inevitably entail its weakness, its total inability, in face of world-occurrence and its elements.

Precisely in this weakness, however, there dwells and stirs—we refer again to 2 Cor. 12⁹ᶠ·—its strength or ability. That it has no little ability may be seen in a very simple fact, though this is not to be taken as more than an intrinsically ambiguous symptom, namely, that even amidst those who have settled dwellings and in face of the constants of world-occurrence this nomadic people of aliens has been able not merely to maintain itself but also continually in its own way to express itself, and not merely to express itself but constantly, and both inwardly and outwardly, to grow, i.e., to upbuild, reform and renew itself, and thus continually to set before the eyes of other peoples the problem and riddle of its existence where everything would seem to suggest that a phenomenon like this pilgrim people, which is so contingent in relation to those great constants and does not seem in any respect to be necessary, might perhaps enjoy a transitory existence but ought long since to have shown itself to be genuinely transitory. The truth of the matter is that in both its Israelite and its Christian forms the people of God has in its own way shown itself to be enduring, not, as has often happened, by partial or more thoroughgoing attempts to secure and maintain itself by adaptation to the world, but in strange proportion to the way in which, with relative unconcern as to its fidelity or infidelity, it has actually accepted, and has been constantly led back to, and has thus willy-nilly had to confess, its alien status and therefore its weakness, on the basis of its election and calling, of its Lord and therefore of the invisible side of its being. Its witness has often been muffled, or confused by loud but false notes, but it has always persisted and been heard at least by the world when it has accepted its marginal existence. Its voice has often been almost completely submerged by the clamour on every hand, but it has always been able to rise again and to sound out with some degree of purity. In the light of its visible history and present reality, it can hardly be denied that in the Christian community there dwells a hidden but uniquely effective power which enables it to persist in spite of all expectation. But what kind of a power or strength is it which is effective in its total weakness ? By its very nature it must obviously stand in the closest connexion with its homelessness and marginal existence.

We may begin with the ancillary consideration that the strength which is effective in weakness, i.e., in the alien character of the Christian community, is perhaps quite simply the strength of the truth of the general human situation which is hidden in other peoples because they cannot or will not see it but which irresistibly emerges in this people. For is it really the case that the surrounding peoples in their dwellings, supported by constants of world-occurrence, are quite as much at home and secure and sheltered as might appear ? The man who no longer lives at peace with God, his neighbour and himself, because he does not recognise or grasp the peace proffered to him, is one who does not have, but merely seeks and does not find, a true place of shelter and permanent home. Since the days of Cain he has been " a fugitive and a vagabond in the earth " (Gen. 4^{12}). Thus in the marginal existence of the Christian community homelessness is surely brought to light and representatively revealed as the true situation of Cainite humanity. In the discipleship of Jesus Christ the community has to confess its solidarity with this Cainite humanity which is yet loved and therefore preserved by God like its progenitor. It does this by uncomplaining acceptance of its alien status and therefore of the total weakness of its visible existence. And in so doing, in virtue of its invisible nature, it may still act in such a way that even in its alien status it may typically hear and attest the Word of God, participate in the peace granted to Cainite humanity, and to that extent be the first of all peoples here and now to be genuinely at home and secure in world-occurrence because in the house of the Father, which by its existence it may attest as the true home which is waiting for other peoples too. Hence the strength secretly dwelling in it is to be understood as the strength of the dawning truth of the general human situation under the judgment and the grace of God.

Yet even if we take this aspect into account, we can understand this strength only as that of God at work in the community, only as that of the revelation of His truth concerning the human situation, of His judgment on and grace towards Cainite humanity. We shall now try to show this directly. In the weakness of the community we have to do with the strength of God. That the constant preservation and renewal of the community in spite of every probability to the contrary is due to the effective power of God is plainly declared in the fact that it is this which so singularly marks it off and distinguishes it from all else in world-occurrence that lives by other powers. so that even though the community is ranked with other peoples it is constantly obliged either to leave the ranks altogether or, if it does not do so, to make clear its uniqueness within them. The powers at work in other peoples are those, or some of those, of the cosmos which God has created. And what distinguishes the life of the community from their life, allowing it only this alien existence among them, is the fact that the force which upholds and activates the community is not a cosmic force. If nevertheless it lives by a power which is at work in it and upholds and activates it in this way, this can only be recognised as the power of the Creator which has been put forth anew in Jesus Christ and in the establishment of the order of grace, and which has thus set up a new reality within world-occurrence. If it is the power of God, then we do not merely see the fact but we also understand the necessity of the strange isolation of the community in face of the products of other powers, the necessity of its alien nature and marginal existence, and therefore of its weakness. We also understand, however, the superiority of the strength in which it may exist. How can the power of the Creator fail to be wholly superior to the united powers of His creature, of the cosmos ? We also understand, however, that the community which lives by this superior power is not only a match for the life of the world, for the strength of other peoples living by other powers, but that it, too, is absolutely superior. God is for it—and therefore the power of the Creator God who in Jesus Christ has roused Himself and intervened in the new act of the reconciliation of the world to Himself. The only thing is that this is the strength which is effective in weakness, the ability which works in inability. Quite apart from maintaining and renewing itself, what can it not do in this strength ? Over what walls (Ps. 18[29]) can it not leap, not in its own strength, but in that of the God who elects and calls it ? We do not forget that it is the strength of its invisible being. Its visible is determined and characterised by its weakness. But in its visibility and therefore its weakness it lives by the invisible power of the will and work and Word of God for whose service it is created as a " new creature " (2 Cor. 5[17]). This strength makes it invincible in the weakness which alone is visible.

In relation to its weakness and strength we must now consider the problem of its work and the success of its work in world-occurrence. Its weakness in this respect is obvious. It is inexorably set in a position where its instrument and weapon, if it is to do its proper work, and to do it effectively, can consist only in the witness which it has to make by its paradigmatic existence, or, to put it more comprehensively, in the ministering word which it has thereby to declare. It cannot impart any strength to this word. It can only pronounce it in obedience and with confidence that it will be mightily confirmed by its content, by the work of God Himself, which is the meaning of its existence. For even quantitatively, how small is the volume of the work done in this ministry compared with the mass of work done in the world around, and even by its own members in the sphere of their economic, social, cultural and political existence! And what a disproportion there is between the unmistakeable majesty and impressiveness, the obvious importance and necessity, of at least many of the works undertaken and already accomplished outside its own particular sphere, and the triviality of that which even with its greatest efforts it can set alongside these works in the form of its feeble witness!

What significance does the existence of the Church really have in the more or less tumultuous life of this city or the more or less peaceful industry of that village? What significance does the modest Sunday service or mass have compared with what humanity usually sets up and deifies as the content of the rest of Sunday? What significance does the tiny theological faculty have in the context of the great *universitas litterarum*? What public interest is there in a conference of this or that Christian organisation, or even of the World Council of Churches, as compared with the arrangement and holding of a winter Olympiad or even the decision of the football championship of the world?

Then there is the problem of success. What can the community of Jesus Christ produce in this regard? What is the result of all its regular or irregular external or internal activities as faithfully and zealously executed? What does it achieve, and more particularly whom does it reach, by means of them? And if, as it desires and sometimes thinks, it does reach the people, what does this signify or really accomplish? What is altered in great or little world-occurrence, in the life of society and individuals, by the fact that among and with other factors the Church is also present and active? Compared with great or little but always notable achievements in other spheres, from the hay harvest in the country to the constant discoveries of science and inventions of technology, what is really accomplished by it for the good or ill of man and in a visible and tangible form in which it can be concretely demonstrated and can even be of sufficient importance to be described in an illuminating and interesting way in the popular press? To be sure, the activity and achievements of the Christian community may actually be seen, but how small and modest and above all problematical they are in comparison with what is constantly achieved in the other works of man ! What is done by man generally may be small or great, but it is at least done in the light of day. But what Christianity does in the world in all its uniqueness never appears on the surface. This is its obvious weakness.

We again have to recall the appearance in which this weakness can conceal itself without really doing so, as though the community did not exist, or did not have to exist, in this weakness of its activity and efficacy. There are impressive mitigating factors in respect of the invisibility of its activity and the results of this activity. Reference may be made to the peculiar spiritual, moral and ideal purpose and quality of Church work, and therefore to the appropriate inner and spiritually apprehensible value and effectiveness which it displays. Yet are there not other enterprises and institutions in whose activities there is an even more evident and successful concern for the spiritual, moral and ideal elevation and fostering of humanity than in those of the Christian community ? And in any case, is not this only in a very casual sense the real work demanded of the community in attestation of the Word of God ? The question is how this true work compares with the works of the rest of humanity. When it is a matter of this true work, does not the community have to confess its utter weakness ? Again, we can point to the influence of its special activity on what is done by others in the world around. Not without pride, for example, we may speak of the part played by it in the rise and development of our so-called European civilisation and culture. But in this rise and development who or what had and has the direction and the decisive word ? Greek and Roman antiquity ? The spirit of primitive Europe ? The idealistic realism or realistic idealism of so-called modern man as he emerged in the later Middle Ages and the 16th century ? Or Christianity ? Well, Christianity played its own important—but not too important—part. Yet to the extent that it worked parallel or in conjunction with other factors, did it not cease to be Christianity ? To what extent did it or does it work in this field in its true form as the historical bearer of the message of Christ, of the free grace of God ? This is the question, and when we put it, seeing the work of the Church in this function confronted by the works of these other factors and powers, the littleness of its work and achievement is seen once more. Again, it may be said that constantly, and with heightened emphasis and on the broadest front in our own age, there has been a concern for the intensification and extension of Church work and therefore for a strengthening of its power to compete with other human works and achievements. Intrinsically there can be nothing against this ; indeed, there is much in its favour. It would go ill with the community if on the very basis of its election, calling and commissioning it were not constantly on the look-out for new ways of prosecuting its cause in the world better to-day than yesterday, and, it is to be hoped, better to-morrow than to-day. And it is fitting that in this respect it should not be shamed and despised by comparison with the children of the world, who according to Lk. 16[8] usually show much greater wisdom in the ordering of their affairs than the children of light. The cause of the community, however, is the witness which it must bear to the kingdom of God drawn near in Jesus Christ, and to prosecute this cause better can only mean as *ecclesia reformata semper reformanda* to bear this witness with ever greater faithfulness to its origin, theme and content, in ever deeper and more manifold unfolding of this basic subject-matter, and yet also in ever clearer, sharper and simpler contours, not least in the form of unequivocal and binding practical decisions. What does all the intensification or extension of its work amount to if the motive which both impels and retards is not its own inner and outer reformation in relation to the service which it must render ? If it is really a matter of being the living community in this sense in every time and place and situation, then it will soon find out how little it can compete with the enterprises and achievements of others in the world. It will soon realise that in relation to the rest of the world it can exist only as a small and strangely gesticulating minority driven into a corner. It will not be deceived, therefore, by the occasional appearance of worldly impressiveness and relevance which may for a time seem to be the immediate result of its efforts.

Yet it is in the weakness of its efforts and achievements that there is concealed and active its strength, its superior ability to all other powers. The people of God need not be ashamed of its weakness. It can renounce all attempts to give itself the appearance of strength. It can count it an honour that in this respect, too, it may share the weakness of Jesus Christ, being unimpressive and unsuccessful in company with Him. It can thus be conscious of its hidden but very real power, and rejoice with a merriness of heart of which other peoples with their deployment of power can have no inkling. And inevitably these other peoples, whether they notice this power or not, will experience it either quietly or with the inexplicable force of a minor earthquake. The strength of what the Christian community does in world-occurrence consists in the fact that in all its obvious weakness it is not concerned plainly and noticeably with the highest and most important of all matters, as on the airy pinnacle of the pyramids, but rather, in a way which is more subterranean and can therefore be easily overlooked or forgotten, with the presupposition and basis of all that man does or refrains from doing, with the matter which, whether they know and accept it or not, is absolutely determinative and therefore significant for all men. The origin, theme and content of its witness is the divine decision which has been taken in Jesus Christ in favour of all men and for their deliverance from sure and certain destruction, namely, the decision that they are free and not slaves, that they may love and are not compelled to hate, that they shall live and not die, that all this is given to them, that it is true and ready for them without any co-operation on their part and against all their deserts. This decision and its revelation are that which inwardly holds the world together, whether it realises it or not. But with this decision and its revelation no other human work, however great or imposing its performance may seem, has anything whatever to do. The Christian community may do what it does in the service of this cause. If others refer to the periphery, it concerns the centre of human existence. This is its secret strength, and the strength of its work. How can it be ashamed of its work and its weakness when it may do it with this strength ? It would have cause for shame if it were not wholly confident and joyous. As we may and must put it, its strength consists in the fact that it and it alone is occupied with that which alone within world-occurrence is full of promise and originally and finally has the future for it. In Jesus Christ there is before it the new reality of all great or small world history as this moves towards its manifestation. It may serve the Word which God has spoken in His omnipotent mercy and in which the defeat and destruction of the antithesis between God's providence and man's confusion is heralded. In all its weakness it may speak this Word of hope. Even the most imposing works of other peoples, even the achievements of politics, science and art, do not serve this Word, this hope. What other work can be done, then, with such uplifted head because with such unlimited confidence that it will be finally vindicated ? What Christianity does, may and should be done with confidence. It does not need to deny this confidence, nor to be timidly afraid of it. It does not need to compare, equate or confuse its work with that of others directed to merely provisional and limited ends. It has only to hold its direction, to look to the eternal goal of its action, to keep the head well up instead of letting it sink, and the community will then find that in all its weakness it is sustained by a strength compared with which all other strength is really weakness. As to the results of its action—and this is the best and finest thing of all—it is totally dispensed from the duty and necessity of having to give any answer, for this can be left to God Himself. It has simply to do what it has been commissioned and commanded to do. As it does this obediently, it need not have any anxious concern as to what the outcome will be or what will or will not be accomplished. Nor in face of the great or little things which may or may not result has it to decide whether its action is to be adjudged a success or a failure. It may sometimes seem to be the one and sometimes the other. But the community need not be weighed down with worry which it really is. It cannot try to be the judge of its own activity. It can only let God be the Judge, the same God who from the very first has assumed responsibility for the meaning of its activity and placed it in His service. It takes its own responsibility seriously as it keeps to His direction, to the meaning which is definitely given to its action by the fact that it is assigned by Him. But this responsibility also includes the fact that it should refrain from acting as the lord of its works, as though it could itself fix their value or lack of value either in advance or in retrospect. God Himself has fixed this, and will .do so. If only it is obedient, it is sheltered in Him in relation to its work. This holy and responsible irresponsibility in respect of the success of its activity is the strength concealed in its weakness. No work of other peoples has this strength. All other works are done under the pressure of the anxious question as to their consequences. The Christian community does not stand under this pressure. This is not because of its lack of illusions and therefore its sobriety as regards its successes. It has this too. But this has nothing whatever to do with the weariness, scepticism and faintheartedness which may sometimes and perhaps definitively overwhelm all men in respect of their work. The Christian community is free from that pressure because it may know and trust and love and praise and confess and expect good things, indeed, the very best, from the One who has called it to His service, who has thus assumed from the very first responsibility for the meaning and rightness of its work, and who step by step will be the only good and righteous and gracious Judge of what it attains thereby. That it may hold by His disposing and decision, that it is allowed and commanded to give itself with the most concentrated attention and yet without care to the matter entrusted to it, is the secret strength of its work which is strangely effective for all that it is so secret, so that in spite of all its obvious weakness amid other world occurrence its work is one compared with which all other human works might well seem of no consequence.

How does the Christian community exist or live or continue within world-occurrence? This is our third and final question in this context. What we are asking is how it comes about, how it becomes event and reality, that there not only can be but is the kind of people tacitly assumed in our answers to the first two questions, namely, a people elected and called to attest God and His Word and thus able to see and understand world-occurrence, and itself within it, as we have just described? Have we merely been spinning a hypothesis behind which the question of the existence of this subject is still open? To what extent have we good grounds to reckon with its existence and therefore to be sure of what we have heard concerning it? To what extent does this people, the Christian community, really exist?

We shall give an immediate and direct answer to this question. (Cf. for what follows, *C.D.*, IV, 1, pp. 660–668 and *C.D.*, IV, 2, pp. 651–660.) In a first general and comprehensive formulation our answer is to the effect that the Christian community exists in virtue of its secret. This means by way of delimitation that it does not exist in virtue of its own controllable power, freedom or capacity. It neither exists of itself nor can understand itself of itself. The power, freedom and capacity in virtue of which it exists cannot be understood as an element in general cosmic being. Or, as we may say more positively, the Christian community exists as it is called into existence, and maintained in existence, by its secret. It exists in this way alone, but in this way truly, indisputably and invincibly. It lives by its secret. Without it, it could only fall. But it cannot fall, for it stands with its secret. Its secret is its ontic and noetic basis, its noetic as its ontic and its ontic as its noetic, and in both cases its clear basis in the sense that it may be indicated and described in terms of its efficacy. This basis is identical with the will and work and Word of God. Hence it neither need nor can be established on the part of man, and for this reason and to this extent it cannot be perceived or explained. Yet it is identical with the will and work and Word of God as effectively addressed to the world and specifically to the community, and for this reason and to this extent it may be known in its operation for all its inscrutability and inexplicability. It may thus be indicated, named and described as its ontic and noetic basis. We can thus point to it. In virtue of it, the Christian community is what it is in the world, visible and yet invisible, in the world and yet not of it, dependent and yet free, weak and yet strong. In the light of it, it sees world-occurrence and understands itself. In relation to its effective operation we can point to it and point back to it, denoting, defining and describing. With this reference, then, we can answer our third and final question.

Two exalted names are both indispensable and adequate to denote and describe the basis and secret of the people of God in relation to the efficacy not concealed from it. Both in different ways are identical with the name of the God who has turned to it. Hence neither can be separated from the other, but each is necessary to elucidate the other. They are the names of Jesus Christ and the Holy Spirit. Jesus Christ acts and works and creates in and in relation to the Christian community by the Holy Spirit and therefore again in the mystery of God. The one effective action of God in this twofold form is the basis and secret of the Christian community. In making this reference and therefore in answering our final question, we may thus make two strictly related statements which mutually complement and elucidate one another.

The first is that the Christian community exists as called into existence and maintained in existence by Jesus Christ as the people of His witnesses bound, engaged and committed to Him. It exists in virtue of His calling. The power of His calling is the power of the living Word of God spoken in it. And the power of this Word is the power of His Holy Spirit. As this power shines as divine power and is at work in the world, there takes place in the world and its occurrence the new and strange event of the gathering, upbuilding and sending of the Christian community. As Jesus Christ in the power of the Holy Spirit, or the Holy Spirit as His Spirit, creates recognition, establishes knowledge, calls to confession and therefore quickens the dead, the existence of the community begins and endures. Hence its existence is absolutely given, imparted or presented to it by Him as the One who in the power of His enlightening Spirit, the *creator Spiritus*, is at work on it and in it. In relation to Him it has neither right nor claim to existence, and therefore no control over it. It cannot control its existence and therefore it cannot control itself. It does not exist in virtue of its own ability but only of His. It lives only as He, the living One, has controlled and still controls it. Its power and freedom and ability to be and live and persist in world-occurrence, it can treat only as His property for which it is responsible to Him, by the assignment of which it is set in His service, for the exercise and application of which it must render an account by continuing to be what it is and accepting and discharging its ministry. It exists as it belongs to Him, listens to Him and is obedient to Him. It really does exist, but only in this way, as the Christ community, as the branches in the Vine. " Without me ye can do nothing " (Jn. 15[5])—indeed, ye can be nothing except perhaps a pile of broken and withering branches that can only be burned. He is the secret, the basis, the Creator and Lord, of the existence of His people.

Thus the being of the people of God is grounded only in its God, and the being of the Christian community only in Jesus Christ as its Lord. We continually had to refer to the content of this statement in our previous deliberations, and especially in answering our second question as to the self-understanding of the community. How can it really understand itself in the first and final instance except as the people elected, called, commissioned, maintained and ruled by Him ? Yet in relation to the question of the basis of its existence this statement needs to be decisively deepened, as is indeed demanded even by its provisional form. For it is neither an accident nor an act of divine caprice that Jesus Christ first calls certain men out of the common mass and constitutes and maintains them as the community of His witnesses in common adherence to Him. And while it is true and important that as His possession this community is wholly His creature called to existence and maintained in existence by Him, yet as a statement concerning the community, concerning this people in its relationship to Jesus Christ, this can only be the second and not the first and original thing that has to be said at this point. For the reconciliation of the world to God accomplished in Jesus Christ is first the history of a breaking through of God to man, and only secondly and in consequence a history of the relationship and intercourse between man and God. This order in the content of the witness entrusted to the community must also apply and emerge, however, in our present question as to the basis of its existence. That " ye shall be my people " is the consequence of the true and basic evangelical revelation : " I will be your God." If we might put it that way, it is the indispensable aspect of Law. The community exists as the people called by Jesus Christ and created by His call on the basis of the fact that first, i.e., in God's eternal election of grace, He has made Himself its Head and therefore made it (" elect in him," Eph. 1[4]) His body, so that He now exists as its Head, as such is its Lord, and as such acts and works in and on it in the enlightening power of His Holy Spirit, and it for its part has its being, the being of His body, in and with His being as its Head. Hence it is from what He is in relation to it that what it is in relation to Him acquires its significance and weight and specific character, and not *vice versa.*

We say further that the Christian community exists as He, Jesus Christ, exists. It does not exist merely because He exists, because its existence is established and created by His election, vocation and governance. This is also true. But there is more to it than this. The first point, which includes the second, is that it exists as He exists, as to His being as its Head there belongs its own creaturely, earthy, human, historical and therefore distinct being as His body. It exists as its being is a predicate and dimension of His, and not *vice versa.* The being of Jesus Christ, then, is not, as Schleiermacher in his own brilliant fashion understood and explained, the supreme, decisive and distinctive predicate of His community, the model and historical point of connexion for its living piety. To be sure, it exists as it believes in Him, loves Him and hopes in Him. But the fact that it does these things is not the basis of its existence. It does not live by them, i.e., by its own activity, by its faith and love and hope. It does not derive from them. Nor does Jesus Christ for His part exist only as the community is what it is and does what it does. No, the community exists only as He exists. "Because I live, ye shall live also" (Jn. 14¹⁹), is the right order. Hence we can and must venture to say that the being of the community is a predicate or dimension of the being of Jesus Christ Himself. In this full and strict sense it belongs to Him and is His property. This is the source of its life and existence. Hence it has no option but to exist in faith in Him, love for Him and hope in Him. It exists as He exists. For He does not exist without it. He alone is who and what He is. But He is not alone as who and what He is. He is it for Himself, yet not only for Himself, but also with His own, and by anticipation with all who will become His own when His own shall be manifested in accordance with their determination as such. He is it together with them, being not only very God but also very man, and as such representing all men to God and God to all men. As very God *solus* He is also very man *totus,* so that His being does not exclude but includes within itself that of His own. In Him it is true and actual that God alone is God, yet that as the only God He is not alone, but that as the Creator, Reconciler and Redeemer of His creature He has ordered and bound Himself to this other which is so wholly distinct from Himself. To this great context belongs our statement that the Christian community exists as Jesus Christ exists, that its being is a predicate, dimension and form of existence of His.

We must emphasise and maintain that it is a predicate. It is not, then, the only one. We have said already that He does not exist only as it exists. Otherwise the statement might be reversed in the sense of Schleiermacher, and there would be a great temptation to concentrate on the reversed formulation. Jesus Christ exists also, secondarily, in a definite sequence, but not exclusively, as His community exists. Primarily—and this is the first predicate of His being which we must always remember—He is the One who He alone is : not in isolation, for He is it for humanity and in the first instance for His community ; but alone, and not together with it. In His baptism in the Jordan and on the cross of Golgotha He is again quite alone : in both cases for humanity and His community ; yet in neither case with them. He alone is the eternal Son of God, who for our sake became flesh of sin like us, and for the reconciliation of the world to God was crucified and slain. He alone is the justification of man before God and his sanctification for Him. He alone is the life of all men and the light of their life. He alone is the Resurrected from the dead in revelation of the glory of His mission, of the act of God accomplished once and for all in Him. He alone is the Prophet, the Word of God. He is all these things for all humanity and in the first instance for His community which has to attest Him to humanity as this One, which He has called and equipped to do so by the enlightening power of His Holy Spirit. But He is not these things together with humanity nor together with His community. He was all these things in His once-for-all enacted work, in His person ; and He is them now, in the time after His first *parousia* and before His second, up above in heaven at the right hand of the Father —He alone, i.e., with God alone, hidden in God, accessible to no aggression nor control from below on the part of the creaturely world, distinct from the being of humanity and His community as the Creator and creature are distinct. Clearly He is all these things in another and first predicate or dimension or form of existence of His being. For all these things which must be said of His being in this primary form of existence cannot be said of the being either of humanity or His community. How can it be said of the community that it was the incarnate Son of God, that it did what He did as such, that it represents humanity or even itself to God and God to humanity, that it is the justification and sanctification of man or even of the Christian before God and for Him, that it already has death behind it and that it has thus to reveal the glory of God and of Jesus Christ as its own ? From its own depths within world-occurrence it can only lift up its eyes to Him in this first predicate of His being as man on earth lifts up his eyes to heaven, praying earnestly for His Spirit from above : *Veni, creator Spiritus !*, for the coming and revelation of His kingdom. To Him in this form of His existence it can only look and move as, " absent from the Lord " (2 Cor. 5[6]), it waits with all creation for His appearance from heaven, for His coming forth from the hiddenness of God. It is comforting, alarming and helpful enough that it may and can do this. But it is obviously with reference to another predicate and form, to the first and basic form of existence of His being, that it does.

It may be asked parenthetically whether we do not have to take into account a third form of existence in addition to these two. What are we to make of what is said in Col. 1, namely, that " all things were created by him, and for him," that " he is before all things, and by him all things consist," or have their *ουστάς* (vv. 16–17), and that " it pleased the Father . . . having made peace through the blood of his cross, by him to reconcile all things unto himself ; by him, I say, whether they be things in earth, or things in heaven " (vv. 19–20) ? How about the alteration of the whole situation of man and his cosmos as already accomplished in Jesus Christ in execution of this resolve ? How about the remarkable step from the statement in Col. 1[18] that Jesus Christ is the Head of His body the community, to that of Eph. 1[22] that as the Head of all things He is given to the community ? How about Jesus Christ as the new reality of world-occurrence to which we referred in answering our first question and which is still concealed in contrast to His present aspect ? Does He really exist only as the One He is with God, and then as the One He is with and in His community ? Does He not already exist and act and achieve and work also as the *Pantocrator*, as the *κεφαλὴ ὑπὲρ πάντα*, as the One who alone has first and final power in the cosmos ? Concealed though He may be in the cosmos and not yet recognised by it as by His community, does He not already exist in it with supreme reality, with no less reality than He does at the right hand of God the Father or in His community ? In this respect we may recall the striking doctrine of Calvin, on which research has thus far shed little light, concerning the Holy Spirit as the principle of life which rules not merely in the history of the saved community but also in the whole created cosmos as such. Will not the future coming forth of Jesus Christ from heaven, from the hiddenness of God, mean also and at the same time His coming forth from His hiddenness in world-occurrence ? A strange stanza in the strange Advent hymn : " O Saviour, rend the heavens apart," seems actually to reckon with this possibility. Obviously based on Is. 45[8], it was retained in the tentative version of the new Swiss hymnbook but deleted from the final version as presumably open to question on dogmatic grounds. It runs as follows : " O earth, break out, break out, O earth, Let green on hill and vale come forth, This little flower to birth then bring, Out of the earth, O Saviour, spring." Do we not have here something true and important which ought to be seen and sung ? But if so, then do we not have to conceive and declare a third form of existence of Jesus Christ, a third predicate of His being, i.e., His being as the *Pantocrator* who already reigns, as the principle of lordship in world-occurrence ? Our present concern, however, is with the relationship of His being to that of His community, and therefore we may raise but cannot answer here this stimulating question.

In relation to the people of God existing in worldly form in terrestrial and human history, and therefore in relation to the Christian community, we certainly have to say that the being of Jesus Christ is not restricted to His being in the height and distance and transcendence of God, that it is not exhausted by this first predicate, that it has more than this first dimension and form, that in His being that of God Himself shows itself to be one which is not merely otherworldly, but which also condescends mercifully to this world. In the community it takes place that Jesus Christ Himself, the living Word of God, is present and revealed to certain men together in world-occurrence as the One He is above in the height and hiddenness of God. And it also takes place that by these men together He is acknowledged, recognised, and confessed as this Word from the height, as their heavenly Head, and that He is confessed by them together as the Lord of all humanity. These men in their own time and place here find themselves commonly ruled and determined by the fact that in speech and action He always comes to their time and place. In other words, they find themselves ruled and determined by the common recollection of His accomplished coming and the common expectation of the awaited coming which He has still to fulfil. In the witness commonly entrusted to these men there still shines here and now in world-occurrence the light of Easter Day, and there already shines the light of the last of all days, the one light of His life both behind and before. It is as this takes place that the community exists. It takes place to it and in it. It takes place in the form of the very human life, choices, speech and activity of the men united in it. It takes place in their particular human history which as such is also an element in human and secular history generally. It takes place in movements which are wholly creaturely and indeed, being made by sinful men, both capable and guilty of error. Yet it takes place as these movements, as the life, choices, thought, speech and activity of the men united here, follow the life movement of Jesus Christ as their model, either well or badly imitating, reflecting, illustrating and attesting it. It is precisely as this takes place that His community exists. It thus exists precisely as He Himself as its model is first present and alive in it, evoking, ordering and guiding its movements by His own, and as He Himself is also secondarily, or in reflection, illustrated and attested by the movements and in the being and activity of His community. We are thus forced to say that the community has its being as a predicate and dimension, and in a distinctive force, of His being. It exists as He alone lives with God, and yet as He who alone lives with God lives also in it, reflecting Himself in it, so that as the primarily active Subject He is not only above but also below, and below as the One He is above, present within it not merely as its recollected and expected but also as its present life. It exists as He does not exist abstractly in heaven, as a Head without a body, but is also with the community on earth, the heavenly Head of this earthly body. It thus exists as it, too, does not exist abstractly as a body existing only in worldly fashion in the world, but as it is His body, the body of this heavenly Head, a predicate or dimension of His being representing the merciful condescension of God to the world, His earthly-historical form of existence. This unity of its being with that of Jesus Christ, the existence of Jesus Christ in His singularity but also His totality, is the basis and secret of its existence.

According to the familiar Pauline formula, the community exists ἐν Χριστῷ. It exists as a fulfilment of the promise : " Where two or three are gathered together in my name, there am I in the midst of them " (Mt. 18²⁰), and : " Lo, I am with you alway, even unto the end of the world " (Mt. 28²⁰). Now obviously the first " I " does not indicate merely a third or fourth added to the two or three, and therefore a numerical increase ; for we are significantly told : " I am in the midst." Again, the second cannot indicate merely the presence of a by-stander or spectator who might give occasional support, for as the final saying recorded by the Evangelist it is linked with the commission given to the disciples and is obviously intended to show how it will be carried out, namely, as during the intervening time which now commences Jesus is not far from His community but directly present with it. In both cases the " I " is the true and primary acting Subject in the Christian gathering and fellowship, constituting, maintaining and directing it by His presence and action. Hence those who hear it, hear Him ; those who reject it, reject Him (Lk. 10[16]). Similarly, in the last judgment all the peoples gathered around the Son of Man enthroned as King will be asked and judged according to their conduct to His brethren, His own (Mt. 25[31-46]). In the time which now draws to its close, He the King was hungry and thirsty and a stranger and naked and sick and in prison as His brethren were. What did the peoples either do or not do to them ? They did it, or did not do it, to Him, their King. Similarly, it is said to the persecutor of the community (Ac. 9[4]) : " Saul, Saul, why persecutest thou me ? " Similarly, the giving of His body and shedding of His blood for the many is the true action, and He as the Doer of this work of atonement is the true Actor, in the human event of the distribution and reception, of the common eating and drinking of bread and wine in the Lord's Supper. It is He who truly nourishes those who there receive and eat and drink bread and wine together. The establishment and realisation of His fellowship with them, the κοινωνία of His body and blood (1 Cor. 10[16]), is the true reality of their fellowship with Him and with one another as achieved in the Lord's Supper. In this action they proclaim His death till He comes (1 Cor. 11[26]). Hence this action as the reflection of His own can be directly equated with it : τοῦτό ἐστιν (Mt. 26[26] and *par.*). The Lord's Supper is truly the κυριακὸν δεῖπνον (1 Cor. 11[20]), as the first day of the week, the day of the resurrection of Jesus Christ and therefore the day of their assembling together, is the κυριακὴ ἡμέρα (Rev. 1[10]). How else can we describe the relationship between Him and the community but by saying that He exists also in this predicate or dimension of His being, that therefore in this predicate or dimension, without ceasing to be the heavenly κεφαλή in the heights on the right hand of the Father, He Himself is also in the depths of world-occurrence, and that He is therefore σῶμα, this σῶμα, His ἐκκλησία. Hence it can be said quite clearly and definitely in 1 Cor. 12[27] : " Ye are the body of Christ." As this His σῶμα, as this His earthly-historical form of existence, the community also exists as He does. It does not exist otherwise. But in this way it exists really, and indeed *realissime*. As the *unus Chrisus, solus* yet also *totus*, He is the basis and secret of its existence.

This first christologico-ecclesiological statement is to be understood as an elucidation of the second and more familiar pneumato-logico-ecclesiological statement with which we began, namely, that the " Holy Ghost calls, gathers, enlightens and sanctifies all Christians on earth, keeping them in the true and only faith in Jesus Christ." The power of the act thereby denoted, of this dynamic event, of this mighty act of the Holy Spirit, is the power of the being of Jesus Christ in its relationship to that of the community as just expounded. In our statement that the Christian community exists as Jesus Christ exists, we have described the solid sphere and setting in which this act takes place, in which it becomes possible and actual. There is thus excluded any false idea that chance or caprice is at work in this happening. The order which underlies the free event of the grace which calls the community is thereby revealed, namely, the order of grace as the order of being.

Conversely, however, we can and should understand the second statement concerning the mighty work of the Holy Spirit, which is the basis of the existence of the community, as an explanation of the first and christological statement. Itself excluding a misunderstanding, the second statement tells us that the relationship of the being of Jesus Christ to that of His community is not static nor immobile, but mobile and dynamic, and therefore historical. As the act of the Holy Spirit which underlies the existence of the community takes place in the order of the being of Jesus Christ and His community, the latter existing as He exists, so this order of the being of Jesus Christ and His community is the order of grace, the order of the act of the Holy Spirit, the community existing as Jesus Christ causes it to exist by His Holy Spirit.

Both statements denote one and the same reality. But neither renders the other superfluous. Neither can be reduced to the other. Hence neither is dispensable. Again, neither can be separated from the other. Neither can be understood to be true except as elucidated by the other. In the present context, our concern is to formulate and fill out in detail the second, pneumatologico-ecclesiological statement in description of the one reality of the basis and secret of the existence of the Christian community in world-occurrence.

The Holy Spirit is the power of God proper to the being of Jesus Christ in the exercise and operation of which He causes His community to become what it is. In the power of His Holy Spirit as the creative power of the Word which calls it, it takes place that it exists as He, Jesus Christ, exists. As He wields this divine power of His in relation to it, its being eventuates as the second and earthly-historical predicate, as the second dimension and form of existence, of His own being, and He makes it in the strict and intimate sense the people of His possession, the Christ community.

What is this power of God? Our first point in characterisation is that this power, and therefore the Holy Spirit, is the power of the grace of God addressed to the whole world in the one Son of God and Son of Man in free, creative action in and on this people. As God is gracious to humanity, He creates, upholds and governs within it this particular people of witnesses, causing it to come to be and to exist as such, to exist as Jesus Christ exists, giving it a share in His being, endowing it with the power, freedom and capacity to do its human work, to bear the witness entrusted to it. If it enjoys and exercises this power, it is not is own, but an alien power addressed and ascribed to it, the power of the free grace of God being great enough—for this is the point of it—to impart, address and ascribe its own power to this people as its witness among other peoples. The event in which this takes place is the work of the Holy Spirit.

As it takes place, this people exists, existing as Jesus Christ exists. As it takes place, its being is the predicate, dimension and form of existence of His being. As it takes place, it has the power to become His people and to take up and discharge its ministry of witness. It is thus also the free grace of God that it may exist as witness of this grace to all humanity and serve it with its human action. To the question how it comes to be this people, we may thus answer that the coming is not on its side at all. Its existence as this people comes freely to it. It could never become such of itself. Of itself it is only a people of blind, vain, stupid, perverted, defiant and despondent men like any other people. What is there to prefer it, what merit or dignity does it display, that it should have the right or the power to become and be this people?

If it were not the case as described in Ezek. 16$^{4-14}$, that as an abandoned infant, poor, naked and suffering, it is invested with this power as with the robe and insignia of royalty, then it could only continue to be that naked infant and die and perish as such. But the fact that it is invested with the robe and insignia of royalty, which are not its own, which it has not itself provided nor fashioned nor won, is the work of the Holy Spirit. The Holy Spirit is the divine power of free grace to clothe this infant. And the action or mighty work of the Holy Spirit is the event or occurrence of the clothing of this infant. It is the action in which the Christian community arises and consists by the creative Word of Jesus Christ, acquiring existence and being maintained in it.

This action of the Holy Spirit as the work of the free grace of God in Jesus Christ is the basis and secret of the existence of the Christian community. This is the second statement to be made in answer to our third and final question. We shall now try to shed light on it.

The Holy Spirit is the power, and His action the work, of the co-ordination of the being of Jesus Christ and that of His community as distinct from and yet enclosed within it. Just as the Holy Spirit, as Himself an eternal divine " person " or mode of being, as the Spirit of the Father and the Son (*qui ex Patre Filioque procedit*), is the bond of peace between the two, so in the historical work of reconciliation He is the One who constitutes and guarantees the unity of the *totus Christus*, i.e., of Jesus Christ in the heights and in the depths, in His transcendence and in His immanence. He is the One who constitutes and guarantees the unity of the first and the second predicates, of the primary and the secondary dimensions and forms of existence of His being. He is the One who constitutes and guarantees the unity in which He is at one and the same time the heavenly Head with God and the earthly body with His community. This co-ordination and unity is the work of the active grace of God. Its freedom, the freedom of God and His action and operation, should not be overlooked nor forgotten for a single moment when we venture, as we must, to see and confess Jesus Christ as the same on both sides, as the Head at the right hand of the Father and as the body in the being of the community in its temporal and spatial present and situation, and therefore as the *Kyrios* in His totality. His being in this unity, and therefore the secret and basis of the existence of His community, is not a datum or state. It is a history which takes place as Jesus Christ exercises His power, as this power is operative as the power of His calling Word, and therefore as the gracious power of the Holy Spirit.

The work of the Holy Spirit, however, is to bring and to hold together that which is different and therefore, as it would seem, necessarily and irresistibly disruptive in the relationship of Jesus Christ to His community, namely, the divine working, being and action on the one side and the human on the other, the creative freedom and act on the one side and the creaturely on the other, the eternal reality and possibility on the one side and the temporal on the other. His work is to bring and to hold them together, not to identify, intermingle nor confound them, not to change the one into the other nor to merge the one into the other, but to co-ordinate them, to make them parallel, to bring them into harmony and therefore to bind them into a true unity. In the work of the Holy Spirit there takes place that which is decisive for the calling and therefore the existence both of the individual Christian and of the Christian community, namely, that the light of the crucified and risen and living Jesus Christ does not merely shine objectively, but shines subjectively into fully human eyes and is seen by them ; that His Word as the Word of God does not only go out into all lands and even to the ends of the world (Ps. 19⁴), but here and now is heard by very human ears and received and understood by very human reason ; that God's revelation of His accomplished act of reconciliation has its counterpart here and now in human faith and love and hope and knowledge, its echo in human confession at this specific time and place ; that its creative freedom finds an equivalent in real creaturely freedom. In the work of the Holy Spirit it takes place that Jesus Christ is present and received in the life of His community of this or that century, land or place ; that He issues recognisable commands and with some degree of perfection or imperfection is also obeyed ; that He Himself actively precedes this people ; that in its action or refraining from action there is more or less genuine and clear reflection, illustration and attestation of His action, more or less faithful discipleship in the life of this people, and therefore a fulfilment of its commission. In the work of the Holy Spirit there takes place in the Lord's Supper, in a way which typifies all that may happen in the life of this people, that which is indicated by the great τοῦτό ἐστιν, namely, that unity with its heavenly Lord, and the imparting and receiving of His body and blood, are enacted in and with their human fellowship as realised in the common distribution and reception of bread and wine. None of this can be taken for granted. It is all most strange and improbable. Indeed, from the human and even the Christian angle it is impossible. Yet on God's side it is not only possible but actual. If it may be perceived only in faith, which is itself the first of these counterparts or correspondents, in faith it may be perceived with clarity and certainty. In other words, it all takes place in the gracious act of the gracious power of the Holy Spirit which co-ordinates the different elements and constitutes and guarantees their unity. In virtue of this gracious act it is always true and actual that the Head does not live without His body nor the body without its Head, but that the Head, Jesus Christ, lives with and in His community, and the body, His community, with and in Him. In virtue of the gracious act of the Holy Spirit, who is Himself God, *Dominus, vivificans, cum Patre et Filio simul adorandus et glorificandus*, there exists and persists—this is the second answer to our third and final question—the people of His witnesses in world-occurrence.

2. THE COMMUNITY FOR THE WORLD

The community of Jesus Christ is for the world, i.e., for each and every man, for the man of every age and place who finds the totality of earthly creation the setting, object and instrument and yet also the frontier of his life and work. The community of Jesus Christ is itself creature and therefore world. Hence, as it exists for men and the world, it also exists for itself. But it is the human creature which is ordained by nature to exist for the other human creatures distinct from it. It is what it is, and exists for itself, only in fulfilment of this ordination. Even within the world to which it belongs, it does not exist ecstatically or eccentrically with reference to itself, but wholly with reference to them, to the world around. It saves and maintains its own life as it interposes and gives itself for all other human creatures.

In this way it also exists for God, for the Creator and Lord of the world, for the fulfilment of His purpose and will for and to all human creatures. First and supremely it is God who exists for the world. And since the community of Jesus Christ exists first and supremely for God, it has no option but in its own manner and place to exist for the world. How else could it exist for God? The centre around which it moves eccentrically is not, then, simply the world as such, but the world for which God is. For God is who He is, not *in abstracto* nor without relationship, but as God for the world. The community of Jesus Christ is the human creature whose existence as existence for God has the meaning and purpose of being, on behalf of God and in the service and discipleship of His existence, an existence for the world and men.

That it exists for the world because for God, follows simply and directly from the fact that it is the community of Jesus Christ and has the basis of its being and nature in Him. He calls, gathers and upbuilds it. He rules it as its Lord and Shepherd. He constitutes it ever afresh in the event of His presence and by the enlightening power of His Holy Spirit. He is the centre around which it moves eccentrically. In Him and by Him it is won for God and claimed for His discipleship and service. For in Him God is not for Himself but for the world. In Him God has given Himself to and for the world to reconcile it to Himself. In Him God, supremely and truly God, has become man. This decides the orientation, meaning and purpose of His community. As the people created by Jesus Christ and obedient to Him, it is not subsequently or incidentally but originally, essentially and *per definitionem* summoned and impelled to exist for God and therefore for the world and men. In this way but only in this way, as the human creature thus orientated, can it and will it also exist for itself, in correspondence with the fact that the God who acts and speaks in Jesus Christ expresses His own true divinity precisely in His true humanity.

The disciples as a whole, namely, as the body of disciples or Christendom, are the " salt of the earth " (Mt. 5¹³), the " light of the world " (Mt. 5¹⁴), and, as " sons of the kingdom," the good seed sown in the field which is the world (Mt. 13³⁸). It is to be noted that we are not told that it is proper to them, or required of them, to be this, or that they are to become salt, light and seed in extension or completion of some very different determination of their existence. As they are disciples of Jesus, ordained to be with Him, it belongs originally and essentially to their existence that " he might send them forth " (Mk. 3¹⁴). Paul, too, writes indicatively and not imperatively that " ye shine as lights in the world " (Phil. 2¹⁵). As a city on a hill they cannot be hid from the world around, nor be of no significance to it (Mt. 5¹⁴). Τὸ φῶς ὑμῶν, the light which they have and are, which as such is not put under a bushel but naturally on a candlestick, actually shines among men. To be sure, there is a powerful element of exhortation in the λαμψάτω : they are to become what they are. But how can this fail to happen ? They would necessarily be something very different, and not the disciples of Jesus, if they were not salt, light and seed. Their sending forth, first to Israel (Mt. 10⁵ᶠ·), then to the nations (Mt. 28¹⁹ᶠ·), simply explains their being and nature. As the disciples of Jesus, from the very outset they do not exist for themselves, or they do so only as they exist for the world according to the tenor of these images.

To be sure, the community is the people which is called out of the nations by the Word of God, which is separated from the world, which is separately constituted within it and which is thus set over against it. To be sure, it is in this distinction that its particular glory is displayed as the glory of the firstborn to whom is entrusted what is to the world the absolutely new thing of the self-declaration and knowledge of the omnipotent mercy of God. To be sure, it acquires and has, with all its members, its own full share in this good thing. How could it be light without itself being bright, or seed without

itself being living ? It is in the community first, and in the life of the
men called to it and gathered in it, that salvation, reconciliation,
the covenant, the justification of man before God and his sanctification for Him, can and should be expressed *de facto*, that the peace of
God which passeth understanding should be experienced, tasted and
felt as an event. As it exists for the world, neither it nor its members
who belong to it and also exist for the world can or will go away
empty. But this is true only as and to the extent that it is for the
world, i.e., only in the sphere and power of the determination in virtue
of which, transcending itself, it is what it is. Called out of the world,
the community is genuinely called into it. And the reality of its
calling out depends upon there being no gap between it and the
calling into which ineluctably follows, upon the separation from
and the turning to the world taking place in a single movement.
The glory of the firstborn is at once invalidated and forfeited if he
rejoices in or boasts of it otherwise than in an absolutely binding
relation to his brethren. The light which is not set on a candlestick
but under a bushel could not be bright, nor could the seed which is
not sown in the field of the world but left to itself remain alive. The
peace of God experienced in the community and by its members
could only be a false peace if limited to this circle and enjoyed only
within it. For the justification and sanctification of man accomplished in Jesus Christ did not take place in order that so many
Christians should be its privileged beneficiaries and should mutually
strengthen, comfort and admonish one another as such. It is true
that even as individuals Christians will not be deprived of their share
in a life on this foundation. But this does not mean that the purpose
and goal of their calling are exhausted by this participation. The
work of the Holy Spirit in the gathering and upbuilding of the community (*C.D.*, IV, 1 § 62 and IV, 2 § 67) cannot merely lead to the
blind alley of a new qualification, enhancement, deepening and enrichment of this being of the community as such. Wonderful and
glorious as this is, it is not an end in itself even in what it includes
for its individual members. The enlightening power of the Holy
Spirit draws and impels and presses beyond its being as such, beyond
all the reception and experience of its members, beyond all that is
promised to them personally. And only as it follows this drawing
and impelling is it the real community of Jesus Christ.

In the patristic and scholastic, and then again in the Reformation and post-
Reformation doctrine of the Church, there is a gap at this point which in spite
of the many correct insights makes it seem theoretically unconvincing from the
standpoint both of Holy Scripture and of the matter itself, and which makes it
veritably suspect in its practical outworking. Like the classical doctrine of the
calling of man to Christ, which suffers from the same deficiency (cf. § 71, 4), it
cannot and should not be affirmed and passed down to the future in this
form.
As in the famous *Article* VII of the *Augsburg Confession*, the Church is defined

on the one side as the *congregatio sanctorum, in qua evangelium pure docetur et recte administrantur sacramenta.* Granted that the individual terms need to be more closely defined and filled out, is not this a true and excellent statement as a general and formal definition of what should take place in, or rather be done by, the Church ? And it is surely understandable and in order that in his *Apology* (*Art.* VII and VIII, 5) Melanchthon tries to fill out and deepen this purely formal description by one in which the main aim is to characterise the *sancti* united in the Church, the Church not merely being a *societas externarum rerum ac rituum* like other public societies, but consisting supremely in " fellowship in eternal goods in the heart, such as the Holy Spirit, faith and the fear and love of God," which as such have externally visible *signa* or *notae* in the pure preaching of the Gospel and the corresponding use of the sacraments. As deepened or corrected in this way, *Art.* VII of the *Augustana* then takes the following form in the so-called *Variata,* namely, that the Church is *proprie* the *congregatio membrorum Christi, hoc est sanctorum, qui vere credunt et oboediunt Christo.* Calvin deepens this still further (*Cat. Genev.*, 1542) when he defines the Church, which is the fruit of the body of Christ, as *la compagnie des fidèles* which God has ordained and elected for eternal life, or as the militant fellowship (*Conf. de Foi,* 1559) united in following the Word of God, in trying to be faithful to the *religio* thereby determined, in seeking, as required, *de s'avancer et marcher toujours plus outre,* to find the forgiveness which they constantly need, to increase in the fear of God and to strengthen one another. As normatively and decisively defined in the school of Calvin along this second line, the Church is described by the *Confessio Scotica* (1560, *cap.* 16) as the *unus coetus et multitudo hominum a Deo electorum, qui recte ac pie Deum venerantur et amplectuntur per veram fidem in Jesum Christum.* Or, as the *Conf. Belgica* (1561, *art.* 27) puts it, it is the *congregatio sancta seu coetus omnium vere fidelium Christianorum, qui totam suam salutem in uno Jesu Christo expectant, sanguine ipsius abluti et per Spiritum eius sanctificati et obsignati.* Or, according to the *Heidelberg Catechism* (1563, *Qu.* 54), it is the elect community which from the beginning of the world to its end will be gathered, protected and preserved by Jesus Christ through His Spirit and Word in the unity of true faith to eternal life. Basically, and again allowing that greater precision may be needed in relation to the individual terms, we can obviously only approve what was more or less emphatically presented and developed along this second line in the 16th and then in the 17th centuries. A comprehensive definition may be quoted from the period of high orthodoxy : *Ecclesia est coetus seu collectio hominum electorum, vocatorum et fidelium, quos Deus per verbum et Spiritum e statu peccati in statum gratiae, ad aeternam gloriam vocat* (H. Heidegger, *Med. Theol. christ.*, 1696, 23, 3). It is indisputable that the Church is, or is also, such a fellowship of those who have been made participant in the salvation of Jesus Christ by Himself and His Word and Spirit.

In the theology of the later 17th century the two lines in defining the Church, the formal and the materio-personal, were brought together (e.g., by Quenstedt, *Theol. did. pol.*, 1685, IV, *cap.* 15, *sect.* 1, *th.* 5) under the concept of the *ecclesia synthetica.* And to this there could then be opposed the definition of the Church from a third standpoint as the *ecclesia repraesentativa,* namely (as in F. Turrettini, *Inst. Theol. el.*, III, 1685, *loc.* 18, *qu.* 2, 10), as the *coetus rectorum et pastorum ecclesiae, qui legitima vocatione et potestate instructi sunt ad verbum in ea praedicandum, sacramenta administranda et sanctam disciplinam exercendam.* The Church is thus that which might also be denoted by the term *regimen ecclesiae* or Church government. (This is a more than doubtful *theologoumenon,* whether we think in Lutheran terms of the sacred office of pastors or in Reformed terms of the no less sacred college of the presbytery, classis or synod. Either way, the community is divided into two subjects, a smaller, superior, active and directly responsible, and a greater, subordinate, passive and only indirectly responsible, the mediaeval scheme being thus revived in a new clergy and laity. In other words, a theological basis is found for the misunderstanding which is still so fatefully powerful even to-day, causing countless people not to think of themselves when they speak of the Church but only of the parsons and theologians and other leading members. It ought never to have been even admitted, let alone dogmatically formulated, that by the Church we are to understand, as *in parte pro toto*, certain persons or bodies which are exalted above the rest and particularly prominent and to that extent representative in its activity, both internally and externally. The Church may never in any tolerable sense be identified with a rank of pastors and other ecclesiastical dignitaries. It is enough for these that with their special gifts and tasks they should be in the Church with all other Christians.)

If we exclude this final element in the traditional doctrine of the Church, we may well approve, accept and meaningfully maintain what has been said along the first two lines. The Christian Church is indeed inwardly constituted by the election, calling and gathering of certain men to faith in Jesus Christ with all that this may mean for the fellowship of these men and their personal lives by way of endowment, commission and eternal promise. And it is characterised externally by the proclamation which goes forth and is heard within it, by the administration of baptism and the Lord's Supper which takes place in it, according to the standard and under the control and criterion of the Gospel which underlies, maintains and overrules it. There can be no doubt that all this is the Church.

Apart from that dubious addition of later orthodoxy, there was nothing doubtful in what was said but only in what was not said. We have only to put the question for what purpose is all this, to be aware at once of the yawning gap. It is not merely legitimate but imperative that we should also ask concerning the meaning and purpose of the existence of the Christian community which may be described along these two lines. But in the traditional doctrine *De ecclesia* there is either no answer at all, or only an unsatisfactory answer, to this question. Is the Church, then, an end in itself in its existence as the community and institution of salvation ? We are led to this impossible hypothesis if the question is not taken into account. It is an impossible hypothesis because on it there is ascribed to the Church that which can be rightfully attributed only to the being of God for man and the being of man for God ; on it the Church is brought into rivalry with Jesus Christ and indeed surpasses Him as an actualisation of the divine-human being made possible only in Him and by Him ; on it the Church is as such the kingdom of God. Theoretically, of course, the Church of the Reformation never understood itself in these terms. But the question is whether it has not actually done so in some ages and forms.

It is plain that in the depictions of the 16th and 17th centuries we do not find any goal of its existence which transcends the Church itself, its ordered activity and the temporal and eternal life of its members. According to Calvin (*Inst.*, IV, 1, 1) its only function is to be, as Cyprian put it, the mother of believers as God is their Father, to nourish them as infants and children, to surround them with motherly care as adolescents, and to bring them to the goal of their faith. And if at the beginning of the 17th century J. Gerhard (*Loci*, 1609, XXII, *cap.* 12, 303), and at the end A. Quenstedt (*op. cit.*, *th.* 20), both obviously under the influence of Aristotelian logic, do finally and briefly take up the question of the *causa finalis ecclesiae*, they both give what amounts in substance to almost the same answer, namely, that we have to distinguish between a *finis principalis*, the glory which God procures for Himself in the existence of a particular people which rightly knows and worships and magnifies Him, and a *finis subordinatus*, the translation of certain men, the members of this people, out of darkness into light, out of a state of wrath into a state of grace. But even if we put both these together, what else do they amount to but that the existence of the Church as such, and that of its members, is the ultimate goal of the ways of God ? Thus the *regnum gratiae* and the *consortium ecclesiae* seem to be interchangeable terms for J. Gerhard. F. Turrettini, too, was plainly of this opinion (*op. cit.*, 18, *qu.* 1, 3), the Church being for him the *primarium S. S. Trinitatis opus*, the *objectum adventus et mediationis Christi* and the *subjectum applicationis beneficiorum eius. Siquidem non alia de causa in mundum venit et officio mediatoris functus est, quam ut ecclesiam sibi acquireret et acquisitam ad communionem gratiae et gloriae vocaret.* The implication is that on the one side the whole act of reconciliation and salvation accomplished in Jesus Christ and self-revealed in the power of the Holy Spirit, and on the other the existence and activity of the Church, constitute a closed circle and a perfect world apart in the midst of the rest of the world in all its imperfection. It is rather strange that Calvin's meritorious and significant rediscovery of the prophetic office of Jesus Christ did not work itself out either in his own doctrine of the Church or in that of his followers. *Il a été messager et ambassadeur souverain de Dieu son Père pour exposer pleinement la volonté d'iceluy au monde,* is what he wrote in this connexion in the *Geneva Catechism.* How far does this *au monde* extend in practice? Has not the work of this divine messenger and ambassador actually ceased in the blind alley of the Church as an institution of salvation for those who belong to it? Does not God seem to have been content to found this institution, to establish the community of salvation, and to be the gracious God to those united in it? What has become of the decisive New Testament saying in 2 Cor. 5[19] that it was the world which God reconciled to Himself in Jesus Christ, or of the well-known Jn. 3[16] that it was the world which He loved so much and in such a way that He gave for it His only begotten Son, or of the statement in Col. 1[16] (cf. Jn. 1[3], Heb. 1[3]) that He created the world δι' αὐτοῦ καὶ εἰς αὐτόν? The classical doctrine seems not to envisage any relationship, or at least any basic and essential relationship of the institution and community of salvation to this world outside. As though there could be no question of any such relationship, in explanation of the description of the community as *ecclesia militans,* it was often maintained that on earth and in this age the Church has to fight not only against the flesh and the devil but also against the world. To be sure, it has also to fight against the world. But above all does it not have to exist for it? The classical doctrine of the Church suffers from the same " holy egoism " as we had occasion to deplore in our critical consideration of the classical doctrine of man's vocation. The fact that the Church exists for the world and not for itself does not appear at all, let alone the fact that it does so originally and essentially. Was it for this reason that in the 16th and 17th centuries the Protestant world was characterised by that pronounced lack of joy in mission, and even unreadiness for it, which we had occasion to notice at the beginning of this third part of the doctrine of reconciliation? Or conversely, were the lack of joy and the unreadiness the basis of this striking deficiency in the self-understanding of the Church during this period? Or are both explanations true, so that we have here a true vicious circle? However that may be, there can be no doubt that we are here confronted by a noticeable gap in the Evangelical dogmatic tradition, nor is the case much better, so far as I can see, with the traditional self-understanding of the Roman Catholic Church, even though it does have an undeniable advantage over the Protestant in respect of missionary purpose. For did not and does not the practice of this Church stand rather under the slogan: The world for the Church, than its opposite: The Church for the world? Among the accounts of its doctrine we do, however, find a few and for the most part modern references which seem to point in the second direction, as, for instance, the passage in the encyclical " Satis cognitum " of Pope Leo XIII (June 29, 1896, Denzinger, 1955), according to which *partam per Jesum Christum salutem simulque beneficia omnia, quae inde proficiscuntur, late fundere in omnes homines atque ad omnes propagare aetates debet ecclesia.* We must always take this *late fundere* seriously if we are not to acquiesce in that gap.

The true community of Jesus Christ is the community which God has sent out into the world in and with its foundation. As such it exists for the world. It does so, not in virtue of any dignity, authority or power immanent to its creaturely nature as one people among others, but in virtue of the plenary power with which it is invested, and which is thus proper to it, in and with its particular foundation as this people. No creature as such can exist for others. Even the Church is a creature. How, then, can it exist for the world, for the totality of creatures, for all men ? To the extent that it can, it is not " of the world " even though it is " in the world " and itself a creature (Jn. 17¹¹), just as the One who sends it forth with plenary divine power is not " of the world " (Jn. 17¹⁶). And the fact that it can exist for the world is the plenary power with which it is invested by Him in and with its foundation and as He sends it forth. It is invested with it in the context of His divine sending and in correspondence with the plenary divine power proper to Him. We can and must speak of it as strongly as this, but not more strongly. Its sending is not a repetition, extension or continuation. His own sending does not cease as He sends it. It does not disappear in its sending. It remains its free and independent presupposition. Its sending is simply ordered on its own lower level in relation to His. The power with which it is invested is comparable with His, as is necessarily the case since He Himself gave it, but neither quantitatively nor qualitatively is it equal. He is sent to precede it on the way into the world. It is sent to follow Him on the same way. These are two things. But the two sendings are comparable because they have the same origin. The one God who sends Him as the Father also sends them through Him the Son. Again, they are comparable because they have the same goal. He and they are both sent into the world, which means very generally that they are directed to the world and exist for it.

At this point we naturally have in mind Jn. 20²¹ : " As my Father hath sent me (ἀπέσταλκεν), even so send I you (πέμπω) " ; and also Jn. 17¹⁸ : " As thou hast sent me into the world (ἀπέστειλας), even so have I also sent them (ἀπέστειλα) into the world." The adverb καθώς used in both verses indicates the interconnexion, parallel, analogy and comparable nature of the two processes. The emphatic κἀγώ at the beginning of the second statement in both cases underlines, of course, the fact that Jesus is conscious that He with His sending is to be ranged alongside the Father who sends Him. He sends them in execution of His own sending. If the two processes are put in the perfect and present in Jn. 20 and the aorist in Jn. 17, the different nuances required by the contexts simply serve to emphasise their character as a historically interconnected event. In Jn. 20 the use of the two verbs ἀποστέλλειν and πέμπειν, which in any case are hard to distinguish in Johannine terminology, enables a distinction to be made between the sending of Jesus Himself and that of His disciples. In both cases, however, " sending " means to be invested with δόξα, to participate in the dignity, authority and power given to the one commissioned to go to a third party for the discharge of his mission. Hence we note the point, which is important in the present context, that it is twice emphasised in Jn. 17 that the goal of the sending both of Jesus and of His disciples is the cosmos. The world is the third party to which they are sent, Jesus by the Father and the community by Jesus. Both His and their fully accredited embassy is to the world.

In the third sub-section we shall have to speak of the mission to the world which the community has to accomplish as sent by Jesus Christ. It is not idly, but as it performs this, that the community exists for the world. This action, however, has a hidden yet not unrecognisable preliminary form in which it may be concretely described. It has as it were a living root in which it does not seem to be action, nor to take place for the world, but in which already there does take place something decisive for its empowering and actualisation. There, not in the inactivity but in the quietness of this basis, there begins the obedience of the community to its commission. What does not begin there will either not be action at all or only disobedient and therefore powerless and unfruitful action. If the community sent into the world is active towards the world at all, not like a fire of straw which suddenly flares up and as quickly dies down again, but rather like a constantly kindling, shining, warming and even consuming flame, then it is from the quietness of this basis where the movement is prepared and intimated, from which it derives its impulse, direction and law and by which it will be continually renewed, corrected and transcended. In this second sub-section we must now indicate the more essential elements concerning this basis of the active execution of the commission linked with its sending into the world.

We may begin by stating that the true community of Jesus Christ is (1) the fellowship in which it is given to men to know the world as it is. The world does not know itself. It does not know God, nor man, nor the relationship and covenant between God and man. Hence it does not know its own origin, state nor goal. It does not know what divides nor what unites. It does not know either its life and salvation or its death and destruction. It is blind to its own reality. Its existence is a groping in the dark. The community of Jesus Christ exists for and is sent into the world in the first basic sense that it is given to it, in its knowledge of God and man and the covenant set up between them, to know the world as it is. We may well say that, itself belonging also to the world, it is the point in the world where its eyes are opened to itself and an end is put to its ignorance about itself. It is the point in the world where the world may know itself in truth and reality. From this basic sense in which the community exists for and is sent into the world there necessarily proceeds what it may do on its behalf. If it did not have this knowledge, how could it do anything for it, or how could it do the right thing for it? But to know it, because to know God and man and the covenant between them, is given to it from the very outset in and with its founding, gathering and upbuilding, seeing that it has its origin in the prophecy of Jesus Christ and is created by the revelation and in the knowledge of the divine act of reconciliation accomplished in Him. The revelation and knowledge of this divine act is at the same time the revelation and knowledge of the world as it really is, as ordered, reformed and renewed by this divine act, of its origin, state and goal, of its possibilities and limitations, of its nature and perversion, of its need and promise. It is first and basically in the knowledge thus grounded that the community confronts the world, or rather assists it as itself belonging to it.

But to know the world means concretely to know man, to see with free and untrammelled eyes who, what, where and how men exist. It thus means to be constantly aware, both as a whole and in detail, both inwardly and outwardly, of what is involved in man's existence and situation as determined by the good creation of God, by the disruptive factor of his own intervening transgression and its consequences, and decisively and predominantly by the grace of God. To know man is to see together all these conditions of all human life, to see each of them only in its positive and negative relations to the others, and therefore to see each individual man, or each natural or historical group of men, on the basis of the fact that God's good creation, man's own sin and the reconciling grace of God may all determine his being and nature, its action and inaction. To know men is respectfully to weigh their great and little, collective and individual achievements and works in their positive significance, neither dramatising nor underestimating their limitation and corruption, their aberration and cruelty, but quietly and yet firmly seeing them in the limits of their guilt and therefore as intolerably evil, and above all knowing both human good and human bad in its limitation by what God is and has done for them all. To know man is to see and understand, how in fact all men, the strong and the weak, the clever and the foolish, the able and the needy, the leaders and their willing or unwilling followers, the indolent and the industrious, the religious and the irreligious, the apparently or genuinely law-abiding and the crude or refined transgressors, the Western and Eastern orators, newspaper men and liars, the men whose interests and orientation are academic, technical, aesthetic, political, or ecclesiastical, and the men who have no interests or orientation at all—it is to see and understand how all of them are both impelled and restricted. To see and understand men is to perceive, that is, how all of them are impelled by some normal or abnormal faith in a life which is thought to be meaningful for them and by the more or less justifiable or at least understandable concern that they should seek to do this or lest they might miss it ; and yet how all of them are restricted by the limitations of the *condition humaine*, by the brevity of their day, by the contingence of their environment and their own potentialities, by the relationships imposed upon them or more or less fashioned by themselves, and by their various distinctive or unknown personal rivals and opponents. Nor should it be forgotten that all these men who are impelled and restricted are also active to impel and restrict. Yet to know man is not merely to see and understand all this. It is to see and understand above all that God is the God of all these men, that His omnipotent mercy rules over all without exception, over both their heights and their depths, their glory and their misery, that no matter how lost they are they are not lost to Him, that no matter how hard they fight against Him they cannot break free from Him, that as they are created so they are also guided and upheld by His hand. To know men is to see and understand that, as surely as Jesus Christ died and rose again for all, the grace of God has reference and is promised and addressed to all. To know men, to be aware of them, in this critical and comprehensive way is to know the world as it is. For the world as seen in all its distinctions, antitheses and inner contradictions and yet as seen in relation to Jesus Christ and therefore originally and definitely with God, is the world as it really is. The world as seen and understood in any other way is not the world as it is ; it is a mere picture of the world projected idealistically, positivistically, or existentially, scientifically or mythologically, with or without a moral purpose, pessimistically or lightheartedly, yet always with an unhealthy naivety and one-sidedness. The world thinks that it knows itself when it draws and contemplates a book of such pictures, whereas in truth, or rather in the most radical untruth, it misses its own reality and is simply groping in the dark as it turns the various pages. In these pictures men and the world are not seen nor understood. For how can they be when, as in these pictures, they are played off against each other in terms of their different ways and conditions instead of being generously seen together from every angle ? But how can we acquire the generosity of this common view unless originally and definitively we see them together with God ? And how can we do this both critically and comprehensively, with any real cogency or clarity, unless we do so on the sure basis and ground of God's covenant with man, with all men, concluded in Jesus Christ ? As the world is neither able nor willing for this, so it is in no position to know itself in its true reality.

The community is the place in the world where man and therefore the world may be known as they are with the free and untrammelled and universal gaze, with the critical and yet comprehensive generosity, which we have just described. But are man and the world really known as they are in this place ? The gift of this knowledge implies the question of its realisation. Is the task thereby set perceived and tackled ? In other words, do we have the true community of Jesus Christ ? It may well be affirmed that we have to do here with a true *nota ecclesiae*, with an external sign by which the true community of Jesus Christ may be infallibly known. In this as in every other respect the true community of Jesus Christ does not exist esoterically and invisibly but visibly and exoterically, so that it may be noted by the world around. To be sure, those around cannot see that it is the enlightening power of the Holy Spirit, the constraining love of Jesus Christ, which enables them to know the world as it is. But even the community and its members cannot see this; they can know it to be true and actual only in faith. On the other hand, the knowledge which has this hidden basis, if it is not merely given to men but realised by them, must and will be noticeable even to those without in the manner in which the community comes to them, acts towards them, thinks of them and speaks to and concerning them, and finally in the manner in which it discharges its commission to them. It necessarily emerges in the being and activity of the community, whatever their attitude to it. It necessarily impresses itself upon them, causing them to consider that in the community it has to do with a society of men who are at least honestly attempting, and are also able, to see and understand them in their own place and manner, in their worldliness. They cannot possibly be seen and judged and addressed and treated by the true community of Jesus Christ as strangers by strangers, but rather as those who are well acquainted. If the basis of the critical and comprehensive generosity with which they are approached by the Christian community, if God Himself as the secret, origin and goal of the community's view of them, is hidden from them, yet they cannot fail to note this generous view as such, puzzling though it may be. This can and should be accepted as a criterion, and indeed as a fundamental criterion, whether all is well with the Church to which we belong and for which we are in part responsible, and with ourselves as responsible members of this Church. Where the freedom, the openness, the universality and the generosity of this knowledge of the world as it is cannot be seen, noted and detected without, where the community does not give those around something to think about in this regard, where the impression is rather given that they are not really known but are merely preached at in ignorance, this may well be a bad and supremely alarming sign that something is decisively wrong in the inward relation of the community to its own basis of existence and that under the cover of sacred zeal there is a process of defection from its Lord. Everything is perhaps lacking to the community, and all that has still to be said about its existence for the world is perhaps built on sand or in the air, if there is a deficiency or failure at this central point, and if in its surrender to a picture of the world in place of the reality it ranges itself with the world in its groping.

We continue our description of the basis and origin of the obedience of the community to its task by stating that the true community of Jesus Christ is (2) the society in which it is given to men to know and practise their solidarity with the world. Not their conformity to it! The community cannot be conformed to the world; the salt is not to lose its savour (Mt. 5¹³). On the contrary, it is very unlike the world inasmuch as in distinction from it its eyes are open— opened by Jesus Christ, by the enlightening power of the Holy Spirit —to the light of the life given in Jesus Christ as this also shines in Him. But as it may see this light, it must see and express its own solidarity with the world. What shines for it, and illumines it when it is given to it to see it, is the love (Jn. 3¹⁶) with which God has loved the world to such a degree and in such a way that He has given His only Son for it. If it is to share this love, where can it find itself set, or try to set itself, but at the side and indeed in the midst of this world which God has loved? It necessarily closes its eyes again to the light which it may see in distinction from the world, and therefore conforms again to the world, if it tries to ignore or to deny in practice the fact that it belongs to the world, thus attempting not to be in solidarity with it. It necessarily flees the love of God if it tries to flee the world and not to be wordly within it. In this attempt it necessarily becomes unfaithful to its sending, not to a place alongside or above the world, but to the world itself, before it has even taken the very first step. Solidarity with the world means full commitment to it, unreserved participation in its situation, in the promise given it by creation, in its responsibility for the arrogance, sloth and falsehood which reign within it, in its suffering under the resultant distress, but primarily and supremely in the free grace of God demonstrated and addressed to it in Jesus Christ, and therefore in its hope. How can there be any question of a generous view and understanding apart from this participation? The community which knows the world is necessarily the community which is committed to it. This brings us to the second basic sense in which it exists for the world. Of what value would be all it might do for it if it were done with no share, or with only a reserved and partial share, in its existence, if it were only done to it externally and from a distance? If the community acts, and acts meaningfully, then it does so as it sees and finds its own cause in that of the world, and that of the world in its own.

Here, too, our concern is with men. Now there can be no doubt that in the discharge of its mission to them the community has in a sense to keep its distance, and even to contradict and oppose them. Without saying No it cannot really say Yes to them. But of what value would be all its well-founded and solemn withdrawal, or its well-meaning and justifiable contradiction and opposition, if it did not proceed from the profoundest commitment to the whole of humanity and each individual man?

The No of the Pharisees to those around was undoubtedly sincere, but it could not be significant nor fruitful because, as their name indicates, it was the No of separatists, of those who separated themselves and were separate from the rest of men by the fact that they did not think that they had any share in their transgressions and corruption and the impending wrath of God, that they were not prepared to accept any responsibility for the actions and impulses of this *'am ha'aretz*, that they would not share the consequences of its folly and wickedness, and therefore refused to participate, of course, in the hope which dawned precisely for this *'am ha'aretz*, this *profanum vulgus*.

What is telling and important from the standpoint of the community is not the true or false principles or the lack of principle which confront it in men, but the man himself who is controlled or not controlled by these principles and of whom it knows that as such he belongs to God. What is telling and important is the indestructible destiny of this man, his aberrations and confusions, and the universally applicable Word of his justification and sanctification accomplished in Jesus Christ. From this man it cannot separate itself. It belongs to him. It must share unreservedly in his existence. " When he saw the multitudes, he was moved with compassion " (Mt. 9[36]). And the fact that He was moved with compassion means originally that He could not and would not close His mind to the existence and situation of the multitude, nor hold Himself aloof from it, but that it affected Him, that it went right to His heart, that He made it His own, that He could not but identify Himself with them. Only He could do this with the breadth with which He did so. But His community cannot follow any other line. Solidarity with the world means that those who are genuinely pious approach the children of the world as such, that those who are genuinely righteous are not ashamed to sit down with the unrighteous as friends, that those who are genuinely wise do not hesitate to seem to be fools among fools, and that those who are genuinely holy are not too good or irreproachable to go down " into hell " in a very secular fashion.

Les saints vont en enfer (G. Cesbron). The solidarity of the community with the world means to give as little offence as possible to Jews and Greeks as well as fellow-Christians (1 Cor. 10[32]). Even more strongly, it means to be as a Jew to Jews and as without law to those who are without law (1 Cor. 9[20]). Or, to put it more strongly still, it means to be all things to all men (1 Cor. 9[22]).

The solidarity of the community with the world consists quite simply in the active recognition that it, too, since Jesus Christ is the Saviour of the world, can exist in worldly fashion, not unwillingly nor with a bad conscience, but willingly and with a good conscience. It consists in the recognition that its members also bear in themselves and in some way actualise all human possibilities. Hence it does not consist in a cunning masquerade, but rather in an unmasking in which it makes itself known to others as akin to them, rejoicing with them that do rejoice and weeping with them that weep (Rom. 12^{15}), not confirming and strengthening them in evil nor betraying and surrendering them for its own good, but confessing for its own good, and thereby contending against the evil of others, by accepting the fact that it must be honestly and unreservedly among them and with them, on the same level and footing, in the same boat and within the same limits as any or all of them. How can it boast of and rejoice in the Saviour of the world and men, or how can it win them—to use another Pauline expression—to know Him and to believe in Him, if it is not prepared first to be human and worldly like them and with them?

It manifests a remarkable conformity to the world if concern for its purity and reputation forbid it to compromise itself with it. The world only too easily sees itself in a community which has no care but for its own life and rights and manner and which thus tries to separate itself from those around. The world itself constantly divides into individual cliques, interested groups, cultural movements, nations, religions, parties and sects of all kinds, each of which is sure of the goodness of its own cause and each anxious within its limits to maintain and assert itself in face of all the rest. The world will not accept the inward interconnexion of its whole striving, activity and suffering, but seems naively or with conscious superiority to assume that it should not think or speak or act or conduct itself in terms of universality and solidarity. To be sure, there is no lack of philosophical, moral, political and even religious insights which clearly point in this direction in principle, nor of the corresponding well-meant reminders and admonitions. Quite obviously, however, there is no basic impulse necessarily driving in this direction. And it can quietly acquiesce in this lack and find justification for its sectarianism if it discovers that the community of Jesus Christ finally suffers from the same deficiency, that it takes the form only of another and perhaps even more radical separation, that it does not accept the solidarity of its particular humanity with all other good or bad human manifestations, that it is not, in contrast to the world, determined and controlled in practice by a basic impulse irresistibly driving it to the breadth of that great interconnexion. As distinct from all other circles and groups, the community of Jesus Christ cannot possibly allow itself to exist in this pharisaical conformity to the world. Coming from the table of the Lord, it cannot fail to follow His example and to sit down at table with the rest, with all sinners.

What we said concerning the *nota ecclesiae* which is to be affirmed in this context must now be developed and deepened. The community is the noteworthy point in the world at which the latter not only sees and understands itself as it is but at which, in spite of its inner distinctions and contradictions, it is permitted and commanded in a way which is exemplary to achieve inward peace and unity. What are all the internal antitheses of the world compared

with that in which the community as the people of Jesus Christ confronts the world in its totality ? Yet that which separates the community from the world also binds it to it, and that with a strength
which has no peer in the various alliances, brotherhoods and unions
known also to the world. For in it there rules the One who, verily
distinct from the whole world as the eternal Son of the eternal Father,
unreservedly gives Himself to it to reconcile it in His person to God,
making common cause with it, not avoiding its sin but bearing it
and making it His own. How can the particularity of the human
fellowship established and ruled by Him fail to manifest itself in the
fact that, without being able to do for it what He has done, it follows
Him in this attitude of His to the world ? By the enlightening power
of His Holy Spirit it is not led out of the world but into the world.
Its singularity cannot express or declare itself in separation from the
world but only in the most genuine attachment to it. This means,
however, that precisely in the spirituality of its existence, in its whole
being and action it can only approach the world in a sincerely worldly
character, making it obvious that in good and ill alike it belongs
to it. What it has to do in the world saves it from being lost in the
world even though it is worldly. But only as it does this in truly
worldly fashion, does it do so as the true community of Jesus Christ.
The world cannot see, of course, in whose service it stands or whom
it follows and obeys in its worldly being and action in the world.
But it can and should see the community as the place where it is
given to men to do in an exemplary way that of which it is not itself
capable in its internal contradictions, not tearing down bridges but
building and traversing them, being with others and like them for
all their singularity, sharing and bearing as their own all the hopes
and burdens in the existence, situation and constitution of others.
And again, if the community is neither able nor willing to do this,
we are faced by the menacing question whether it is really adapted
to perform that which it has been commanded to do in the world
in and with its mission. Might it not be that, if it holds back at this
point, being like the world instead of unlike it in an exemplary way,
it basically lacks no less than everything for the discharge of its task ?

  In description of the basis on which the community executes its
commission, it must be said finally and decisively that as the true
community of Jesus Christ it is (3) the society in which it is given to
men to be under obligation to the world. As they know it, and are
united in solidarity with it, they are made jointly responsible for it,
for its future, for what is to become of it. Jesus Christ their Lord,
when He was in the world, suffered with it and for it, and acted for it
and to it. And the prophetic Word of this work of His, as the Word of
truth about its new reality established in Him, is the Word of renewal
which here and now applies to the world and affects it. Hence His
community cannot be content contemplatively to know the world

in all its heights and depths. The God who acts in Jesus Christ does not Himself confront it in this way, merely as an omniscient spectator. Nor can it be content to participate only passively in its being and corruption, its nature and degeneration, its history and destiny. God Himself has not associated with it in this way, in idle co-existence. To be sure, the community as the people of God in world-occurrence is not burdened with the commitment and responsibility which God has assumed and carries towards it. It has neither created the world nor reconciled it to God. Itself a creature among others, it belongs to the world. Hence it cannot be its task to rule it as does the God who reconciled it to Himself in Jesus Christ and who will finally do so as the coming Redeemer in the last revelation of Jesus Christ. Nevertheless, it is called and appointed to the active service of this God. Within the limits of its creaturely capacity and ability it is ordained and summoned to co-operate with Him in His work. And since His work is on and in the world, in its own place and manner it, too, is pledged to the world and made responsible for what is to become of it. Different though its action may be from His, in its own definite function and within the appointed limits it, too, is summoned and freed and commissioned for action in and towards the world. Hence in the course and movement of the world, in its rises and falls, in its progressions, retrogressions and pauses, it cannot possibly be neutral or passive, nor withdraw into itself, into its profounder knowledge of it, or into a sincere but inactive participation in its situation. It is sent to the world to play its own part in its own way, not merely knowing it better in its good and evil, its greatness and misery, nor merely hoping and suffering with it, but also waiting with it for its future and with it hastening towards this future. To the basic sense in which it exists for the world there belongs as a third and as it were culminating element the consciousness, which excludes any possible quietism, that it is committed to it, i.e., that it is sent in order that it may zealously do for it that which is required and possible in the light of this future.

In the world it has to do with men. It could perhaps ignore and pass by as non-essential both the world and what takes place in it if it were not that in the world, whether in small things or in great, we are always concerned with the existence, enterprises and experiences, the acts of commission and omission, the triumphs and defeats, the joys and sorrows, the short life and bitter death of men. It is because this is so, because the call comes to it from the man whom God has elected and loved, that the community of Jesus Christ and the men united in it are bound to the world and everywhere summoned to action in relation to it. For God's active intervention for man, His eternal election of all men in the One, His giving of this One for all, His Word which goes out to all in this One, is the basis of its own being and existence. Whether it knows and values and accepts and confirms the fact or not, the brothers of this One, those who in Him are justified before God and sanctified for Him, are all fellow-men with the men united in the community. Hence an inactive or neutral faith in relation to them could not possibly be faith in the God who has done this for all in that One. It is thus impossible that the community which believes in this God should pass by those who are without as the priest and Levite passed by the man who had fallen among thieves. All those who are without are waiting not only for the understanding and solidarity and participation, but for the helping action of the Christian community, for that which it alone in the whole world can do for them. Whether they are aware of it or not, their whole being and striving and existence utters the cry of the Macedonian : " Come over . . . and help us " (Ac. 16⁹). To be sure, they do not realise that they await and need what the community of Jesus Christ can do and is called to do for them if God acknowledges its activity. If they did, why should they look around for so many different means with which they think they can help themselves ? Yet this does not alter the objective fact that they do actually need and lack and seek and expect to find the one thing which the Christian community of all creatures is called to do for them. In spite of every appearance or subjective experience to the contrary, this is true of every man, since none can evade what God is and has done for him in Jesus Christ and what it is appointed that he, too, should know in His Word. Therefore : " Behold, I say unto you, Lift up your eyes, and look on the fields ; for they are white already—not in four months but already—to harvest " (Jn. 4³⁵). This is why the community is under obligation to the world. It cannot possibly refrain from meeting, within the framework of its task and ability, the actual and existing request of humanity. It cannot leave it in the lurch, nor to its own devices. It has no option but to follow the saying of Jesus to His disciples in Mk 6³⁷ : " Give ye them to eat," and therefore to give hungry men that which they need and in spite of every appearance to the contrary demand. It is true, of course, that they cannot do this without first allowing Him to fill their own hands that they may give. How could they do it if it were not really given them to do it, and therefore if they themselves had not to ask for that which is necessary thereto ? Only the *ecclesia orans* can and will be the *ecclesia efficaciter laborans*, the community which really corresponds to its responsibility. It is also true that when what is given to it passes through its hands it does not go hungry but is itself fed. Yet when it asks for it, it is given in order that it should pass through its hands to men, and that it should thus do and accomplish what it is sent into the world to do.

Again the community would be guilty of too close conformity to the world if it were to exist within it for its own sake, refusing the active assistance which it ought to give. The world indeed thinks that it can and should nourish and sustain itself as each and all satisfy themselves, playing the role of their own neighbours, assistants and helpers. It is a profoundly hungry world just because the way of the priest and Levite is only too characteristically its own. What it needs is not to be confirmed and strengthened by another variation of its own way, but to be pointed beyond it in unambiguous practice. It waits for a Good Samaritan to appear within it who will not act for himself, who will not be his own neighbour, assistant and helper, who will relieve it of the burden of being left to itself and having to save and preserve itself. A community alive and interested and active only in and for itself, and inactive towards those around, might well be familiar in its conformity to the world, and to that extent acceptable, but in the long run it could only prove a source of disillusionment. The Christian community cannot encounter the world in this conformity. To be sure, it is not itself the Good Samaritan who has come into the world as the Saviour, active not for Himself but only for it in the manner and the power of God. And it is well advised not to try to play this role. But it is gathered and upbuilt by this Good Samaritan for active service on His behalf, and it is actually sent out into the world in this service. If it cannot do what He does, and it should not pretend it can, it may and should follow Him in what He does. It may and should be obedient to His command. It exists to do this, and therefore to set up in the world a new sign which is radically dissimilar to its own manner and which contradicts it in a way which is full of promise. In all its creaturely impotence and human corruption, it is required to do this. It is indeed made responsible for doing it, and therefore, for all the modesty incumbent upon it, it must not fail to do it.

We are thus given a fuller and sharper understanding still of the *nota ecclesiae* visible in this context. The true community of Jesus Christ does not rest in itself. It does not merely contemplate the striving of the world with its better knowledge. It does not refrain from active participation. It exists as it actively reaches beyond itself into the world. It acts and works within it. Not by a long way does all its supposed or ostensible ecclesiastical outreach into the world validate it as the real community of Jesus Christ, as the true Church. It might well reach beyond itself in denial or falsification of its task, or with shortsightedness, ignorance or arrogance. In its undertaking, as in that of the builder or the king of Lk. 14[28f.], the question might seriously arise whether it has sufficient to finish. It is not a matter of any activity in the world, but of that which is required, of that which corresponds to its commission, of that for which it is empowered by the One who gives it. In no circumstances, however, may it or should it try to evade this task. In discharging it, it will always need the forgiveness of the sins which it commits, and therefore correction, and therefore constant self-criticism. But even the most stringent self-criticism must never be a reason or occasion for prudently doing nothing. Better something doubtful or over bold and therefore in need of correction and forgiveness, than nothing at all! If even in the most holy reserve and modesty and prudence it prefers to fold its hands and therefore to rest in itself, it is certainly not the true Church. The true Church may sometimes engage in tactical withdrawal, but never in strategic. It can never cease wholly or basically from activity in the world. It does not exist intermittently, nor does it ever exist only partially, as the sent community, but always and in all its functions it is either leaping out or on the point of leaping out to those to whom it is sent. In every respect, even in what seems to be purely inner activity like prayer and the liturgy and the cure of souls and biblical exegesis and theology, its activity is always *ad extra*. It is always directed *extra muros* to those who are not, or not yet, within, and visibly perhaps never will be. It exists in this venture which is no more than the simple and unassuming venture of its obedience. It is recognised as the true Church by the fact that it is engaged in this venture of obedience. Self-criticism in the Church is meaningful and fruitful only if it does not arrest it in this venture but stimulates and impels it afresh and as never before. And only as it makes this venture can it be sure of the forgiveness of its sins. The world exists in self-orientation ; the Church in visible contrast cannot do so.

The true community of Jesus Christ is the society in which it is given to men to see and understand the world as it is, to accept solidarity with it, and to be pledged and committed to it. We have made these statements in development of the proposition that the Church as the true community exists essentially for the world and may thereby be known as the true Church. But the presupposition that it is the society in which these things are given to men requires certain elucidations, and above all it needs a solid foundation.

We may begin with three elucidations. We are dealing (1) with men to whom it is *given* in their adherence to the fellowship of the Church to exist in the way described, i.e., as those who know the world, who accept solidarity with it, and who are committed to it. It is not self-evident, nor does it belong to their human nature, that they should have either the commission, the will or the power for this. But they have not ascribed or arrogated to themselves the commission to exist in this way for the world. Nor have they conceived of themselves the resolve to execute it. Nor do they set to work in an immanent power. The freedom to exist for the world is given to these men. As they exercise it, they enjoy a gift which is made to them. Their liberation is the reality of a grace which is not proper to them, which they have not won, but which is shown to them.

We are dealing (2) with a society or *fellowship* in which men are freed to exist for the world, and therefore not with certain isolated individuals who exist alone, but with those who are called by the same Lord, who enjoy the same knowledge, who share in the same promise and who stand in the same order. It is in fulfilment of the promise which applies in common to all, and in expressions of obedience to the order which is equally binding on all, that it is given to them to exist for the world as described. To be sure, the freedom to see and understand the world, to accept solidarity with it and to be committed to it, is a freedom which is given to them personally and which has to be expressed in personal responsibilities and decisions. It is not given to them, however, as a freedom for their personal enrichment and adornment, to be used according to their personal judgment in accordance with their individual standards and goals. It is as members of the community, and to empower them for participation in its work, that they are given it as a freedom which each is to exercise in accordance with the promise which applies equally to all and the order which equally determines all. It is in order that each in his own place and manner, but all in the same sphere and therefore in unity and concord, may represent the society as such and act on its behalf, that they are thus endowed to exist for the world.

With intentional restraint, we have said (3) that it is given to *men* in this society to exist as described in this way for the world. At this point we must be rather more explicit. The gift or endowment or grace of liberation for this knowledge of the world, this solidarity with it and this responsibility for it, are ascribed and allotted and promised to the Christian community. The Christian community as such and all its members exist under the promise of this grace. The fulfilment of this promise, however, may not be flatly equated with the existence of the Christian community ; we cannot simply say that the grace of this liberation belongs to all its members in virtue of their adherence to this collective and without their needing specifically to request, receive and exercise it. Even within the framework of their membership of the people of God, the dealings of God with men are always free. God unites with men but He is not bound to them. And the union of men with God, as the purpose of their history with Him, has always to be specifically and personally realised by each of them. This is not less true in relation to the fulfilment of the promise made to the community as such and to all its members in respect of its existence for the world, i.e., the promise of the grace which liberates and capacitates it for this existence. Hence our formula could not be to the effect that the Christian community is the society in which it is given to all men, in virtue of their membership, to exist for the world in the sense described. This would imply that the fulfilment of the promise might be understood as an automatically created state which leaves no room either for the freedom of divine grace or for that of its human recipients. And in this case there would be need neither of a special divine giving nor a special human receiving of this gift, neither of a special human requesting of it nor a special divine hearing of the request. This is not the way of things between God and man even in the sphere of membership of His people and even in respect of man's enablement as a member of this people to exist for the world. On the contrary, the liberation for this takes place in the history of this people, which is also the history of the dealings of God with the individuals gathered in it. In practice, therefore, the fulfilment of the promise does not take place either contemporaneously or in equal measure in the being and action of all these men, but always in a specific measure and manner in the being and action of some of them, many perhaps in some cases and few in others. Hence our formula must be that it is given to *men* in this society to exist for the world as described. Since the promise of this grace applies to the Christian community as such and to all its members, it is evident that none is debarred from receiving it and therefore that none may regard himself as not adapted to and therefore dispensed from participation in its sending to the world. How can a man be gathered to this people if he thinks he has no share in its mission, if he does not refer to himself the promise of the grace of liberation, if he does not pray for the fulfilment of this promise in himself? Yet, since the fulfilment of this promise is a matter of the free dealings of God with him and *vice versa*, it is no less evident that there will always be difference in the participation of individual Christians in the sending of the community. In the one community participant in that promise and existing under the order established by it, there will always be Christians who are temporarily, provisionally and transitorily more advanced and those who are temporarily, provisionally and transitorily more retarded in respect of their knowledge of the world, their solidarity with it and their responsibility for it. This does not mean that there are two ranks: on the one side an institutionally and once-for-all privileged circle which is responsible for the whole and represents it; and on the other a class which is finally deprived of this privilege and can and should leave it to the other group to act responsibly and representatively in matters of the community's mission. What it does mean is that there is a fluid distinction between those to whom it is given here and now in a specific way to exist for the world in the sense described, and those to whom it is not given here and now in this specific way, who have thus to look forward, or rather eagerly and humbly to move forward, to the hour of their own particular equipment for it. In this respect all are directed to the work of the enlightening power of the Holy Spirit, to the free grace of God, to their own prayer for it and to their own willingness in relation to it. And we may be confident that the power of the Holy Spirit will see to it that the distinction is really fluid, that those who were last to-day may be first to-day or to-morrow, and that those who were first yesterday may be last to-day or to-morrow. Fulfilled in this history, however, the existence of the community for the world will always be realised with this fluid distinction or differentiation between those who have a more direct and those who have a more indirect part in its mission.

In relation to this third point it may be noted historically that the older Protestant theology was concerned about a distinction between different members of the Church, describing the Church as a *corpus mixtum* which in its visible form is composed of true and serious believers on the one side and unfruitful and hypocritical believers associated with them on the other, the former being understood in Calvinistic circles as the elect of God and the latter as the reprobate who may also be found in the Church. What gave rise to this distinction was the problematical aspect which even the renewed Christianity of the 16th century presented and which was bound to cause deep concern and to occasion the most serious misgivings. It is to be found already in the *Augustana* (VIII), and in view of it the definition of the Church as the *congregatio sanctorum* in which the Gospel is purely preached and the sacraments are rightly administered (VII) acquires almost a purely formal and technical character. Yet the Church is the *congregatio sanctorum*. And we have seen how a fuller concept of these *sancti*, i.e., that those united in the Church are the *membra Christi* who truly believe in Him and truly obey Him, was brought to the forefront by Melanchthon in the *Apology* and the *Aug. variata*, and became the decisive element in the conception of the Church advanced by Calvin and the Reformed. If, then, the more mixed and questionable aspect of the men united in the Church could not be overlooked, and if it was still desired to maintain the distinction between believers and unbelievers, the elect and the reprobate, within it, then in explanation of the implied contradiction there was no option but to make the further distinction that the true *sancti*, i.e., those who truly believe and obey, the elect, constitute the true but invisible Church, whereas in the visible Church they are admixed with the others who are quite different inwardly but cannot yet be differentiated outwardly.

Neither individually nor in combination can these distinctions be called a particularly fortunate element in Reformation and post-Reformation doctrine. On the basis of the one Lord and the calling of His one community we could never arrive either at the distinction between the believing and unbelieving or the elect and reprobate among its members, or at the distinction between an invisible Church comprised only of believers and a visible comprised of both believers and unbelievers. We become entangled in these distinctions only if in our definition of the Church we look abstractly at the men assembled in the community rather than at the Lord and His action. But who tells us to do this ? And if we do, what right or competence have we either to make the first distinction, dividing the community into two groups, and then to go on to identify the first group as the real Church which is invisible and the second as the mixed and improper Church which is visible. On the basis of the one Lord, the one calling of His community and the one promise and order which He has given it, we can only see and understand all those united in it as elected by Him and therefore as summoned and ordained to faith and obedience, but also as participant in the forgiveness of sin in all its forms, and therefore as those who deny faith and withhold obedience, as those who in some way are all both generally and individually recalcitrant in relation to the One who calls them. Again, on this basis, i.e., of what they are in and by Jesus Christ, we can only describe all of them as the invisible Church, i.e., the Church which in its reality is directly visible only to God and to its own members only in faith, but also—in respect of the warfare of the spirit against the flesh and the flesh against the spirit in which they are all involved—as the visible Church which both they and the world may know. With all men generally each of those assembled in the community is in Jesus Christ a *justified* and *sanctified* sinner, yet also a justified and sanctified *sinner*. The only point is that as a Christian, as a member of the community in distinction from the rest, each is both these things in the particular sense that he may know that he is a man of whom both these things are true, yet not in equilibrium, but in a definite order of superiority and inferiority. This is the positive fact which makes the older Protestant distinctions impossible.

We, too, have made a distinction within the one community of Jesus Christ in our third elucidation of the concept of a society in which it is given to men to exist for the world in the sense described. We have not made it in relation to the men gathered in it as such, but in relation to the work of the Lord which takes place in their society. We have referred to all the promise of the grace which capacitates these men to participate in the sending of the community to the world. Hence we have not presumed to differentiate between believers and unbelievers, the elect and the reprobate, within the community, as though we could and should do this in the light of what they all are in and by Jesus Christ. Nor have we had any cause to differentiate between a pure, invisible Church embracing qualified Christians on the one side, and a mixed, visible Church embracing both qualified and unqualified Christians on the other. The distinction which we have made is not to be equated, therefore, with the distinctions made in the older Protestant theology. On the other hand, there remains the *tertium comparationis*, and the resultant element of truth in the older distinctions, namely, that we cannot see and understand the community of Jesus Christ as a monolithic block, as a collective of which the individual elements, as mere parts of the whole, are all equally and in the same way blessed, endowed and determined contemporaneously and to the same degree. The One who gives to it the grace, endowment and determination for its existence for the world is its living Lord, and it for its part, as the recipient of His grace and endowment and determination, is His living community. It exists in His history with it, and its with Him. And this history takes place in a series of free fulfilments of the promise given to it and all its members, and therefore in a fluid and not a static distinction between persons who participate more directly or more indirectly in its mission. There is no cleavage of the community into qualified and unqualified members. We are all qualified and all unqualified. In the ongoing common history of the community, there may have arisen yesterday, and there may arise to-day, a juxtaposition of those who participate more directly and those who participate more indirectly in its mission, but this may also reverse itself and become very different to-morrow. All members participate in the mission of the community. A distinction arises, however, in the different times and forms in which there is a realisation of this participation in specific men. It is for this reason that we must exercise restraint and describe the community, not as the society in which it is given to all men, but rather as that in which it will be given to men, i.e., to some men, to exist for the world.

Having made these elucidations, we now turn to the question of the basis of our presupposition that the Christian community really is the society which exists for the world as it is given to some of those united in it practically to fulfil this existence. Where do we derive this assumption? How far is it possible, because necessary and responsible, to count on it that we may start with the fact, and continually return to it in what we say concerning the sending of the Christian community, that this endowment and therefore the execution of its mission actually take place ? How do we ourselves know that when we begin with the statement that the Christian community exists for the world we are not just idealising its reality, or announcing a programme, but realistically describing the historical actuality of the one Church which is at one and the same time both invisible and visible ?

We may begin with the general assertion that this is a statement of faith. This does not mean—for otherwise it would be a strange statement of faith—that we make it only on the basis of a postulate, of a more or less probable assumption, or at least of a conceivable speculation, and therefore with some degree of uncertainty. Hence we must be careful not to say that, as distinct from statements grounded in some kind of *a priori* or empirical knowledge, it is " only " a statement of faith. Precisely as a statement of faith it is a statement of certain knowledge established with a force which cannot be excelled or even equalled. When the Christian community believes that it exists for the world, it knows what it believes. What it says in this regard, therefore, can be said only with unconditional, assured and joyous certainty if it is really made as a statement of faith. That it is a statement of faith means that like all such statements, in the context of and in relation to all the rest, it speaks of a particular form of God's action towards man and in and on the world for the world's salvation and His own glory. That the community exists for the world is true in the same sense in which it is true—to mention just a few examples—that God has loved the world from eternity, that He has created it as the world thus loved by Him, that in His Son He has given Himself to it and for it, that Jesus Christ in His death has reconciled it to Himself, justifying man before God and sanctifying him for Him, that He as the Servant of God is Lord over all men and all things. That the Christian community exists for the world is one element in the one comprehensive truth of this divine activity. And the statement which expresses this aspect, like other statements expressing different aspects and in indissoluble connexion with them, is one of the true human answers to the true Word in which the God who acts for the salvation of the world and His own glory has declared and revealed Himself, both making Himself known and continuing to do so. This statement, too, cannot be fashioned or uttered otherwise than in hearing this divine Word, i.e., otherwise than in the knowledge of faith awakened by this divine Word and obedient to it. But fashioned and uttered in this hearing and obedience, it has a genuine and supreme content of knowledge, and is established with a force that cannot be surpassed or even equalled. We must now consider the basis which its particular declaration has in the Word of God.

That the community of Jesus Christ really exists for the world is something which, as hearers of the divine Word and therefore with the sure knowledge of faith, we affirm at the very same moment at which we also affirm that God lives, or concretely that Jesus Christ is risen again from the dead. As surely as God lives, and lives indeed as the Creator, Reconciler and Redeemer of the world made by Him, and for the man to whom He has turned as His covenant-partner ; as surely as Jesus Christ lives, the One who has fulfilled His will and been raised by Him from the dead, and lives indeed for the world which has been reconciled by Him but is still moving to its consummation ; as surely as this is not a mere opinion or hypothesis or arbitrary theory but God's revelation of the reality of His action and therefore the truth, so surely does the community of Jesus Christ really exist for the world. As God exists for it in His divine way, and Jesus Christ in His divine-human, so the Christian community exists for it in its own purely human. All ecclesiology is grounded, critically limited, but also positively determined by Christology ; and this applies in respect of the particular statement which here concerns us, namely, that the Church exists for the world. The community neither can nor should believe in itself. Even in this particular respect, there can be no *credo in ecclesiam*. Yet as it believes in God the Father, the Son and the Holy Ghost, it can and should believe and confess its own reality : *credo ecclesiam*, and therefore the reality rather than the mere ideal that it exists for the world. In what follows we shall seek to develop this knowledge of the basis of our presupposition from the most important standpoints which claim our attention.

The Christian community knows (1) that it owes its origin and continuation to a very definite power, to the constant working of which it is totally directed for its own future. The power of its own human and creaturely being and action, which it also has, is not to be recognised in this basic power, nor is any other power which it might even partially control. It can only acknowledge, recognise and confess it as the free power of God which does in fact establish and direct it in superiority from without. But it recognises it as the free power whose operation is its own freedom to be exercised by it. For what it sees to be the working of this power is not that it is mastered, naturally or mechanically moved, and as an object pushed and forced and driven by it, but rather that it is placed by it in the freedom of a definite, genuinely human and spontaneous thought, volition, decision and activity in which it is created, nourished and sustained by it as an active subject. The operation of this power is that it finds itself summoned to give its own corresponding, and to that extent appropriate, and to that extent obedient answer to the Word of God spoken to and reasonably received by it. The power which establishes, directs and upholds it is the power of this divine Word. This Word makes it what it is as a creature among creatures. To it, it owes both the fact and the manner of its existence. For the Word spoken to and received by it has and exercises the power to give it this freedom. We refer to the powerful operation of the Holy Spirit. If it knows itself, it knows itself in its existence on this basis. The Word of God, by whose Holy Spirit, i.e., by whose free and liberating power the community is established and continually sustained, is, however, the Word of joy, omnipotence and mercy by which God has made heaven and earth or the world as His own possession. It is the Word of Him who has loved, loves and will love the world. As the light of this God and His love, the Word shines into the world, causes men to receive it, awakens them to hearing and obedience, calls them together and mirrors itself in the being of their fellowship. The community as the gathering of these men finds itself illumined by the eternal light of this God and His love, being itself set alongside His light in the world as a created and indirect light wholly dependent upon and nourished by Him, yet nevertheless a true light. By this God and His love it is liberated for its distinctive being, for its common human thought, volition, decision and activity according to His mind and will and along the lines indicated by His love. This means, however, that it can see and understand itself, its own existence in this basic sense, only in the light of the illumining and therefore constitutive power of the Holy Spirit as the power of the Word of God, and therefore only in relation to the world created and actively loved by this God. Hence it is not the case that its task to be a light in the world is only an immediate or more distant deduction from the gift of its being and existence. On the contrary, in and with the gift of its specific being, and therefore in and with its creation, it receives, not from itself but from its Creator, this determination and task. In this sense it is originally and essentially light, i.e., the light which by the power of God and therefore of the Holy Spirit may reflect His eternal light in the world. In this sense, it has fundamentally no option but to exist for the world as it reflects the light of God and is itself light. It necessarily understands itself otherwise than in faith, otherwise than in the light of the Word of God which establishes it, and therefore in a radical self-misunderstanding in which it tries to ascribe to itself a being in contradiction, if it seeks to ascribe to itself any other existence than that in which it actualises the gift of this existence, and therefore fulfils this determination and task. If and to the extent that it does this, in great and little things alike it is constantly opposed by its own reality.

The Christian community knows (2) that what it can do and effect and accomplish of itself in its human and creaturely spontaneity, as empowered by the power of the Holy Spirit, can consist only in its confession of Jesus Christ. To confess Him is its business. This includes many things in many different forms. The one thing which includes the many and by which it is established and nourished is the simple fact that it exists as the assembly of those who commonly confess Jesus Christ. It does, of course, know other good and evil lords and helpers and powers and forces. It exists in their sphere. It wrestles with them, either joyfully and thankfully on the one side or with alarm and repugnance on the other. But it cannot wrestle with Jesus Christ. It exists as He exists. It belongs basically and from the very outset to Him. He is its being at its very root. He is the Word in which God addresses it, gives Himself to be known by it and causes Himself to be received by it. He is the self-proclamation of His creative, reconciling and redeeming act. And because it cannot look past Him or go behind Him to compare Him with others and to choose between them, He alone is its being with the singularity of God Himself and the power of His Spirit. It has not chosen Him as this One ; He as this One has chosen it. All vindications of its exclusive attachment to Him can consist only in the assertion and description of this fact that He as this One has chosen and established it. It stands or falls with Him. If it were possible, it would prefer to fall with Him rather than to stand without Him. For without Him, it could only exist, if not necessarily as a collection of atheists in the technical sense, yet factually and practically " without God in the world " (Eph. 2^{12}), i.e., without the One who by His action shows Himself to be the only true God. It can stand only as it stands by Jesus Christ. It is not accidentally or incidentally that it bears His name ; His name is the revelation of its basis. Again it would have to ascribe to itself an existence in contradiction with itself if it were ashamed of this basis and were not prepared to confess that it is the community which bears this name and this name alone. It cannot possibly disguise the fact that not only much or most of what it has to represent, but everything, has its specific weight and meaning and power in the fact that originally and properly it has Him in view, recalls Him, points to Him and proclaims Him. Hence it does not merely confess in themselves and as such various Christian truths such as the love of God, the love which man must then show to God and neighbour, grace and its triumph, forgiveness, sanctification, the life of the future world. It confesses the truth of the person of Jesus Christ in His work, and the truth of His work in His person, as the substance in which all these truths are truth but without which they are only empty religious ideas and principles, not to say mere rhetorical flourishes. It confesses reconciliation as it has taken place in Him, the covenant as it has been concluded in Him, Him as peace and hope, Him as the Way, Him as the Lord. It is sent to do this. As it does it, it lives by its root, existing and knowing itself in its reality.

But the Jesus Christ whom it confesses, thus living by its root, is in His person as very God and very man, and in His work as the

Mediator of the covenant, the God who acts in and for the world and reveals Himself to it. And in this One God is not merely the Brother of some but of each and all men, having taken their part and bound Himself to them for blessing and cursing, for life and death. The living Lord who acts and reveals Himself in this One is thus the God who is absolutely interested in the world, who in spite of all the theoretical and practical godlessness of men is never without man, but always was and is and will be with him and for him. Hence the community called and built up by this One can confess Him only as it confesses to the world, to men, and to all men without distinction, that He is the One in whom God is their God. This is what differentiates its confession from an accidental, arbitrary or optional action. This is what makes its confession of Jesus Christ imperatively necessary on the basis of its being. Might it not be content to exist of Him and by Him and with Him only for itself, to understand His name only as the sum and His action only as the origin and guarantee of the salvation experienced in Him, and His Word only as the ever necessary direction to be assured and worthy of its salvation in Him ? We recall the classical definition of the Church according to which it might actually be content with this. Why does this definition need to be completed and corrected ? Why does the community have to be the confessing community, confessing Jesus Christ, not only *intra muros* but to all men without distinction (Mt. 10³²) ? Why is it set under the unmistakeable threat that otherwise He as the one true Son of the one true God will not confess it as His community before His Father in heaven and therefore in the final and supreme decision ? To this question there is obviously only one answer, namely, that it must confess Him before men because the Father in heaven, as whose Son He founds and gathers and upbuilds it, is the God of all men and therefore of others beside itself, because He causes His sun to shine on the good and the bad and His rain to fall on the righteous and the unrighteous (Mt. 5⁴⁵), because His community can know Him only as the Son of this Father, because it cannot possibly keep to itself or suppress or not confess the fact that it knows Him thus, because it would *ipso facto* deny the One whom it knows as the Son of this Father if it did not confess Him as such, because, to be His community, it has no option but to reach out beyond its own circle and to confess Him to all men. Its most inward being has an irresistible impulse towards that which is without, its most proper being towards that which is alien. In its very exclusiveness its knowledge demands universal confession. Precisely the name revealed to it, as the name which is above every other name, demands proclamation as such. It exists as it is pledged to the one Jesus Christ and therefore basically and without reservation to the world. It would not exist in the reality established by Him if it were not prepared to exist in this commitment to the world.

Nor would it know itself if it were unwilling to see its reality in its existence in this commitment, or to try to exist as in any sense a non-confessing community.

The Christian community knows (3) that its confession of Jesus Christ as the distinctive action for which it is empowered by the Holy Spirit can only be, in all its human and natural spontaneity, a grateful response to the fact that first and supremely Jesus Christ has confessed it, does confess it, and will continually do so. It is its own free action, yet not an arbitrary but an obedient action. It is a venture of the first order, yet not an independent or unauthorised venture, if among all the many lords in question it confesses Him as the Lord of all lords, if substantially and decisively it chooses to remember and vindicate and proclaim Him alone. As we have seen, it chooses Him as the community chosen by Him which cannot but choose Him. It is the people personally and therefore supremely preferred by Him, and as such it must give to confession of Him preference over all other possible actions. It is personally and supremely preferred by Him, however, in the sense that He wills to be specifically present with it, to dwell within it, and to speak and act by it, i.e., by its ministry, and in the sense that He actually does these things, not in any external and contingent relationship, but in an intimate and necessary connexion in which He is its Lord and it is the body inspired and directed by Him. He Himself, risen from the dead, does not only exist eternally in heaven at the right hand of the Father as Head, but also in His prophetic office, as the living Word of God, in the power of the Holy Spirit, as the Head of His body, and therefore historically on earth within world-occurrence. As the One He was and is and will be, He Himself goes through the twilight and obscurity of this lingering time with the humanity reconciled to God in Him but not yet redeemed. He did not merely live once ; He also lives to-day with us and like us. He does not merely live, speak and act, the Son of God, as the Lord over time ; He also lives, speaks and acts, the Son of Man, in time and therefore as participant in what takes place as our history in time. Now He certainly does this in other forms as well as in the existence and history of His community. He is not bound to it as it is bound to Him. We fail to see His lordship if we do not reckon with the fact that in His self-proclamation He, the living One, may go other ways than those indicated by the human and creaturely limits of His community conditioned by its constant obduracy. Yet this does not alter the fact that His community, and alone so far as we can see it, has the promise, and may and should live by the truth of the promise, that it is the body of Jesus Christ which in the power of the Holy Spirit He as its Lord has personally called into existence and directs and sustains, so that in its existence it is the earthly-historical form and representation of His own.

" Where two or three συνηγμένοι (are gathered, or constituted a synagogue) εἰς τὸ ἐμὸν ὄνομα (in the sphere of the revelation and knowledge and therefore the confession of His name, in the act of salvation which has taken place in His person and work, and in the revelation of salvation present in Him), there am I in the midst of them " (Mt. 18²⁰). The rather more restrained form in which the saying is handed down in Codex D and other manuscripts is worth noting, but it does not seem to imply any real weakening of content : " Two or three cannot be gathered in my name, except I am there in the midst of them." In neither version, of course, is it meant that because they have come together in His name He comes into the midst as a Third or Fourth, but conversely that they are gathered by Him in and with the fact that He is in the midst of them.

He is the primary and proper Subject acting in and with the community. It is constituted by His confession made not only in heaven but also with power on earth. Its confession of Him gratefully follows His confession of it.

Now the One who constitutes the community by confessing it, this primarily and properly acting Subject in its history, is the One who, in that as very God He became and was very man, did not will to withdraw or to hold aloof from, or to be alien to, either the world as His creation or humanity as the world of His fellows, but who rather willed to intervene and give Himself personally for it in its totality, taking to Himself and therefore away from it the whole burden of its folly and corruption and misery and suffering, and in His person justifying every man against every accusation and sanctifying every man to every good work. Nor is He merely the One who willed all these things, but the One who totally and not just in part accomplished them. Moreover, He is the One who continually attests and reveals and makes Himself known as He who has done such things for its reformation and renewal, so that He is not idle or dumb, but actively with it on the way as the authentic Prophet of its new reality. This is the One who has called the community into being and maintains it in being. This is its Head. His Holy Spirit is the power by whose distinctive activity it is enabled to confess Him. What does this signify for it as His body, as His earthly-historical form of existence ? What can be the meaning and *telos* of its own existence as the predicate of this Subject ? In the light of Jesus Christ as the basis of its existence, obviously it cannot be its own meaning and *telos*, nor can it rest content with its own being as such. In the light of its basis in Him, it is sent in the same direction as He is, i.e., into the world, in order that it may exist, not for itself, but for the world as He did. What He gives to the twos and threes, and to the hundreds and thousands, who, as He is in the midst, are assembled in His name into His circle of light to confess Him, and what they receive from Him, can only correspond to what He Himself is and does in the time which hastens to its end but is still left to the world. It can thus consist only in the fact that He gives it to them to take a ministering part in His prophetic work, claiming them for this service and equipping and directing them in its discharge. The intimate and necessary connexion between Him as the Head and the community as His body would obviously snap if it tried to exist otherwise than in this imitative and ministering participation in His mission to the world. As the community has its basis in Him, and knows in Him its Head, with all its being it can try to actualise only this connexion with Him, and in all its work only this participation in His mission, in His prophetic work. It would completely mistake its one basis in Him, and therefore itself, if it tried to substitute for the way on which He precedes a circular course in which its concern were only for its own confirmation and expression. On the way on which He precedes, however well or badly it can only belong to men and the world, and seek to exist for them, in the strength imparted to it if also in its own impotence.

The Christian community can and should understand itself (4) in the full New Testament sense of the term as a likeness. As such it is a subsequent and provisional representation of the divine-human reality distinct from itself. As this both precedes and follows its own being, the community can only indicate, reflect and represent it subsequently and provisionally. It can only portray and denote it imperfectly and inadequately in a way which obscures as well as enlightens, achieving similar but not the same colours and contours. It can only be its duplicate. Yet as it is essentially proper to it to derive from it and to move towards it, in all its imperfection it has a genuine share in that which it denotes and portrays. The Christian community can and should understand itself as a likeness in this specific sense. The reality distinct from itself which it denotes and portrays as this likeness is the kingdom of God which commences and is already particularly revealed in the resurrection of Jesus Christ as the *terminus a quo* of its own specific history, and which will be definitively and universally manifested in the final appearing of Jesus Christ as the *terminus ad quem* of its own history. And the kingdom of God is the establishment of the exclusive, all-penetrating, all-determinative lordship of God and His Word and Spirit in the whole sphere of His creation. Jesus Himself is this kingdom in all its perfection. In Him this divine lordship is inaugurated. For in Him, this human creature, the Creator and Lord dwells and acts and speaks directly and without restriction in the rest of His creation. In Him the calling of all humanity and indeed of all creation to the service of God, and therefore the unity of all the forms and forces and works of the creature, is already a completed event with a perfection which cannot be transcended. The community has its origin in His revelation, and therefore in the calling which has gone out universally in Him, and therefore in the established divine lordship of the kingdom in the seed form of the Easter event. And it moves towards His manifestation, and therefore the manifestation of the kingdom, in the full visibility of the tree (Mt. 13³²) with birds nesting in the branches. It recognises that this is so, that it has its origin in the one and moves towards the other, as it has its basis of existence, in the manner described under our three heads, in the impelling power of the Holy Spirit, in its empowering for the confession of Jesus Christ, in which it recognises that it is to His confession of it that it may gratefully respond with its confession of Him. And encircled by this origin and future, it resembles Him, and the lordship of God set up in Him, and the calling of all humanity and all creatures to the service of God as it has gone forth in Him. Neither it nor anyone else can or should ascribe to it more than a resemblance to this first and final reality, and to its revelation as it has already taken place and has still to take place. It is not identical with it. It has and maintains in face of it its own reality which is neither divine nor divine-human but a specific form of creaturely and human reality. Yet as the body, as the earthly-historical form of existence, of Jesus Christ, it is His likeness, and may and should recognise that this is so. We need not waste words on the obscurity and confusion with which in its existence it reflects Him and the kingdom of God as revealed already in its commencement but still to be revealed in its consummation. It need not doubt, nor can it be contested, that He reflects Himself in it, that it is created and ordained to be His likeness. As it beholds Him " with open face " (2 Cor. 3¹⁸), it is changed, not into an *alter Christus*, but necessarily into an image of the unrepeatably one Christ. It receives from the Lord, who is the Spirit, a glory which, if it is not the same as His own, corresponds and is analogous and similar to it—the glory of His own image. Hence, although it does not belong to it to set up the kingdom of God in the creation of God, as though it were not already set up, and although it cannot belong to it to manifest this kingdom, as though it had any power of manifestation and as though its manifestation were not the work of the One in whom it is set up, yet it can and should indicate the kingdom and its revelation in its existence. The purpose of its existence is the subsequent and provisional representation of the calling of all humanity and all creatures to the service of God as it has gone forth in Jesus Christ. The origin and goal of the ways of God, which took place initially but perfectly in the resurrection of Jesus Christ, and which will take place definitively and no less perfectly in His final appearing, is the calling of every man and indeed of all creation to the service of God. The function of the community is to follow and yet at the same time to precede His universal call.

" Make a joyful noise unto the Lord, all ye lands. Serve the Lord with gladness : come before his presence with singing. Know ye that the Lord he is God " (Ps. 100¹ᶠ·)—this is the Alpha and Omega of the call of Jesus Christ Himself. It is to this that there corresponds the very imperfect but quite unmistakeable calling of the Christian community between the origin and the

goal, in the time between the times. To it first among all creatures the call of
God has gone forth, and gone forth effectively, as its existence shows. It could
and can hear it. In it, it is recognised by at least some among the great masses
of men and nations, invincibly if only from afar and with considerable obscurity,
that the Lord alone is God. In it, some men, even though they are weary and
heavy-laden because blind and deaf and lame, do come into His presence with
real singing, if only in the form of sighs and croaks. In it, even though under
the severe pressure of human corruption and always on the edge of the abyss of
the Christian and therefore the worst possible deception, and yet always restrained
and called back to reality by His call, the attempt is at least made to serve the
Lord, and to serve Him in the only way possible, i.e., with joy and therefore without murmuring or complaint. In it, even though from the depths and with many
a discord, yet continually lifted out of the depths and brought into an obvious
final harmony, creatures are gathered out of every land and speech and natural
and cultural sphere, and for all their difference and antagonisms united with
one another in this joyous praise.

For all its weak and doubtful character, therefore, there takes
place in it a subsequent and provisional fulfilment of the prophecy
of Jesus Christ which takes up the Easter message and anticipates
the " Behold, I make all things new " (Rev. 21[5]) of the last day,
not with the perfection with which Jesus Christ Himself, risen from
the dead, was once its fulfilment, nor with the perfection with which
He will be at His coming again to judgment, but, in virtue of His
presence and action in the Holy Spirit by which it is constituted in
this time between the times, as a reflection and replica of the glory
which is His alone, in participation in it, and therefore with its own
glory as the representation, indication and likeness of His prophecy.

As the community perceives itself to be this likeness, however, it
can and should see and understand—and this brings us to the same
goal by a fourth path—that it exists for the world. As a likeness
of the prophecy of Jesus Christ, it obviously has itself a prophetic
character. And in its prophetic character it cannot possibly be an
end in itself. According to the purpose and power of the one who
fashions and uses it, a likeness points beyond itself to what he intends
to indicate and represent in using it. What the One who fashions
and uses His community as a likeness of His own existence indicates
and represents by it is His own prophecy in its full sweep, namely,
the calling of the world to the service of God which He has inaugurated
and will consummate but which in this time between the inauguration
and the consummation proceeds in the power of His Holy Spirit and
therefore with the same perfection which characterises it in its origin
and its goal. The ongoing of this calling of the world to the service
of God takes place in the likeness of the community founded, maintained and guided by the power of His Holy Spirit, between the
terminus a quo of its history and its *terminus ad quem*, here and now,
in every hour of our time which is the time between the times. This
time is not, therefore, a vacuum between the other two. It is the
time of the *parousia* of Jesus Christ in its second and middle form,

in the power of His Holy Spirit ; and therefore it is especially the time of the community (*C.D.*, IV, 1, § 62, 3). This time is given the community in order that it may be to the world an indication, representation and likeness of its calling in Jesus Christ to the service of God as it proceeds in this time between. In this sense it is given it for its own supreme joy, which is not, however, its joy in itself, but can only be its joy in this ongoing calling of the world, and therefore in the progress of the mission of its Lord and hence of its own mission to the world, namely, joy in the fact that it may be in and to the world a likeness of the kingdom of God which has come but is still to come, and therefore that in this sense it may exist for the world.

In retrospect, our concern in the four trains of thought just concluded has been to show the basis of the presupposition that the Christian community is the society to which it is given to exist for the world. In relation to this by no means self-evident statement of faith, our concern has been with the *intellectus fidei*, i.e., with the theological establishment of the truth of its content. We could do this only by theological reflection. That is to say, since our concern is genuinely with a statement of faith, or with a specific form of the general statement of faith : *credo ecclesiam*, we could establish it only as along four different lines we dealt with the work and Word of God in the context in which it is also the basis of the reality of the Church and of its orientation to the world. Beginning with its basis in the power of the Holy Spirit, we considered the work for which the Church is thereby empowered, namely, the confession of Jesus Christ, then tried to see that this can only be an answer to His confession of it, and finally sought to interpret its existence as the subsequent and provisional likeness of the prophecy of Jesus Christ described under the first three heads. All four lines of thought, however, have finally brought us to a recognition of the reality of the Church in its address to the world, and therefore to a recognition of its existence for the world, and to this extent, therefore, to an illumination of the basis of the presupposition with which we started and in terms of which we have now to continue. This is what had to be shown, *quod erat demonstrandum*, in this second sub-section.

3. THE TASK OF THE COMMUNITY

It is with a task, and to fulfil this task, that the community is sent into the world and exists for it. We shall consider this task in this third sub-section, and its execution, the service of the community, in the fourth and last.

The Christian community is not sent into the world haphazardly or at random, but with a very definite task. It does not exist before its task and later acquire it. Nor does it exist apart from it, so that there can be no question whether or not it might have or execute it.

It exists for the world. Its task constitutes and fashions it from the very outset. If it had not been given it, it would not have come into being. If it were to lose it, it would not continue. It is not, then, a kind of imparted dignity. It exists only as it has it, or rather only as the task has it. Nor is it a kind of burden laid upon it. It is the inalienable foundation which bears it. Every moment of its history it is measured by it. It stands or falls with it in all its expressions, in all its action or abstention. It either understands itself in the light of its task or not at all. It either takes itself seriously with regard to it, or it cannot do so. Even to the world it can either be respectable in relation to it, or not at all—though it may perhaps make a false impression in virtue of qualities and achievements which it shares with other historical constructs and which have nothing whatever to do with its true and distinctive being. The Christian community lives by and with its task.

And in this task it is concerned with something very definite. This forms its content. It is of this that we must speak first. As a task, however, it is also addressed to specific people. We cannot consider the content at issue without at once having our attention turned to those addressed. Conversely, it is only from the content that we can learn who and what and how they are those that are addressed by it, i.e., only as they are revealed and understood in the light of this content. Finally, we must pose and answer the question of the purity of the task given to the community and discharged by it, namely, the purity of its content and of its relation to those addressed in it.

We begin (1) by defining and describing its content. The community is given its task by Jesus Christ, and it is He who continually entrusts it to it, impresses it upon it and sees to it that it does not slip from it and that the community, deprived of it, does not sink into the abyss—He who, as He declares Himself to it, enlightens it in the power of His Holy Spirit, and whom, as it is enlightened by Him, it may know. As He gave and gives Himself to be known by many different men, they ceased and cease to be an unco-ordinated mass of so many different individuals with different gifts and interests and views and convictions and aspirations. He calls them together. He calls them to the community. He makes of them His people, His body, and makes them its members. As the origin and content of their common knowledge which binds them to the community, however, He is also the origin and content of their commonly given task. As He thus constitutes and fashions them as His community, He awakens them—this is the origin of their task—as a community to *confess* Him. And He gives Himself to be known by the community—this is the content of their task—in order that they may and should confess *Him*. He who gives the community its task, who continually entrusts it to it and impresses it upon it, who in so doing causes it to become and be the community, who preserves and renews it as such, He, Jesus Christ, is *in nuce* but in totality and fulness the content of its task. His person, His work, His revealed name, the prophetic Word by which He proclaims Himself within it, is the matter at issue in its task. To use the simplest and biblical formulation : " Ye shall be witnesses unto me " (Ac. 1⁸). It will be seen already that we are concerned here with something which is quite definite and clear-cut, which is protected on all sides against confusion with anything else, being defined and delimited by the concreteness and uniqueness of His person, work and name. The matter includes a great deal, indeed, a whole cosmos of distinctive reality and truth : the true and living God and true and living man ; their encounter, co-existence and history with its commencement, centre and goal ; the grace of God triumphant in judgment, His life triumphant in death and His light in darkness. But all these things are enclosed first and properly in Jesus Christ. Anything not revealed in His self-declaration and knowledge has nothing whatever to do with what is at issue in its task. We shall have to remember this. For here we have the supreme and decisive criterion in the question of the purity of its task, i.e., of the content of its task.

Leaving aside, however, any critical application, we must first maintain that our concern is with a great and comprehensive affirmation which the community is set in the world to attest, namely, with the Christian position which the community is charged to manifest and indicate. Jesus Christ is this great affirmation or Christian position. Declaring Himself, He pronounces a single and unambiguous Yes. He is this Yes, and therefore not merely its proponent, sign, symbol or cypher. When we call this Yes the content of the task of His community, we do not point beyond Him or speak of something distinct from Him, but with John the Baptist we point to Him. The concrete particularity of this Yes is identical with the concrete particularity of His name which cannot be exchanged for any other, of His person and work. Abstracted from Him, the Yes could not have the character or power of truth. It is as He declares Himself that Jesus Christ pronounces it. And it is as He Himself is the content of the task of His community that it is charged to accept and attest it. It names and proclaims and praises Him in vain if in so doing it does not accept it and pass it on as its witness. The praise of Jesus Christ can only be genuine when filled out by this Yes. Abstracted from it, it can only be powerless even though sung with the tongues of angels.

It is true that in the task or concern of the community we are dealing with a Yes which includes a No. But since it is identical with Jesus Christ, it is predominantly, decisively, originally and definitively a Yes and not a No. It is not a Yes which is limited, constricted, conditioned and therefore weakened or called in question by a No.

It cannot, then, be the task or office of the community to say No, or Yes and No. It fails to discharge its task if, forgetting that it has to do with Jesus Christ, it either says No instead of Yes, or sets a No alongside the Yes with the same dignity and force. Because the Yes which it has to pronounce cannot otherwise be brought out, it can seldom or never abstain from also pronouncing a delimiting No, from also asserting the severity of the Law and the stringency of the call to repentance, from also naming sin, and revealing its consequences, in the form of man's pride and sloth and falsehood, from also warning and criticising and resisting and attacking, from also proclaiming the force of the wrath of God. But it can do all this only in the context and with the meaning which it can have when proclaiming Jesus Christ. Since it has to proclaim Jesus Christ, not even temporarily nor in appearance can it allow this to become its true theme, or a second theme alongside the first. If what it has to represent has to be a No, this cannot be its first or last, let alone its one true word. It can only be an intervening or parenthetical word transcended by the absolutely primary Yes. Whatever else may come between, the morning and the mid-day and the evening of the work of the community must always be unconditionally bright. As and because it has to proclaim Jesus Christ, its task consists first and above all things in attesting the Yes of the true and effective, and therefore the hard and severe, yet the pure goodness of Him who alone is good, i.e., of God. In the measure that it does this, it is true to its task and serves it. In the measure that it does not, it turns from it and works against it. If it does not do it at all, its activity has nothing whatever to do with the matter in hand, it has abandoned its task, and it has ceased to be the Christian community and must be called to life again. For to proclaim Jesus Christ is to attest the goodness of God, no more, no less, no other.

Jesus Christ signifies God, not without man or—which would be even worse—against him, but God with man, and indeed for him, as his Friend and Helper and Saviour and Guarantor. Jesus Christ signifies God Himself become man's Neighbour and Brother, akin and alongside in order in his stead to redeem his ruined cause. Jesus Christ is in person the faithfulness of God which draws near to the unfaithfulness of man and overpowers it as God Himself not only confirms and maintains His covenant with His creature but once and for all leads it to its goal and secures it against every threat. He is the reconciliation of the world to God which does not merely look and go beyond the sin of man but sets it aside. He is the effective justification and sanctification of sinful man, and indeed his honourable vocation to the service of God. He is the kingdom of God which with its comfort and healing has approached and invaded torn humanity suffering from a thousand wcunds, and put an end to its misery. He is in the deepest sense the reformation, i.e., not merely the restoration but the disclosure or manifestation of the purpose and glory of all creation. He is the gift of what it has not merited, its liberation by the free love, the free grace and the free mercy of God in the purity of His will and with the superiority of His power. In a word, He is the goodness of God : the goodness which does not accord with our human thoughts but with His divine thoughts ; the goodness in actualisation of which He does not follow our human ways but His divine ways ; the goodness which may well alienate or startle or terrify us by reason of its inconceivable origin and no less inconceivable manner ; the goodness which judges as it restores, which leads to life through death, and the wonderful commencement of which always entails an irresistible conclusion. Yet in its divine manner it is pure goodness : pure from any indifference of the exalted to the unworthy ; pure from any despising of the unholy by the holy ; pure from any *diastasis* where *diastasis* seems to be the only possibility ; not referred to nor waiting for the goodness of those to whom it is shown but constituting at once its own source and stream. Hence it is a goodness which is not only theory or programme or projection, which has not found only a provisional manifestation, but which is actualised in the act of God, which is already accessible, revealed and perceptible in the Word of God, and which is impregnably grounded in the eternal counsel of God, in His own triune essence. Jesus Christ Himself as Emmanuel, " God with us," is this divine goodness. Hence its knowledge, and life in its knowledge, is not difficult for the creature but easy. And the community is charged to represent and attest it by simply proclaiming Jesus Christ.

But if in Jesus Christ our concern is absolutely with the goodness of God, this implies that man is the content of the task committed to the community. According to the task of the community, man as fellow-man is the one indisputably clear and definite value in creation by which all else that might be called or be valuable is shown to be relatively or indeed absolutely valueless : man in all the forms and at all the stages of his general and individual development ; man triumphant and defeated, honourable and covered with shame, good and evil, noble and hateful ; man himself and not his achievements and products which have their passing day, nor their great or little glory nor inner or outer significance which is also passing ; man himself as in strength or weakness, with good or less good intentions, with joy or sorrow, he achieves this or that in his own time and place as one of the known or unknown soldiers in the great army of humanity ; man who does not perish, who does not live in vain, who is not lost or forgotten ; man himself and not the great or little heap of money or property or fortune which he may gather and enjoy for a time, nor the spiritual, moral, political, economic and artistic principles with the help of which he may try to achieve some understanding, clarity, certainty and guiding lines concerning himself, his cosmos, his history, the chaos which threatens his existence and the best means to guard against it. To be sure, man needs these things. And it is even understandable that when he thinks he has found them he should present them to his fellows and by either gentle means or sometimes not so gentle try to get them accepted. But the validity of all these things is limited. Even in their best and most enlightening and worthy forms it is not they which are originally and conclusively interesting, but man himself as in wisdom or folly, and for the good or ill of his fellows, he produces and propagates them. His validity has no limits. According to the task of the community, man himself is always of value and interest. For God sets value on him, and God in all His power is interested on his behalf. It is not that there is an immanent value or significance in his general manner or specific existence. It is not that God necessarily finds something about him. No individual as such is irreplaceable, nor is the race itself, any more than is the obviously related world of plants and animals (and perhaps not as much). Man is irreplaceable, however, because he is the object of the goodness of God, because he is ennobled by it, because God is his Friend and Guarantor and Brother, because God is for him, because God is his God in Jesus Christ. For the sake of God, therefore, man cannot be omitted either for a single instant or in a single respect from the content of the message entrusted to the community. He who acts together with man and in conjunction with him, as God has done in Jesus Christ, can be the content of its task only in company with him. The community abandons and loses its task and ceases to be the Christian community if all the emphasis does not fall on man, on man only in relation to God, yet also on God only in relation to man. It is required unconditionally and in all circumstances to exist for man because it exists for God. Clean through every possible and justifiable interest in other causes, it is required to take up the cause of man because this is the cause of God committed to it.

To sum up, we may say that there is committed to it the Gospel, i.e., the good, glad tidings of Jesus Christ, of the real act and true revelation of the goodness in which God has willed to make and has in fact made Himself the God of man and man His man. This great Yes is its cause. It has no other task beside this. This task is so profoundly stimulating, so radically impelling, so important, urgent and comprehensive, that it claims it utterly, and it cannot undertake any other. It demands its undivided attention and devotion because with every new gathering of the community and in every new situation in its history it must be taken up with full readiness and concentration, and enquiry must be made into its meaning, its height and depth and breadth, and the proper way to discharge it. To be sure, the men united in the community all have their own varied questions and concerns and cares and aspirations. They would not be men if it were otherwise, and it would be dangerous if they tried artificially to conceal or even to deny this fact, and therefore their divinely given creaturely nature. But united in the community and as its members, they can only pursue and serve one cause, i.e., the Gospel, and the fact that they do this in common must work itself out in the order of their own personal action. Again, the differences in their vocation to the community, and in the temporal and spatial conditions of their Christian existence, necessarily imply that there are differences in their conceptions of the Gospel and their activities in its service, so that its attestation cannot possibly become the uniform and monotonous function of a collective. Nevertheless there are no differences within the community and in the execution of its task which can possibly throw doubt on the unity and totality of its content, i.e., of that which is at issue in it, the Gospel. In every possible variation of execution, always, everywhere, in all circumstances and in every individual form its concern will be with the total content and therefore unconditionally with Jesus Christ, with the great Yes, with the goodness of God, and with man ennobled by God's goodness. In all the freedom which is not left but given to the community and its members to go their own way *hic et nunc* in their own specific manner, they must never deviate nor be jostled away even a hair's breadth from the line very definitely marked out for them in the service of the Gospel. On the contrary, they must always reassemble and be brought into harmony on this line. There is thus no freedom in the community either to call upon or to proclaim other lords than Jesus Christ. There is no freedom to obscure the great Yes by an arbitrary Yes-But. There is no freedom either to begin or end otherwise than with the goodness of God. There is no freedom to substitute for interest in man any other interest, even an abstract interest in God, as though a true and concrete interest in God did not point in the very opposite direction. The freedom which is not just left but given to the community is not license to deviate from the Gospel. It is freedom for the Gospel in its unity and totality. In this exclusiveness and totality conditioned by its content, the task of the community is rich and animated enough to keep its activity from any narrowness or one-sidedness. It is the activity of the community which is disobedient rather than obedient to the Gospel that is always narrow and one-sided.

We now turn (2) to the question of those addressed in its task. To whom does it apply? Who is in the mind of the One from whom it receives and has it? To whom must it turn in its discharge? The answer is not so simple as might at first sight appear. Naturally we may answer: Man as the epitome and representative of the world to which the community is sent, as the creature affirmed by God, as the true object of His goodness. Yet it is not so obvious, but needs clarification, who and what man is, or how he is, in this character and position as the one to whom the task of the community is materially directed.

The question as to those addressed in its task is necessary because, unless we catch a clear glimpse of the man intended, we cannot understand the task itself in its own peculiar nature, and what we have said concerning its content might easily acquire the character of an abstractly objective doctrine, of a *gnosis* boldly circling around the three points of Jesus Christ, God and man. Now there can be no doubt that the content of the task laid upon the community is a matter of revelation and knowledge and therefore of doctrine and *gnosis*. Yet it was not for nothing, but rather with a view to the misunderstanding which might arise at this point, that we described its content comprehensively as Gospel. Its content is message, *kerygma*, proclamation. Indeed, it is message of a special kind, namely, the message which brings and is calculated to awaken joy. This means, however, that if we are to understand its content at all we can do so only as an address which may well contain and declare profound and supreme doctrine and disclose profound and supreme *gnosis*, but which is still an address and as such cheerful by nature. Directly or indirectly, explicitly or implicitly, it is only in the sense and with the tone and emphasis and weight, yet also with the gaiety of such an address that it can be proclaimed. Merely thinking and speaking to oneself, and doing so without joy, one cannot possibly grasp or pass on the content of the task of the community. If we are to confess and declare it, we must be clear that we have to do this in the form of an address, and indeed of an address of radiant content and cheerful manner. If we fail to see this, then even in terms of knowledge, as doctrine and *gnosis*, it escapes us.

This is the basis of the unavoidable affinity between all genuine theology and preaching, especially Christmas and Easter preaching. Theology cannot and should not be ashamed of this affinity. It should not be led astray by those who ridicule it because of this affinity. Nor is this merely because it derives from it its seriousness, and indeed its *pulchritudo*, once rightly extolled by Anselm of Canterbury. For the theme of what we may call its scientific statement, discussion and reflection is the task of the community and the specific content of this task. Theology loses its scientific character if it loses sight of this, if it conceals or even denies it, if it does not take part in its execution, if in its biblical and historical elements it tries listlessly to assume the character of abstractly objective history, and in its systematic elements the character of abstractly objective metaphysics, with the result that when it comes to the practical elements, and therefore back to a consideration of the problem of address, it can only listlessly tack these on as an organically unrelated and foreign body. Theology is certainly not preaching. Even as practical theology it cannot preach ; it can only lead to preaching. And the scientific nature of its activity is guaranteed by the difficulty of its tasks. But in all its elements, historical, systematic or practical, its concern is to understand the task given to the community, so that it is always dealing with the message, the joyful message, entrusted to it. But it cannot be concerned with this without, in its appropriate critical function, participating in the orientation corresponding to its content. Necessarily, therefore, its thinking and speaking about this matter becomes directly or indirectly a speaking from out of it to someone else, thus acquiring and assuming the character of an address, and indeed a joyful address.

Where there is such address, however, there inevitably has to be considered in his own specific character and position the one who is addressed, the one to whom the community is sent, man in his specific form as addressee in the task given to the community. To understand him as such is indispensable in the present context.

We are dealing with man from the standpoint of this task, or rather from the standpoint of the One who constitutes the community by entrusting this task to it, from the standpoint of the Gospel.

At this point we must not allow any general or special anthropology to intervene with its supposedly normative suggestions. We cannot be helped to our goal by any definition of man projected in the sphere occupied by a biological, sociological, psychological or ethical conception. Common to all such anthropologies is the fact that their pictures of man are all products of a human self-understanding. The man intended and addressed in the Gospel, however, is the man who is seen and understood and known, through all the veils of such human pictures, by God Himself, acting and revealed in Jesus Christ. He is the being which man cannot and will not know himself to be by any analysis, investigation or reflection of his own, but only as he is told about himself by the Word of God in the course of God's history with him and his with God. At this point, therefore, no help is to be found even in the most penetrating analyses of what in any given age, e.g., our own, is called " modern " man. It may well be that the concrete pictures in which the Narcissus of any age, e.g., our own, thinks he can know and portray his own reality do sometimes have subsequent relevance in the light they shed on who and what he is before God. But who and what he is before God, as the one addressed in His Gospel, is something which Narcissus as such cannot discover in any age for all the loving exactitude of his self-analysis, self-appraisal and self-description, and something which he cannot accept even in his most ruthless sincerity. To know himself as the one who is intended, addressed and known by God in the Gospel, he must first be radically disturbed and interrupted in the work of self-analysis by receiving the Gospel of God. Then perhaps *a posteriori* he can see whether or how far in his self-analysis he was on the right track, or on one which was quite wrong.

Man from the standpoint of the Gospel is man in his particularity and uniqueness as this man, i.e., man himself, determined no doubt both inwardly and outwardly, both naturally and historically, both socially and individually, yet man himself.

Young or old, man or woman, he has his own share in the psycho-somatic structure of human essence, in its nature and possible corruptions. Child of his own age and place and climate, he is determined by the development and relationships of this particular narrower or wider segment of human society. He is more or less intimately and intensively stamped by the life and action and suffering of others who are his more close or distant fellows. He is more or less narrowly bound to their customs and enterprises, more or less marked by their common qualities and more or less characterised by their common failings. He is one of his family, clan and people. Originally at least he is at home in a specific language which speaks and thinks for him. He exists in a distinctive form at a distinctive stage in a distinctive cultural grouping, conditioned by its science, art and technics. He exists in the sphere, in the specific freedom and bondage, of a political and economic order. His life is conditioned by the ameliorations and advantages which these things carry with them, but also by the limitations and restrictions which they impose. Man as God sees and understands and knows him, as He intends and addresses him in His Word, is always and everywhere man in this cosmically given situation. But in this situation he is himself.

Man never dissolves into, nor is he exhausted by, his determination by his situation. He does not exist as the sum but as the subject, as the mystery of the centre of the co-ordinated system of individual predicates and those deriving from his situation. Hence the man intended by God and addressed in His Gospel may be quite unavoidably a child or an adult, a man or a woman, healthy or sick, eastern or western, European or African, ancient, mediaeval or modern, uncivilised, half-civilised, or highly civilised, riveted to this or that economic and political context ; but always and everywhere, however determined, he is man himself who as such is immediate to God, and therefore to his neighbour. It is this man with his immediate being whom God seeks and finds, not in an empty, but in a specific sphere. It is to him that the task given to the community is directed. Always and everywhere, no matter in what sphere, it is he whom the community must seek and find as such. There is no man to whom it has not to turn in the discharge of its task, just as there is no man who in his particular situation, determined on every hand, is not immediate to God and his neighbour.

But now we must proceed with caution. Who and what is man in his immediate being to God and his neighbour ? Where is the community to seek him when guided by its task ? In what character is it to address him as it keeps before it the content of its charge ? There suggests itself an apparently illuminating consideration which would serve but poorly the attestation of the Gospel, since the character therein ascribed to him is not the same as that in which God sees and understands and knows him, and which is proper to him from the standpoint of the Gospel. Since the community undoubtedly has the task of bringing to man the knowledge of Jesus Christ and the real and true goodness of God directed to him in Him, it is tempting to speak to him first and decisively about his ignorance of this Gospel, about the vacuum which is to be filled by imparting it. His immediate being to God and his neighbour is then primarily and decisively to be understood as a form of human unbelief, superstition or error, or objectively of his human alienation from and hostility to God, of his actual standing outside, or heathenism. What are we to say to this ? There can be no doubt, of course, that what man is before God and from the standpoint of the Gospel includes also, with his situation and the resultant determination, the fact that he has not received what the Gospel makes it possible for him to receive, that he is ignorant in relation to its message, with all that this implies both theoretically and practically. To this degree there can be no question that everyone addressed in the task entrusted to the community—including the Christian to whom it is still directed—is also an unbeliever, a godless heathen who is still outside and has to be brought in. Undoubtedly it is always and everywhere something quite new which is brought to his hearing and knowledge in the Gospel of Jesus Christ, of the unconditional Yes of the eternal goodness of God. Will even the Christian receive it as Gospel, if every time he does not receive it as something new, and therefore as one who has not yet received it ? It is as such that God sees, understands and knows man. But at the very beginning of His encounter with him does He see, understand and know him primarily, decisively, properly and polemically as this one outside ? Is it really the first and final thing in man's being before Him that he does not know about Jesus Christ, about God and therefore about the goodness of God ? When God addresses him as He does in the Gospel, does He really commence with the fact that man thus confronts him in ignorance as a remote and alien and hostile being ? The new thing of the Gospel, in relation to which the one to whom it is addressed is always, and always shows himself to be, a stranger and therefore an unbeliever, a godless heathen, points us quite decidedly, in respect of the new thing at issue, in a very different direction. If Jesus Christ, or the great Yes of the goodness of God, is the new thing disclosed and declared and made known, this carries with it the impartation that his ignorance and alienation and indifference and rejection, his hostility and resistance, constitute an attitude which is out of keeping, which in its confusion has indeed been transcended, antiquated and set aside, so that it can only be described as thoroughly unstable ground on which he cannot stand or move, as a position in which God certainly finds him but in which He does not take any first or final interest, refusing to accept or recognise it as the starting-point of His own dealings with him. God does indeed see the heathen with whom He has to do in him. But in virtue of what He says, He overlooks this remoteness, alienation and hostility, not taking his heathenism seriously, refusing to consider him in this capacity. Is it not truly the case that in and with what He says to him in the Gospel, in spite of all his ignorance and the contradiction and opposition grounded upon it, He considers him already in relation to what he is in Jesus Christ, on the basis of His own Yes pronounced and applicable to him, as the object of His goodness ? Is it not truly the case that in addressing Him He already in anticipation claims and treats this one who is obviously without as one who is within ? God does not believe in the unbelief and therefore He does not believe in the manifest theoretical and practical ungodliness, the deep heathenism, of man. Hence He does not define him polemically. He does not accept the misunderstanding in which man thinks he can exist without and even against Him. He sees, understands, knows and claims him as the one with whom and for whom He Himself was and is and will be. Above all and decisively, in what He says to him, He links him with the work of His own will for man already accomplished in Jesus Christ. Man's immediate being before Him is what he is on the basis of this divine will and work. God presupposes this when He encounters him and wills to be heard and known and believed by him. If we keep to what is said to man in the Gospel—and to what else can or should we keep ? —we cannot understand in any other way the one who is addressed in the task given to the community. If the community discharges its task in accordance with its content, it cannot possibly see and understand him otherwise. But it surely does not wish to live in opposition to the direction given by the content of its commission. To the extent that it is obedient to this direction, it surely does not believe of man what God obviously does not believe. It surely cannot accept his obviously poor self-understanding. It surely cannot take him seriously in his unbelief and ungodliness, in his own clever or foolish opinions. It surely cannot define him polemically. In its encounter with him it surely cannot fail to regard and treat him as the one with whom and for whom God was and is and will be in spite of his evil attitude and acts. How else can it represent to him the new thing of the Gospel which is always so wonderfully new even to its own members ? How else can it be faithful to its task ? How else can it hope to discharge it effectively ? As it is faithful to its task, it will certainly see clearly and realistically that both *extra et intra muros* it is dealing with the man who does not know the content of its message, who to this extent is without, who does not have its knowledge, and who is thus supremely needy. But it will also see clearly and realistically that in his ignorance he stands in a position which has been transcended, antiquated and done away by the will and work of God, so that it is completely untenable. It will see clearly and realistically that in virtue of what it has to attest to him he truly is already what he will be. Only as it grasps the superiority of its own knowledge concerning him can it really meet him as the community of Jesus Christ. Otherwise, entertaining a false respect for his impossible position, it cannot possibly become or be to him a witness of the Gospel.

We take a further step by adopting the formulation just used, namely, that the man addressed in the task given to the community is the man who lacks the knowledge of the Gospel and is thus supremely needy. He obviously is this, too, in the view of the Gospel itself which constitutes the normative content for the community's understanding of man. According to the Gospel, he obviously is it first for God Himself. In his determination by the situation prescribed for him, and decisively because he is always a stranger to the Gospel and finds its content strange, he needs to be brought out of this condition. For in relation to that which from God's standpoint is already his new reality, this condition is not normal, but profoundly abnormal. In it he is entangled in a fatal self-misunderstanding and self-contradiction. It makes no difference whether he knows and wills it or because of external circumstances does not do so. In this entanglement he is not campaigning against an alien law which he might have some excuse, or even some more or less solid justification, for breaking ; he is fighting against his own immediate being before God which also includes his immediate being with his neighbour. He thus wars against himself. He makes himself a sinner and therefore impossible. The man who persists in his alienation from the Gospel harms himself. He needs to be brought out of his abnormal, contradictory and impossible being in sin. For this state, for the rise and continuation of which he is responsible, is as such his plight. It cannot be otherwise. Whether or not he knows and experiences it, and whether or not he acts accordingly, he is most profoundly confused and assaulted and tortured and helpless and troubled. His ignorance, which he obviously experiences in the form of a supposed knowledge of a very primitive or possibly a more refined type, necessarily leads to the most varied and apparently contradictory attitudes and tendencies. In these he may assume very arrogant postures. Both individually and in concert, however, they are symptoms of his lack and need and misery, and expressions of his pain and complaint. They may sound bright and cheerful, but they are urgent calls for help, voicing his total lack of clarity concerning himself, his fellows and his world, his impotence in face of the powers which threaten him in this world, his helplessness in face of his great and little problems, his concealed but overpowering sadness, his need, and his anxious fear of further, and even greater need.

This is supremely true of his conscious or unconscious worship of gods or idols in so many crude or sublime forms. *Primus timor fecit deos.* When man does not accept the Gospel, he is necessarily left with his need, and his anxious fear of further and even greater need. In this state of anxiety, he may become religious. It would be an independent task to consider this in the light of the history and phenomenology of religion (including the Christian), but also of concealed religions. It must be added, however, that in this state man may also become an atheist, a sceptic, a religious, philosophical or political indifferentist. The various ancient and modern revolts against the gods, which usually involve only a change in the forms of gods already concocted and worshipped, are themselves products of the only too well founded anxiety of the man who does not yet know or no longer knows the Gospel. To understand this too, e.g., with the help of Fritz Mauthner's great history of western atheism, would again be an independent task. There can be no doubt, however, that the spiritual and indeed the physical aspect presented by man as he meets us in the history and phenomena both of warm and imaginative superstition and of cold and unimaginative unbelief in every age and place, is the very opposite of calm and peaceful and cheerful. Whether we turn to the prophets and faithful of the different religions, or to those of the different forms of irreligion, we find that all of them seem to be restless, worried and tense, " weary and heavy laden," yet also downright bad. They all seem to be suffering creatures, and yet also rebellious against their suffering. It may be an open question whether their trouble is superstition or unbelief or perhaps both, but we can tell them—or rather, ourselves still superstitious and unbelieving, we had better tell ourselves—that the ignorance of the Gospel which distinguishes man, even the Christian, as the one addressed by it, and therefore his superstition and unbelief, can bring him neither joy nor peace, that in this ignorance he is in need and fearful of even greater need, which he may seek to evade in different ways yet can never succeed in doing so.

As this man who lacks the Gospel he thus stands in supreme need of the knowledge of it. And in relation to this supreme neediness God takes up his cause, speaks with him and discloses Himself to him, declaring to him the news of Jesus Christ, of His affirmation accomplished once for all in Jesus Christ and cancelling every negation, of His own active goodness which creates a new thing, liberating him as the prisoner, healing him as the sick and giving him life as the dead. For this reason, though God sees his ignorance, He overlooks it (Ac. 17[30]) and its works, not imputing them to him, nor nailing him to them and dealing with him accordingly, but taking pity on him in his need and anxiety and his feeble attempts to remove them, and above all in his ignorance as the root of his misery and dejection. For this reason He speaks to him as the one he is on the basis of His will and work, not recognising nor respecting his self-misunderstanding, not regarding his consequent misery, but taking from him the whole burden of his sin and its consequences by showing him that it has long since been taken from him and borne and done away, freeing him from his prison by revealing to him that the door to freedom has long since been opened. God shows him his new reality as He Himself has established it. The man to whom God thus shows mercy, to whose help He comes in his well-deserved need and anxiety, is the one addressed in the task given to the community. What option, then, does the community have but to see and address the man with whom it has to do in the discharge of its task as the creature who is indeed strangely and joylessly entangled in this great need and anxiety, and yet decisively as the creature to whom, in spite of his ignorance, superstition and unbelief and all the other symptoms of his misery, or rather because these are seen and understood as symptoms, God in Jesus Christ is not ill-disposed but kind and good ? How can man be interesting to it except as the creature who hurts God, but to whom God for this very reason turns His mercy, causing him to hear His pardoning Word, awakening him to knowledge and thus leading him to freedom ? The content of its task relentlessly shows this man to be the one addressed by it in its execution. It is again necessarily unfaithful to the Gospel which it must attest

3. *The Task of the Community*

if it does not understand and practise its witness as service in the work of the divine mercy, but arrogantly tries to see and understand man otherwise than as the miserable man who participates in the divine mercy. We may now venture to sum up. The task given to the community is aimed at the human creature which suffers by reason of its ignorance and groans under the burden of its exclusion. But in spite of its contradiction and resistance, and taking pity on its need and anxiety, God has loved and loves and will continue to love this sufferer as His creature, not only from and to all eternity, but in time as well, in man's own time, by becoming like him, his Brother, in Jesus Christ. This, then, is how it stands with the one addressed, with the man to whom the community has to turn and reckon in the execution of its task, according to the content of this task. In the structure of man, therefore, we have to distinguish two elements of existence, a subordinate, static and present, and a superior, dynamic and future. In other words, we have to distinguish between what the Gospel sees man to be in himself in virtue of his ignorance, and what it also sees him to be in virtue of the work of God and the Word of God addressed to his ignorance. In and of himself, he is that self-contradictory and suffering creature. This is his obvious and unforgettable state which he has good reason not to forget. This is his present position in which the community with its task will always find him both *extra muros* and also *intra muros*. Yet, from the standpoint of the Gospel, this is not the superior but the subordinate element in his existence. The superior element, to which the community must have no less regard and which it must no less forget, is the other and dynamic element, which does not proceed from man himself, which is not simply present in him, but which is proper to him as his decisive visitation by God. It consists in the fact that this ignorant and suffering and unloving and loveless man in all the historical forms, in all the twists and turns, in which he tries to be rid of his need and anxiety, is the man whom God loves as His creature, whom He has elected in His Son and therefore in the bosom of His own divine being in the decree of His grace, and whom He has called once and for all in His incarnate Word to Himself, to fellowship with His life, to eternal life. This never-resting love of the living God is the dynamic element in the human existence which in and of itself is so corrupt and harassed. Taking man to Himself, God reveals to him beyond his present state a very different future, and impels and conducts him to his future. " Arise, and take up thy bed, and walk " (Mk. 2⁹), is the law, superior to sickness and even death, and bracketing, transcending and outbidding ignorance and all its consequences, under which man is placed by the fact that God loves him and that in His love He takes him to Himself and will not let him go again. The revelation and declaration of this superior law of human existence is the Word of God, the Gospel. To attest this superior law of man's existence by portraying Jesus Christ to him (Gal. 3¹) is the task of the community. In the discharge of this task it deals on the lower level with the man who is sunk in ignorance, need and anxiety, who is engaged in all the possible convulsions of his mortal sickness, who is going down hopelessly like Don Juan to a well-deserved hell ; and on the upper level with the man who in all his misery and even in his descent to hell is loved by God and impelled by His love in the opposite direction. It must see to it that it knows and addresses him as the one he is in and of himself. But it must see to it even more that it knows and addresses him as the one he is already in process of becoming in virtue of the work and Word of God. In each and every man to whom it is directed it is concerned, not with an actual, but certainly with a virtual or potential Christian, with a *christianus designatus*, with a *christianus in spe*. It is concerned with a creature ordained to know and realise his membership of the body of Christ. It has to encounter him as such. To him as such it has to attest Jesus Christ as his Lord too, the great Yes of God spoken to him too, the goodness of God directed to the whole world and therefore to him too. It only deceives itself concerning what even men in its own ranks need as the new thing to be attested to them, and above all it misconceives and denies the content of its own commission, if it tries to see and understand the one addressed by it in any other way.

Taking a further step, we can now add that the future which even in all the misery of his past and present, of his ignorance, awaits the one addressed in the task given to the community is a future of joy, of the great joy of Christmas, of the Easter message of the kingdom of God already come, and also of the Advent message of the kingdom which is yet to come, i.e., which is yet to be definitively and comprehensively revealed, and in which many from both east and west will come and sit down with Abraham, Isaac and Jacob (Mt. 8¹¹). His future is the refreshment promised to the weary and heavy-laden whom Jesus calls to Himself (Mt. 11²⁸). It is the time of the restitution of all things (Ac. 3²¹). According to the content of the Word of God, what is allotted to and appointed for the man whom God addresses in it is not only the removing of his ignorance, the acknowledging of His Word, his awakening to faith and obedience, his conversion from a potential Christian to an actual, but the meeting of the need in which he engulfs himself with his self-contradiction, with his denial of his new reality already created in Jesus Christ, and the dispelling of the anxiety which as the fear of even greater need both agitates and oppresses him in this need and causes movements of anxiety which in fact produce this greater need. Man's persistence in ignorance and therefore his continuance in misery is indeed the danger under threat of which he stands of himself and to which he would be a hopeless prey if he were only what he is of himself. In virtue of the work and Word of God, however, he has not only not fallen victim to this persistence and continuance, to this fatal progress of his ignorance ; he has actually been rescued from it. And the knowledge of his accomplished liberation from this state, and his consequent action, constitute the future which awaits him even in the misery of his past and present, or which, to be more exact, is already breaking into his present. It is the factual realisation of his being as already established and secured *de iure* in Jesus Christ. God wills to be and will be the sun which will enlighten him as it already begins to shine for him, and in its light he himself will become and be bright. He will have his sickness and suffering behind him and be rid of them. He will stand erect after being bowed down in so many ways. He will have no more cause to fear or flee.

" There shall no evil befall thee, neither shall any plague come nigh thy dwelling. For he shall give his angels charge over thee, to keep thee in all thy ways. They shall bear thee up in their hands, lest thou dash thy foot against a stone. Thou shalt treat upon the lion and adder : the young lion and the dragon shalt thou trample under feet " (Ps. 91[10f.]). " I shall not die, but live, and declare the works of the Lord " (Ps. 118[17]).

Man will be true man. He will no more distort but genuinely realise his humanity before God and his neighbour. He will rejoice in it. He will be able to affirm his existence as God does. This existence itself will be cheerful service of God, magnifying as such God's goodness to him. It will lead to existence in the community and in and with its prophetic ministry. This is the future which awaits man according to the Gospel. And the decisive criterion in the question whether or not the community does justice to its task is as follows. It does justice to it if it sees, addresses and treats the one addressed in it with hope of his knowledge in spite of his ignorance, as one who will be within even though he is now without, as a creature who even in his troubled present is to be relieved and liberated and cheered, as one who is ordained and moves to the cheerful service of God and therefore to a prophetic existence, as one who is open to this future. On the other hand, it does not do justice to its task if it does not regard man from the very outset as one who hastens towards this future of great joy, if it allows itself to be impressed and depressed by the aspect of his past and present, if it regards his ignorance and misery as his fate, as a complex of completed facts, if it accepts the fact that he is without, i.e., if it gives up one whom God obviously does not give up but with whom He is on the way to the future of his knowledge, liberation and joy. For in accordance with the content of its task the community, too, can only be on this way with him and for him as the one addressed by it, with the same expectant and anticipatory joy with which the men united in it hope that they themselves are on it. For if they did not have this joy even for those who are without, there would be serious cause to ask whether they themselves are actually on this way, whether they have this anticipatory joy as Christians, and therefore whether they are real Christians. The Christian community is either the place of this great anticipatory joy in relation to all men and all creation, or it is not the Christian community.

We come (3) to the supremely critical question of this sub-section, namely, the question of the purity of the task entrusted to the community. As it is given to it by its Lord and received at His hands, its content and its orientation to the one addressed are self-evidently pure and genuine and authentic. In relation to its source our question is thus meaningless. But from the pure hands of its Lord its task comes into the hands of the men united in the community whose creaturely limitation and sinful fallibility make it very doubtful what will become of it. His light is broken up in this questionable prism. And this gives rise to our third question. His light might well be distorted in this prism. It might well be falsified in the hands of the community. And since the latter's task is neither incidental nor accidental, since it is constituted by it, since it stands or falls with it, it might well be that, if this task suffers deterioration, distortion or depreciation through the way in which it adopts and executes it, its own total existence in the service of the Word of God will be called in question, its own character as the community of Jesus Christ rendered doubtful and its own mission and existence for the world placed in jeopardy. Nor is this a mere possibility. In all ages and places, in all forms of the Church both past and present, the mission of the community, its character as the Christian community and its *ministerium Verbi divini* have in fact been questioned and threatened by the fact that it consists of men doing their only too human work. In the sphere of conceptions, thoughts and enterprises there has always and everywhere been the actual threat of embellishments and obscurations of the content of its commission on the one side and of its orientation to the addressees envisaged on the other. In face of this threat there is demanded constant critical vigilance accompanying the action of the community in the discharge of its task. In other words, the question of the purity of its task has to be continually put on both sides. And since the community stands or falls with its task, this may be called the question, latently but also acutely posed in every age, of the renewal of the community or the reformation of its existence in the ministry entrusted to it. It necessarily implies the constant consideration of what is becoming of its task in its own hands. It necessarily implies the failure of its work and ministry when measured by the purity with which it has received them from the hands of its Lord, and its readiness to reform and correct them by this standard.

In retrospect of the first discussion in this first sub-section, we begin with the question of the purity of content of the task committed to the community. We have to consider critically two temptations, two possible distortions and falsifications of its content, i.e., of the Gospel, both of which must be rejected with equal energy by a Christian community which is faithful and vigilant in the discharge of its task and therefore worthy of the name. And it is usually the case that the one is as it were the complement of the other, arising as an ostensible reaction to it and probably provoking quite quickly a counter-action. On the one side we are concerned with the failure to see that the Gospel is always the living Word of the living Lord of the community, and on the other with the failure to appreciate that it is always the constant Word of its one Lord. If it loses its living quality in the witness of the community, it will soon be all up with its constancy. And if it loses its constancy in this witness, it cannot become or very long remain a living Word.

If it cannot be seen as a living Word in its attestation by the Christian community, the Gospel of Jesus Christ, of the Yes of God spoken in Him, of His goodness directed to man, may very well lose its character as a call which always goes out to the men of a particular age from the God who reveals Himself in that age, addressing them here and now in their own particular situation. The community may very well forget that it has to hear and attest Jesus Christ as the Lord who is risen again from the dead and therefore lives as the Prophet of God who in the power of the Holy Spirit is not inactive but powerfully at work in the time between Easter and His final appearing both in heaven and on earth. On its own lips the eternal Word from His lips may well become timeless truth. The concrete meaning with which it speaks here and now may well dissolve in its presentation into an abstract signification. The specific point with which His Gospel, notwithstanding its identity in every age and therefore its universality, penetrates each specific historical situation with a specific intention to be specifically received and attested by the community, may be softened and blunted and secretly broken off or rendered invisible in its proclamation. The Gospel as transmitted by it may be changed into a dull impartation which says everything and nothing, proclaiming a supposed but not a real salvation. Formally, such an impartation need not be lacking in a biblical foundation, biblical content and attachment to the best traditions of the ecclesiastical past, such as, for example, those of the century of the Reformation. It can have the appearance of a true message of Christ, a true preaching of the kingdom of God or true praise of free grace. It can ostensibly be a proclamation of justification by faith alone and a warming reference to the spiritual conversion and moral renovation needed by humanity. And why should it not proclaim this with genuine emotion and true zeal ? In this corrupted form only one thing will be carefully left out and therefore lacking. The impartation will not be intended nor go forth as an invitation to or demand for a concrete decision of faith and obedience, at any rate in the sense of a Yes or No which entails a distinction of word and act at a specific time and in a specific situation. In spite of all its profundity and eloquence, at the point where it ought to do this, it will come to a halt and become an inarticulate mumbling of pious words.

There will be talk of inward regeneration by faith, of the struggle for a new awakening by the Spirit of God, of the solemn prospect of a distant " world of Christ," but there will be no demand to grasp the nettle and to make a small beginning of this regeneration and awakening in a specific act of will here and now. There will be prayer for peace, but prayer committing no one. When the time comes for steps to peace which commit anyone, there will be quick withdrawal into neutrality, into a safe avoidance of the fatal problems and the even more fatal freedom from problems of the existing present, followed by a new and powerful and sincerely meant but blunted and generalised and therefore impotent assurance that Jesus Christ is risen, that He will come again at the last day and put everything right, and that faith in Him is the victory which overcomes the world.

The community which wants to adopt this attitude will never be at a loss for practical reasons in its favour. The questions in relation to which it has to pronounce a clear Yes and No as it follows Jesus Christ and attests His living Word are always questions which humanly speaking are not at all simple or easy. They are very difficult and complicated questions which must be answered in terms of reason, though of a bold and enterprising reason in the case of the Christians. The more urgent the questions are, the more true this is. The arguments *pro* and *contra* may often seem to be confusingly even, so that in answering them the bold reason of the community which listens to the living Word of its Lord may often seem to be very isolated and even foolish. It thus has many apparently convincing reasons for either remaining neutral or keeping to generalities. In this or that specific matter, no unequivocal word is given to it, and therefore it must humbly wait instead of speaking. Again, in the burning topics of the hour, even in the community there may be different and sincerely represented views whose champions are summoned to mutual respect and forbearance in love and cannot therefore force or constrain one another by appeal to the common faith. In such a situation, serious though it may be, regard must be had above all else to the preservation of the unity and peace of the community. Finally, account must be taken of the purity of the Gospel. Its universally valid declaration is not to be contaminated by admixture with all kinds of attitudes which do not readily commend themselves to all believers as Christian. What is required to maintain this purity is a wise and safe restriction to the sphere of a general, abstract and neutral Christianity which never compromises itself and is therefore always right. How solid and even illuminating these reasons seem ! But would it not be better if, when at what is perhaps a critical moment for the world and therefore for itself the community finds itself in the disturbing position of not knowing what to say or what not to say, or of being divided on the point, it should at least refrain from regarding itself as excused or even justified for these reasons ?

Is there really any *hic et nunc* in which it may maintain with a good conscience that it cannot hear the living Word of its living Lord spoken to this *hic et nunc* ? Dare it ever make Him responsible for the fact that it obviously does not hear Him, as though to-day He had unfortunately broken off His prophetic work, as though to-day He were either not present at all or only silently within it, as though He had become a dumb Lord in relation to the present time and situation, as though obedience to Him demanded either a respectful silence or the accompaniment of the Yes by an interwoven No ? Assuming that it does not dare to blame its necessity on Him, ought not such an attitude to give it a very definitely disturbed or bad conscience which will not allow it to persist in its neutrality but will impel it rather to become a new and perhaps more attentive hearer of the voice of the Good Shepherd ? It is this disturbed conscience, however, which it does not seem to have so long as it can find such good reasons for its neutrality, its empty generality, and the consequent blunting of its word, of its supposed attestation of the Word of Jesus Christ.

Is it perhaps the case that the comfortable ease with which it can explain its weakness without feeling any need for repentance is a symptom of its general and radical failure to see that in the Gospel entrusted to it its concern is with the living Word of its living Lord ? May it even be that it is thinking in terms of a continuous and not just a temporary silence of Jesus Christ ? Does it perhaps think that since His first coming and for the time being He has left the world and itself to the ebb and flow of human opinions whose alternation He accompanies at a distance but without throwing in His own Word ? May it be, therefore, that it does not expect to hear the Gospel as His living and decisive Word here and now ? Has it long since come to regard it as fanaticism to think that as His *viva vox* it is not an abstract, static and non-binding, but a supremely concrete, dynamic, and binding disclosure concerning God, the world and man, that it is always in every specific time and situation the decisive Word to the world, and that it must be attested by the community as such ? Does it think that it is not committed to repeat a Yes and No which He speaks here and now, because basically it denies that He really speaks it ? Is its true opinion that He whose kingdom is obviously not of this world has nothing to say about what takes place in this world, so that in the time between Easter and His final appearing the community is set in a difficult position in relation to Him, in which it has certainly to believe in Him and therefore in God's good Yes in Him, in which it has to attest Him and therefore God in general, but in which, when it is a matter of the concrete questions of the ongoing history of this time between the times as they press upon both it and the world, it is left to its own opinions and judgments and therefore to its own resultant decisions or non-decisions, which are " free " in the sense that they do not come within the scope of its direct relation to Him ? Does it perhaps envisage its situation and task as one in which it has only to remind itself and the world around of His past coming, and to point itself and the world around to His future coming ? Is it in fact the case that its strange neutrality in relation to the particularly critical times and situations of the modern world, and its strange explanations of this neutrality, are suspicious symptoms that it regards its Lord as One who is absent in a past and future distance, so that it is superfluous to listen for His living Word here and now, and pointless to attest it to the world ? Are we not challenged by the alarming question whether in this relation to Him it does not betray far too close a resemblance to the priests of Baal on Carmel ?

For there can be no doubt that, when its relevance to specific times and situations is taken from it, intentionally or unintentionally the Gospel is no longer preached as the declaration of the risen Jesus Christ who rules at the right hand of the Father Almighty but who also by His Holy Spirit lives and acts and speaks in the ongoing earthly and temporal history of the world and the Church. There can be no doubt that in these circumstances it is emptied of its content and therefore made unserviceable as the eternal Word of the Yes of God's goodness pronounced in Him. The task of the community does not allow but forbids it to mumble it in this way. If it still does it because it cannot receive the concretely spoken Word of its living Lord, then it ought not to excuse its weakness but rather to be ashamed of itself and to begin to listen to Him afresh. If, on the other hand, it does it because it does not think He now speaks such a Word and therefore does not expect to hear it, then it ceases to be His community, the content of its own witness testifies against it, and its only hope is that it will do so powerfully enough to waken it from the tomb.

In virtue of its proclamation of a general, timeless, neutral and blunted instead of concrete truth, it might still claim and even to some degree enjoy a certain validity in the eyes of men as one of the constructs and forces of world-occurrence. In this way it might make it easier for the world to recognise and tolerate if not to accept itself and its function. For what particular objection can the world have to a Church which understands and discharges its task in so innocuous a way ? Its contradiction and opposition will usually be directed only against a community which brings out the concrete relevance of the Gospel. But if the Church does in fact make itself invisible, and the Gospel is being made or has already been made timeless and irrelevant on its lips, it has to realise that it has forfeited its own true right to exist, that it cannot expect any serious respect on the part of the world, that it cannot be sure of its own cause in face of it, and above all that its vitally necessary connexion with its Lord has been hopelessly broken. As salt which has lost its savour (Mt. 5[13]), it is good for nothing but to be cast out and trodden under foot of men.

It is well for the community that it should occasionally see that the world actually understands it better than it does itself. It is well for it that the world should occasionally tremble before the concealed point of the content of its task and therefore before the threatened unsettlement of its own being and activity. It is well for it that its affirmation, recognition and toleration of the community should sometimes come to an end and be replaced by a very different attitude. It is well for it that in spite of and in the calm of its neutrality it should be rudely startled from without and given cause to remember something better, i.e., its living Lord and His living Word, and consequently perhaps to dare to do what in practice or even in principle it has refrained from doing, i.e., to stand with the witness of its lips to the Gospel which it has received and still receives in pristine purity from the lips of its Lord, believing and obeying the well-aimed Word which is spoken by Him here and now.

In two senses, however, it will always be a dangerous moment in its history when in this respect it finds itself both outwardly and inwardly stimulated, summoned and compelled to turn over a new leaf, resolutely leaving the old way and no less resolutely entering the opposite way. For in these circumstances it might fall victim to the opposite temptation and be guilty of the opposite error. Let us assume that it does in fact recognise that the Gospel must not be perverted on its lips into an impartation of general, timeless and irrelevant Christian truth. Let us assume that it sees itself invited and required to accept and understand it very differently, i.e., as the Word of God spoken to a specific time and a specific human situation. It is now seriously disposed to represent it in its prophetic actuality, to unfold it in its power and significence for itself and the world around as the Word of God spoken *hic et nunc*. What is not so self-evident, however, is that it will really undertake the venture of faith and obedience to the Word of the Lord. The question is urgent, for in the zeal of conversion it might well commit, as has often happened, the complementary error in which the Gospel, not as it is in itself but in the prism of its presentation, loses the identity or constancy which is proper to it as the living but one Word of the living but one Lord, as His eternal Word in every age and situation, and which must in all circumstances be maintained in its attestation by the community. Jesus Christ will not be, nor is He to-day, different from what He was yesterday. He is the same yesterday and to-day (Heb. 13⁸), as is also the Holy Spirit in whose power He acts and speaks. Similarly His prophetic Word, though it may have different points demanding our attention, is the same here and now as it was there and then. It remains substantially the same, and shows itself to be such. It is always and everywhere the self-declaration of Jesus Christ, the Yes of the goodness of God towards man. Always, every-where and in all changing circumstances, it is thus to be attested as

the same by the community which serves it. If there must be unconditional openness to its living quality, there must also be
unconditional loyalty to its constancy. But at this point there might
well be a second failure in relation to the content of the task committed
to the community, namely, the falsification of the Gospel in the form
of its transformation into "another gospel" (Gal. 1⁶ᶠ·), i.e., into a
pseudo-Gospel which is not according to the direction of the living
Lord Jesus Christ, which is not under the impulsion of His Holy Spirit,
which is novel in its adoption and conception, which is arbitrarily
and independently interpreted by the community, which is approxi-
mated and adapted to the moods, the modes of thought, the instincts,
the ideas, the needs and the aspirations of a specific age and situation,
which is thus robbed of its original power and significance, and which
will therefore be lacking in the very actuality and force which it is
hoped to create for it.

Now it is strangely but obviously true that this second failure
does not usually spring from an evangelical radicalism but from a
very unevangelical conservatism. It is in this light that we are to
view the falsifications of the content of the task committed to the
community in the great heresies of all ages from the days of ancient
Gnosticism to its rationalistic, romantic, speculative, empiricist and
existentialist variations in the modern age and our own day. For
what is their starting-point but the strange illusion that the Gospel
is a tolerably well-known magnitude, a sum of dogmas, forms of life,
ideals and hopes prescribed in the Bible and tradition and to be
accepted by the community, and as such an object which can be
surveyed and considered as such, weighed against the demands of
the general spiritual or other situation of a given age, translated into
the language and concepts and philosophy and practical notions of
this age, and both critically and positively interpreted, reduced,
explained, deepened and applied? What counts is not what the
Gospel or the living Lord Jesus Christ has to say to the Church or
the world in this age, or what the community has to grasp and
appropriate and attest anew as His living word in this age, but rather,
as though it were a question of putting it to children, how the men
of this age may best be reached with information concerning this
object, how they may most certainly be won over to what it is thought
should be regarded as a sure and certain knowledge which stands
in no need of renewal. With a supposed knowledge of what stands
in the Bible, and even of the common mind of the *communio sanctorum*,
but also with high expectations in relation to the Gospel itself, it is
thought that there may be complete freedom in this respect, namely,
a cheerful adaptation to the order of the day, a contemporary
translation, interpretation and application of the well-known text, a
critical reworking and handling of the well-known object. It is
thought that the content of the Gospel is securely held and may

and should be turned to personal use, just as it is thought that there is certain knowledge of the age in question and the structures and tendencies of its thought and will and life, and that this knowledge may be confidently used as a measure, criterion and instrument in the translation, interpretation and application of the well-known Gospel. It is this twofold indolence, and decisively that which changes the content of the Gospel into a prescribed object and disposable possession, which has made possible and indeed always makes inevitable its greater or lesser falsifications.

What are the necessary consequences of this indolence, of this very unevangelical conservatism? As an object readily accessible in the Bible and ancient doctrine, already known, needing only the interpretation of the community to which it is surrendered, the Gospel obviously cannot be the Word of God which is superior to the community and the world and which must be obediently attested by the community to the world. It can be this only as, documented in the Bible and confirmed by the doctrine of the Church, it is allowed by the community to be spoken directly from His own mouth and therefore with constant freshness. It can be this only as the community maintains an attitude of pure and unassuming receptivity and allows itself to be mastered by it. Otherwise the community is superior to it in the given time and situation, being both free and obviously directed to master it by means of the criteria, principles and methods which impose themselves and are normative in the given time and situation. In these circumstances it is not the Gospel which gives to the community the faith, the mode of thought and the outlook corresponding to it, writing them upon its heart and conscience and laying them upon its lips that it may be attested by it with this correspondence. On the contrary, it is the community which imposes upon the Gospel its own faith, mode of thought and outlook, i.e., those corresponding to the age and situation, causing it to say what it must say, what alone it can say, to be understood and received by the men of its age, and first of all by itself. Is it not inevitable that in what is called the Gospel the community should in truth be attesting only itself in its existing inner and outer reality and limitation?

Thus Jesus Christ Himself, being sought as the living among the dead, i.e., as a figure of the well-known text delivered up to its own interpretation or control, might well be called " the Lord " and willingly understood as such, but He cannot possibly be manifest or recognisable as the real Lord of the community and the world ruling at the right hand of God the Father and acting and speaking by His Spirit in temporal history. He can be this only as the Resurrected, in the event, the act, the occurrence of His act of lordship documented in the Bible and confirmed in the doctrine of the Church, as the Subject acting in exercise of His prophetic office, in face of whom His acknowledgment as the Lord and His confession as such are the only possible and therefore the authentic movement of His community, underlying its witness to the world.

Otherwise, in pious attachment to Scripture and tradition, it may well call Him " the Lord," and call upon Him as such, but in reality He is so, not of God, but by its own favour, as a creature of its own religious fancy interpreting that figure of the Bible and the Church in philosophical or mythological terms. In reality it is His lord and not *vice versa* : the lord of His work ; the lord of the atonement made in Him ; the lord of the covenant concluded in Him. Again, the Yes of God to some degree perceptible as the epitome of this work of His in the well-known text surrendered to its possession and control cannot possibly be understood or represented by it as the divine and therefore the sovereign Yes which is not limited by any No but limits every No. It is this at once if, documented in the Bible and confirmed by the doctrine of the Church, it is received from His own mouth in continual self-disclosure. But placed under the control, evaluation and assessment of the community, how can it maintain its superior, unconditional and impregnable validity, or be confidently received, and with assurance and conviction repeated, transmitted and attested by it ? In this case, it can be pronounced by it only as a broken Yes hedged and qualified by all kinds of doubts and problems. And finally, assuming that it is one of the elements of that well-known text delivered up to its interpretation and control, how can this Yes be the Yes of the eternal goodness of God which is new every morning ? It is this only when, documented in Scripture and confirmed by the Church, it is spoken to it personally by the One who is the goodness of God in person, and entrusted to it by Him for attestation to the world. Otherwise, as the declaration of a Christian conviction which is certainly nourished by the Bible and Church doctrine but which is independent of and even sovereign over the person of Jesus Christ, even the goodness of God stands or falls with the goodness of this conviction, and can thus have on its lips only the form of a rather restricted goodness.

This dissolution of the substance, and therefore this destruction of the identity and breaking of the constancy of the content of the commission of the community, will necessarily result where the community is slack in the vigilance continually demanded of it and in its further instruction in the school of its Lord.

In these circumstances, what will decide the form, or rather the deformation, of the Gospel committed into the hands of the community which is slack in this school, will be the presuppositions on the basis of which, having taken from the Gospel its own freedom of self-exposition, it will make its own attempt to expound, interpret, appropriate and master it.

Among these presuppositions the dominant philosophy of the age and its associated scientific and particularly hermeneutical principles and methods will play an important part, since in the appropriation and domestication—or should we say the imprisonment, martyrdom, execution and burial ?—of the living Word of the living Lord which thus commences, by no means the least concern is with exegesis in the narrower sense, i.e., with the exposition of its documentation in Holy Scripture and its confirmation in the scholarship and confession of the earlier Church, as indeed in the whole sphere of the *communio sanctorum*. The reigning philosophy and the corresponding hermeneutics, which for better or worse must be admitted by the community once the Gospel becomes an object surrendered to its own control, affect and alter the Gospel already in the literary sources normative for its understanding. Yet when there is no longer the ability or readiness to hear the Gospel as the living Word spoken to-day, we have to do with something more than the unavoidable mastering and deformation of the Gospel. Indeed, it may be that what we have in the first instance is not exegesis in the narrower sense and therefore not the disastrous influence of what is regarded as the normative philosophy and its related hermeneutics. It may be that this simply represents the life lived at this period by the fraction of humanity concerned, and the awareness of life experienced by them, their particular culture, civilisation and technics, their historical past and present with the need or glory involved, their national qualities, aspirations and disillusionments, their moral standards and customs, their retrogressive or progressive commercial relations, and somewhere deep down their particular degree of religion or irreligion. Christianity in any age or place has a part in all these things. It is more or less consciously and intensively interested in them. All these things work themselves out in its thinking and volition as at least partially determinative.

If the Gospel, i.e., the content of the commission of the community, becomes a supposedly well-known text and object, subjected to its own interpretation, instead of an eternal Subject, the living Word of the living Prophet Jesus Christ, which reveals itself afresh and establishes fresh knowledge in every age, then it is only to be expected that the community's handling of this object will be radically, totally and at bottom irresistibly influenced by all the presuppositions which it inevitably brings to it from its relationship with the world around. All the sluices are necessarily opened, and all the elements of its participation in the general life of the world naturally make their greater or lesser contribution. There are no philosophical, historical, national, cultural, political or economic factors in its existence in the world which do not help to shape the Gospel as it is delivered up into its hands. No possible deformation of the Gospel is ruled out. Once it has been made an object, and the community's sovereignty over it established, it is not surprising if distortions and falsifications in its declaration immediately follow, if it loses overnight its character as a Word which is superior to the world and man, if the lordship of Jesus Christ in His prophetic office and work as proclaimed in it becomes no more than a notion which is perhaps formally and verbally accepted but totally devoid of reality or practical significance, if on examination its content amounts to no more than the doubtful claim to lordship advanced by the Church and its piety. It is not surprising if the divine and therefore unconditional Yes pronounced in it, although occasionally mentioned, loses its specific force and ring and validity, if it is lost in the muffled dialectic of every kind of Yes and No, if the goodness of God can be declared only as the postulate of a good human conviction and according to the criteria of this conviction. It is not surprising that there are all these dilutions. If the Gospel is no longer heard and attested as a living Word, but has become an *obiectum vile* to be mastered by the community, then, since in the process it is referred to the prescribed conditions of its life in the world, the result can consist only in these dilutions. What it presents under the name of Gospel can then be only a more or less secularised Gospel, deprived of its original meaning and power, i.e., " another " Gospel. For on the presuppositions in question, how could it even understand it in its true and original form, let alone attest it ? On the basis of the history, culture, nationality, political and economic relations and especially the religion of this or that fraction of humanity, it certainly cannot be prepared for or taught the knowledge of the Word of God which is superior to the whole world and the men of every age and clime, and which is addressed to all, of Jesus Christ as the Lord, of the divine and therefore unconditional Yes pronounced in Him, of the free, pure and unmerited and therefore omnipotent goodness of God. Nor on this basis can it be prepared and taught to transmit and attest these things with the clarity with which they are disclosed to it. What the community brings to what it should receive and attest in declaration of them can only turn it from instead of directing it to them. The direction and instruction which it is given by these presuppositions can only be a temptation to divest the Gospel of its true and original form and to give it a form which is more acceptable, tolerable and understandable to the world around and not least to itself, thus bringing about the secularisation, adulteration and obfuscation of the content of its task. In this form, although there may be meretricious reminiscences of the Bible and Church doctrine, it can no longer be the superior Word of God nor the proclamation of the lordship of Jesus Christ, nor can it manifest His unconditional Yes, nor can it express the goodness of God in freedom, purity and omnipotence but only with all kinds of reservations. This means, however, that whether it realises the fact or not the community has lost the Gospel as the content of its task. What it may still preach under this name is no longer the Gospel of Jesus Christ.

But the mutations, interpositions, embellishments and subtractions which inevitably follow from the alien presuppositions brought by the community to the Gospel are only the resultant phenomena of an alienation from it of which it has already been guilty in what we have called the unevangelical conservatism or indolence of its handling of it, this being the basic error which makes of it, instead of a speaking subject, i.e., the living Word of its living Lord, an unspeaking object surrendered to its own control, i.e., its own arts of speech. It is in this way that it is first and decisively secularised and made another Gospel. Its falsification commences, with all the ineluctable consequences, when the community ceases to hear it afresh each new day, and begins to imagine that it is here concerned with a well-known magnitude awaiting its own investigation, exposition and application. It commences with the patronising attitude which it permits itself to take up in relation to it. This dumb object which has to be expressed by the community is no longer the Word of God, the Gospel of Jesus Christ, the superior Yes of the goodness of God. This fact can be revealed only when the community approaches it with its alien presuppositions and tries to appropriate and domesticate it by means of them. It must be conceded, therefore, that as analysis of this object all secularising exposition is in keeping with this object and therefore relevant and correct. Only this perverted exposition really fits that which is already perverted in itself. The Church which does not continue learning in the school of the living Word, which is not thereby continually awakened to life and maintained in life, which is sufficient unto itself in relation to it, i.e., satisfied with its own supposed knowledge how to declare it, is as such the false synagogue whose manifestation as the mother of all heresies, namely, of all disruptions of the unity and constancy of the Gospel as the content of its commission, is only a question of time and opportunity.

At the beginning of this second discussion of the question of the content of the task committed to the community, we spoke of the doubly dangerous moments in its history when it may again begin to realise that Jesus Christ never speaks His prophetic Word generally or in the void, but always specifically in time to different ages, and that the community in its witness must follow Him in this. The first danger is that of its inability or unwillingness to rise up, to cast aside its slothful neutrality and truly to follow Him.

The second danger, which we have been trying to depict, is that it will make this movement, that it will seriously attempt an understanding and confession of the Word of God relevant to the time and situation, but that there will be the fateful substitution of an autonomous for an obedient movement, the Gospel being made relevant to the age and situation in the sense that it is not just spoken to it but spoken in accordance with it, being fashioned by its concerns and needs and aspirations. It is thus made concrete and addressed to the existing situation by its interpretation according to the alien presuppositions of the situation and the resultant loss of its unity and constancy. And we have seen that this second danger no less than the first has its origin in the breaking of the vital direct contact between the community and its living Lord. Without this, its witness, i.e., the Gospel on its lips, can neither be alive and relevant to different times and situations nor can it be in all times and situations the one eternal Word addressed and applicable to all men.

It only needs to be added rather more explicitly that when the second danger, i.e., that of the breaking of the constancy of the Gospel, becomes acute, then, since they have a common origin, there can be little chance of escaping the first. That is to say, if the Gospel suffers degradation as an object, and as such becomes subject to deformation and sooner or later falls victim to it, it cannot possibly have the character of a living Word directed to specific times and situations and bringing about concrete decisions. It lacks all the things necessary for this purpose—the love, the righteousness, the wisdom and the authority. And where is it to find them ? On the lips of the community which transforms the one great and incomparable subject into an object which it has then necessarily to master by means of alien presuppositions, it is not the Word of the living Lord, the "hammer that breaketh the rock in pieces" (Jer. 23[29]). In this form there cannot and will not be the penetration to something concrete which was originally intended and which was sought in this fatal process. Submission to this process with a view to this penetration deprives it of all the power necessary to its achievement. If the Gospel, being understood and treated as an object by the community, loses its constancy, it also loses its living quality. The striving of the community for relevance merely plunges its witness more truly and deeply into the sphere of the impartation of general, neutral and blunted truths. For the Gospel can be on its lips a concrete and pointed Word relevant to specific times and situations only when it is proclaimed in its unity and constancy as the eternal Gospel. The first error has called forth the second, and the second can only call forth a repetition of the first. If " they have forsaken me the fountain of living waters " (Jer. 2[13]), this is inevitable.

The question of the purity of the task committed to the community is also to be put, however, in relation to the one addressed, namely, in relation to the manner in which the community sees, understands, addresses and treats the men among whom and to whom it is sent. In the relation of the community to this counterpart we are also concerned with temptation in a twofold and complementary form deriving from a single source. The first form is that of neglect of the counterpart, the second of patronising him. The purity of the task of the community as given by the Lord and received at His hands is necessarily lost if it gives way to either form of this temptation. Its task and therefore its existence as the Christian community is forfeit if it treads either way to the bitter end. The common feature shared by both mistakes, as also by the failure to recognise either the living quality or the constancy of the content of the commission, is the withdrawal of the community from the sphere of the immediate direction of its Lord who has laid the task upon it. If the community does not hang continually and ever anew on the lips of the Lord, it will necessarily either neglect or patronise the one addressed in its task, probably switching backwards and forwards from the one error to the other. Guided by the direction of its living Lord, it will not fail those to whom it is sent either in the one respect or the other. In obedience to Him, it will approach closely the men among whom and to whom it is sent, yet not too closely, preserving the no less required distance even in the required proximity, and indeed being rightly near at the right distance. Both are included in the purity with which the community receives and executes its task. But unfortunately it cannot be taken for granted that it will be executed with this purity.

The addressee whom the community neglects is the man who, as it has become lazy, or sleepy, or even independent in relation to its living Lord and hard of hearing or even deaf in respect of His living Word, is no longer the representative of the world for whom it exists and for whom it must do so totally and unconditionally if it is not to surrender its existence as the Christian community. In this case it forgets that it is what it is among the other creatures of God, only as this man is so unreservedly and unalterably ordered in relation to it, and it to him, that it can itself exist only in co-existence with him, only in relation and indeed a positive and as such an actualised and actual relationship to him. This relationship is broken and threatened with dissolution. It becomes for it only an incidental and basically accidental or arbitrary or contingent determination of its own existence. It is no longer prepared to stand or fall with it. Its positive actualisation also becomes optional. It may practise it or it may not, and in any case it will do so only on the left hand. It has no direct, no vitally necessary and positive relationship to the fellow-man. It can withold everything from him. In the strict and proper sense, it has no interest in him. He may be bound to it in some way, and it to him. He might also be lacking as a counterpart. But it can exist very well without him. Indeed, it might even be better off without him, or with only external and occasional contacts with him.

The man of the world seen in this way is the addressee neglected by it. In the light of its task, and, since it lives by its commission, of its very existence, it cannot see him in this way. Such neglect of the addressee of its mission, such remoteness from him, is a sign of its own most radical disorder and most dangerous aberration. Impressive secondary reasons may be found for this aberration.

It may be that the man of the world outside seems to be so different, so alien and even threatening in his attitude and conduct that it is repelled and startled and can only set him at a distance. To maintain itself, to guard and preserve inviolate what is proper to it, it thinks it preferable not to give itself fully or seriously to him, but to keep its relationship to the bare minimum of what is necessary and unavoidable, for the rest commending him to God in a disturbed and anxious way, so that even prayer for him involves no commitment and does not alter the relationship to him. It thus prefers not to exist for him truly or seriously, since this is too much to ask and might entail too great a risk. On the other hand, it may be that the community finds so great joy and satisfaction in what is proper to it, yet also so many problems, e.g., of worship, pastoral care, social life and theology, so many tasks, so many claims in what has to be experienced, considered and done in its own inner circle, that it simply has neither time nor energy for those who are without, and therefore thinks it better either to proceed without them or to maintain only that loose relationship which can be easily broken. Along these lines a good deal may be said in justification or at least in excuse of the aberration.

Yet it is still an aberration. For the primary cause which produces, conditions and motivates all the apparently good secondary causes is definitely a bad one. It is an overlooking, ignoring and forgetting of the task without which the community does not exist at all, by which alone all that is proper to it has meaning and substance, but by which that counterpart is for good or evil brought necessarily into relation with it and it with him.

In Jesus Christ the community and the rest of humanity constitute a differentiated, yet in this differentiation firmly integrated, whole.

This means on the one side that, elected by God, reconciled to Him and called to His service in Jesus Christ, humanity cannot in practice escape confrontation and co-existence with the community which is actually brought into relation with it and established among it by Jesus Christ. It must always accept its presence and action and be reminded of its existence. In a very different way, however, the community on its side is also referred to its co-existence with the rest of humanity. True, the rest of humanity does not need the community in respect of its new and true reality, to the establishment of which the community can contribute as little as itself, and which the community also can gratefully recognise, presuppose and respect only as the act and work of God. It is only in respect of its perception of this new reality that the world is referred to the community to the extent that this is commissioned by Jesus Christ to attest it and in this sense to make it known to the world. It cannot be said that even in this respect the world is referred absolutely and inescapably to the existence of the community. It is not the community, but Jesus Christ Himself in His prophetic office and work, who mediates this perception. The community has a part in this occurrence, yet not in the form of an independent enterprise, but only in ministering participation in His action. We may thus venture the three statements : 1. the world would be lost without Jesus Christ and His Word and work ; 2. the world would not necessarily be lost if there were no Church ; and 3. the Church would be lost if it had no counterpart in the world. It is an act of free grace that Jesus Christ wills to claim its service in this matter. He is not bound to it in His prophetic action. He is not restricted to what He can and does accomplish by means of its ministering work. Who is to prevent Him from going His own direct way to man without it in His self-declaration ? This does not set aside the necessity with which humanity does actually belong together with the community and has to co-exist with it. But it relativises this necessity.

It is with a very different necessity, however, that the community belongs together with humanity. Of the community it must be said that it is referred absolutely and inescapably to its co-existence with humanity. Its existence finds not merely its meaning but its very basis and possibility only in its mission, its ministry, its witness, its task and therefore its positive relation to those who are without. It stands or falls with this relation. Woe to it if it abandons instead of actualising this relation, if it does not confess before men what it specifically may know among them, if for the many and good reasons which it may adduce it neglects the men of the world in the sense already described ! In so doing, it is not merely guilty of ingratitude in relation to the grace, distinction and honour undeservedly shown it in its induction to this ministry ; it also questions and even denies that which it may know before all others of the election, reconciliation and vocation of all. In the light of the content of its commission, how can it hold aloof from any, or try to be the Christian community without any to address, without the accompanying world ? In so doing it holds aloof from Jesus Christ Himself who is the Saviour of all men. To the degree, therefore, that through laziness or self-will it neglects the man of the world, either seeing him no more or only at a distance, and preferring to be without him, it is brought into mortal peril. For this other is absolutely indispensable to it. It is thus really in danger of perishing without hope of salvation if it succumbs to this temptation.

The complementary temptation to falsification of its task in relation to the addressee is that of patronising him. The addressee who is patronised by the community is the man who, as it thinks it super-fluous to listen to the voice of its living Lord, as it arbitrarily and arrogantly interposes its own rights and presence instead, as it refuses to see and understand him solely from the standpoint of the Gospel, becomes for the community the material for its own art and the object of its own deployment of power. It has somehow discovered that it must understand and express itself in relation to him. It thus turns forcefully enough to him. It conceives a genuine interest in him. It cannot continue its introversion. The pendulum swings in the opposite direction. The hour is full of promise. Perhaps it will be the moment of its awakening from sleep, of its renunciation of self-will. But it is certainly a dangerous moment. The imminent and opposing danger is that the community which once felt itself to be and acted as its own mistress *ad intra* will now do so *ad extra*, posing in extraverted form as the mistress of the situation in its relationship to the target of its commission. It now approaches the man of the world as the owner and proper disposer of higher and indeed the very highest goods, with superior knowledge and will, always knowing better and willing better than he does, and especially understanding him better than he does himself, plumbing the very heights of his glory and depths of his misery, and prepared for his own good to give him the most authentic information concerning himself. It is no longer embarrassed, puzzled, alienated or repelled by him. It is only too sure of itself in relation to him. It does not need to avoid him. It is in a position to look kindly on him and with benevolent patronage to draw his attention to that which he lacks but which applies unconditionally to him. It see and treats him now according to the very definite picture which it forms both of himself as one who is without but who is to be brought in, and of his position, of his positive and negative possibilities, of his destiny and limitations, of what might be more or less good for him. It is in relation to this picture that it feels that it is called and equipped to address him. In possession of it, it thinks that he is commended to it and to that extent committed to its hand. Armed with it, or rather with the assumption that he corresponds to it, it believes that it can reach him, that it can strike home, that it can reveal to him from within what it has to reveal to him as the answer to his well-known question to it. From the height secured by the possession of this picture, it thus thinks that it can do what it ought to do in relation to him as the one addressed in its task.

There can now be no question of neglect ; he is now specially favoured. The community does not hold itself too aloof ; it now approaches too closely. And once again its task is falsified. For the figure of the addressee imprisoned in this picture and approached in the form of this picture is not envisaged in its task. Proceeding thus, it again deviates from its task and shows itself guilty of aberration. The attention, the zeal, the boldness and the participation with which it now turns to the man of the world are all good. But what has really happened ? Why does it think it can play the role of providence, of *praevenire*, in relation to the one addressed by it, instead of simply discharging its commission ? Why does it think it must first discover and know how far he may be reached and affected by what it has to tell him, how far he is addressable ? Who has commanded or authorised it to try to dispose concerning him, to stand poised over him in the discharge of its commission ? Who ordains that it should make that picture of him and therefore at root turn to the picture rather than himself ? Who gives him the superiority, and what kind of a superiority is it, with which he undertakes to treat him in this way ?

To be sure, it has no difficulty in adducing reasons for its action. Does it not really know more than those without ? Does it not know what they do not know at all ? Is it not commissioned to share this knowledge with them ? To do this, does it not have to form a view, a notion, a concept, a picture and pictures of them ? Is it not active in the necessary work of love when it patronises them in this sense ? It might well explain and justify itself along such lines as these.

Nevertheless, there has clearly been a quiet but fateful substitution. For what it has to impart to the man of the world is not its own superior knowledge, but rather what it actually knows. What it has to attest, not from above downwards but alongside in unity and solidarity, is the Gospel which is absolutely superior both to the man of the world and itself. If this is what it does, there can be no question of an attitude of patronage. Nor does it have any need whatever of a prior picture, since he is clear enough in the light of the Gospel, namely, as the man who is already elected, reconciled and called in Jesus Christ, as the one who is already loved by God, as the one who is thus far ignorant and therefore weary and heavy laden, but also as the one who is on the way to knowledge and appointed to great joy, as *christianus designatus*, and therefore as one who can be reached and addressed as such. Nor can it ever dream of directing him to his own good according to its own fancies, since it now keeps to what it has to attest as the Gospel addressed to him, namely, that he is already in the best hands, so that if he simply entrusts and abandons himself to their guidance, he will not fail to find and tread the right way of himself, in the freedom which he is given and which is therefore his own. If, however, it does not attest the Gospel, or Jesus Christ, but its own knowledge of the Gospel and of Jesus Christ, its own little Christianity—which is the πρῶτον ψεῦδος in this matter—then, to reach him with this, it has to have a picture of him, and if it has none it has to make one, and it has, of course, to direct him, to manœuvre him out of his ignorance into its own knowledge. It is then inevitable that it should patronise him in this sense. Patronage means the human exercise of power by men against other men as though they were objects. It means the treating of others, however benevolently, as so much material for one's own abilities. The community, however, has no power of its own to exercise in relation to others. It has not to cause them to experience its abilities. It has not to handle them. It has to attest to them the power of its Lord and the art of His grace. It has to call them unassumingly and without reserve to the freedom of faith and obedience. If it handles or patronises them, it falsifies its task no less than when it neglects them.

The community of Jesus Christ, cleaving to Him as it hears His voice, can be great and rule with Him in the world and among men only as it performs its ministry with no concern to assure or create results, but leaving it to Him whom it attests to make of it what He wills. In the discharge of this ministry, it cannot possible assert or maintain itself in relation to the target of its mission. It cannot possibly try to gain power over him or even with the best intentions to patronise him. It ought to know that it can accomplish nothing along these lines, because the power which it is given for the discharge of its ministry cannot be used but will definitely be withheld where there is any such attempt. If it were a matter of mastering and ruling, it would always be outstripped by the world, which can do this much better. But even if it had the capacity, what would be the value of the attempt? In relation to the man of the world it has no cause of its own which it must represent, for which it must make propaganda, and to which it must win him. It has to represent the cause of Jesus Christ, but this will slip through its hands if it confuses its ministry with the attempt to secure certain advantages, successes or triumphs for itself in relation to it. It can represent His cause, if at all, only with decided selflessness and therefore the firm renunciation of any self-assertion or self-promotion. His glorious, omnipotent and triumphant prophetic Word is itself a ministry to the world. It is not a demonstration of His superiority to it, but an expression of the divine mercy shown to it in Him. If the community may serve this Word of His, then it can only try to serve and not to control the world, which needs service and not dominion, liberation and not enslavement, elevation and not suppression. It is thus forbidden and not commanded to point the object of its commission in any sense to itself, to present to him and impose upon him in any sense its own law, even though it be that of its faith and love and hope, to try to win him in any sense for itself. It is in grace that it is spared all the painful exertion of any such attempt. The fact that it is painful is shown by the way in which it quickly tires of it, and the pendulum automatically swings back again, and it thinks it might do better to adopt towards the one addressed in its task an attitude of neglect and withdrawal rather than patronage. If it is only patient and cheerful in the school of its Lord, it will not be exposed to this unprofitable and dangerous choice. It does not have to be betrayed into this dark strait. Hence it can never be too carefully on guard against the deviation which necessarily leads to the strait of this choice

4. THE MINISTRY OF THE COMMUNITY

The ministry of the community is very definite, and therefore limited, but also full of promise. This must be our next theme.

It is definite (1) because its consists quite simply in the fact that as the community of Jesus Christ it has to exist actively for the world, as we saw in the second sub-section, and therefore to execute its task within it by attesting to it the Word of God, as we saw in the third. It is for this that it is sent by God to men. It is in this, in its whence and whither, that it has its specific basis of existence. There took place there the gracious work of God, as there still takes place its disclosure in His gracious self-revelation. And there exist here the men for whom it took place and to whom it is revealed, but who have not yet received it, who do not yet know that it took place for them and is revealed to them, for whom it seems to this extent to have taken place and to be revealed in vain. Between the two, in the service of God and serving men, there strides Jesus Christ in His prophetic office and work. As the living Word of God in the calling, enlightening and awakening power of the Holy Spirit, He marches through the history of humanity which hastens to its goal and end, continually moving from our yesterday, through our to-day into our to-morrow. Yet He does not do so alone. He is accompanied by the community gathered, built up and sent by His attestation. He is surrounded by the people established and characterised by the ministry laid upon it. Thus the ministry of this people also takes place in the course, in the constantly changing stages and situations, of ongoing human history. And its ministry of witness, ordered in relation to that of Jesus Christ, is also both a ministry to God and a ministry to man : a ministry to God in which it may serve man ; and a ministry to man in which it may serve God ; and therefore a ministry to the God who speaks to man in His Word, and to the man who is already called and now summoned to hear, perceive and accept the Word of God.

The ministry of the community is given this concrete definiteness as a ministry to God and man by its institution and ordination as such in the discipleship of Jesus Christ. He, or the Gospel which He proclaims and which proclaims Him, is the content of the witness which is alone at issue in its ministry : He as very God and very Man ; He as Mediator between the two ; He as the Executor of the divine work of grace accomplished for men ; He as the man in whom it has already reached its goal and is already valid for all ; He as the one Word of God and its one Hearer, Witness and Guarantor in advance of all others. Other service can be offered both to God and man, some of it real and some only apparent. But the mark which distinguishes all other such service from the ministry of the community is the lack of necessity and certainty with which it is genuine service of both God and man, the latter as the irresistible consequence of the former and the former as the root of the latter. On the one side, it may perhaps be merely genuine service of God, and only apparently so in this abstraction. On the other side, it may perhaps be merely genuine service of man, and only apparently so in the corresponding abstraction. Or the connexion in virtue of which it either is or pretends to be both is perhaps on the one side or the other so slight, contingent or arbitrary that it cannot really and truly be either the one or the other. The ministry of the great, primary and true Minister Jesus Christ is with clear and indissoluble unity both service of God and of man, and both truly and properly. Now the community ministers, however imperfectly, in His school and discipleship. It is orientated by His ministry. It continually orientates itself by it. And inasmuch as it does so, its service of God and man is distinguished by its recognisable and basic unity from all other true or pretended service. Executed in the name of Jesus Christ, it is thus a definite ministry in this concrete sense. Executed by it as His community, it cannot fail to be in movement wholly from God and wholly to man. More clearly in some cases and less clearly in others, but always at least in outline, the essential and characteristic action of Christendom in all the forms and formations of its history is always distinguished in this way from all other human action and indeed from all other creaturely occurrence.

As concerns its definiteness more specifically as the service of God, it is to be noted that it can be discharged as such (in the service of man) only as it continually becomes this, i.e., only as the community does not cease to pray, and so does not cease to be granted, that its ministry, which it can execute only in very human fashion, may continually acquire the character of service of God without which it cannot be true service of man, and that it may be acceptable to God as such. It cannot be taken for granted that it really has and does not merely seem to have this character. It cannot count on this as a given factor. If and when it has it, this is always the gift of free grace which God has certainly promised and always does promise to His community, but which He does not owe it, which it has rather the responsibility of continually seeking from Him and receiving at His hands. That its ministry as true service of man should primarily and supremely become service of God is something which can only happen in its ongoing encounters with the source of its knowledge and confession, in its vitally necessary listening to the voice of the Good Shepherd, which means in practice its constant listening to the prophets and apostles called by Him, and therefore its constant investigation of Scripture and instruction by it. Because the Spirit which enlightens the community is not its own spirit but the Holy Spirit, what matters is that there should be heard the sigh which it must never neglect at any stage or at any turn of the way : *Veni, Creator Spiritus !* God Himself, His presence and action, are required if its service of man is not to be only this and therefore not very good as such, but is to take place with the character of service of God which is decisive for its soundness as service of man, i.e., if it is to be really on the way from God to man in its witness.

As concerns its definiteness more specifically as service of man, it is to be noted that there can be no doubt that it is true service of man if it is true service of God. It may be pointed out, however, that as true service of man and therefore true ministry of witness it will be addressed first and supremely to the men who do not share the knowledge of the community and are thus strangers to it, but then necessarily in this connexion to those who do share its knowledge and thus belong to it. It is thus a ministry both *ad extra* and *ad intra*, and the two in a very definite order. In the light of what we have said in the previous sub-sections concerning its existence and task, it need hardly be established that it is comprehensively and decisively a service of mission and therefore a ministry *ad extra*. It has to be light to those who in some way are still in darkness, drawing their attention to the light of life which shines for them. It has to call them to knowledge and obedience, attesting to them the Word of God. In principle it stands in this service and therefore in the service of unbelievers and rebels of all kinds, from lapsed or dead Christians at home to pure heathen abroad, from practical and crude atheists and enemies of the race to theoretical and refined. It stands in the service of those who in fact live in the world without God and their fellows, and therefore in forfeiture of their own true selves. To such it is sent. When active in this field it is what it truly is. Yet its resolute outward service has necessarily an inner dimension. Its witness must also be addressed to its own members and continually made perceptible to them. None of the Christians united in it so shares in its knowledge and confession that he does not need every day to be enlightened and awakened afresh to this participation, and therefore nourished, comforted and admonished as a living Christian. The same Word which the community has to attest to the world will and must be continually heard afresh by it to its own constant gathering, upbuilding and sending. In this sphere as well, therefore, its witness must never cease. If it were to fail here, its outer witness might be compared to the empty bed of a stream which has been sealed at its source, or to the sowing of bad or shrivelled seed. Christians can obviously be serviceable in the ministry of the Word to those without only if they find themselves constantly placed under the same Word. This relationship is not to be reversed. The indispensable ministry of the community must not become, as has happened and still happens on innumerable occasions, an end in itself, the true and dominant purpose of the service to be rendered by it. If its inward service is not to become an institution for private satisfaction in concert, or a work of sterile inbreeding, it must accept the priority of its sending to the world, of its task in relation to those without. Yet for the sake of the execution of this task, in order that the missionary community may be the living and authentic Christian community which is able and willing to execute it, its witness must also be directed inwards to its own members. In this respect we may think of the circular motion of the heart which in order to pump blood through the whole organism not only goes out in the diastole but also has to return in the systole, yet only to go out again in the renewed diastole. In this relationship of outward and inward action, the ministry of the community will always be both true service of God and true service of man. We need not waste words in showing how seldom this relationship between its outer and its inner ministry has been correctly perceived, understood and achieved by Christianity in our hemisphere right up to our own times. It is to be hoped that it may be led to a fresh realisation by the existence and example of the so-called young churches of Asia and Africa, assuming that the latter do not age too quickly and come to be churches with a decisive inward and only an occasional outward orientation.

In this definiteness, the ministry laid on the community has (2) its limitation. We shall consider this from two angles. It is determined by the fact that it is ministry, and more specifically by the fact that it is ministry of witness.

It is ministry—ministry to God and to man, no less, no more, no other. It is no less, and therefore in no conceivable form is it either a neutral co-existence with God and man or a domination and control on the one side or the other. Ministry means active subordination. As the ministry of the community, this means its active subordination to God from whom it derives and therefore to man to whom it turns and whom it is to serve if it serves God. God demands, and man may expect of it, no less than faithfulness in this active subordination. That which it has to do in obedience to its mission and task must not sink below this level.

Yet no more is demanded nor to be expected. It can only serve God and man. It can neither carry through God's work to its goal nor lead men to the point of accepting it. It transgresses the limits of its mission and task, is guilty of culpable arrogance and engages in a futile undertaking if it makes this the goal and end of its activity, assuming responsibility both for the going out of the Word of God and its coming to man. If this takes place at all, it does so in the power of the Holy Spirit over whom it has no power. Its task is simply to serve this happening, i.e., to assist both God and man. This task is serious and difficult enough. It can and should be grateful that it is committed to it and that it is spared anything more. It can and should be humble enough to be content with it. It is called and engaged to faithfulness in service and not to mastery.

Finally, it is not commanded to do anything other than render its specific service to God and man, and therefore it is not commanded to pursue *allotria* which, quite irrespective of their possibility, importance or necessity, cannot be its concern and can only disturb and confuse the action demanded of it. It can, of course, be said of all organic and inorganic creation that secretly but very really it stands in the service of both God and man, and that it probably does so in its own way far more effectively and gloriously than the poor Christian community. Yet in the context of this great and comprehensive ministry of all creation the Christian community has its own specific function and service. In this context it is indeed distinguished to the extent that in it and in it alone is it a matter of the service of reconciliation, and this in the direct and concrete following of the prophetic work of the One in whom God has accomplished it. It is also distinguished to the extent that as such it does not take place secretly like that of the rest of creation, to be manifested in its reality only in and with the final revelation of Jesus Christ, but that even in its weakness and corruption, in anticipation of the disclosure of the secret of all creation, it is already revealed to be service of God and man here and now in time and space. It is as well for the community to keep to the ministry assigned it. If it is the creature of God in exemplary fashion, it is not the only creature. If its ministry has central significance for the whole, it cannot comprehend or replace or even transcend and improve all that takes place as the quiet service of God and man offered by creation in nature and history. And if the measure of what is required of it certainly cannot be foreseen and fixed in advance and in general, because new and very unexpected tasks might constantly be asked of it within the sphere of its service, what is demanded will never be immeasurable, but always measurable. In no time or situation is the Church called to do anything and everything, but always and everywhere there are other things which do not fall within the sphere of its service and which it is well advised to leave alone if it is rightly to do what it should. One constant criterion for distinguishing other things from what is demanded is perhaps as follows. Where it is not clear in a given case that it has to render service of both God and man in that strict connexion, where under any title it is a matter of a supposed service of God to which the character of service of man is totally alien, or where under any title there is question of a supposed service of man which has nothing to do with the service of God, there a plain warning is given, and, as in the case of the " too little " and the " too much," it is clearly shown the limit of its ministry which it must not transgress.

Its ministry is also limited, however, by the fact that it is materially determined as a ministry of witness. For the sake of comprehension, and in order not to overlook anything of importance, we may again say that it is no less, no more and no other than the ministry of witness required of it and constituting it.

It is no less. The community is the people of Christians who even as individuals are decisively and essentially witnesses. It is the company of those who could and can hear the Word of God spoken in the existence of the great, active and primary Witness in His prophetic office, of the Mediator between God and man. It is the company of those who could and can hear His Word of the atonement made in Him, of the divine covenant concluded and sealed in Him, of the divine lordship established in Him, and therefore of the new and true world reality. It is the company of those who could and can hear it in order to represent it to all other men. Their ministry consists in causing this divine Word of this divine work to be heard in the world, and therefore in confession to the world as His witnesses that Jesus Christ is the One in whom it has taken place and is revealed. Beneath the level of the witness determined by its origin, theme and content the ministry of the community must never sink if it is to be true and genuine service of both God and man. The matter in which it is engaged is no less than this.

It must not happen, for example, that it should have to propose only a particularly radical criticism of human existence and the human situation in its disintegration and destruction. What it has to attest is the light which has broken into the world in Jesus Christ, not the darkness into which it falls in order to dispel it. For the same reason its concern cannot be merely with human questions, longings and hopes for an expected alteration of the world, but only with that which is already accomplished in Jesus Christ, which is already reality, and which hastens towards its full and definitive manifestation. For the same reason again it cannot be concerned only with abstract doctrines, principles, ideas and ways of salvation. It has to attest the crucified and risen Jesus Christ who in His person is salvation and its self-declaration. Certainly God and man might be served by critical analyses of existence, by the expression of serious human questions and longings, by the proclamation of correct ideas of salvation. Nor is there any reason why such undertakings with all their doubtful features should not be secondarily accepted by God in His grace along with many other human thoughts and words and works, and therefore sanctified and made helpful to men. The only thing is that these things are too small in relation to the witness required of the community. The community of Jesus Christ cannot rest content with them. It must not transgress the lower limit marked by them.

Again, however, no more is demanded or expected than this definite witness. The reconciliation of the world to God, the divine covenant, the kingdom of God, the new reality of the world, cannot be its work. Nor can the manifestation of these things. It is not itself Jesus Christ either acting for the world or speaking to it. It is only the particular people which on the basis of His gracious self-declaration may know about Him, believe in Him and hope in Him. It has to confess Him, therefore, according to the knowledge granted to it. It has to attest Him to the world as the work of God accomplished for it and the Word of God going out to it. What is demanded and expected therewith is glorious enough to render superfluous any grasping at higher possibilities. It is also serious and difficult enough to claim all its attention, fidelity, courage and resources.

But it is not commanded to represent, introduce, bring into play or even in a sense accomplish again in its being, speech and action either reconciliation, the covenant, the kingdom or the new world reality. It is not commanded even in the earthly-historical sphere to take the place of Jesus Christ. In so doing it would only arrogate to itself something which is absolutely beyond its capacity, in which it could achieve only spurious results, and which would finally involve it in failure. In so doing it would do despite to Jesus Christ Himself as the one Doer of the work of God and the primary and true Witness of this work, becoming a hindrance to what He Himself wills to do and accomplish. Its prophecy would *ipso facto* become false, unauthorised and misleading prophecy. It lives as true prophecy by the fact that it remains distinct from His, that it is subject to it, that it does not try to replace it, but that with supreme power and yet with the deepest humility it points to the work of God accomplished in Him and the Word of God spoken in Him, inviting to gratitude for this work and the hearing of this Word, but not pretending to be claimed for more than this indication and invitation, nor to be capable of anything more.

In the sphere of Romanism and Eastern Orthodoxy we have examples of the transgression of this upper limit of the ministry of the community to the extent that in them the Church ascribes to itself, to its life and institutions and organs, particularly to its administration of the sacraments and the means of grace entrusted to it, and in Romanism to its government by the teaching office, certain functions in the exercise of which it is not only not subordinate to Jesus Christ but is ranked alongside and in practice even set above Him as His vicar in earthly history, its ministry of witness being left far behind as it shares with Him an existence and activity which are both human and divine, and human in divine reality and omnipotence. Yet even outside these particular historical spheres there is no lack of notions and enterprises in which Christendom inclines more or less clearly and definitely to what is attempted along these lines, trying to give to its resolutions the character of semi-divine decisions, to its offices a semi-divine dignity, to its proclamation the quality of semi-divine revelation, to its sacraments the nature of once-for-all established channels of grace, to its efforts *ad extra* the character of the establishment and extension of the kingdom of God, and in short seeking to understand and set up itself, the Church, as a direct representation of Jesus Christ, its existence as a vicariate, its action as a direct repetition and continuation of His. This is the very thing which it must not do whether on a large scale or a small, or indeed the very smallest.

The community does not achieve less but more, i.e., it fulfils the truly high ministry required of it, if it observes the limit set for it by the fact that, like John the Baptist, it is not worthy to loose the shoes' latchets of Him who comes, being willing to shine, not as itself the light, but as its witness and therefore in the brightness of the one true light. On the other hand, it does not accomplish more but less, and is indeed in danger of serving darkness instead of light, if it will not follow this example and observe this upper limit.

We may again conclude by saying that it is not commanded to

do other than render this definite ministry of witness.   Alongside
Jesus Christ and the world reality renewed in Him there may well
be other realities demanding to be recognised, acknowledged, confessed and attested.   There may well be spiritual and natural forces
which also, and to some degree perhaps with good reason, claim our
notice and will to be proclaimed in their dignity and importance.
This may and perhaps must be done, though we must be careful
to see that they deserve it and also to consider the consequences if
we do hear and obey them.   It is indisputable, however, that in the
ministry of the community there can never be any question of the
attestation of these other realities and forces even in the sense of an
ancillary task subordinate to the main one.   This work is to be left
to their own authorised or unauthorised prophets.   They may, of
course, be significant to the community and worthy of its consideration.
Nothing human can be wholly out of place in the sphere of its own
task.   According to the circumstances of the case all the factors and
lights which under God's providence are operative in the sphere of
His creation and important to man deserve its serious and even
zealous attention.   But it does not stand in the service of any of the
factors or lights in question.   It cannot combine the witness to which
it is engaged with the attestation of the reality, dignity and significance
of these other lights and factors.

Alongside its proclamation of the message of Jesus Christ, it cannot, for
example, work also for the dissemination of the knowledge of this or that higher
or lower world, nor for a particular understanding of nature or culture, nor
for the establishment of this or that western or eastern philosophy of history,
society or the state and the corresponding ethics.   It cannot attach itself to any
world-view, nor can it produce, propagate and defend any supposed Christian
world-view of its own.   It can accompany all efforts in this direction sympathetically and more or less hopefully, but in no circumstances may it make common
cause with them.   It can respectfully acknowledge their results.   But it cannot
accept any responsibility for them.   It cannot appropriate them nor inscribe
them on its own banner.

Why not ?   Because in so doing, even though there might be
occasional and temporary success, or at least not total failure, yet
it would squander the time and energy which are demanded by
its own task with its call for the strictest concentration and the
most strenuous effort.   Again, in so doing it would enter uncertain
ground on which for the sake of the trustworthiness of its own witness
it might be compelled to revoke to-morrow what it maintains to-day
or maintain to-morrow what it thinks it should deny to-day.   Again,
in so doing, by linking its witness with the attestations of such
conceptions, however good in themselves, it would make it suspect
to those who are perhaps quite disposed to hear it but who for solid
or less solid reasons cannot accept the conception in question.   Again,
in so doing, it would forget or even deny that whatever is true or

enduring in these conceptions is much better expressed and honoured in its own witness if this is given its full scope and content than by their proclamation as a subsidiary task outside the context of its witness. Finally, in the service of the attestation of Jesus Christ it cannot even with the best intentions serve two different lords, no matter who the second may be. It can serve Him only whole-heartedly or not at all. In this respect as well it must thus observe the limit of its ministry of witness.

In its definiteness and therefore limitation as witness and ministry of witness, however, it has also (3) its promise. It needs it. The community, feeble people that it is, needs the assurance that as it undertakes and seeks to fulfil its ministry its cause is righteous, that as it discharges it according to the measure of its knowledge and resources it is not left to its own knowledge and resources, and that it does not finally act in vain. It stood and stands so isolated in relation to the world, to the godless, the indifferent and the pious, to the ancient and the modern, to the western and the eastern, to the middle-class, proletarian and bohemian world. In the exercise of its ministry it sees itself confronted by so many unmistakeable positions of power and not altogether illegitimate claims that it might be genuinely assailed by anxiety as to the justice of its own cause when it is called in question and even contested by so many. In addition it is troubled by the modest and unassuming and even pitiable nature of its own ability and the means at its disposal, and especially by the almost irresistible temptations which come to it and the resultant failures and distortions. Again, it has to face the question whether its whole concern for the witness borne by it, whatever the effects of its activity in this ministry, is not after all a crying in the storm, a writing in the sand or even the water, a futile running up against a cliff. What can it oppose to these many and varied anxieties ? How can it keep its courage and the power to endure under this pressure ? Is there not cause for astonishment that, with all the defeats and failures and mistakes which it has made in its history and still makes at every point to-day, Christianity has not completely strayed from its ministry and given up the struggle ? Is there not cause for astonish-ment that there have always been new men and generations ready and willing to take up its ministry with new courage and pursue it along new ways, all sooner or later oppressed by the same anxieties, all followed yet again by others who notwithstanding have still been ready and plainly constrained to take up the same cause, but all obviously needing the assurance to make it possible ? A powerful counter-pressure is needed if the ministry of the community is not to prove impracticable and to crumble under the pressure of these not unfounded anxieties, if it is to be continually sustained and renewed in the work of its ministry and therefore in its existence.

Nor is this counter-pressure lacking. It is, in fact, stronger than the pressure of the anxieties. It is strong enough to make it possible for the community to discharge its ministry, continually sustaining and renewing this ministry and therefore itself. We refer to the promise which is no less characteristic of its ministry in its definiteness than is the limitation. It is not proper to it in the sense of a security which it possesses as it discharges its ministry, or a quality inherent to it, like the great or small position in the world, the members and institutions, the codified or uncodified historical traditions, which it thinks it possesses, as though all these things, too, were not really on loan to it. What is true of all these things, however, is particularly true of the promise which sustains, protects and renews it. It is not a state in which its ministry is automatically and once and for all protected against and superior to the questioning which assails it on every hand. It is rather the mystery of the history of its ministry which is free and always remains free. It characterises it as it is given to the community and received by it. Its ministry of witness is neither divine nor semi-divine. It is the unequivocally human speech and action of a people like all others. It stands always in supreme need of assurance. It never shows itself in any respect to be assured in advance. If the question is raised what it has to set against all the anxieties, the answer is that it has nothing of its own to set against them. Of itself it could only be hopelessly defeated by and subjected to them. What it needs, but what it is also given, is the promise which marks its ministry. It is to be noted and grasped that as a free promise it is the needed assurance which actually comes and is therefore proper to its ministry. Nor is it a purely verbal and external assurance. It is a supremely real and internal. This is shown by the fulfilments which it brings with it. Yet it is a free promise which comes to characterise the ministry of the community only in the form of a gift, so that it can never have it at its disposal but only hope for it as it discharges its ministry. Yet it is really proper to it just because it is free and can never be more than the subject of its prayer and thanksgiving. In its very freedom it does in fact secure the ministry of the community, protecting it against all those threats and the consequences of the insecurity in which alone it can discharge it in relation to the world and especially itself. It thus exerts the counter-pressure which is more than a match for the pressure under which the community discharges it.

The promise which always does this, and by which the ministry of the community is thus always assured, is, however, quite simply the origin, theme and content of its witness, namely, that which is said and entrusted to the community in and with its gathering, upbuilding and sending in order that it may repeat it to the world to which it is sent according to the measure of its knowledge. What is said to it, i.e., the Word of God concerning reconciliation, the covenant, the kingdom and the new reality of the world as spoken to it in and by Jesus Christ in the truth and power proper to Him in every dimension, is as such the promise and assurance given to the community, sustaining its witness, and victoriously encountering the pressure under which it stands. The risen and living Jesus Christ Himself, who is the origin, theme and content of its witness, who is indeed the Word of God to be attested by it, gives it this promise and assurance. It will be seen that it is truly free because it is His personal promise. It cannot say to itself what is said to it and entrusted to it to repeat. It can only allow it to be said to it, and in its ministry of witness repeat it as that which is said to it. Similarly it cannot give to itself the promise and assurance in the power of which it may and should attempt its ministry of witness. Nor can it seize it as its own even when it is given. It cannot dispose of it as though it were its own possession and under its own control. It does not have it institutionally. It does not have it even in the power of its own faith and knowledge, its own love and inspiration, or indeed its own prayer. It has it as it is given to and received by it in the power of the Holy Spirit as the power of the personal Word of Jesus Christ. It does receive and have it, however, as the promise and assurance of the living Jesus Christ coming to it in all its incommensurability as the work and Word of God. As such it characterises its ministry from one day and century to another. Hence it can and should know that it is held and carried by it, and be of good courage in the execution of its ministry. The promise which marks its ministry guarantees that, no matter how threateningly they may open up on every hand, the gates of hell (Mt. 16[18]) shall not swallow it up.

It is true that the promise which establishes and preserves its ministry is always a promise in relation to everything which it is and does in this ministry. It is true that it has always to reach out for it with empty hands. Yet another aspect has also to be incidentally recalled, namely, that the promise does not stand like a closed and brazen heaven above it, but can always demonstrate and confirm itself in specific fulfilments. In the history of the community there have never been lacking distinct individual experiences of the truth of the promise given to it and the reliability of the assurance granted therein. Nor need there be any fear that it will ever be in want of such experiences. Never and nowhere, or at least never for long or in every place, has there been a complete absence of more or less clear signs, signals and demonstrations of the action of the Holy Spirit accompanying its way, again confirming its ministry, and encouraging it to perform it. Not infrequently, and sometimes most impressively, it will come to taste and see " how gracious the Lord is " and to realise that it is not so isolated in the world as might appear (like Kierkegaard's individual illumined by a beam shining vertically upon him from above), but that in its threatened and indeed lost position in this dark valley it does at least—and this is a great deal—find itself in the good fellowship of angels and sometimes in the good fellowship of men, who make it plain that its mission to the world is not the absurdity which it might often seem to be. That its cause is just, i.e., that it is on the right way in its serving of the cause of Jesus Christ, may in certain encounters and phenomena shine out with the brightness, if also the transience, of a flash of lightning, so that it can never again be forgotten. It may equally suddenly, if perhaps as transiently, find itself in all simplicity stimulated to and enabled for thoughts and words and acts and movements which it could never have ascribed to itself, and in the boldness and power of which it could not easily recognise itself, i.e., its own vacillation and impotence. Fruits may fall into its lap and results accrue which it could never seriously expect. It may sometimes happen, as often described in Acts, that in spite of the dominant secular and religious obduracy there are in the world around small penetrations, that cracks suddenly appear in the wall of general ignorance and mis- understanding before which it has perhaps stood for a long time in complete helplessness but which is now seen not to be eternal. It may be that something begins to happen to all kinds of people around, so that they look and speak differently and take up new attitudes and tread new ways. It may be that here and there in some in- explicable way a new wind begins to blow and to impel whole groups of men like yachts in a new direction. Are these really fruits and results of its ministry of witness? Yes, even though we cannot perhaps speak of any causal connexion, they are along the lines and according to the intention of this witness, being obviously the sprouting of an unmistakeably evangelical seed. At any rate, there can be no doubt that in the world around the community, and among the men among whom it renders its service, everything does not have to remain the same, nor does it actually do so. The depressing aspect of the impotence, insignificance, uselessness and hopelessness of the activity of the community can suddenly change, nor does the change per- ceived by the community always have to be an illusion. Its ministry consists not only of much apparently hopeless weeding, ploughing and sowing, but sometimes also of joyful reaping. There are ful- filments of the promise by which it is sustained and borne in its ministry.

It is to be noted, of course, that the community does not live by such fulfilments, nor should it set itself to experience them nor seek to live by them. They cannot be more than signs. If it were more loyal and disciplined in the execution of its ministry, and if it had more open eyes and hearts, there would certainly be more of them and it could be more joyful and cheerful and pertinacious in the cause in hand. But it is not by the signs that it is sustained, protected, borne and secured in the discharge of its ministry. Even in the best conceivable circumstances they are no more than instructive, helpful, comforting, encouraging and admonishing indications of the promise itself which as such is the assurance needed by the community and actually given to it. They cannot, then, be equated with the latter. They are not the support unconditionally needed by the community. It must be prepared often to carry on without their support. It cannot reckon on it. Even when given, it will never be unconditional. It will always be limited, provisional and temporary. The community may be deceived in respect of it. It cannot be contested that there are false as well as genuine experiences of this kind. There are also times and situations when they are perhaps most desired but seem to be almost completely lacking or at least not to be experienced by the community. It will never in any respect place its confidence in either the possibility or the actual emergence and manifestation of such fulfilments. It will rejoice when they come and may be perceived, but it will not demand that they should. And it must see to it that it does not spoil everything by aiming at the emergence and manifestation of such fulfilments in the rendering of its service. Their appearance or non-appearance, the experiencing of them or not, is neither the purpose of its ministry, nor its power, nor the test of its authenticity, nor can it possibly be the measure of the faithfulness, the joy and the willingness with which it has to discharge it.

The reality which bears or rather glorifies it through all inward and outward assaults is the distinctive promise itself and as such. Not even the finest and most genuine fulfilment bears and glorifies it, but, as we may now put it, He whom it has to attest in its ministry, He whom it cannot emulate nor master, He with whom it cannot identify itself, He whom it can only follow as it renders its service, He who is within it only as its sovereign Lord. He is the secret of its history. It stands and goes as the people elected by Him from all eternity and called by Him in time in the power of His eternal electing. In so doing, it stands and goes on solid ground. It works in the power of His work, of the name hallowed in Him, the kingdom come in Him, the will of God done on earth as in heaven in Him. Not in its own power but in His, its work is neither meaningless nor futile. It serves in His task and under His responsibility. Hence it is more sure of its cause and more cheerful than any other people. In its modest function it works in connexion with the occurrence set in train, kept in motion and conducted to its goal by Him. In all modesty it thus has an active part in the overriding origin, meaning and scope of all creaturely history. It attests the one true Witness, and is thus covered and guaranteed, not by the immanent truth of its own witness, but by that of His witness. Appointed by Him, it may stand and go with Him, work with Him, serve with Him, achieve results with Him and be His witness. This is the promise which characterises its service and by which it may live.

In Jesus Christ this is a fulfilled promise. It is fulfilled with a height and breadth and depth before which the community in the discharge of its ministry can only be astonished and give thanks and pray, and of which all the fulfilments granted to it, and all that it may experience, can only be indications and reminders. The community can live neither by what it achieves and produces in its service nor by the fulfilments granted to it. It may live, however, and it can and should do so, by the promise of its ministry fulfilled in Jesus Christ. This cannot and will not fail as such. In relation to it, what can be the significance or power of the questions and anxieties which oppress it, of the lostness of its own position and right in face of the world, of the all too narrow limits of its own equipment and achievements, of the follies and errors of which it will always be guilty, of the dubious past, the pitiable present and the questionable future of its ministry ? As ought to be written on its heart and conscience by these questions and anxieties, it should never trust in itself nor try to draw on its own resources. But it can and should trust in the promise which it is given as it is impressed into service and which is fulfilled in Jesus Christ. The promise is unshakeable and infallible. It may also be clearly seen and firmly grasped. It exerts a superior counter-pressure against every pressure. It is its security in the insecurity, its strength in the weakness, its health in the latent or acute sickness, its wealth in the poverty, and its glory in the gloom of its service. It causes it to awaken out of every sleep, to take new courage in every hesitation, to venture new steps in every weariness. It thus enables it to endure and its history to go on from one day and generation to another. It allows and commands it to exist, for all its timidity and humility, with an unparalleled assurance, to persist in the cause which it does not bear but by which it is borne, to hasten forward in its ministry. Fulfilled in Jesus Christ, the promise of its ministry justifies the motto which it has been given : *fluctuat nec mergitur*.

In a second discussion we now go on to describe the nature of its ministry. We shall then have to speak of its forms. But first we ask concerning that which remains the same in every form. What is it that always takes place when its ministry is performed in accordance with the purpose of its existence in the world and task towards it ? The concept of witness has suggested itself in the whole of this section, as indeed in the preceding section on the vocation of the Christian. But what is meant by witness as the sum of what the Christian community has to render ? We may first answer in a word that witness as the sum of what must always take place in Christian ministry is declaration, exposition and address, or the proclamation, explication and application of the Gospel as the Word of God entrusted to it. We choose this sequence of the three elements for the sake of perspicuity. The emphasis can and must always fall equally definitely on all of them. They are all implicit and explicit in one another. The nature or essence of the ministry of the community as witness is one and the same in all three.

The ministry and therefore the witness of the community is essentially and in all forms and circumstances (1) the declaration of the Gospel. Whatever else the community may plan, undertake and do, whatever else it may or may not accomplish, it has always to introduce into the sphere of world-occurrence and to disclose to men a human historical fact which, not itself the kingdom of God but indicating it as a likeness, corresponds and points to the divine historical fact which constitutes the content of the Gospel. The point is that alongside and over against everything else that takes place in the world the witness of the community also occurs, that what God says in the Gospel concerning what He has done and does and is for man is accepted, answered and proclaimed by certain men. It is not in the power of the community to produce or even to reproduce the divine historical fact. Nor is it in its power to disclose it. It lives itself by the fact that God has created and reveals it, that He is actively and eloquently present in it. Yet it does lie in its power, in the power which it is given, to receive with human ear and heart and reason the Gospel which has this divine historical fact as its content, and to declare it with the human means at its disposal, thus introducing the human historical fact which corresponds to it and setting it alongside and over against everything else which takes place in the world. It has the power " in the name of our God to set up our banners " (Ps. 20⁵), to establish a sign, to say powerfully or weakly, but at any rate in the light, what Jesus has said to it in darkness, to proclaim skilfully or unskilfully, but at any rate openly on the housetops, what it has heard in the ear (Mt. 10²⁷)—a task which in itself, as a human movement, is no other, neither easier nor more difficult, than what other men and human groups are always doing in a different sense and for a different purpose. Its ministry is to make this indicatory movement as well or badly as it can.

The sign which it establishes thereby must not be lacking in the world. The world needs the human historical fact of the declaration of the Gospel. It differs from the community in that the Gospel as news of the decisively important divine historical fact is still unknown to it. The community has to receive this news, and to do so in order to pass it on to others, from men to other men. It can only acquaint them with it. It cannot be its task to manifest it to the world in such sort that the world may believe and know it. This can only be the work of the prophecy of Jesus Christ Himself, of the Holy Spirit. The demand is not too severe, however, that it should acquaint others with what the Gospel says to the extent that it has itself received it, just as others communicate that which is new. Its ministry of witness is to do this. Nor is the demand too severe that it should declare the Gospel, or its content as received by it, in a way which is not muffled or confused or embarrassed, but in clear and strong and unhesitating indicatives, just as clear and strong and unhesitating proclamations of other supposed or real facts are also made to it. It need not be ashamed of its own declaration (Rom. 1[16]). It need not be afraid to place it alongside and over against others. Compared with what others have to say, the substance of its own proclamation is better. Indeed, it alone is good. Again, it need not grumble that it can fulfil the task laid upon it only with human instruments. No more is demanded than that it should actually make use of what is humanly possible with all its energies and in a way appropriate to the cause in hand. Finally, it need have no anxiety concerning the success of its witness. Its Lord rules ; its own task is to serve Him. Its Lord triumphs, even though it does not perceive it ; its own task is simply to assist with its own word and therefore its witness. This is, however, demanded of it.

To declare and thus to proclaim the Gospel means, however, to utter and to cause to be heard in the world, with no less distinctness than many other things, and with incomparably greater peace, certainty, freedom and joy, the grace of God addressed to man as His creature, the covenant concluded and sealed between Him and man, the act of God in which it took place that He reconciled an opposing and gainsaying world to Himself, in short, the existence of the living Jesus Christ yesterday, to-day and to-morrow as the content of the Gospel. As it does this, it sets up that banner. This is what must take place no matter what the cost, the result or the circumstances, and to the postponement and even the exclusion of all other purposes and enterprises. For it cannot do this and yet at the same time plan and attempt and do all kinds of other things. The one thing can be done in many different forms, directly or indirectly, explicitly or implicitly, in some kind of human speech or in eloquent silence, in specific acts and modes of conduct or in intentional and well-considered abstentions from action. But the one thing must take place unequivocally and unconditionally if the community discharges its ministry. The Christian community may be known by the fact that it is concerned to do it. Individual Christians may also be known by the fact that as members of the community they have a direct or indirect part in this action, their very lives actually declaring the Gospel. The community as such and the community in its members fulfils its responsibility that the grace, the covenant, reconciliation, the life of Jesus Christ and there-fore the kingdom of God should be indicated and shown to the world, that the knowledge of them should be shared with it. If it did not do this, it would not be the Christian community. It may be that to some extent it attains this appointed goal, which is a near and not a distant goal. It may be that with its declaration it simply sets the world an annoying riddle, or leaves it indifferent. But its whole being and action in every aspect and form has the sterling content of witness in the simple or varied proclamation : " Jesus Christ is risen, He is risen indeed." Otherwise it does not have any sterling content at all, and therefore, though it may not be lacking in majesty and possibly results, it has no promise. To be sure, the community cannot fulfil as such the task laid upon it without at once, as we shall see, indicating the meaning and scope of what is attested by it and to that extent necessarily striding on to explanation and address, to exposition and reference, to explication and application of the Gospel. Nevertheless, it is vital that whatever it may attempt and achieve along the lines of these two other elements in its witness must have its compass, backbone and specific weight in the simple declaration of the Gospel as such. It is vital that in all its explication and application it should simply proclaim it, repeating, confirming and emphasising its declaration, and giving it the true mark of a likeness of the self-declaration of Jesus Christ. Certainly the authenticity, dignity and power of its witness do not consist in the naïve force of its proclamation, as they do not consist in the fulness of its explication or the earnestness and emphasis of its application. Yet if its witness is to be authentic, dignified and powerful, then it must also have the naïve force of a simple proclamation of the Gospel permeating and sustaining all its activity. Lacking this, its whole ministry would not merely suffer a partial but a total lack.

The ministry and therefore the witness of the community is also essentially and in all circumstances and forms (2) the explanation or explication of the Gospel. To explain is in general terms to point to the proper clarity or immanent light of something. It is to show how, without ceasing to be one and simple, it articulates and unfolds itself, and therefore makes itself perceptible and intelligible. The community's ministry of witness also consists directly in this explaining and unfolding of the Gospel, in making it intelligible. Now the divine historical fact which constitutes its content is not dumb and does not therefore conceal its meaning or fall victim to ambiguity. It is a fact which shines forth from within, which speaks for itself, which indicates and unfolds its own meaning. We remember that the work of God is as such His Word also. The history of the covenant, of reconciliation, is as such the history of revelation as well. The new life of the world created in Jesus Christ is also as such its light. And so that divine-human fact, declaring itself, establishes knowledge. This knowledge is the knowledge of faith. But it is true knowledge. It creates the *intellectus fidei*, *fides* necessarily being *fides quaerens intellectum*. The Gospel gives itself to be understood, and wills to be understood. Hence the human historical fact which corresponds to its content, and which it is the task of the ministry of the community to introduce, consists not only in the declaration of the Gospel but also in its explanation. It has to follow the elucidation which constantly issues from the self-declaration of Jesus Christ, from the content of the Gospel itself. It has to copy with the human means at its disposal the work of the prophecy of the divine-human Mediator.

Two basic points are to be noted in this connexion. First, the self-enunciating content of the Gospel does not permit a mere unfruitful acquaintance, i.e., a purely formal and mechanical reception, and therefore a proclamation which may be loud and clear but is empty because it is undeveloped and unarticulated declaration or mere assertion. It is not itself empty in its encounter with the community. It develops, articulates and explains itself. And it demands to be proclaimed accordingly, i.e., in such sort that it is understood and seeks understanding. Hence the community cannot escape the implied task of explanation.

Secondly, the self-enunciating content of the Gospel does not permit any autonomous explanation, i.e., any interpretation other than according to its own direction and from its own chosen standpoints. It is not to be mastered. It is not to be invested with fulness and articulation. It is not to be treated as if it did not explain itself and make itself intelligible. The community is given the task of listening to its self-explanation and then of using the human means at its disposal, not to proceed independently, but to follow it. It has not to shape it according to its own needs or whims, but to follow the shape which it has already assumed. It is when it follows in this way that it fulfils its declaration as *intellectus fidei*. If it cannot refuse the Gospel the ministry of explanation, this can only be a ministry, and indeed a ministry of witness. Pledged to the Gospel, it cannot fail to set up the sign which it has to give to the world by serving its understanding and by leading to its understanding. Yet in so doing it can only set up *its* sign or banner and not try to set up its own.

The world has need that the Gospel should be explained to it as it is declared. By the world we mean the men to whom it is addressed but who as yet have no acquaintance with it, let alone knowledge. The community has no power to create this knowledge. But it has to acquaint them with it, or to set them on the way at the end of which—by the work of the prophecy of Jesus Christ Himself, or of the Holy Ghost—this knowledge will be opened up to them and there can take place for them, too, the *intellectus fidei*. The way to this goal always consists in the fact that, whatever they may or may not make of it, the content of the Gospel becomes intelligible, perspicuous and evident to them, so that they realise what is at issue in it, what it has to believe, and in faith to know, as truth. Otherwise they are not really made acquainted with it, and there is no point of reference for the work of the Holy Spirit which leads them to knowledge. The man in whom this work takes place is the man to whom the Gospel is both told and also explained. It can and should be explained to him. This is where the ministering witness of the community comes in to the extent that it includes a second element. There can and should be taken from man the illusion that knowledge is possible only in the form of a *sacrificium intellectus*, and the excuse that he is neither capable of this nor willing to make it. While the community will not presume to try to accomplish what is not its work, it can show him that even from the human standpoint this knowledge is quite as much in order as any other human knowledge. In other words, it understands what it is saying as enlightened and guided by the origin, theme and content of its witness. A people like others, it can and should make perceptible to other peoples what it declares in it. This, then, in connexion with its declaration and borne by it, is the second inalienable mark of its witness. It will be careful not to overestimate what it can do in this direction. It will see to it that it does not regard its little explanation as divine revelation, that it does not make it out to be such, only to be disappointed and perplexed when it does not have the appropriate effect. But it will also be careful not to bury its talent, not to withhold from the Gospel and those to whom it is directed the limited but definite service which it can render in the form of an explanation of its declaration and therefore of the Gospel. Here again it is true that no more is demanded, but this is demanded. It is obvious, of course, that whatever it can do in this direction can only be a human work and therefore an attempt which will always be imperfect and call for further more serious and careful attempts. What else is the whole of Church history but a constant attempt on the part of the community not only to declare the Gospel to the world but to make it intelligible and therefore to explain it, to bring out the perspicuity of its content? In this form its witness can never cease. And it is important to affirm that, while this limited ministry may often be a failure in practice, it does not have to be. If this proximate goal is not attained, the fault lies neither with the content of the Gospel, with its lack of the necessary clarity and therefore at bottom with its lack of rationality and perspicuity, nor with the human means at the disposal of the community, which are adequate in themselves to reveal clearly in human terms that which is intrinsically clear. If it does not succeed in showing some at least that what it proclaims to the world is not an absurdity but a communication which, however it may be received, is self-consistent and to that extent meaningful, it is also at fault if it throws the responsibility for its failure on the men to whom it is sent. For it is surely possible for even the most obstinate of unbelievers, whether or not they can come to a knowledge of the truth, at least to appreciate the inner consistency and to that extent the meaning of the evangelical message. If they do not, the community is well advised to ask itself whether this is not because of a deficiency in its own attention to the inner clarity, rationality and perspicuity of the Gospel on the one side and neglect of the human means at its disposal on the other. It is thus advised to seek the fault in itself rather than the wicked world, and therefore with new zest and seriousness to make new and more energetic efforts in this direction. The Gospel is not generally knowable. But it is generally intelligible and explicable. For its content is rational and not irrational.

To explain the Gospel is to trace the points and lines and contours of its content in the relations and proportions in which it discloses and explains itself, and to do so, not with divine skill and power, but with the human skill and power given to the community as the people of God. To explain the Gospel is to define and describe the nature, existence and activity of God as Creator, Reconciler and Redeemer, the grace, the covenant and the work of reconciliation with all that these include and in the living terms of the manifestation, life, death and resurrection of Jesus Christ. It is to do all this, according to the measure of God's own Word, in the constantly changing forms of human consideration, thought and expression. It is to introduce this whole occurrence on to the human scene in a way in which it is not knowable but at least intelligible and perspicuous. It is to cause it to be told to men in human terms. The vital thing in so doing is that the whole content of the Gospel in all its elements and dimensions should be allowed to be its own principle of explanation, that under no pretext or title should alien principles of explanation in the form of metaphysical, anthropological, epistemological or religio-philosophical presuppositions be intruded upon it, that it should not be measured by any other standards of what is possible than its own, that answers should not be given to any other questions than those raised by itself, that it should not be forced into any alien scheme but left as it is and understood and expounded as such. To explain the Gospel is generally and very simply to narrate the history which God Himself has inaugurated, which He rules, in which He has taken the world and man to Himself, and in which man finds himself taken up into intercourse and fellowship with Him. And it means in detail to indicate all the individual elements, moments and aspects of the content of the evangelical message, not as a collection or mosaic of static Christian truths, nor as mere parts of a Christian or other system, but dynamically as elements, moments and aspects of that history, i.e., of the history of salvation and revelation. The history which has here taken place is as such (Lk. 2^15) the fact at issue. We have called it the divine historical fact in correspondence with which the community, turning to the world in which it lives, has to introduce the analogy of the human historical fact of its witness. In the measure that it wearies of the general and detailed task, perhaps taking up or accepting other tasks, it ceases to be a witness, neglecting or even betraying its ministry, and continuing to owe to God and the world what is due to them. On the other hand, in the measure that it gathers all the means at his disposal and seeks patiently and zealously to "teach," i.e., to recount that history as such, it is a witness, performing its ministry and justifying its existence before God and man. To explain the Gospel is to expound, unfold and articulate its content, with no effacement of its unity and simplicity, but rather in enhancement of its unity and simplicity. It is to assert and honour it synoptically in all its richness, displaying the place and manner of each individual part. It is to make known the periphery in each section as that of the true centre, and the centre as in every respect that of the distinctive periphery. When the community is occupied with this explanation of the Gospel in every form of its ministry, there arises as its human work the likeness of the kingdom of God, to represent which is its modest but definite task and the meaning of its existence and ministry. When it does this, or rather tries to do it according to its ability, it makes the Gospel perceptible, perspicuous and intelligible to the world, since the world can see and recognise and understand this sign as such. The community leaves it to God whether or not, or how far, it may also be knowable to the world and actually known by it. It can and should leave this to him. As we read in 1 Corinthians 3[7], it may plant and water, but God gives the increase. And as we read in 1 Corinthians 4[2], no more is demanded of stewards than that they should be found faithful. But this is demanded.

The ministry and therefore the witness of the community is also essentially and in all forms and circumstances (3) evangelical address, i.e., proclamation and explication in the form of application. For this reason it cannot achieve its declaration and explanation in a vacuum. For it does not itself live in a vacuum. In every age and situation it stands in definite relations to the world around, i.e., non-Christians, who like its own members are above all living men who have in some way gone astray and are therefore under assault. What it does, it does in these relations, or else it only seems to do something as the community, but in reality does nothing. Similarly it cannot achieve its declaration and explanation in a vacuum, for in so doing it would not really declare or explain. It can do so only as it genuinely turns to the men of the world around. It has to speak to them, and to explain to them. It has to have them in mind when it introduces that likeness of the kingdom of God. It would not really represent this likeness if in its action there were not heard the echo of the Word and call of God Himself, which does not go out into the void, but is directed to the whole human race and every man. When it speaks, therefore, it, too, must have men not only in view but also in mind and heart in its whole action. It cannot speak past them or over them. It must know them, not merely to gather from its knowledge how best it may declare and explain the Gospel to them, but to utter and to cause to be heard as applying to them the Gospel which they do not know and which is indeed continually new even to the community itself as it declares and explains itself. It must really know them, the presupposition in view of which it speaks to them, the right with which it does so, the point where they really are what they are and where they may be reached when addressed. This point consists in the fact that God has made and loves them too, that Jesus Christ has died and risen again for them too, and that reception of the Word of God and obedience to it is their first and final destiny too. It is for this reason that the Gospel applies to them. It is on this basis and with this in view that the community has to address them, and indeed to appeal to them, since it cannot be taken for granted that they can or will hear what they really are. The only relevant and legitimate answer to the question how this is to happen, the answer which does not exclude but includes and dominates as a *conditio sine qua non* all other conceivable answers, is to the effect that the witness of the community must be evangelical address, i.e., address in which men are claimed in advance for what is to be made known to them as the content of the Gospel. This content must form not only the declaration and explanation but the appeal with which the community turns to the world. What option has the community but to love, and to address in love, the men whom it knows to be loved by God ? In the form of bitter and threatening accusation spreading alarm and terror, the proclamation of the Gospel, even though it has made an impression, has never really reached the world or set it on the way of knowledge to which it should be called by the community. Without either deviations or reservations, its appeal must call men to the rest and peace of God, inviting them to the feast which is prepared (Mt. 22⁴, Lk. 14⁷) and thus summoning them to joy. As this evangelical appeal it can never go out in a way which is sufficiently loud or pointed.

The world needs this appeal. It needs to be given a jolt and moved in a particular direction by the witness of the community and its declaration and explanation of the Gospel. It has no lack of jolts and pushes in other directions. It is constantly engaged in other movements, but not in this one movement—for how is it to start and who is to summon and impel it ? Yet this is the movement to salvation, to its new reality already given by God its Creator. In fulfilment of this movement it has to believe, and in so doing to know " the things which belong unto its peace " (Lk. 19⁴²). No man can create for it this faith and knowledge. Even the Christian community, which is only a human people, cannot do so. The call and impulsion to this movement can be only the work of God, of the prophecy of Jesus Christ, of the Holy Spirit. But the Christian community can and should serve God and man by at least calling man to the way of knowledge with its witness, by at least giving an indirect push in the direction of salvation and peace. It does this as it does not merely present but proclaims the Gospel, making it known with the obvious intention of winning the ears and heart to which it is directed for the resolve and venture of faith. The likeness of the fatherly love of God which it has to offer is completely spoiled, and its witness does not perform its service, if its declaration and explanation of the Gospel are not as such a dynamic, if only a humanly dynamic, invitation and wooing, a summons to faith, and therewith a sign of the nearness of salvation, of the accomplished removal of human error, wickedness, confusion and need, of the most radical alteration of its nature and situation, of the invading kingdom of God. The community has to set up this sign by not merely presenting to men its declaration and explanation of the Gospel but by laying it right in front of them, addressing them on the assumption that it is valid and effective for them too, on the assumption of the truth of the Gospel. As the human historical fact of its witness has the nature and character of an appeal, it becomes a fact which at least sets the world concretely in the reflection of the divine promise given to it, thus concretely affecting and limiting the other facts of world-occurrence, concretely challenging the necessary sequence of its course and concretely opening up a new horizon of its whole being and existence. In its form as an appeal addressed to men, the ministry of the community becomes and is itself a real if peculiar world factor which does not transcend the nexus of others but does point beyond and secretly revolutionise it. The community cannot give the world more than an intra-worldly jolt of this kind. Even with the most powerful and heartfelt appeal which it may make to them, it cannot change men. But with its appeal it can set before them the act of the love of God in which He has already changed them. It can make them aware that the revelation and knowledge of this act are awaiting them. It can thus make an impact in their lives and in world-occurrence. It can encourage their movement in the direction of faith and knowledge— —a movement which as such will already imply a small provisional change in the form and structure of their being. Where the community really fulfils its ministry, it calls men to faith, makes this impact in their lives and in world-occurrence, and excites a readiness which as such implies a small and provisional but real change in their being and action. It is God alone who by the light of His revelation can bring them to the goal of knowledge. The work of the community, however, is to encourage readiness for it and thus to set them on the way to the goal. It does this as it does not spare either itself or them evangelical address.

To address men evangelically, however, is decisively to present to them the great likeness of the declaration and explanation of the Gospel in such a way that they come to see its crucial application to them, that so far as any human word can do so it pricks their hearts

(Ac. 2[37]), that it brings them to realise that the reference is to them, or to a supremely general truth which as such demands their personal cognisance and knowledge. To address men evangelically is to challenge as strongly as possible their illusion that this is something peculiar which applies only to special individuals needing and capable of religion, and to make as clear to them as possible that they have to do with the reality which is the secret of the existence of all men and the whole world, and which as such is directly their own secret and that of their whole life. Evangelical address as the community's ministry of witness means the inclusion of all men near and far, from the very first and without fastidiousness even as the great sinners they are, like all members of the community. It means the bringing of all into the picture in the most literal sense. It means their incorporation into the likeness of the kingdom of God which is to be offered, into the circle of the validity of the content of the Gospel and therefore of grace, of the covenant, of reconciliation, of God's humiliation accomplished for the world in Jesus Christ in order that man might be exalted. In evangelical address the community, with a full awareness of what it is attempting, but constrained to make the attempt, strides across the frontier which separates non-Christian humanity from itself as the elect and calling people of God, taking the frontier seriously in the sense that, neither optimistically nor pessimistically but in faithfulness to its mission, it does not regard or address them as Jews or various kinds of heathen, as atheists, sceptics or indifferent, as victims of error, superstition or unbelief, nor as the total or partial hypocrites they may seem to be, but as the people of *christiani designati*, so that while the barrier between them is not destroyed it is removed in the act of encounter and common ground is occupied. How can it really address them if it will not make this attempt ? As it does so, it serves God and man as commanded. If it did not, it could serve neither God nor man. Thus evangelical address finally consists quite simply in the fact that at every point, in every form of its ministry and with all that we have described as its existence for the world, the community realises its existence concretely, not shunning the world but entering it and dealing with it as required. Even in its most effective address to men, it cannot exist for the world, enter it and deal with it as God does in Jesus Christ. It is for God and not His people to show them that they are in the sphere of lordship of His grace and thus to translate them into the state of faith and obedience. It is for His people, however, to give to the divine call, by which it is itself enlightened and translated into this state, the human response of taking it up with the human means at its disposal and passing it on to other men. If the community cannot make these men know what it knows, it can and should not merely proclaim and explain the Gospel but summon men with all its power to make ready for this knowledge.

Its situation and function are those of John the Baptist. As " the voice of one crying in the wilderness," it can and should " prepare the way of the Lord " and " make his paths straight " (Mk. 1³). More than this, i.e., baptising with the Holy Ghost (Mk. 1⁸), is not required of it. But it is required to baptise men with water, i.e., to summon them to readiness for the knowledge of the mightier One who comes after, to readiness for the baptism of the Spirit and thus for faith and obedience. Yet it is always conscious, and never forgets to make clear, that it is " not worthy to stoop down and unloose his shoes " (Mk. 1⁷).

It is commissioned and empowered to render to God and man this service of calling. It can and should render it. It should do so with great humility but also with great resolution.

The third and most far-reaching discussion which we have to undertake in relation to the ministry of the community concerns its forms, the differences and peculiarities of its orientation as these are characteristically expressed in, though not conditioned by, the distinctions in the human means and possibilities of which it may avail itself. On the basis of its origin, theme and content, the unity of its witness is concrete, and in its concreteness it is unity in the multiplicity of orientation. At every point and in all the functions of its life the Church is concerned to offer that great likeness of the kingdom of God. There can and should be no question of a cleavage in its activity. If it is ever concerned to do other than to offer that likeness and therefore to declare and preach the Gospel and appeal for faith and obedience, it neglects and denies and betrays its ministry. Nevertheless, its activity neither can nor should be uniform. If it is to be faithful in its ministry, it must be integrated and manifold. This inwardly necessary multiplicity of its activity carries with it the differentiation of human means which it uses to do what it is commissioned to do, and also the differentiation of aspects under which it presents itself externally to the world to which it is sent. This differentiation, then, is not a matter of accident or caprice. Nor is it an imperfection of which the community must be ashamed and which necessarily leads to defection. It is not a painful remnant of earth. On the contrary, its activity would be not merely imperfect but basically corrupt, because irrelevant, if it lacked this multiplicity, if it did not really entail the use of different human means, if it did not lead it to present itself under different aspects. The primary reason for this is that God Himself, the Lord of the community as the people called to His service among men, is absolutely one God as Father, Son and Holy Spirit, yet not with an undifferentiated, lifeless and motionless unity, but as the eternally rich God who is the basis, source and Lord of an infinitude of different divine possibilities. The secondary reason is that the community called by Him and created by His call is also absolutely one, yet not as a monolithic block or a collective such as that of the ant-heap or bee-hive, but, in correspondence with the being and life of God, as a living people gathered and continually upbuilt and set in the service of God by the special callings and endowments of individuals. It is not, of course, the differentiation of the human individuals assembled in it, but that of the callings and endowments imparted to them in the context of the one task of ministry laid on the whole community, that underlies the multiplicity with which the community has to execute its task. It is the latter which gives rise to the individuation, differentiation and multiplicity which do not disturb but rather give strength to the unity of its witness.

We shall now consider this multiplicity of the ministry of witness which is normal and legitimate because created and therefore justified and sanctified by the power of the Spirit of the eternally rich God enlightening the community. Limited by it, and also unfortunately limiting it, there is also an abnormal multiplicity which jeopardises and perhaps to a large degree actually hampers this ministry. This does not derive from above but from below, from human nature and its perversion. Those united in the community are all human individuals and live their own lives with their own particular natures, capabilities, weaknesses, inclinations, aversions, needs and aspirations. This is inevitable. It need not stand in the way of their individual calling and endowment in connexion with the commitment to service of the one community, nor need it disturb the work of the one community. It might well be subject to it and thus become serviceable and fruitful material for the performance of their particular service in the setting of that of the one community. Nevertheless, it is true that in fact the specific calling and endowment of individuals in the community does usually tempt them to an independent assertion of what is peculiar to them in its naturalness but also in its perversion, to the unavoidable detriment both of their specific activity and of that of the whole community in the ministry laid upon it. Even in the New Testament there are indications that this temptation already proved to be powerful and menacing in the first communities. In these circumstances multiplicity implies not merely differentiation but actual division in the ministry and witness of the community. Yet we maintain that in itself and as such this multiplicity has nothing whatever to do with the sinful corruption of Christians. In itself and as such it is inwardly proper and even indispensable to their ministry. The Holy Spirit does not enforce a flat uniformity. Hence the Christian community, quite apart from the natural individuality of its members and the consequent dangers, cannot be a barracks, nor can its members be the uniformed inhabitants, nor can their activity be the execution of a well-drilled manœuvre. Their divine calling and endowment are as such manifold. They are always new and different. They are specific in each and every case. They demand of each and all specific attention, specific obedience and specific faithfulness. And the more openly they are received by each and all, the more will the ministry and witness of the community necessarily display *de facto* as well as *de iure* an integrated multiplicity. This implies that the " communion of the Holy Ghost " (2 Cor. 13[13]) which constitutes the whole community, in which alone individuals can seriously participate in its ministry and witness and from which they cannot in any circumstances separate themselves, will always express itself concretely in the form of specific communions which within the sphere of the one action of the community are called and equipped in detail for the same or similar action. It can and should develop special working fellowships to which all Christians cannot and will not necessarily belong but in which, in execution of the activity demanded of all Christians, a particular service is rendered in common in a particular form of thought, speech and action, Christian witness being given in a particular way. Care must be taken that the formation of such trends and groups within the Church is really based on divine gifts and endowments received in concert, and not on the arbitrariness and self-will of common whims and impressions. Care must also be taken that it really takes place within the " communion of the Holy Ghost " which embraces the whole community, expressing rather than disrupting this communion. Separations, schisms and the founding of sects cannot arise if everything is in order in this matter. Finally, care must be taken—and this is the criterion of the true churchmanship of these particular fellowships—that they do not consist of inactive groups of like-minded people concerned only to satisfy certain needs of soul which they experience in common, but rather of genuine working fellowships, of particular forms in which the aim is simply to achieve in closer fellowship the ministry and witness of the community in the world. Where these presuppositions are present, no objection need be raised ; we may welcome and encourage the rise and continuation of particular fellowships of the few or the many within the general fellowship of all Christians. In the plurality of such fellowships of work and service and witness the unity of the living community of the living Jesus Christ will be the more powerful and visible, speaking the more clearly for that which it has to express with its existence in the world.

In what we have here said generally concerning the different forms of the ministry of the community, we have merely been restating what Paul in particular says about the matter in 1 Cor. 12[4f.], Rom. 12[3f.] and Eph. 4[1f.]. (We cannot undertake, of course, to unfold all the literary, historical and material problems associated with these passages, but only to consider them from the standpoint which particularly concerns us.)

In all three passages Paul makes emphatic use of an image which was for him, and which is in fact, more than an image, namely, that of the body and its members. In the Church as the fellowship of all Christians in ministry and witness Paul sees a body, and in what we here call the different forms of ministry and witness visible in individual Christians and Christian fellowships he sees the members of this body. At the beginning of the particularly explicit presentation in 1 Cor. 12 he describes it by means of three terms obviously meant to be synonyms, i.e., χαρίσματα, διακονίαι, and ἐνεργήματα. What is the relation of the unity of the community and its ministry to this plurality ? And what is the relation of this plurality to the unity ? There were two insights which constantly forced themselves on Paul in this matter and which he constantly tried to make clear and explicit to the readers of his letters by means of this image. They are both stated alongside one another in 1 Cor. 12¹² : " The body is one, and hath many members, and all the members of that one body, being many, are one body." We shall now attempt briefly to grasp the meaning and the mutual relationship of these two basic statements.

The first is that the body is one, and that as such it has many members. This expresses the clear and forthright recognition that the plurality of gifts of grace, of powers and of ministries in the Christian community is not an evil, not even a necessary evil, but right and good and inwardly necessary. For good or ill the one body lives in the plurality of its members. The one ministry of the community is performed both *de facto* and *de iure* in the multiplicity of the ministries discharged in it. " The body is not one member, but many " (1 Cor. 12¹⁴). " If they were all one member, where were the body " (v. 19). Nor is this merely *de facto* the case ; it is also *de iure*. " Now hath God set (ἔθετο) the members every one of them in the body, as it hath pleased him," and none with the same office (πρᾶξις, Rom. 12⁴). " God hath set some in the church, first apostles, secondarily prophets, thirdly teachers, after that miracles, then gifts of healing, helps, governments, diversities of tongues. Are all apostles ? are all prophets ? are all teachers ? are all workers of miracles ? have all the gifts of healing ? do all speak with tongues ? do all interpret ? " (1 Cor. 12²⁸f.). Obviously not, but God set them all. In the first enumeration (1 Cor. 12⁸f.), there are also mentioned under the name of gifts of the Spirit the word of wisdom, the word of knowledge, rather strikingly faith, and the discernment of spirits. The διακονία, which in 1 Cor. 12⁵ is a kind of master concept to describe all these particular ministries, is one among others in Rom. 12⁷, where παρακλεῖν and μεταδιδόναι also occur for the first time (v. 8). In the corresponding enumeration in Eph. 4¹¹f. there are added to the apostles, prophets and teachers of 1 Cor. 12 the evangelists and pastors. " All these worketh that one and the self-same Spirit, dividing to every man severally as he will " (1 Cor. 12¹¹), i.e., according to the measure of faith dealt to each (Rom. 12³), with different gifts (χαρίσματα διάφορα) according to the grace commonly given (Rom. 12⁶). We read exactly the same in Eph. 4⁷ : " But unto every one of us is given grace (institution to a particular ministry) according to the measure of the gift of Christ." The decisive affirmation is clear. First, it is a matter of particularities, not in the well-being of the community and its members, but in its activity, the apostles and prophets notably coming first in all three passages. Then, too, the particularities in question, whatever or however many there are, and therefore the specific fellowships conditioned by them, do not arise accidentally or capriciously, nor are they discovered and established by individuals for reasons of practical convenience. On the contrary, they are works of God, of Jesus Christ, of the Holy Spirit. As χαρίσματα, they are forms of the one χάρις addressed to the community as such and operative in it. The very unity of the ministry of the community demands and creates its multiplicity. On this assumption the existence of particularities is not to be contested but unreservedly affirmed and taken seriously.

The second basic statement made in 1 Cor. 12¹² is that the many members are one body. Complementing the first statement, this tells us no less clearly and forthrightly that the right and necessity of the many particular activities and fellowships within the community are shown in the fact that the latter in its unity and each of the former in its particularity do not arise or exist for themselves but for all, for the totality of the life and work of the community. " Now there are diversities (διαιρέσεις) of gifts, but the same Spirit. And there are differences of administrations, but the same Lord. And there are diversities of operations, but it is the same God which worketh all in all " (1 Cor. 12⁴ᶠ·). " By one Spirit we are all baptized into one body " (v. 13). No member can cease to belong to the body on the ground that it is not another member (v. 15 f.). Again, none can be the body alone (v. 17). It is not for self-exaltation, but πρὸς τὸ συμφέρον (literally, to make a contribution), that the manifestation of the Spirit is given specifically to each (v. 7). " Whether one member suffer, all the members suffer with it; or one member be honoured (δοξάζεται), all the members rejoice with it." In this sense Rom. 12 sums everything up in the admonition (v. 3) that none is to think of himself more highly than he ought to think, but every man is to think soberly (σωφροσύνη), which in the context, in characteristic application of this classical term of Greek philosophy, means with a view to mastery, to full deployment within the very limitation imposed by his participation as a member in the life of the whole. Thus in their mutual relations all are to mind one and same thing (τὸ αὐτό, v. 16). Similarly, the exposition in Eph. 4 is also dominated by this second basic principle, the σπουδάζειν or endeavour of the whole community in the differentiation of action described later being to keep (τηρεῖν) the unity of the Spirit (v. 3 f.). " One body, and one Spirit, even as ye are called in one hope of your calling ; one Lord, one faith, one baptism, one God and Father of all, who is above all, and through all (διά πάντων, probably meaning operative in the ministry of all), and in you all." Hardly any other admonition is so frequent in Paul's Epistles as that which urges Christians to seek one and the same thing, to be of the same mind, and to serve one another in humility. These are not general moral exhortations to unity, peace and neighbourly love. They refer to the plurality of their activities and special fellowships within the commonly imposed ministry. Nor is it merely a matter of human imperfection, but it rests on the divine will and order, that all these particularities as such should both have and keep their limits. In virtue of their origin in God, in Christ and in the Holy Spirit, it is made impossible that any one of them, i.e., of their particular representatives in the community, should break loose and swallow the others, finally making itself out to be the one ministry or the one fellowship of ministry, and acting as such. All of them, i.e., of the few or many Christians who find themselves commonly called to this special action and equipped for it, have to serve together " the edifying of the body of Christ " (Eph. 4¹²) and have thus to be modest in their mutual relations. As they do this, not a jot of that which is particularly entrusted and committed to them will be lost, nor will anything of their particular law or freedom have to be denied or surrendered. But all these groups with their particular tendencies must keep rigidly to the rule that they have not to exist or act for themselves, self-sufficiently, aggressively, in attempted mastering and subjugation of others, but with the selfless desire to serve and with openness on every side to all others and to the whole. It need hardly be said that no calling and endowment accepted and practised on this understanding can lead to schism or to the formation of sects or parties, but rather that all of them, as they arise and continue within the community, can only serve to confirm and strengthen its unity.

Naturally the two basic principles of 1 Cor. 12¹², and their complementary relationship to one another, can only be fully clear and necessarily illuminating when it is understood that for Paul, as he develops them with the aid of the image of the body and its members, there is in this image not merely an image but something real, indeed, primarily and ultimately the only real thing in the world. He has the community before his eyes as the body and members of the Head Jesus Christ. " Now ye are the body of Christ, and members in particular " (or in your particularities, ἐκ μέρους, 1 Cor. 12²⁷). Before he thinks of any human ministries or witness, Paul thinks first of the one ministry and witness of the one Son of God and Son of Man ; and before he thinks of the wider and yet also narrower working fellowships, he thinks of the fellowship which God in this One has generally established between Himself and man. It is as he looks up to this Head that he understands as he does the community, the unity and plurality of its ministry and witness, and the relation of the fellowship to the fellowships, and that he is so certain of the one Spirit and yet also of the multiplicity of His gifts. The " communion of the Holy Ghost " (2 Cor. 13¹³) is for him neither a prison nor a maze of human caprice, invention, freedom of opinion and thirst for adventure, but the σύνδεσμος τῆς τελειότητος (Col. 3¹⁴) which neither represses nor withholds the perfect bond uniting the community (and called the bond of peace in Eph. 4³), since it is for him exactly the same as the " fellowship of his Son Jesus Christ our Lord " (1 Cor. 1⁹). Remarkably and yet unmistakeably the two basic statements, by means of the καθάπερ of 1 Cor. 12¹², both lead to the words οὕτως καὶ ὁ Χριστός. The total meaning of the verse is thus as follows : " As the body is one, and hath many members, and all the members of that one body, being many, are one body : so also is Christ." The obvious teaching is that it is first Christ Himself as the Head of this body and its members who is in this way, who exists—we are reminded of the terminology of Rom. 5¹²ᶠ·— from all eternity and in His temporal being and action as the One for the many, for the many as the One. Hence He is the original of the relations of unity and multiplicity described in the two basic statements. And it is only in correspondence to Him that the community follows as His reflection and likeness. Here, then, is the basis of the significance which the two statements acquire and have for Paul. Because Christ cannot be divided (1 Cor. 1¹³), there cannot and must not be disruption any more than there can or should be uniformity in the community. But from Him " the whole body fitly joined together and compacted by that which every joint supplieth, according to the effectual working in the measure of every part, maketh increase of the body unto the edifying of itself in love " (Eph. 4¹⁶). From Him ! By this there stand or fall the right and necessity of all distinction and therefore particularity, and yet also of interrelationship and therefore harmony, in the ministry and witness of the community. The Holy Spirit of χάρις with the unity and integration of His χαρίσματα is the Spirit, and only the Spirit, in whom it is known and confessed that Jesus is the Kyrios (1 Cor. 12³). Where this Spirit is and works, there the union arises in which as such freedom rules, and there freedom rules which as such creates union.

If we finally turn to the question of the different forms of the Church's ministry as such, i.e., in their concrete particularity and distinction, it must be stated above all that we can and must ask concerning the different basic forms, i.e., the specific forms of the witness of the community, which, conditioned and demanded by its nature as declaration and explanation of the Gospel in the world and evangelical address to it, will characterise it in every age and place and in all circumstances if it is the work of obedience, and which cannot indeed be lacking in so far as they are generally posited by God. In this connexion, therefore, we cannot undertake a historical survey and critical analysis of all the variations of these divinely posited basic forms which have occurred at different times in different places, nor can we try to make a positive system of one such variation supposedly normative and binding in our own age and place. There is perhaps room for a historical survey and critical analysis in Church history and confessional study. Such a system, however, in the sphere of practical theology, could have only limited and passing validity. For even to-day the history of the community moves on from century to century. And under the influence of different traditions, but also of the different places and circumstances in which it exists, the community might well find itself inspired and summoned to new variations of the basic forms, and endowed for them. Our concern, then, is with the forms of differentiated ministry which persist in both past and present.

Clearly the biblical and especially the Pauline distinctions which we have already considered are themselves, in concrete manifestation, variations of these basic forms. The lists given in the three passages do not tally exactly. Nor are they introduced dogmatically, but rather assumed to be effective and visible and therefore mentioned for the sake of illustration—in Corinth thus, in Rome thus and in Ephesus (?) thus—in the context of an evaluation of their meaning, justification and limitation. In relation to them the only sensible course to pursue is to ask concerning the different basic forms of the Church's ministry already revealed in them, not to treat and expound them as norms of the differentiation of ministry which are valid once and for all, always and in every place. The generally valid law for this differentiation is not to be taken from them except perhaps indirectly. Both in themselves and in their context they do, of course, give us important stimulation and direction to an understanding of the generally normative law of this differentiation which it is our task to discover. Yet they cannot themselves represent this law, nor are they to be applied as such.

In our quest for this general law of the differentiation of the Church's ministry, it is advisable and indeed necessary to begin a little further back than Paul with the directions given to the disciples in the Gospels when they were sent out by Jesus Himself. We have these in two forms, the one indicating the unity and the second the plurality, or rather in the first instance the basic duality, of the activity demanded of them as witnesses of Jesus.

As concerns the unity, we have studied this so closely in our previous deliberations that no more than a restrospective summary is needed. The disciples are sent into the world to make known to it the One who, sent by God, has first called them to Himself and gathered them as the people of His own, and in so doing to proclaim to the world that He also calls it, that He is on the point of gathering it, that He wills to enlighten and awaken it to know Him, and in Him to know its reconciliation with God and the accomplished justification and sanctification of all men in faith, i.e., in active conversion and obedience. This one thing is at issue in the various forms of its ministry and witness.

It is in the Gospel record of the so-called missionary or baptismal command in Mt. 28¹⁸⁻²⁰ that we have our first emphatic documentation of the unity of the direction to service given by Jesus to the disciples. On the assumption manifestly present in the resurrection of the Crucified : " All power is given unto me in heaven and in earth," one thing is required of the disciples, namely, that they are to help all nations to become what they themselves are, i.e., disciples of Jesus. They are to conduct them to membership of the one people of God. They must μαθητεύειν. What is added in the participle clauses is not a second or third thing alongside the first, but its elaboration. They are to make disciples

4 The Ministry of the Community

by calling them, in the name of the Father, the Son and the Holy Spirit, and therefore in appeal to the authority of God to which they know that they themselves are subject, to true conversion, to the forsaking and forgetting of their former way, to a new beginning, to the state of hope, to prayer for the Holy Spirit, in short to the baptism which is then to be administered : βαπτίζοντες. And they are to make disciples by teaching them what they themselves have been taught by Jesus, by causing them to participate in the knowledge granted by the self-declaration of Jesus : διδάσκοντες. Thus μαθητεύσατε . . . βαπτίζοντες . . . διδάσκοντες—but this one and indivisible whole in the light of and in reliance on the fact that as they do this He, Jesus, is not far from them but present among them to the end of this age as the One who primarily and properly speaks and acts. In all forms of its ministry it must be assumed, therefore, that He is risen and there must be confidence in His continuing and lasting presence.

Distinctively underlining the first, a second record of this unity of the Church's ministry is to be found in the saying which is specifically directed to Peter in Mt. 16¹⁹ but to all the disciples in Mt. 18¹⁸ and Jn. 20²³ : " Whatsoever ye shall bind on earth shall be bound in heaven : and whatsoever ye shall loose on earth shall be loosed in heaven." If this reflects the language of the synagogue, binding and loosing means forbidding and permitting. In Jn. 20²³, however, the two concepts are linked with the forgiving or non-forgiving of sins. Since this agrees more closely with the image of the keys which open or shut the kingdom of heaven in Mt. 16¹⁹, it would probably be more accurate to use the terms " retain " and " release " in the verses in Matthew, since these would also include forbid and permit. The saying has obviously played a decisive role in the theory of later penitential or Church discipline, as unfortunately explained and applied, e.g., in the *Heidelberg Catechism, Qu.* 83–85. Indeed, Mt. 18¹⁸ seems in the context to point in this direction. Nor can it be contested that it has an inward significance for the Church, if hardly perhaps in the technical sense later acquired. The solemn connexion with the founding of the community in which it occurs in Mt. 16¹⁹ and Jn. 20²³, however, makes it probable that primarily and properly it is to be referred to the function of the community in and in relation to the world. If so, it speaks of that which, as the community is at work, either takes place or does not take place in the world and among men, including the members of the community itself. If everything is in order and its work is well done, there must be a great opening, permitting and releasing, i.e., the promise and reception of the forgiveness of sins. If its work is not done or done badly, then contrary to its task the community closes the kingdom of heaven and excludes men from it instead of pointing them to the door which is open to all. It holds where it should release. The remission which is the content of its witness is kept from men. Was it and is it not a strangely perverted mode of interpretation to think that the community may actually be commissioned to choose this negative alternative, using some standard (but which ?) either to open on the one side or to close on the other, either to proclaim forgiveness or to withhold it, and thinking that this dual action is even given heavenly sanction ? Unless it neglects or corrupts its ministry, can it possibly use the keys of the kingdom of heaven committed to it to close the kingdom to men ? " Woe unto you, scribes and Pharisees, hypocrites ! for ye shut up the kingdom of heaven against men : for ye neither go in yourselves, neither suffer ye them that are entering to go in " (Mt. 23¹³). " Woe unto you, lawyers ! for ye have taken away the key of knowledge : ye entered not in yourselves, and them that were entering in ye hindered " (Lk. 11⁵²). How can we follow these sayings and yet think that Jesus has recommended and commanded the community, at least in the form of an alternative, to do the very thing which is here condemned ? If this interpretation cannot be accepted, then the point of the sayings is that what takes place or does not take place between the community and the world or the community and its own members, its opening or shutting, its forgiving or non-forgiving, i.e., its obedience or disobedience, its action *per fas* or *per nefas*, has more than earthly significance. In one way or the other heaven is at stake in what it does or fails to do on earth. By its work God Himself is either glorified or compromised and shamed in His work. God Himself rejoices or weeps over what it does or fails to do, over its lawful opening or unlawful closing. It is not in vain that He has made His cause that of the community in calling it to His service. If God in heaven is not bound to what is done or not done by it on earth, He shares most intimately in it. Understood in this way, the saying serves to emphasise, as does also in its own way the reference to His triune name in the baptismal command, the infinite relevance, the sacred and inestimable responsibility, the promise yet also the violability of the one ministry and witness to which the community is engaged. What it does among men according to the command of Mt. 28$^{18-20}$, it not only does among men but also directly before God, and what it fails to do among men, it fails to do before God.

In its other version, the direction to service given to the disciples with their sending forth has a twofold form in the differentiation of which may be clearly seen the root of the multiplicity of Christian witness. According to the Gospels even the active life of Jesus, especially from the standpoint of the crucifixion which crowned it, is differentiated, though not divided, into speech which is also action on the one side, and action which is also speech on the other.

" He preached the gospel of the kingdom, and healed every sickness and every disease among the people " (Mt. 9^{35}). The accent may be placed on either the one aspect or the other according to the texts. In John's Gospel the speech predominates. Again, in Lk. 4$^{43f.}$ we read : " I must preach the kingdom of God to other cities also : for therefore am I sent. And he preached in the synagogues of Galilee." In Ac. 10^{38}, however, there is no mention of preaching ; we are simply told that He " went about doing good, and healing all that were oppressed of the devil ; for God was with him. And we are witnesses of all things which he did . . ." Similarly, the second aspect is emphasised in Lk. 24^{19}, where He is described as a " prophet mighty in deed and word before God and all the people." The deed and word or the word and deed of Jesus are twofold in their unity. In both we have His self-declaration, the indication of the kingdom of God drawn near in' Him. He gives it both in the form of words of proclamation and instruction and in that of acts of power and aggression and assistance set up as signs in the midst of sinful and suffering humanity and giving distinctive emphasis to the picture as we have it in all four Gospels. For the most part the Word precedes and the act follows. But neither is lacking even where one or the other alone is mentioned or receives prominence.

A corresponding differentiation may be seen in the witness demanded of the disciples. They, too, must speak, not in self-witness, but as those who have to receive and pass on His self-witness, the revelation of the kingdom of God drawn near in Him. In this secondary position and function their human words are also needed. And their speech is to be linked at once and directly with a distinct human action, becoming an active life in unity with it. Hence they too, not independently but in His discipleship and according to His example, and therefore in all seriousness, are also to act, i.e., not merely to do something, but to say the same thing in another way, with the speech of their acts, with their hands as well as their lips.

According to Mt. 10⁷ they, too, instructed by Jesus, are to proclaim : " The kingdom of heaven is at hand." But their proclamation is also to have the other form : " Heal the sick, cleanse the lepers, raise the dead, cast out devils " (v. 8). And these two things are what they actually did when they were sent out, as we learn from Mk. 6¹²ᶠ· and also from Lk. 9⁶ : " Preaching the gospel, and healing every where."

No matter how we understand speaking or proclamation on the one side and acting or healing on the other in the ministry of the community, and no matter what the community may think it is commanded to do and may actually try to fulfil along these two lines, there can be no doubt that in the light of its origin, of the Giver of its task who is also its content, its ministry and witness have always to move along these two lines : not merely along either the one or the other, but along both ; and no less along the one than the other, but with equal seriousness and emphasis along both. It is not as though it were concerned with something different in the two, but wholly with the same thing though in different ways in both. For its speech is also action and its action speech. And for this very reason they are distinct. There is a work of the lips and also of the hands. There is speech and also action, proclamation and also healing ; though it must be remembered, of course, that the direction given by Jesus to His disciples displays a clear sequence, the speech always preceding the action, as emerges in what we are told of their actual work.

Thus it is no accident that in the various lists prophecy (Rom. 12⁶), the word of wisdom and knowledge (1 Cor. 12²⁸) and the ministry of the apostles and prophets (Eph. 4¹¹) are preferred above all other *charismata*. To be sure, they and their recipients and bearers are only members of the body and not the head. They, too, live by the fact that other members have at the same time their distinctive ministries. Nevertheless, it is quite unmistakeable that in them, in the *ministerium Verbi* in the narrower sense, and in its particular bearers, Paul found as it were the *praecipua membra* of the whole.

In this sequence there is obviously revealed an order which is not reversible and which does not therefore allow us to find the main force of the witness of the community in its specific activities. The first if not the only thing in its witness is the ministry of the *viva vox Evangelii* to be discharged *voce humana* in human words. It is its declaration, explanation and evangelical address with the lips. This does not mean, however, that a higher value is to be assigned to speech and a lower to action. The burden of both the speech and the action of the community is that men are called to knowledge, yet not to empty but to active knowledge. Because it is a matter of knowledge, speech must come first. But because it is a matter of active knowledge, the element of action must not be lacking. Nor may this be only an incidental characteristic, as though it were optional, *ad libitum*, whether it need accompany the speech of the community, or as though it might do so perhaps in a very rudimentary and imperfect form.

Who can say off-hand that the community may not often speak and therefore call to knowledge more clearly and forcefully with its action than with the verbal speech which must necessarily, of course, precede and indicate the meaning of the action ? What would be the value of verbal speech if it were not followed and accompanied by analogous action of like value and dignity ? The example of the life action of Jesus Himself, the direction given to His disciples according to the Gospels, the indications at least which we are given of its work, and finally the Pauline description of the ministry of the community, all tell us plainly that two great and distinctive elements must always be present in it independently and yet in concert, namely, the elements of word and deed. The right order is that it should first speak. But with the same seriousness and emphasis it has also to act in correspondence with its word. In this unity and differentiation it represents what it is its task to represent to the world, namely, the likeness of the kingdom of God.

We shall now try, from the two main standpoints thus presented, to grasp in detail the interconnexion of what is demanded in the ministry of the community. We remember that as we consider the differentiated speech and differentiated action of the community we are concerned only with what is demanded always, everywhere and in all circumstances. All the emphases which we must attempt are thus to be judged by the standard whether they really represent the basic forms or necessary and generally valid elements of the Church's speech and action and whether they are thus serviceable as norms by which to estimate and finally to judge the variations in which the one ministry of the community has developed, or possibly not developed, or done so badly, in the form of different ministries both past and present. It must also be said by way of introduction that the right to understand the whole from these main standpoints—a right which is secured by its origin in the directions of the Jesus of the Gospels and of the apostle Paul—will find confirmation in the fact that we cannot discuss the speech of the community in detail without realising in detail that in it we are always concerned with a concrete action, and conversely that we cannot discuss its action without having to maintain that it is impossible without concrete speech. If we ever come across a form of the Church's ministry in which there is neither speech on the one side nor action on the other, it may be affirmed with certainty that at least this is not a basic form. Finally, the basic forms which call for mention may indeed be named separately and *a parte potiori* described in detail, but they cannot possibly be separated from one another. There is hardly one which does not impinge upon the others, and many of them actually intersect. This is perhaps an additional argument for the utter impossibility of a system of Church ministry constructed on analytical and synthetic lines.

As is only proper, we begin with the different ministries in which the community has especially to act by its speech, and in the first instance (1) we indicate a special ministry when we maintain that it is our office to praise God. To praise God, as a function in the ministry of the Christian community, is to affirm, acknowledge, approve, extol and laud both the being of God as the One who in His eternal majesty has become man, and the action in which He has taken man, all men, to Himself in His omnipotent mercy. It is to magnify the God who in this being and action of His is our God, Emmanuel, with us and for us. It is to confess Him publicly as the only true God. Now obviously the existence of the community as such and of all Christians has to serve this praise of God. Its existence as such is a distinctive world factor, newly created and of independent significance in relation to all others, to the extent that in it, in the work of its ministry, there takes place the affirmation, acknowledgment, approval, extolling, laud, magnifying and confession of this God. It does not praise this God in vain, nor merely to its own satisfaction. To be sure, its praise of God would be intrinsically worthy even if it took place in secret. To be sure, the uplift associated with its praise of God is to the advantage of itself and all its members, and to this extent brings them satisfaction. Yet when it praises God its particular concern is to set up that banner, to raise a standard, to lift up an escutcheon, in the ministry of its witness. The community's ministry of witness has to fill a yawning gulf in the life of the world. What is more worthy or urgent for any man than to praise God ? But the great majority of men seem not, or not yet, to do this. The community does, not reproaching others for their failure, nor of course posturing before them, but provisionally, in their place, anticipating what in the light of the consummation will one day be the work of all creation. And it naturally does it in the sense of the summons of Ps. 150⁶ which is unhesitatingly addressed to it too : " Let every thing that hath breath praise the Lord." It has the freedom, and sees that it is commanded, to praise God. All its ministries, whether of speech or action, are performed well to the extent that they all participate in the praise of God enjoined upon it. We may also add that if its praise of God as a specific act of speech is well done it is also itself quite definitely a saving, helpful, purifying and restoring action, and as such an act of witness to the world.

But if the speech of the community is also action, and if its whole speech and action are a praise of God, this does not exclude but includes the fact that this praise also has its own specific place and form in the ministry of the community, and indeed in that of its speech. Its particular place is the assembling for divine service in the specific sense, in which the community is constantly reminded of the task or witness committed to it, and in which it prays constantly for the insight and strength with which to perform it, and for the world to which it has to direct it, and to which it does in fact direct it,

C.D.—IV.–III.–II.—28

by so doing. The community does not speak only in divine service ; but it does also speak in divine service. To its fulfilment there belong not only preaching and prayer, which for their part cannot be well done without the praise of God, but also this praise in the most concrete sense, i.e., as the particular element by which the whole action of divine service is orientated in accordance with its meaning, shaped, not as something artificial, but as a " liturgy," as the concrete and public performance of service, and fashioned under the control of the affirmation, acknowledgment, and approval, not of any god, but of Emmanuel, so that it takes the form of worthy and salutary confession ; and therefore even more particularly as the element in which the community says expressly to itself and the world that the main concern in its whole existence, and therefore its assembling too, is with this affirmation and confession. The praise of God will not be merely a tacit presupposition of the life and assembly of the community. The intrinsically fine and true saying : " Thou art praised, O God, in stillness," is to be found only in Luther's Bible (Ps. 65^1). Nor will the praise of God be only the formal principle of assembly for divine service which gives its action the shape of liturgy. While it is this, it also demands expression, and this not only in the hearts of members of the community and the decisions which they are constantly summoned and led to make when they assemble.

We remember what we are told in Mt. 7^{21} concerning those who say to Jesus " Lord, Lord " without doing the will of His heavenly Father. This does not contradict but rather presupposes the fact that according to Phil. 2$^{10f.}$ every knee shall one day bow at the name of Jesus and every tongue confess Him as Lord. According to Rom. 10^9 confession with the lips is no less demanded here and now than faith in the heart. The very fact that Christians are like-minded according to the will of Christ leads them directly to the extolling with their lips of God the Father of their Lord Jesus Christ (Rom. 15^6). Similarly, in Col. 3$^{16f.}$ it is not merely insisted that the community should allow the Word of God to dwell in it richly, nor that Christians should sing to God in their hearts, nor that they should do everything in word and deed in His name and therefore with thanksgiving to God the Father, but also quite expressly that in wisdom they should teach and admonish one another " in psalms and hymns and spiritual songs." And is it not worth noting that in Mk. 14^{26} we are told that the disciples sang a hymn immediately after the last highly significant meal with Jesus and just before the commencement of His passion ?

The praise of God which constitutes the community and its assemblies seeks to bind and commit and therefore to be expressed, to well up and be sung in concert. The Christian community sings. It is not a choral society. Its singing is not a concert. But from inner, material necessity it sings. Singing is the highest form of human expression. It is to such supreme expression that the *vox humana* is devoted in the ministry of the Christian community. It is for this that it is liberated in this ministry.

It is hard to see any compelling reason why it should have to be accompanied in this by an organ or harmonium. It might be argued that in this way the community's praise of God is embedded by anticipation in that of the whole cosmos, to which the cosmos is undoubtedly called and which we shall unquestionably hear in the consummation. The trouble is that in practice the main purpose of instruments seems to be to conceal the feebleness with which the community discharges the ministry of the *vox humana* committed to it. There is also the difficulty that we cannot be sure whether the spirits invoked with the far too familiar sounds of instruments are clean or unclean spirits. In any case, there should be no place for organ solos in the Church's liturgy, even in the form of the introductory and closing voluntaries which are so popular.

What we can and must say quite confidently is that the community which does not sing is not the community. And where it cannot sing in living speech, or only archaically in repetition of the modes and texts of the past ; where it does not really sing but sighs and mumbles spasmodically, shamefacedly and with an ill grace, it can be at best only a troubled community which is not sure of its cause and of whose ministry and witness there can be no great expectation. In these circumstances it has every reason to pray that this gift which is obviously lacking or enjoyed only in sparing measure will be granted afresh and more generously lest all the other members suffer. The praise of God which finds its concrete culmination in the singing of the community is one of the indispensable basic forms of the ministry of the community.

Within it, yet also independently alongside, there belongs also (2) the explicit proclamation of the Gospel in the assembly of the community, in the midst of divine service, where it is also heard directly or indirectly by the world, i.e., in what is denoted by the overburdened but unavoidable term " preaching." This, or the pulpit, has been called the true arena of the kingdom of God. But it can be this only in the form of event, and not automatically. On the other hand, in relation to what was undoubtedly the first task of the first witnesses, there can be no doubt that in preaching we have a truly basic and therefore highly important element in the action not only of the assembled community as such but of its whole ministry. What is at issue in preaching ? Decisively that the community, and with it the world, should remind itself or be reminded explicitly of the witness with which it is charged, that it should find reassurance as to its content, that reflected in it Jesus Christ Himself should speak afresh to it, that it should be summoned afresh to His service in the world.

This decisive task of preaching in divine service seems to suggest that the presence of artistic representations of Jesus Christ is not desirable in the places of assembly. For it is almost inevitable that such static works should constantly attract the eye and therefore the conscious or unconscious attention of the listening community, fixing them upon the particular conception of Jesus Christ entertained in all good faith no doubt by the artist. This is suspect for two reasons. The community should not be bound to a particular conception, as inevitably happens where there is an artistic representation, but should be led by the ongoing proclamation of His history as His history with us, so that it moves from one provisional Amen to another, in the wake of His living self-attestation pressing on from insight to insight. Supremely, however, even the most excellent of plastic arts does not have the means to display Jesus Christ in His truth, i.e., in His unity as true Son of God and Son of Man. There will necessarily be either on the one side, as in the great Italians, an abstract and docetic over-emphasis on His deity, or on the other, as in Rembrandt, an equally abstract, ebionite over-emphasis on His humanity, so that even with the best of intentions error will be promoted. If we certainly cannot prevent art or artists from attempting this exciting and challenging theme, it should at least be made clear both to them and to the community that it is better not to allow works of this kind to compete with the ministry of preaching.

As a solemn direction first to the community itself of the message entrusted to it, preaching as it goes forth is an action, its witness being a pregnant reminder and confirmation of the vocation to which it owes its gathering and upbuilding and indeed its very existence. To this extent all preaching is on the human level a new constitution, and outwardly a new manifestation, of the community as a fellowship of ministry and witness. For in all true preaching there is made a new and specific reference to that which, according to the Gospel which it has to attest, has been accomplished by God and is manifested to be real and true. True preaching is, in fact, preaching of Jesus Christ, of the radical alteration of the situation between God and man, between heaven and earth, as it has been effected in Him. Hence by the content of its declaration preaching is at once and primarily distinguished from all other forms of human declaration and communication, and if it takes place in obedience it is safeguarded against becoming general talk or special talk chosen only at random. Yet a secondary distinction and guarantee are also to be found in the fact that it takes place in concrete connexion with the original witness concerning Jesus Christ and therefore the kingdom of God, namely, with the Old and New Testaments, so that it is to this extent a communication of the biblical message. Two things are to be related but also distinguished at this point. Preaching is attesting communication of the biblical message on the assumption and under the stimulation and guidance of investigation of the biblical writings. Thus biblical studies, i.e., the investigation and exposition of the biblical writings, belong also to the ministry of the community. We shall return to this when we have to speak about the special tasks of instruction and theology in the Church. Preaching rests on biblical studies. It is not, however, identical with them. Shaped always with special reference to a special part and aspect of the biblical witness, nourished by it as its " text," it is preaching of Christ, of the kingdom, of salvation, of grace. On the basis of listening to the declaration of Scripture, preaching is an independent declaration and explanation of the Gospel, an independently ventured evangelical appeal. It is not more than simple exposition of Scripture. It is not better. But it is certainly different. Scriptural exposition belongs to those other ministries to which we shall come later, but preaching is a special ministry which can only be neglected or disrupted if it seeks to be only or even predominantly exposition. Preaching has to speak out of the Bible, but not concerning it.

Much that is indispensable to exposition as such, and therefore to the background of preaching, has thus to be withheld from preaching, or to be introduced into it only by way of brief indication, since it could only disrupt the specific ministry of preaching. Discussions of relations in Jerusalem at the time of the war between Syria and Ephraim, or of the nature and activities of the scribes, Pharisees and Sadducees at the time of Jesus, or of the errors and confusions of the community at Corinth, together with the relevant literary, historical and archaeological data, must certainly occupy the one who has to preach on the texts concerned, but they must be left on one side in the actual event of preaching, where the concern is direct communication and address and where they could only disturb and distract both the preacher and the listening community.

Again, preaching is no more a work of systematic than of biblico-historical theology. Preaching does not reflect, reason, dispute or academically instruct. It proclaims, summons, invites and commands. Naturally it must be full of dogmatics, i.e., dogmatic culture, i.e., thoroughly worked and applied and practised rather than explicit dogmatics. Naturally in speaking *ad hominem* it must never become an *exposé* in lecture form of such psychological, sociological, ethical and political learning and convictions as the preacher may also have. Naturally it is even more important that it should be faithful to the inner lines of its particular ministry, that it should express truly and exclusively, not an alien, constricting and questioning train of thought or law, but the Gospel itself and its command and claim and judgment and above all its promise, the Yes of God to man and the world in which His No is enclosed, but genuinely enclosed so that it cannot be an independent theme, the atonement made in Jesus Christ in all its dimensions, and not something different, contradictory or neutral. When preaching does not proceed deviously but comes quickly to the point ; when it does not engage in confusing analysis or tedious expansion but to the glory of God and the joy of man is concise and pointed ; when in this way it declares and expounds the Gospel and addresses man and appeals to him on the basis of it, then it, too, is a liturgical act and it fulfils its ministry in the context of the totality of the ministry of the common Christian community and of all its other forms. It then speaks explicitly of what applies to all. It calls each and all to decision for faith instead of unbelief, to obedience instead of disobedience, to knowledge in the battle against ignorance. It sets up in the life of all a sign which divides at first but which, in virtue of the decision already taken concerning them and thereby declared to them, is positive in its significance—the same hopeful sign both in the community to which it brings a fresh realisation of its task and to the world which also hears either close at hand or at a distance. Preaching as the work of human speech is the human action by which the fact of this divisive but positively significant sign is established. Poor community whose ministry is deficient in this basic form! The fault might lie with the speakers who ought to be dedicated to the discharge of this ministry or with the hearers who ought to be actively willing and able to support this ministry. But either way, if this ministry is indeed lacking, then there is specific need of the reformation in head and members which is always needed by the community; and the prayer must go out with particular urgency that the Lord will send forth labourers, or better, wiser and more cheerful labourers, into His vineyard (Mt. 9[38]).

We are still looking in the same direction when we describe as another basic form of the Church's ministry (3) the instruction which is to be given in the community, first to its own members, but also to the world at large. The Christian community is more than a school, but it is also a school.

The overestimation of this element of its action in the days of Protestant orthodoxy with its teaching sermons and catechetical drill was no doubt mistaken, but so, too, is the underestimation which has become customary and popular in more recent times in the form of the well-known but rather trivial antithesis between doctrine, which supposedly appeals only to the understanding or even the memory, and life, which it is thought can be made immediately accessible apart from these. In both cases the basic error is a confusion of that which God alone can do and does with that which it is the business and task of the community to do. The real knowledge which wins and claims the whole man and therefore his understanding, disposition, will and heart, can be only the work of God. It belongs, however, to the witness of the community which serves this work of God that in a limited but definite way it should contain instruction, which in the first instance is addressed to the understanding and memory, concerning that which might arise as living knowledge, as its theme and its fulfilment.

To attest the Gospel in the world, there is serious though not exclusive need in both speaking and hearing of definite information which it is the duty of the community carefully to impart to both the young and old, the educated and uneducated, within it. All are, and in the strict sense all remain throughout their lives, catechumens who as such need to be catechised or instructed. It is here that biblical studies with all their problems have their legitimate place. To know the literary source not merely of preaching but of the whole ministry of the Church, and to have a part with all one's powers in the attempt to understand it, is not merely the affair of a few specialists but fundamentally of all members of the community. For none is infallible, and all need to be subject to the control of the rest. And again, it might some day be asked of any Christian to give an answer

to those without concerning " the hope that is in you " (1 Pet. 3¹⁵).
For this no little knowledge of the Bible, and indeed some understanding and therefore study, are indispensable. The statement :
" I am a mere layman and not a theologian," is evidence not of
humility but of indolence. The Christian must also be exercised,
however, in the act of Christian thinking as it is to be demonstrated
libro clauso, in the fulfilment of the decisive movement from the
centre to the periphery and back to the centre, from above energetically
down and no less energetically up again. He must also be in a position
to see his way clearly and not to be constantly bewildered in the
dramas, tragedies and comedies of the past and present history of
the community. He must be able in some degree to discern between
spirits, which is obviously a special gift according to 1 Cor. 12¹⁰. As
concerns his own life, he must be able to know what is the " good,
and acceptable, and perfect will of God " (Rom. 12²). He cannot
simply do these things. He must learn to do them. Hence there is
need of the catechism and even of some memory work. The Holy
Spirit, who is the true and proper *doctor ecclesiae* creating faith as
well as giving information and therefore establishing real knowledge,
sets up in the community the specific and sober ministry of instruction.
To be sure, there can be no instruction in the community without a
concurrent element of proclamation. To be sure, Christian instruction
in all its forms must always for this reason have something of the
manner and tone of preaching. But as preaching should not degenerate
into mere instruction, so instruction for confirmation—or should we
say baptism ?—should not degenerate into preaching. Nor should
the Bible hour, the lecture, or the discussion. In this sphere there
should be a place for questions and answers which are out of keeping
in the assembly for worship. For Christians have both the right and
the duty soberly to inform themselves, or to gain information, concerning what is at issue in that which is entrusted to them and
represented by them in concert. The most careful possible introduction
to knowledge is thus the meaning and purpose, the pedagogic goal,
of the instruction to be imparted in the community. This instruction
will be linked with the praise of God and preaching, but it will also
be an independent and non-liturgical element alongside them, and as
such it will show itself to be one of the indispensable basic forms of
the ministry of the community when it too, achieving mastery in
limitation, keeps its specific goal as precisely as possible in view and
seeks faithfully and consistently to attain it. It, too, will then be not
merely the speech but the action of the community—an indispensable
and unique contribution to the introduction and confirmation of the
fact of a people of God capable of bearing witness to the world and
actually bearing it by its very existence. For if it did not know what
is at issue, in what other part of its witness could it bear clear and
sharp-cut witness ? It is for this reason that instruction is a function

which is so important and can never be taken too seriously. It is for this reason that the Church must also be a school.

We come to the speech and action of the community which are for the most part directed outwards to the world, and are therefore characteristically apostolic, when we turn (4) to the task which might be and usually is excellently summed up in the term " evangelisation."

In the Synoptists εὐαγγελίζεσθαι is one of the general terms used to describe the public speech of Jesus Himself and His disciples as directed primarily to the people of Galilee. It is distinguished from κηρύσσειν and διδάσκειν (cf. on these three terms, *C.D.*, IV, 1, p. 195f.) by the nuance that the content is emphasised. What they bring to these people as " the lost sheep of the house of Israel " is good or glad tidings, the message of the coming of the kingdom of God which is identical with the coming of Jesus Himself. In Ac, 21⁸ Philip, one of the " deacons " of the first community mentioned in Ac. 6⁵, is called an εὐαγγελιστής. In 2 Tim. 4⁵ Timothy is told to fulfil his διακονία in " the work of an evangelist." And in Eph. 4¹¹ the εὐαγγελισταί come in the centre of the list which begins with the apostles and prophets and ends with the pastors and teachers. In none of these passages are we given instruction as to the more precise meaning of their function. There can be no doubt, however, that we are here concerned with a ministry of proclamation and teaching closely linked with that of the apostles in the narrower sense.

Materially, it is perhaps legitimate to take the word evangelisation in the usual modern sense, in which it is distinguished from missions or related to what we now call home missions, and means the directing of the message to those who stand in the more immediate environs of the community. It is true, of course, that to-day this nearer group often has in many respects a character different from that of the immediate external world surrounding the New Testament community. It consists in the main of men who can be distinguished from the community in the more serious sense only by a shifting frontier, and strictly only by taking each case on its merits, since on the basis of the curious notion of a *corpus christianum* which includes both the Church and the world, and on the basis of the even more curious custom of infant baptism, they seem to belong to the community and yet do not really belong to it to the extent that they have no obvious part in either the knowledge or the resultant ministry of the community. They are thus men who, being " Christians " before they know what is at issue or have have made any resolve or expressed any desire to be such, are just as much strangers to the Gospel, or have only the same hearsay knowledge, as if they belonged to the heathen races to whom the disciples are sent. And yet it is only in a very dubious sense that we can really classify them as heathen. Since the dawn of the post-apostolic period, and then more clearly in the Middle Ages, and in the earlier as well as the later modern period, there has always been this as it were non-Christian Christendom, and it no doubt exists also even in the sphere of the so-called younger churches of Asia and Africa. Evangelisation was and is specifically addressed to men of this kind. It is the particular task, undoubtedly laid upon the Church in every period, of ministering the Word of God to the countless men who theoretically ought long since to have heard and accepted and responded to it, but who in fact have not really done so at all, or only at a distance and therefore in a way which is meaningless as regards their participation in the cause of the community. Evangelisation serves to awaken this sleeping Church. It is obvious that the worship, preaching and teaching of the community, which the world also hears in some sense, or at least may hear, in its form as the Christian world, must always have also the character of evangelisation, of a call to those who are within in theory but not in practice. And the same is true to different degrees of all the other basic forms of ministry which we have still to mention. Evangelisation, however, is still a task which needs a special name and is to be specially attempted. Those countless nominal Christians are undoubtedly the immediate neighbours of the community as the assembly of serious Christians. Do not even the latter continually find that they themselves are nominal Christians and urgently need to receive the Gospel afresh ? The concern of evangelisation is precisely to sound out the Gospel on this shifting frontier between true and merely nominal Christians. Do we not have to understand all the New Testament Epistles, with the exception of the Pastorals, formally at least as records of evangelisation in this sense ? Its task is made particularly difficult, in a way which does not apply to foreign missions, by the fact that its work is continually hindered by the notion that all nominal or serious Christians are already at the place to which they are summoned by the Gospel. In evangelisation the concern must be, not so much to engage negatively in the necessary criticism and destruction of this notion, but rather to disclose positively that both neighbours without and those within are indeed at this place as seen by God in Jesus Christ, that the love and grace of God apply to them from the very beginning, that their salvation is assured and present to them, and that on this basis they are invited, not to pass by this reality in their blindness and deafness, but to accept it from their hearts and with all its consequences, in other words to believe and to obey, coming to this place in practice and becoming in practice what they already are, not just in theory, but according to the resolve of God and on the basis of His act of reconciliation, namely, those who are also called, who also know, who also witness, who also have a part in the responsibility of the community. Everything depends upon evangelisation worthy of the name, upon the community taking the required step of speaking to those without by actually saying this to them. It can say it in many ways, with many variations or combinations of preaching or instruction, or in new and particular modes of specifically evangelistic speech and address of which one may be the more suitable and serviceable in one case and another in another. It must say it in connexion with the other ministries of the community, and particularly in conjunction with what is to be called its diaconate in the narrower sense, as the latter must also have an evangelistic character. What is vital is that the evangelising community should say what it has to say to those around in a glad and spirited and peaceful way corresponding to its content, the Salvation Army setting a good example in this respect. What is vital is that it should really say this, i.e., the Gospel, and not something else. What is vital is that concern for spurious results should not cause it to make the proclamation of freedom into propagation of a law, the promise of life (ostensibly on pedagogic grounds) into threatening with the terrors of hell, the declaration of what is eternally undeserved into incitement to praiseworthy moral rearmament, the artless indication of the truth into clever or attractive apologetic. If it is clear that only by simple means can men be won for that which is intrinsically simple, then it will know how to seek and find its way in this respect. Certainly it owes it to its task and to the world of men around it that it should enter and tread this way. Certainly a Church which is not as such an evangelising Church is either not yet or no longer the Church, or only a dead Church, itself standing in supreme need of renewal by evangelisation.

The other function in which the community has to speak apostolically in the more specific sense is (5) that of mission in the narrower sense which is also the true and original sense, in which sending or sending out to the nations to attest the Gospel is the very root of the existence and therefore of the whole ministry of the community. In mission the Church sets off and goes (πορευθέντες, Mt. 28¹⁹), taking the essentially and most profoundly necessary step beyond itself, and beyond the dubiously Christian world in which it is more immediately set, to the world of men to which, entangled as it is in so many false and arbitrary and impotent beliefs in so many false gods of ancient or most recent invention and authority and reflecting its own glory and misery, the Word which God has pronounced in Jesus Christ concerning the covenant of grace which He has concluded with it is still alien and must therefore be taken as a new message. The vocation which constitutes the community is directly the command to take this message to this world, to the nations or the "heathen." As it is obedient to this command, it engages in foreign missions.

We must first maintain that even missions to the heathen, and they particularly, can be pursued meaningfully only on the presupposition of the clear promise and firm belief that everything which was needed for the salvation of all, and therefore of these men who have fallen victim to these false beliefs in false gods, has already taken place, that Jesus Christ died and rose again for these heathen too. Thus the task of mission can consist only in announcing this to them. It is on this basis that they are to be addressed from the very outset.

Secondly, the community itself and as such is the acting subject in foreign missions too, or else it is not the Christian community. That in practice there may be definite circles or unions or societies which initiate missions corresponds to the practical discharge of many other ministries in the Church. But no such society should claim to be a particular missionary community composed of friends of missionary work. For this work cannot be their own special preserve. The rest of the community is not to be released even in appearance from the missionary obligation laid upon it in its totality. The missionary society can only act representatively for the whole community which is as such a missionary community.

Thirdly—and this has still to be considered, though perhaps it is more widely perceived to-day than fifty years ago, and therefore need not be emphasised so strongly—the only purpose of missions must be to make known the Gospel to foreign peoples, and they must be pursued only to the glory of God and the salvation of men. Everything is falsified if other purposes either predominate or are even admitted. Neither the aim to strengthen confessional positions, nor to extend European or American culture and civilisation, nor to propagate one of the modes of thought and life familiar and dear to the older Christian world by reason of its antiquity, can be the motivating force behind true Christian missions, and certainly not the desire to support colonial or general political interests and aspirations.

Fourthly, in the false beliefs in false gods, in the so-called religions from the sphere of which the nations are to be called into the light of Jesus Christ and the divine election of grace and the divine covenant, we are always concerned, even in the primitive forms as well as the higher and especially in Islam, with constructs which are in their own way psychologically, sociologically, aesthetically, ethically and from the general human standpoint both interesting and imposing. Missions presuppose both that they will be valued and taken seriously, with a complete absence of the crass arrogance of the white man, and yet also that they will not be allowed to exercise any pressure on the Gospel but that this will be opposed to them in all its radical uniqueness and novelty, with no attempt at compromise or at finding points of contact and the like. Missions are valueless and futile if they are not pursued in strict acceptance of these two presuppositions, and therefore with a sincere respect and yet also an equally sincere lack of respect for the so-called religions.

Fifthly, missions, in spite of the one-sidedness of their particular task, are concerned with the establishment of the whole ministry of the Church. They must be carried through in the form not only of preaching and evangelisation but also of instruction and diaconate. Hence it is unavoidable that in many places if not universally, and in the early stages if not permanently, they should also contribute to the education and upbringing of the nations where they operate in the form of missionary schools, and also to the improvement of their physical health in the form of medical missions. These tasks cannot become an end in themselves, so that missions cannot be conducted solely along the lines of the work of Albert Schweitzer, nor need there be any regrets when sooner or later these tasks are taken out of their hands, since this enables them to apply themselves with greater concentration of energy to their proper work.

Sixthly, the goal of missions is not to convert heathen in the sense of bringing them to a personal enjoyment of their salvation. Neither at home nor abroad can it be the work of the community to convert men. This is the work of God alone. When God does convert a man by His call, then he does, of course, come to personal salvation, but supremely and decisively he becomes a witness in the world. Hence the goal of the missionary work of the community must be to attest to the heathen the work and Word of the God who, as He has created them by His call, wills to make them, too, His witnesses, and to equip them as such.

Seventhly, missionary work among the nations cannot take the form of mastering and ruling, but only of serving, both in its commencement and its continuation. It has to lead the heathen themselves to become witnesses, to become the community, by the awakening call of God. Nor can the mission, which owes its own creation, existence and stability to the same call of God, range itself above this community. It can only integrate itself with and subordinate itself to it, advising and helping on the ground of its longer experience. And it can do this only up to the point when the new and young community can do without it, when the European or American mission has rendered itself superfluous, when it can thus hand over the missionary task to the new and young and native community. Epigrammatically, one might almost say that the purpose of missions is to make themselves superfluous by the establishment of new missions carried on by the former heathen. The fact that missions can prosper only as a truly selfless work in this concrete sense has been widely recognised to-day, but it still needs to be seen and accepted more radically in the so-called home churches, nor should it ever be forgotten. Hence there is good reason to recall it in this connexion.

The relationship of the Christian community to the Jews, to the Synagogue, to Israel, requires separate treatment at this point. Obviously its witness is owed also to this part of the surrounding world which is at once so promising and yet so alien, so near and yet so distant. For its content was enacted in Israel, and on the lips of Jesus and His first disciples, and indeed of Paul, it was first directed to Israel as the witness of this event. How can it fail to be addressed to Israel, and indeed to Israel first, in the ages which follow ? Yet the nature of this recipient, a consideration of the beginnings of the encounter of the community with it, and finally the reciprocal relationship of the community to it, all compel us to say that its witness will have to be highly singular in this direction. We attach what we have to say in this regard to what has been said concerning the missionary task of the Church only to add at once by way of antithesis that in relation to the Synagogue there can be no real question of " mission " or of bringing the Gospel. It is thus unfortunate to speak of Jewish missions. The Jew who is conscious of his Judaism and takes it seriously can only think that he is misunderstood and insulted when he hears this term. And the community has to see that materially he is right. Mission is not the witness which it owes to Israel. When Paul sought to be a Jew to Jews, it was not just formally but materially *toto coelo* different from when he sought to be a Greek to the Greeks. Two decisive considerations are to be held in view in this regard.

First, in relation to the Synagogue there can be no question of the community proclaiming the true faith in place of a false, or opposing the true God to an idol. The God whose work and Word it has to attest to the world was the God of Israel before the community itself ever came forth from this people, and to this day He can only be the God of Israel. To the Jews belong (Rom. 9⁴ᶠ·) the υἱοθεσία (the appointment of men to be the children of God), the διαθῆκαι (the covenant in all its renewals and confirmations), the νομοθεσία (the grace of the divinely given order of life), the λατρεία (the true worship of God), the ἐπαγγελίαι (the sequence of the divine promises), and the πατέρες (the fathers in the communion of the one true faith). Above all, it was of their flesh and blood that Jesus Himself was born, so that κατὰ σάρκα He is first their Christ. They are the people of God loved by Him in free grace, elected and called to His service, and originally sent into the world as His witnesses. " Salvation is of the Jews " (Jn. 4²²). And this κλῆσις of theirs (Rom. 11²⁹) is ἀμεταμέλητος, irrevocable and unrevoked. It is we Christians called out of the nations who have been associated with them. It is we who as wild shoots have been grafted into this cultivated tree (Rom. 11¹⁷ᶠ·). The Gentile Christian community of every age and land is a guest in the house of Israel. It assumes the election and calling of Israel. It lives in fellowship with the King of Israel. How, then, can we try to hold missions to Israel ? It is not the Swiss or the German or the Indian or the Japanese awakened to faith in Jesus Christ, but the Jew, even the unbelieving Jew, so miraculously preserved, as we must say, through the many calamities of his history, who as such is the natural historical monument to the love and faithfulness of God, who in concrete form is the epitome of the man freely chosen and blessed by God, who as a living commentary on the Old Testament is the only convincing proof of God outside the Bible. What have we to teach him that he does not already know, that we have not rather to learn from him ?

Secondly, however, there is the shattering fact that at the decisive moment the same Israel denied its election and calling, that when the hour struck it did not know the fulness and goal of its history, that when it eventuated it did not receive the promised consolation, that when it was fulfilled it did not believe the Word of God spoken to it by Moses and the prophets, that when its King appeared among it He was despised and rejected and delivered up to the Gentiles. It was thus on the road from the Jew Caiaphas by way of the half-Jew Herod to the Gentile Pilate that He became the Saviour of the world and therefore our King too. Meantime the Synagogue became and was and still is the organisation of a group of men which hastens towards a future that is empty now that He has come who should come, which is still without consolation, which clings to a Word of God that is still unfulfilled. Necessarily, therefore, the Jew who is uniquely blessed offers the picture of an existence which, characterised by the rejection of its Messiah and therefore of its salvation and mission, is dreadfully empty of grace and blessing. Necessarily he reflects the same existence without grace to which we poor heathen would be hopelessly abandoned apart from that which has taken place for us and has been manifested to us in the person of the one Jew. What object is there here for missionary activity ? What we have to see, and sympathetically to fear, is the judgment of God in His love. We certainly can and should hold talks with the Jews for the purpose of information. But how can the Gospel help as proclaimed from men to men when already it has been repudiated, not just accidentally or incidentally, but in principle, *a priori* and therefore with no prospect of revision from the human standpoint? And in the long run what is the use of conversations? If the Jew is to go back on the rejection of his Messiah and become a disciple, is there not needed a radical change in which he comes to know the salvation of the whole world which is offered to him first as a Jew and in which he thus comes to read quite differently his own Holy Book? Is there not needed the direct intervention of God Himself as in the case of the most obstinate of all Jews, Paul himself? Can there ever be a true conversion of the true Jews, therefore, except as a highly extraordinary event? Can we ever expect a gathering of all Israel around the Lord who died and rose again for this whole people of Israel except, as Paul clearly thought in Rom. $11^{15, \ 25f.}$, in and with the end of all things and as the eschatological solution of this greatest of all puzzles?

Does this mean that the Christian community has no responsibility to discharge its ministry of witness to the Jews? Not at all! What it does mean is that there can be only one way to fulfil it. To use the expression of Paul in Rom. $11^{11, \ 14}$, it must make the Synagogue jealous (παραζηλῶσαι). By its whole existence as the community of the King of the Jews manifested to it as the Saviour of the world, it must set before it the fact of the event of the consolation of the fulfilled Word of God, confronting it with the monument of the free election, calling and grace of God which have not been despised but gratefully accepted and grasped. It must make dear and desirable and illuminating to it Him whom it has rejected. It must be able to set Him clearly before it as the Messiah already come. It must call it by joining with it as His people, and therefore with Him. No particular function can be this call, but only the life of the community as a whole authentically lived before the Jews. It need hardly be said that the life of the community as a whole neither has been nor is this call. To this day Christianity has not succeeded in impressing itself upon Israel as the witness of its own most proper reality and truth, of the fulfilled Word of God in the Old Testament. It has certainly not succeeded in making it jealous, in making clear to it the nearness of the kingdom as the kingdom of tne Son of David, in making Jesus of Nazareth dear and desirable and inviting to it. In this sense the Church as a whole has made no convincing impression on the Jew as a whole. It has debated with him, tolerated him, persecuted him, or abandoned him to persecution without protest. What is worse, it has made baptism an entrance card into the best European society. It has seriously sought the conversion of individuals. But for the most part it has not done for the Jews the only real thing which it can do, attesting the manifested King of Israel and Saviour of the world, the imminent kingdom, in the form of the convincing witness of its own existence. And thus it still owes everything to those to whom it is indebted for everything. This failure, which is often unconscious, or perhaps concealed by all kinds of justifiable or unjustifiable countercharges against the Jews, is one of the darkest chapters in the whole history of Christianity and one of the most serious of all wounds in the body of Christ. Even the modern ecumenical movement suffers more seriously from the absence of Israel than of Rome or Moscow. The Church must live with the Synagogue, not, as fools say in their hearts, as with another religion or confession, but as with the root from which it has itself sprung. But it cannot and will not live with it in the only way possible. For the penetrating pain of this hurt it should not seek false alleviation, even though it may be faithfully at work in all other branches of its ministry. The recurrent Jewish question is the question of Christ and the Church which has not been and cannot be answered by any of its ministries. It stands as an unresolved problem, and therefore as the shadow behind and above all its activity in foreign missions.

In relation to the speaking community, we come finally (6) to the ministry of theology which is of special interest in these pages. There would be no theology if there were no ministry specially committed to the witness of word. It is not in a vacuum, but in relation to this ministry, that there is posed for theology the central problem by which it is constituted a science among others. If we abstract its origin in the ministry of the community, all its problems are either irrelevant or they lose their theological character and may be relegated to the sphere of general and more particularly historical scholarship. Conversely, the community cannot dispense with theology, more especially in relation to the witness of its word, but on a broader view in relation to the whole of its ministry in every form. In theology the community gives a critical account, both to itself and to the world which listens with it, of the appropriateness or otherwise of its praise of God, its preaching, its instruction, its evangelistic and missionary work, but also of the activity which cannot be separated from these things, and therefore of its witness in the full and comprehensive sense and in relation to its origin, theme and content. In the ministry of theology the community tests its whole action by the standard of its commission, and finally in the light of the Word of the Lord who gave it.

In classical Greek θεολογία means generally the investigation of God and divine things. The New Testament does not use the term except that in a few unimportant manuscripts the title of the Book of Revelation calls the author θεόλογος. The thing itself was familiar enough in the New Testament communities, not in the weak general sense, but as the question of the shaping of Christian thinking, speech, action and life in the light of its origin, theme and content. Not merely the Pauline and Johannine but all the New Testament writings are obviously records of varied theological reflection and activity in this sense, and it is expected by the authors of their readers. In the factual accounts as in the doctrines of the apostles and Evangelists there is a by no means negligible amount of such reflection. As the received texts everywhere bear witness, they all put the question of the meaning and legitimacy of what they say as measured by the object presented, and each in his own way, with a view to the community around and in dialogue with the better or worse theology pursued within it, gives his own answer and passes it on to his successors, as we see from the Pastoral Epistles. It may be suggested that Paul perhaps has this special ministry in view when at the head of the list of special gifts in 1 Cor. 12[8] he mentions the λόγος σοφίας and the λόγος γνώσεως. For to what else could he refer but to some kind of action at least along these lines? In some manner and to some degree theology has always and everywhere been pursued in the Christian community. There have naturally been unfortunate relapses into the ambiguous Greek conception. But there has always been a return to the connexion with the community's ministry of witness and therefore to its specifically critical task as Christian theology.

What is the issue? First and basically, it is a matter of expressing the witness to Jesus Christ, and therefore the New Testament in the context of the Old, in ways which are always fresh, yet always more exact and authentic, because based upon a more attentive hearing. This is biblical or exegetical theology. Again, it is a matter of considering and understanding in its dialectic the history of the Christian community right up to our own day as the alternating history of its relationship to the original witness which constitutes it and therefore to the subject of this witness, as its history under and with the Gospel recorded in this witness, and therefore as the history of its loyalty or disloyalty to it. This is ecclesiastical and dogmatic history, including the study of symbols and confessions. Again, it is a matter of the attempt by means of this original witness, and the records of the theoretical and practical understanding which it has hitherto enjoyed (or not enjoyed), to point the community of a given time to the norm of its thought and speech, and implicitly of its whole action, which imposes itself upon it in this time. It is thus a matter, not of trying to exhaust or even to canalise the fulness of Christian knowledge, but of bringing it once more under a suitable denominator, and by this means indicating at least that as a kind of star of the Magi there is such a thing as universally and permanently valid " dogma " which Christianity cannot control but to which it must conform. This is what we now call systematic theology or dogmatics. Finally, it is a matter of seeking the directions which investigation of the original witness, of the previous history of the community, and of the norm which is disclosed to it to-day, shows to be normative for the practice of its ministry in every branch. This is practical theology. None of these four elements may be omitted, nor should any fail to be brought into connexion with the other three, if theology is to be at every point critical scholarship in the context of the ministry of the community, and therefore the fulfilment of the self-criticism which is so bitterly necessary in every age and place.

Theology as a whole and in all its disciplines is a threatened and dangerous undertaking, since it is menaced by every kind of human pride. Can we and should we really attempt it, is a question which may well be asked, and which is in fact asked in many Christian circles. We recall the sigh of Faust that alongside and after many other things he had unfortunately studied theology too. Indeed, its only purpose is to make itself superfluous. But since the rest of Christian ministry is also a human undertaking and therefore in need of criticism and correction, it differs from foreign missionary work in the fact that it can become wholly superfluous only in the *lumen gloriae.* Meanwhile it has necessarily to be pursued, though on account of its vulnerability with the greatest prudence and caution.

It is sound and healthy when in all its four elements it keeps its eye fixed on its problem and theme, and brings these to light. It is unhealthy and more dangerous than useful when it falls victim to human pride and loses sight of its problem and theme, when in different ways it posits itself absolutely in the sense of Greek investigation of God and things divine, and when there is a consequent disintegration of its four elements into a relation of mutual indifference or concealed or open hostility. Biblical and exegetical theology can become a field of wild chasing and charging when it bows to the idol of a supposedly normative historicism and when therefore, without regard to the positively significant yet also warning experiences of ecclesiastical and dogmatic history, or to its co-responsibility in the work of systematic theology (in which it may perhaps make a dilettante incursion), or to the fact that ultimately theology in the form of practical theology must aim to give meaningful directions to the ministry of the community in the world, it claims autonomy as a kind of Vatican within the whole. Similarly ecclesiastical and dogmatic history, if it does not take up the question of the meaning and *telos* of this history, may well cut itself off and become for both systematic and practical theology no more than an unimportant list of strange facts or of arbitrarily undertaken constructions which seek to pass for facts. Similarly, and most of all, systematic theology, if it isolates itself from the biblical witness and its history in the community, or if it thinks it should master them and thus does violence to them, will seek and find in them only a little material for the different stones of its arbitrarily conceived and unfounded system of thought, from which practical theology will certainly not be able to gather any binding directions. Finally, practical theology itself will seriously degenerate if it becomes only a working doctrine which is orientated by every conceivable practical consideration but not by Scripture, history and dogma, and which is therefore theologically empty. These are the many sins of which one might well be guilty in theology.

In the light of what we have already said, it is surely clear that before the end of all things there is no age whose work cannot be taken up again and continued and improved. Together with the whole ministry of the community, the critical scholarship of theology itself stands in constant need of criticism, correction and reform. For the same reason, it is inevitable that in constant self-testing it should be involved in continual warfare not so much with individual errorists as with the countless evil spirits of false or semi-false theology. To be sure, its weapons are those of " righteousness on the right hand and on the left " (2 Cor. 6⁷), yet there can be no doubt as to the conflict. Always there must be serious questioning, analysis, argumentation, construction, discussion and therefore directly or indirectly, and preferably only indirectly, polemics. From time to time, though not all the time, a little of the notorious *rabies theologorum* is thus in place. This does not alter the fact, however, that in itself and as such theology is supremely positive and peaceable, that it fosters peace, and that it is thus to be pursued soberly, good-humouredly, without any nervous excitement, and particularly without too much petty, self-opinionated bickering. It is to be noted further that it is a modest undertaking which like missionary work can only aim to serve rather than to dominate by rendering a certain limited and transitory assistance to the cause of the community and therefore of all Christians and the world as a whole. It is to be noted further that when it is conceived and executed correctly and resolutely, yet also freely and modestly, theology is a singularly beautiful and joyful science (cf. *C.D.*, II, 1, p. 656f.), so that it is only willingly and cheerfully or not at all that we can be theologians.

Two points may be made in conclusion. The first is that in solidarity with the community theology in all its movements must always have in view the surrounding world and its thought and aspiration, its action and inaction, not to draw from it its standards, and certainly not to parley and compromise with it, but in order to maintain a constant awareness of whom and what it speaks when it speaks of man, and also in order that it may bring the *fides* before those who happen to come to its notice in its inner consistency as the *intellectus fidei*, thus making its own contribution to the presentation of the likeness of the kingdom of God. Since it cannot do more than this, it will spare both the world and itself the pain of a specific apologetic, the more so in view of the fact that good dogmatics is always the best and basically the only possible apologetics. Those who are without or partly without hear theologians best when these do not speak so ardently to them but pursue their own way before their eyes and ears. Correctly conceived and executed, theology will present itself even to the community and its members in such a way that it cannot fail to be noticed. For it will not be an alchemy remote from life, but *nostra res agitur*. All indolent talk of non-theological laymen will thus be quietly refuted. For if theology understands and regards itself as an integrating element in the ministry of the community, the conclusion is natural enough that every Christian is responsible for it and has indeed to think of himself as a theologian.

We now turn to the basic forms of the Church's ministry in which it is predominantly action in its varied concretions. If all is well, the speech of the community in all its forms must also be action. Similarly, action will also necessarily be both implicitly and indeed explicitly speech. Nevertheless, there is a second series of forms of ministry in which it is primarily and predominantly action. It is these which we must now consider.

As is perhaps fitting, we begin (7) with prayer. The community works, but it also prays. More precisely, it prays as it works. And in praying, it works. Prayer is not just an occasional breathing of the soul, nor is it merely an individual elevation of the heart. It is a movement in which Christians jointly and persistently engage. It is absolutely indispensable in the accomplishment of the action required of the community. It cannot possibly be separated from this action.

To take only one example, theological work is surely inconceivable and impossible at any time without prayer. All the gulfs and contradictions which occur in it have their final cause in the fact that it is not everywhere carried through in the fellowship of prayer. And what is true of theology is equally true of all the other functions of the Church's ministry.

Prayer is a basic element in the whole action of the whole community. " Pray without ceasing " (1 Thess. 5^{17}). Hence prayer—

we are reminded of the first person plural in the Lord's Prayer—
is a work of the community. In and with the community all the
members can and should also pray individually.

Prayer includes in inseparable union both thanksgiving and
intercession : the one in relation to the past for the free grace of God
already received in it ; the other in relation to the future for the same
grace which will be needed in it. Prayer is, therefore, the acknowledgment that the community which exists in time, as it has performed
and does and will perform its ministry, has lived and does and will
live by the free grace of God addressed to it rather than by the inner
meaningfulness and power of its own action. If God had not freed
it for this action, and were He not to do so again, what freedom or
ability would it have ? In praying, it acknowledges that its whole
action can only be a ministry of witness which as such is totally
referred to its confirmation by the One whom it has to attest, to His
good-pleasure to which it has no claim, which it has not deserved
and cannot deserve, which in past, present and future can only be
His free gift. Yet both as thanksgiving and as intercession prayer is
offered in the certainty of being heard, and therefore in a humble
but bold bid for the divine good-pleasure which will give meaning and
power to its action. Hence in prayer as its confession of God's free
grace we do not have a purely subjective exercise of piety with only
subjective significance. Such an exercise might well lead into the
void. In prayer the community keeps God to His Word, which is
the promise of His faithfulness as the Word which calls, gathers,
upbuilds and commissions it. It keeps Him to the fact that its cause
is His. Appealing to His free grace, it expects quite simply that He
will let Himself be kept to His Word and therefore that its cause
which was His yesterday will be His again to-morrow. In its thanksgiving and intercession it thus enters without doubt or hesitation,
not hypothetically but confidently, into the dealings which God has
initiated between it and Him, becoming an active partner in the
covenant which He has established. Hence prayer is no mere gesture
of elevation. It creates in the world a fact which has this significance
and which speaks for itself, whether it is heard and accepted by the
world or not. Where else in the world does it take place that God is
thanked for the love with which He has turned to the world and asked
that He will turn to it again with this love ? Where else in the world
is there the unreserved confession that we can do nothing in our own
strength but that all things are possible to Him ? Above all, where
else in the world does there operate the certainty which enables us
to keep God to His Word and therefore not merely to feel and think
and say but actually to do and accomplish something in our dealings
with Him ? Does not the whole world need that this very thing
should take place in it, that together with the many other things
which it does prayer should be offered ? And it is the community

which with its prayer no less than its praise can act representatively for the world, going on before and introducing as a witness this fact, this obvious likeness, of reconciliation, the covenant and fellowship between God and man.

This must be done, however, in all its action in every part and element. Where it does not pray, it does not work, its whole action being hollow and futile. If it is to pray without ceasing, neither in its life as a community nor in the life of its individual members should this become an excuse for not giving concrete form to its thanksgiving and intercession. And the proper place for this, as for praise, is in the assembly for divine service in which it continually constitutes itself afresh as the Christian community. The prayer of the Church, which must have quite unconditionally the character of both thanksgiving and intercession, is not from the formal standpoint a ritual addition to liturgical action but an integral part of it, of no less dignity than praise and preaching, with which it cannot be brought into too close or evident conjunction. Indeed, with the praise of God it is prayer particularly which for its members and the listening world unequivocally distinguishes the gathering of the community from a lecture society and characterises it as action, as divine service which as such is also in the innermost sense human service. Restoration of the widely and seriously threatened dignity, importance and effectiveness of the whole liturgical action depends not least upon whether it succeeds in recapturing the character of prayer, of common thanksgiving and intercession, and therefore of an activity.

In detail it has to be considered whether the prayers before and after preaching ought not to be brought into much closer connexion with it even externally, not being separated by congregational singing or organ music, but forming a threefold complex opened and closed by singing. Again, it ought to be considered whether these prayers should not always be worked out afresh, so that, instead of recurring in stereotyped fashion from a printed book or sheet, they are newly fashioned and therefore prepared with the sermon for each Sunday in honour of the living Lord of the living community. Again, it must be considered whether the antithesis of the confession of sin and the promise of grace—naturally in the reverse order—would not be better placed in the context of preaching rather than in the opening prayer or the rather questionable little drama which serves as the commencement of divine worship in many places, the opening prayer being reserved for thanksgiving for the call of God which gathers the community and intercession for the presence and activity of the Holy Ghost. Again, it has to be considered whether the Lord's Prayer, best repeated by the whole congregation, would not better come at the end, or even at the beginning, of the opening prayer than at the conclusion of the final prayer. Finally, it must be asked whether this final prayer should not for the most part and decisively, instead of occasionally or not at all, follow the example of the Liturgy of Chrysostom and consist in intercession for the whole state of Christ's Church, for all the semi-Christian or non-Christian world, for all the men who err or sin or suffer in so many ways, and especially for those who hold positions of responsibility, so that at the climax of the service, and in transition to administration of the Lord's Supper, there is the necessary opening of the doors and windows to the outside world, and this in the best possible form, namely, of calling upon God.

By the cure of souls (8) we understand the activity of the community as a sign and witness to individuals both within itself and in the nearer or most distant world around.

In the language of the Bible and that of Christian understanding the term " soul " (*nephesh*, and sometimes *ruach, ψυχή*, and occasionally *πνεῦμα*) means the totality of a human being in his individual personal existence, and therefore this or that man in his unique and incomparable individuality grounded in the fact that as this or that man he is the object of the love of God which is not merely universal but particular in its universality, and therefore of the promise and claim of God which are not merely general but wholly specific ; that he is a creature of the Spirit of God quickening and sustaining him (cf. *C.D.*, III, 2, § 46). The cure of souls, *cura animarum*, thus means in general concern for the individual in the light of God's purpose for him, of the divine promise and claim addressed to him, of the witness specially demanded of him. God is the One who is primarily and properly concerned about souls. They are always in His hand. Yet in His service, in the ministry of witness committed to His people, there is a corresponding human concern, a cure of souls to be exercised by men to men, a *mutua consolatio fratrum*. The theological foundations of this are considered by Eduard Thurneysen in his book *Die Lehre von der Seelsorge*, 1946.

The cure of souls, too, has to be understood and exercised as a form, and indeed a basic form, of the divine and human service of the community. Within the community it may indeed, like all the other functions, be the concern of those specially called and gifted in this regard. Yet no Christian can escape responsibility for it. Preaching, instruction, evangelisation, missionary work and theology all have to do with it. It is also exercised indirectly by the community in common prayer. The witness enjoined on the community would be blunted if it were merely a general call, if it were not everywhere directed immediately and personally to individuals *intra et extra muros*, if it did not remind them of the specific form in which the kingdom has drawn near for them, in which the promise and claim of God addressed to all have them particularly in view, if in virtue of their declaration individuals are not helped and restored and freed and invited and summoned. Who does not need this reminder, and therefore who does not need this ministry ? In everything that it does the community has also to exercise the cure of souls, *mutua consolatio fratrum*.

But here, too, the general includes rather than excludes the particular, i.e., the turning of one brother to another, or to one who is not yet a brother but may be claimed as such only *in spe*, as this is actualised concretely and specifically in fulfilment of the ministry of the community. The cure of souls understood in this special sense as the individual cure of souls means a concrete actualisation of the participation of the one in the particular past, present and future of the other, in his particular burdens and afflictions, but above all in his particular promise and hope in the singularity of his existence as created and sustained by God. It means the active interest of the

one in the divine calling and therefore in the being and nature of this
specific other. In the cure of souls, he accepts responsibility for his
new or newly confirmed membership of the community of knowledge
and witness. He does so by inviting him to be open, by listening in
a spirit of openness, and by assisting him by pointing to the Word
of God which nourishes him also to temporal and eternal life. It
means helping another by making clear to him that he is ordained a
witness of Jesus Christ and that he is usable as such. To this extent
it is the attempt to fill a gap in the life and witness of the community
which has either arisen or which threatens in the person of the other.
It is thus a legitimate exercise of the Church discipline which in the
past has been a more painful than profitable undertaking on the part
of the Christian Church. Here in the cure of souls there can and should
be confession with the promise of the remission of sins, and the
invitation to the resultant amendment of life, not as an institution
bound to certain clerical officials, but as an event. Here in the cure
of souls, in certain extraordinary conditions of emergency and conflict,
and as made possible by highly specialised calling and endowment,
there may be actions analagous to the healings and exorcisms which
receive such emphasis in the charge to the first disciples. It certainly
cannot be questioned that such emergencies and also such callings and
endowments do in fact exist. The only thing is that we cannot
postulate them and incorporate them into a regular programme.

All who can and should exercise the cure of souls must be clear
that they are not merely serving man but both God and man : God
for the sake of man and man for the sake of God ; neither God
according to the standard of an arbitrarily conceived picture of God
nor man according to a similar picture of man ; but both God and
man according to the standard of the image of Jesus Christ, of the
covenant between them established and sealed in Him ; and therefore
God as the merciful Father, Friend and Helper of man and man in
the light of the fact that in his specific time and situation he is called
and ordained to be a hearer of the Word of this covenant and a witness
of this Word. Whether he knows it or not, to become this is that
which is determined for every man as the salutary thing which he
profoundly and finally needs. To be serviceable to him in this respect,
to show him the way to it, is the unique beginning of what the community can do for him in the cure of souls. Seldom or never will this
occur without the unconscious—and why not the conscious ?—
presupposition and sometimes application of various forms of general
or secular and therefore neutral psychology, psychogogics and
psychotherapy. This does not alter the fact, however, that the
problems of the cure of souls begin where those of a neutral psychology
and the neutral art of healing based upon it cease. It can thus understand the problems of the latter and include them in its own discussions,
but it cannot take them over or try to solve them. This means that

the community's pastoral care must have such a knowledge of its own modest and restricted function that it really knows what it is after and can the better achieve it so far as there can be any question of achievement. Everything depends upon its constant practical discharge in the Christian understanding of God and man and the divine calling and ordination of man. Everything depends upon its fidelity in doing what it does in this understanding. If it knows its own business and acts accordingly, there can be no fear of its becoming a superfluous religious duplication of the neutral science and art, and it will have both in its own narrower circle and in the world around the power of a sign of salvation and witness of the kingdom which only the community can set up.

In connexion with our exposition or sketch of the cure of souls it must also be said, if it is difficult to say with precision, that to the active witness of the community there belong (9) the production and existence of definite personal examples of Christian life and action.

Perhaps it is along these lines, as a demonstration of the depth and power of faith exemplified in individuals within the community, that we are to understand the striking inclusion of πίστις in the Pauline list of *charismata* in 1 Cor. 12⁹. For how else are we to explain it ? There was a time not far distant, which began in the earlier and later stages of Romantic Pietism and which culminated in the Liberalism of more radical Ritschlians and kindred groups, when the concept of prominent Christian personalities played an unfortunate role, and under the influence of Carlyle with his heroes and hero worship even threatened to become almost the central Christian concept to men like Paul Wernle. In theology as a whole this age now seems to be past. But can we simply abandon what lay behind this trend ? Are there not in fact Christians whom like the Pietists we can describe as " chosen vessels " (Ac. 9¹⁵) in relative distinction from others, and whose existence is absolutely necessary to the life and witness of the community ? If this brings us inevitably into close proximity to Roman Catholic doctrine and practice, we should not let this prevent us from perceiving a serious problem and tackling it as such. It is naturally intolerable that, in obvious opposition to both the spirit and the letter of the New Testament, we should describe these models of Christian existence as " saints " in distinction from others, that we should call upon these sometimes very singular saints as guardians and helpers, that by curious processes we should ascribe to them the honour of altars and that we should direct upon them a whole mass of popular superstition. Yet we should still recognise the genuine concern concealed behind these confused developments.

It was the case in New Testament days, and has been so in all subsequent periods, that the voice of the community, surrounded, accompanied and sometimes overwhelmed by many others, is very largely that of individuals impressing their life and witness on their own time and place and beyond, and giving characteristic and representative expression to the message of their day either in strength or weakness, clearly or not so clearly, in a way which invites or possibly repels. The life of the community would not be healthy, nor its witness eloquent, if it did not have such proponents. It makes no odds what higher or lower function or office these men have. It makes no odds whether they have any official function at all. It is not a matter of the form or quality of their character, culture, morality, or human appearance and achievement. In this field the last may often be first and the first last. What counts is that the general perception of the community, its general speech and action, the word entrusted to it and the action demanded, should in some way emerge in these persons in such sharp contours and glowing colours that not the significance of their persons, but the validity in their persons of what is common to all Christians, should be in some sense illumined and for a time and in certain circles both *ad intra* and *ad extra* acquire in them an exemplary, directive and canonical character. The process naturally entails certain dangers.

It can be the ground of fatal attachments and these can lead to fatal mis-conceptions. In virtue of its one-sidedness personal light of this kind can easily be or become the light of error. Such prominent characters are constantly ex-posed to the temptation to glorify themselves in their individuality by means of the Gospel rather than to glorify the Gospel in their individuality, perhaps even beating their fellow-servants and eating and drinking with the drunken (Mt. 24⁴⁹). Even if they honestly and successfully resist this temptation, who is to protect them against the narrower or wider groups of personal followers, the -ians, with their impulse to address them as master, father, leader and the like (Mt. 23⁸ᶠ·), and to make them the object of a personal cult by which the light of the community, as has obviously been found in the Soviet community, is in fact placed under a bushel rather than set on a candlestick ? And who is to protect Christianity and its witness even in the eyes and judgment of those around from the confusion of its cause with the unique greatness of these figures and their conduct and enterprises, which will also in their own way contain something at least of pettiness and therefore of vulnerability ? For this reason it is as well that these trees should not grow to heaven and that the time and sphere of such prominent Christian figures should usually be limited.

We should also consider, however, the less dangerous aspects. In spite of all the fears and reservations to be noted in this regard, it is not merely a matter of experience, but fundamentally true, that the Holy Spirit is not a friend of too doctrinaire democracy, that the community living in the ministry of its witness can never remain a uniform multitude of believers (Ac. 4³²) within which at most the pastors or bishops or other ecclesiastical dignitaries may be separated from the rest in virtue of their office. It does not in any way contradict the priesthood of all believers in the community, nor the equality of all Christians before God as poor and lost sinners saved and kept only by grace, that the community always needs and may point to the existence of specific individuals who, without leaving the multitude of believers, within it, and therefore in relation to the world around, stand out as models or examples in their special calling and endowment, its witness being more clear and comprehensible and impressive in their persons and activity than in those of others. Certainly in none of them do we see it in fulness, but only in one or another of its elements and aspects. Yet in these we see it with a certain concentration which at least indicates its fulness, which makes them in distinction from others the inciters and initiators of greater or lesser movements in the life of the community, which enables them to admonish, instruct, encourage and comfort the community again in some regard and therefore as a whole, and thus to impel it in the ministry of its witness. The one may do this in virtue of his radiant warmth of Christian love and self-sacrifice, the other in virtue of his particularly compelling and stimulating Christian hope. The one may do it in virtue of the energy of his Christian thinking and knowledge, the other in virtue of his particular perspicacity, boldness and steadfastness in the temptations and trials which assail the community, and him within it, both from within and from without. What impresses may be the Christian earnestness or the Christian serenity of his attitude and conduct. He may be an example of Christian freedom or Christian commitment. He may arouse respect in his Christian isolation, or awaken interest in his Christian breadth and openness to people. To be sure, none is without his definite and perhaps very obvious limitations and faults and transgressions. None is by a long chalk a second Christ. But each in his particularity is a witness of Christ to be greeted with particular thanksgiving. For what would the community be if it were referred only to the Christian mediocrity in which all these possibilities might finally be open in a mild form to all ? What would it be if it had no place for shining exceptions ? What would its external witness be if there were only that Christian mediocrity and none of these lights which, even if only transitorily, shine with particular brilliance ? As the representatives of a special action of God in the community they are also the special representatives of the action of the community. We cannot postulate their existence. They cannot be part of a programme. It can only be an event if they are present. The community cannot, therefore, seek to produce them. It can only do so in fact. That it does so ; that such special Christians continually come and go in Christendom as examples to others and as outstanding executives of its action in the world ; that the community may continually repose some measure of confidence in them, accepting their guidance for a while in a specific sphere and specific respects and thus being grateful for their existence, is absolutely indispensable. Hence we have always to think expressly of them, too, when we consider the basic forms of the ministry of the community.

We come to a hotly disputed point in the more specifically active ministry of the community when we turn (10) to what is called its diaconate in the more special sense. Diaconate means quite simply and generally the rendering of service. Hence it does not denote only a specific action of the community but the whole breadth and depth of its action. For with its witness it always serves both God and man. It is only customarily and never unconditionally that the term has come to be used to denote a special ministry, namely, the helping of those in physical or material distress both within the community and outside. In this sense, however, it has proved to be both meaningful and useful.

The origin of the diaconate in this special sense is to be found in the account in Ac. 6[1f.] of the solemn selection and institution of seven men, whose names are given, to undertake the διακονία of the daily provision particularly for widows (though probably this word is meant to cover all in material want) within the circle of the infant Christian fellowship in Jerusalem, thus freeing the apostles for prayer and for the διακονία τοῦ λόγου. It is to be noted, however, that they are not yet expressly called διάκονοι. Nor do we hear any more of the discharge of their particular task. Five of the seven are never mentioned again. And what we are told of the first two, namely, Stephen (Ac. 6[8f.] and 7[1f.]) and Philip (8[5f.] and 21[8]), has to do for the most part, and rather surprisingly, with their participation in the proclamation of the Word. In the rest of the New Testament the word διακονία usually indicates quite generally the relationship of service in which especially the apostles stand, but also all other Christians, and Jesus Christ Himself at their head (Rom. 15[8]). Certainly in Rom. 12[7] (unlike the parallels in 1 Cor. 12[8f.,] 28[f.]), διακονία is mentioned as one of the various *charismata*. Again, in Rom. 16[1] a woman Phoebe appears as διάκονος of the community of Cenchrea, and deacons are mentioned with bishops in the introduction to Philippians (1[1]) and also in 1 Tim. 3[8f.,] 12[f.] as the bearers of specific functions in the Church, though we are not told exactly what their particular tasks are. It is only in the 2nd century that the term is clearly used to link social and liturgical obligations. In the Roman Catholic sphere this is still reflected in the fact that the diaconate is the final stage in the preliminary orders which precede the sacerdotal ministry as the full spiritual office. In the older Reformed Churches the term " deacon " or " assistant " was often used to describe the second pastor in a congregation in distinction from the first, the dignified *archidiaconus* or " chief assistant " being used in the case of the Minster Church at Basel. But this is a reactionary deviation from the renewal of a social diaconate attempted in the course of the 16th-century Reformation by Bucer in Strassburg and both theoretically and practically by Calvin in Geneva.

The breadth and depth of the matter, which are evident even from the history of the term, should not escape us even though we rightly think of it to-day in its narrower character. For what specific action of the community can ever be anything but διακονία, *ministerium*, the rendering of service ? And conversely, is it not inevitable that what is called diaconate in the narrower sense should touch and intersect and link up with the action of the community in all its branches ? Is there any preaching, evangelisation or cure of souls which is not necessarily an act of diaconate, or which does not directly or indirectly include such an act ? Is there any form of diaconate which is not implicitly or explicitly preaching, evangelisation and cure of souls ?

There is good reason, however, to describe more specifically as service or diaconate the form of the action of the community in which *a parte potiori* relief is brought to the materially needy both within and without the community. For many forms of its action, such as the work of a powerful preacher or evangelist, a dignified leader of worship, a successful pastor or a learned theologian, can so easily be encircled by an ambiguous glory in which their character as service is easily lost and the Christians active in these ways seem rather to achieve a superior mastery and control over men and situations. But the things done in diaconate, e.g., caring for the sick, the feeble, and the mentally confused and threatened, looking after orphans, helping prisoners, finding new homes for refugees, stretching out a hand to stranded and shattered fellow-men of all kinds, can obviously never be more than drops in a bucket and are usually done in concealment, so that by their very nature no great glory can attach to them, and they can be undertaken and executed only as pure, selfless and unassuming service which might well be hampered or even totally spoiled by even occasional attempts at domination. In this respect the community has a unique chance unequivocally to accomplish and manifest its witness as a ministry of witness. This is what makes the diaconate formally so important and indispensable as a basic form of witness.

But the material point has also to be considered that in diaconate the community explicitly accepts solidarity with the least of little ones, with the ἐλάχιστοι (Mt. 25[40, 45]), with those who are in obscurity and are not seen, with those who are pushed to the margin and perhaps the very outer margin of the life of human society, with fellow-creatures who temporarily at least, and perhaps permanently, are useless and insignificant and perhaps even burdensome and destructive. In the diaconate these men are recognised to be brothers of Jesus Christ according to the significant tenor of the parable of the Last Judgment (Mt. 25[31f.]), and therefore the community confesses Jesus Christ Himself as finally the hungry, thirsty, naked, homeless, sick, imprisoned man, and the royal man as such. In the diaconate the community makes plain its witness to Him as the Samaritan service to the man who has fallen among thieves—a service fulfilled in company with Him as the true Neighbour of this lost man. In the diaconate it goes and does likewise (Lk. 10[29f.]). And woe to it if it does not, if its witness is not service in this elementary sense! For if not, even though its proclamation of Christ is otherwise ever so powerful, it stands hopelessly on the left hand among the goats. If not, even though its zeal in other respects is ever so ardent, it is on the steep slope which leads to eternal punishment. Without this active solidarity with the least of little ones, without this concrete witness to Jesus the Crucified, who as such is the Neighbour of the lost, its witness may be ever so pure and full at other points, but it is all futile.

A further material point is that here in the diaconate it has the opportunity to reveal at least in sign the cosmic character of the reconciliation accomplished in Jesus Christ, of the kingdom, of love for God and one's neighbour and therefore of the content of the witness which it has to give to men in its preaching, evangelisation, cure of souls and missionary work. It has this opportunity at the point where it intervenes for man more specifically in his physical and material existence and therefore for the whole man. For here it escapes the misconception that in its message its final concern is only with words, thoughts, ideas, feelings and moral injunctions. To be sure, even here it will not act without granting the Word as well to the least of little ones, without calling them urgently and explicitly to God who, as He is the primary and proper Preacher, Teacher, Evangelist, Pastor and Theologian, is also the primary and proper Deacon. Nevertheless, its distinctive action here is to hold out a helping hand, indicatively and in part at least causing the good deed which corresponds to the good Word to be tasted and felt, and thus enabling the good Word to be understood in the fulness of its truth. It is here that medicine in all its branches has its theological origin and place. Specifically in the diaconate the community, whether or not it is given greater or lesser power to heal and to cast out demons, can be obedient to the second and easily overlooked element in the direction for service given by Jesus to His disciples, thus serving the whole truth which otherwise is divided and reduced to a purely intellectual, moral and sentimental form, so that it is no longer the truth of Jesus Christ at all. On this side, too, the vital necessity of the diaconate is obvious.

Consideration must now be given to three particularly urgent problems in the theory and practice of the Christian diaconate.

First, its distinctive task of giving help to the needy in the totality of their human existence cannot be undertaken in the long run unless the community realises that the need of individuals is also and indeed decisively, though not exclusively, grounded in certain disorders of the whole of human life in society, so that at certain points a limit will be set to what it can do or try to do by prevailing social, economic and political conditions. The community must not close its eyes to this fact, nor try to evade its partial responsibility for it. Does it not also belong to the human society in which there can be these disorders? Has it not contributed to their emergence at least by its silence? This recognition will not cause the diaconate to refrain from fulfilling its task at the frontier set by these relationships. But it cannot refrain from expressing this recognition, from imparting it to the community in order that the latter may raise its voice and with its proclamation of the Gospel summon the world to reflect on social injustice and its consequences and to alter the conditions and relationships in question. In this situation there is need for the open word of Christian social criticism in order that a new place may be found for Christian action and a new meaning given to it.

The way must be trodden whose main direction (the helping of God, of the brethren and of the state) was indicated in Germany in the latter part of the 19th century by the successive thinkers J. H. Wichern, F. v. Bodelschwingh, A. Stoeker, F. Naumann and C. Blumhardt Jr. Every step taken involved a host of difficulties, objections, genuine and spurious problems, differences of opinion and conflicts. These were all in some way connected with the fact that in this as in so many other matters the community had been too long asleep or inactive, and that it needed the competition of godless Marxist Socialism with its evangelisation and diaconate, combined under the name of Home Missions, to set it moving in the necessary direction. The same difficulties will arise in the altered relationships of the present. But they should not prevent the Christian diaconate, even at the risk of being accused of singing a political and therefore an unwelcome tune, from reaching out in this direction, while not of course neglecting its proper task.

The diaconate and the Christian community become dumb dogs, and their service a serving of the ruling powers, if they are afraid to tackle at their social roots the evils by which they are confronted in detail.

Secondly, it may happen, and has recently done so to an increasing degree, that the state, perhaps under an original Christian impulse but mostly in its almost irresistible development to a more or less openly totalitarian and therefore a welfare state, has taken over the tasks which were once discharged by the diaconate (under the title of *Caritas* in Roman Catholicism), assuming responsibility for them one after the other, so that first education and now pastoral care in the widest sense have come under its wing, being transformed into a varied apparatus of social security and assistance backed by all the material and financial resources of the state, embracing all known and patent cases of need, and working with incomparably greater efficacy. Does this mean that there is no further need for Christian diaconate ? Is it simply clinging to a lost position which it will finally have to surrender ? The answer is in the negative. It has still to recall its own particular possibilities and to look for new ones. For instance, the pastoral care which the state gives can tackle the various evils only from outside, and therefore in the main only from physical and material standpoints, and therefore only partially, so that there is no care for the whole man. However much it may do for him, what has it really to say to him ? There is also the threat that its action will become the functioning of officials doling out pensions rather than the service which forms the nerve of true assistance from man to man. Again, we have to remember the innumerable hidden cases of need which cannot be provided for in any state scheme, but which the community must have the detective skill and imagination to discover, and to meet which it must find the appropriate new ways and methods. Finally, it is surely the business of the diaconate to assist the state by placing suitable men at its disposal to act within it in this particular way. When we take all these factors into account, we certainly cannot conclude that the welfare state renders the diaconate superfluous.

Thirdly, the diaconate, like missionary work, is an affair of the community as such. The community without responsibility of diaconate would not be the Christian community. Nor can it delegate this responsibility to individual members, unions, societies, organisations and groups. It is right enough that in fulfilment of this responsibility there should be in the community deacons and deaconesses specially called and fitted and endowed for this purpose, that those particularly concerned with the matter, again in the community and in fulfilment of its responsibility, should find themselves specially associated, e.g., in fellowships of deacons and deaconesses, that special organisations should thus be formed for the purpose, and finally that these special societies should develop distinctive modes and orders of life in accordance with their special nature and orientation. It is not right, however, if the law of these working societies makes itself out to be different from that which guides the whole community, or if their distinctive form either has or adopts any other purpose than that of expressing concretely the obligation of service laid on the whole community. Nor is it right if other Christians think that the existence of such individuals or groups even partially relieves them of their full responsibility for the ministry laid upon them in their totality. There may be something to be said for accepting an almost monastic discipline in the special discharge of the diaconate, but if so this must not be allowed to give rise to the fatal idea that the existence of deacons is a peculiar one in a peculiar status or order rather than normal Christian existence specially adapted to a special purpose. Is it not possible and necessary that this idea should be carefully avoided ? And from the opposite angle is it not possible and necessary that both theoretically and practically the community should play a much more forceful role in what takes place in its name in the diaconate, e.g., by transforming the collections at divine service, which are often for charitable purposes, into what they used to be in the early Church, namely, an action in which it consciously places itself behind those members who according to their special vocation are active in the diaconate, not just buying itself off with a few coins, but itself engaging in the concrete work of diaconate ? Is there not, indeed, a great deal that can be done by way of quiet personal diaconate among Christians or between Christians and non-Christians or semi-Christians in their own homes ? A final and to-day very relevant question in this respect is as follows : What is the real defect if, as we are constantly told, there is in the community so little readiness for the diaconate in the narrower sense, i.e., for service as deacons or deaconesses, so that there has to be continual retrenchment in the work of the diaconate ? Does it lie only in the worldliness and materialism of the younger generation on which the blame is often far too hastily fixed ? Does it lie only in the fact that the working societies of deacons have not always been successful in so fashioning their ministry of the Gospel in accordance with the Gospel itself, and therefore in so discharging it with the freedom and cheerfulness of the Gospel that direct participation in it is effectively invited ? We do well to refrain from rash accusations either on the one side or the other. For either way this deeply unsettling question is addressed to the whole community. The action of the community in the ministry of its witness is (11) a prophetic action, i.e., an action based on perception into the meaning of the current events, relationships and forms both of its own history and that of the world around in their positive and negative connexion to the imminent kingdom of God attested by it and therefore in their significance for the concrete form of this witness.

It can and should be left open whether this is a correct interpretation and exhaustive definition of what is called προφητεία in the New Testament. It cannot be shown that it is not. The true interpretation and definition are certainly to be sought in this direction. What we know for certain is simply that according to Acts there were in the widely varying communities of the first period both male and female prophets, including some false ones (Mt. 24¹¹, 1 Jn. 4¹), that prophecy is the only *charisma* mentioned in all the lists (Rom. 12¹, 1 Cor. 12 and Eph. 4), that Paul expressly ranks it above all other gifts in 1 Cor. 14¹: μᾶλλον δὲ ἵνα προφητεύητε, that it was thus an indispensable element in the life of those communities and can claim even to-day to be regarded and estimated as one of the basic forms of the ministry of the community. In 1 Cor. 14 it is distinguished to its advantage from speaking with tongues—the special topic of discussion—by the fact that the particular πνεῦμα which moves the prophet does not simply overmaster and control him (v. 5) but remains under his control (v. 32), that what he utters can be understood at once and should also be judged by others (v. 29), that his word serves to edify, admonish and comfort the community (v. 4, 24), and finally that if it is genuine prophecy it will always confirm the apostolic word (v. 37). We also learn from this passage that the exercise of prophecy can and should be the affair of all for the instruction and admonition of all (v. 34) and that by it all may have the ability to speak convincingly to unbelievers too (v. 24). These are important hints towards a proper understanding. The only thing which we are not told in 1 Cor. 14 is what is concretely at issue in New Testament προφητεία and how it is to be distinguished from ἀποκάλυψις, γνῶσις and διδαχή, with which it is associated in v. 6. Since what we say in this regard must correspond to the obvious importance of the matter in the New Testament (as distinct from *glossolalia*), we follow in our presupposed definition what we learn from the Old Testament concerning the function of prophets. Prophecy rests on a special apprehension and consists in a special declaration of the Word of God that is continually spoken in His work, namely, in the history of His people and the world as directed by Him. It rests on a special apprehension and consists in a special declaration of the Word in which God does not replace, amplify nor supersede what He has said once and for all in the establishment of the covenant, but in which He does repeat and confirm it at a given time with a new clarity and in a way which demands new attention and obedience.

In the prophetic element and character of its ministry the community looks and grasps and moves in and from its present into the future, not arbitrarily nor on the basis of analyses, prognostications and projects, but in attention to the voice of its Lord who is also the Lord of the world, who repeats what He said when He called, established and commissioned it in what now takes place within it and the world as spheres of His lordship, who thus points and leads it to the future, and lays on its lips in a new form, though with no material change, the witness entrusted to it. To-day and here is heard the voice of the One who was and is and is to come. To-day and here it is to be heard by His community and attested as His voice. But "to-day and here" means in His work, in the divinely controlled history of the community and the world in its present form. To be sure, this is a puzzling form for Christians as for others. But it cannot be only this for Christians and the community. It cannot be a night in which all the cats are grey. It is surely necessary that in every present the community should not only be engaged in fresh self-examination and self-amendment as *ecclesia semper reformanda*, but also that it should be at least a length or half-length ahead of the world, instead of far behind, in its awareness of the "signs of the times" (Mt. 16³) and its sensing of things which must come to pass. Why should it not be able and equipped to do this when it is granted and permitted in the confusion of so many Christian or semi-Christian or non-Christian voices always to hear also the very different voice of the living God acting and speaking in Jesus Christ, always to hear His Word, the same Word as it heard yesterday and the day before in a very different form, and as it will hear to-morrow and the day after in a new form again, as a new promise and direction? If it hears it to-day as it is uttered to-day, it detects and sees and distinguishes that which must or should not obtain in its own life and in the world, that which should no longer or not yet do so, that which is waiting its turn, that which is ripe to be received or discarded, to be done or not done, in short, the free but clear decision which has now to be taken because it is now the will of God and therefore good and acceptable and perfect (Rom. 12²). As it recognises the necessity of this decision, and makes it, and proclaims it in the world, its witness is prophetic. It acquires the concrete thrusts of which we spoke earlier. In these it points in and from the present into the future. It was along such lines at least that there took place the witness and activity of the Old Testament prophets. And it is hard to imagine that the community of Jesus Christ can exist except under the necessity and in the freedom of such prophetic witness.

It is only to be expected that in giving it, it will come up against a threatening and apparently impenetrable wall of suspicion, rejection, contradiction and opposition both within and without. In the prophetic element and character of its witness, it must and will become concretely and painfully clear that in its content we are concerned not only with the new work and Word of the grace of God but also with a new world reality in face of which the old cannot continue but only perish. It is this which, in the prophetic witness of the community to the Word of God which here and now demands new attention and obedience, is reflected and delineated with the greatest possible clarity and in a way which prevents any confusion with mere plerophoric and disruptive pronouncements of a supposedly eschatological character. In the one call to advance, to be received and followed here and now, there is here compressed the whole Gospel as a message to the community and through it to the world. What will happen if the community appropriates this call, not timelessly and in general, but here and now in particular, here and now in detail, and indeed in the most specific detail ? Will it not ruthlessly show that, while the Christian and even perhaps the non-Christian may perhaps be prepared for serious faith in a well-known God from whom nothing new is to be expected to-day, among both Christians and non-Christians alike joy in the Gospel, or its toleration, reaches the limits where, deciding and calling for decision with this prophetic thrust, it points to the present, and beyond it to the future ? What will be the result ? Probably there will be division even in the community itself. The tares will be sifted from the wheat. Many, and perhaps the majority, will take offence and hold back and become incensed and turn accusingly away from or even against the few who believe that they should not deny or conceal the prophetic character of the Christian witness. And in the world around it will probably happen that most folk, awakened as by the unusual sound of a trumpet, will be roused from the indifference with which they are prepared to accept as tolerable within limits the singing, prayer, preaching, pastoral care and diaconate of the community, and even its evangelisation and missionary work, and will find again in the community, or at least in this resolute part of it, the opponent whom they have perhaps long since suspected. In other words, when the conflict between the Christian witness and the world comes to be unmistakeably concentrated in this command to advance, and perhaps only so, it will become unavoidable and patent. And it may well be that, since the prophetic command is no more acceptable to many Christians than to semi-Christians and non-Christians, there will be concluded the same kind of unholy but very effective alliance between priests and false prophets on the one side, and rulers and people on the other, which offered such determined resistance to the prophets of the Old Testament. The results are incalculable when the community, or even an important section within it, dares to take its ministry of witness seriously in its prophetic character.

This is no reason for failing to take it seriously in this character. It is indeed a test of the genuineness of its minstry in every other function that in them too, in its preaching, prayer, diaconate, theology etc., its ministry should have this prophetic character regardless of the consequences, and that it should therefore attest this call to advance. Prophetic does not mean ecstatic, enthusiastic or violent. On the contrary, prophetic witness implies the sober disclosure of the sublime and exciting truth that two times two are not now five, as the crowd always thinks, but that in a new sense and with a new power they are still unexpectedly four, This witness cannot possibly be given in the community in a way which is only incidental, capricious or accidental. It cannot possibly be a matter only of the foolish freedom of the few, at best merely tolerated by the remainder. Here, too, our concern is with the ministry of the whole community, with a gift and possibility of which at bottom all Christians are invited and summoned to make use. Again, of course, it is natural and right enough that certain individuals should have special abilities to sense or detect what is coming in the present, and special freedom to pursue the road from yesterday through to-day to to-morrow. It is natural and right, then, that they should precede in this matter and the rest follow. But it is neither natural nor right that there should not be in the whole community a dominant openness to this prophetic call, and a readiness and willingness to obey it. For if there is not, then it is inevitable that there should be a sifting in the community, a painful division and even conflict, entailing the necessity of reformation and reconstitution in both head and members.

There can be no doubt that the witness of a community can have little or no promise if the Spirit is quenched, prophecy despised and the searching question of the good allowed to stagnate (1 Thess. 5[19f.]). The remarkable observation of 1 Cor. 14[24f.] is also to be recalled in this connexion, namely, that, on the assumption that all members of the community are as such witnesses in this character and therefore prophets, all may have the power to address those whom they meet outside with such direct understanding of the secrets of their hearts that they will be immediately caused to fall down on their faces, to worship God and to report " that God is in you of a truth." To my knowledge there is no other function of the community's ministry which is said by the New Testament to have anything like the same power of witness. Does not this force us to a serious consideration of the decisive significance of the prophetic activity of the community ? Yet it is of the prophecy of all Christians, of the whole community, that this tremendous affirmation is made.

The Christian community acts (12) in the fact that it establishes fellowship. It does this comprehensively by attesting as the first and final mystery of its message the supreme fellowship, namely, that of the Father with the Son and the Son with the Father in the Holy Spirit, and on this basis the particular fellowship of Jesus Christ as the Head with the community as His body and each of its members, and on this basis the more general fellowship which God has newly and definitely established between Himself and the whole world as created by Him. In virtue of this content the witness of the community as such is the act which establishes fellowship, namely, between men. The establishment of divine and divine-human fellowship, i.e., fellowship between Jesus Christ and itself, or God and the whole world, cannot be its act. But as this is its content, in sign at least it can certainly establish fellowship between men. For in recognition of the one kingdom which has drawn near to all, of the one covenant concluded in the name of all and to the salvation of all, it calls all to free thanksgiving for the one grace of God addressed to all and to the one free service in the sphere of lordship of this grace. It thus brings and rivets and holds them all together, binding them more strongly to one another than anything else could do. This binding of men to one another is also an indispensable element and mark of all the forms and functions of the Church's ministry. Certainly this cannot be executed without all kinds of separations, without the disrupting and destroying of false, corrupt and fatal human fellowship. In all that is done by His community, the sword of Jesus Christ (Mt. 10^{34}) will continually prove to be necessary and powerful. Yet in no form nor function is its ministry rightly performed unless it aims at unity even in separation and peace in conflict, and therefore unless its performance results in the visible emergence and operation of new and true and fruitful and lasting fellowship between men.

As the community goes to the nations, to all nations according to Mt. 28^{19}, calling them to discipleship, it certainly does not remove the frontiers and differences between them. On the other hand, it does not sanction them. Rather it constitutes right across them a new people in which the members of all peoples do not merely meet but are united. Gathered to it, men are first members of this new people, i.e., Christians, and only then, without disloyalty to their derivation but above all without compromising their unity, are they members of the different nations. A Church whose members sought to regard and conduct themselves first and decisively as members of their own nation and only then as Christians, i.e., a national Church in the strict and serious sense, would necessarily be a sick Church, since it would resist the witness to the fellowship of all nations, not helping to achieve this but making it if anything more difficult. The community which is true to its witness, while it does not question its particular membership of and responsibility to this or that nation, recognises the primacy of its own citizenship over all others, and *eo ipso* is not merely one of the uniting factors in the common life of humanity, but *the* such factor.

The same is true as regards its attitude to the racial question, which in many parts of the world has become so acute to-day. All that one can say concerning this is that it naturally arises within the sphere of the community too, but that the answer is found quite easily as soon as it is raised, and therefore, no matter how others may handle it, it cannot be any real question for the community. Obviously, both in the sphere of the community and outside it racially different people are to be seen and understood and taken seriously as such and therefore in their particularity. But this cannot in any sense or circumstances mean that appeal can be made to supposed orders of creation or sin, or even to Christian love, for the legitimate or even necessary dividing of the community into special white, black and brown congregations. This cannot and must not happen because the community owes to the world a witness, not to the equality, but to the mutual fellowship of men, which in its final and decisive foundation only the community can give, and which it must not suppress even in the racial question, no matter how great may be the cost. That Churches which are not prepared to settle this question within themselves in the only possible way should have the audacity to engage in missionary work with hope of success is something which can only cause us astonishment.

The same is also true, however, in relation to cultural differences. It is one thing that the community should be aware of these and take them into account in its ministry of witness. It is quite another, and something wholly illegitimate, that it should appropriate and sanctify them. There is not one Gospel for the cultured and another for the uncultured. Necessarily both groups intermingle in the community in a way which is exemplary for the world around. If its witness becomes so artificial that the uncultured cannot follow it, or so crude that the cultured stop their ears, it is sick. In this respect, too, there must be no cleavage in the community and its ministry. Its duty both to its own members and to those around is to bring out the Gospel both in its immeasurably astonishing depth and its no less amazing simplicity, so that all are led to the place where the wise of this world are made fools before God and the fools of this world are made wise. In this respect, too, it must establish fellowship.

Self-evidently, the same is also true in regard to the economic classes, their differences and antitheses, their conflicting interests and ideologies. The community cannot ignore these sociological divisions, whether in the world around or within itself. We have seen that in its ministry of diaconate it is brought right up against them and against the problems they raise, and it is precisely in relation to them that it must be shown whether or not its activity and speech are prophetic. The first decisive thing to be said in this regard is that in no circumstances must it sanction these class distinctions, or absolutise them, or take them seriously. It would be mortally sick if it were to identify itself with a class, or its concerns with the interests, its faith with the ideology or its ethos with the morality of such a class. Whenever it has apparently done this, the judgment of God has brought upon it the alienation, scorn and hatred of other classes. And, though there is perhaps little danger of this, it is equally senseless and unrealistic to try to identify itself alternately with different classes. In its own sphere first, but in a way which is exemplary for the world around, it has to establish fellowship between the men of different classes. It has to do this by leading them in the knowledge of the Gospel of the kingdom of God which is concerned with the reality by which the unsolved social problems which separate men are transcended, relativised, enclosed and challenged, in which their removal is manifested if only from afar, in which they are always summoned to seek a new and third way. It has thus to address the middle classes neither positively nor negatively in terms of their capitalistic ideas and attitudes, nor the proletariat in terms of their socialistic, but both zealously on the basis of the fact that as men they are called and may be the children of God, that as such they may expect all good things only from His hand, that as such they are responsible only to Him, but that as such they are thus united and belong to one another. The more resolutely and fearlessly it confronts both with the cause of God and writes it on their hearts and consciences as their own most proper cause, the more confidently it invites both to a common hearing of the Word, to common praying of the Lord's Prayer and to the common table of the Lord's Supper, and the more joyful may be its assurance that with its invitation to participation in these unassuming actions it is setting up even in the conflict of classes a sign which points unmistakeably to the goal and end of this conflict and therefore to its hidden meaning.

We have been reminded of the Lord's Supper. But in this connexion reference should be made in the same sense and with the same emphasis to baptism. In baptism and the Lord's Supper we are concerned in a uniquely dramatic way with the action of the community, and indeed with the action by which it establishes fellowship. In baptism we have the once-for-all and conscious entry and reception, manifested in the sign of purification, of the individual man into membership of the people of those who are called by God in free grace to be His witnesses, to participate in the work of His witness. And in the Lord's Supper we have the repeated and conscious unification of this people, manifested in the sign of common eating and drinking, in new seeking and reception of the free grace which it constantly needs and is constantly given in its work of witness. There is more to be said concerning baptism and the Lord's Supper. But it certainly has to be said concerning them that they are significatory actions in which men, instead of being merely alongside or even apart, both come and are together. They are thus actions which establish fellowship. In baptism and the Lord's Supper an invisible action of God—the fellowship of the Father and the Son in the Holy Ghost, the fellowship of God and man in Jesus Christ, the fellowship of Jesus Christ the Head with His body and its members, and finally the fellowship of God with the world created by Him and reconciled to Him—is the prototype, the meaning and the power of the visible and significatory action of the community and therefore of the unification of men therein attested. But on this basis and as likenesses of this original, baptism and the Lord's Supper are not empty signs. On the contrary, they are full of meaning and power. They are thus the simplest, and yet in their very simplicity the most eloquent, elements in the witness which the community owes to the world, namely, the witness of peace on earth among the men in whom God is well-pleased.

THE HOLY SPIRIT AND CHRISTIAN HOPE

The Holy Spirit is the enlightening power in which Jesus Christ, overcoming the falsehood and condemnation of sinful man, causes him as a member of His community to become one who may move towards his final and yet also his immediate future in hope in Him, i.e., in confident, patient and cheerful expectation of His new coming to consummate the revelation of the will of God fulfilled in Him.

1. THE SUBJECT OF HOPE AND HOPE

We have now come to the end of this third part of the doctrine of reconciliation. We have been treating of the prophetic office and work of Jesus Christ, of its nature and execution. As He is life in His death, so is He light in His resurrection. He is the God who not only acts for and to man, but also speaks to him in Him. He is the One who accomplishes not only the reconciliation of the world to God accomplished in Him, but also its revelation. Corresponding to this, or rather contradicting it, the sin of man is the falsehood by which he perverts the truth. Along the same lines, however, the justification of man before God and his sanctification for Him as accomplished in Jesus Christ also include his election and vocation to be the witness of God, and in and with the gathering and upbuilding of the community there takes place its sending to His service in the world.

In this context, too, as at the end of the two earlier parts of the doctrine, we come up against the question of the participation of the Christian, of the individual member of the community of Jesus Christ, in this action of His. In the first part we spoke of faith, in the second of love. The question in the third part is how it is actually possible for the man who is called to be a witness of Jesus Christ in and with His community, i.e., for the Christian, to become and be a child of light (Jn. 12³⁶) following, obeying and corresponding to the light of the world (Jn. 8¹²), to serve the Word of God in the world and in his own small way to exist prophetically in the school and discipleship of the one great Prophet. We anticipate our answer by stating at once that this is not only made possible but actually achieved as Jesus Christ causes the Christian to become a man who may stride towards his future in hope in Him.

Our first concern must be to gain a clear conception of the question which is answered by this statement about Christian hope.

Its final and decisive basis lies in the fact that the prophetic action of Jesus Christ, and therefore the revelation of the name of God already hallowed, the kingdom of God come and the will of God done in Him, and therefore the revelation of the man already justified and sanctified in Him, while it is complete in itself, is only moving towards its fulfilment, i.e., not to an amplification or transcending of its content or declaration, which is neither necessary nor possible, but to a supremely radical alteration and extension of the mode and manner and form of its occurrence. Jesus Christ has spoken in His resurrection. He speaks in the enlightening power of His Holy Spirit. And what He has spoken in His resurrection and continually speaks in the enlightening power of His Holy Spirit, is the one total and final truth as it may be heard already here and now by the ears and reason and heart of those who are awakened by Him to faith and love, since the one and total and final act of divine reconciliation accomplished in Him, and He Himself as the one and total and insurpassable Mediator between God and man, was and is the content of this declaration. Nevertheless, He has not yet uttered His last Word in this matter. For He has not yet spoken universally of Himself and the act of reconciliation accomplished in Him. He has not yet spoken of it in such a way that the ears and reason and hearts of all must receive it. He has not yet spoken of it immediately, i.e., in such a way that even those who are awakened by Him to faith and love can hear His voice in perfect purity and to the exclusion of every conceivable contradiction and opposition and above all participation in human falsehood. He has not yet spoken of it definitively, i.e., in the final Word of the Judge at which every knee must bow, both of things in heaven and things on earth (Phil. 2[10]). He has not yet spoken of it in such sort that for Christians and non-Christians, for the living and the dead, there can be no option but " to live under Him in His kingdom, and to serve Him in eternal righteousness, innocence and blessedness." This last, comprehensive, immediate and definitive Word has certainly been announced in His resurrection and is declared in the power of His Holy Spirit, but it has not yet been spoken. In this manner and form His revelation has not yet taken place, nor does it yet take place. In this third and final and eternal *parousia*, presence and action of His He has not yet come. In relation to it, it is perfectly plain that His prophetic work has powerfully commenced and continues, but is not yet completed.

And it is this Not Yet which is at a first glance the most striking determination of the time in which the Christian now exists on the basis of his vocation to be a witness of Jesus Christ in the context of the sending of His community. This time is the last time, i.e., the time which from the resurrection of Jesus Christ moves towards its end, but has not yet reached it, because the prophetic work of Jesus Christ has not yet reached its goal even in the mighty operation of His Holy Spirit. It is not really true, of course, that this time of

ours is primarily and decisively determined by this Not Yet and therefore negatively. Primarily and decisively it is positively determined
by that which Jesus Christ already is and means in it, by its beginning
in His resurrection and its continuation in the mighty operation of
His Holy Spirit. For this reason, as we must note in explanation of
our statement about Christian hope, it is not a vacuum, nor a day of
small things, nor a time of the delay or suspension of the *parousia* or
personal presence and action of Jesus Christ. On the contrary, in its
first and second forms His *parousia*, namely, the fact that He has risen
and lives, is the decisive presupposition of all that is and occurs in this
time of ours. It is the basis of the existence of the community and each
of its members. Yet this time is also determined by the fact that the
coming of Jesus Christ in His complete revelation has not yet taken
place in it, that His last, universal, immediate and definitive Word has
not yet been spoken. And if we are to understand the question answered
by our statement concerning Christian hope, we must pay particular
attention to the fact that it is the time characterised by this Not Yet.
This means that in and with the whole Christian community the Christian is relatively lonely, isolated and apart in relation to the majority
of men to whom Christ is not yet manifest. It also means that, since
Jesus Christ has not yet spoken immediately to him either, he may well
be sure of his faith and love, but only in contradiction with himself
and under the shadow of the sinister possibility that after all he might
become or still be a liar against the truth. It means finally that, no
matter with what intentions of loyalty or zeal he may fulfil his service,
Jesus Christ has not yet spoken His last Word as Judge and therefore
his service cannot by a long way claim to be that service " in righteousness, innocence and blessedness." These are the limits set for Christian
existence, in spite of its greatness, by the fact that it is existence in the
last time, in which the prophetic work of Jesus Christ certainly takes
place but has not yet reached its goal, in which the *parousia* of Jesus
Christ in its third and final form, His completed revelation of the will
of God fulfilled in Him, is certainly announced and promised but is
not yet an event. It is only in the imagination of a non-Christian and
only too human arrogance and folly that the Christian can try to
leap over these limits, and in so doing he will always land on his
feet, or more probably his back, on this side of the barrier. For the
limit set to Christian existence can be removed only with the coming
of Jesus Christ Himself to complete His revelation.

It is at these set limits that there arises in its characteristic form
the question of the possibility and reality of this existence. There
can be no doubt as to its foundation, since the Christian derives
securely from the resurrection of Jesus Christ. Nor can there be any
doubt as to its present constitution and the step which the Christian
has to take at the moment, since every action may be performed within
the sphere of lordship of the Holy Spirit. What was and is deeply open

to question is the manner and measure of faith, obedience and love, in short, of the gratitude with which the Christian has thus far responded and even yet responds to so great grace. But for all its seriousness this question is made irrelevant by the fact that, even as the sinner he was and is, he knows that in Jesus Christ he is justified before God and sanctified for Him, that he may live by this knowledge, that every morning afresh he may cling to the divine remission and direction. The grace by which the Christian may become and be a Christian cannot itself be called in question, notwithstanding the feebleness of the Christian's response to it. But what about the future existence of the Christian, which is the true theme of our discussion? Will he still have the possibility and reality of being a Christian then? How is it that Paul can say that neither things present nor things to come can separate us from the love of God which in Christ Jesus our Lord (Rom. 8[38])? Necessarily, since Jesus Christ has indeed spoken and speaks but has not yet spoken His last Word, since His prophetic work has commenced in His first *parousia* and continues in His second but has not yet reached its completion in His third, since His consummating, universal, immediate and definitive revelation has not yet taken place, the existence of the Christian cannot yet have attained its goal, but he is still on the way into a future which seems to be for him an absolutely open and wholly unwritten page, or even an impenetrable sea of mist. There in the dark morning nothing seems to be clear or decided for him and his existence as a Christian. To what extent can and will the grace of God be addressed to him to-morrow as it was yesterday and to-day? To what extent can and will he live by it to-morrow as he did yesterday and to-day? To what extent can and will he be awakened and quickened and nourished and sustained and protected to-morrow by the presence and action of Jesus Christ as he was yesterday and to-day? To what extent can and will these things take place to-morrow, seeing that Jesus Christ has not yet brought to its goal this last time of ours, or rather that He has still retained for Himself a future in this time? What will His resurrection and the power of His Holy Spirit mean then, in the unknown land which is still ahead and which seems as yet not to be lighted at all by the light of His Word? This is, in provisional form, the question answered by the statement about Christian hope.

We are well advised, however, to put it more sharply even in this provisional form. For this purpose, let us consider the situation in which the Christian looks and moves towards the existence which is still before him. We may take it as presupposed by our very definition that if he has any future at all as a Christian he can only be a witness of Jesus Christ and exist as such. But how can and will he exist in the future as the one he has become and is, and therefore as a witness of Jesus Christ? How can this be possible and real in this last time of ours in which Jesus Christ has still retained for Himself the completion of His prophetic work, in which witness to Him cannot therefore relate directly to its completion but can only point to this, in which it may be given on the assumption of its commencement and continuation but also of the fact that it is not yet completed? In these circumstances, what can the Christian see and expect of future existence as His witness? If he gives serious consideration to the question, he can see himself only as one of a fast disappearing minority amongst the great mass of men to whom Jesus Christ seems so far to have spoken and still to speak in vain and for whom His resurrection and the power of His Holy Spirit seem to be no more than idle tales and empty words rather than manifest and significant reality. How can this be otherwise so long as Jesus Christ has not spoken his last Word which all will receive? Again, the Christian can see himself only in his own contradiction which has not yet been set aside, in the lasting conflict between his new but not yet exclusive being in the righteousness and holiness of Jesus Christ and his old and rejected but not yet excluded being in the flesh, in his own perishing nature which is also that of the world as a whole. Is not this inevitable, seeing that Jesus Christ has not yet spoken to him the last Word which removes all contradiction? Finally, the Christian will see himself confronted in the future with the mystery of the decision, not yet made, whether or not his ministry of witness has been well done and is thus an object of the good-pleasure of God definitely approved and accepted. How can this be otherwise, seeing that Jesus Christ has not yet spoken His last and definitive Word, nor come as Judge of the quick and the dead? There is no point in concealing the fact that it is in this very doubtful and vulnerable way that the Christian must see himself as a Christian and therefore as a witness of Jesus Christ both to-morrow and the day after and in every conceivable future. And this aspect is made the more dreadfully acute by the fact that the only thing he can know for certain about his future is that one day time, so far as it is his time, will be up, and then his Christian existence and witness will only have been that which it was able to be in its dubiety and frailty.

To be sure, there are other and important considerations which cut across and mitigate this aspect. For his future does stand in the light of the origin of his Christian existence and witness in the resurrection of Jesus Christ and of his present as determined by the power of the Holy Spirit. Again, he is received and accepted by the grace of God in his totality, not only as the one he has become and is, but also as the one he will be, including the fact that one day he will die and will only have been that which he could be within these limits. Necessarily these factors are also to be put in the scales. The future of the Christian stands also under this aspect and sign, i.e., in the light of his derivation from Jesus Christ and fellowship with Him, and of the commencement and continuation of the grace of His revelation, of His prophetic work. But how does this apply, to what shall he cling, how is he to see and understand his future and with what attitude and mind is he to march towards it, in view of the unmistakeable fact that it no less plainly stands under this very different sign and aspect, i.e., in the shadow of the oppressive question which results from the fact that the revelation of Jesus Christ is not yet completed ? Can the result be any other than a twofold, ambivalent, equivocal future dominated by a dangerous dialectic, a future which is both bright and dark, and which he can await either with calm and confidence or with uncertainty, doubt, anxiety, depression and even despair ? Is he not forced to ask how in the obvious vacillation between the one future and the other he can possibly be a true and loyal and usable witness of Jesus Christ ? Is he not forced to ask whether and how far his future existence in these circumstances will really be that of such a witness and therefore of a Christian ?

What happens when to the question as thus provisionally formulated we oppose our statement about Christian hope ? Assuming that the hope opposed to it is really Christian hope, it is obvious that the question can only be provisional and cannot be put with ultimate seriousness. If we understand our statement about Christian hope as a reply to this question, then it answers it quite simply by negating the assumption on which it rests and thus radically calling the question itself in question, forcing us to put it, if at all, in a very different way. For if anyone truly and seriously saw before him that twofold, ambivalent and equivocal future, and thus came to ask concerning the possibility and reality of his existence as a witness of Christ in the future, he could do so only by forgetting and denying that which makes him a Christian, i.e., his derivation from the resurrection of Jesus Christ and his present in the sphere of power of the Holy Spirit, and therefore by suspending himself, deserting and abandoning his ministry as a Christian. His future as a Christian is in no sense open, neutral and therefore divided. Hence his expectation for the future, in spite of appearances to the contrary, cannot be one which vacillates between confidence and uncertainty, between calm and despair. Hence he does not have to ask how he can possibly be a Christian and therefore a witness of Jesus Christ in this future which sometimes resembles the dawn, sometimes the end of day, but is always wrapped in twilight.

What the Christian who is entangled in the question as previously put has especially to learn from its confrontation with the statement about Christian hope is that his hope has nothing whatever to do with that twilight and therefore with the divided expectation which is the presupposition of the question as thus formulated. His hope, as Christian hope, marks this divided expectation as one of the products of the falsehood of sinful man which perverts the truth of God. It forbids it to the Christian at the very root. It keeps him from it. And in so doing it releases him from the condemnation which threatens as a result of this falsehood. What the man who hopes as a Christian expects is not twilight. It is not light and also shadow, good and also evil, salvation and also destruction. It is unequivocally and uninterruptedly light and good and salvation. For the One whom he sees before him is unequivocally and uninterruptedly God, the living God in His grace and righteousness and mercy and glory, the God towards whom he can go, not with a mixture of confidence and suspicion, but only with confidence.

We do not say this at random but in the light of what is called hope in Holy Scripture, i.e., the expectation of the man elected by God, justified before Him, sanctified for Him and called by Him to His service. We say it concretely in the light of the concept of hope in the Old and New Testaments, with its typical distinction from the meaning and use of ἐλπίς and ἐλπίζειν in classical Greek. (Cf. on this distinction the examples given by R. Bultmann in Kittel, II, p. 515f.) In classical Greek the word group denotes the optimistic or pessimistic expectation of man. It thus denotes his vacillating because intrinsically dubious and pragmatic attitude to the future still concealed from him. Hence it is closely related to the fact that, whether he be confident or fearful, his concern is with the bright or dark pictures of the future projected by man himself. In face of these, there is indeed room for caution, since only a god does not go astray in his expectations. But this ambivalence of the future, this hesitation and the warning against all security in face of it, can have no place in relation to expectation of the future as understood in Holy Scripture. For the Subject of expectation, i.e., the One expected, has nothing whatever to do with the theme and content of a human picture of the future, and therefore He has nothing whatever to do with the necessary ambiguity and uncertainty of such a picture. The term ἐλπίς as used in the one case, and the same term as used in the other, denote human modes of thought and attitudes which are not merely dissimilar in structure but totally unlike and even opposed in view of their very different origin. Hence Paul is not guilty of polemical exaggeration but is making a sober statement of fact when he says of the heathen that they have no ἐλπίς (1 Thess. 4¹³, Eph. 2¹²). From what they know as hope there is no bridge to the hope of the Old and New Testaments, nor *vice versa*.

The man who hopes in the Old Testament sense does not await the fulfilment of his own comforting or comfortless prognoses and dreams, and therefore he need not be on guard against threats to his expectation. He looks to that which in virtue of His self-declaration the God of Israel was and is and will be and mean and do in the history of this people both for Israel and for himself as a man united with it as a member. This God is the God of his future as of his origin and present. He thus expects His guidance, protection, help and blessing. He expects Him as his Saviour, as the source and sum of the salvation granted to his people and therefore to himself in person. It is to be noted that his personal expectation of the blessing and salvation granted to him as a member of this people, being his expectation of the being and action of this God, is enclosed and upheld and guaranteed and ordered by the expectation of the salvation which God has promised and which He will grant to this people as the goal of its history. He expects that in the small and detailed matters of his own life-history he will receive from Israel's God by way of anticipation that which in accordance with its election and calling is finally promised and will finally be granted by God to Israel in its totality as the goal of its history, to its own salvation but also as a sign of salvation for all peoples. In this sense, too, his hope takes a given form and is very different from subjective wishful thinking. The only warning to be found in the Old Testament is that he should not seek his hope anywhere but in the God of Israel, nor expect his salvation from any other factor, e.g., wealth, or his own righteousness, or other men, or the gods of the nations, or Egypt, or the temple in Jerusalem, or even the temple in Bethel. The only warning is not against too great but rather too little confidence of hope in the One in whom it is meaningful, legitimate and incumbent to hope.

Saying this, we have already described in outline what *mutatis mutandis* emerges as the hope of New Testament man. It is to be noted that here, too, it is simple and concrete expectation of a new being and action of God, of the God already known to the Christian by His past and continuing self-declaration. 'Eλπίς thus derives from the act of God and looks forward to His new act which unforeseeably but infallibly dispels the obscurity of the future still before man, and delivers, redeems, fulfils and overrules to salvation this future too. The only point is that this expectation is now determined by the fact that the divine self-declaration from which the man who hopes derives is a single event of salvation at the goal of Israel's history, and that what is still awaited but will infallibly follow is none other than the same event in a new form, its whole significance and relevance for the future being included in the fact that it is a repetition of the first in this different guise. It is to be noted further that the New Testament hope which looks to this new event is also exclusive hope in God Himself as the one source and sum of all expected blessing and salvation. The only point is that God Himself, the " God of hope " (Rom. 15¹³), in the glory still to be manifested, is not an abstraction but bears the features of a specific human countenance well known to the one who hopes, namely, the countenance of the One who has come already in the event which fulfils the hope of Israel, and who will Himself come again in that future event in full revelation of His salvation and glory. It is to be noted further that the hope of New Testament man, too, is upheld and enclosed and guaranteed and ordered as his personal fulfilment of the hope of the community of which he is a member. The only point is that this hoping community and he who hopes in and with it already exist in virtue of the first event in direct fellowship with the One for whose new coming they may hope, and that they have received, and must continually pray for and receive again, directly from Him the freedom to hope for His future coming. Finally, hope is here again absolutely unequivocal, unbroken and therefore certain hope. The only point is that the unambiguity and certainty are now clearly a reflection of the divine authority, of the κυριότης, of the Subject of hope, so that even as the unambiguity and certainty of human expectation they clearly bear the character of grace thankfully received and expressed. It is as and because His being in the future is certain that Christian hope may also be certain.

It will be seen that the basic features of hope are the same in both cases. It will also be seen, however, that they come into sharp focus only in the latter case. It will be seen why this is so. In the transition from the Old Testament to the New there has come about a concentration in respect of the origin, theme and content of hope. Jesus Christ, who has come already and is to come again, who is thus the Subject of hope and the Creator of hope in Him, has taken the central place which seems to be empty in Old Testament expectation. Above all, it will be seen that the hope presented in the Bible of the Old and New Testaments is not an ambivalent expectation of the future, but a very definite and wholly positive expectation. We necessarily alienate ourselves from its witness, and from the presupposition of all theological thought and utterance, in the direction of a pre-Christian and even extra-biblical outlook, if we try to give to the concept a dialectical content in the sense previously described. The Christian expectation of the future cannot be uncertain, nor unsettled, nor sceptical, but only assured and patient and cheerful expectation.

In the light of this, we must return to our starting-point. Not on the basis of anthropological construction, but on that of definite and theologically valid, i.e., christological insights, on the basis of the revealing work of Jesus Christ which has already commenced and continues but is not yet completed, we take up again the question of the future possibility and reality of Christian existence which we first formulated on the assumption of an expectation which mere anthropology would suggest to be divided and therefore ambivalent. This assumption has proved to be impossible in the light of hope as understood in Holy Scripture, and therefore our first formulation naturally falls to the ground. Grounded in God, namely, in the God who acts in Jesus Christ, and orientated on Him, Christian hope is an uninterrupted and unequivocally positive expectation of the future, and it is only on this basis that we may legitimately and meaningfully raise the question of the future possibility and reality of Christian existence. Yet we have still to consider and clarify the attitude to be taken in face of what seem to be contradictory christological insights, of the difference between the revelation of Jesus Christ as it has already taken place in its commencement and is still taking place in its continuation, and the revelation of Jesus Christ as it has not yet taken place in its consummation. In face of this difference, how far is the way barred to that divided expectation, and how far is the way directly opened to the consistently positive expectation which seems to be imperatively suggested by Holy Scripture ?

If we are to accept the teaching of Scripture, it is obvious that there can be no question of contradiction between the christological Already and Even Now on the one side and the christological Not Yet on the other, valid though both may be. To be sure, there is a plain and irremovable distinction ; but there is no flat contradiction. The Already and the Even Now are no less forms of the one *parousia*, presence and action of Jesus Christ in His prophetic action than the Not Yet. The commencement, continuation and consummation of His prophetic activity are all equal in this respect. Even if in a different manner, it is the same person who was yesterday, is to-day, and will come to-morrow and for ever : εἰς τοὺς αἰῶνας (Heb. 13⁸). This means, however, that the One who rose from the dead and came to His first disciples on Easter Day was already, unrecognisably as far as they were concerned, the same as He who then encountered them in the outpouring of His Holy Spirit and who is present with His community to this day in the power of the same Spirit. And in this commencement and continuation of His revelation in which Christianity participates between the times, as the One who came once and is present to-day, concealed from the world and His community yet well known in faith and love, He was and is no other, but exactly the same, as He who has yet to come in the consummation. As, therefore, the Then of His resurrection did not exclude but included the Now of the event of Pentecost and of all the time, our time, which follows, so this Now, looking back to the Then, does not exclude but includes by way of anticipation the One Day of

His future coming. And it is the One Day already anticipated in the Then and Now which will then reveal and fulfil what is implied by the Then and Now, namely, that in the resurrection of Jesus Christ God was already mighty, holy, merciful and glorious, and that in the power of His Holy Spirit He is so to-day in this time of ours which is the time between and the last time.

It is for this reason that 1 Pet. 1³ᶠ· can say that God of His great mercy, by the resurrection of Jesus Christ from the dead (then), has begotten us again to a living hope, and then that, begotten to this hope, we are " kept " by the power of God through faith (now) for the salvation which has already taken place but awaits its revelation ἐν καιρῷ ἐσχάτῳ (one day). Similarly, we can be told in 1 Thess. 1⁹ᶠ· that, converted from the worship of idols to the living God (now), we await the risen Jesus from heaven as our Deliverer from future wrath (one day) ; or again in Rom. 8²⁴ that, as we have this hope (of the one day), we are saved without seeing what we hope for (now). We can also be told in Heb. 6¹⁹ᶠ· that we have hope as a sure anchor of the soul (now) which reaches into the inner court beyond the veil (one day) where Christ has already entered as a Fore-runner (then) ; or again in Col. 1²⁷ that χριστὸς ἐν ὑμῖν, Christ among and in us Christians as such, is the hope of not yet manifested glory, the great mystery already revealed to the nations in the existence of His people. Hope can be defined in 2 Thess. 2¹⁶ as a gift of Jesus Christ and in Gal. 5⁵ and Rom. 15¹³ as a work of His Holy Spirit. It can be described in 1 Jn. 3³ as hope in Him, or in 1 Pet. 1¹³ as hope in the grace to be brought us at His future revelation, or in 1 Tim. 1¹ (as in Col. 1²⁷) quite simply as Jesus Christ Himself described in a single breath both as our Hope and our Deliverer. It will be seen that the lines between the Then, the Now and the One Day everywhere intersect. It is true that we may be dealing with different New Testament theologies which it is by no means easy to present as a consistent whole. More relevant than this hypothesis, however, is the sure conclusion that within the totality of New Testament thinking on hope, and without bursting the limits of this totality, there are so many variations which in their very variety indicate the persistent unity of the christological basis.

It is always unity in variety. If the Now cannot be separated from the Then in which it is grounded, nor the One Day from the Now, nor the Then from the Now and the One Day or *vice versa*, each of these different forms of the one *parousia* of Jesus Christ maintains its individuality and is inseparably bound to the others in this individuality. To this there corresponds the individuation of the being and attitude of the Christian in his relation to Jesus Christ in the different forms of His *parousia*. To be sure, we again have only distinctions and not irreconcilable contradictions. But in a general and non-exclusive way we can and should say that the Christian believes (*a parte potiori*) in the One who came then, that he loves (*a parte potiori*) Him as the One who is present now and that he hopes (*a parte potiori*) for His new coming one day. He cannot do any of these things without the others. Each is moved and sustained by the others. Yet none can be wholly identified with the others. Our present concern is with hope in its particularity as the relation of the Christian to his future and therefore his existence in its connexion with Jesus Christ as the One who is still to come. To be sure, if we do not believe in Him as the One who came then, nor love Him as the One who is present now, we cannot hope in Him as the One who will come one day. The *Benedictus qui venit in nomine Domini !* is not then in our hearts, and therefore it will not come to expression on our lips. Yet this *Benedictus qui venit !* indicates, and hope in its distinction from faith and love as a resolute look ahead constitutes, a particular dimension of Christian existence without which there can be no solidity in faith and love even though they are not identical with it. Any identification would entail an impoverishment of the understanding of Christian existence and indeed its christological foundation. It would entail an overlooking or expunging of the inner movement proper to Christian existence on this foundation in favour of a uniformity which is a threat to truth quite apart from the fact that in the long run it is so dreary and uninteresting. We should thus refrain from attempts in this direction, which smack more of philosophy than of the Bible.

What I have in view is the broadening of the concept of the eschatological which has become so popular in the last decades. In its earlier sense this was usually related to the particular sphere of hope as Christian expectation of the future. Now it has suddenly been extended to cover and explain the transcendent character of all the subjects and contents of theological discussion. In addition, it has come to be either completely or almost completely equated with the strangely empty because negative concept of the uncontrollable. But everything is uncontrollable and therefore everything is eschatological—the crucifixion, the resurrection, faith, love, the *kerygma*, the Church, baptism, the Lord's Supper, the Christian ethos and even the good Lord Himself as " my future." The only trouble is that little importance can now be attached to a particularly eschatological sphere of hope as Christian expectation of the future, or to hope itself as a particular dimension of Christian existence. But does not this give us a flat and uniform rather than a sharply contoured understanding of the Bible on the one side and proclamation of the Gospel on the other ? The time has surely come when we should awaken from this pan-eschatological dream to see and understand things, in this case the one relationship of the Christian to the one God in the one Jesus Christ, in their differentiation. And this means that, while we should not separate, we should certainly distinguish the Then, the Now and the One Day, and therefore that we should assert as particular dimensions of Christian existence the faith and love and hope which Paul never thought to be identical for all their unity (1 Thess. 1³, 1 Cor. 13¹³).

In detail, of course, it is not always easy (cf. Rom. 4 and Heb. 11) to understand especially ἐλπίς and πίστις as two dimensions distinct even in their interconnexion and unity. The faith of Abraham, for instance, is explicitly called his πιστεύειν παρ᾽ ἐλπίδα ἐπ᾽ ἐλπίδι (Rom. 4¹⁸), his hope where even as a believer he could have no hope of a successor. Again, Heb. 11¹ defines faith as ἐλπιζομένων, ὑπόστασις πραγμάτων ἔλεγχος οὐ βλεπομένων, i.e., a lasting confidence and conviction in face of things which are invisible and therefore can only be hoped for. Similarly, in Heb. 11⁹ we are again told that by faith Abraham went out into a strange land, looking for " the city which hath foundations, whose builder and maker is God." As an act of obedience to a demand made of man which as such is also a promise to him, faith includes and gives rise to hope in the fulfilment of this promise. This is obvious from both passages. Yet their whole drift, as is clearly shown by the details of Heb. 11, is to the effect that faith as such is the obedience which man gives to the Word and command of God by receiving and respecting this as the Word of promise quite apart from banking on its fulfilment. He does not believe because he hopes, for he has no ground for hope apart from believing. But as and because he believes, putting active trust in the Word spoken to him as God's Word, he also hopes. Thus faith and hope are closely related. They belong inseparably together. Yet they are two distinct things. In the very phrase παρ' ἐλπίδα ἐπ' ἐλπίδι it may be seen formally how hope springs from faith yet also how it is relatively new and distinct beside it. Even in Heb. 11¹ faith is not actually defined as hope but is rather described as its basis and presupposition (ὑπόστασις, ἔλεγχος) in Christian existence.

In one of the most striking passages in the *Institutio* (III, 2, 42) Calvin has clearly shown the unity and yet also the distinction of the two : " Wherever this living faith exists, it must have the hope of eternal life as its inseparable companion, or rather must of itself beget and manifest it ; where it is wanting, however clearly and elegantly we may discourse of faith, it is certain we have it not. For if faith is . . . a firm persuasion of the truth of God—a persuasion that it can never be false, never deceive, never be in vain, those who have received this assurance must at the same time expect that God will perform his promises, which in their conviction are absolutely true ; so that in one word hope is nothing more than *eorum expectatio, quae vere a Deo promissa fides credidit.* Thus, faith believes that God is true ; hope expects that in due season he will manifest his truth. Faith believes that he is our Father ; hope expects that he will always act the part of a Father towards us. Faith believes that eternal life has been given to us *(datam nobis vitam aeternam)* ; hope expects that it will one day be revealed. Faith is the foundation on which hope rests ; hope nourishes and sustains faith. For as no man can expect anything from God without previously believing his promises, so, on the other hand, the weakness *(imbecillitas)* of our faith, which might grow weary and fall away, must be supported and cherished by patient hope and expectation. For this reason Paul justly says, ' We are saved by hope ' (Rom. 8²⁴). For while hope silently waits for the Lord, it restrains faith from hastening on with too much precipitation, confirms it when it might waver in regard to the promises of God or begin to doubt of their truth, refreshes it when it might be fatigued, extends its view to the final goal, so as not to allow it to give up in the middle of the course, or at the very outset. In short, by constantly renovating and reviving, it is ever and anon furnishing more vigour for perseverance *(perseverantia)*." How much need faith has of hope may be seen from the innumerable temptations which assail and shake those who would cling to the Word of God, from the delay of God in the fulfilment of His promises (cf. Hab. 2³), from the hiding of His face, from the *aperta indignatio* with which He can sometimes startle even His own people, from the scoffers who ask where is His coming, who argue that all things remain as they were, and who can so easily insinuate their doubts into ourselves and the world around (2 Pet. 3⁴) ! Only a concentrated faith which is sustained by hope, and raised up by it to the *contemplatio aeternitatis*, realising that one day is with the Lord as a thousand years, is a match for this kind of mocking question.

It is with this individuality and particularity in relation to faith and love that Christian hope has the power of that uninterruptedly positive and certain expectation of the future and therefore the power to give to Christian faith and love the assistance so extolled by Calvin. But it has its particularity, and therein its power, as it takes place that man may and must actually venture to realise it in his own free act, looking and moving forwards as a free man. It does not have it of itself as a kind of quality of soul residing in this man and needing to be practised by him. It does not have it in such a way that with faith and love it is something existential to man. That a man is saved in hope (Rom. 8²⁴) does not mean that he saves himself by it, that by it he liberates himself for an unequivocally positive outlook on the time still before him including the hour of death. He does not guarantee his future by hoping any more than he justifies himself by believing or sanctifies himself by loving. The kind of hope of which man as such is capable, and in achievement of which he is referred to his own power and the readiness to use it, will sooner or later, and certainly *in articulo mortis*, prove to be one of those arbitrarily projected expectations of the future which may occasionally and temporarily but not necessarily and lastingly have a positive character, but which may just as well assume the contrary. In other words, it will prove to be one of those hopes which are not orientated on God and therefore cannot be certain but only ambivalent, and which are thus very likely to make fools of us. It is like the self-grounded and self-produced faith and love by which man thinks that he is justified before God and sanctified for Him, only to find out sooner or later, and certainly *in articulo mortis*, that he is newly and truly accursed and enslaved.

Can we read the passage quoted from Calvin without being just a little bit disturbed by the question how the hope which he so finely depicts, since it seems finally only to enhance or deepen faith by leading it to the *contemplatio aeternitatis*, is really to be distinguished from the capacity and readiness for such a human and therefore very doubtful elevation and programme for the future ? To be sure, Calvin did not regard it as such. Like faith and love, it was for him a gift of the Holy Ghost. But the question remains how far and on what basis it is distinguished as such from a work of supreme human endowment and skill the result of which certainly cannot be that absolutely guaranteed and therefore sure expectation of the future. How far can it be *expectatio*, and remain such, even when no fulfilment of the promise is as yet to be seen and the Christian has to do only with a God who hides His face from him ? How far is it the Christian hope against which the arguments of 2 Pet. 3⁴ have absolutely no force whatever ?

If Christian hope has this power, then it is as and because it has a power which Calvin unfortunately did not refer to explicitly in the passage adduced, namely, the power of the One hoped for who is its basis, who is not absent from it but present in it even though it still looks and moves to Him, and who is powerful and active in it, determining both its particular form and also its relevance for the whole of Christian existence. Its clear and unshakeable basis, which makes it certain because unilaterally positive expectation, is not the Christian awaiting his future, but God in Jesus Christ who is his future, and who therefore creates his expectation. As He is his future, He makes the man who hopes a man who is saved as he hopes, who is simply and unequivocally liberated even in relation to the life and death which are still ahead, who is delivered from all his dreams both good and bad. The case of hope is exactly the same as that of faith and love. It is not his Christian faith which justifies him, but the One in whom He may believe as his righteousness. Nor is it his Christian love which sanctifies him, but the One whom he may love as his holiness. He hopes, indeed, on the basis and in the power and righteousness and holiness of the One in whom he may believe and whom he may love. He thus hopes in grateful awareness of his reconciliation to God perfectly accomplished in Him, of his membership of the divine covenant of grace and peace. He hopes on the basis of the Then of His resurrection, and therefore " now " in virtue of His presence and action in the power of the Holy Spirit. How could he hope in Him if he did not believe in Him in that commencement of His prophecy and love Him in its continuation ? How could he wait for His last Word if he had not yet received and taken to heart His first and second Words ? This One not merely was and is the same yesterday and to-day, but He will be to-morrow. As the One He was and is, He will also come and be for ever and therefore in all future time. Even in its commencement and continuation His prophecy is secretly but very really full of completion. It is already the presence and pronouncement of His last Word. The one *parousia* of the one Jesus Christ in its first and second forms is like an arrow pointing to the third. It moves irreversibly in the direction of His final coming. Its Word is in every respect a promise of His not yet manifested universal, exclusive and ultimate glory, of His appearing as Judge of the quick and the dead.

Of relevance in this connexion is the *catena aurea* of Rom. 8²⁹ᶠ· in all its links : " For whom he did foreknow, he also did predestinate to be conformed to the image of his Son, that he might be the firstborn among many brethren. Moreover whom he did predestinate, them he also called : and whom he called, them he also justified : and whom he justified, them he also glorified (τούτους καὶ ἐδόξασεν)." It is to be noted that in and with, i.e., in consequence of, their election, calling and justification, fashioning them into the likeness of the Son of God even to this extent, He has already addressed to them that which is future by its very nature, so that its presence has not yet been manifested to them, but they are only looking and moving to its manifestation.

As the Subject of the faith and love of the Christian, Jesus Christ is also the Subject of his hope. As He came for the justification and sanctification of the Christian, so, according to the equation of 1 Tim. 1¹, He is objectively already his hope, i.e., the theme and goal and basis of his subjective hope. Nor is it that He merely *is* his hope. He was, and is, and, as the One who was and is, He will be. The Christian can only believe in Him and love Him as in so doing he also hopes in Him. Hence Jesus Christ rather than the Christian, as the One who came and comes, is also the One who is to come, who gives to Christian existence its third no less than its first and second dimensions. Jesus Christ, who does not merely precede and accompany him in time, who also comes to meet him from its end and goal, makes possible and actual his being as a Christian and a witness even in the apparently dark and empty time which is before him, including the hour of death. Even as he goes into this future of his, Jesus Christ gives him clarity without obscurity, certainty without doubt, steadfastness without hesitation, hope which as His gift is unambiguous and " maketh not ashamed " (Rom. 5[5]). It is not the Christian trying to help out his feeble faith and love with a little hope, but Jesus Christ already present now as the One He will be in the consummation of His revelation, who actually makes his hope the power which sustains his faith and gives wings to his love to-morrow no less than to-day. Nor is it that in hope the Christian anticipates that which he is not yet and does not yet have ; it is rather that, hoping in Jesus Christ, he is anticipated by Him. In other words, as he may hope in Him, in all the dubiety and frailty of his existence he may have a preliminary part in the knowledge of the universality, definiteness and finality which will one day characterise the full and total revelation of the will of God accomplished in Him, but of which he cannot as yet be a direct witness. As Jesus Christ Himself is objectively his hope, it is infallibly guaranteed that his witness to Him as witness of subjective hope in Him will actually be possible and real to-morrow no less than to-day, so that even in the future he may live and die as a Christian.

We must be clear that it is in all the dubiety and frailty of his existence that the Christian is given freedom for this. It is under this veil that he has to hope as well as to believe and love. The veil is not taken away. This can happen only when his future is present, when his present has no more future, when time comes to an end with the last *parousia* of Jesus Christ, when His consummating revelation takes place, when the fulfilment of what God has done in Him is redemptively revealed, when the rising sun chases all shadows, and irradiates, removes and dispels all dubiety and frailty. In hoping in Jesus Christ, the Christian hopes for the glory of God investing the whole creation of God of every time and place with unspotted and imperishable glory. This glory, the redemption which will take place in the consummation of His revelation, which will bring with it His last Word, is not yet seen by him. Nevertheless, since he can already believe in and love the One who will create and bring it, it cannot be alien to him. Knowing that He came yesterday and is present to-day, he need not doubt but can have full assurance that He is coming again, that the One Day of Jesus Christ with all its consequences will become quite simply His Now together with the Then. Already, in celebrating Easter, the Christian may celebrate the dawn of the Last Day on which the veil will be taken away and everything that ever was and is and will be will be set in the light of God, divested of its dubiety and frailty and therefore redeemed. The power of the Holy Spirit in which Jesus Christ is already near and present is not merely awakening and quickening but illuminating power in the fact that already, as the first glow of eternity, He shows and promises the dawn of this day, proclaiming it in His operation and already being to him the pledge and earnest of its coming (Rom. 8[23]) and therefore of the nearness of His redemption.

Yet the fact remains that the consummating revelation of Jesus Christ and its redemptive work have not yet taken place. The One Day is not yet a Now like the Then. His prophetic work still offers us the picture of a fragment which is certainly meaningful and pregnant with the future but which still calls for the completion lacking to it. Thus even Christian hope, for all its clarity and certainty, for all its participation in the One hoped for, cannot be more than hope. It is clear and certain in the power of the One hoped for who is its origin, theme and content. And in its clarity and certainty it threatens all the present elements which contradict it. Yet it is also threatened by these elements. If thus resembles Albrecht Dürer's Horseman, who knows his defensive and offensive strength and may thus ride calmly between death and the devil, but who has in fact to venture this perilous passage. For the One in whom he hopes, and therefore that which he hopes for, is not yet manifest, whereas he can see quite clearly that which contradicts his hope, in the midst of which he has to protect it, against which he has to maintain and practise it as hope.

He still exists in the time which has not yet ended. He still walks διὰ πίστεως, i.e., in the power of the promise grasped by him in the obedience of faith, and not διὰ εἴδους, i.e., in the power of a manifestation of the glory of God which has already come to him in fulfilment of the promise (2 Cor. 5⁷). He is still constantly reminded that he could never live except under the threat of death, and that he can still live only under this threat, " that we should not trust in ourselves, but in God which raiseth the dead : who delivered us from so great a death, and doth deliver : in whom we trust, i.e., have hope, that he will yet deliver us " (2 Cor. 1⁹ᶠ·). " That the excellency of the power (ἡ ὑπερβολὴ τῆς δυνάμεως) may be of God, and not of us," " we have this treasure in earthen vessels " (2 Cor. 4⁷), i.e., as those who are distressed, perplexed, persecuted and cast down, always bearing in our bodies the dying of Jesus, according to the verses which follow.

Christian hope has yet to be confirmed in its essential and unalterable character as an unambiguous, uninterrupted, unilateral and therefore absolutely positive expectation of the future, because expectation of Jesus Christ and therefore hope in God and His salvation. What is true in itself has yet to become true. Thus the possibility and indeed the reality of Christian existence given in hope has yet to work itself out as salvation in life and from death even in the time ahead and ultimately in death. For Jesus Christ, and in and through Him God— we must not forget the ultimate basis of all these Yets—has yet to speak His last Word of redemption putting an end to all conflict. We are yet in the sphere of warfare, though in hope and not without hope like the heathen. What is implied as we thus look back again to our starting-point, and particularly to the unmistakeable and insurmountable barrier of Christian existence, the concrete form of its dubiety and frailty, as revealed by this great Not Yet ?

What is hope, and what does it mean for the Christian who, since Jesus Christ has not yet spoken His universal, generally perceptible and conclusive Word, finds himself in that dwindling and almost hopeless minority as His witness to the rest of the world ? If the great Constantinian illusion is now being shattered, the question becomes the more insistent, though it has always been felt by perspicacious Christians. What can a few Christians or a pathetic group like the Christian community really accomplish with their scattered witness to Jesus Christ ? What do these men really imagine or expect to accomplish in the great market, on the battle-field or in the great prison or mad-house which human life always seems to be ? " Who hath believed our report ? and to whom is the arm of the Lord revealed ? " (Is. 53[1]). And what are we to say concerning the countless multitudes who either *ante* or *post Christum natum* have had no opportunity to hear this witness ? *Hic Rhodus, hic salta !* The Christian is merely burying his head in the sand if he is not disturbed by these questions and does not find his whole ministry of witness challenged by them. He buries it even more deeply if in order to escape them, forgetting that he can be a Christian at all only as a witness of Jesus Christ, he tries to retreat into his own faith and love or that of his fellow-Christians. Nor is there any sense in trying to leap over this barrier with the confident mien of a Christian world conqueror. The meaningful thing which he is permitted and commanded and liberated to do in face of it is as a Christian, and therefore unambiguously and unfalteringly, to hope, i.e., in face of what seems by human reckoning to be an unreachable majority to count upon it quite unconditionally that Jesus Christ has risen for each and every one of this majority too ; that His Word as the Word of reconciliation enacted in Him is spoken for them as it is spoken personally and quite undeservedly for him ; that in Him all were and are objectively intended and addressed whether or not they have heard or will hear it in the course of history and prior to its end and goal ; that the same Holy Spirit who has been incomprehensibly strong enough to enlighten his own dark heart will perhaps one day find a little less trouble with them ; and decisively that when the day of the coming of Jesus Christ in consummating revelation does at last dawn it will quite definitely be that day when, not he himself, but the One whom he expects as a Christian, will know how to reach them, so that the quick and the dead, those who came and went both *ante* and *post Christum*, will hear His voice, whatever its signification for them (Jn. 5[25]). This is what Christian hope means before that insurmountable barrier. This is what the Christian hopes for in face of the puzzle which it presents. But the Christian has not merely to hope. He has really to show that he is a man who is liberated and summoned, as to faith and love, so also to hope. And if he really hopes as he can and should as a Christian, he will not let his hands fall and simply wait in idleness for what God will finally do, neglecting his witness to Christ. On the contrary, strengthened and encouraged by the thought of what God will finally do, he will take up his ministry on this side of the frontier. He will thus not allow himself to be disturbed by questions of minorities or majorities, of success or failure, of the probable or more likely improbable progress of Christianity in the world. As a witness of Jesus Christ, he will simply do—and no more is required, though this is indeed required—that which he can do to proclaim the Gospel in his own age and place and circle, doing it with humility and good temper, but also with the resoluteness which corresponds to the great certainty of his hope in Jesus Christ.

To press our enquiry, we ask what is Christian hope and what does it imply—since Jesus Christ has not yet spoken His last and exclusive Word to the exclusion of all contradiction—in face of the great contradiction in Christian existence which has not yet been removed but is renewed each day, i.e., in face of the conflict in which the Christian necessarily finds himself as one who seriously believes and loves, as *simul peccator et iustus*, yet also as *simul iustus et peccator*, whose righteousness and holiness are before him in Jesus Christ, but whose own unrighteousness and unholiness are still behind him in ever new forms and with only too powerful a grasp ? How can he be a strong and active witness to Jesus Christ in this conflict ? He certainly cannot close his eyes either to the facts or to the question which they pose for his Christian life. Nor can he find help against the immeasurable burden which they might be to his Christian ministry of witness in too confident an interpretation of the well-known Lutheran formula. The only legitimate and meaningful answer to the question —and it really is legitimate and convincing—is that he has the freedom to hope even in this conflict. Naturally it is not a matter of hoping in himself in view of possibilities which he may realise more fruitfully than before. It is not a matter of expecting that things will turn out better, or that sooner or later, if he makes a greater effort, he will resolve the conflict and thus become a more useful witness to Jesus Christ. Such expectation would not be Christian hope, and even at best it could lead only to illusory results, and to these not for long, let alone definitively. The real point is that he has the freedom to hope unconditionally and uninterruptedly for the coming of Jesus for the consummation of His revelation in which that will be unequivocally clear which is as yet obscure, namely, that what is before him, i.e., his righteousness and holiness in Jesus Christ, his being in the Spirit, is not counterbalanced by, but completely over-whelms, what is behind him, i.e., his own unrighteousness and unholiness, his being in the flesh ; that the issue between them is not undecided but a definitive decision has been reached ; that, even if as yet only in a hidden way, what he is in and of himself has already been excluded, superseded, destroyed and removed by what he is in and of Jesus Christ ; that it is now only behind him and therefore cannot have any true power over his present ; that it belongs wholly to the past and has fallen from him like a withered leaf. It is obvious that this is not yet visible to him, least of all the exclusiveness of his being in Jesus Christ and his life in His righteousness and holiness. It is obvious that all appearances are against it. Yet even now, and in spite of all appearances, he hopes that this will become un-equivocally visible in the light of the last day of Jesus Christ which is also the first day of redemption, like the Sabbath which is the last day of creation and the first day for man. He hopes for this fulfilment of the promise given him in and with the Word of the accomplished reconciliation of the world to God on the ground of which he may already believe and love. He hopes for it in face of this other aspect of the insurmountable barrier placed around his Christian existence, in face of the second riddle by which he finds himself confronted. The only thing is that he must use this freedom to hope. If he does, this will not mean that he need do no more in view of what God will do to remove the conflict. Certainly he himself is neither com-missioned nor empowered to remove it. Yet if he truly hopes in God, he will find himself summoned and enabled daily to play the man in that conflict, to fight a good fight for the cause of the righteous-ness and holiness of Jesus Christ and against his own unrighteousness and unholiness, and above all against the worst form of this, namely, his evil desire to justify and sanctify himself. It is not required that he should be victorious in this fight. What is required is that he should fight it honestly and resolutely. And power is given him to do this as he may hope in the true Victor. If he makes use of it, then as a warrior who sometimes triumphs but sometimes falls he will certainly be a useful witness to Jesus Christ in this warfare even in the future.

We now come to the third and at a first glance the most difficult question. What is the Christian's hope, and what does it mean, since Jesus Christ has not yet come as Judge of the quick and the dead and has not yet spoken His ultimate Word as such, in face of the mystery whether or not his Christian existence will stand in His judgment, i.e., whether or not that which makes him a Christian, his ministry of witness, will be properly fulfilled by the standard of the One whom he has to attest, whether it will be approved and accepted by Him or repudiated and rejected? This is something which will be manifested to all eyes and therefore to his own in the consummating revelation of Jesus Christ, but which is still completely concealed from him.

Paul described the moment of this final Word not merely as the day when God will judge the hidden things of all men by Jesus Christ according to the Gospel (Rom. 2[16]), but also as the time when with specific reference to Christians, himself included, the coming Lord will " bring to light the hidden things of dark-ness, and will make manifest the counsels of the hearts : and then shall every man have praise (ἔπαινος, in the sense of appraisal) of God " (1 Cor. 4[5]). We should also remember 2 Cor. 5^{10} : " For we must all appear before the judgment seat of Christ (as before the judgment throne of God, Rom. 14^{10}) ; that every one may receive the things done in his body . . . whether it be good or bad." We should also think of I Cor. 3$^{12f.}$ (with reference to Apollos), in which Paul tells us that it will be revealed in the fire of this day whether what we have built on the one foundation of Jesus Christ will stand as good, silver, precious stones, or whether it will perish as wood, hay, stubble. From this it follows (I Cor. 4$^{3f.}$) that even the apostle Paul is in no position to judge himself, i.e., to decide the final question of the worth or worthlessness of his life's work. Even if he is not conscious of any defect, this does not justify him. The One who already exercises competent judgment (ἀνακρίνει), but has not yet pronounced His verdict, is the Lord. But it also follows that those who obviously wish to arrange a little judgment day for the apostle must be told : " Judge nothing before the time (the καιρός), until the Lord come " to pronounce what He alone can pronounce but what no one as yet knows concerning either himself or others.

Here again we have a limit which the Christian can neither overlook nor overleap. He cannot overlook it because not even he can conceal from himself the fact that even his most loyal concern and strenuous effort to maintain his existence as a witness of Jesus Christ is always a human work like that of his fellows, so that, although he is charged to fulfil it, it cannot be his business to decide whether this fulfilment is good or bad, valuable or worthless, meaningful or meaningless. Nor can he overleap it, because he could do so only by grasping at that which does not belong to him, seating himself on the throne of Lord, judging both himself and the servants of another (Rom. 14^4), and thus trying to anticipate what the Lord has reserved for Himself. Again, it is an intolerably bitter thing for him to be confronted by this limit. For what courage or confidence can he have in the execution of his service when, even though he has the best possible conscience, he can have no knowledge whether even that which he has done with the best intentions and in exercise of his finest powers will finally be approved as serviceable or rejected as worthless, whether he will be accepted or repudiated in that which makes him a Christian ? The severity of the question is to be considered. For the issue is quite simply whether the Christian has any option but in his own most proper concern to be like the poor heathen who optimistically or pessimistically can proceed only with uncertainty into a neutral, ambivalent and therefore obscure future. If he could not hope as a Christian, it would be all up with him. But since he may, all is not lost but won. He must not hope in himself. He must not hope that as a worker in the Lord's vineyard he will finally do enough at least to assure his promotion, not perhaps *cum laude*, but at any rate *rite*. He must not hope in a friendly or not too exacting world which might finally hold out the prospect of a *magna* or *insigni* or even *summa cum laude*. He must not be distracted by such illusory possibilities. Here again : *Hic Rhodus, hic salta !* The Christian hopes in Jesus Christ, in Him alone, but in Him confidently. For He alone, but dependably, is the origin, theme and content of his hope, as of his faith and love. Can it hope in Him as the coming Judge ? Yes, in Him as such, since as Judge He is the same as the One who then came in His resurrection and who is now present in the enlightening power of His Spirit. Not an unknown judge of fable, but He who is well-known to the Christian comes as Judge of the quick and the dead and therefore as his Judge. Not the Christian himself, nor the contemporary world, nor posterity, but He will judge and decide concerning his Christian witness, whether it is good or bad, valuable or worthless, meaningful or meaningless, gold, silver, precious stones, or wood, hay, stubble. He will judge and decide concerning the sincerity of heart and integrity of mind with which he has discharged it. There can be no doubt that His judgment is the future of the whole world and therefore of the Christian too. There can be no doubt that the heart and mind and work of the Christian too, with all that all other men have either been or not been, done or not done, will then come truly and ultimately into the fire of a radical and incalculable testing. There can be no doubt that even among Christians many of those who are apparently first will be last and last first, and much of that which is thought to be first in the way of Christian thought and speech and action will be last and last first. Above all, there can be no doubt whose fire will burn and purify and sift, whose standard and judgment will reign and find application, who will set all men and all things, not in any light, but in His own light. There can thus be no doubt that those who know Him will look and move forward to His judgment, fire and testing, not with hesitant but with assured, unequivocally positive and therefore joyful expectation. If they wait for His grace which judges, and which cuts with pitiless severity in this judgment, they still wait for His grace. If they wait for His grace which is absolutely free, unmerited and sovereign in the execution of His judgment, they still wait for His grace. If they wait for His righteousness, as is inevitable since it is His coming which is expected, they wait for the righteousness of His grace.

For this reason they are not afraid, but hope for righteousness (Gal. 5⁵). In the words of *Qu.* 52 of the *Heidelberg Catechism* (cf. Calvin's *Geneva Catechism, Qu.* 86–89), the Christian finds comfort in the return of Christ to judge the quick and the dead, because with uplifted head he waits for the Judge from heaven who has already exposed Himself to the judgment of God for him, and taken away all cursing from him, in order that He may receive him with all the elect—note the less satisfactory part of this fine statement—into heavenly joy and glory.

Those who hope in Him cannot possibly droop or shake their heads ; they can only lift them up. No spark of presumption can pervert the expectation of those who hope in Him, for whence could they derive it in this hope ? Nor can any spark of resigned anxiety or anxious resignation disturb it, for how could such be possible or permissible in this hope ? If they hope in Him, as they may and should in their moving towards this Judge, then it is He Himself, the Subject of this hope, who lives and thinks and speaks and acts in it. It is He Himself, the Judge towards whose fiery, purifying and sifting, yet gracious judgment they look and move. As He Himself lives and thinks and speaks and acts in this hope, the Christian for his part acquires and enjoys the freedom, even on this side of the insurmountable frontier set by the mystery of His ultimate judgment, to be confident and to count upon it that it will not be spoken against him but for him. How else but in the grace of his Lord can he know that he himself and his action will be affirmed, approved and accepted ? But from the very outset he can be confident of this grace. Hence, even though he leaves the last judgment to the One to whom alone it belongs, he can and should discharge his ministry with the quiet confidence that it will be performed under the clear and positive promise of the One who has laid it upon him and who does not cease to claim him for it. The righteousness and holiness grounded in Him and imparted in His grace will be decisive and determinative, not only for his present, but also, because the One who imparts them is also his hope, for his future as His witness. To discharge his ministry he needs no more than that the Gospel which he has to attest in the future should illuminate this future, availing for him and his action as its future witness. This is the indicative of his hope. Nor is more required of him than that he should accept its validity in every future and on this basis do what is commanded. This is the imperative of his hope. Jesus Christ as the One in whom His witness hopes is in His own person the hope in which to-morrow as to-day he can and should do as he is bidden.

These, then, are the three limits which are sharply and insurmountably set up for the Christian by the fact that Jesus Christ has not yet taken the last step in His prophetic work, that His consummating, i.e., universal, exclusive and ultimate revelation has not yet taken place, that he may and should attest Him in the light of His resurrection and the power of His Holy Spirit but cannot yet do so with the face to face knowledge (1 Cor. 13[12]) corresponding to and following after the knowledge with which he may already find himself known and loved and elected and justified and sanctified and called. For this adequate knowledge and therefore for the true and full form of his witness, the Christian waits. And it is his hope that he may do so, and not do so in vain or in the void, but with a measure of participation already in the One in whom he hopes and in what he expects from Him. On this side of the limit, his hope is already the dimension of Christian existence which points into the future and therefore beyond the limit. In hope, that which the Christian cannot reach is already near for all its farness. In hope, that which is unknowable is not alien but already known. In hope, that which he cannot realise is already real ; indeed, it is the most real thing of all in presence of which he may stride from to-day into to-morrow. In hope, he is apprehended already by that which he cannot apprehend nor even comprehend. In hope, his there is already here, this then already now, even though here and now he cannot be there and then. In hope, he continually dares to venture the next step ahead, even though Jesus Christ has not yet taken His last step which is decisive for his future. In hope, he may take it resolutely, unhesitatingly and joyfully, because the One who in His own time will take this last step, the Subject of hope, is not a remote object but the present and living basis of his hope. What it means to live with this promise of His in face of those limits, and in answer to the questions thereby posed for the Christian, may perhaps be summed up in the brief statement that in every future he not only can but will be a witness of Jesus Christ. It is with this sure expectation that he looks and moves towards the future.

But what we have said implies that a distinctive and disturbing edge is given to our initial question of the Christian's future, answered in our statement concerning Christian hope, by the fact that what is before him contains also his end. At some future hour, whether in his death prior to the end of all time with the consummating revelation of Jesus Christ, or in and with this happening, there awaits him the one concrete event which he and all other man can count upon to arrive with absolute certainty, namely, the conclusion of his temporal existence and therefore of his function as a witness of Jesus Christ.

This conclusion may be the event of his death. But if we are to keep to the line of thought of the New Testament, we best describe it as his end. His end does not have to be the event of his death. The syllogism : All men must die, Caius is a man, therefore Caius must die, is no doubt an illuminating statement of pagan wisdom. But it is not a statement of Christian wisdom, any more than the obvious moral of the mediaeval dance of death.

It cannot be, because it overlooks the *parousia* of Jesus Christ, which in its last and as yet outstanding form carries with it an alternative so far as concerns the end of the man living in it, so that his end does not have to be his death. We recall that in all its forms, and therefore in the last form too, the *parousia* of Jesus Christ is a new and unforeseeable divine event in face of all human experience and expectation. This is true of His resurrection and of His coming and acting in the power of the Holy Spirit. It is no less true of His final Word which brings history to its goal and end. Hence : " Ye know not what hour your Lord doth come " (Mt. 24⁴²). Now with the end of time generally, and the raising again of those already dead, His new coming will undoubtedly entail the conclusion of the temporal existence of those still living. But this conclusion will not be their death. Hence 1 Cor. 15⁵¹ : " We shall not all sleep, but we shall all be changed." Instead of dying, Christians who are still alive will be caught up with those already dead and raised again from the dead (ἅμα σὺν αὐτοῖς, 1 Thess. 4¹⁷), who will have the precedence, and they will be brought to an immediate encounter with the returning Lord and an immediate and enduring being with him (πάντοτε σὺν κυρίῳ ἐσόμεθα, 1 Thess. 4¹³f.). Materially, this is obviously the same process as Paul has in view in 1 Cor. 15⁵¹ : " We shall not all (i.e., including those then alive) sleep, but we shall all (i.e., including those who sleep already but are raised from the dead and are thus alive) be changed," i.e., invested with a new, incorruptible and immortal being (v. 53 f.). Whether we describe it as rapture or change, a direct transition to participation in the glory which comes to the creaturely world in and with the coming of Jesus Christ can be the end of the Christian instead of dying—the same transition to the same participation in the same glory which is awaited indirectly, in the passage from life through death to the resurrection, by those already dead, but in this other form by the Christians who will then be alive. No one knows, of course, the hour of this final appearing of Jesus Christ. Hence no one knows whether it will come in his own lifetime, whether his end will come in the one form or the other, or whether death will necessarily be the form of this end. *Venturus est iudicare vivos et mortuos,* is confessed by the early Church at the end of the second article of the creed (cf. 1 Pet. 4[5], 2 Tim. 4[1]). It thus reckons with the fact that when Jesus Christ appears in His consummating revelation and therefore to judgment, alongside the many dead who will then be raised, there will also be those who are still alive and who thus reach their end in this way.

The same procedure is described by the term " change " in 1 Cor. 15[51, 52]. Those who are already dead, but raised from the dead, will share this with some who are still alive. In the Thessalonian Epistle, often thought to be his earliest, Paul was obviously assuming that he himself and others (ἡμεῖς οἱ ζῶντες, 1 Thess. 4[15, 17]) might still be amongst those who are alive. The same assumption may be seen in the expression which he uses with reference to the same event in 2 Thess. 2[1]: ἡμῶν ἐπισυναγωγὴ ἐπ' αὐτόν. It is not so apparent in the later Epistles. We cannot be sure that he abandoned it. This has been assumed with reference to 2 Cor. 5[1], in which he speaks of the coming dissolution of his earthly tabernacle. But does this necessarily refer to his death ? Even in this passage (v. 4) we still read of his desire, not to " be unclothed, but clothed upon." And the same assumption is surely quite evident in 1 Cor. 15[52] with his express balancing of the statement that " we shall be changed " against the assertion that " the dead shall be raised." To be sure, in Rom. 14[8] he considers the alternatives : " For whether we live, we live unto the Lord ; and whether we die, we die unto the Lord : whether we live therefore, or die, we are the Lord's." Similarly in Phil. 1[20] it is his firm expectation and hope that Christ will be glorified in his body εἴτε διὰ ζωῆς, εἴτε διὰ θανάτου, so that in the following verse he can even speak of his death as gain, and then go on to speak in v. 23, with this gainful death in view, of his desire to depart and be with the Lord. If his personal expectation to be amongst those who would be alive at the day of Christ's coming, and would not therefore die but come to their end and goal some other way, did not entirely disappear in the later Paul, it did no doubt become less prominent. It could easily do so. For even in Thess. it was not a predicate of his apostleship and formed no part of his message. What could not become less prominent, let alone disappear, was his picture of the day of the Lord, which will certainly be a day of the general resurrection of those who have already died and thus reached their end by dying, but also a day when those who are still alive will reach their end in a very different way, Jesus Christ appearing as Judge of both the quick and the dead, in order that, in correspondence with His own death and resurrection, " he might be Lord both of the dead and the living " (Rom. 14[9]).

If the triumph of hope is to be clear and understandable in face of this most bitter of all limits, namely, the ineluctable end of human and therefore Christian existence, then it is not merely advisable but quite indispensable to realise that the end which is before all of us can come with death but may also come directly with the coming of Jesus Christ, with His coming again in the final form of His *parousia* as Judge of the quick and the dead, with the end of all time and things and men in Him, yet also in Him with their true beginning in reconstitution, with their investiture with eternal life, with the rapture or change in which it will be made manifest that the will of God for His creation and for each individual is actually done in Him. Now it may well be, and the New Testament takes this into account, that any one of us may reach his end by dying. It is rather a dubious circumstance, however, that the Christian world has long since come to think of death, and therefore of the moral of the mediaeval dance of death, as the normal case, or even as the iron rule, for the end of human existence. According to the New Testament death has no such monopoly in principle. It is limited by that other form, which is also a form of the end, but of the end which as such will be a new beginning bordered by no further end, since in it a term is set and a veto opposed not only to the existence of all the men then living but also to their death with its threat to them as to their predecessors, the lordship of death over them as over all creation of every age and place being broken. It is advisable and even indispensable to realise that dying is in fact only one form of the end, confronted in free superiority by the very different form of departing to be with Christ, because only on this basis and in this association can we really see the meaning of death as the end which overtakes us. If death is the more obvious and apprehensible and relevant form of the end, we must set alongside it the fact that the coming of Jesus Christ Himself, the occurrence of His consummating revelation, may bring and be the same end, namely, the end which is also the goal and therewith the beginning without end, the resurrection of the flesh, eternal life in eternal light. The end can also come in the form of death. In this form it did in fact come for Paul and for all our Christian predecessors. In this form—though we cannot really know—it may well come for us. But the end in this form is lit up as seen in association with and on the basis of the alternative of that very different form. In its character as the end of human and even Christian existence it is confirmed but also relativised by the fact that in that other form its end is so clearly shown to be a beginning. Seen in this light, can death as the first form of the end be anything more than a provisional substitute or mask of the true end, or indicate otherwise than in a glass darkly (1 Cor. 13^{12}) the original of this true end which comes with the coming again of Jesus Christ ? In other words, even if the end is still before us in the form of our dying, can we look or move towards it otherwise than in hope ?

There can be no doubt, nor should we try to evade the fact, that the end which will certainly come in one form or the other might well seriously compromise, threaten or darken the Christian's expectation of the future, giving to it the character of expectation which either hovers between hope of good and fear of evil, or is simply fear of evil. No matter how it comes, even for the Christian the end means thus far and no further. You have had your time and no more remains. You have been given your chances, possibilities and powers of varying degree and nature. It is now all up with them, and you can expect no more. This was your life as a witness of Jesus Christ. This was what you made of it according to the measure of your faith and love, in acceptance of the task laid upon you, in the use of the powers granted for its execution, within the limits of your obedience and faithfulness. You cannot alter anything, or improve anything, or rectify anything. With the totality of whatever you have done, of your completed life work, you must now encounter your Lord, come before His judgment throne, and pass through the fire in which it will be definitively shown who and what you are, and what you have done or not done as such. Been and done ! *Non plus ultra !* " Forth thou must go, thine hour hath run its course ! " This is what the end means in itself and as such, whether in the form of dying or in the other form in which apart from death it will coincide with the end of time and all things in the consummating revelation of Jesus Christ. Do we not have here the most painful of all the limits of Christian existence, and the acutest possible form of the question to which they give rise ? For this unquestionable end ahead of us means quite simply that our Christian ministry of witness, when we are one day called away from it as from our temporal being generally, will even at best be only a torso or the fragment of a torso which is quite disproportionate to the height and depth and breadth and fulness of the Gospel which we are commissioned to attest. What is the significance of the few years or decades in which, painfully and by way of so many mistakes and misconceptions, we have come to know and understand our task and made our puny efforts to fulfil it ? Have we ever done more than make a toilsome and pitiable beginning, which on close inspection is perhaps no more than a false start ? Is all this really over ? Is it finally too late to do anything more about it ? How can the Christian possibly live and work with the prospect of this end which in some form is certain, if in itself and as such, even though he has made the best and most zealous and careful use of his time and powers, his end necessarily implies this bitter Too Late ?

But we move too fast. If we were concerned with an end in itself and as such, then there would be good cause indeed to fear that only this bitter Too Late awaits even the Christian. In all circumstances, however long delayed, this end could only come too soon and be awaited with a terror difficult to suppress. When the Christian hopes, however, he does not expect an end in itself and as such. His end, in whatever form it comes ; the end to which he looks and moves, is the consummating revelation and judgment of Jesus Christ. There is for him no triumphant Father Time to hold up the empty hour glass, to crow his *Non plus ultra !*, to thrust in his sickle and to make an end. On the contrary, it is the One whom he is free to trust and love and attest who, when he has proceeded thus far according to His gracious plan and disposing, will pronounce His unconditionally good and right and saving Halt !, telling him that he has done enough, that no more is expected of him, that he does not need any more chances or possibilities or powers, that the measure of his life work, whatever it contains, is full, that his service either good or bad is rendered, that his time is over. But if this is so, then surely the conclusion of Christian existence expected from Him can never come too soon, nor give cause for that bitter Too Late. Coming from Him, it can only be an unequivocally welcome, because gracious, event.

Those whom He calls out of their temporal existence and ministry, He does not set in the darkness of no more being. He rather takes them out of the darkness of present not yet being into the light of His consummating revelation, in which, together with all that will only have been when He comes, their concluded existence, though it be only a torso or the fragment of a torso, will be seen as a ripe fruit of His atoning work, as a perfect manifestation of the will of God fulfilled in Him, being thus illuminated, having and maintaining its own light, and bearing witness to God in this renewed form in which it is conformed to the image of the Son of God. Strict justice will then be done to them, but it will be the justice of His grace. They must go through the fire, and therefore, in respect of the as yet invisible form of their being and activity, they will suffer loss (1 Cor. 3^{15}), undergoing reduction and subtraction. Yet they will be saved through the fire as those they have been, not in their own eyes nor those of men, but in the eyes of God, from all eternity and in their own lives. Hence in and with their life work, whether alive or awakened from the dead, they will be caught up and changed by the One who calls them away from their temporal existence and ministry, being clothed upon by His true and incorruptible and immortal being, so that they are restored and set in that service " in eternal righteousness, innocence and blessedness." This end which is also a goal and as such a new beginning—the beginning of the exalting of his temporal existence and all its contents to eternal light and therefore eternal life —is what the Christian expects, and may expect, when either as one who dies or one who still lives he encounters his Lord. It is in this expectation, therefore, that he moves into his future which at some point unknown to him will be the future of his end. In this expectation he has the freedom not to fear his end in whatever form it comes, but to rejoice in it. How can he fail to rejoice in it when in this final parting he expects his Lord, and with Him, as concerns his completed existence and ministry, exaltation to the eternal light of eternal life ? He cannot really look or move to his end except in hope. Whatever it brings me can only be the fulfilment of the promise in the preceding light of which, even though I be a pilgrim on the earliest stages of the path, I may already believe, and witness, and cry, and live either well or badly in His service so long as time is given me.

2. LIFE IN HOPE

We started with the question how the Christian may maintain himself as such, i.e., as a true and faithful and serviceable witness of Jesus Christ, when he moves towards a dark future full of conflicting possibilities and thus seems to have ground only for a divided expectation fluctuating between confidence and uncertainty. In answer to this question we have formulated our statement about Christian hope, of which we have given at least an outline. We have seen that this statement implies the radical destruction of the question of the future and the resultant attitude to it as originally posed, since it removes the assumption on which it rests and replaces it by a very different one which shapes the question in a way that is meaningful, legitimate and fruitful in this context. The statement concerning Christian hope tells us negatively that the future to which the Christian looks and moves is not an obscure, or neutral, or ambivalent future. There can thus be no question of the Christian having to maintain himself in face of such a future. Neither relatively nor absolutely is it relevant to him as a Christian. But the statement about Christian hope also tells us positively that the future to which only the Christian as such can look is the *parousia* of Jesus Christ in its final form, His coming in completion of His prophetic work and to His consummating manifestation. The Christian's expectation of the future is the expectation of this event. Hence his question, critically corrected by the statement about Christian hope, can only be that of his self-authentication in the light of this future and therefore in expectation of this universal, exclusive and conclusive Word of Jesus Christ. This question is meaningful, legitimate and fruitful, and demands an answer. And we must now attempt at least an outline of the answer to be given. It is not answered by the statement concerning Christian hope as such. This merely raises the question. Nor does its answer consist in a further statement, but only in the fact that the Christian lives with that which the statement denotes, i.e., in Christian hope, not theoretically, but with a dynamically practical actuality corresponding to its own dynamically practical actuality, so that it becomes in all seriousness his own expectation in contrast to all pagan expectation. The answer can consist only in his own being, thinking, speaking and action in hope, in this better expectation. Striding as a Christian into the future, he approves himself as a witness of Jesus Christ when what he does, the work of his life both as a whole and therefore in detail, becomes a work, or an unbroken series of works of hope, testifying to the Lord who has not only come and is not only present but will come again in the future. Since He in whom he hopes is already present as the basis of his hope, he owes Him this active witness. And as he discharges it, he gives proof of his Christian existence in this third dimension. " Begotten again unto a lively hope " (1 Pet. 1³), he has the ability to discharge it as and because he is liberated thereto by the Subject of his hope, by His presence and action. He not only may and should hope ; he is able to do so. We must now give a few indications concerning his life in hope.

It is obvious that at this point we are already given a glimpse, or at least a partial glimpse, as of the field of eschatology in the previous sub-section, so now of the ethics of reconciliation which we shall have to treat in the fourth part-volume. Even in this partial glimpse, however, we can only deal with certain elements which generally characterise Christian life and action, or the divine command which controls them. Three general determinations in particular are important and noteworthy in this regard, and therefore, in conclusion and transition, we shall briefly mention and describe them.

1. As in the development of the problems of faith and love in the first two parts of the doctrine of reconciliation, so in relation to that of hope we have been thinking of the individual Christian as a member of the Christian community. We have posed and answered it as the problem of his personal future and expectation of the future, as the question how and how far his Christian existence is possible and real as he strides from the present into the future. We have already laid down how the Christian does in fact live in his hope which is orientated on Jesus Christ because grounded by Him in the enlightening power of His Holy Spirit and participant in His own presence and action ; how his Christian existence in itself and as such does in fact acquire and have a dimension which transcends its present and points and presses to its future ; how the individual Christian as a member of the Christian community may thus actually live in prospect of his good and saving and blessed end. This is a way of considering the question which is theologically legitimate and obligatory, and we shall have to return to it under the third head of our introductory study of life in hope. How can it be otherwise ? *Tua res agitur.* In hope no less than faith and love, the Christian is always personally concerned and involved.

Not in opposition to this understanding, but to give to it greater critical precision, we must now go on to say, however, that in hope, as in faith and love, he is not acting for private ends and therefore in prosecution and propagation of a private cause. Religion is no doubt a private affair, but Christian existence, which is radically distinct from all religion, can never be the private affair of the Christian. To be sure, in his life action both as a whole and in detail he is acting in supreme *Inter-Esse*, i.e., in supreme personal participation and commitment. For this reason the problems of faith, love and hope must certainly be raised and answered as personal or " existential " questions of the Christian individual. It is as and because Christian existence as such is a supremely " interested " existence that the *Tua res agitur* applies. What is everywhere envisaged does indeed have a personal reference. Nevertheless, this does not mean that the human person of the Christian as such is what is primarily envisaged or ought to become or be the true and central object of interest. From time to time the Christian does no doubt see himself on the margin as a minor character in undeservedly resplendent and gratifying relationship with that which is truly and centrally at issue. But he cannot possibly have any concern for his own glory, or his own glorious being in this relationship, if he has in view what is really envisaged in Christian faith, love and hope, and if he does not wish to risk the dissolution of his own participation. In relation to what is envisaged in Christian faith, love and hope, personal interest means the personal acceptance by the Christian of the function assigned to him rather than the concentration of his will and desire and striving on personal advantages which might accrue. We are not really Christians, or we need to be renewed as such ; we do not yet believe or love or hope as Christians ; we do not participate in what is truly envisaged even as secondary figures ; we therefore lose our proper glory, if we are concerned about ourselves, if in believing and loving and hoping we are not pointed beyond ourselves, if we are not liberated from all futile and burdensome glancing aside at the personal glory or rewards or advantages that we might secure.

Our specific topic at the moment is Christian hope. What does the Christian really expect as he hopes ? What, then, will specifically determine and characterise his life in Christian hope ? We have seen that he expects the coming of Jesus Christ in glory, i.e., His consummating revelation of that which is still hidden, namely, that the will of God has been definitively, irrevocably and unassailably done by Him on earth as it is done in heaven. This implies something forceful and decisive even for his own personal future and expectation of it. It means even for him, too, glory and reward and gain. It means pardon in the final and strictest sense. It means his departing to be with Christ. It means his translation out of the darkness around into the great coming light. It means his transformation, his investiture with a new being which is neither exposed to corruption nor subject to death, his restoration and the beginning of his eternal salvation and life. But it means all these things only in the comprehensive context of the final redeeming act of God in full manifestation of the reconciliation of the world accomplished in Jesus Christ, of the conclusion of peace between the Creator and the creature established in Him, of the kingdom or establishment of the rule of God over all men and all things enacted in Him, of the alteration of the whole of human and cosmic reality effected in Him. This event of revelation expected by him in hope will not be particular but universal. Not his eyes alone, but those of the whole community which has hoped in Him in every age and place, and indeed of all the men who have lived, or live, or will live, will see this great light, will be terrified by it, but will also be made to rejoice by it. Not he alone, but all the known and unknown members of the community exalted to be brothers and sisters of Jesus Christ and therefore children of God, and indeed all the men among whom the community has had to proclaim the Gospel of divine sonship in this age, will then have to pass into the burning, searching, purifying fire of the gracious judgment of the One who comes, and to pass through this fire no matter what the result may be. Not to him alone, therefore, but to the whole community of which he is a member, and indeed to all men and all creation, there will then come the great change of the overthrow of all the contradiction in which they now exist and the necessary bending of every knee to Jesus Christ and the confessing of Him as Lord by every tongue. This, then, is what the Christian expects. It is wonderful that he himself belongs and will belong to the community and all humanity and the whole cosmic order which has this before it. But how can he expect it as a Christian in the hope grounded in Jesus Christ Himself as the Subject of hope, if his gaze is limited to or even concentrated upon his own personal part in this event, so that he forgets that it is only within the community and the whole of humanity and the whole cosmic order that he will participate in this light and can thus look and move towards it ? How can he try to make private an event which is so essentially public, as though that which does indeed lie before him lay before him alone or preferentially ? If his hope is really a private hope of this kind, then he needs to be told quite bluntly that he definitely loses the prospect of his own personal participation in this event and forfeits his own glory, reward and advantage by such restriction to himself in his life action.

This brings us to an insight which is decisive for the whole of this third part of the doctrine of reconciliation which we now bring to a close, namely, that *per definitionem*, and therefore not incidentally nor subsequently but essentially and from the very first, in virtue of his special election in Jesus Christ to be a member of the people of God, the Christian is a witness of Jesus Christ, who as such is not engaged in a private enterprise, however beautiful, important or salutary, but lives and works in a public ministry. His calling is to service. It is calling to a ministry of witness to the Word of God which is directed not only to himself or a few but to all men. It is calling to the ministry of the divine Word concerning the work which God has done not merely for himself or a few but for all men. It is calling to attest Jesus Christ as the Saviour of the world who is also the great Prophet speaking to the world. It is calling to personal participation in the ministry of the Christian community sent into the world. The Christian is not only ordained to this function but instituted in it. What other meaning or goal could his life have as that of one who may hope, but to look and move forward in present participation, though within the world, to the future fulfilment of the divine Word, to the consummating revelation of the Saviour of the world, which is the future of the world ? What determines and characterises his life and action is that he does not therefore hope at his own risk, that he does so with certainty and unconcern in face of all appearances because he does not follow his own judgment, nor have regard to what he himself might expect in this fulfilment of the Word of God. He hopes for God, " unto the praise of his glory " (Eph. 1[14]). God wills that among those who have no hope he should exist as one who has. And when he keeps to the promise given him with this divine disposing he hopes for others too, for those who are without hope, i.e., for those who do not yet know that God's Word applies to them too and that its fulfilment is before them, who are strangers to the previous revelation of Jesus Christ and are therefore unable to find comfort in His coming again to judge and restore, to rejoice in His consummating revelation and therefore to move to their own future with heads erect. The Christian hopes in order to show thereby that there is good cause and ground for all men and the whole world to hope with him. Even when he hopes in his own cause —for his public ministry of witness is his own cause—he hopes because, in virtue of his election and vocation, he has no option but to spring into the breach between Jesus Christ, whom it is given him to know, and those to whom it is not yet given to know Him, showing them by his existence that what he expects is really before them too. Thus, even though he is certain of the glory, reward and advantage which will accrue to him, he does not hope for his own sake, but for God's sake and for the sake of the men to whom he is bound and pledged as one who believes and loves and therefore hopes as a Christian.

The Christian who hopes is thus from two angles a representative. On the one side he keeps the post or watch apart from which God does not will that occurrence should proceed in the world which is reconciled to Him in Jesus Christ but which as yet is only moving from this event to its end and goal. There have to be in the world men who even in the night, perhaps only at midnight or before, or possibly in the hour of early dawn, look forward to the morning, to the rising sooner or later of the Sun of righteousness, to the end and goal of all things and therefore to their new beginning in light, which no further end can follow. There have to be men by whose irrepressible and constant unrest at least a few and even perhaps quite a number of their fellows are prevented from falling asleep as though nothing had happened and nothing out of the ordinary could happen in the future. In so doing, they do provisionally, and in great weakness and frailty, that which He Himself will finally do with unequivocal and irresistible power when His day comes. To this extent they are His representatives. Yet in the act of hope we can and should also understand and describe Christians as on the other side representatives of the surrounding humanity which seems for the most part to slumber. One day the whole of the human race must awaken, not of its own volition or resolve, nor in consequence of the clamour and tumult of great catastrophes, but as the trumpet is sounded which no one, not even the Christian, can now blow, but which one day will be blown in such a way that neither the Church nor the world can fail to hear it. The Christian now can only wake up for others, for the sleeping Church and world around. He can only appear to them from time to time as a watchman. Provisionally the Church and the world hope in him as their representative. To this extent, even though he may be an isolated figure, he is a representative on this side as well. To gather up the two concepts in a rather different metaphor, the Christian life in hope, where it is genuinely found, is the seed of eternity already sown in the present world, or rather the seed of the coming salvation of the whole world. It is only seed, and therefore still alone and concealed from the rest by a hard and wintry crust of earth. Yet it is living seed, which must die as such, but which will come to life again in the springtime, and like the grain of mustard seed in the Gospel (Mt. 13[31]) grow greater than all plants and become a great tree, so that " the birds of the air come and lodge in the branches thereof." The only thing is that the Christian must not delay to take up his post, to keep his watch, to become this seed, and therefore truly, i.e., not at all for his own sake but primarily for the sake of the ministry in the discharge of which alone he can be a Christian, to live in the hope for which he is liberated.

2. His life in hope is his existence in expectation of the coming of Jesus Christ to judgment, and therefore of the end, and therefore of the dawn of eternal light. It is his step out of the present into a future of which this still outstanding event of revelation is the horizon, so that he cannot enter it except in expectation of its coming. The goal to which he looks and moves is this horizon, i.e., the redemption of the created world which will also include his own and which will consist in the fact that every veil is lifted and there is manifested, to the freeing of what is bound, the healing of what is sick and the correction of what is perverted, that which Jesus Christ has accomplished for the salvation of the whole world and therefore for his salvation, namely, the hallowing of the name of God, the coming of the kingdom of God and the doing of the will of God in Him. His looking and therefore his moving to this goal does not mean, however, that he already sees it as his own future, and already strides up to it as he marches into the future. He looks and moves towards it. This is the very different thing called hope. What he sees is what is before the eyes of all, i.e., the veils which are not yet lifted, the created world which is not yet illumined and irradiated by the coming light and therefore not yet redeemed, the ongoing history of this world with all its confusions and entanglements under the sign of this Not Yet, and within it his own confused and tangled life history. He sees the continuing sin of men and above all of himself among them, as though his and their sin were not yet forgiven and done away and obliterated on the cross of Jesus Christ. He sees the death of men, and sooner or later his own death, as though he and they were not already risen again in Jesus Christ. As he moves into the future in hope, he lives in spite of these appearances and without seeing the goal or horizon towards which he looks and moves. What does hope mean under this sign ? This is the second point to be elucidated. For a second decision has here to be made which is of

the utmost importance for the meaning and character of his being and activity in hope.

Once again, as in the case of the possibility or impossibility of making hope a private affair, we have to delimit ourselves sharply from an illegitimate and absurd possibility or impossibility. In a strange perversion, hope might tend to become hopelessness in face of the existing world of appearances. It might tend to become resignation in face of the future in so far as this is still a temporal future and not the eternal goal and end. It might tend to become resignation in face of the veils which are not removed so long as time endures, in face of the form of the world which still persists and renews itself in time, in face of the unredeemed nature of world history, and especially Church history, and the individual history of the Christian, in face of the limits of the thinking, speech and action possible under these circumstances. Hope might tend to become the rigid orientation of the Christian on what is finally expected but is obviously not yet present nor visible nor attainable in his movement from the present to the future, and therefore his equally rigid turning aside from what is visible and attainable as he engages in this movement. Hope might tend to concentrate only on the one final thing which by its very nature is invisible and unattainable before it comes, i.e., on the future appearing of Jesus Christ, and in and with it eternal light and life and therefore the redemption of the created world. This might become the sole object of the Christian's thinking and yearning and rejoicing. He might live only in expectation of this final thing, living wholly in this expectation but in this expectation alone. He might thus close his eyes to what is now visible in time, on this side of that goal and horizon, as to something unpleasant. He might fail to do what might be done on the ground that it is meaningless and even dangerous. He might refuse to have anything to do with the world in its present form and history, resigning in face of it. Hope as the total but also exclusive expectation of the one great, eternal and definitive thing would thus extinguish every small, temporal and provisional expectation. Transfixed by thought of the last goal and end of his own future and that of the world, the Christian would move toward the future, in so far as it is still temporal and not the goal and end, with the more fixed and exclusive hopelessness. Any expectation in this regard, if it is not resigned from the very outset, could only be a restriction and even a denial of the expectation which is permissible and required, because alone true and full of promise. And even if on this understanding he is still aware that as a Christian he is bound and committed to be a witness to Jesus Christ in the world, his witness might summon to faith in Him and love for Him, but to hope in Him only in respect of the final appearing which is yet to come, a definite warning being given against all hope in Him as regards the present. Prior to the sounding of the last trump and the pronouncement of His final Word, all hope must be abandoned.

Now there have been many and varied attempts to fix Christian expectation so exclusively on the ultimate dénouement that a hopeless view is taken of penultimate developments. Seldom, if ever, however, has the matter been thought out or practised with the consistency of the above representation. If many Christians have tried to live with such exclusive concentration, it may be safely assumed that none has succeeded. The attempt is in fact an impossible one at its very root, and not merely in its consistent outworking. No one is able to concentrate so rigidly on the ultimate dénouement or to turn so resolutely from penultimate developments. The whole enterprise is a pious illusion. To be sure, in a way which is free and not rigid the Christian can and should expect wholly and exclusively his Lord, his light, his salvation, and the salvation of the world, at the moment when His promise, and therefore the Christian's expectation, is fulfilled at His coming. Yet in His coming there will also be fulfilled all the expectations which he has had of Him in his life in time if he is a good Christian. Again, in a way which is free and not rigid the Christian can and should, with the coming of judgment and redemption, turn from the goals in respect of which he has previously waited for Him, since his awareness of the ultimate dénouement means that all the penultimate developments expected of Him in time, while they are not destroyed, are set aside and stand in no further need of expectation. Yet no one should imagine, or proclaim to the world as the way of Christian hope, that prior to the goal and end regard should be had only to the ultimate dénouement and not to penultimate developments. If we ever come to believe that prior to the goal and end, and therefore at the next step out of the present into the future, we can and should hope in this way, then we must see to it that we are not the victims of a gross deception, that we do not have only a warm love for the eternal and a cool contempt for the temporal, that we do not finally come to the painful realisation that the supposed ultimate subject of our expectation really means nothing to us and the rejected penultimate means everything. If the sphere of the penultimate is left empty by pure hope of the ultimate, and is therefore made a place of hopelessness, there will exult and dance and triumph in it demons of the crassest because uncontrolled and undisciplined worldiness which has always proved to be the consequence of too rigidly eschatological versions of Christianity. Only a Christian hope which is strong in this sphere, too, is a match for these demons. And if the Christian, even while he has his ultimate hope, does not in relation to it have this penultimate hope as well, then it is highly probable that he has long since forfeited and lost his freedom even for the ultimate. It has always proved to be the case, however, that while this mortally dangerous illusion may suggest itself to the Christian, and even become a temptation to him, it can never become a reality. He can never achieve either exclusive concentration on the ultimate on the one side, nor rejection of the penultimate on the other. The dimension of Christian existence in which the Christian looks and moves in hope from his present into his future points not only to the ultimate dénouement of eternal light and life but also initially to the sphere of penultimate developments in the temporal life still lived by the Christian and the world. It is this corruptible which is to put on incorruption, this mortal which is to be clothed with immortality (1 Cor. 15^{53}). If the Christian has hope of this future, how can the corruptible and mortal be for him a sphere of hopelessness which he can only abandon as a temporary station to be vacated as quickly as possible and with the most vociferous exclamations of horror ? If he does not serve the Lord here and now in the time still given to the world and himself, what prospect is there for his future service " in righteousness, innocence and blessedness " ? Is it not his ministry in this world which is to be exalted to eternal light ? But how can he serve Him in this time if, in addition to concrete faith and concrete love, he does not have concrete hope, namely, in his movement from the present into the immediate future ? If Jesus Christ is the goal and end of time, then necessarily this time as such with all its contents, though it is not yet the day of redemption, is at least partly determined by the fact that it moves towards this as its end and goal. It is the last time. For all its obscurity and ambiguity, for all the temptations and dangers which it entails, it is the time of penultimate happenings immediately preceding the ultimate and definitive. It is the time which derives its irresistible impetus and flow from this ultimate occurrence, like a river moving towards a cataract. If this is the case, however, it is quite impossible that the Christian awaiting the coming of Jesus Christ should not in his movement from the present to the immediate temporal future look hopefully for the visible signs of His coming, for indications of the impetus or flow of time to its goal and end. Expecting the ultimate each new day and in each new situation in which the day may set him, he expects of each new day and every situation before him intimations of the ultimate even in this part of the sphere of the penultimate. What is before him as he steps into the future is in itself no more or other than what may be before all other men, namely, events and forms and relations and movements of world-occurrence, and his own deeply implicated life history, as these are apparently abandoned to their own law or contingency as if there could not possibly be anything new or singular. What is before him, and is no less clear but probably more so to him than to others in all its lost and restless character, is surging life on the market or battlefield, in the prison or mad-house, of as yet unredeemed existence as this is ruled by sin and marked by death, both serving and falling victim to them. But he cannot close his eyes to these events, nor seek escape in thoughts of heaven or the wonderful Last Day, because he can find more than those who have no hope even in that which exists and takes place before his own eyes and the eyes of all. He knows that in these penultimate things he is not dealing with the ultimate, with the judgment and redemption of the world. But he also knows that in them he is dealing with the negative and positive indications of the ultimate. What he expects in time is to come up against these indications, to perceive them as such, to be comforted and yet also startled by them, to be directed by them to the coming of the Lord, and to be prepared for it. Just because the Christian hopes for the ultimate and definitive, he also hopes for the temporal and provisional. Just because he hopes with joy for the dawn of the great light, he hopes with provisional joy for the little lights, which may come and go, but which will not come and go in vain, since as a temporary illumination they will help him to look and move more properly towards that which they can only indicate, but which in their time they can in fact indicate. Just because he hopes for the Last Day, for the eternal year, he hopes for the next day and the new year, from which, whatever they may bring, he can always expect at least new indications of the coming of Jesus Christ. Three concluding observations may be made in relation to this point.

The genuineness of this Christian hope for the ultimate in the penultimate will first be shown by the fact (*a*) that it is not bound to either the lighter or the darker side which existence may alternately display, let alone to the optimistic or pessimistic view which the Christian may have of a given situation or his own personal position. Even in relation to aspects which are absolutely black and desperate from the human standpoint, he may still dare to hope for indications of the ultimate. Nor is this true only of those aspects of the future which seem to threaten death and destruction. It is no less true of apparently or relatively more kindly aspects which in contrast to so much menacing gloom invite him here and now to see a feeble light and in the reflection of it to think of the great light. The provisional hope of the Christian is one which is free in face of both possibilities. In this freedom it may confidently expect signs of salvation both in that which is pleasant and that which is unpleasant. As such it is genuine hope.

Its genuineness is proved again (*b*) by the fact that, as distinct from idle contemplation, it assumes at once the form of an action corresponding to its concrete object. The Christian hopes as he serves, and as he thus expects provisional and temporal encouragement, equipment and direction for his service. He expects those feeble lights as lights on his temporal way. And because he expects them in intimation of the great light, he will not sit down waiting for something to come and snatch him away, but will manfully go forward hoping for the concrete help needed to enable him to do so. In this respect, too, Christian existence is existence in movement. Hope takes place in the act of taking the next step. Hope is action, and as such it is genuine hope.

Its genuineness is proved finally (c) by the fact—and here we take up again our first main point—that even in time and in relation to indications of the coming of Jesus Christ the Christian does not think or act as a private individual. It is only last of all that he hopes for himself. He stands in the public ministry of witness to Jesus Christ. In this function of his he hopes not only for the ultimate dénouement but for all kinds of penultimate developments as intimations of the coming judgment and redemption. In the service of God he hopes in and with the community, and in and for the world, that there will not be lacking to the world, even in all its needs and perplexities, provisional lights, concrete aids and deliverances and preservations and advancements, but also salutary crises. For each new day and year the Christian hopes. He hopes that throughout the Christian world and the world at large there will always be relative restraints and restorations and reconstructions as indications of the ultimate new creation to which the whole of creation moves. And as he hopes for these indications, he knows that he has some responsibility for them. He knows that he himself is claimed, not as an idle spectator, but actively. While his hope will include some hopes for himself, if it is genuine it will far transcend what it may mean for himself, becoming a light which shines out amidst so much individual and corporate, secular and even ecclesiastical hopelessness. In other words, his Christian existence will be a prophetic existence. Where it is given to us truly to hope, life in hope is as such a declaration and summons to all who hear it : " We bid you hope "—namely, in that which is ultimate, and therefore in spite of everything in the sphere of the penultimate.

3. Life in hope is life which derives from God. Of himself, in consequence of intellectual, theological, moral or religious effort or concern, or in spontaneous elevation of his inner or emotional life, no man has ever lived in hope, whether in the service of God for the world or for himself, whether of the ultimate dénouement or of its indication in time in the sphere of the penultimate. What derives and proceeds from man can never be Christian faith, nor Christian love, nor Christian hope. There may perhaps come forth a more or less comprehensive or restricted philosophy or mythology of the world to come, or the system or programme of a more or less deterministic or indeterministic philosophy of nature, history, culture or life. There may perhaps be produced the more or less naive or profound expectation of heavenly or earthly satisfaction in private future bliss. But there can never emerge true Christian hope, the clarity and certainty of the expectation of eternal life in eternal light which is

grounded in Jesus Christ as its origin, theme and content, a strong and inspiring confidence in relation to even the immediate temporal future. The expectation of the future which derives and proceeds from man himself can never escape the vacillation of its gaze between the inward and the outward, the cosmos and the individual, an abstract beyond and an equally abstract present. It is always exposed to the possibility of relapse into the scepticism of an ambivalent, inwardly divided and therefore obscure expectation. It can never have a prophetic character. This is true, of course, even in relation to the Christian. Even the expectation of the future produced by him, and nourished perhaps by imposing theological considerations, and even characterised by many biblical reminiscences and contours and colours, can never be prophetic and therefore truly Christian hope. Our present concern is not with the idea or concept of Christian hope in its characteristic distinction from all other expectations of the future. It is decisively with its reality, with the Christian's act and life in this hope. It is with his existence in the corresponding orientation, peace and movement. It is with a hope which is not occasional or intermittent but which is given solidity by its origin, theme and content, and thus perpetuates itself in an unbroken series of corresponding acts of human thought, speech and action. It is with a life which is either not lived in hope at all, or wholly in hope. Christian life is a life lived wholly in hope as well as faith and love. But no man has this whole life in hope of himself. Not even the Christian can produce it of himself. The Christian, however, is the first to realise that neither he nor any other man can do this. If a man is to live a life in hope, it must be a life derived from God. This is the assertion with which we must, or may conclude.

For it is not so much a command as a privilege to keep before us the fact that the Christian is summoned by Phil. 2$^{12-13}$ to work out (in " fear and trembling ") his salvation, or, as we may say, his life in hope, because it is God who works in him to will and to do of His good-pleasure. To be sure, his hope, like his faith and love, is a work which he himself has to perform either well or badly. It is a work which is required of him, so that he is responsible for its proper fulfil-ment. If a man looks for the day of the Lord, he must hasten unto it (2 Pet. 3^{12}). Of his own desire, according to his own judgment or whim, of his own ability or impulse ? None has ever done this. On the contrary, he hastes or works or hopes with all his heart and soul and mind and strength, being concerned at all points, and with " fear and trembling " in view of the magnitude and importance of the task, for the genuineness of his hope, because the free God awakens him who in himself is unwilling and incapable to freedom, to freedom of thought and will and movement and action, and therefore to hope. Because the free God awakens him to this freedom, he has no other freedom. He has thus no option but to make use of this freedom, i.e., to will and achieve that for which he is elected, called, ordained, enabled and equipped, to serve Him therefore as His witness in and for the world by hoping in Him in His ultimate but also penultimate action, by living wholly in this hope. How can he lack the ability to do this when God Himself has freed him for it ? How can he wish or attempt to do anything else when God Himself has freed him for it ? This means that he need not care whether he is worthy of the work of such a life or able to achieve it. It means that he need not care whether or not, though very willing to hope, he might slip back into all kinds of non-Christian, ambivalent and therefore despairing, self-seeking, abstractly otherworldly or thisworldly expectations of the future. In the freedom to which the free God awakens him, he will select and desire and achieve the work of what is on every hand genuine Christian hope. In this freedom, however, he will only desire and be able to live in this hope. What he has to keep in fear and trembling can only be this freedom, or, more exactly, his readiness continually to let himself be awakened by God to this freedom. In it he can and will live infallibly in hope, and wholly in hope.

To what do we refer ? Certainly not to a miracle which can be understood only with the help of a mythology which includes all kinds of magical notions, and which is then to be rejected when it is found impossible to accept these notions. No, our reference is to the mighty activity of the Holy Spirit. It is He who awakens a man to be a Christian, to be the kind of Christian who may hope in God, who in the service of God in and for the world, in the sphere of the penultimate, may hope for the ultimate. The Holy Spirit, however, is not a good daemon intervening between God and man like a *Deus ex machina* to make possible the impossible by a kind of magic. As there is no human skill, so there is no supernatural magic, to make possible the impossibility of a human life in hope. There is thus no daemon to grant this impossibility. Nor do we refer to a mere possibility, but to the actuality of such a life. The only One who can secure and introduce this reality of the Christian who hopes is God Himself in whom he may hope with reference both to the ultimate and the penultimate, and whom he may thus serve in his prophetic existence in the world, The reality of this prophetic existence of the Christian is not any kind of human or supernatural mystery. It is the mystery of God Himself. And God Himself is the Holy Spirit who awakens the Christian to life in hope.

God is *Spirit*, and therefore He truly awakens man to freedom. That He causes His divine power to come on him does not mean that he overtakes and overwhelms and crushes him, forcing him to be what He would have him be. He does not dispose of him like a mere object. He treats him, and indeed establishes him, as a free subject. He sets him on his own feet as His partner. He wills that he should stand and walk on his own feet. He thus wills that he should believe and love and hope. He wills his hope as his own spontaneous act. He awakens him to this hope. The breath of the living God raises him up a living man. The Holy Spirit is God in the power of His eternal and incarnate Logos, of His Word spoken in Jesus Christ. He is thus God in His power which enlightens the heart of man, which convicts his conscience, which persuades his understanding, which does not win him physically or metaphysically from without, but "logically" from within. Hence His work can only be man's freedom for life by Him and therefore for life in hope. Far from the Christian being mastered and taken out of himself when he is awakened to hope by the power of the Holy Spirit, it is in this life in hope awakened by the power of the Holy Spirit that he really comes to himself and may be himself. The man born of God or the Spirit, called to service and living in hope, is the man who is no longer self-alienated, and therefore he is real man.

But we must also say that God is the *Holy* Spirit, so that even when He awakens the Christian to the freedom of a life in hope and permits him to live by Him as a real man, He remains the free God. His mighty action on and in man is the work of His good-pleasure which He neither owes to any, nor comes to owe when it takes place. "I will have mercy on whom I will have mercy" (Rom. 9¹⁵). He would not be God if it were otherwise. Hence He does not fall into the power of the Christian, nor does He become superfluous when He makes him a free man and sets him on his own feet. If the Christian in his own spirit may be His witness together with the Holy Spirit and in fellowship with Him (Rom. 8¹⁶), the Holy Spirit never becomes his spirit but is always the Spirit of God. "I cannot take a single step alone." From what we have seen, Christian hope is too high a thing for the Christian not to have to seek afresh each new day and hour the freedom which he has and uses. Only the breath of the living God makes him a living man. That God should not take His Holy Spirit from him, but constantly grant him a new and right spirit (Ps. 51¹¹⁻¹²), must be the continual if confident sigh and cry of the Christian. How else can he do that whereto he is called? "Not slothful in business; fervent in spirit; serving the Lord; rejoicing in hope; patient in tribulation" (Rom. 12¹¹⁻¹²), the Christian will stride out of the present into the future if according to the last link in the chain he continues "instant in prayer." If he does, then he will not be found wanting in the third and fourth links which have been our particular concern. For he will definitely be serving the Lord, and he will do so rejoicing in hope.

INDEXES

I. SCRIPTURE REFERENCES

II. NAMES

Adenauer, Konrad, 694.
Althaus, Paul, 370.
Anselm of Canterbury, 32, 85 f., 802.
Apostolicum Symbolum, 90, 925.
Aristotle, 524.
Athanasius, 5, 178.
Augustana, Confessio, 22, 764 f., 783.
Augustine, 5, 32, 568, 571, 658.

von Balthasar, Hans Urs, 173.
Barmen, Synod of, 36, 86, 102.
Bartmann, Bernhard, 16.
Bauer, Walter, 9, 292, 600.
Belgica, Confessio, 765.
Bellarmine, Robert, 24.
Berkouwer, G. C., 173 f.
Bernanos, Georges, 33.
Bernard of Clairvaux, 549, 551, 553
Beza, Theodore, 24.
Biedermann, Alois Emanuel, 509.
Blumhardt, Christoph, 29, 170, 892.
Blumhardt, Johann Christoph, 168 ff.,
    172, 175 f., 261, 569 f.
von Bodelschwingh, Friedrich, 892.
Boniface VIII, 631.
Bready, J. Wesley, 27, 500.
Bucer, Martin, 26, 36, 890.
Buess, Eduard, 174.
Bultmann, Rudolf, 9, 295, 908.
Bunyan, John, 506.
Burmann, Franz, 14.

Calixt, G., 24, 36.
Calvin, John, 5 f., 13 ff., 17 f., 23, 26,
    33, 38, 62, 69, 137, 189, 484, 499,
    506, 514, 539, 541, 549 ff., 567, 756,
    765 ff., 783, 890, 913 f., 922.
Carey, William, 25.
Carlyle, Thomas, 887.
Cesbron, Gilbert, 774.
Charlemagne, 529, 694.
de Châteaubriand, François René, 33.
Churchill, Winston, 694.
Claudel, Paul, 33.
Constantine, 524, 918.
Contarini, Caspar, 551.
Cyprian, 766.

Decius, Nikolaus, 712.
Diekamp, Franz, 15.
Dittus, Gottliebin, 169 f.
Dort, Synod of, 17.
Dulles, John Foster, 694.
Duraeus, Johannes, 24, 36.
Dürer, Albrecht, 615, 917.

Egede, Hans, 24.
Elert, Werner, 370.
Eliot, John, 24.
Ephesinum, Concilium, 13.
Erasmus of Rotterdam, 36.
Ernesti, Johann August, 5.
Eusebius of Caesarea, 13.

Feuerbach, Ludwig, 72 ff., 78, 82 f.,
    85, 564.
Francis of Assisi, 514.
Francis Xavier, 23.
Francke, August Hermann, 25, 33,
    568 f.
Frank, Franz Hermann Reinhold, 6.
Frommel, Gaston, 569.

de Gaulle, Charles, 694.
Gerhard, Johann, 16, 24, 766 f.
Gerhardt, Paul, 393, 396, 414, 426
    673.
Gesenius, Justus, 302.
Goethe, Johann Wolfgang, 147, 171,
    266, 424, 880.
Gollwitzer, Helmut, 371.
Günther, Cyriakus, 302.
de Guyon, Jeanne Marie, 568.

Heermann, Johann, 302.
Hegel, Georg Wilhelm Friedrich, 171,
    703.
Heidegger, Heinrich, 15, 562, 765.
Heidegger, Martin, 473.
Heidelberg Catechism, 13 ff., 17, 290,
    357, 537, 654, 765, 861, 922.
Heintze, Gerhard, 371.
Herman, Nikolaus, 302.
Hermann the Cheruscan, 694.
Hiller, Philipp Friedrich, 928.
Hirsch, Emanuel, 20.
Hitler, Adolf, 102, 438.
Hölscher, Gustav, 399, 424.
Hofmann, Johann Christian Konrad,
    676.
Hollaz, David, 6, 505 f., 562.

Ignatius Loyola, 23.

Joest, Wilfried, 370.
John Hyrcanus, 13.
John of Monte Corvino, 23.
Josephus, Flavius, 13.
Julius Caesar, 694.
Jung, Carl Gustav, 384.
Jung-Stilling, Johann Heinrich, 33.

III. SUBJECTS